In Quest of the Historical Pharisees

In Quest
of the Historical Pharisees

Edited by

JACOB NEUSNER AND BRUCE D. CHILTON

BAYLOR UNIVERSITY PRESS

Cover Design: Pamela Poll
Cover Image: "Large Standing Stone Vessels," courtesy of James F. Strange.

Library of Congress Cataloging-in-Publication Data

In quest of the historical Pharisees / edited by Jacob Neusner and Bruce D. Chilton.
    p. cm.
  Includes bibliographical references and index.
  ISBN 978-1-932792-72-0 (pbk. : alk. paper)
  1. Pharisees. 2. Judaism--History. 3. Rabbinical literature--History and criticism. I. Neusner, Jacob, 1932- II. Chilton, Bruce.

  BM175.P4I5 2007
  296.8'12--dc22

                              2007001713

Printed in the United States of America on acid-free paper with a minimum of 30% pcw content.

CONTENTS

PART THREE
THE PHARISEES IN MODERN THEOLOGY

PART FOUR
CONCLUSION

PREFACE

The essays in this book describe the pictures of the Pharisees that emerge from the several ancient documents that refer to them. These are, in order of chronological proximity, (1) the gospels and references in Paul's writings, (2) the writings of Josephus, and (3) the later rabbinic compositions, beginning with the Mishnah and the Tosefta; hence, ca. 65–90 CE for the gospels, ca. 90–100 CE for Josephus, and ca. 200–300, extending through the Talmud to as late as 600 CE, for the later rabbinic compilations, respectively. We include a discussion of the relationship between the Pharisees and the Judaic religious system adumbrated by the library of Qumran.

We do not undertake to homogenize the distinct sources' pictures or reconstruct a coherent account of how things really were. Prior generations of scholars have signally failed at that task. We begin afresh in a more critical spirit. In these pages each source is described in its own terms and framework.

What about other writings of Judaic origin? A number of books in the Apocrypha and Pseudepigrapha of the Old Testament are attributed to Pharisaic writers, but none of these documents positively identifies its author as a Pharisee. Secure attribution of a work can only be made when an absolutely peculiar characteristic of the possible author can be shown to be an essential element in the structure of the whole work. No reliance can be placed on elements that appear in only one or another episode, or that appear in several episodes but are secondary and detachable details. These may be accretions. Above all, motifs that are not certainly peculiar to one sect cannot prove that sect was the source.

No available assignment of an apocryphal or pseudepigraphical book to a Pharisaic author can pass these tests. Most such attributions were made by scholars who thought that all pre-70 Palestinian Jews were either Sadducees, Pharisees, Essenes, members of the "Fourth Philosophy," or Zealots, and therefore felt obliged to attribute all supposedly pre-70 Palestinian Jewish works to one of these groups. That supposition is untenable. That is why, in this account of the Pharisees, we omit all reference to the apocryphal and pseudepigraphical books.

Who were the Pharisees and why should we care? The Pharisees formed a social entity, of indeterminate classification (sect? church? political party? philosophical order? cult? none of the above?), in the Jewish nation in the Land of Israel in the century and a half before 70 CE. They are of special interest for two reasons.

First, they are mentioned in the synoptic gospels as contemporaries of Jesus, represented sometimes as hostile, sometimes as neutral, and sometimes as friendly to the early Christians represented by Jesus. Thus, in the history of Christianity they play a role.

Second, they are commonly supposed to stand behind the authorities who, in the second century, made up the materials that come to us in the Mishnah, the first important document, after Scripture, of Judaism in its classical or normative form. Hence, the Mishnah and some related writings are alleged to rest on traditions going back to the Pharisees before 70 CE. So, in the history of Judaism they are supposed to represent the formative component.

How do we know anything at all about the Pharisees? No writings survive that were produced by them; all we do know is what later writers said about them. The three separate bodies of information are quite different in character. The first—Josephus—is a systematic, coherent historical narrative. The second—the Christian contribution—is a well-edited collection of stories and sayings and firsthand letters. The third—the rabbinic documents of the late second through seventh century—consists chiefly of laws, arranged by legal categories in codes and commentaries on those codes.

Moreover, the purposes of the authors or compilers of the respective collections differ from one another. Josephus was engaged in explaining to the Jewish world of his day that Rome was not at fault for the destruction of the Temple, and in telling the Roman world that the Jewish people had been misled, and therefore were not to be held responsible for the terrible war. The interest of the gospels is not in the history of the Jewish people, but in the life and teachings of

Jesus, to which that history applies. The rabbinic legislators show no keen interest in narrative, biographical, or historical problems, but take as their task the promulgation of laws for the government and administration of the Jewish community.

What do the discrete sources have in common? The several sources concerning pre-70 Pharisaic religion and law were generally shaped in the aftermath of the crisis of 70 CE. With the Temple in ruins it was important to preserve and, especially, to interpret, the record of what had gone before. Josephus tells the story of the people and the great war. The gospels record the climactic moment in Israel's supernatural life. The rabbis describe the party to which they traced their origin, and through which they claimed to reach back to the authority of Moses at Sinai. All three look back upon events deemed decisive: what are we to learn from those events?

To Josephus the answer is that Israel's welfare depends on the success of its aristocratic leadership in administering the constitution given by Moses, as also on peaceful and dignified relations with the world power, Rome.

The gospels claim that, with the coming of the Messiah, the Temple had ceased to enjoy its former importance, and those who had had charge of Israel's life—chief among them the priests, scribes, and Pharisees—were shown through their disbelief to have ignored the hour of their salvation. Their unbelief is explained in part by the Pharisees' hypocrisy and self-seeking.

The rabbis contend that the continuity of the Mosaic Torah is unbroken. The destruction of the Temple, while lamentable, does not mean Israel has lost all means of service to the Creator. The way of the Pharisees leads, without break, back to Sinai and forward to the rabbinic circle reforming at Yavneh. The Oral Torah revealed by Moses and handed on from prophet to scribe, sage, and rabbi remains in Israel's hands. The legal record of pre-70 Pharisaism requires careful preservation because it remains wholly in effect.

Clearly, putting together into a single coherent framework these wildly diverse accounts of the Pharisees presents a challenge to coming generations, the legacy of the generation that took things apart to see how they work.

The editors acknowledge with thanks the support of Bard College for their scholarly enterprise, support that encompasses not only ideal material conditions but constant encouragement and appreciation. They further thank the contributors to this volume, who gave us their best work, on time, in first-class form. And they acknowledge, finally, the editorial collaboration of Carey Newman, Baylor University Press, and his staff of consummate professionals. They have made possible this composite account of the state of learning and the issues of scholarly debate on the subject at hand.

Jacob Neusner
Bruce D. Chilton
Institute of Advanced Theology
Bard College
Annandale-on-Hudson, New York

PART ONE

FIRST-CENTURY ACCOUNTS

CHAPTER 1

JOSEPHUS'S PHARISEES: THE NARRATIVES

Steve Mason

What do we really know about the Pharisees? A hallmark of Jacob Neusner's scholarship is the maxim "What we cannot show, we do not know." More than three decades ago, he demonstrated that impatience in resolving historical questions about the Pharisees had led scholars to approach the evidence—that is, the literary sources—in a jejune manner.[1] The result was a bewildering array of mutually exclusive hypotheses, each requiring assent to certain prior assumptions, and none susceptible of proof in a meaningful sense.[2] Neusner insisted rather that we first attend to the portrait of the Pharisees in each text, as a construction suited to the work's interests, date, and audience—a principle he has applied systematically to rabbinic literature, with profound consequences for interpreters and historians alike. Only when the evidence is thus understood in situ can we reasonably formulate historical hypotheses to explain it.

In the spirit of Neusner's distinction between interpreting texts and historical reconstruction, my work has focused on understanding Josephus's narratives, most recently in the context of post-70 CE Flavian Rome, where Josephus's first audiences were to be found. This is itself a historical kind of interpretation, and a necessary propadeutic to efforts at reconstructing the history behind the texts. Yet it tends to sharpen the distinction between interpretation—focused on the text as medium of communication—and reconstruction of realities behind the text.

This approach commends itself because reconstruction of the underlying history or the external referents, which remains an aspiration for most readers of Josephus, must be conducted with a rigor sufficient to explain all relevant evidence, whether literary or material.[3] In Josephus's case, the very richness and subtlety of the evidence

3

render perilous efforts to get behind it, to events as we might have seen them. Archaeology or parallel literary accounts may provide independent confirmation of certain scenic elements (sites, buildings, distances, provincial administration, military practices, names of key figures) mentioned by Josephus; very rarely do we have such other material for reaching behind Josephus's accounts of who did what, when, and why.

My two contributions in the present volume are therefore about *Josephus's* Pharisees, not about *the* Pharisees as they understood themselves, or as one might have encountered them. This first chapter examines the role of the Pharisees in Josephus's narratives. Those passages in which he halts the action to present the Pharisees as a philosophical school, alongside Essenes and Sadducees, we shall reserve for the second chapter.

Any interpretation of Josephus's Pharisees must reckon with a basic fact, all too often overlooked. Namely, the group figures only incidentally in his thirty volumes: one could write a fairly detailed account of Josephus and each of his four compositions without mentioning the Pharisees. They are not even as prominent as other minor supporting players—Herod's executed sons, Parthian rulers (even Adiabenians), Arabians, Pompey the Great, the Egyptian queen Cleopatra—let alone the major figures of Josephus's stories: biblical, Herodian, Hasmonean, or revolutionary.

In the *Judean War*, the Pharisees are named in seven sentences in books 1 and 2. Although they shape the narrative in perhaps fifteen sentences all told, they do not appear in the main story (viz., books 3–7). In the leisurely twenty-volume narrative of *Judean Antiquities*, they get more space, though again not in the trunk of the work anticipated in the prologue (*Ant.* 1.5–26), that is, books 1 through 11 or 12. As in *War*, Pharisees appear mainly in connection with the Hasmonean and Herodian sections of *Antiquities*. They account for some 20 of the 432 sections in book 13 (thus, one part in forty-two in that volume) and receive glancing mention in book 15, a paragraph at 17.41–45, plus a couple of sentences in book 18 (outside the school passage there). In the 430 sections of Josephus's one-volume *Life*, an appendix to the *Antiquities*, Pharisees appear at two crucial points (*Life* 12.191–198; incidentally at 21). The *Against Apion*, which explains and defends the

Judean constitution and laws, omits them along with the other two schools.[4]

The four philosophical-school passages, subject of chapter 2 of the present volume, do not alter this impression of the Pharisees' narrative marginality. In *War* 2.119–166, Pharisees and Sadducees are both dwarfed by the Essenes. In *Ant.* 13.171–173, each school receives one sentence. In *Ant.* 18.12–15, the Pharisees again receive less attention (and praise) than the Essenes (18.18–20). And in *Life* 10–11, all three schools yield immediately to Josephus's beloved teacher Bannus.

We should realize from the start, then, that Josephus could have had no serious axes to grind concerning the Pharisees, or none that he expected to communicate to audiences who lacked our technologies for locating and assembling "Pharisee passages." A Roman audience could have been forgiven if, after hearing or reading Josephus, they did not remember much about this group. This does not mean that Josephus had no view of the Pharisees, which we might still discern in what he wrote—*because* we are interested in the question and it is easy for us to gather the material. But given the textual data, we should be wary of theories that make the Pharisee passages drive interpretations of Josephus's works or even his thought in general.

It may be tempting to elevate the historical worth of the few Pharisee passages in Josephus on the principle that, precisely because the group is not significant in his narratives, he had little stake in massaging their image; thus, his incidental remarks likely reflect the historical situation. Yet Josephus is an artful writer, entirely capable of exploiting for momentary purposes even the smallest bit-player— whether a youthful hothead, a courageous fighter, or a would-be tyrant.[5] We cannot so easily escape the web of his narrative world, even in the case of minor players.

Here, then, is a survey of the Pharisees in Josephus's narratives.

IN THE *JUDEAN WAR*

Since the Pharisees appear almost exclusively in the Hasmonean and Herodian stretches of the *War*, my sketch of the relevant context will focus on those sections in books 1 and 2, which are preparatory to the book's main story.

Josephus wrote the *Judean War* in the difficult environment of
Rome in the 70s. The recent victory of Vespasian and his son Titus
was being exuberantly celebrated (in the triumph, the new monumen-
tal buildings, coins, arches, and literature) as a primary legitimation of
Flavian authority.[6] Predictably, the conflict was being reported in
fawning pro-Flavian "histories," to the severe detriment of the
Judeans. Josephus responds to this situation with a work that will, he
claims, attempt to restore some balance (1.1–2, 6–8). The first sentence identifies him as a proud aristocrat and priest from Jerusalem,
who fought against the Romans at the beginning and was then com-
pelled to watch from their side (1.3). This rare *curriculum vitae* allowed
him enviable claim to the balance of perspectives that had been
prized as the key to impartiality since Herodotus invented "history"—
objectivity in the modern sense being not yet on the horizon—as well
as the eyewitness access required by Thucydides and Polybius.

In a complex and often brilliant narrative, Josephus develops the
following thematic lines, among others: the essential virtue of the
Judeans and the dignity of their leaders; their long suffering under
incompetent and corrupt Roman equestrian governors; the Judeans'
manly virtue and contempt for pain and death (often contrasted with
the behavior of hapless legionaries); the gravitas of their aristocratic
leaders, who, had they lived, would either have fought a more successful war or reached respectable terms with the Romans; the civil war
that threatened and finally erupted when a few tyrants managed to
overturn aristocratic control and so precipitate the final disaster.

The unifying theme of all this is the question of the Judean ethnic
character. In antiquity it was widely assumed that behavior issued
from one's innate character: both individuals and groups behaved the
way they did *because* of their character. In the case of individuals, this
principle may be seen in the rhetorical structure of legal defenses: the
frequently used argument from "probability" appealed to the ancestry, familial glory, education, and virtue of the accused, with surprisingly little attention directed to the facts of the case: "The accused
could not plausibly have done what he is charged with because of his
character (including ancestry and glorious deeds)!"[7] Similarly, ethno-
graphers, geographers, and historians tended to see correlations
among the characters or natures of whole peoples, their environmental conditions, their political constitutions, and their national behav-

ior.[8] Thus, when Tacitus sets out to describe the fall of Jerusalem in 70 CE, he thinks it important to supply an explanation of the Judeans' origins, culture, and character (*Hist.* 5.1–6, esp. 2). Because the revolt against Rome was taken to be the expression of a rebellious and misanthropic nature, Josephus understood his task in similar terms but from the other side: to furnish a more accurate picture of that national character, along with a better explanation of the war's origins and outcome.

It is curious that Josephus should begin his account of the war in 66–73 CE with the Hasmonean revolt 250 years earlier, following that with a detailed portrait of King Herod (40–4 BCE) and Archelaus (1.31–2.116). This is all the stranger because he then glides over the three decades from 4 BCE to the mid-20s CE with almost no material. Among the many reasons one might adduce for this interest in Hasmoneans and Herods (beyond the formal justification in *War* 1.17–18) we should include the following. The Hasmonean story, remembered annually at Hanukkah, had provided inspiration for those dreaming of independence from Rome in the recent war.[9] Himself cherishing roots in the Hasmonean-priestly dynasty (*War* 5.419; *Ant.* 16.187; *Life* 1–6), Josephus retells the story so as to argue that the Hasmoneans actually created a Judean state only in alliance with the superpower Rome (*War* 1.38). Therefore, their storied and paradigmatic "freedom" was astute, but never absolute. In Josephus's narrative the Hasmoneans and King Herod (also Herod's father, Antipater) demonstrate rather the *diplomatic skills* that the author attributes to members of the elite such as himself, a remarkable adaptability in making alliances as needed with almost anyone (e.g., various Seleucid pretenders or the successive strongmen of the Roman civil wars), *for the welfare of the Judean state.* Given that world powers come and go under inscrutable divine providence, as Jeremiah and Daniel had understood long before, this was the only feasible way of life for peoples such as the Judeans.[10] As it happens, Josephus's approach intersected well with contemporary political reflection among other elites in the eastern Mediterranean.[11]

Further, because the government of the Hasmoneans and then Herod saw the concentration of political power in one person, their cases brought to light the very problem that plagued all monarchies and Rome herself since the rise of dictators in the first century BCE, and especially since Augustus had carefully developed a de facto monarchy: if one person is entrusted with supreme power, how to secure a peaceful succession? What do we do for an encore? John Hyrcanus, though a successful and beneficent administrator, foresaw that his less pious and less fortunate sons would quickly trigger the downfall of the dynasty (*War* 1.68–69). In a similar vein, although Herod's reign was consumed by the making and canceling of wills, when he died in 4 BCE the succession saga dragged on at great length in the hands of Augustus—whose own problems in finding and keeping an heir were notorious (2.1–116).[12] The problem of monarchy and its Achilles heel, succession, will become a still more prominent issue in the *Antiquities*.[13] In the *War*, this issue is tied up closely with the work's central questions of political "freedom" and governance.[14] The whole project of the so-called tyrants, who will seize the revolt from the nation's aristocracy, is allegedly based on the monarchical principle: each one seeks to be supreme ruler for the basest of reasons, with no genuine concern for the welfare of the nation, no training in or understanding of governance, and no provision for the sequel.[15]

We first meet the Pharisees of *War* when the Hasmonean dynasty is already well into its downward spiral, following the death of Hyrcanus I. This degeneration began with Aristobulus I, who assumed the diadem and thus transformed the state into a monarchy (*War* 1.70; 104–103 BCE). In keeping with this tyrannical turn, he lost no time in murdering family members (1.71–84). His brother Alexander Jannaeus had a much longer and in some respects successful reign (103–76 BCE), but it, too, was marred by tyranny (1.97). Josephus remarks that although Alexander seemed (δοκεῖν) to be moderate (1.85), he faced a mass rebellion of the people, which he put down brutally by killing some fifty thousand (1.91).

When Alexander died, his wife Alexandra assumed the throne as queen. She was a ray of hope for the dynasty because she utterly lacked her husband's brutality (the narrator authoritatively reports): she not only had a *reputation* for piety (δόξαν εὐσεβείας); she really was a precise observer of the laws (1.108). This piety, however, was also her downfall, for it caused her to give far too much power to the Pharisees, whom Josephus now introduces as a group with a reputation for, or image of (δοκεῖν), precision in the laws (1.110). Josephus describes their relation to the queen with a striking verb, normally used of plants growing from the same root: the Pharisees grow alongside (παραφύονται) Alexandra and encroach on her authority parasitically.

Indeed, the Pharisees become the de facto government in many respects, exploiting the queen's naiveté to settle their own scores: they arrange for their enemies to be bound and banished, their friends to be recalled and liberated. Josephus remarks that whereas Alexandra bore all the costs of rule, the Pharisees enjoyed the real authority behind her protective screen (1.112). Although they were not mentioned in the Alexander narrative, they are evidently on the side of those who opposed Alexander, for they take revenge on the late king's advisers and friends; therefore, the eminent and distinguished classes (would Josephus locate his kind of people here?) have the most to fear from their revenge (1.113–114). Whereas Alexandra succeeded in controlling neighboring nations through shrewd military planning, Josephus opines, the Pharisees controlled her (1.112).

This account of Alexandra and the Pharisees moves the narrative along by offering an explanation for the continuing decline of the Hasmonean house. After the deep wounds inflicted on the body politic by Alexander, yet before the dynasty reaches its nadir in the rivalry between Alexandra's sons Hyrcanus II and Aristobulus II (which ushers in Roman rule), the potential of this just and pious queen to turn things around is undercut by her alliance with vindictive and aggressive Pharisees.

More specifically, the passage carries forward a number of key Josephan themes. Chief among these is the contrast between seeming and being, reputation and truth, illusion and reality, names or titles and actual authority. This sort of dialectic is Josephus's métier.[16] Just as the historical man lived and wrote in a world of "doublespeak," dissonance, irony, and indirection in imperial Rome, so Josephus the writer often has his characters (including himself) say things that the audience knows to be either completely or substantially false. It is a world of unsettling and constant double games, where nothing is what it appears to be. In Josephus, as in Tacitus, we see vividly the "rhetoricized mentality" fostered by Greco-Roman education for elite males.[17] In the story of Queen Alexandra, the image-reality dialectic is everywhere at work. Her husband had given the *impression* of moderation, but this turned out not to be the reality. She really *was* moderate and pious, but this led her mistakenly to yield power to the *seemingly* moderate Pharisees. Their invitation to power allowed the Pharisees, in turn, to assume the *real* authority of the state, leaving her the outward shell and *title*.

Other characteristic language of Josephus has to do with "precision" (ἀκρίβεια), or apparent precision, in interpreting the laws. He will return to the Pharisees' reputation for legal precision in several places, even in his autobiography when describing Simon son of Gamaliel.[18] Although it was long conventional for scholars to relieve Josephus of responsibility for hostile attitudes toward the Pharisees by attributing them to his (undigested) sources,[19] these connections of language and perspective preclude such maneuvers. Indeed, we already see here one likely reason for Josephus's hostility toward the group: himself a member of the priestly elite, which has been charged with preserving and interpreting the Judean laws ever since the time of Moses (see notes 30 and 55 below), the sudden rise to power of a popular and populist group, whose members lack the aristocratic culture that creates elite statesmen and who undertake to rid the state of their aristocratic enemies, could not but attract his ire.

This debut of the Pharisees in Josephus's narratives, which is also their fullest scene in the *Judean War*, is at best inauspicious. Their two fleeting appearances in the later story confirm their ongoing influence with the people, but our author is not interested in exploring this phenomenon for his audience.

In the *War*, King Herod is mainly a virtuous figure: a tough, proud, generous, and wily Judean who constantly shows other nations what his people can do in military and diplomatic spheres alike. He is plagued by succession worries, however, and his downfall is attributed by Josephus to the women in his life (1.431, 568). It is in the latter half of the Herod story, which explores his domestic woes, that the Pharisees turn up as *agents provocateurs*. Josephus as narrator plainly disapproves of Herod's sister-in-law, the unnamed wife of Pheroras, who behaves insolently in public and conspires to turn the king's son Antipater against him (1.568–570). At a hearing of Herod's *consilium*, one of the charges brought against the woman is that she has "furnished rewards to the Pharisees for opposing him" (1.571). We should like to know much more, and *Antiquities* (below) develops the story, but here in *War* Josephus is not interested in explaining further: he merely cites this among several examples of the woman's alleged impudence.

As for the Pharisees, who played such a large role in Alexandra's reign, it is clear only that they remain a significant presence and a source of trouble for Herod. Although we might expect Josephus to admire those who oppose kings, given his stated preference for aristocratic rule, his narrative is much more textured than such simple dichotomies would require. The Pharisees can oppose eminent citizens as well as kings, and in this case are allied with a troublesome woman; they do not seem to be Josephus's kind of people.

In *War* 2, Josephus mentions the Pharisees twice: first in the philosophical-school passage that features the Essenes (2.119–166), which we shall consider contextually in chapter 2; second in a brief notice about the constituency of the leading citizens at the outbreak of the revolt. Seventy years have passed in real time since the death of King Herod in 4 BCE—Josephus does not, however, write in chronological proportion—and a lot has happened. Under the deteriorating maladministration of the later equestrian governors sent by Nero, predictable tensions threaten to explode in violence and civil war, while members of the elite struggle to keep a lid on things in order to avoid Roman intervention. A series of riots induces Queen Berenice and her brother King Agrippa II to try oratory, the ancient statesman's best friend, in order to calm the masses; but this ultimately fails (2.342–407). Some younger aristocrats, led by the Temple commander, insist on suspending all sacrifices by foreigners and the daily sacrifice for Rome and its *princeps* (2.409–410). This defiant action advances the movement to war.

At this point Josephus remarks (*War* 2.411) that "the elite [or 'the principal men, the powerful': οἱ δυνατοί] came together in the same place (εἰς ταὐτόν) with the chief priests (τοῖς ἀρχιερεῦσιν) and those who were eminent among the Pharisees (καὶ τοῖς τῶν Φαρισαίων γνωρίμοις)," to discuss the brewing crisis. Brief though it is, the itemization is suggestive: the principal men or aristocrats, based in the priesthood and so naturally accompanied by the super-elite chief priests, are now also joined by the most prominent men of the Pharisees. Elsewhere, Josephus almost formulaically pairs the elite (οἱ δυνατοί or similar) with the chief priests as Jerusalem's leaders (2.243, 301, 316, 336, 422, 428, 648), without mentioning the Pharisees. In one other place he adds to this formula (οἱ τε ἀρχιερεῖς καὶ δυνατοί) a vague third term, "and the most eminent [stratum] of the city"

(τὸ τε γνωριμώτατον τῆς πόλεως; 2.301). If leading Pharisees were
in his mind as he wrote that, however, he chose not to burden his
audience with this information. So the notice at 2.411, that the standard pair of priestly elite groups met with the leading Pharisees at
that crucial point, seeming to stress that they also convened in the *same
place*, hints that such a coalition was unusual in more normal times—
necessitated here, we infer, by the emergency.

Although we later learn that it was quite possible to belong to the
priestly caste and be a Pharisee (*Life* 197–198), membership in the
Pharisees being a voluntary affiliation, members of the hereditary
priestly aristocracy needed no school affiliation to give them status,
and many apparently had none. It was by definition the elite class,
comparable to other aristocracies in the Greek cities of the eastern
empire, to which the Roman governors turned (or were supposed to
turn) for collaboration in administering the province.[20] Inclusion of
the Pharisees' leading representatives in this emergency council thus
appears to be a diplomatic necessity, part of the elite's effort to calm
the masses. Such a conclusion anticipates what will be spelled out in
the *Antiquities* (13.297–298; 18.15, 17): that the Pharisees had avenues
of access to the masses that the priestly aristocracy as a body lacked.

Josephus's first known work does not, then, give the Pharisees
much play. And yet the author's disdain seems clear. He gives the
impression of mentioning them only when he must in order to tell his
story, while leaving many obvious questions unanswered. What
exactly was their social status and composition? Who were their leaders? How did they acquire such powerful enemies, whom they purged
under Alexandra? Why were they so popular among the masses, and
such a threat to Herod? How did they acquire their reputation for
piety and careful observance if they were so politically cunning (as
Josephus claims)?

Recounting Herod's final days, Josephus describes a popular uprising led by two influential "sophists," who also had a *reputation* for precision in the ancestral traditions (δοκοῦντες ἀκριβοῦν τὰ πάτρια) and
consequently enjoyed a reputation of the highest esteem among the
whole nation; they were personally courageous in defending the laws
against Herod's clear violation—placing a golden eagle atop the sanctuary (1.648–650; 2.5–6). Although Josephus's characterization leads
those of us with concordances to suspect that he understood the pop-

ular teachers to have been Pharisees,[21] he again fails to convey any such connection to his Roman audience (who therefore could not have known it). He will not include moral courage among the traits of his Pharisees.

A similar case concerns two leaders of the people whom Josephus admires for their indignation against the Zealots' atrocities, and their opposition to the Zealots' appointment of an illegitimate high priest (4.159–160):

> For those among them [sc. ὁ δῆμος] with a reputation for excelling (οἱ προύχειν αὐτῶν δοκοῦντες),[22] Gorion son of Joseph and Symeon son of Gamaliel, kept exhorting both the gathered assemblies and each individual in private consultation that it was time to exact vengeance from the wreckers of freedom and to purge those who were polluting the sanctuary; the most eminent of the chief priests, Jesus son of Gamalas and Ananus son of Ananus, while castigating the populace for lethargy, in the meetings, roused them against the Zealots.

This cooperative venture is presented in an intriguing manner: some very popular teachers, with rhetorical skill and special access to individuals as well as groups, join the chief priests in trying to calm the masses. One of the two men named is none other than Simon son of Gamaliel, whom Josephus will describe in a later work as a leading Pharisee (*Life* 190–91), and his illustrious family is well known from other sources (Acts 5:34; 22:3; *m. Sotah* 9.15 et passim). Josephus must have known that Simon was a Pharisee, but again he chose not to reveal this to his audience—just where he is praising the man's behavior without demurral. When he later decides to label Simon a Pharisee, in the *Life*, the context will be very different and harshly critical (see below).

Thus, Pharisees hardly appear in Josephus's *War*, though for the historian they have a tantalizing presence behind the scenes. A dispassionate observer might have related much more than Josephus does: he seems to forgo every opportunity to say more than is required for a coherent story, in which the Pharisees feature mainly for their negative (antiroyal, antiaristocratic) traits. Although *War* is filled with digressions of various kinds (note especially the lengthy celebration of the Essenes in 2.119–161, as well as the topographic and geographic excursuses), the Pharisees are not a group on which he cares to lavish attention. What he chooses to disclose about them to his audience is rather one-sided and derogatory: they latch on to the powerful in order to cause trouble for the nation, though their influence *must* be reckoned with.

In the *Judean Antiquities*

Whereas the *War*, written in the darkest days of postwar Rome, tried to portray the admirable Judean character in and through an account of the war's origin and course, Josephus's magnum opus, published about fifteen years later (93/94 CE; cf. *Ant.* 20.267), takes advantage of the additional time and space to explore Judean culture on a larger canvas, in particular the constitution (πολιτεία) of the Judean people (1.5, 10).[23] A nation's mode of governance was generally considered an expression of its character: people get the constitution they deserve.[24] This axiom stood in some tension with the recognition that constitutions change over time, from monarchy to aristocracy or oligarchy to some form of "democracy" and back again, as also with discussions of the optimal constitution,[25] which presupposed that peoples had an element of choice in their mode of governance. Rome itself had famously emerged from ancient kingship through the "mixed constitution" of the Republic to the current *principate*—a de facto monarchy, though crucially not yet called kingship in Rome itself. Although Roman authors seem to have largely given up the sort of abstract constitutional discussions that Herodotus, Plato, Aristotle, and Polybius had indulged (but note Cicero's *Republic* and *Laws*), Josephus's younger contemporary Tacitus reveals the ongoing concern in elite circles with relations between a *princeps* (or emperor) and an aristocratic Senate.[26] All tied up in that discussion was the question of true *Roman* character. Contemporary Greek writers also devoted considerable attention to the problem of local constitutions and aristocracies in the context of a Roman superpower.[27]

In his *Antiquities* as in his *War*, Josephus shows himself fully aware of such questions (e.g., What sort of "freedom" should nations desire—untrammeled or conditioned by political necessity?), which had become pressing among Roman and Greek elites, especially in the waning years of Domitian's reign, when Josephus was writing. His detailed portrait of the Judean constitution and the vicissitudes through which it had passed reveals abundant parallels with the Roman experience, which have been examined in detail elsewhere.[28] Crucially, both nations decisively reject kingship, as the inevitable precursor of tyranny, and Josephus is vocal in his insistence that the Judean constitution is aristocratic-senatorial.[29] The nation is properly run, its ancient laws preserved and rightly administered, by people like his good self: the hereditary priests, who have always constituted—already in the time of Moses and Joshua!—the governing council or Senate (βουλή, γερουσία).[30] The essay known as *Against Apion* (2.145–196) will develop in moving, idealized terms this image of a hereditary priestly college under the orchestration of the high priest as the most sublime form of constitution imaginable.

In the *Antiquities*, which assumes the obligations of history writing, the picture is messier than in the *Apion*. After the principle of aristocratic governance has been enunciated by Moses and his successors, the masses nonetheless clamor for a king (*Ant.* 6.33–64). It was widely acknowledged in Josephus's day that the masses of all nations preferred powerful monarchs—even if these vaulted to power through bloody coups—to the vagaries, corruptions, and inefficiencies of aristocratic bodies.[31] Kings tended to be more solicitous of their popular base: they found it much easier to keep the tiny aristocracy in check than to deal with overwhelming popular animosity. So, although Josephus's Samuel forcefully advocates aristocracy (*Ant.* 6.36), he must yield to popular demands; and the era of kings, with its inevitable decline into tyranny, begins (6.262–268). The destruction of the First Temple and with it the monarchy of Judah clears the way for a new aristocracy (11.111), but this is undone by the later Hasmoneans (13.300), who once again assume the diadem and quickly lead the nation to disaster. Roman intervention restores the aristocracy yet again (14.91), though this gives way to the Herodian monarchy—as a function of the Roman civil wars, which featured their own (Roman) contenders for supreme power. In the symmetrical structure of the *Antiquities*, the two great king-tyrants of Judean history, Saul (book 6) and Herod (15–17), occupy corresponding positions.

Josephus devotes a surprising amount of the *Antiquities*' final quarter to parallel constitutional crises: the Judean problem of finding a successor to King Herod and the Roman succession woes following Tiberius and Gaius Caligula.[32] For the Judeans, after the debacle of

Herod's son Archelaus, matters are resolved for some decades when a native aristocracy (including our author) is allowed to govern Jerusalem under the remote supervision of a respectable, senior-senatorial Roman legate based in Syria, to which province Judea is joined (17.227, 355; 18.1–3; contrast *War* 2.117). This arrangement preserves Judea's native traditions and collective local leadership while at the same time securing the people's freedom—that is, *freedom from native tyrants*. When the *Antiquities* closes, however, this arrangement is beginning to unravel with the first rumblings of civil strife (e.g., 20.205–214), which the *War* has described in detail. The Roman constitutional crisis, for its part, is *never* resolved, leaving open the possibility that the *Antiquities* functions in part as a critique of Rome's increasingly monarchical governance in Josephus's time.[33]

Because some of the Pharisee passages of the *Antiquities* develop items mentioned briefly in the *War*, we need to bear in mind that Josephus frequently recounts in *Ant.* 13–20 and *Life* stories already told in *War* 1–2. In virtually every case of overlap, however, the retelling is markedly different. He is a zealous practitioner of what ancient rhetoricians called *paraphrasis* or *metaphrasis* (παράφρασις, μετάφρασις)—changing the form of expression while retaining the same thoughts (Theon, *Prog.* 62–64, 107–110; Quintilian, *Inst.* 1.9.2; 10.5.4–11)—and he certainly pushes the limits of "retaining the same thoughts." Changes run from the trivial to the comprehensive: dates, relative chronology, locations, dramatis personae and their motives, details of scene, and numbers.[34] Given Josephus's demonstrable freedom in retelling stories, and in view of parallel phenomena in other contemporary literature from the gospels to Plutarch,[35] efforts to explain such changes programmatically—with reference to putative shifts of historiographical outlook, religious affiliation, moral convictions, personal allegiances, or political necessity[36] —seem a waste of scholarly energy. If Josephus changes more or less every story that he retells, we have more to do with the rhetoricized mentality mentioned above than with a new ideological program.[37] He seems to abhor the prospect of boring his audience, at least by retelling stories verbatim, and so he experiments with new literary and rhetorical configurations, careless of the historical casualties.

Typical of such changes is our first encounter with the Pharisees in *Antiquities*, in a brief statement about the three schools' views on

Fate (13.171–173). Even this concise presentation is irreconcilable with the sketch of the schools' positions on Fate in *War* 2.162–166, though Josephus refers the audience to the earlier work for details (see chapter 2).

In assessing the role of Pharisees in *Antiquities*, we must again maintain some narrative perspective. They do not figure in the main part of the work (books 1–12), which outlines the origins of the aristocratic constitution, its contents, and early changes. This absence cannot be merely a function of chronology—that is, because there were no Pharisees in the time of Moses or Saul—for Josephus does not hesitate to mention other current issues or figures in the course of his biblical paraphrase (e.g., 1.94, 108, 151; 4.146, 161; 7.101; 8.46). If he had any interest in doing so, he might well have extolled the Pharisees' legal tradition, or at least mentioned it, while elaborating on Moses' laws and constitution, which he elaborates precisely because they form the *living code* by which Judeans of his day govern their lives. His failure to mention Pharisees or the other schools in the core of the *Antiquities* is noteworthy.

After the brief philosophical aside of *Ant.* 13.171–173 just mentioned, the Pharisees next appear in connection with the greatest crisis in the Hasmonean dynasty: the transition from the illustrious period of "senatorial" self-rule, led by the virtuous hero and high priest John Hyrcanus, to the destructive monarchy-cum-tyranny initiated by his short-lived and tragically self-absorbed son, Aristobulus I (13.301). Like *War*, *Antiquities* presents Hyrcanus I as the Hasmonean ruler most favored by God, the apogee of the glorious family (13.300). Following a detailed account of his exploits (e.g., successful manipulation of Seleucid rivals, Judaization of Idumea, renewed treaty with Rome, destruction of Samaria), Josephus tells a story with no parallel in *War*, but one that helps explain the mysterious "growth" of the Pharisees alongside Queen Alexandra in *War*, as well as the Pharisees' behavior toward Alexander's friends as recounted in the earlier work. Yet the new episode has a ripple effect on the whole Hasmonean story, changing its contours in significant ways.

The scene is a banquet, to which Hyrcanus invites "the Pharisees" (all of them?) because, our author notes, the virtuous high priest was one of their students (13.289). Because they "practiced philosophy" (see chapter 2), and because he wished to live a just life, which training in philosophy should produce, he invited them to offer criticism of anything untoward in his behavior (13.290). They all praised his conduct, but a certain Eleazar, also present at the dinner, boldly demanded that he relinquish the high priesthood on the ground—a false rumor, Josephus claims—that his mother had been a captive, and so presumably raped (13.290–292). At this, *all* the Pharisees become indignant (13.292). Josephus does not say that Eleazar was a Pharisee, and we soon learn that non-Pharisees were also present. For certain Sadducees in attendance cleverly exploit this opportunity by asking the Pharisees what punishment they deem suitable for the offending man. When the Pharisees call for (merely) severe corporal punishment—lashes and chains, rather than death (Josephus notes editorially that the Pharisees by nature take a moderate position in relation to punishments [φύσει πρὸς τὰς κολάσεις ἐπιεικῶς ἔχουσιν; 13.294])—the Sadducees are able to convince Hyrcanus that their rivals *approved* of the man's outburst, in spite of what our narrator plainly says. The Sadducees' device for proving this, asking the Pharisees how they would punish Eleazar's outburst, after their unanimous condemnation of his words, appears to confirm that Eleazar was not one of their school.

In any case, the Sadducees' gambit is successful and leads the prince to abandon his affiliation with the Pharisees. His new embrace of the Sadducees is dramatic: it results in his "dissolving the legal precepts established by [the Pharisees] among the populace" (τὰ τε ὑπ' αὐτόν κατασταθέντα νόμιμα τῷ δημῷ καταλύσαι) *and punishing those who continued to observe them* (13.296). This radical turn sets off a public uproar.

A Roman audience might reasonably wonder what practical difference the change would make, and so Josephus hastens to explain that the Pharisees follow a special set of legal prescriptions (νόμιμα) "from a succession of fathers" (ἐκ πατέρων διαδοχῆς) *in addition to the laws of Moses*—the latter being famously followed by all Judeans; the preceding narrative of *Ant.* 1–12 has explored this common constitution. This supplementary legal tradition is rejected by the Sadducees, who recognize only the "inscribed" laws (of Moses).

Although this passage has been adduced as evidence for the rabbinic doctrine of תורה שבעל־פה,[38] or "Oral Law," Josephus does not mention such a thing. He first characterizes the Pharisees' special ordinances as "not written *in the laws of Moses*" (ἅπερ οὐκ ἀναγέγραπται ἐν τοῖς Μωυσέως νόμοις), attributing them rather to a succession of fathers. Although the following phrase, describing the Sadducees' view (viz., "it is necessary to respect only those ordinances that are inscribed," ἐκεῖνα νόμιμα δεῖν ἡγεῖσθαι τὰ γεγραμμένα), might appear to suggest an oral law, if it were wrenched from its context, in context it plainly assumes the qualification in the preceding part of the sentence: the laws of Moses are contrasted not with *oral laws*, but with laws "from a tradition of the fathers."[39] The Sadducees reject the Pharisees' tradition not because no one thought to write it down somewhere, but because it is not part of Moses' constitution, which has been elaborated at great length. Josephus has never mentioned such a special tradition before, and he will not do so again outside of *Ant.* 18.12 (recalling this passage in a later description of the Pharisees). When he speaks elsewhere of "the ancestral customs or laws" (οἱ νόμοι, τὰ νόμιμα, τὰ πάτρια [ἔθη, νόμιμα]), as he frequently does, he plainly means the laws followed by all Judeans, given by the lawgiver Moses, which he compares and contrasts to the laws of other nations.[40]

In this explanatory gloss on the Pharisees' tradition from "a succession of fathers," Josephus also makes explicit what the audience might already have inferred from his brief notices on Pharisees in the *War*: whereas the Sadducean base is tiny and found only among the elite, the Pharisees have the support of the masses (13.298). This point will turn up repeatedly in the few lines devoted to Pharisees in the sequel. If Josephus wishes to leave any image of the Pharisees with his audience, it is that they have popular access, support, and influence.

Hyrcanus's break with the Pharisees and Josephus's explanation about their influence receive space at this juncture, apparently, because they are programmatic for the balance of the Hasmonean story. This rift was not merely a personal one: it had ramifications for the constitution of the state because it meant the dissolution of the Pharisaic jurisprudence that had been in place throughout Hyrcanus's reign. Although Josephus does not pause to explain why Pharisees were so popular, or the nature of their legal precepts, he does drop an important hint in the banquet story: their penal code was milder. He will confirm this point in a later note to the effect that Ananus II, the high priest who executed Jesus' brother James, was a Sadducee and *therefore* "savage" in punishment (*Ant.* 20.199).

A brief historical reflection may illuminate Josephus's biases. At face value, biblical law seems raw, unsystematic, and potentially severe. The various apodictic and casuistic declarations throughout the Pentateuch offer little by way of a real jurisprudence: rights of the accused, a system of courts, principles of advocacy, or procedures for hearing and sentencing.[41] Any self-consciously interpretative tradition, therefore, simply as a function of articulating general legal principles and procedures of prosecution and defense—such as that a certain number of judges must hear cases, with advocates for the accused— would tend to mitigate the Law's potential severity. Perusal of the Mishnah-tractate Sanhedrin, which reflects one kind of elaboration, suggests that few accused persons could face capital punishment under its provisions. The school of Hillel, represented in the first century by Rabban Gamaliel and his son Simon, is particularly associated with leniency.[42] Without assuming any identification between Pharisees and tannaitic rabbis, we may still observe that Josephus's remarks on the leniency of Pharisaic jurisprudence seem antecedently plausible.[43] Anyone who wished to live by the Law had necessarily to interpret it, to resolve its various prescriptions in some way.[44] If the Sadducees took a deliberately minimalist approach, rejecting any explicit body of authoritative legal principle or case law, claiming to observe *only* what the Law specified, it stands to reason that their interpretations would be more severe. If so, it is telling that our aristocratic reporter has no interest in explaining the popular Pharisees' legal principles, much less in embracing or celebrating them.

But why would the Sadducees prescind so pointedly from the Pharisees' tradition, or apparently any other body of ordinances not in the laws? And how might Josephus's audiences have understood this difference? In premodern societies—recall even Dickens's *Tale of Two Cities*—it was inevitably the poor who faced the full force of severe laws. Aristocrats might worry with cause about committing political offenses, but they were largely immune from the legal cares of the masses because of their social position, connections, and pre-sumed noble character. *They* were not likely to be accused of theft or assault. In Rome, the position of city prefect (*praefectus urbis*) was created under Augustus mainly to deal with the petty crimes of slaves and freedmen, not the nobles.[45] The elite author Josephus himself claims to *favor* severity in law, even celebrating this as a virtue of the

Judean constitution in contrast to the ever-softening codes of other peoples: whereas others wiggle out of their laws' ancient demands, Judean law *still* exacts the death penalty for adultery and rebellious children (*Ant.* 1.22; 4.244–253; 4.260–264; *Apion* 2.276). It is understandable that in such contexts the masses would favor the party with the more lenient penal code, but the aristocrat Josephus takes a typically piteous view of the masses: the rabble or the mob, who are fickle and vulnerable to persuasion by almost anyone.[46] He explains only, and rather dryly, that Hyrcanus's break with the Pharisees and his dissolution of their jurisprudence resulted in popular opposition to the Hasmonean dynasty.

His disdain for the Pharisees, no matter how popular they may be (or *because* of a popularity he considers unfortunate), becomes obvious in the way he frames the story of their rupture with Hyrcanus. The episode itself, which is borrowed from oral or written tradition,[47] seems neutral or sympathetic toward the Pharisees. It leaves the affiliation of the troublemaker Eleazar uncertain, while emphasizing that the Pharisees as a group praise John's conduct, and *all* of them (πάντες) condemn Eleazar for his impertinence (13.292). It is the *Sadducees* who mischievously implicate all Pharisees in Eleazar's views (13.293). On the basis of the account itself, therefore, it makes little sense for Josephus to blame the Pharisees. Yet he chooses to introduce the episode with a remarkable indictment: popular envy of the Hasmoneans' success was expressed *through the Pharisees in particular*; they were *especially hostile* to him, and "they have such influence with the rabble [note present tense] that even if they say something against a king and a high priest, they are immediately trusted" (τοσαύτην δὲ ἔχουσι τὴν ἰσχὺν παρὰ τῷ πλήθει, ὡς καὶ κατὰ βασιλέως τι λέγοντες καὶ κατ᾽ ἀρχιερέως εὐθὺς πιστεύεσθαι; 13.288). The animus of our aristocratic author apparently leads him to stretch his material out of shape. Since he will use very similar language when characterizing the Pharisees in later episodes, he seems to have an *idée fixe* concerning the group—no matter what the evidence he can adduce.

Although Pharisees do not appear by name in Josephus's account of Alexander Jannaeus's actions (as also in *War*), the king's deathbed scene in *Antiquities* clarifies for the first time that much popular resentment toward him has been generated by this popular group:

Alexander realized that "he had collided with the nation because of these men" (13.402). If we read the Hasmonean narrative as a unity, this makes sense. The Pharisees and their legal system have been repudiated by Hyrcanus I, so that under Aristobulus I and Jannaeus the milder and more popular legal regimen has remained outlawed. This has been a factor in the masses' hatred for Jannaeus, to which the king has responded with extreme brutality. Only by such a coherent reading can we explain why Jannaeus now advises his wife, who is terrified at the volume of popular hatred she is about to inherit, to grant power once again to the Pharisees—in an ostentatious manner. Invite them even to abuse my corpse, the wily politician declares, for all they really desire is power, and if you give them this they will immediately turn sycophant and allow me a grand funeral (13.403)!

This hardheaded appraisal of "those *reputed to be* the most pious and most scrupulous about the laws" is patently disparaging, and yet Josephus as narrator does nothing to ameliorate it. On the contrary, Jannaeus's cynical prediction is borne out by the story: invited to share power with the widow queen, the Pharisees give her husband a magnificent send-off, proclaiming what a just or righteous (δίκαιος) king they have lost, and exploiting their demagogic talents to move the masses to mourning (13.405–406).

The fuller narrative here vis-à-vis *War* thus creates a significantly different atmosphere. Whereas the Pharisees' growth appeared sudden in the *War*, minimally explained as if the pious Alexandra had simply been duped by an unscrupulous band, in the *Antiquities* the Pharisees' popular influence has been a central concern to the Hasmoneans all along. The queen becomes a fellow schemer in the calculus advanced by her dying husband in order to help quiet the people.

Josephus makes the connection with the earlier rupture explicit: Queen Alexandra "directed the rabble (τὸ πλῆθος) to submit to the Pharisees, and *she reestablished whatever legal measures* (νόμιμα) the Pharisees had introduced in keeping with the 'fatherly tradition,' *which her father-in-law Hyrcanus had dissolved* (ὁ πενθερὸς αὐτῆς κατέλυσεν)" (13.408). This note signals the complete reformation of the legal code to the status quo ante. Josephus further strengthens the connection with Hyrcanus's break from the Pharisees by reprising his editorial observation of *Ant.* 13.288, now placing it on the lips of dying Jannaeus (13.401–402):

. . . for he declared that these men had vast influence (δύνασθαι δὲ πολύ) among the Judeans, both to harm those they hated and to benefit those in the position of friends (βλάψαι τε μισοῦντας καὶ φίλους διακειμένους ὠφελῆσαι). "For they are especially believed among the rabble concerning those about whom they say something harsh, even if they do so from envy (κἂν φθονῶσιν)." Indeed, he said that he had collided with the nation because of these men, who had been outrageously treated by him.

Though Jannaeus confesses his crimes here, strangely none of it helps the Pharisees' image. Josephus is too artful a writer to work with simple oppositions, such that where he is critical of a certain ruler, opponents of that ruler must therefore receive his favor. There are many shades of virtue in his narrative: a Jannaeus or a Herod can have serious flaws but still receive due credit for certain virtues, or sympathy for his plight. Yet the Pharisees consistently come across as unprincipled demagogues.

With more space available in the generous proportions of *Antiquities*, Josephus can elaborate on the Pharisees' disruptive activities under Alexandra, crisply asserted in the *War*. Now we are told that they personally cut the throats of numerous powerful men who had advised King Jannaeus in his actions against opponents, systematically hunting down one after the other (13.410). This purge by Pharisees causes a counterreaction amongst the elite (οἱ δυνατοί), who evidently include the military leaders: these rally around the queen's younger son, Aristobulus II, whose intercession wins them at least the privilege to live securely in royal fortresses, safe from the Pharisees (13.415). Significantly, Aristobulus himself makes a bid for supreme power *because* he foresees that if his ineffectual older brother, Hyrcanus II, should assume the throne, the family would be powerless to stop continued control by the Pharisees (13.423; cf. 408). But Hyrcanus II, who is already high priest, will *indeed* become king (14.4), leaving the audience to infer that Alexandra's reinstatement of Pharisaic jurisprudence remains in force.

Given all of the nuanced exchanges that Josephus crafts in describing Aristobulus II—he with the friends of his father, Alexandra with her Pharisaic cohort—one might wonder whether the narrator really intends us to sympathize with the influential men now hiding from the Pharisees, for had they not overseen the brutal regime under

Jannaeus? Josephus removes any doubt about this, however, in his obituary on the queen in *Ant.* 13.430–432. With the omniscient narrator's voice, he adopts the sentiments expressed by Aristobulus II (13.416–417): Alexandra should not have insisted on ruling, out of a personal power-lust (ἐπιθυμία) inappropriate to a woman, while she had grown sons more suited to the task (13.431). Without mincing words, Josephus declares that Alexandra's rule caused *all* of the disasters and catastrophes that would subsequently fall on the Hasmonean house and lead to its loss of authority (13.432). This happened because she preferred present power to what was noble or right (οὔτε καλοῦ οὔτε δικαίου) and because she invited into government *those who held her house in contempt* (namely, the Pharisees), leaving the leadership bereft of anyone who was concerned for its well-being (τὴν ἀρχὴν ἔρημον τῶν προκηδομένων ποιησαμένη; 13.432). Again, Alexandra's rapprochement with the Pharisees allegedly had lasting ill effects.

Among the seven remaining volumes of the *Antiquities*, the Pharisees appear as narrative actors in only three further episodes. These occur during the administration of Herod's father, Antipater, the Roman-appointed governor while Hyrcanus II is high priest and quasi-royal *ethnarch*; under King Herod himself; and then at the annexation of Judea to Roman Syria.

The first episode shows Hyrcanus II in the unenviable position of trying to assert the national laws, in his responsibility as ostensible ruler, yet thoroughly intimidated by an already tyrannical young Herod (14.165). At first persuaded by the Judean elders and the mothers of Herod's victims that Herod has been practicing extrajudicial killing, Hyrcanus summons him to trial (14.164–169). Upon Herod's arrival, however, the council serving as Hyrcanus's court is intimidated into silence. Only one Samaias (not further identified here) rises fearlessly to declare that if the council does not punish Herod, the young man will come back to punish them. Josephus adds that this indeed happened later, and paradoxically only Samaias would be spared—for he, realizing that they could not avoid divine retribution, would advise the people of Jerusalem to admit Herod as king (14.172–176).

When we next hear of Samaias, though, the story has changed. At 15.3 we learn that he is *the student* of a Pharisee named Pollion,[48] and that it was *the Pharisee* who had made the original prediction about

Herod! Herod's gentleness toward the Pharisees, even when they resist his directives, is spelled out again at 15.370. Leaving aside the manuscript problems at 15.3, we may observe two important points here. First, in Josephus's narrative, Pharisees remain an influential part of the vestigial Hasmonean (effectively Roman-Herodian) government under Hyrcanus II—just as Aristobulus II had feared while his mother, Alexandra, lived. Even Herod, once he is in ostensibly absolute control of Jerusalem, thinks it necessary to persuade (συμπείϑω) Pollion and Samaias to take an oath of allegiance to him along with their fellow Pharisees (15.370).

Second, however, Josephus continues to avoid clarifying the situation for his audience. While he is describing Samaias's personal virtues as a fearless speaker, he declines to identify him as a Pharisee; this identification he reserves for a later setting that highlights Pollion's advice to admit Herod to Jerusalem. There, however, the bold and accurate prediction (now by Pollion) of future punishment is recalled as a mere afterthought (15.4). Our aristocratic author shows no interest in explaining the continuing presence and popularity of the Pharisees. He certainly does not advertise them, though *we who are interested* can discover from such incidental clues that they remain in the background of his narrative.

Josephus's failure to identify Samaias as a Pharisee while he is admiring his actions may be comparable to the cases of the teachers in *War* 1 and the popular orators of *War* 4 (above), as well as another instance in *Ant.* 20. That is the story of the high priest Ananus II's execution of James, brother of Jesus, which I have already mentioned. Josephus attributes the action by Ananus (whom *War* 4.319–325 lauds for his behavior during the early phase of the revolt) to the high priest's alleged youthful rashness and daring, as well as to his membership in the school of the Sadducees, "who are savage in contrast to all other Judeans when it comes to trials, *as we have already explained*"—an apparent reference to the banquet with Hyrcanus I, at *Ant.* 13.296. Josephus goes on to say that "those in the city who were *reputed to be most fair-minded and most precise in relation to the laws*" (ὅσοι ἐδόκουν ἐπιεικέστατοι τῶν κατὰ τὴν πόλιν εἶναι καί περί τοὺς νόμους ἀκριβεῖς), both phrases recalling earlier descriptions of the Pharisees, were deeply offended by the Sadducean high priest's action.

Whereas scholars often suggest that Josephus *means to indicate* Pharisees here, I think that we must respect his compositional choices. He could not plausibly expect his audience—any audience other than scholars with concordances—to read "Pharisees" here in *Ant.* 20, without his spelling it out. Although his narrative might lead *us* to expect that he was *thinking* of Pharisees when he described these popular non-Sadducean exegetes, yet again he opts not to apply the label "Pharisee" just where he is praising the behavior of the group in question.

In the next *Antiquities* episode in which the Pharisees appear, Josephus is openly hostile. After Herod has killed his sons Alexander and Aristobulus (ca. 8 BCE), another son, Antipater, rises to prominence while the beleaguered king, exhausted by intrigues, begins to fail (*Ant.* 17.18, 32). Antipater reportedly gains control over Herod's brother Pheroras, partly by influencing that man's wife and her relatives (17.34). Immune to Antipater's designs, however, was the king's sister Salome. She dutifully reported the conspiracy to her brother, though he was reluctant to believe her exaggerated accounts (17.38–40). So, a stalemate for the moment.

At this sensitive juncture, the Pharisees appear as the decisive factor in prompting the king to action against all these conspirators. In the crabbed Greek that Josephus adopts throughout *Ant.* 17–19:

> There was also a certain faction of the Judean people priding itself on great precision in the ancestral heritage (ἐπ᾽ ἐξακριβώσει . . . τοῦ πατρίου) and, of the laws, pretending (προσποιουμένων) [regard] for those things in which the Deity rejoices. To them the female bloc was submissive. Called Pharisees, they were quite capable of issuing predictions for the king's benefit, and yet they were plainly bent on combating and also harming him (εἰς τὸ πολεμεῖν τε καὶ βλάπτειν). (*Ant.* 17.41)

This editorial perspective, with its reference to harming those in power, recalls *Ant.* 13.288, 401, and continues the well-established theme of the Pharisees' contentious disposition.

Josephus's attempt to justify such strong language in this case borders on the bizarre. First, when some six thousand Pharisees reportedly refuse to take an oath of loyalty to Herod—whether this is the same event as in 15.370 is debatable—the troublesome wife of Pheroras pays their fine (*Ant.* 17.42). In gratitude, they manufacture predictions not for the king's benefit, but for *her* pleasure. They emptily promise that Herod and his descendants will forfeit the rule, which will fall to Pheroras and to her (17.43). Josephus claims that Herod heard about this quid pro quo through his sister Salome, and now was enraged enough to execute those Pharisees who were to blame, as well as a eunuch named Bagoas and one Karos, the former object of the king's desire (17.44). Most interestingly, the king also executed "the entire element of his domestic staff that had supported *what the Pharisee was saying*" (πᾶν ὃ τι τοῦ οἰκείου συνειστήκει οἷς ὁ Φαρισαῖος ἔλεγεν). The rhetorical personification in "what the Pharisee was saying" is especially striking because at *Ant.* 18.17 (below) Josephus will use the same unusual turn of phrase.

He explains that Bagoas was executed because the eunuch foolishly embraced the Pharisees' prediction that *he* would be enabled to marry and father children, and that *he* would be called father of a future king-messiah figure (17.45). The prediction to Bagoas makes clear the vacuous and promiscuous nature of Pharisaic prediction in Josephus's hands: they happily stir up those who should be most loyal to the king with promises of incredible, mutually exclusive, outcomes. The effect on the audience of Josephus's portrait here would presumably have been much like that created by his younger contemporary Juvenal when he spoke about Jewish fortune-tellers in Rome (*Sat.* 6.546): "a Judean will tell you dreams of any kind you please for the minutest of coins." Tacitus comments more generally, in the context of imperial court astrologers, about the deceptions of those who bring the science into disrepute by describing what they do not know (*Ann.* 6.22).

For all its interest and oddness, this remarkable story of Pharisaic prediction is dropped quickly and Josephus returns to the main narrative. The Pharisee incident seems to be mentioned mainly because it provides the trigger for Herod to act more forcefully against Pheroras's wife, who is the main character in this part of the story (*Ant.* 17.46–51). This episode in turn opens the way for Pheroras's retirement from Jerusalem, and death, as well as Antipater's momentary rise and protracted, desperate fall (17.52–145, 184–187).

To give a sense of proportion: many individual speeches in that ensuing narrative are longer than this paragraph mentioning the Pharisees. It is in the psychological analysis of motives, virtues, and vices, to which speeches lend themselves, that Josephus's main interest as a historian lies. His description of the Pharisees is by contrast vague and impersonal: individual Pharisees are not named; they act as a sort of nefarious Greek chorus, en bloc and without benefiting from rounded portraiture.

Here again, Josephus passes up the opportunity to answer inevitable audience questions about the Pharisees: Where does their ability to predict come from? Why is Josephus so cynical about this ability? In what sense could they have manufactured predictions "for the king"? It is clear only, because he emphasizes the point, that the Pharisees' popularity keeps them near the center of power and able to cause serious problems for those who govern, no matter how ostensibly powerful the rulers may be. In Herod's case, the Pharisees are entirely on the wrong side, with the impious son Antipater, the disloyal brother Pheroras, his scheming wife, and their conspiratorial bloc.

Although the final discussion of the Pharisees in *Antiquities* (18.12–15, 17) has mainly to do with their philosophical tenets in relation to those of the other schools, and so will be considered in chapter 2, three statements in and around that passage complete *Antiquities*'s treatment of the group.

First, as at *War* 2.118–119, Josephus's introduction of the three schools is prompted by his mention of Judas the Galilean (here Gaulanite), who initiated a popular rebellion when Judea came under direct Roman rule: in *War* as a province in its own right, here as a territory annexed to the province of Syria (17.355; 18.1–2). With extra space at his disposal, Josephus dilates on the novelty, strangeness, and inescapably dangerous outcome of Judas's absolute conception of "freedom" (ἐλευθερία): this notion sowed the seed of every kind of misery, starting a movement that would spin out of control, sparking civil war and the murder of fellow citizens, especially those of high standing, and resulting in the destruction of the Temple (18.4–9). Curiously, though, Josephus now explains the popular appeal of Judas's message by explaining that the rebel leader won the support of a certain Saddok, a *Pharisee* (18.4): together they appealed to the nation (τὸ ἔθνος), and the people (οἱ ἄνθρωποι) heard what they said with pleasure (18.4, 6). Josephus reinforces this link among rebels, the masses, and Pharisees at the end of the school passage, where he asserts that the ironically described "Fourth Philosophy"—this is not a *real* group, who called themselves by such a name (see chapter 2)—

agrees with the Pharisees in everything *except* the rebels' more absolute devotion to freedom (ἐλευθερία, 18.23).

Against the old scholarly view that this connection with the Pharisees contradicts War's isolation of Judas's rebel philosophy and newly dignifies the rebels,[49] Josephus's language implies the opposite relationship: it is rather the Pharisees who are *tainted* by their new association with rebels. Josephus's rejection of rebellion and *stasis* does not abate in his later writings: he writes as the aristocrat who, like Plutarch, is ever alert to prevent civil strife and unrest (cf. *Life* 17–22 et passim). *Ant.* 18.3–11 is even more adamant than *War* 2.118 in repudiating Judas and his heirs. Therefore, Josephus's new identification of a prominent Pharisee at the source of Judas's rebel program can work only to associate the Pharisee with despicable behavior. Saddok exploits the Pharisees' popularity with the masses, which is by now familiar to the attentive reader, to stir up the always pliable rabble for unworthy goals. Significantly, it is a chief priest, Joazar son of Boethus, who must work to pacify the people against such rebel leaders (18.3)—*here* is the representative of Josephus's values in the narrative—though Joazar's statesmanlike work is largely undone by Judas and the Pharisee.

Second, at *Ant.* 18.15 Josephus remarks that "because of these [their philosophical views], they happen to be extremely persuasive among the citizens (τοῖς τε δήμοις πιθανώτατοι τυγχάνουσιν), and divine matters—prayers and sacred rites—happen to be performed according to the manner of interpretation of those men (ὁπόσα θεῖα . . . ποιήσεως ἐξηγήσει τῇ ἐκείνων τυγχάνουσιν πρασσόμενα)." Next comes a difficult clause about the cities' testifying to the Pharisees' potency (or virtue, ἀρετή) by pursuing, in both their regimen of life and their speech, the way that prevails over all things.[50] Note the double "happen to be," which applies more than the usual amount of distance between author and object of discussion: Josephus conspicuously withholds any personal investment in the group's popularity.

Third, any doubt about Josephus's evaluation of the Pharisees' popularity is removed by his further notice concerning the Sadducees. Recalling his earlier observation about the small elite base of the Sadducean school (13.297–298), he now remarks:

> This [Sadducean] doctrine has reached only a few, albeit those who are highest in standing (τοὺς μέντοι πρώτους τοῖς ἀξιώμασι), and almost nothing is accomplished by them. For whenever they enter into governing positions (ὁπότε γὰρ ἐπ᾽ ἀρχὰς παρέλθοιεν), though unwillingly and under compulsion, they therefore [i.e., as a condition of public office] side with *what the Pharisee says* (προσχωροῦσι δ᾽ οὖν οἷς ὁ Φαρισαῖος λέγει), because otherwise they would not be tolerable[51] to the masses.

Although one or more of Josephus's references to the Pharisees, especially the more overtly hostile ones, have traditionally been ascribed wholesale to his undigested sources,[52] it is clear now that he is responsible for all of them. The striking similarity of language between this relatively neutral school passage and the preceding episode (in speaking of "what the Pharisee says/said"), along with the conspicuous share of both passages in the peculiar language experiments of *Ant.* 17–19, and then the links between these passages and *Ant.* 13 (e.g., the Pharisees' determination to "harm" rulers and their influence with the masses), show that we are dealing with a consistent authorial hand—no matter how varied Josephus's underlying sources may (admittedly) have been.

To summarize thus far: Josephus features the Pharisees only briefly in the *Antiquities*, and only after the main story (*Ant.* 1–12) is finished, in his narrative of the Hasmonean dynasty's decline. There he sets up a situation that will apparently endure until his own time; namely, although John Hyrcanus threw over the Pharisees' legal prescriptions (νόμιμα) in a fit of pique engineered by the Sadducees, the popular animosity that this generated, which reached its height under Alexander Jannaeus, could not be sustained. Alexander's widow restored Pharisaic jurisprudence, and the group's hold on popular opinion has remained formidable ever since. Even King Herod could only execute a few of their leaders when they created serious difficulties for him; he had still to deal with the group, and by the time his son Archelaus was removed in 6 CE at least one of their leaders was ready to exploit their influence again for rebellious ends. Tellingly, Josephus's summary comments on the Pharisees' popularity are in the present tense, including his description of the Judean philosophies at 18.12–22. He gives no narrative reason to think that the Pharisees' influence waned appreciably through the period of his history.

What must impress the reader interested in the Pharisees is Josephus's lack of interest in the group: *we* must go looking for Pharisees in Josephus. He does not highlight their presence or answer obvious questions about their leaders, activities, legal principles, group structure, social composition, relationship to the ancient priestly senate (as Josephus presents it), entry requirements, claims to special powers, or popular appeal (contrast the Essenes of *War* 2.119–161). That they are able to manipulate the masses for whatever end they wish, and often use this influence to harm the eminent—this is enough of an indictment for our aristocratic author. Apparently, he fails to answer obvious questions because he disdains the group and regrets their popularity, like that of the countless other demagogues in his stories (e.g., *Ant.* 4.14–20, 37; 7.194–196; 18.3–6; 20.160, 167, 172; cf. Sallust, *Cat.* 37.3).

In the *Life of Josephus*

Josephus's autobiography adds a fascinating personal dimension to the picture of the Pharisees developed in his two historical accounts. This one-volume work is an appendix to the magnum opus, a celebration of the author's self-acclaimed virtue (*Life* 430) elaborated against the standard ancient rhetorical criteria of noble ancestry (1–6), youthful exploits (7–19), military and political achievements (20–413), and benefactions given and received (414–430).

This self-introduction first mentions the Pharisees quite neutrally in conjunction with the other two schools (*Life* 10), only to say that in his youthful quest for philosophical training, self-improvement, and toughening (ἐμπειρία, σκληραγωγέω, πονέω), Josephus did not find any of these groups satisfactory; he refers the audience to his "frequent" (πολλάκις) earlier discussions for details. Fleeting though it is, this constitutes the final "school passage" (see chapter 2). For present purposes, however, we must deal with Josephus's claim that his lack of satisfaction with the schools led to his retreat to the desert to live with the extreme ascetic Bannus for three years. It was this experience that finally answered his philosophical yearning (ἐπιθυμία, *Life* 11).

What comes next (*Life* 12) requires careful attention, for English-speaking scholars have almost always taken it to mean that Josephus either joined or wished to claim that he joined the Pharisees. Yet such a claim at this point would make no sense of the immediate context, where he has found the Pharisees and the other schools insufficient; only Bannus (whose ardent student, ζηλωτής, he became) has shown him the way. A sudden lurch toward the Pharisees would, moreover, come as a shock after Josephus's few and disdainful references to the group throughout *War* and *Antiquities*. And most important, such a reading cannot be sustained by the sentence in question (*Life* 12).[53]

At the age of eighteen to nineteen, when his Roman contemporaries would have completed their higher studies in philosophy and/or rhetoric and begun to take up responsibilities in public life, this is precisely what Josephus claims to have done. He returned to the *polis* of Jerusalem (εἰς τὴν πόλιν ὑπέστρεφον) and, "being now in my nineteenth year, I began to involve myself in public life" (ἠρξάμην πολιτεύεσθαι). Although in Jewish and Christian literature the middle verb πολιτεύομαι can have the meaning "govern *oneself*" or simply "behave," it is clear from the immediate context here (preceded by *polis* and followed by his diplomatic trip to Rome; *Life* 13), from Josephus's usage of this verb elsewhere,[54] and from the closest parallels in contemporary Greek authors of Josephus's class (Plutarch, *Mor.* 798d–e, 800d, 800f, 813a, 804f), that he is describing his embarkation on *adult political life*, something expected of all members of his class. Thus, "[after three years with Bannus], I returned to the city. Being now in my nineteenth year, I began to involve myself in *polis*-affairs [or 'become politically involved']."

But that is not the end of the sentence. Dependent clauses add: "following after [or "following the authority of"] the school of the Pharisees (τῇ Φαρισαίων αἱρέσει κατακολουθῶν), which is rather like the one called Stoic among the Greeks." Clues about the intended sense of the first and crucial subclause include the following: First, the κατα-prefix on the main participle suggests "following *after* someone's lead or following an authority"—rather than joining or becoming zealously involved with a group (contrast Josephus's experience as Bannus's *devotee*, ζηλωτής). Second, since this clause is dependent, Josephus's entry into *polis* life provides the basis or reason for his following the lead of the Pharisaic school. Third, we have seen that it is a minor theme of the later *Antiquities*, however grudgingly divulged, that the Pharisees and their program hold complete sway

over the masses and therefore over political life. At *Ant.* 18.15, 17
Josephus has said pointedly that whenever anyone comes into public
office, he must—*even if unwillingly* and by necessity—side with "what
the Pharisee says." Just as his mention of the three groups at *Life* 10
refers the audience to earlier discussions, so also this notice about following the lead of the Pharisees in public life reminds the audience of
what he has said just three volumes earlier. If even Sadducees coming
into office must support the Pharisees' agenda, Josephus's observation
that his own entry into public life required following the Pharisees'
prescriptions does not imply any closer affiliation with the group than
the Sadducees had.

Like *War* 2.411 (above), *Life* 21 makes only passing mention of the
"principal men of the Pharisees" (τοῖς πρώτοις τῶν Φαρισαίων)
alongside the chief priests, in the coalition trying to manage the
clamor for war. Even more pointedly than *War*, *Antiquities* has insisted
that the hereditary priesthood and its leaders constitute the proper ruling elite of Judea.[55] Since the time of Queen Alexandra, although
Josephus has preferred to speak of hereditary aristocratic-priestly leadership, he has grudgingly acknowledged that the immensely popular
lay movement of the Pharisees must always be reckoned with by those
in power. Since Alexandra, at least, leading Pharisees have been able
to exert considerable influence on those in power; we glimpse their
presence in the highest councils under Hyrcanus II and Herod. As the
war against Rome takes shape, *War* 2.411 and *Life* 21 furnish hints of
what seems a closer, more deliberate and diplomatic alliance: leading
Pharisees are specifically identified in the ruling coalition. This makes
sense in Josephus's narrative world: in the national emergency created
by popular and demagogic demands for rebellion, the chief priests
need the influence of prominent Pharisees to help calm the masses.[56]

The next cluster of references to the Pharisees, which is the last
among Josephus's known writings, may illustrate the sort of relationship between chief priests and leading Pharisees that he has suggested
until now. Observe even here, during the early revolt, the divide that
remains between even the most eminent Pharisees and the chief
priests. This narrative section confirms that Josephus does not number
himself among the Pharisees. Some of his most determined adversaries, however, are Pharisees or close friends of Pharisaic leaders.
Josephus's career as Galilean governor-commander has placed him in

roughly the same position—that is, a successful leader undermined by jealous Pharisees—that he has repeatedly described as the typical situation for other rulers.

By *Life* 189–191, Josephus's Galilean command is facing increasingly energetic opposition from John son of Levi, from Gischala in Upper Galilee, who will eventually become one of the two chief "tyrants" of Jerusalem in the war against Rome. The strongman of his hometown, John at first tried to restrain his fellow Gischalans from revolt against Rome (*Life* 43), much as Josephus tried to restrain the Jerusalemites (17), but John became outraged when nearby Greek cities launched attacks. These led him to fortify the walls of Gischala against future incursions (44–45). This taste of militancy, Josephus implies, paved the way for John's later emergence as rebel leader—solely, we are told, for the sake of personal power (*Life* 70). This change brings John into direct confrontation with Josephus, who has been sent by the Jerusalem council to govern all Galilee (*Life* 29, 62). The main expression of this conflict before the passage that interests us has been John's effort to inspire the major city of Tiberias to defect from Josephus (*Life* 84–104, 123); John had considerable success there, as also at Gabara (123–124).

The next we hear of John (*Life* 189–190), he is pulling out all the stops to contrive Josephus's removal from Galilee. He sends his brother Simon to Jerusalem, to ask the renowned Pharisee Simon son of Gamaliel to persuade the council to demand Josephus's recall. Josephus introduces this famous Pharisee in grand style: Simon son of Gamaliel was from Jerusalem (the greatest stage for any Judean aristocrat: cf. *Life* 7), of illustrious ancestry, and from the school of the Pharisees, "who have the reputation of excelling others in their precision with respect to the ancestral ordinances" (οἳ περὶ τὰ πάτρια νόμιμα δοκοῦσιν τῶν ἄλλων ἀκριβείᾳ διαφέρειν)—Josephus's standard description of the group (cf. *War* 1.110, 2.162; *Ant.* 17.41). But we have seen that such an introduction does not indicate his favor, for in the other cases the ensuing narrative undermines the Pharisees' reputation. So it is here. Although he acknowledges that Simon was a most capable politician (191), Josephus continues: "Being a long-time friend and associate of John [son of Levi], however, he was then at odds with me." The following account describes the eminent

Pharisee's efforts to have Josephus removed, in terms that amount to a serious indictment of Simon's character.

Simon first tries a direct approach: attempting to persuade the chief priests Ananus and Jesus, who evidently retain executive authority even in the wartime coalition, to replace Josephus with John. But these priest-aristocrats, whose wisdom and probity Josephus had celebrated at length in the *War* (4.314–325), dismiss the leading Pharisee's ploy as both unjust ("the action of sordid men"), since Josephus was an able and well-regarded leader, and impracticable— for the same reason (*Life* 194). When Simon fails with this forthright approach, he confidently promises John's men that he will nonetheless achieve his aim: not to worry! His new, secret plan is for John's brother Simon to bribe Ananus and his group with gifts (*Life* 195–196). This tactic succeeds, alas, so that even the chief priests now become complicit in seeking Josephus's ouster from Galilee.

Needless to say, we might easily entertain doubts that the story represents historical reality: it plainly serves Josephus's interests to protest the chief priests' unwillingness to countenance the dishonorable process pushed by Simon. Yet we are trying to *interpret the narrative*, and Josephus's portrait is clear enough: this famous Pharisee cannot direct policy himself, but must *try* to use his influence (deriving from the Pharisees' popular prestige) to convince the chief priests, the most powerful leaders, of his views. Remarkably, Simon is the only named Pharisee in Josephus besides Pollion (Samaias may be judged a Pharisee by association), and he benefits from a touch of Josephus's typical effort at rounded characterization of individuals. In spite of Simon's otherwise admirable qualities, his close friendship with Josephus's adversary John drives the prominent Pharisee to move against Josephus, even though the undertaking is patently unjust. Simon corrupts even the chief priests.

As a result of the head Pharisee's machinations, three other prominent Pharisees are recruited to act unjustly against Josephus. It is not clear whether the chief priests themselves comply with the whole appeal and agree to replace Josephus with John (*Life* 190), because they send a four-man delegation with armed escort to bring Josephus back dead or alive, and apparently to provide a substitute collective government (202). This delegation is on John's side (203), to be sure, but the council has sent four men in order to persuade the Galileans that somewhere among them will be found whatever qualities they admire in Josephus(!). In Josephus's sardonic enunciation of the comparison, we learn that all four are Jerusalemites like him; all are highly trained in the laws, as he is; and two of the men are priests, one of chief-priestly ancestry, thus more than compensating for the one priest Josephus (198). They ostensibly have the better of Josephus on all fronts.

Yet, before he spells out this comparison, Josephus has also informed us that *three* of the four men—two of the laymen and the ordinary priest—were Pharisees (197). Significantly, Josephus does *not* adduce membership in the Pharisees as a point on which this group can be favorably compared with him. He does not say: "They were three Pharisees in contrast to me, only one," though he does compare himself with them in ancestry, origin, and legal training. Why, then, does he identify the three as Pharisees? Obvious reasons are (a) to explain how they all had a claim to education in the laws, given that two of them were not priests as he was (note the reminder that Pharisees enjoy a reputation for legal precision); and (b) to connect them with the leading Pharisee Simon, as opponents of the legitimate leadership of Josephus. His own position, by contrast, is connected with the nation's revered chief-priestly leadership under Ananus and Jesus (cf. *War* 2.563–568).

Once they arrive in Galilee to execute their mission, the behavior of this mostly Pharisaic delegation confirms—and helps explain— Josephus's consistent portrait of the popular school as hostile toward the nation's priestly/royal elite. Josephus portrays the actions of their leader Jonathan, one of the three Pharisees (*Life* 197), as particularly reprehensible. He and his group lie and deceive, slander, engage in violence (202, 216–218, 237–238, 274–275, 280–282, 290–292), and even abuse the sacred Law (290–291) in their single-minded pursuit of Josephus—in spite of our author's self-reported uprightness and popular affection. Another Pharisee, Ananias, Josephus describes as "a vile and wretched man" (πονηρὸς ἀνὴρ καὶ κακοῦργος; 290). In the end, Josephus's divine protection and resourcefulness, complemented by the grateful devotion of the Galilean masses whom he has managed to win over by every possible stratagem, enable him to defeat the Pharisaic delegation and send them back cowering to

Jerusalem (332). The council eventually dismisses the attempt of Simon the Pharisee to remove him (311–312).

CONCLUSIONS AND COROLLARIES

Although my work since the published revision of my 1986 dissertation on Josephus's Pharisees (1991) has taken many new directions in exploring his rich and vast corpus—his rhetoric, the structure of his works, his audiences in Flavian Rome—these new perspectives mainly confirm my original sense of the way the Pharisees function in these narratives. Now more than ever I would stress how marginal the Pharisees were to Josephus's principal concerns: they do not appear in the main stretches of *War* (3–7) or *Antiquities* (1–12), or in the summation of the Judean constitution we know as *Against Apion*. Throughout his writings run many coherent lines of interest, concerning the character and constitution of the nation, and his own character as the Judeans' shining representative. To these interests, the Pharisees are more or less irrelevant.

Josephus assumes the position of a proud aristocrat, the spokesman for his nation after the disastrous war against Rome. He writes with sophistication, showing deep familiarity with the repertoire of elite political themes that was cultivated from Polybius through Diodorus and Dionysius to Josephus's contemporaries Plutarch and Dio Chrysostom, and on to Cassius Dio.[57] This is a world of discourse in which men of breeding and culture (παιδεία) are the only ones capable of leading their people with wisdom and restraint, resisting the reckless, emotional impulses that drive lesser characters: the mobs, youthful hotheads, barbarians, and women. The job of the statesman (ὁ πολιτικός) is to protect the body politic from disturbance (στάσις), and Josephus's accounts are filled with the measures taken by his people's rightful leaders, from Moses and Aaron to himself and his aristocratic peers, to ensure the peaceful life of their citizens under the world's finest constitution.

In this narrative world, Pharisees appear as an occasional aggravation to the elite. They are a nonaristocratic group with enormous popular support and a perverse willingness to use that support demagogically, even on a whim, to stir up the masses against duly constituted authority—Hasmonean, Herodian, or Josephan. In *War*, the moment of Pharisaic ascendancy is the reign of Queen Alexandra, though Josephus says as little as possible about the group after that. In *Antiquities*, Alexandra's reign is again a watershed, but now Josephus offers a backstory, the preceding interval from Hyrcanus I to Alexandra, as a failed experiment in governance *without* the popular Pharisaic jurisprudence. Ever since Alexandra's reign, therefore— under Herod's government and through the first century until Josephus's time—the Pharisaic program has again been in place: one who accepts office must listen to "what the Pharisee says." We do not know, because Josephus does not explain, how his audience should have understood the mechanisms of Pharisaic influence, let alone the content of the Pharisees' jurisprudence or how it was implemented. He seems uninterested in moving from complaint to clarification. During the earliest phase of the war, at least, leading Pharisees are more deliberately welcomed by the priestly elite, as the latter use the popular party's influence to try to stem the tide of rebellion. Still, the priests retain control through the early phases, before the "tyrants" seize power following the murder of Ananus and Jesus (*War* 4.314–344). (N.b.: I continue to speak of the story, not of the real past.)

Conspicuously, to us who are able to scrutinize the narratives (a pleasure not shared by many ancients), Josephus passes up many opportunities to mention Pharisees, especially in contexts that might have elicited his praise (e.g., the anti-Herodian teachers, Simon son of Gamaliel in *War*, Samaias, or those who opposed James's execution by a young Ananus II). Nor does he elucidate their group structure or explain their popularity. We must connect some dots if we wish to understand. When he does mention them as players in the narrative it is usually to express annoyance at their influence and tactics. He retains the last word over his own mischievous Pharisee opponents in Galilee, however, in the self-aggrandizing *Life*.

Although my aim has been to construct an adequate synthesis of the Pharisees *in Josephus's narratives*, if this interpretation is successful it obviously undermines hypotheses about the historical Pharisees that are based on significantly different interpretations of Josephus. For example, an influential theory has held that the Pharisees attained some power under Alexandra, then faded from political life under Herod (or earlier), to resurface only on the eve of revolt in 66. This theory depends on the impression that Josephus's narratives (viewed rather positivistically, as if proportional records of events) highlight the Pharisees only at these points.[58] But we have seen that Josephus portrays the reestablishment of Pharisaic jurisprudence under Alexandra as a necessary condition of governance, which has persevered until his own time.[59] The theory of decline and reawakening is usually tied up with a surprisingly durable claim about Josephus's biases: that in the *Antiquities* and *Life* he aligns himself with the Pharisees and advocates their (post-70, Yavnean) program—and so the fuller attention to Pharisees in *Antiquities* amounts to his endorsement of them as a new post-70 elite.[60] If the foregoing analysis is even roughly correct, however, such an assessment of Josephus's aims is impossible. He limits discussion of the Pharisees and generally ignores them (even in the *Antiquities*), only occasionally exposing them as examples of the demagogic type that he and his audiences deplore.

It is worth stressing that Josephus was a uniquely positioned reporter who may have had special reasons for disliking such a group as the Pharisees. His aristocratic biases should therefore be checked, if possible, by sources closer to the popular levels where the Pharisees found their supporters. Even Luke-Acts, the two-volume work that is among the best (in literary terms) produced by the first generations of Jesus's followers, is more favorably disposed toward the Pharisees than is our elite priest. That work will be examined in chapter 4 of this volume.

One might object that excision of the school passages for separate treatment (chapter 2) skews the picture. There, if anywhere, Josephus achieves near neutrality in portraying the Pharisees; his comments about *their beliefs* are not hostile. And surely the school passages are also part of the narratives. This is all true. My proleptic response is that, while it has seemed efficient to accept the editor's proposal to reserve the school passages for a separate chapter, I have also commented here on the *narrative function* of those passages. They do not significantly alter the general portrait I have described. As we shall see in the next chapter, brief comparative sketches of two or three philosophical schools, especially on the central question of Fate and free will, were a literary convention, found also in other elite writers. They are too schematic to be of much use, and of doubtful accuracy or consistency anyway: they seem to function mainly as display pieces for the author's erudition, providing a narrative diversion. They also place him above the fray of interschool squabbles, showing that he is not bound by a particular doctrine. It was a natural option for some-one of Josephus's presumed stature to describe in brief compass the range of Judean philosophical schools. Yet just as Cicero can be harshly critical of Epicureans in other contexts (*Pis.* 68–72) and still grant them a neutral place in his philosophical spectrum, so, too, the fact that Josephus can epitomize the Judean schools in such set pieces without overt judgment says nothing about his view of the Pharisees. That view is more likely to emerge in his narrative descriptions and moral evaluations of this group alone, which we have examined here.

CHAPTER 2

JOSEPHUS'S PHARISEES: THE PHILOSOPHY

Steve Mason

In the previous chapter, treating the roles of the Pharisees in Josephus's narratives, we noticed a telling remark. In his story about the banquet at which John Hyrcanus repudiated the Pharisees and their legal code, Josephus observes that the Hasmonean prince, then a student of the Pharisees, was intent on living a just (δίκαιος) life and on pleasing both God and his beloved teachers (*Ant.* 13.289). Josephus offers the editorial explanation, "for the Pharisees philosophize" or "practice philosophy" (οἱ γὰρ Φαρισαῖοι φιλοσοφοῦσιν).

Two points impress one immediately. First, the offhand way in which he makes this remark suggests that Josephus's understanding of Pharisees as philosophers is ingrained, and not an artificial construction for the "school passages" (below). It is hardly plausible, in spite of long-standing scholarly assumptions,[1] that Josephus's sources are responsible for portraying as philosophical schools what were really "religious" groups, and that Josephus took over these sources in spite of his own knowledge and perspective. Those passages fit too well with his general and even incidental tendencies as an author.[2] Second, the explanation itself—Hyrcanus asks Pharisees for help in his pursuit of just or righteous living and in pleasing God *because they are philosophers*—drives home signal differences between modern philosophy and ancient φιλοσοφία or *philosophia*. (Can we imagine inviting the local philosophy department to dinner, to solicit their help in our quest to live a decent, God-fearing life?) Yet "justice" in all its valences—political, criminal, moral, religious—was indeed a central preoccupation of ancient philosophy.[3]

These observations already generate three tasks for this chapter, which attempts an adequate contextual reading of Josephus's Pharisees *as a philosophical school*, namely: to survey the landscape of "philosophy" in Josephus's time; to investigate the larger uses of philosophy in Josephus's works; and then to examine the school passages in those works.

By "school passages," I mean those in which Josephus compares the Pharisees, Sadducees, and Essenes as philosophical schools, with generic terms such as αἱρέσεις (schools) or φιλοσοφίαι (philosophies). There are four such units in Josephus—*War* 2.119-66; *Ant.* 13.171–173; 18.12–22; *Life* 10–11. Although the last of these adds little, referring the audience to "frequent" earlier discussions (see chapter 1), we shall consider it briefly by way of introduction to the theme. Another pericope, the "footnote" to Hyrcanus's banquet story (*Ant.* 13.297–298), nearly qualifies as a school passage, since it explains important differences between Pharisees and Sadducees; but we have examined that clarification as a narrative product in chapter 1. Here, then, we shall focus on the three school passages of *War* and *Antiquities*, after initial sketches of philosophy in the Roman world and in Josephus. Although our focus will remain on the Pharisees, we cannot avoid considering this school in relation to the other two, because Josephus does so.

PHILOSOPHY IN ROMAN ANTIQUITY: SOME SALIENT FEATURES

I have noted that Josephus's brief reference to the three schools in his autobiography adds little *content* to our picture of their respective systems. Yet the passage does highlight an essential difference between ancient and modern categories, for it describes his youthful experimentation with the Judean schools in terms of discipline, training, and even toughening (*Life* 10–11):

> When I was about sixteen years old, I chose to gain expertise (or experience, ἐμπειρία) in the philosophical schools[4] among us. There are three of these: the first, Pharisees; the second, Sadducees; and the third, Essenes, as we have often said. . . . *So I toughened myself* and, *after considerable effort* (σκληραγωγήσας οὖν ἐμαυτὸν καὶ πολλὰ πονηθείς), passed through the three of them.

Hellenistic *philosophia*, "devotion to wisdom," was oriented toward discovering happiness or well-being (εὐδαιμονία, *felicitas*). But if one's well-being were to be secure, everyone realized, it needed to be grounded in reality.[5] Philosophy's great advantage was that it claimed to offer a safe, solid, reliable way to live one's life, neither reacting impulsively to circumstances, animal-like, nor resorting to unreasonable, superstitious coping mechanisms (Plutarch, *Mor.* 171e; Epictetus, *Diatr.* 3.23.34; Lucian, *Menipp.* 4; Justin, *Dial.* 8.1). As Aristotle's vast legacy illustrates, the ancient precursors of most modern disciplines, from physics, biology, mathematics, agriculture, and astronomy to political science, anthropology, psychology, language, and theology—not to mention metaphysics, logic, and ethics—fell within the purview of the ancient philosopher. At least by the Hellenistic and Roman periods, however, the more abstract aspects of philosophy had become harnessed to the quest for the virtuous and therefore happy life. In spite of the many differences among Greek philosophical schools concerning the workings of the cosmos, they largely agreed on the moral disposition that should result from philosophical study.

The label "philosopher" came, therefore, to describe a type of person: a man (usually) committed to simplicity of lifestyle, rational mastery of the desires and fears that drove other mortals, and direct, frank speech. Already for Cicero in the first century BCE, the categories "philosophy" and "philosopher" were more important than the doctrines of any particular school: he speaks of worthily undertaking the heavy obligations of "philosophy" (e.g., *Pis.* 58, 71–72; *Phil.* 8.10; *Red. sen.* 13). This recognition of philosophy as a pursuit requiring one's whole commitment appears frequently in authors of the first and second centuries CE.[6] Probably the closest ancient parallel to modern evangelical conversion was the sharp turn to embrace the philosophical life, with its rejection of worldly values.[7] The existence of identifiable persons who had taken up such a life explains how Vespasian and Domitian could expel "philosophers" from Rome—when the latter had begun to express with annoying candor their views on the developing monarchy (Dio 66.13.1; Suetonius, *Dom.* 10). And it was not Stoicism or Epicureanism but *philosophy* that would later console Marcus Aurelius (*Med.* 1.6, 14, 16–17, etc.) and Boethius (*Cons.* 1.3.2, 5; 4.1.1).

One index to the comprehensive claims of ancient philosophy is what we might call the "Spartanization" of philosophy's image, by which I mean a resort to the highly disciplined community of classical Sparta as a paradigm of moral and political philosophy. We see a

glimpse of this already in Xenophon's (fourth-century BCE) portrait of
the Spartan leader Agesilaus, alongside whom he had fought. Observe
his points of emphasis (*Ages.* 8.8; 9.5; 10.1–2):

> No doubt it is thought to be noble to build walls impregnable to the
> enemy. But I at least judge it nobler to prepare for the *impregnability of
> one's own soul*: in the face of material gain and pleasures and fear [as did
> Agesilaus]. . . . It brought him great cheer also that he knew he was
> able to *adjust ungrudgingly* to the way the gods had arranged things,
> whereas he saw the *other man fleeing the heat and fleeing the cold alike*, through
> weakness of soul, emulating a life not of good men but of the weakest
> animals . . . . The man who is foremost in *endurance* (καρτερία) when the
> time comes for labor, in *valor* when it is a contest of courage, in *wisdom*
> when it is a matter of counsel: this, it seems to me at least, may rightly
> be considered *an excellent man* overall. . . . The virtue of Agesilaus
> appears to me to be a model for those wishing to cultivate manly excel-
> lence (καλὸν ἂν μοι δοκεῖ εἶναι ἡ Ἀγησιλάου ἀρετὴ παράδειγμα
> γενέσθαι τοῖς ἀνδραγαθίαν ἀσκεῖν βουλομένοις).

Tellingly, Xenophon's description elsewhere of the philosopher
Socrates' virtues hardly differs from this: philosophy enabled him to
be a master of endurance in all seasons and situations (*Mem.* 1.2.1;
cf. 2.1.20; 3.1.6), always able to control his passions, following a
tough regimen (*Mem.* 1.3.5), relentlessly training his body and rejecting all forms of luxury and softness (*Mem.* 1.2.1–4). He lived in
extreme simplicity, eating and drinking only the minimum necessary,
and fleeing sexual temptation along with other harmful pleasures
(*Mem.* 1.3.5–15). Well-trained soldiers, such as Agesilaus, thus often
possessed the virtues that philosophy aspired to inculcate by other
means.

Later Cynics, Stoics, and others found the characteristics of classical Sparta's adult males—rigorous training, simplicity of diet and
lifestyle, disregard for marriage and family, communal male solidarity,
rugged adaptability to all hardships, disdain for conventional goods,
keen sense of personal honor at all costs, and unflinching courage in
the face of pain and death; stripped, as necessary, of objectionably
bellicose traits (Plato, *Leg.* 626c–d; Aristotle, *Pol.* 1333b)—the living
enactment of their philosophical aspirations (cf. Plutarch, *Lyc.*
31.1–2).[8] Roman moralists, too, found the Spartiate model singularly
appealing and so exempted Spartans from their typical characterization of Greeks as effeminate, preening windbags. Old Sparta,

notwithstanding its subsequent decline, seemed a model of Cato the Elder's Roman virtues enacted through the male elite of a whole society.[9] Polybius discussed Spartan-Roman parallels, Poseidonius speculated about genetic links between Spartans and Romans, and the Hasmoneans played up a genetic connection with Sparta.

Sparta was so attractive because it was a basic goal of ancient philosophical training to make the practitioner impervious to physical hardship, weakness, and desire, to the emotions and human suffering (two senses of τὰ πάθη). Many philosophers, including Seneca's teacher Attalus, prescribed harsh physical regimens with respect to food, drink, and sex; he even required his students to sit on hard seats (Seneca, *Ep.* 108.14).[10] Though possibly exaggerating, Lucian's *Nigrinus* observes that students of philosophy are commonly subjected by their teachers to whips, knives, and cold baths, in order to produce toughness and insusceptibility to pain (στέρρον καὶ ἀπαθές); students often expire, he claims, from the physical exertions required by other philosophers (*Nigr.* 28). At *Nigrinus* 27 he seems to quote a slogan about philosophical training, "with many compulsions and efforts" (πολλαὶς ἀνάγκαις καὶ πόνοις), which as it happens closely matches Josephus's language above. The final test of all this training, and so of one's worth as a philosopher, was the ability to face death itself with equanimity (e.g., Epictetus, *Diatr.* 3.26.11–14, 21–39).

Significantly, the only other occurrence in Josephus of the verb σκληραγωγέω, which he uses to describe his "toughening" through philosophy, concerns his Pythagorean-like Daniel and friends, who observe a vegetarian diet in Babylon (*Ant.* 10.190). Josephus claims that these young men thereby avoided making their bodies soft (μαλακώτερα). He has said nothing so explicit about such tough training elsewhere in his descriptions of the Judean schools, though his Pharisees (*Ant.* 18.12) and especially Essenes (*War* 2.122–123; *Ant.* 18.20) reportedly practice the simple life, avoiding luxury and softness.

The tendency that we have observed in the Roman period toward eclecticism among philosophers[11] was mirrored and facilitated by standard assumptions about the education of aristocrats. These men were cultivated to be all-around leaders, ready to meet any public need that might arise: as orators, lawyers and magistrates, governors, generals, landowners, priests, historians, poets, and philosophers. In the mix of training needed to produce members of the elite, Plutarch comments on the importance of philosophical education (*Mor.* 10.8a–b):

> One must try, then, as well as one can, both to take part in public life (τὰ κοινὰ πράττειν), and to lay hold of philosophy [note the generic category] so far as the opportunity is granted. Such was the life of Pericles as a public man (ἐπολιτεύσατο) [same verb as in Josephus in *Life* 12; cf. chapter 1].

Cicero's intensive youthful training among several philosophical schools (*Fam.* 13.1.2; *Fin.* 1.16; *Brut.* 89.306–91.316), an exercise thought to instill the Roman-elite virtue of *humanitas*,[12] had become a model of liberal education. Going the round of the philosophies to gain breadth and perspective may not have been possible or desirable for everyone, but it was a typical course for certain determined young men of means (Lucian, *Menipp.* 4–5; Justin, *Dial.* 2; Galen, *De anim. pecc. dign. cur.* 5.102). Such worldly cultivation in all the schools precluded any gauche or possibly dangerous devotion to a single ideology: as Ramsay MacMullen observes,[13] "Specialization in one school . . . belonged to pedants, not to gentlemen." Both the quest itself and the folly of embracing any single school's doctrines were satirized, two generations after Josephus, by Lucian in his *Philosophies for Sale*.[14] Thus, Josephus's determination to equip himself by training in the several Judean schools, in preparation for a public career, was a familiar experience in the Roman world.

Inevitably, to put it another way, philosophical perspectives became another element of the juggernaut of *rhetoric*. Whereas the principles of rhetoric had once fallen under the polymath-philosopher's scrutiny,[15] by Josephus's time philosophical themes had long since been fully incorporated under the mandate of rhetoric. Expertise in rhetoric was the ultimate goal and highest good of elite education in the Hellenistic-Roman world,[16] and the first-century rhetor Aelius Theon complains that too many students approach it without even a modicum of training in philosophy (59.1–7):

> The ancient rhetoricians, and especially the most renowned, did not think that one should reach for any form of rhetoric before *touching on philosophy in some way* (πρὶν ἁμωσγέπως ἄψασθαι φιλοσοφίας), thereby being expanded with a breadth of intellect. Nowadays, by contrast, most people are so lacking in paying attention to such teachings that they rush into speaking without taking on board even much of what are called general studies.

So those who had some claim to philosophical training might understandably flaunt their credentials, as Josephus does (*Life* 10–12). Philosophical issues such as those described above had become for them, just like the historiographical principles originally designed by Thucydides and Polybius to *distinguish* history from rhetoric,[17] rhetorical commonplaces or *topoi* (*loci*): stock items in a speaker's or writer's repertoire, around which accrued standard techniques of elaboration, illustration, and evaluation.

Because elite students were trained by rhetoric to write and speak in all genres (cf. Theon, *Prog.* 60, 70), and because philosophy was part of the elite repertoire, a cultivated man should be able to speak of it knowledgeably but without unseemly devotion. An important part of rhetorical training was mastering different kinds of what were called *ekphraseis* (ἐκφράσεις): focused, vivid digressions on key persons, environmental conditions (geographic or climatic), battle preparations and scenes of conflict, or objects such as building structures (Theon, *Prog.* 118–120; Hermogenes, *Prog.* 10). Though not as common as these other forms of digression, the comparison of philosophical schools shares the essential requirements of *ekphrasis*: diversion from the main narrative to make vivid some particular issue, in language suited to the subject. Philosophical comparison is a kind of *ekphrasis* that includes within it a theoretical *thesis* (Theon, *Prog.* 120–123): it is a matter of abstract controversy not involving specific persons or circumstances. Thus, a smattering of philosophical understanding and especially a repertoire of philosophical anecdote were useful items in the speaker's or writer's arsenal.

Like other members of his class, Josephus employs philosophical language not as a specialist or devotee, but as a man of the world who took the harder path and immersed himself in philosophy—Judean and Greco-Roman—as part of his education. One upshot of this eclectic training was that authors who had enjoyed an aristocratic education felt comfortable tossing off the sort of philosophical discourse that Josephus writes for himself at Jotapata (*War* 3.361) or providing urbane asides for their audiences.

In particular, schematic comparisons of the various philosophical schools could be useful subjects for digression. Cicero, after his strenuous efforts to acquaint himself with Greek philosophy, describes the main Greek schools for his Roman audiences: Epicurean (*Fin.* 1–2),

Stoic (*Fin.* 3–4), and Platonist (*Fin.* 5). He could also range the schools along a spectrum according to their views on Fate (*Fat.* 39; cf. *Nat. d.* 1.1–2):

> It seems to me that, there being two opinions among the older philosophers, the one held by those who believed that everything occurred by Fate in such a way that Fate itself produced the force of necessity (this was the view of Democritus, Heraclitus, Empedocles and Aristotle), the other by those to whom it seemed that there were voluntary motions of the mind without Fate, Chrysippus wanted to strike a middle path, as an informal arbitrator. . . .

Among historians, Tacitus, while commenting on Tiberius's devotion to astrology, pauses to remark on the various philosophical approaches to the same questions (*Ann.* 6.22):

> Indeed, among the wisest of the ancients and among their schools you will find conflicting theories, many holding the conviction that the gods have no concern with the beginning or the end of our life, or, in short, with mankind at all; and that therefore sorrows are continually the lot of the good, happiness among the lesser sort. Others, by contrast, believe that, though there is a harmony between Fate and events, yet it is not dependent on wandering stars, but on primary elements and on a combination of natural causes. Still, they leave to us the choice of a way of life, maintaining that wherever the choice has been made there is a fixed order of consequences.

Like Cicero, Tacitus identifies the Fate/free will problem as fundamental: some deny that Fate determines human life at all; others find a certain (vaguely explained) symbiosis between Fate and events, while allowing freedom of human choice; most think that a person's future is astrologically fixed at birth (*Ann.* 6.22). Later, Galen the polymath-physician will routinely compare three or four schools on a given issue (*De anim. pecc. dign. cur.* 5.92, 102; *Hipp. Plat.* 7.7.22; *Ord. libr. eug.* 19.50.14), and Diogenes Laertius will plot the Greek schools along two lines of "succession" from ancient masters (1.13), or between the two poles of affirmative or dogmatic and negative or skeptical beliefs about the workings of the cosmos (1.16).[18] We have a parallel to this kind of comparison even from Greek India: when in the early second century BCE King Menander goes in search of a wise man to help resolve his doubts, his Greek entourage informs him that there are six philosophical schools in India, each with its own master (*Milindapanha* 1.11).[19]

This is all (perhaps disappointingly) similar to Josephus's comparisons of the Pharisees, Sadducees, and Essenes, which also hinge on
their views of Fate (below). In all of these texts, such summaries have
the effect of elevating the author as a man of broad philosophical
awareness far above the parochial views of any particular school. But
we should not expect much illumination from Josephus's learned
digressions, any more than we do from Tacitus's brief reflections on
the various approaches to Fate. Josephus's three-school schematics are
formulaic and, in relation to his larger narratives, of negligible size or
significance.

In sum, the broad values of philosophy had by Josephus's time
become fully assimilated to aristocratic Roman social values: personal
honor, courage, simplicity of life, incorruptibility, frankness, liberality,
mastery of the emotions by reason, imperviousness to the allure of
pleasure, and contempt for suffering and death. Only men of such
virtues (i.e., the elite) were thought capable of steering the ship of state
and preserving it from the impulses of the masses or from rogue demagogues. An author of Josephus's standing should know and be able to
explain the particular philosophical schools of his culture, yet with the
requisite detachment from any particular one. He might be excused if
during his idealistic youth he had indulged himself in philosophical
devotion (as he did).[20] Yet civic-*polis* life required him to lay aside such
indulgence. (See the analysis of *Life* 11–12 in chapter 1.)

GENERAL PHILOSOPHICAL CURRENTS IN JOSEPHUS

To provide some perspective for Josephus's three school passages, we
should first consider the broader philosophical themes that permeate
his writings. Judean culture had for a long time appeared to some outside observers as distinctively philosophical, because of its acceptance
of a single invisible God, its lack of regional temples and sacrifice, its
devotion to the study and interpretation of ancient texts, and the conspicuous daily regimen—in diet, calendar-based observance, and
social restraint—of its representatives (Theophrastus *ap.* Porphyry,
Abst. 2.26; Megasthenes *ap.* Clement of Alexandria, *Strom.* 1.15.72;
Diodorus Siculus, 40.3.4; Strabo, *Geogr.* 16.2.35; *Apion* 1.179).[21]
Tacitus, though no admirer of the Judeans in general, concedes the

philosophical character of their piety in contrast with that of the
Egyptians (*Hist.* 5.5):

> Egyptians worship many animals and made-up images, but Judeans
> *conceive* of one deity, and *with the mind* only (*Iudaei mente sola unumque
> numen intellegunt*). Those who fashion representations of a god from per-
> ishable materials in human form [they consider] impious, for that
> which is supreme and eternal is neither susceptible of imitation nor
> subject to decay. Therefore they do not allow any images to stand in
> their cities, much less in their temples: not for kings this flattery, nor for
> Caesars this honor.

Judean insight into the ineffable nature of the divine plainly commands Tacitus's respect. Corresponding to such admiration among
foreign observers—even if this was occasionally grudging—was a tendency among Greek-language Jewish-Judean writers from at least the
second century BCE to interpret their own tradition in philosophical
terms (Aristobulus *ap.* Eusebius, *Praep. ev.* 13.12.1, 4, 8; *The Letter of
Aristeas*; 4 Macc 1:1; 5:4, 8, 23; Philo passim). In considering this issue,
we must bear in mind that ancient writers did not have the option—
-open to us—of speaking about either *religion* or *Judaism*. Greek (as
Latin and Hebrew) lacked either a word or a concept matching our
post-Enlightenment category "religion"; therefore, there could be no
"Judaism" as such—and indeed there is no corresponding term in the
extensive writings of either Philo or Josephus.[22] What we consider religion was woven into many different categories of life (e.g., cult, politics, family life, sports, games, and theater). Prominent among these
categories, and one that included crucial aspects of modern religion
(viz., moral exhortation, exposition of texts concerning ultimate questions, an ethical system based thereon, and freely chosen adoption of
["conversion to"] that system), was *philosophia*. Josephus is among
those writers who vigorously promote the philosophical interpretation
of Judean culture.

Though present from the beginning of the *War*, this is clearest in
his later works. Josephus claims that, because the constitution of
Moses reflects natural law, anyone wishing to inquire more closely
into the basis of Judean law will find the exercise "highly philosophical" (*Ant.* 1.25). He laces the *Antiquities* with detours on geography,
ethnography, astronomy, mathematics, plant and animal life, historiography, language, and other such tools of the savant's trade. He crit-

icizes the Epicureans, a favorite target of Roman authors too,[23] for believing that the divine does not interfere in human affairs (*Ant.* 10.277; 19.28), and he occasionally shares his own editorial observations on Fate and free will, the soul, and the afterlife (1.85; 6.3; 8.146; 12.282, 304; 19.325). He separately compares Essenes with Pythagoreans (*Ant.* 15.371) and Pharisees with Stoics (*Life* 12). In keeping with his claim to be thoroughly trained in the "philosophy" of the Judeans' ancient books (*Apion* 1.54), he even asserts that the Judean law itself "philosophizes" on the vexed problem of Fate and free will (*Ant.* 16.398).

Particularly noteworthy is Josephus's emphasis on "happiness, well-being, prosperity" (εὐδαιμονία), a term whose importance to moral philosophy we have seen above. From the prologue onward, *Antiquities* insists that only the legal constitution bequeathed by Moses brings happiness (*Ant.* 1.14, 20). Josephus introduces this word some forty-seven times into his biblical paraphrase (*Ant.* 1–11), though it had not appeared at all in the other major effort to render the Bible in Greek, the Septuagint. What Moses received from God at Sinai promised, according to Josephus, "a happy life and an orderly constitution" (βίον . . . εὐδαίμονα καὶ πολιτείᾳ κόσμον; 3.84). The Judean nation is singularly happy (εὐδαίμων), Josephus's Balaam says, happier than all other nations (πάντων εὐδαιμονέστεροι τῶν ὑπὸ τὸν ἥλιον), because it alone has been granted God's watchful care (πρόνοια) as an eternal guide (4.114).[24] This related theme of God's watchful care, or providence, was a preoccupation of contemporary Stoicism (e.g., Epictetus, *Diatr.* 1.6, 16; 3.17). In a number of places Josephus more or less equates God with Providence, Fate (εἱμαρμένη), and even Fortune (τύχη).[25]

Accordingly, Josephus portrays key figures in early Judean history as philosophers. Following Seth's descendants, who discovered the orderly array of the heavenly bodies (*Ant.* 1.69), Abraham inferred from the irregularity of these bodies that there was one ultimate God (1.155–156). With the mind of a true philosopher, Abraham visited Egypt intending that "if he found it [what their priests said about the gods] superior, he would subscribe to it, or, if what he himself thought was found preferable, he would reorder their lives according to the more excellent way" (1.161). Anticipating Socrates, he employed a dialectical method to listen carefully to them, and then expose the vacuity of their arguments (1.166). So it happened that it was he who taught the elements of mathematics and science to the renowned Egyptians (1.167–168).

Moses, the peerless lawgiver, himself studied nature in order to achieve the proper foundation for his laws (*Ant.* 1.18–19, 34). Like Plato (*Rep.* 3.386–417), the Judean lawgiver rejected out of hand the unseemly "myths" about the gods (*Ant.* 1.22–24). His greatness of intellect and understanding were apparent even in childhood (2.229–230). He "surpassed in understanding all who ever lived, and used his insights in the best possible ways" (4.328).

King Solomon, for his part, "surpassed all the ancients, and suffered in no way by comparison even with the Egyptians, who are said to excel everyone in understanding; in fact, their intelligence was proven to be quite inferior to the king's" (*Ant.* 8.42). His knowledge covered not only the whole range of natural science—encompassing every creature in existence—but extended even to occult science: the techniques for expelling demons and effecting cures (8.44–49). These powers remain the unique legacy of the Judeans in Josephus's day (8.46). Josephus's Daniel is yet another kind of philosopher: he and his companions adopt a Pythagorean-like vegetarian diet, by which they keep their minds "pure and fresh for learning" (*Ant.* 10.193).[26]

It was apparently the philosophical character of the Judean laws, for Josephus, that facilitated the movement by other nationals to come and live under them—what we frame as "conversion." Josephus contrasts the Judeans' openness to receiving those who wish to come and live under their laws with Athenian and Spartan jealousy of their own respective citizenships (*Apion* 2.255–263). In his glowing account of the Adiabenian royal house's "having been brought over" (μετακεκομίσθαι) to the Judean laws and customs, he acknowledges that these laws were foreign, and this created great risk for the royals. Standard English translations, such as the Loeb's "Jewish religion" for τὰ Ἰουδαίων ἔθη (lit. "the customs of the Judeans"; *Ant.* 20.38) or "Judaism" for τὰ πάτρια τῶν Ἰουδαίων (lit. "the ancestral [laws, heritage] of the Judeans"; *Ant.* 20.41), disguise this ethnic-national context, replacing it with comfortably modern categories such as "religion" and "conversion." Yet Josephus stresses the "foreign and alien" character of Judean laws in relation to the Adiabenians (*Ant.* 20.39: ξένων καὶ ἀλλοτρίων ἐθῶν; cf. 20.47), and it was precisely this issue of foreignness that bothered his Roman contemporaries: Tacitus and Juvenal considered it impious for Romans to adopt foreign laws, because it meant abandoning their own ancestral traditions in the process (*Hist.* 5.4–5; Juvenal, *Sat.* 14). The anomie involved in adopting the laws of another *ethnos* is partly resolved in Josephus by resort to the Judean constitution's uniquely *philosophical* character, for one cannot be faulted for converting to the philosophical life. Josephus's Abraham provides the model of the missionary philosopher (above), and the whole discussion of comparative constitutions that Josephus hosts in *Apion* 2.146–196 is philosophical in nature.

In the *Judean War*, Josephus's first work, he exploits philosophical themes in a subtler way. Without much using the explicit language of philosophy, he nevertheless crafts two erudite speeches, for himself and Eleazar son of Yair, on life, death, morality, and suicide—with demonstrable debts to Plato (*War* 3.362–382; 7.341–388).[27] Throughout the entire *War* he drives home the Judean-philosophical virtues of courage, toughness, endurance, and contempt for suffering and death. But the most compellingly philosophical section of the work, and a primary contextual reference point for the Pharisees and Sadducees of the *War*, is Josephus's lengthy description of the Essenes in *War* 2.119–161.

Although there is much to say about *War*'s Essene passage, I wish to make only two points here. First, Josephus's Essenes exhibit the comprehensive life regimen of a philosophical school that we have now come to expect. In describing so many aspects of this school— initiation requirements and oaths, disciplinary and expulsion procedures, daily regimen, leadership structure, treatment of private property, sexual relations and attitude toward children, dress, dining and toilet habits, purity measures, objects of study, manner of worship, view of the soul and afterlife—Josephus gives us the clearest picture anywhere in his writings of a Judean "school." And it emerges that they live out the highest aspirations of philosophy in the Roman world. We considered above the Spartanization of Greco-Roman philosophy. Very much like the Spartiates, Essenes live their whole lives under the strictest discipline, avoiding even the use of oil in personal grooming (*War* 2.123; cf. Plutarch, *Mor.* 237a; *Lyc.* 16.6; *Ages.* 30.3), which is otherwise ubiquitous in the Greco-Roman world. They, too, remove women from their company, hold all possessions in

common, and share a common meal. They disdain equally the pleasures (2.122) and the terrors (2.152) that motivate most others.

Second, the Essene passage is a condensed version of Josephus's
claims about *all Judeans*. We see this partly in *War* 2.152–153, where
the Essenes display the same virtues of courage and toughness in the
face of torture that characterize Judeans throughout the work (2.60;
3.357, 475; 5.88, 458; 6.42; 7.406), but most clearly in a comparison
with the *Apion*. There, what Josephus has said about the Essenes in
War 2 is applied to all Judeans: *the whole nation* observes the laws with
the strictest discipline and solemnity, lives in utmost simplicity, values
virtue above all else, holds death in contempt (same phrases used as
for Essenes), and keeps women in their place. Sex, among Essenes
(*War* 2.161–162) as for all Judeans, is thus for procreative purposes
only, and not for pleasure.[28] It is conspicuous, in light of the discussion
above, that the *Apion* compares the Judeans favorably with the
Spartans, driving home the point that the glory days of that universally admired state are only a distant memory, whereas Judeans have
continued to practice these virtues for many centuries until the present, as the recent war has demonstrated (*Apion* 2.130, 172, 225–231,
259, 272–273). Josephus has entered the Judeans in the competition
for most philosophical nation.

The third-century Platonist philosopher Porphyry seems to have
seen these connections clearly. In the fourth book of his work *On
Abstinence* (from animal food), soon after discussing the Spartans
(4.3–5) he treats the Judeans (*Abst.* 4.11–14) as further models of a disciplined regimen. For evidence about the Judeans he devotes most of
his account to *War*'s Essene passage (4.11.3–13.10, almost verbatim),
although he claims to get his information from both *War* 2 and the
Apion. Since the *Apion* does not mention the Essenes, it appears that
Porphyry saw the striking similarities and so confused the Essene passage in *War* 2 with what Josephus ascribes to all Judeans in *Apion*, perhaps on the assumption that a whole nation could not sustain such a
disciplined regimen.

The school passages, to which we now turn, are therefore only one
example—a minor and perfunctory one—of the philosophical interests that run throughout Josephus's works. As an author he is much
more interested in those larger issues of moral character, in relation
to the Judeans as a people, than he is in the petty doctrinal differences

of the schools. When he fleetingly compares the schools' positions on Fate and the soul, he is only doing what a man of his education should be able to do: explain to foreign audiences that his people, too, have schools, with such and such views. But the result smacks of conventionalism and suitable vagueness. Josephus does not have Cicero's taste or patience for detailed philosophical analysis.

PHARISEES AMONG THE THREE JUDEAN SCHOOLS

Let us, then, consider in turn the three school passages identified above. Such an examination is more useful for understanding Josephus than for investigating the Pharisees: we shall find what seem to be quite deliberate inconsistencies. At the very least, however, a responsible assessment of the Pharisees among the school passages should provide some criteria for using these passages in historical reconstruction.

War 2.119–166 is paradoxical. On the one hand, Josephus appears to regard it as his definitive statement, for he will refer the audience to it in both of the later school passages, *Ant.* 13.173 and 18.11, as also at 13.298. On the other hand, the form of the passage is not standard. Since the Essene component of the description (*War* 2.119–161) consumes more than twenty times the space given to either Pharisees (2.162–163, 166a) or Sadducees (2.164–155, 166b), the Essenes cannot properly be considered part of a three-way comparison.

Because Josephus has chosen to feature the Essenes so elaborately, as towering examples of Judean virtue, instead of using a Ciceronian three-point spectrum he opts here for the sort of binary contrast between affirmative and skeptical positions that Diogenes Laertius (above) will employ: Pharisees affirm what Sadducees deny.

> **162** Now, of the former two [schools], Pharisees, who are reputed to interpret the legal matters with precision, and who constitute the first school, attribute everything to Fate and indeed to God: **163** although doing and not [doing] what is right rests mainly with the human beings, Fate also assists in each case. Although every soul is imperishable, only that of the good passes over into a different body, whereas those of the vile are punished by eternal retribution.

Affirmed by the Pharisees—after the reminder that they are reputed to be the most precise interpreters of the laws (*War* 2.162)—are the connection of "all things with Fate and indeed with God" (εἱμαρμένῃ τε καὶ θεῷ προσάπτουσι πάντα); the immortality of the soul (ψυχήν τε πᾶσαν μὲν ἄφθαρτον); the passing of the good soul into another body (μεταβαίνειν δὲ εἰς ἕτερον σῶμα τὴν τῶν ἀγαθῶν μόνην); and the eternal retribution facing the vile (τὰς δὲ τῶν φαύλων ἀιδίῳ τιμωρίᾳ κολάζεσθαι). The Sadducees (2.164–165) deny Fate, remove God from the scene (n.b.: Epicurean-like), and reject survival of the soul with postmortem judgment.

We lack the space here for a proper exegesis of these statements, but a few points are noteworthy. First, when it comes to the most important arena of Fate's intervention, namely in human behavior, Josephus qualifies the Pharisees' alleged pan-fatalism in a significant way (*War* 2.163): "although doing and not [doing] what is right rests mainly with the human beings, Fate also assists in each case" (τὸ μὲν πράττειν τὰ δίκαια καὶ μὴ κατὰ τὸ πλεῖστον ἐπὶ τοῖς ἀνθρώποις κεῖσθαι, βοηθεῖν δὲ εἰς ἕκαστον καὶ τὴν εἱμαρμένην), whereas the Sadducees recognize human choice alone. This formulation preserves the ubiquity of Fate's activity for the Pharisees, allowing them to occupy the affirmative pole, but also reveals a degree of sophistication.

According to Cicero, the Stoic Chrysippus distinguished two kinds of causes: principal or antecedent (*causae perfectae et principales*) and "helping" or proximate (*causae adiuvantes et proximae*, *Fat.* 42).[29] When one pushes a drum down a hill, for example, the antecedent cause of its rolling is its particular nature (its rollability, so to speak). The push that starts the roll is an immediate, "helping" cause—and in every case of action such an initiating cause will be found. So for Josephus's Pharisees, humans have a certain nature, but Fate "helps" *in each action* by applying a sort of prod to that nature.

Of course, the relationship between determinism and free will has, in various guises (nature vs. nurture, heredity vs. environment), remained a central problem of philosophy. Plato deals in several contexts with the problem of causation in human affairs (e.g., *Phaed.* 80d–81d; *Resp.* 614b–621d; *Tim.* 41d, 42d, 91d–e). Aristotle credits nature, necessity, and chance with much influence, but he holds that the choice of virtue or vice lies "in ourselves" (*Eth. nic.* 3.3.3–5.2). From rabbinic literature, a parallel to Josephus's statement is often drawn from a saying attributed to R. Aqiva in *m. Avot* 3.15: "*All is fore-seen*, yet freedom of choice is given" (Danby translation). But the key phrase (הכל צפוי) may mean only that all is *observed* (by God), and so one ought to be careful how one exercises free choice.[30]

These observations about Fate and human virtue in Josephus's Pharisees prompt a second point: that his language is wholly conventional in relation to Greek philosophy. Diction and phrasing alike are well attested in other writers on similar subjects: "doing . . . what is right" (Aristotle, *Eth. nic.* 1105b; Lucian, *Anach.* 22), "rests . . . with the human beings" (*Eth. nic.* 3.1.6, 5.2), "every soul is imperishable" (Plato, *Meno* 81b), "passes over into a different body" (Plato, *Meno* 81b; *Phaed.* 70c, 71e–72a), "eternal retribution" (Philo, *Spec.* 3.84; cf. the classical Greek examples offered by Josephus himself at 2.156).

Josephus's language is not only classic-philosophical, however. It also turns up often in other parts of his narratives: describing Essenes, for whom he uses nearly indistinguishable language concerning the soul and punishments (2.154–155, 157; *Ant.* 18.18); describing Sadducees, for whom he uses the same language concerning human volition (2.165; *Ant.* 13.173); describing Pharisees in other passages (especially *Ant.* 18.12–15); and describing a number of other figures, including his own views as character and as narrator.[31]

Finally, although Josephus uses conventional philosophical language, his description remains vague enough to hint at a unique twist in the Pharisees' view of the afterlife, for the soul of the good "passes over into another body" (singular). According to the parallel passage on Pharisees in *Ant.* 18.14, the souls of the virtuous find "an easy path to living again" (ῥαστώνην τοῦ ἀναβιοῦν). On this point the Pharisees appear to depart from the Essene position, which envisions a spiritual home beyond Oceanus for the souls of the righteous—a view that Josephus explicitly compares with Greek notions (*War* 2.155). The difference may be only apparent, however, since elsewhere he speaks of good souls going *first* to a heavenly place and *from there* to "holy new bodies," in the revolution or succession of ages (ἐκ περιτροπῆς αἰώνων, *War* 3.375; *Apion* 2.218). Those passages envisage an intervening period of the soul's existence before its reincarnation.

In any case, Josephus's emphases in all these passages on the holiness and singularity of the new body, its nature as *reward* for a good life (whereas reincarnation tends to be either generic necessity or punishment in Greek thought), and the notice that the transfer will occur (once?) in the succession of ages—so not as an ongoing process—create affinities with current pictures of *resurrection* (e.g., Paul in 1 Cor 15:35-51). If Josephus has bodily resurrection in view, he chooses not to make himself clear: his vague but evocative language would no doubt make such a view of the afterlife sound more familiar to his audience. Whether this language reflects his own views or he obfuscates because straightforward talk of "bodily resurrection" might make audiences uncomfortable (cf. Acts 17:31-33; Celsus *ap.* Origen, *C. Cels.* 5.14; Augustine, *Civ.* 22.4–5) is impossible to say.

As in the other school passages, in *War* 2.119–166 Josephus neither condemns nor praises the Pharisees' views. Affirmers of Fate, the soul, and judgment after death, they come off better than the Sadducean deniers of these things—since we know that Josephus also affirms them (*War* 2.158). But in this passage he has given much fuller attention to the Essenes' views, though these are quite similar to those of the Pharisees on key points, with unambiguous endorsement and admiration (2.158). Even his positive closing remark that, whereas the Pharisees are mutually affectionate (φιλάλληλοι) and cultivate harmony in the assembly, the Sadducees are harsh even to one another (2.166), is relativized by 2.119: the Essenes outshine all others in their mutual affection (φιλάλληλοι . . . τῶν ἄλλων πλέον).

In the *Antiquities*, the first school passage (13.171–173) gives us precious little content, though it again reveals interesting traits in our author. Restricting the comparison to the single issue of Fate, Josephus here constructs a simple three-point spectrum like Cicero's:

> **171** At about this time there were three philosophical schools among the Judaeans, which regarded human affairs differently: one of these was the [school] of the Pharisees, another that of the Sadducees, and the third that of the Essenes. **172** The Pharisees, then, say that some things but not all are the work of Fate, whereas some—whether they happen or do not occur—fall to our account. The order of the Essenes, by contrast, posits Fate as the governess of all things, and [holds that] nothing whatsoever happens to humans that is not according to her determination. **173** Sadducees do away with Fate, reckoning that there is no such thing, and that human affairs do not reach fulfillment on her account, but everything rests with us, that indeed we were responsible for what is good and received evil from our our own thoughtlessness.

But concerning these things I have provided a more precise explanation in the second volume of the work *Judaica*.

As in *War* 2, Sadducees "do away with Fate" altogether, but now the Essenes take up the other pole position ("Fate is the Governess of everything, and nothing happens without her vote"). Where does that leave the Pharisees? To say that "some things but not all are the work of Fate, whereas some—whether they happen or do not occur—fall to our account." Clearly, Josephus needs three schools for the spectrum, and the Sadducean position (denial of Fate) is a given. Whereas the Pharisees had been the Sadducees' polar opposites in *War* 2, that role must now be played by the Essenes, since they have been brought into the direct comparison, which leaves the Pharisees to find a middle way between the poles. Instead of taking *War*'s route, however, claiming that the Pharisees find Fate in every action *along with* human will, Chrysippus-like, Josephus now unhelpfully has them attribute *some* things (which?) to Fate and some to human choice. That these changes do not bother him, and indeed do not seem to matter (since he refers to *War* 2 for a more precise explanation), shows how little he wishes to be seen as the pedantic sort of philosopher. Broad strokes, changeable as needed for presentational reasons, suffice.[32]

Josephus's final school passage aside from *Life* 10–11 (above) is the only one that ostensibly combines proportion (i.e., roughly equivalent space for each school) and a degree of comprehensiveness (i.e., several items are considered for each). Closer inspection shows, however, that very little is offered there concerning the metaphysical positions of either Sadducees or Essenes; Josephus focuses rather on the practices and social position of those two schools. Only the postulates of the Pharisees receive any sustained treatment.

The most peculiar feature of *Ant.* 18.12–22 is the addition of a "Fourth Philosophy" (18.23–25)—the party of radical freedom represented by the followers of Judas the Galilean/Gaulanite—generated when Judea was annexed to the Roman Empire in 6 CE. As for the Fourth Philosophy, Josephus both abhors the innovation in the national heritage they represent, which will allegedly result in the destruction of Jerusalem, and admires the indomitable courage of its practitioners, in much the same way that he esteems the fearlessness of all Judean fighters and Essenes in the *War*[33] and the nation as a whole in the *Apion*.

Although scholars have often taken Josephus at face value and spoken of the Fourth Philosophy as if it were a real entity, we should rather consider it an ad hoc literary construction. Reasons: (a) To have a "fourth philosophy," one must first have three, and Josephus is the only one we know to have positioned the three philosophies thus. Imagining the representatives of the Fourth Philosophy as a real group whose members understood themselves by such a description would be akin to expecting film characters to step off the screen into real life. (b) Before, during, and after this passage, Josephus insists that there are (only) *three* Judean philosophies, even though he has always known about Judas the Galilean and his followers (*War* 2.119; *Ant.* 13.171; 18.11; *Life* 10–11). It does not occur to him elsewhere to mention a Fourth Philosophy. (c) Blaming the Fourth Philosophy for Judea's later ills is an ex post facto exercise, possible only with hindsight. It is unreasonable to imagine that later *sicarii*, Zealots, economic rebels, and other groups that emerged from particular conditions in the 40s through 60s (2.254, 651; 4.160–161) *understood themselves* to be members of such a philosophical school. (d) The Fourth Philosophy is not comparable to the others in having a distinctive set of views, way of life, admission procedures, and membership requirements. Rather, Josephus claims that they agree with the Pharisees on all philosophical questions except the meaning of freedom (18.23). It seems, then, that he constructs a Fourth Philosophy for at least two reasons: as a novel means of exposing the aberrant character of the rebel mentality and as a way to drive home the ongoing theme of Judean courage (under the rubric of philosophy).

Like the other school passages, then, *Ant.* 18.12–25 is thoroughly conditioned by the demands of immediate narrative context. One decisive element of this context, rarely discussed by scholars, is the peculiar style of writing that Josephus adopts in *Ant.* 17–19, which Thackeray had credited to a literary assistant he dubbed the "Thucydidean hack."[34] Thackeray's notion that for the *Antiquities* Josephus employed an array of literary assistants with different propensities has been rightly rejected, however, and we seem to be dealing with the author's own experimentation with the literary possibilities of Greek.[35] In any case, *Ant.* 18.12–15 (on the Pharisees) uses the same stilted, quasi-poetic prose that one finds throughout these three volumes. Old Attic was characterized by "poetical colouring, forced and strange expressions, bold new coinages and substantivized neuters of participles and adjectives."[36] That *Ant.* 18.12–25 shares fully in the style of books 17–19 is another indicator that Josephus has written the passage himself or thoroughly reworked any sources used. The school passage could not have been inserted bodily from another source.

What this language means for us is that, although Josephus devotes more words here than elsewhere to the Pharisees' views, we struggle in near futility to understand him. The strangely poetic character of his language may be seen in his new treatment of the Pharisees' unique tradition (*Ant.* 18.12b–c):

> They follow the authority of those things that their teaching deemed good and handed down;
> they regard as indispensable the observance of those things that it saw fit to dictate.
> Out of honor do they yield to those who precede them in age;
> Nor are they inclined boldly to contradict the things that were introduced.

All of this appears to mean no more than what we learned from *Ant.* 13.297–298, that the Pharisees observe a special "tradition from [their] fathers" (see chapter 1). Obviously, embracing such a tradition assumes that they revere those predecessors. It may be that the third panel also indicates respect for *living* elders (though that would qualify the synonymous parallelism); if so, it only underscores the point made in *War* 2.166 that they live harmoniously, unlike the argumentative Sadducees; so also *Ant.* 18.16 has the Sadducees disputing even their own teachers. We do not have access to the historical reality of the Sadducees, but such a harsh evaluation might have been explained by insiders as nothing more than a tradition of vibrant exegetical debate.

The only straightforward statement in this paragraph is the one that opens it, and it is new: "the Pharisees restrain their regimen of life, yielding nothing to the softer side" (*Ant.* 18.12). Josephus does not contrast the Sadducees on this point, though their base among the elite might imply wealth (18.17; cf. 13.197–198; chapter 1). Translating for the Loeb Classical Library, Louis Feldman notes a rabbinic parallel (*ARN* 5): Pharisees deprive themselves in this world—foolishly, the Sadducees believe, because there is no other world. In the narrative of Josephus, it is striking that Josephus does not make more of this universally recognized virtue of simplicity in the case of the Pharisees, the way he does with the Essenes—both in this final school passage (18.20: they surpass all others) and in *War* 2. Shunning luxury certainly qualifies the Pharisees to be included among the philosophers (cf. *Ant.* 13.289), though Josephus does not celebrate this in their case.

On the issue of Fate, Josephus's language is so garbled as to have caused copyists and translators much confusion:

> They reckon that everything is effected by Fate;
> Yet they do not thereby separate the intending of the human element from the initiative that rests with them [humans] (οὐδὲ τοῦ ἀνθρω-πείου τὸ βουλόμενον τῆς ἐπ᾽ αὐτοῖς ὁρμῆς ἀφαιροῦνται),
> It having seemed right to God that there be a fusion [or judgment or weighing against] (δοκῆσαν τῷ θεῷ κρᾶσιν [κρίσιν]),
> And in the council-chamber of that one [Fate?] and [in] the one having willed of the humans, a siding with—with virtue and vice (καὶ τῷ ἐκείνης βουλητηρίῳ καὶ τῶν ἀνθρώπων τὸ ἐθελῆσαν [τῷ ἐθελ-ήσαντι] προσχωρεῖν μετ᾽ ἀρετῆς ἢ κακίας).

Although making sense of this confusion may be a worthwhile text-critical challenge, it is difficult to see the rewards for those who simply wish to understand Josephus's portrait of the Pharisees. The language appears deliberately crabbed and obscure, and we have no compelling reason to believe that there is much substance to be discovered. Apparently, Josephus abandons the simplified three-point scheme of *Ant.* 13.171–173, where the Pharisees hold a middle position of attributing "some things" to Fate and "some" to human volition, to return to the cooperation model of *War* 2.162–163. Fate is somehow involved in *every* action: her collaboration with human will is fancily framed but ultimately unfathomable. Since Josephus will not comment in this passage on the view of Fate held by either Sadducees or Essenes, he need not be concerned with maintaining a position for the Pharisees along a spectrum.

His description of the Pharisees' theory of souls is also awkwardly constructed, a sentence lacking a finite verb (finite verbs given below are either added for English translation or they represent infinitives in Josephus), though the general sense is clear (*Ant.* 18.14):

> That souls have a deathless power is a conviction of theirs (ἀθάνατόν τε ἰσχὺν ταῖς ψυχαῖς πίστις αὐτοῖς εἶναι),

> And that subterranean punishments, and also rewards (ὑπὸ χϑονὸς δικαιώσεις τε καὶ τιμάς), are for those whose conduct in life has been either of virtue or of vice:
> For some, eternal imprisonment is prepared (ταῖς μὲν εἱργμὸν ἀίδιον προτίϑεσϑαι),
> But for others, an easy route to living again (ταῖς δὲ ῥαστώνην τοῦ ἀναβιοῦν).

Here, too, the new quasi-poetic verbiage adds little to the spare prose of *War* 2.162–163. The eternal punishments (and possibly rewards), we now learn, are dispensed beneath the earth—the equivalent of Hades—and the envisaged eternal punishment is explained as an imprisonment or binding. This would come as no great surprise for Roman audiences, who would easily recall Odysseus's famous vision of Hades (*Od.* 11.576–600), where Sisyphus, Tantalus, and Tityus face unending torture in the netherworld. At *War* 2.156, indeed, Josephus mentions precisely those figures, including the similar character of Ixion, while elaborating the *Essene* view of postmortem punishment.

War's "passing over into a new body" is now described by the similarly ambiguous "an easy route to living again." It is on this point only that Sadducean philosophy will be briefly contrasted (18.16): "The doctrine of the Sadducees makes the souls disappear together with the bodies"—ironic phrasing, as if a doctrine could *make* souls disappear.[37] The closer parallel to the Sadducees, however, is the Essene doctrine, for with reciprocal irony those men "render souls deathless" (ἀϑανατίζουσιν δὲ τὰς ψύχας; 18.18).

The relationship between Josephus's portraits and any actual Pharisee's articulation of his views must remain an open question, though we have good reason—in his accommodation of this passage to the style of *Ant.* 17–19 and in his generally free rearrangements—to think that literary artifice accounts for a great deal. In relation to *War* 2, there is nothing substantially new here.

A comparison of Josephus's Pharisees with his Sadducees and Essenes in this passage turns up three matters that deserve brief discussion. First, although his language for the other two groups has a similar poetic quality, it is more straightforward in structure and meaning. Second, and this is probably related, his descriptions of Sadducees and Essenes focus on ethical and practical questions:

Sadducees recognize only what is in the laws and they are men of the highest standing (though Josephus dilates on the necessity of their public capitulation to Pharisaic law, 18.16–17); Essenes maintain special sacrifices and therefore are barred from the Temple, but otherwise he praises their agricultural pursuits, unsurpassed virtue, common possessions, rejection of marriage and slavery, and provisions for leadership (18.18–22). Even the Fourth Philosophy, whose doctrine of radical political freedom Josephus repudiates, he mainly praises for the courage it evokes (18.23–25). Third, and the reverse of the same coin: Josephus says very little about the other schools' metaphysical views, mentioning only briefly the Sadducees' dissolution of the soul at death, the Essenes' attribution of all things to God and immortalization of souls, and the Fourth Philosophy's agreement with the Pharisees.

Is there any connection among these three features? If the impression of symmetry in this school passage, which Josephus deliberately encourages—by proportionate sections, by the recurrence of "the doctrine" (ὁ λόγος) at the beginning of the first three descriptions, by certain structural features (e.g., Σαδδουκαίοις δέ . . . Ἐσσηνοῖς δέ), and by a family resemblance of diction and word form—turns out to be undermined by such differences of content and emphasis, one might reason as follows. As Josephus shows on nearly every page of the *Antiquities*, he is preoccupied with the Judean laws (or "constitution"), with those who observe or flout them, and thus with virtue and vice. He is no abstract philosopher. In the cases of Essenes and even Sadducees, he can easily identify praiseworthy aspects of their practical philosophy. With the Pharisees (18.15, 17; cf. chapter 1), however, in spite of their enormous popularity and although he recognizes them as a philosophical school, he finds little to praise. After briefly noting their rejection of luxury, he uses their space, as it were, for highly abstruse formulations of their positions on intractable questions of metaphysics. Although this surely does not constitute overt criticism, it fits with the lack of sympathy for the Pharisees that we found in chapter 1.

CONCLUSIONS AND COROLLARIES

In this chapter we have seen that Josephus's occasional presentations of the three Judean philosophical schools along a spectrum of meta-physical beliefs are the sort of thing one should expect from an elite representative of Judean culture. From a rhetorical point of view, they are much like his other digressions—on geography, military tactics, or botany. They display his erudition, resulting in part from his thorough training in all three schools, and yet at the same time his urbane superiority to any *parochialism, fanaticism, or pedantry*—even if he had forgivably indulged philosophical yearnings in adolescence. Like a Cicero (though with rather less philosophical intensity overall) or a Tacitus, this eastern nobleman can throw in such descriptions at opportune moments, as pleasant rest stops in the onward march of his historical narrative. The broadly philosophical character of the whole story, however, is much more prominent and important than such brief and murky outlines of the schools' beliefs.

In Josephus's case, because we have three such passages in his thirty-volume oeuvre, we can also see how freely he manipulates his material for momentary needs. In *War* 2, where he singles out the Essenes in order to extol the manly virtue that is the unifying theme of the book, Pharisees and Sadducees are left to occupy formulaically the pole positions of affirmers and deniers. In *Antiquities* 13, where he opts to break the narrative with a short schematic of the three philosophies *On Fate*, he must rearrange the pieces. Essenes and Sadducees now occupy the extremes, with Pharisees attributing "some things" to Fate and "some things" to human volition. In *Antiquities* 18, in the middle of his regrettable experiment with bold style, Josephus tries his hand at describing the schools in the new poetic prose—as in *Antiquities* 13 referring to *War* 2 for greater precision. The many added words for the Pharisees are largely redundant, however, because of their opacity and the synonymous parallelism within this passage. They do confirm the notice in *Ant.* 13.297–298 concerning the Pharisees' special tradition, which had not appeared in *War* 2, and they include a new comment about the Pharisees' simple life. The rather technical-sounding descriptions penned for the Pharisees, however, stand in marked contrast to Josephus's open assessments of virtue among the other schools.

Josephus's handling of the three Judean philosophical schools should make us wary about using his descriptions of the Pharisees in these sketches for historical purposes.[38] Some aspects of Sadducean and Essene thought and life can be confirmed by, respectively, the New Testament and Philo (also Pliny): we may conclude from such independent witnesses that Sadducees rejected the afterlife and that Essenes lived in highly regimented "philosophical" communities that stressed simplicity of life (Philo, *Prob.* 75–91; Pliny, *Nat.* 5.73). Of the Pharisees, the New Testament confirms that they observed a special legal tradition "from the fathers"[39] and that they believed in the afterlife; Josephus's language permits the notion of resurrection, even though he does not spell it out. Rabbinic literature on *perushim* and *tzadukim* presents considerable difficulties, both internally and in relation to the Pharisees and Sadducees of Josephus and the New Testament.[40] For the finer details of life and practice among these groups, however, we are frustrated partly by the general dearth of evidence, partly by an author who uses them as set pieces to be manipulated along with the rest of his material.

CHAPTER 3

MATTHEW'S AND MARK'S PHARISEES

Martin Pickup

The gospels of Matthew and Mark are recognized as key sources of information on the Pharisees, yet any analysis of their data is fraught with difficulty. We are dealing with highly tendentious documents whose interest in the Pharisees lies solely in the fact that, as key opponents of Jesus' ministry, the Pharisees serve to set forth Jesus and his teaching in vivid relief. Scholarly debate on the historicity of the material in Matthew and Mark continues, both in regard to what they relate generally about Jesus and his ministry, and in regard to what they relate specifically about the Pharisees. Are we to regard the accounts of encounters between the Pharisees and Jesus as faithful remembrances of actual events, or are we reading idealized material that reflects the issues confronting Christians at the time of the gospels' composition?

The dates assigned to these documents play a significant role in this historicity debate. If Mark was written ca. 65–70 CE (the common view), it becomes a valuable source of information on the Pharisees prior to 70, even if its specific claims about the Pharisees' encounters with Jesus are considered "idealized." The case is more dubious for Matthew, a gospel which is commonly dated in the 80s or 90s at a time when the Pharisees appear to have risen in prominence and power (though to what extent remains debatable), and a time when the relationship between Jews and Jewish Christians collapsed. That late first-century setting provides a possible *Sitz im Leben* for Matthew's gospel, which suggests to many scholars that, rather than providing historical information about the Pharisees of Second Temple Judaism, Matthew's portrayal of the Pharisees is really a representation of the Jewish leadership toward the end of the first century.

Complicating the matter is the lack of scholarly certainty about the compositional history of Mark and Matthew. The vast majority of scholars agree that some kind of literary interdependence exists between the synoptic gospels, but how so? Was Mark the earliest gospel and did Matthew and Luke use it as a source? Did they also use a collection of Jesus' sayings? Or did Luke use Matthew, and Mark condense them both? (Most scholars would affirm the former position, but the latter has its defenders.) Also, what part might other Christian traditions, in written or oral form, have played in each evangelist's final product? Uncertainty about these matters impedes any historical inquiry about the Pharisees.

What then shall we do? In this essay I will focus attention on the picture of the Pharisees that each gospel offers. In deference to the fact that the majority of scholars affirm Matthean dependence on Mark, my methodology will be to analyze Mark's portrait of the Pharisees first and, when analyzing Matthew, to take note of how Matthew's portrait of the Pharisees compares and contrasts with Mark's. Nevertheless, the emphasis here will not be on redactional debates. Instead, I will analyze each pericope where Pharisees appear so that readers may have ready access to the data. I will draw conclusions about what each document presents about the Pharisees' role in Palestinian society and their level of interaction and influence among the Jewish populace. I will highlight data about the Pharisees' religious views and practices that emerge from the accounts of their confrontations with Jesus. The ultimate purpose of this study is to reveal the portraits of the Pharisees that Mark and Matthew have produced so that these portrayals may be compared and contrasted more effectively with those of other ancient sources.

The Pharisees in Mark

Survey of the Data

Four successive pericopes in Mark (2:15–3:6) introduce the Pharisees as opponents of Jesus during his ministry in Galilee.[1] Their antipathy toward Jesus increases with each encounter. In 2:15-17 "the scribes of the Pharisees" question Jesus' disciples about the fact that their master dines with tax collectors and sinners. Upon hearing of the matter, Jesus replies, "Those who are well have no need of a physician, but those who are sick; I have come to call not the righteous but sinners." In 2:18-22 Jesus is asked why his disciples do not fast like the disciples of John the Baptist and the (disciples of the) Pharisees.[2] Jesus responds by comparing himself to a bridegroom whose companions naturally rejoice when in his presence; their time of fasting will come when the bridegroom is taken from them (a foreshadowing of the fate that awaits Jesus at the end of the gospel). Comparing his teaching to new cloth and new wine, Jesus further contrasts himself with John and the Pharisees: his teaching is new, whereas their instruction is no longer relevant for the current times, the dawning of the kingdom of God.

In the last two pericopes of this fourfold grouping, the Pharisees confront Jesus personally over alleged Sabbath violations. In 2:23-28 they criticize him for allowing his disciples to pluck grain as they pass through fields on the Sabbath day. Jesus defends his disciples' action by appealing to the precedent of David and his men being allowed to eat the priest's showbread (1 Sam 21:1-6). "The sabbath was made for humankind," Jesus says, "and not humankind for the sabbath; so the Son of Man is lord even of the sabbath" (vv. 27-28). Then in 3:1-6 Jesus initiates a debate in the synagogue over the issue of healing on the Sabbath day.[3] "Is it lawful," Jesus asks the Pharisees, "to do good or to do harm on the sabbath, to save life or to kill? (v. 4)" The section concludes with the notation that the Pharisees "went out and immediately conspired with the Herodians against him, how to destroy him" (v. 6).

The authorial intention of these four pericopes is to present the Pharisees as major opponents of Jesus, and to explain why, from this point on in Jesus' ministry, they tirelessly confront him. C. S. Mann is correct when he says, "We have reached a climax in the ministry [of Jesus]. From this point in the narrative the threat of death is never far away."[4]

Pharisees confront Jesus again in 7:1-22, the gospel's longest pericope involving the Pharisees. In the region of Gennesaret, as Jesus' popularity with the crowds is growing, "the Pharisees and some of the scribes who had come from Jerusalem"[5] ask Jesus why his disciples eat without first washing their hands. An editorial insertion in verses 3-4 explains to Mark's Gentile audience that the question stemmed from

the Pharisees' dedication to "the tradition of the elders," which mandated the ceremonial washing of hands before eating. Mark says that
this tradition (παράδοσις) was practiced by "the Pharisees, and all the
Jews," and he explains that whenever they return from the marketplace they are careful to wash their food as well as various food con-
tainers. The narrative continues with Jesus rebuking the Pharisees for
being "hypocrites," having committed the error of Isaiah 29:13: their
commitment to human traditions supersedes obedience to the commandment of God.

Mark records three more confrontations between the Pharisees
and Jesus, each initiated by the Pharisees in order "to test him." In
Mark 8:9-12 the Pharisees seek out Jesus while he is in the region of
Dalmanutha, and they ask him to show them a sign from heaven.
Jesus says that "no sign will be given to this generation," and he subsequently warns his disciples to "beware of the yeast of the Pharisees
and the yeast of Herod" (vv. 14-15). In Mark 10:2-12, when Jesus is
teaching in "the region of Judea and beyond the Jordan," Pharisees
come and ask him about the lawfulness of divorce, citing the case law
in Deuteronomy 24:1-4.[6] Jesus counters by saying that God's original
intention for marriage was that it be a permanent union, so a couple
joined by God should not be separated; putting away one's wife and
marrying another amounts to adultery against one's wife. Mark's final
reference to the Pharisees comes in 12:13-17 as Jesus is teaching in
the Temple during the final week of his ministry: "Then they [appar-
ently the chief priests, scribes, and elders of 11:27, mp] sent to him
some Pharisees and some Herodians to trap him" by asking whether
it was lawful to pay taxes to Caesar.[7] The question addresses a Jewish
religious issue with highly political ramifications, and one surmises
that the Herodians' presence is intended to represent the latter concern, the Pharisees' the former. Jesus' response amazes all: "Give to
the emperor the things that are the emperor's, and to God the things
that are God's."

Analysis: The Pharisees in Jewish Society

From the above survey we can see that Mark portrays the Pharisees as
major opponents of Jesus. Their opposition centers upon various

issues relating to the Law—most notably, table fellowship with reputed sinners, the proper keeping of the Sabbath commandment, and ritual purity. Of special significance to the Pharisees is the keeping of "the traditions of the elders."[8] The fact that Mark connects (some) scribes with the Pharisees fits in with the Pharisaic stress on legal issues. Each time Mark associates scribes with Pharisees, it is an occasion of disputation with Jesus or his disciples over alleged violations of the Torah. The later confrontations between the Pharisees and Jesus—those pertaining to heavenly signs, the legality of divorce, and Roman taxation—are not presented in the text as feuds over doctrines fundamental to Pharisaic thinking, but as issues broached merely because of their potential to mire Jesus in controversy and minimize his growing popularity with the Jewish people.

Mark's Pharisees are located primarily in Galilee, but they are willing to seek Jesus out in other regions in order to confront him. The text is not completely clear as to whether the Pharisees who confront Jesus are permanent residents of Galilee or whether they are sent there from Jerusalem. The scribes who act in conjunction with the Pharisees do come from Jerusalem (7:1; cf. 3:22).

Mark does not present the Pharisees as a group possessing political authority or holding religious office. They must conspire with the Herodians (the aristocratic supporters of Herod Antipas) to try to bring about Jesus' demise (3:6; 8:15).[9] Mark's Pharisees never send any other group to confront Jesus; rather, they themselves are the ones who are sent (along with the Herodians) at the behest of the chief priests, scribes, and elders to interrogate Jesus (12:13). Particularly striking is the fact that the Pharisees have no direct involvement in Jesus' arrest and trial. The chief priests, scribes, and elders carry out that function (15:1), which implies that this triad wields the political power and not the Pharisees. Nor do we see anything in Mark to indicate that the Pharisees have control of the synagogues. The evangelist mentions synagogue officials (ἀρχισυνάγωγοι), but not in connection with the Pharisees (5:22-38). In the synagogue the Pharisees' opinions on the Law are weighty and freely offered (3:2-4), but scribes are the ones whom Mark places in "the best seats in the synagogues" (12:38). It is clear, then, that the Pharisees in Mark are not political or religious officials.

Nevertheless, Mark's Pharisees do have a tangential connection to those who are in power. Mark presents the Pharisees as a highly respected and influential group, not only among the general populace, but especially with governing officials and religious leaders.[10] The Pharisees are able to initiate discussions with those in power over matters that concern them, and they are willing to function as unofficial ancillaries of the Jewish leadership.

Mark's gospel mentions the Pharisees in conjunction with several other groups: scribes, Herodians, and (by way of comparison) the disciples of John. Yet, it is the scribes whom Mark associates with the Pharisees in a special way. To appreciate the relationship between the scribes and the Pharisees in Mark's gospel—and to understand the subsequent use that Matthew makes of this Markan material—we need to survey and analyze Mark's data about the scribes.

Scribes and Pharisees

Mark presents the scribes (not the Pharisees) as the formal teachers of Scripture to the Jewish people. Early on, the gospel contrasts the instruction of Jesus with that of the scribes: the multitudes are astounded, for Jesus "taught them as one having authority, and not as the scribes" (1:22).[11] Furthermore, it is the scribes who have taught the people what the Scriptures say about the advent of Elijah (9:11-13) and the nature of the Messiah (12:35-36).

Mark presents the scribes as the ones who first object to Jesus as he ministers in Galilee. When Jesus pronounces a paralytic's sins forgiven, the scribes say to themselves, "Why does this fellow speak in this way? It is blasphemy!" (2:6-7). The first time that Mark mentions the Pharisees, it is in association with scribes; the text speaks of "the scribes of the Pharisees" (2:16). In 3:22-30 scribes from Jerusalem publicly accuse Jesus of casting out demons by the power of Beelzebul. Jesus denies the charge and warns them about committing blasphemy against the Holy Spirit. In 7:1-23 scribes again come from Jerusalem and join the Pharisees in condemning Jesus for allowing his disciples to violate the tradition regarding hand-washing. Scribes dispute with Jesus' disciples when a father brings his demon-possessed son for healing (9:14-29; cf. 3:22).

In 11:27-33, when Jesus is in the Temple during the final week of his ministry, "the chief priests, the scribes, and the elders" ask Jesus by what authority he acts. Jesus declines to answer their question because they refuse to commit themselves publicly on the matter of whether John the Baptist acted with divine authority. These appear to be the same persons who subsequently become provoked by Jesus' parable of the wicked tenants (12:1-12): "When they realized that he had told this parable against them, they wanted to arrest him, but they feared the crowd" (v. 12). Mark's Jesus recognizes these individuals as the leaders of the Jews when he uses the words of Psalm 118:22-23 to designate them as "the builders" who reject God's cornerstone.

In 12:28-34 we read of an unusually irenic discussion between Jesus and a scribe as Jesus teaches in the Temple at the end of his ministry. When the scribe asks about the greatest commandment in the Law, Jesus replies that the love of God and the love of neighbor are the two greatest commandments. Agreeing with Jesus' analysis, the scribe says that obeying these two precepts "is much more important than all whole burnt offerings and sacrifices." He receives Jesus' commendation: "You are not far from the kingdom of God." Following this conversation, however, Jesus publicly questions the understanding of the scribes regarding the Messiah's Davidic sonship (12:35-37). He then issues a warning to the crowd in the Temple:

> Beware of the scribes who like to walk around in long robes, and to be greeted with respect in the marketplaces, and to have the best seats in the synagogues and places of honor at banquets! They devour widows' houses, and for the sake of appearance, say long prayers. They will receive greater condemnation. (12:38-40)

Mark consistently lays direct responsibility for Jesus' arrest and execution upon the heads of "the chief priests and the scribes" or "the chief priests and the scribes and the elders" (8:31; 10:33; 11:18, 27; 14:1, 43, 53; 15:1). The Pharisees, as we noted earlier, are not involved. Mark's final reference to the scribes comes in 15:31, where the chief priests and scribes mock Jesus while he is on the cross.

Our survey reveals that Mark's gospel gives even greater attention to the scribes' opposition to Jesus than it does the Pharisees' opposition. Mark portrays the Pharisees either in contrast or in conflict with Jesus on nine occasions. He portrays the scribes in contrast or in conflict with Jesus on eighteen occasions. Scribes in Galilee are the ones whom Mark first presents as objecting to Jesus (2:6-7). As Mark relates the Galilean ministry of Jesus, both Pharisees and scribes confront him, and they sometimes do so together. For the most part, these scribes come from Jerusalem. When Jesus goes to Jerusalem at the end of the gospel, the Pharisees recede from view and we read of scribes—along with chief priests and elders—bringing about his arrest and execution.

The precise relationship between the scribes and the Pharisees in Mark's gospel is difficult to unravel. Mark does not regard "the scribes" and "the Pharisees" as two completely separate groups with common interests, but rather as two groups that to some extent have an overlapping of members. The term "scribes" is best understood as the designation of a professional class, and the term "Pharisees" as the designation of a religious party. The first time the Pharisees are mentioned (2:16), Mark speaks of "the scribes of the Pharisees" (οἱ γραμματεῖς τῶν Φαρισαίων).[12] This construction must refer to certain scribes who were regularly associated with, or were members of, the Pharisaic party. The phrase serves to prepare a reader for the potential overlap of those persons whom the author will subsequently designate as "scribes" or as "Pharisees." Semantically, the evangelist distinguishes the scribes from the Pharisees (e.g., "the Pharisees and some of the scribes who had come from Jerusalem," 7:1), but he clearly sees the two groups of people designated by these terms as having a strong integration. His initial reference to "the scribes of the Pharisees" indicates that some scribes could be further classified as Pharisees.[13] It is also evident that there were other scribes who were not Pharisees, so we cannot think of the scribes in Mark's gospel as a monolithic group in terms of party affiliation.

But questions remain. What of those pericopes where Mark speaks only of "scribes" (sans "Pharisees") opposing Jesus? Are these scribes to be understood as *Pharisaic* scribes? Perhaps, but the text is not clear about this matter. Also, since the scribes associated with Pharisees are said to come from Jerusalem (7:1), is a reader to understand that these Pharisaic scribes are included among "the scribes" connected with the chief priests and the elders in Jerusalem (e.g., 8:31, 10:33, 11:18)? Again, this is quite possible, though the evangelist never explicitly makes the point, nor does he ever connect the Pharisees per se with the triad of leadership at Jerusalem.[14]

Pharisaic Disputes with Jesus: Analysis of Individual Pericopes

As noted earlier, Mark's conflict stories in which Pharisees bring a charge against Jesus provide the best potential data on the doctrines and issues that the Pharisees deemed important. In addition, some of these texts yield information about the extent of the Pharisees' interaction with the Jewish populace and religious influence over them. A close analysis of these pericopes is therefore required. Mark's focus, of course, is always on Jesus' responses to the Pharisees' charges; the text never includes any Pharisaic rejoinder. But a clear understanding of Jesus' responses to the Pharisees provides us with insight into the religious thinking of the Pharisees, as the author of Mark portrays it.

Mark 2:16-17, Eating with Tax Collectors and Sinners

> [16]When the scribes of the Pharisees saw that he was eating with sinners and tax collectors, they said to his disciples, "Why does he eat with tax collectors and sinners?" [17]When Jesus heard this, he said to them, "Those who are well have no need of a physician, but those who are sick; I have come to call not the righteous but sinners."

Mark informs us that the Pharisees objected to Jesus' willingness to eat with tax collectors and sinners. *Tax collectors* (τελώνης) were generally regarded as having forsaken their Judaic heritage in that they sided with the Romans over against their Jewish countrymen, collected pagan coinage, and often did so unscrupulously.[15] The term *sinners* (ἁμαρτωλοί), seeing that it is consistently coupled with *tax collectors* in this pericope, must be intended in a technical, rather than generic sense.[16] The word has often been explained as a designation for the *'ammê ha-'arets*, the "common people" among the Jews who did not follow the special regulations that the Pharisees observed.[17] But that understanding cannot be sustained; the term is equivalent to *resha'im* "the wicked" and in this context it is best understood as a reference to Jews who had abandoned the moral and religious lifestyle of the Mosaic Law.[18]

The objection that Mark's Pharisees make to Jesus' choice of table companions could lie on two (not mutually exclusive) levels: (1) Jesus' apparent acceptance of people who practiced a rebellious, immoral lifestyle. In this case, the act of eating per se is not so much the issue for the Pharisees, but rather what it seemed to imply—namely, an endorsement of lawless behavior.[19] (2) Jesus' lack of regard for Jewish traditions of ritual purity, since the houses and tables of such rebellious Jews would undoubtedly be rife with ceremonial uncleanness.[20] In favor of the latter view is the fact that, according to Mark 7:3-4, traditions of ritual purity with regard to food were of great importance to the Pharisees. On the other hand, the present passage does not explicitly mention the matter of ritual purity; it is not until chapter 7 that such issues are introduced to the reader. That fact suggests that our author did not perceive the Pharisees' objection to eating with tax collectors and sinners to be (primarily) related to table impurity. (Of course, it is also true that Pharisees themselves might weigh matters differently than does the evangelist.)

It seems best to view the data broadly and to see the issue for Mark's Pharisees as one fundamentally about Jesus' fellowship with rebellious Jews, with his lack of concern for purity traditions making his actions even more objectionable. Jesus' statement about the sick needing a physician could apply to both of these matters, since Scripture applied sickness and healing metaphors to moral as well as ritual issues (e.g., Ps 41:4; 2 Chr 30:18-20; 2 Kgs 2:21). Interestingly, Jesus' statement is both a compliment and a criticism of the Pharisaic scribes: they are correct in their evaluation of his dinner companions' unrighteous condition, but they themselves show no desire to help these persons overcome their spiritual disease.

From this pericope we learn that Mark's Pharisees never practice table fellowship with perceived rebels against the Law, and they have no reservations about confronting anyone who would do so. It must be noted, however, that this pericope cannot be used to support the idea that the Pharisees were such a highly exclusive sect that they had little or no interaction with common (non-Pharisaic) Jews.[21] Tax collectors and sinners were not common Jews; they were Jews who no longer observed the Mosaic lifestyle. The refusal of Mark's Pharisees to eat or associate with such persons tells us nothing about how much interaction Pharisees may or may not have had with observant Jews who were not Pharisees.

Mark 2:23-28, Plucking Grain on the Sabbath

> [23]One sabbath he was going through the grain fields; and as they made their way his disciples began to pluck heads of grain. [24]The Pharisees said to him, "Look, why are they doing what is not lawful on the sabbath?" [25]And he said to them, "Have you never read what David did when he and his companions were hungry and in need of food? [26]He entered the house of God, when Abiathar was high priest, and ate the bread of the Presence, which it is not lawful for any but the priests to eat, and he gave some to his companions." [27]Then he said to them, "The sabbath was made for humankind, and not humankind for the sabbath; [28]so the Son of Man is lord even of the sabbath."

The reason for this criticism of Jesus' disciples appears to be that the Pharisees viewed the act of plucking grain as equivalent to harvesting a crop and, thus, a violation of the Sabbath commandment. Such thinking was not limited to Mark's Pharisees; Philo explained the Sabbath day of rest as a time when "it is not permitted to cut any shoot or branch, or even a leaf, or to pluck any fruit whatsoever" (*Vit. Mos.* 2:22). Of course the Law of Moses permitted poor people in Israel, or aliens, to glean crops in a landowner's field since needy individuals like these did not have fields of their own to grow food (Lev 19:9-10; Deut 24:19-22). One could pluck by hand the grain in a neighbor's field or the grapes on his vines, though harvesting with a sickle or basket, as if one owned the property, was not permitted (23:24-25; cf. 4Q 159). The latter restrictions prevented a person from storing up food for the following day(s), yet the Law's overall purpose was that of benevolence—namely, to guarantee that a needy person had a means of obtaining sustenance each day.

But was this opportunity to be suspended on the Sabbath day? According to Mark, the Pharisees had concluded that it was. Though the disciples' act of plucking grain while walking through a field would have been their right to do on any other day of the week, in the opinion of the Pharisees this right had to cease on the Sabbath day.In the view of some interpreters, the point of this pericope is to demonstrate Jesus' authority as the Son of God to annul Torah statutes; the "lord of the Sabbath" statement is understood as an explicit affirmation of this point.[22] But that interpretation fails to do justice to Jesus' appeal to Scripture in support of his disciples' actions. Jesus' response to the

Pharisees is best understood as a challenge to Pharisaic halakha.[23] Specifically, he presents the case of David's eating of the showbread (1 Sam 21:1-6) in order to illustrate a legal principle regarding the implementation of God's laws.

The Law of Moses commanded that the showbread be removed from the sanctuary each Sabbath and given to the priests to eat (Exod 40:23; Lev 24:5-9). But in the Samuel narrative, when David comes to the sanctuary as a fugitive from Saul, the priest allows David and his men to eat this bread since it was the only food available.[24] The only condition was that the men had to be ritually clean, not having had recent sexual relations. I understand Mark's Jesus to be making the following argument. Ordinarily, it would be a violation of Torah for a nonpriest to eat the holy bread. But the high priest's decision indicated that David's partaking of the bread was justified in this case because "he and his companions were hungry and in need of food" (2:25). Thus, the point here is an issue of how the Law should be applied in such a case. For Jesus, the teaching of the Law regarding ritual holiness and Sabbath-keeping is the same: these statutes were not to be interpreted in such a way that their implementation brought harm to a person, for to do so would be a misuse of the Torah. The prohibition against plucking a neighbor's grain with basket in hand effectively prevented a needy person from preparing in advance for the Sabbath day. Hence, the Pharisaic interpretation of the Sabbath commandment meant that, in effect, a poor person who on other days could receive benevolence from his neighbor would have to go hungry on the Sabbath. For Mark's Jesus, this was an unthinkable interpretation of the Law.[25]

The principle of interpreting a Torah statute always under the canopy of humanitarian obligation appears to be the underlying point of Jesus' maxim, "The sabbath was made for humankind, and not humankind for the sabbath" (2:27). The following statement, "the Son of Man is lord even of the sabbath," could reinforce the same point if the phrase "the Son of Man" (ὁ υἱὸς τοῦ ἀνθρώπου) is understood as a general reference to a human being. Or, if ὁ υἱὸς τοῦ ἀνθρώπου is an oblique reference to Jesus himself (as is more likely in view of how the expression is used elsewhere in Mark), the point would be that Jesus is the authoritative explicator of the Law (cf. Mark 1:22).[26]

It is noteworthy that, according to 1 Samuel 21:4, the priest stipulated that David and his men had to be in a state of ritual cleanness to eat the holy bread. That stipulation would have been seen as an enforcement of Leviticus 22:3, which declared that any Israelite who came in contact with a holy item while in a state of uncleanness was to suffer *karet* (death by divine agency).[27] The fact that the priest bound this stipulation upon David and his men would indicate that he was not ignoring the Torah, but only applying it to an exceptional circumstance. Thus, the case of David and the showbread had halakhic import.

Another factor may also explain why Mark's Jesus appeals to the showbread incident: Jews may have understood David's eating of the showbread to have occurred on a Sabbath day.[28] The Law said that the showbread in the sanctuary was to be replaced every Sabbath, and the replaced bread given to the priests (Lev 24:8; 1 Chr 9:32). So the words of 1 Samuel 21:6—"So the priest gave him the holy bread; for there was no bread there but the bread of the Presence, which was removed from before the LORD, to be replaced by hot bread on the day it is taken away"—could suggest that the incident with David occurred on a Sabbath day. Jews of the rabbinic period understood the passage in this way (*b. Menah.* 95b). Such an understanding would give the passage greater pertinence to the current issue between Jesus and the Pharisees. For Mark's Jesus, it was a fundamental misunderstanding of the significance and purpose of the Sabbath to think that the divine command to rest would prevent persons in need from obtaining the very food that the Law provided for them.[29] That this is how the author of Mark sees the issue is suggested by the subsequent pericope where Jesus heals on the Sabbath because he understands it to be fundamentally "lawful to do good" on the Sabbath (3:4-5).

It is important to recognize that Mark's gospel never portrays Jesus as rejecting Sabbath observance per se, but only a very particular application of Sabbath observance that came from the Pharisees. Mark's account of Jesus' debates with the Pharisees over Sabbath halakha shows that a strict observance of the Sabbath day is a paramount concern of Mark's Pharisees, and so emphatic are they about resting from labor on the Sabbath that they even view it as a necessity for legally mandated provisions of benevolence to cease on the Sabbath. Moreover, they strongly seek to enforce their views on other Jews.

Mark's gospel gives information only about Jesus' side of the dispute. But Mark suggests to us that the key halakhic philosophy that guided the Pharisees' thinking in this matter was the issue of dedication to God versus service to man. Mark's Pharisees view Jesus' philosophy of Torah observance as something that minimizes dedication to God. For them service to God is paramount and the fulfillment of human needs has to be sublimated to the necessities of divine service or else God is insufficiently honored. Mark's Jesus, on the other hand, sees the failure to fulfill human needs as a violation of service to God. In other words, one cannot really fulfill the greatest commandment if it means nullifying the second greatest (Mark 12:28-34). Mark's Pharisees, however, believe that one cannot nullify the greatest commandment in order to fulfill the second greatest. The halakhic difference between the Pharisees and Jesus comes down to the issue of how love of God and love of one's fellow man are to be integrated. This, at least, is what Mark's (one-sided) presentation of the debate suggests. In the eyes of both disputants, the consequences of these two differing philosophies of Torah observance are crucial, for the Kingdom of God is at stake (12:24).[30]

Mark 7:1-23, Eating with Unwashed Hands

[1]Now when the Pharisees and some of the scribes who had come from Jerusalem gathered around him, [2]they noticed that some of his disciples were eating with defiled hands, that is, without washing them. [3](For the Pharisees, and all the Jews, do not eat unless they thoroughly wash their hands, thus observing the tradition of the elders; [4]and they do not eat anything from the market unless they wash it; and there are also many other traditions that they observe, the washing of cups, pots, and bronze kettles.) [5]So the Pharisees and the scribes asked him, "Why do your disciples not live according to the tradition of the elders, but eat with defiled hands?" [6]He said to them, "Isaiah prophesied rightly about you hypocrites, as it is written, 'This people honors me with their lips, but their hearts are far from me; [7]in vain do they worship me, teaching human precepts as doctrines.' [8]You abandon the commandment of God and hold to human tradition."

[9]Then he said to them, "You have a fine way of rejecting the commandment of God in order to keep your tradition! [10]For Moses said, 'Honor your father and your mother'; and, 'Whoever speaks evil of father or mother must surely die.' [11]But you say that if anyone tells

father or mother, 'Whatever support you might have had from me is Corban' (that is, an offering to God)—[12]then you no longer permit doing anything for a father or mother, [13]thus making void the word of God through your tradition that you have handed on. And you do many things like this." [14]Then he called the crowd again and said to them, "Listen to me, all of you, and understand: [15]there is nothing outside a person that by going in can defile, but the things that come out are what defile."

[17]When he had left the crowd and entered the house, his disciples asked him about the parable. [18]He said to them, "Then do you also fail to understand? Do you not see that whatever goes into a person from outside cannot defile, [19]since it enters, not the heart but the stomach, and goes out into the sewer?" (Thus he declared all foods clean.) [20]And he said, "It is what comes out of a person that defiles. [21]For it is from within, from the human heart, that evil intentions come: fornication, theft, murder, [22]adultery, avarice, wickedness, deceit, licentiousness, envy, slander, pride, folly. [23]All these evil things come from within, and they defile a person."

In this pericope the conflict between the Pharisees and Jesus over oral tradition comes to the forefront—in particular, the tradition of cleansing one's hands of ritual defilement before eating. The evangelist inserts into his source material several editorial comments for the benefit of his Gentile audience: an explanation of Pharisaic traditions (vv. 3-4), an explanation of the Aramaic term "Corban" (v. 11), and an explanation of Jesus' statement about the nondefiling nature of foods (v. 19). In addition, redaction criticism has yielded several competing suggestions as to what verses may have existed originally as independent units of material before being joined together in this Markan format.[31] Verses 9-13 (the matter of Corban) are usually viewed as having an origin independent from the stratum containing the Pharisaic criticism on hand-washing (vv. 1-2, 5). Jesus' comments on defilement (vv. 15-23) are usually separated as well, on the grounds that a discussion of what enters a person and defiles him has nothing to do with the purification of hands. (But see the discussion below.)

In the pericope as it stands before us, Pharisees and scribes reproach Jesus for his disciples' breach of oral tradition. In verse 3 only the Pharisees are mentioned. This, and the fact that the evangelist places the Pharisees first in order, indicates that he saw the Pharisees as more prominent in such discussions of oral tradition. Or, it may be an indication that he envisioned these particular scribes as

Pharisees themselves (cf. 2:16). Little is said here about the oral traditions in general; they are designated simply as "the tradition of the
elders" without further explanation. Nothing is said about these traditions originating at Sinai (as the rabbinic myth of the dual Torah
would later maintain),[32] yet it is clear from what Mark says that the
Pharisees view these traditions as authoritative and they are dedicated
to observing all of them.

Verses 3-4 are an editorial insertion that explains the tradition of
hand-washing before meals as a practice of "the Pharisees and all the
Jews" (οἱ Φαρισαῖοι καὶ πάντες οἱ Ἰουδαῖοι), and then lists other
purification traditions pertaining to food and food vessels.[33] Mark may
intend to attribute to "all the Jews" only the practice of hand-washing,
for if the understood subject of ἐσθίουσιν in verse 4 is simply "the
Pharisees"—the author's mind having refocused on them as the real
protagonists of the pericope—then the intention may be to assign the
additional cleansing rituals of verse 4 only to the Pharisees. The key
point, in any case, is that the evangelist wants his Gentile readers to
understand the basis of the Pharisees' criticism. Since the Pharisees
regarded the traditions of the elders as authoritative and since ritual
hand-washing was a tradition that even non-Pharisees were willing to
observe, the failure of Jesus' disciples to wash their hands before eating opened them up to the charge of committing presumptuous sin.

This is the situation as Mark presents it. But did *all* Jews really
practice ritual hand-washing? Even the most conservative of scholars
would admit that the evangelist's statement is somewhat exaggerated.
But can we even accept it as a fair generalization? E. P. Sanders
rejects Mark's assertion as inaccurate and claims that we cannot
imagine that most Jews would have practiced rituals of table purity,
for such concerns were the defining feature of a specific segment of
Jews—those known in rabbinic literature as the *haberim*.[34] So, against
Mark, Sanders asserts that only a small number of Palestinian Jews
would have practiced such rituals. He proposes that the evangelist was
misled by the practice of Diaspora Jews who washed before engaging
in prayer and Torah study.[35] Yet, Mark never mentions washing before
prayer or Torah study; the text is talking about washing before eating
(vv. 2-5). It seems unduly incredulous to think that the author of this
gospel, a Jew in the opinion of most scholars, would have made so
glaring a mistake.[36] Moreover, John 2:6 says that at the wedding cere-

mony at Cana there were on hand "six stone water jars for the Jewish rites of purification, each holding twenty or thirty gallons." So the author of Mark is not alone in his claim about the widespread nature of this Jewish ritual practice. As noted above, the evangelist sees it as a crucial part of his explanation of the Pharisees' criticism of Jesus' disciples. Otherwise, the criticism amounts to nothing more than the rather inane complaint that Jesus' disciples do not follow Pharisaic praxis—that is, they are not Pharisees. Mark presents the incident as a more substantive controversy than that.

Sanders even rejects the idea that most Pharisees practiced ritual hand-washing, or that it was a particularly vital matter. Pharisees, he says, may have washed their hands after handling Scripture, or to maintain the cultic purity of a heave offering. But washing before eating ordinary food was practiced by only a few Pharisees and then only for Sabbath or festival meals.[37] Mark, of course, says nothing about this incident occurring on a Sabbath or festival day, nor does he limit the purification traditions to such occasions. Mark's record of Jewish cultural practice—early testimony that it is—merits more weight than Sanders is willing to give it.[38]

What was the purpose of Pharisaic cleansing rituals? John Poirier suggests that we can find the answer by looking at the custom of Diaspora Jews who washed their hands as a preparation for prayer or Torah study; perhaps this was the thinking in Palestine too.[39] Strong evidence for this suggestion is lacking, however. It seems to me that the text of Mark, while not addressing the question explicitly, is nevertheless quite clear about the matter. The reason for washing one's hands before meals was so that one would not risk ingesting impurity.[40] Verse 4 states that, after coming from the marketplace, Pharisees do not eat anything unless they first wash it (καὶ ἀπ' ἀγορᾶς ἐὰν μὴ βαπτίσωνται οὐκ ἐσθίουσιν).[41] It is not hard to imagine how scrupulous Jews in Roman-controlled Palestine might develop a concern over contracting ritual impurity from food that, although meeting all the Torah requirements of *kashrut*, was liable to have come into contact with impurity at the marketplace or similar public venues. Mark implies that the ritual cleansing of one's hands was another safeguard along the same line of concern. Before one touched his food to eat it, potential impurity on the hands needed to be cleansed.[42]

This is how the author of Mark conceives of the matter. Only the concept of hand-washing to avoid ingesting impurity would explain why he includes verses 14-23 in the pericope.[43] In these verses Jesus addresses the crowd with a rebuttal to Pharisaic thought, saying, "Listen to me, all of you, and understand: there is nothing outside a person that by going in can defile, but the things that come out are what defile" (vv. 14-15).[44] The pertinence of this statement as a response to the Pharisees' initial charge is obvious. The reason why some scholars want to separate these verses from the initial verses of the pericope seems to be due, in part, to a reticence to accept the portrait that Mark presents of Pharisaic ritual concerns. But according to the information that Mark presents, Pharisaic cleansing rituals such as hand-washing before meals and the cleansing of food and food vessels were all intended to prevent ingesting ceremonial impurity.[45] Moreover, Mark indicates that the Pharisees' thinking along this line had become pervasive among the Jewish populace, at least to the degree that the Pharisees had influenced the spread of ritual hand-washing among the people. The entire pericope serves to highlight Jesus' attempt to dissuade the crowds from focusing on matters of ritual cleansing as the Pharisees do.

What is the point of Jesus' teaching on defilement? When he says that "that there is nothing outside a person that by going in can defile, but the things that come out are what defile," does this mean that Jesus is annulling the Mosaic laws on food uncleanness? Many commentators think so.[46] They believe that this was the understanding of the author of Mark, as indicated by verses 18-23 which provide Jesus' private explanation of his aphorism to the disciples:

> [18]"Do you not see that whatever goes into a person from outside cannot defile, [19]since it enters, not the heart but the stomach, and goes out into the sewer?" (Thus he declared all foods clean.) [20]And he said, "It is what comes out of a person that defiles. [21]For it is from within, from the human heart, that evil intentions come: fornication, theft, murder, [22]adultery, avarice, wickedness, deceit, licentiousness, envy, slander, pride, folly. [23]All these evil things come from within, and they defile a person."

The editorial insertion in verse 19, "Thus he declared all foods clean" (καθαρίζων πάντα τὰ βρώματα), has seemed to many commentators to be a clear abrogation of the Mosaic precepts of *kashrut*, and Jesus' words themselves are understood accordingly. More recent scholars stress the need to interpret Jesus' words within their Jewish cultural setting. From that perspective it becomes more plausible to understand Jesus to be emphasizing the point that moral purity is of greater importance to God than ritual purity—without trying to nullify the latter.[47] Jesus is saying that since ritual impurities enter the body from outside and are eliminated, they cannot defile a person in his heart. Instead, moral evils are what originate from within a man's heart and thus are able to defile the heart.

The point of Jesus' teaching, therefore, is not to reject what the Torah says about ritual cleanness and uncleanness, but to correct a misplaced Pharisaic emphasis on ritual cleanness to the neglect of the more serious matter of moral cleanness. Support for this view comes from the fact that when we consider the early church's struggle with the issues of Gentile inclusion and food laws (e.g., Gal 1–2; Rom 14:1-23; Acts 10–11, 15), we find no evidence that this teaching of Jesus was ever brought to bear on the issue. "The logion was simply not thought to imply a cancellation of the Levitical ordinances. It was rather construed as an exhortation (cf. the list of vices). The Jesus tradition did not determine the purity issue precisely because it was silent on the subject."[48]

Even commentators who acknowledge the above interpretation as Jesus' actual meaning will often affirm, in view of the editorial insertion of verse 19, that the author of Mark failed to perceive Jesus' point accurately and, altering the sense of Jesus' words, affirmed to his Gentile audience that Jesus had annulled the Mosaic food laws. This seems to me to be a strange and unnecessary position to take in view of the evangelist's use of the Jesus tradition throughout the gospel. Moreover, if Jesus' words in this unit of material are indeed indicating that cleanness/uncleanness distinctions regarding foods were not inherent, absolute states and that only moral matters fell into that category, then the rules of *kashrut* addressed relative states of purity that were set up by the Mosaic Law only for those who were under it. Thus, it is quite plausible that the author of Mark concluded from Jesus' teaching that the Gentile Christians to whom he wrote would not themselves be bound in their diet by Jewish food classifications. This may be all that is intended by the editorial comment of verse 19.[49]

If Jesus' teaching in this pericope is understood as described above, then his dispute with the Pharisees on this occasion perfectly conforms to their earlier halakhic dispute over Sabbath observance. Jesus' difference with the Pharisees regarding hand-washing before meals was not a matter of whether the Mosaic holiness legislation should be practiced by Jews, but a matter of how that legislation should be applied. For Mark's Jesus, it was an egregious error to elevate ritual holiness to such a level of importance that human tradition surrounding it attained a binding, authoritative status. Such actions not only treated human traditions as if they were the word of God, but in this particular case, the end result was a flip-flopping of the hierarchical categories of holiness. Moral holiness—that which was inherently absolute and essential—was superseded in priority by ritual holiness—that which was inherently relative and nonessential. The difference between Jesus' approach to Torah observance and the Pharisees' approach could not have been more substantial.

The controversy between Jesus and the Pharisees in this pericope is quite dense, because the issue over ritual hand-washing is made to highlight a larger dispute over oral tradition in general. For Mark's Jesus, part of the issue is that dedication to oral tradition frequently causes one to violate moral injunctions of Scripture. Citing Isaiah 29:13 against the Pharisees, Jesus says, "You abandon the commandment of God and hold to human tradition." Jesus sees this as a form of hypocrisy (vv. 6-8). The hypocrisy charge against the Pharisees is found twice in Mark's gospel: in this passage and in 12:15. Current interpretation commonly understands it as a charge that the Pharisees are duplicitous and do not live in accordance with their own teachings—i.e., that they purposely do not bother to "practice what they preach." But the pericope's subsequent discussion and illustration of the hypocrisy charge does not fit that mold. Mark's Jesus says that the Pharisees give the impression of Torah observance by diligently keeping their traditions, but they are hypocrites (ὑποκριταί) in that the keeping of their traditions causes them, in effect, to violate the Torah (v. 8).[50]

The subsequent section of material, verses 9-13, provides an example of the problem: the way that the Pharisaic tradition mandated the application of vows. Jesus says that, despite the injunctions of the Torah that obliged the financial support of one's aged parents (Exod 20:12; 21:17), the Pharisees' tradition sometimes causes one to disobey that injunction: "You say that if anyone tells father or mother, 'Whatever support you might have had from me is Corban' (that is, an offering to God)—then you no longer permit doing anything for a father or mother, thus making void the word of God through your tradition." The Mishnah contains numerous halakhic discussions on vows, and some of these address circumstances where one could be released from a vow.[51] Jesus, however, is complaining about a case where Pharisaic tradition enforced a vow too strictly, such that one's parental obligations were effectively negated.

It may be that the text is talking about a person intentionally declaring funds or property Corban so that he might spitefully prevent his parents from receiving the use of them.[52] M. Nedarim contains examples of vows that prevented others from sharing in one's wealth (see 5.6; 8.7; 9.1). Or, Jesus could be talking about a case where a person had declared as Corban the future proceeds of a business venture, but later was faced with aging parents who needed that assistance.[53] If so, Jesus would be criticizing the Pharisees for enforcing a voluntary act of religious service to God to the point where one could not adequately fulfill explicit Torah commands to care for one's parents. Both of these views of the Corban matter fit with what Mark already has presented as the chief issue between Jesus and the Pharisees regarding the proper approach to the Law— that which was illustrated by the earlier Sabbath controversies: one cannot bind a precept of the Torah in a way that causes one to neglect humanitarian or (in this case) familial responsibility.[54] Jesus regards it as invalid to think that God is pleased with an act of religious service that causes harm to another human being, whereas the Pharisees affirm that their tradition demonstrates a proper prioritizing of piety toward God.

Pharisaic Disputes with Jesus: Conclusions

Our analysis of Mark's presentation of the major disputes between the Pharisees and Jesus, though one-sided accounts, causes a picture of the religious philosophy of the Pharisees to take shape. Mark's Pharisees are experts in the Law of Moses and they are very concerned about the proper fulfillment of Mosaic statutes. They show a

special concern with the strict fulfillment of the Sabbath commandment, the maintenance of ritual purity, and the enforcement of
Corban—all of which pertain to matters of piety toward God. It is
here that Mark's Pharisees place their religious emphasis.

The strictness with which the Pharisees implement their understanding of the Law is seen in several areas. They view plucking grain
by hand while walking through a field as the virtual equivalent of harvesting crops, and therefore they classify such an action on the
Sabbath as "work" that the Law prohibits. So strong is the Pharisaic
dedication to Sabbath observance that Sabbath-keeping may even
suspend the benevolence aims of Torah statutes. Honoring God on
the Sabbath day is what is important, which is why in the Pharisees'
concept of Torah observance, needy persons on the Sabbath may not
exercise their normal right to pluck grain in a neighbor's field, and
healing someone on the Sabbath day is an impious offense against
God. For similar reasons, Mark's Pharisees strictly enforce Corban
vows even to the point where the keeping of the vow supersedes
humanitarian and familial obligations.

Mark's Pharisees are also strong proponents of the "traditions of
the elders," which they see as necessary if one is to fulfill the Law
properly. Of particular importance to Pharisees are purity traditions
regarding food. The Pharisees wash their hands before eating, and
after coming from the marketplace they perform other washing rituals lest by chance they ingest foods that have contracted ceremonial
defilement. Such concerns over ritual purity suggest an extreme dedication to the concept of holiness before God, perhaps in imitation of
priestly levels of holiness, and these practices comport with the dedication to piety that we observe in Mark's Pharisees in other matters.
It is here that the Pharisees and scribes come into major conflict with
Jesus. He criticizes the Pharisaic traditions because they are of human
origin and do not rise to the level of the word of God. Dedication to
the Pharisaic traditions causes a person to pay less attention to the
moral principles that form the very foundation of the Torah.

The attitude of Mark's gospel toward the Pharisees is indicated by
the things that Jesus says about the Pharisees' character. They manifest a "hardness of heart" in their acceptance of divorce (10:5) and in
their opposition to healing on the Sabbath day (3:5). They are "hypocrites" in that they violate God's moral principles while they practice

religious traditions that outwardly make them appear pious toward God (7:6).[55] Their pervasive influence on the Jewish people is corrupting, and one needs to "beware of the yeast of the Pharisees" (8:15).

It is clear that Mark's Pharisees have a significant amount of influence over the Jews of Palestine. This is due in large part to the fact that certain of the scribes—the formal teachers of the Law who enjoy being "greeted with respect in the marketplaces, and to have the best seats in the synagogues and places of honor at banquets"—are affiliated with the Pharisaic party (12:38-39; 2:16). The Pharisees are therefore able to influence the Jewish populace to observe some of their traditions, particularly those relating to ritual cleansing. They are also quite ready to charge someone with a breach of Torah (as they would apply it), particularly a teacher like Jesus who was having an influence of his own upon the Jewish people.

There is nothing in Mark to suggest Pharisaic exclusivity in a sectarian (i.e., soteriological) sense. If we use E. P. Sanders's definitions, Mark's Pharisees would seem to be a "party" rather than a "sect."[56] They do not associate—particularly in table fellowship—with nonobservant Jews whose lifestyles indicated an abandonment of the Mosaic covenant. But there is nothing in Mark to suggest that the Pharisees were an exclusive table-fellowship sect, if what is meant by that idea is that they refused to associate or eat with non-Pharisees. All that Mark suggests is that the Pharisees would have been sticklers for the maintenance of table purity among those with whom they dined. As long as non-Pharisees were observant Jews and ritually pure at table, nothing in Mark's gospel suggests that Pharisees would have declined to eat with them. Mark's Pharisees "possessed a character which was elitist," but "not soteriologically exclusivistic."[57]

THE PHARISEES IN MATTHEW

Turning now to the Pharisees in Matthew's gospel, I first will survey Matthew's use of material that is found in Mark, observing similarities and differences. Then I will analyze Matthew's non-Markan material on the Pharisees, noting that which is found also in Luke (a relatively small amount of material), and that which is unique to

Matthew. Our purpose is to ascertain the portrait of the Pharisees that Matthew produces and to compare it with that of Mark. Does the author of Matthew alter, in any substantive way, what Mark presents about the Pharisees? Does he embellish what Mark says? Does he subvert it?

Markan Material on the Pharisees

Matthew uses all of the Markan pericopes relating to the Pharisees, in the same order, yet with several notable variations. Matthew 9:11-13 presents the pericope where Jesus is criticized for eating with tax collectors and sinners (= Mark 2:16-17). Rather than using Mark's phrase "the scribes of the Pharisees," Matthew simply says that "the Pharisees" raise the objection. Matthew includes Jesus' response about the sick requiring a physician, but with an additional statement: "Go and learn what this means, 'I desire mercy, not sacrifice'" (v. 13). The quotation is from Hosea 6:6 and it is crucial for Matthew's gospel; on two occasions Matthew's Jesus cites the passage. It is a text of Scripture that encapsulates what Mark presented as Jesus' fundamental philosophical difference with the Pharisees regarding the Torah: for Jesus, showing mercy to sinners and implementing other moral principles is more important to God than even the Temple cult and similar aspects of the Mosaic system.

Matthew 9:14-17 recounts the query about the disciples' failure to fast (= Mark 2:18-22). The only formal difference with Mark's account is that Matthew portrays the question as coming from John's disciples themselves.

In Matthew 12:1-8 we read of the Pharisees' criticism of Jesus' disciples for plucking grain on the Sabbath (= Mark 2:23-28). Matthew's Jesus makes the familiar argument regarding David and the showbread, but he adds two additional arguments:

> [5]Or have you not read in the law that on the sabbath the priests in the Temple break the sabbath and yet are guiltless? [6]I tell you, something greater than the Temple is here. [7]But if you had known what this means, "I desire mercy and not sacrifice," you would not have condemned the guiltless.

The first argument makes the point that the Sabbath restriction cannot be understood to mean that every kind of work is prohibited on that day, for it was obvious that God did not intend the suspension of priestly sacrificial duties on the Sabbath. The quotation (again) of Hosea 6:6 complements the prior argument, for if sacrifice is not forbidden on the Sabbath, and yet mercy (ἔλεος) is more important to God than sacrifice, then deeds of mercy on the Sabbath could not be forbidden.[58] This type of *qal v'homer* argumentation fully comports with the thrust of Jesus' halakhic argumentation in Mark. Curiously, Matthew omits (as does Luke) the Markan phrase, "The sabbath was made for humankind, and not humankind for the sabbath," but he does include the climactic aphorism, "The Son of Man is lord of the sabbath."

Like Mark, Matthew (12:9-14) immediately follows the above pericope with the incident of Jesus healing a man's withered hand on the Sabbath (= Mark 3:1-6). Matthew specifies that the Pharisees are the ones closely watching Jesus in order to accuse him, something that was only implicit in Mark. But in Matthew the Pharisees actually voice the question, "Is it lawful to cure on the sabbath?"—to which Jesus responds with the following argument:

> [11]Suppose one of you has only one sheep and it falls into a pit on the sabbath; will you not lay hold of it and lift it out? [12]How much more valuable is a human being than a sheep! So it is lawful to do good on the sabbath.

Jesus' words presume a knowledge of Pharisaic practice—specifically, that they would have granted an exception to the Sabbath restriction in the case of a trapped animal.[59] Jesus is accusing the Pharisees of inconsistency in their application of the Torah. More than that, he sees it as an inconsistency that fails to give proper place to the humanitarian requirements of the Law. At the end of the pericope Matthew includes the Markan statement about the Pharisees conspiring to destroy Jesus, but Matthew omits the reference to the Herodians, saying merely that "the Pharisees went out and conspired against him, how to destroy him" (v. 14).[60]

Matthew 15:1-20 recounts the Pharisees and scribes' criticism of Jesus' disciples for not washing their hands before eating (= Mark 7:1-23). Whereas Mark leaves the Pharisees' provenance vague, Matthew indicates that they and the scribes both come from Jerusalem.

Matthew's version of the incident corresponds fairly well with Mark's, the most notable departure being that Matthew omits Mark's explanatory insertions regarding Jewish purification rituals and the cleanness of all foods (Mark 7:3-4, 19). These omissions reflect the Jewish background of Matthew's audience.[61] Matthew does add, however, a discussion between Jesus and the disciples about the impact of his teaching on the Pharisees, and this discussion prompts Jesus to issue a harsh rebuke of the Pharisees:

> [12]Then the disciples approached and said to him, "Do you know that the Pharisees took offense when they heard what you said?" [13]He answered, "Every plant that my heavenly Father has not planted will be uprooted. [14]Let them alone; they are blind guides of the blind. And if one blind person guides another, both will fall into a pit."

At the conclusion of the pericope, Jesus states that moral evils originating within one's heart "are what defile a person, but to eat with unwashed hands does not defile" (v. 20). These words tie the entire pericope together by focusing attention back on the Pharisees and scribes' initial complaint regarding ritual hand-washing.

Matthew 16:1-4 records the occasion where Jesus is asked to perform a miraculous sign (= Mark 8:11-13).[62] Whereas Mark portrays the request as coming from the Pharisees, Matthew says that "the Pharisees and Sadducees" (οἱ Φαρισαῖοι καὶ Σαδδουκαῖοι) are the ones who ask for a sign. This coupling of the Pharisees and Sadducees is a characteristic feature of Matthew's gospel.[63] Matthew also adds a rebuke from Jesus concerning his questioners' inability to discern the signs of the times: "An evil and adulterous generation asks for a sign, but no sign will be given to it except the sign of Jonah" (v. 4). The "sign of Jonah" is an allusion to Jesus' third-day resurrection from the dead (cf. Matt. 12:38-40).

Matthew 16:5-12 contains Jesus' warning about "the yeast of the Pharisees" (= Mark 8:14-21). In Mark's account Jesus warns about "the yeast of the Pharisees and the yeast of Herod," but Matthew omits the reference to Herod and once again connects the Sadducees with the Pharisees: "[Jesus said,] 'Beware of the yeast of the Pharisees and Sadducees.' Then they understood that he had not told them to beware of the yeast of bread, but of the teaching of the Pharisees and Sadducees" (vv. 11-12).

Matthew 19:3-12 records Jesus' discussion with the Pharisees about divorce (= Mark 10:2-12). The account corresponds in substance, though not in precise detail, with Mark.[64] Matthew includes two significant additions. First, an exception clause is inserted into Jesus' statement about the adulterous nature of divorce and remarriage: "And I say to you, whoever divorces his wife, *except for unchastity* [μὴ ἐπὶ πορνείᾳ], and marries another commits adultery" (v. 9).[65] Matthew also includes a question by Jesus' disciples as to whether one should marry at all, to which Jesus responds by saying that some men may choose to forgo marriage and make themselves "eunuchs for the sake of the kingdom of heaven" (vv. 10-12). Like Mark, Matthew gives no information concerning Pharisaic views on divorce other than that they permitted the issuing of a bill of divorcement on the basis of the case law in Deuteronomy 24:1-4. Despite the addition of an exception clause, Matthew follows Mark in treating Deuteronomy's case law on divorce as nothing more than a legal toleration of the act of wronging one's spouse. Jesus rejects the Pharisaic practice of using this case law as if it were a model of morality.[66]

Matthew 22:15-22 presents the incident where Jesus is questioned about paying taxes to Caesar (= Mark 12:13-17). Matthew accords with Mark throughout, even including the Markan data about the Herodians joining with the Pharisees in an attempt to entrap Jesus. This is curious, because earlier Matthew omitted two of Mark's references to the Herodians.[67]

Markan Material on the Scribes

Just as Matthew uses all of the Markan pericopes relating to Pharisees, he also uses all of the Markan pericopes relating to scribes.[68] Of special significance, however, is the fact that on several occasions where Mark refers to scribes, Matthew designates them as Pharisees. Mark's reference to "the scribes of the Pharisees" (2:16) is simply "the Pharisees" in Matthew 9:11. The "scribes" of Mark 3:22 (who "came down from Jerusalem" and claimed that Jesus exorcized demons by the power of Beelzebul) are called "Pharisees" in Matthew 12:24.[69] Though Matthew 15:1 agrees with Mark in naming both

Pharisees and scribes as the ones who criticize the disciples' neglect of hand-washing (Mark 7:1, 5), the critics are subsequently designated simply as "Pharisees" (v. 12).[70] The "chief priests, the scribes, and the elders" who (based on Mark 11:27, 12:1-12) become provoked by Jesus' parable of the wicked tenants and seek a means of arresting him are identified in Matthew 21:45 as "the chief priests and the Pharisees." The individual scribe of Mark 12:28-34 (who discusses with Jesus the greatest commandment) is identified in Matthew 22:34-40 as a Pharisee and (in many manuscripts) as a lawyer (νομικός).[71] Matthew's version contains none of Mark's positive portrayal of this individual.[72] Jesus' question about the Messiah that in Mark 12:35-37 is posed to the Temple crowd (which included scribes) is presented in Matthew 22:41-46 as a question addressed specifically to Pharisees. Finally, whereas Mark 12:38-40 records Jesus' stern rebuke of "the scribes, who like to walk around in long robes, and to be greeted with respect in the marketplaces, and to have the best seats in the synagogues and places of honor at banquets" (12:38-40), Matthew 23 gives an expanded version of the rebuke wherein Jesus adds a list of woes against the "scribes and (the) Pharisees" (23:2, passim).

It is not the case, however, that Matthew designates every Markan scribe as a Pharisee. In Matthew's use of pericopes where Mark speaks of scribes associated with the chief priests and elders, Matthew normally either retains Mark's designation "scribes" (16:21; 20:18; 26:57; 27:41) or omits the Markan reference to scribes altogether (21:23; 26:3, 47). Matthew also retains Mark's designation "scribes" whenever they are mentioned simply in their capacity as formal teachers of the Law, rather than in confrontation with Jesus over alleged breaches of the Law (7:29; 17:10). The Markan scribes whom Matthew designates as Pharisees are always scribes who question or confront Jesus about matters of the Law. In four out of five such instances, Matthew identifies Mark's scribes as Pharisees; the single exception is in Matthew 9:3 where the scribes of Mark 2:6-7 (who charge Jesus with blasphemy for claiming to forgive sins) are still referred to as "scribes."

Several points emerge from this survey of the data. First of all, it is quite apparent that Matthew gives more emphasis to the Pharisees as opponents of Jesus than he does to scribes. This Matthean trait stands in contrast to Mark's gospel, in which the scribes' opposition to

Jesus receives more attention. The Markan scribes who oppose Jesus' approach to the Torah are almost always identified in Matthew as Pharisees. Never does the reverse occur—that is, never is a Markan reference to Pharisees presented in Matthew as a reference to scribes. Clearly, the author of Matthew believed that while not every Pharisee was a scribe, certain scribes in Mark's gospel were in fact Pharisees and these Pharisaic scribes tended to be the ones who objected to Jesus as a teacher of the Law. This idea may have been part of the Christian tradition at the evangelist's disposal, but it may also have been a deduction derived from Mark's gospel itself. As we have seen, Mark's early reference to "the scribes of the Pharisees" opposing Jesus (2:16) suggests to a reader that subsequent references to scribes who oppose Jesus might also denote Pharisaic scribes. While Mark's text does not make that point absolutely clear, the author of Matthew may have drawn that inference. It perhaps is significant that the one Markan pericope where "scribes" oppose Jesus on a matter of Law and Matthew does not change the designation to "Pharisees" is the pericope of Mark 2:6 (= Matt 9:3), which comes prior to the reference to "the scribes of the Pharisees" in 2:16. Perhaps the author of Matthew could not be certain whether the scribes of Mark 2:6 were also Pharisees and so, when using this pericope, he retained Mark's original "scribes."[73]

At any rate, it appears that the author of Matthew tried to identify Jesus' opponents as Pharisees every opportunity that he could. Nevertheless, the textual data do not indicate that he did so capriciously; there was a reason to think that most of the Markan scribes who confronted Jesus and his teaching were Pharisees. The emphasis that Matthew's gospel gives to the Pharisees, therefore, seems intended to show that the halakhic approach to the Torah that conflicted so seriously with the teaching of Jesus was that of the Pharisees.[74] Did the author of Matthew presume that all of the Markan scribes who acted in concert with the Pharisees were Pharisees themselves? It would seem so. He recognized (as did the author of Mark) that a number of the scribes from Jerusalem were affiliated with the Pharisaic party, and he presumed that the scribes who acted in concert with the Pharisees in opposing Jesus' halakha were Pharisaic scribes.

It is possible (but not certain) that the author of Matthew believed that some of the scribes whom Mark identified with the Jerusalem political leadership were Pharisees. This possibility is suggested by the reference in Matthew 21:45 to "the chief priests and the Pharisees" as the ones who become offended by the parable of the wicked tenants. In Mark's account, the identity of the offended parties is somewhat ambiguous, but they would appear to be "the chief priests, the scribes, and the elders" of 11:27. As noted earlier, on two occasions Mark's gospel identifies the scribes associated with the Pharisees as "scribes who came down from Jerusalem" (3:22; 7:1). This suggests the idea that some Pharisaic scribes may have belonged to the group of scribes who were a part of the Jerusalem political leadership.

We turn our attention next to Matthew's non-Markan material that relates to the Pharisees, which consists of (1) pericopes that are also found in Luke, and so would be classified by most scholars as belonging to Q, and (2) material that is unique to Matthew's gospel. There is very little of the former (and what there is we shall note as we proceed in our survey), but there is quite a bit of the latter, and both appear in *narratives* and *discourses*. As we shall see, Matthew's non-Markan narratives offer a relatively small amount of data relating to the Pharisees, but in Matthew's discourses the scribes and Pharisees often take center stage.

Non-Markan Material: Narratives

Matthew's first mention of the Pharisees is in 3:7-10, a non-Markan addition to the narrative on John the Baptist wherein John condemns the impenitence of persons seeking baptism.

> [7]But when he saw many Pharisees and Sadducees coming for baptism, he said to them, "You brood of vipers! Who warned you to flee from the wrath to come? [8]Bear fruit worthy of repentance. [9]Do not presume to say to yourselves, 'We have Abraham as our ancestor'; for I tell you, God is able from these stones to raise up children to Abraham. [10]Even now the ax is lying at the root of the trees; every tree therefore that does not bear good fruit is cut down and thrown into the fire."

This material is also found in Luke 3:7-9, and so it is usually assigned to Q. In Luke's version the Baptist directs his words to "the crowds," but in Matthew he specifically addresses "many Pharisees and Sadducees" (πολλοὺς τῶν Φαρισαίων καὶ Σαδδουκαίων).[75] It is normally thought that Luke preserves the original form of the tradition.

In Luke, John's speech is addressed "to the crowds that came out to be baptized by him" (τοῖς ἐκπορευομένοις ὄχλοις βαπτισθῆναι ὑπ᾽ αὐτοῦ), implying that the persons addressed intended to submit to John's baptism. Matthew's alternate wording—Ἰδὼν δὲ πολλοὺς τῶν Φαρισαίων καὶ Σαδδουκαίων ἐρχομένους ἐπὶ τὸ βάπτισμα αὐτοῦ—may indicate the same thing with regard to the Pharisees and Sadducees, but the idea that these two groups would have been willing to submit to John's baptism seems problematic due to what this gospel, and the other gospels, indicate about the antipathy of the Pharisees and Sadducees toward John and Jesus.[76] Luke 7:30 specifically states that the Pharisees and lawyers rejected John's baptism. Since Matthew never says that the Pharisees and Sadducees are actually baptized, perhaps the reader is to understand that John's insistence on repentance and acknowledgment of one's sins is what causes the Pharisees and Sadducees to change their minds about submitting to John's baptism and thereafter turn away from him. Some interpreters seek to resolve the problem in another way. They regard the Matthean words ἐρχομένους ἐπὶ τὸ βάπτισμα αὐτοῦ to be indicating only that the Pharisees and Sadducees were coming to the site of John's baptismal activities, as critical observers.[77] This understanding of the phrase, however, seems discordant with the nature of John's speech, since the speech appears to presume that the ones addressed are seeking baptism.[78]

Matthew 12:38-42 relates an occasion where "some of the scribes and Pharisees" ask Jesus to perform a sign. Though this pericope is unique to Matthew, it is quite similar in content to Matthew 16:1-4 (= Mark 8:11-13). The phraseology "the scribes and Pharisees," with scribes placed first in order, is not found in Mark, but (as we will observe shortly) it is used consistently in the unique material of Matthew's gospel (cf. 5:20; 12:38; 23:2, 13 et passim).

Matthew's non-Markan narratives do contain a couple of references to scribes apart from any Pharisees. In 2:4 "the chief priests and scribes of the people" are summoned to provide scriptural information concerning where the Messiah will be born. This passage presents the scribes as the nation's formal teachers of the Law, just as we see in the Markan material. In Matthew 8:19-20 (= Luke 9:57-58) a scribe affirms his desire to become a disciple of Jesus.

> [19]A scribe then approached and said, "Teacher, I will follow you wherever you go." [20]And Jesus said to him, "Foxes have holes, and birds of the air have nests; but the Son of Man has nowhere to lay his head."

Luke's account does not identify the individual as a scribe; it merely says that "someone [τις] said to him, 'I will follow you wherever you go.'" Matthew's presentation of a scribe who views Jesus favorably and actually wants to follow him is striking, though it can be argued that Jesus' response to the scribe is something of a mild criticism; the scribe does not appreciate the demands of discipleship (cf. vv. 21-22). Still, Matthew's real concern is with Pharisees and the scribes associated with them. This particular scribe is not of that classification. Therefore, this pericope further evidences what we already have observed as the Matthean agenda: portraying the Pharisees and their approach to the Torah as the real threat to Jesus' teaching and influence among the people.[79]

Non-Markan Material: Discourses

The unique material in Matthew's gospel consists primarily of Jesus' instructional discourses, and it is here that we see further evidence of Matthew's great interest in portraying the Pharisees as Jesus' opponents. Once the evangelist begins narrating the ministry of Jesus, he intersperses the narrative sections with five major discourses of Jesus, each one ending with the transitional phrase "when Jesus had finished [these words]." Thus, these discourses have a structural connection with one another. The first discourse (5:1–7:29), commonly known as the Sermon on the Mount, is directed to the disciples while the crowds listen in, and it presents beatitudes and other instruction regarding kingdom righteousness. The scribes and Pharisees provide the negative example that is not to be followed. The fifth discourse (23:1-39) is a stern warning to the crowds and the disciples about the poor example of the scribes and Pharisees, and the discourse culminates with a list of seven woes pronounced against them. These woes seem to provide a counterpoint to the beatitudes that begin the Sermon on the Mount.

Matthew 5:17-48 (Sermon on the Mount), "You Have Heard . . ."

Turning first to the Sermon on the Mount, we see that in Matthew 5 Jesus intentionally juxtaposes his own teaching about the Torah with that of the scribes and Pharisees.

[17]Do not think that I have come to abolish the law or the prophets; I have come not to abolish but to fulfill. [18]For truly I tell you, until heaven and earth pass away, not one letter, not one stroke of a letter, will pass from the law until all is accomplished. [19]Therefore, whoever breaks one of the least of these commandments, and teaches others to do the same, will be called least in the kingdom of heaven; but whoever does them and teaches them will be called great in the kingdom of heaven. [20]For I tell you, unless your righteousness exceeds that of the scribes and Pharisees, you will never enter the kingdom of heaven.

[21]You have heard that it was said to those of ancient times, "You shall not murder"; and "whoever murders shall be liable to judgment." [22]But I say to you that if you are angry with a brother or sister, you will be liable to judgment; and if you insult a brother or sister, you will be liable to the council; and if you say, "You fool," you will be liable to the hell of fire. [23]So when you are offering your gift at the altar, if you remember that your brother or sister has something against you, [24]leave your gift there before the altar and go; first be reconciled to your brother or sister, and then come and offer your gift. [25]Come to terms quickly with your accuser while you are on the way to court with him, or your accuser may hand you over to the judge, and the judge to the guard, and you will be thrown into prison. [26]Truly I tell you, you will never get out until you have paid the last penny.

[27]You have heard that it was said, "You shall not commit adultery." [28]But I say to you that everyone who looks at a woman with lust has already committed adultery with her in his heart. [29]If your right eye causes you to sin, tear it out and throw it away; it is better for you to lose one of your members than for your whole body to be thrown into hell. [30]And if your right hand causes you to sin, cut it off and throw it away; it is better for you to lose one of your members than for your whole body to go into hell.

[31]It was also said, "Whoever divorces his wife, let him give her a certificate of divorce." [32]But I say to you that anyone who divorces his wife, except on the ground of unchastity, causes her to commit adultery; and whoever marries a divorced woman commits adultery.

[33]Again, you have heard that it was said to those of ancient times, "You shall not swear falsely, but carry out the vows you have made to the Lord." [34]But I say to you, Do not swear at all, either by heaven, for it is the throne of God, [35]or by the earth, for it is his footstool, or by Jerusalem, for it is the city of the great King. [36]And do not swear by

your head, for you cannot make one hair white or black. [37]Let your word be "Yes, Yes" or "No, No"; anything more than this comes from the evil one.

[38]You have heard that it was said, "An eye for an eye and a tooth for a tooth." [39]But I say to you, Do not resist an evildoer. But if anyone strikes you on the right cheek, turn the other also; [40]and if anyone wants to sue you and take your coat, give your cloak as well; [41]and if anyone forces you to go one mile, go also the second mile. [42]Give to everyone who begs from you, and do not refuse anyone who wants to borrow from you.

[43]You have heard that it was said, "You shall love your neighbor and hate your enemy." [44]But I say to you, Love your enemies and pray for those who persecute you, [45]so that you may be children of your Father in heaven; for he makes his sun rise on the evil and on the good, and sends rain on the righteous and on the unrighteous. [46]For if you love those who love you, what reward do you have? Do not even the tax collectors do the same? [47]And if you greet only your brothers and sisters, what more are you doing than others? Do not even the Gentiles do the same? [48]Be perfect, therefore, as your heavenly Father is perfect.

In this discourse, Matthew's Jesus vehemently denies the charge that the aim of his teaching is to nullify (καταλύω) the Torah (v. 17). He affirms that the Law must be followed in every way, but he says that the scribes and Pharisees are poor teachers of the kind of righteous behavior the Law advocates: "For I tell you, that unless your righteousness exceeds that of the scribes and Pharisees, you will never enter the kingdom of heaven" (v. 20). Jesus then cites six cases where the commonly heard teaching on the Law fails to receive proper application (5:21-48). He employs a paradigmatic introduction, "You have heard . . . But I say to you" ('Ηκούσατε . . . ἐγὼ δὲ λέγω ὑμῖν). But what is the nature of the contrast?

Some scholars have understood Matthew's Jesus to be contrasting the Mosaic Law with the new-covenant system of Christianity.[80] But this view ignores the immediate context of the discourse in that it interprets Matthew's Jesus to be doing the very thing he explicitly says he is not doing: abrogating the Mosaic Law (vv. 17-20). To the contrary, Matthew is not portraying Jesus as a teacher outside of the Mosaic system, but rather as an insider who has strong disagreement with what the most influential teachers, the scribes and Pharisees, are indicating about the Law.[81] Therefore, we should understand the six examples Jesus gives as six cases of Torah instruction from the scribes and Pharisees—all of which are applied in ways that result in an inadequate level of righteousness (v. 20).

In each example, the issue for Jesus is that the Pharisaic application of the Law fails to go far enough.[82] The people hear from the scribes and Pharisees that the Law condemns murder, but bitterness and estrangement are tolerated (vv. 21-26). They hear that adultery is forbidden, but the problem of lusting after another man's wife is ignored (vv. 27-30). They hear that a bill of divorcement must be provided to legally divorce one's wife, but what is not evaluated is whether the divorce itself is a truly moral act (vv. 31-32). They hear that the Law commands a person to keep his vows, but integrity in what one says is deemed necessary only on occasions where a formally worded vow is uttered (vv. 33-37). They hear about the judicial principle of *lex talionis*, but its use in personal vengeance is permitted (vv. 38-42). Finally, they hear about the obligation to love one's neighbor, but the principle is not extended to one's enemies so as to emulate the righteous behavior of God (vv. 43-48).

Several of the above cases concern issues of Pharisaic legal praxis that, as we have seen, find critique elsewhere in Matthew: for example, the Pharisees' acceptance of divorce as long as it conformed to Deuteronomy 24:1-4 (cf. Mark 10:2-12; Matt 19:3-12); their enforcement of Corban vows (cf. Mark 7:9-13; Matt 15:5-7); their failure to extend love as broadly as they should (cf. Mark 2:16-17; 2:23-28; 3:1-6; Matt 9:9-13; Matt 12:1-8, 9-14). It is important to note that in none of the six cases does Jesus say that the scribes and Pharisees' explicit teaching of Scripture is wrong. The Law did indeed condemn murder, adultery, and unfulfilled vows, and it did speak of a bill of divorcement, the principles of *lex talionis* and love of neighbor. The problem is that the scribes and Pharisees put these precepts of Scripture into practice as if the precept expressed the limit of moral consideration rather than its starting point.

Several of the things Jesus says in this discourse clearly go beyond what the Law enforced for Israelite society.[83] For example, the Law did not actually state that a person should be brought before magistrates and punished for angrily calling his neighbor a bad name, or for harboring adulterous thoughts in his heart, or for refusing to lend to someone in need. Yet, Matthew's Jesus condemns all these behaviors as, in some sense, contrary to the Law (5:22, 28, 42). What he is saying is that the express regulations of the Mosaic Law pointed to underlying moral principles that were incumbent on a person if he would truly be like God (5:48). Yet, the scribes and Pharisees failed to demonstrate this. For Matthew's Jesus, the "righteousness" of the scribes and Pharisees is not an adequate example for the Jewish people to follow (v. 20).[84]

Matthew 23:1-33, "Woe to You, Scribes and Pharisees"

Structurally, Matthew 23 consists of three sections: a warning about the scribes and Pharisees being inadequate teachers (vv. 1-12); woes pronounced upon the scribes and Pharisees (vv. 13-33); and a lament over Jerusalem because it must receive God's judgment (vv. 34-39). The responsibility for that judgment, says Jesus, lies largely with the scribes and Pharisees who provide poor religious role models. The underlying problem, of course, is that they reject Jesus and his messianic status. But the discourse presents the matter as something more than the "Pauline" question of whether one believes in Jesus. It is, rather, a halakhic issue. As we have seen throughout Matthew, the differences between Jesus and the Pharisees consistently center around the matter of whose explication of the Torah is correct. The thrust of Matthew's gospel is this: Jesus properly teaches and exemplifies the Torah, while the scribes and Pharisees do not.

It is important to note to whom the discourse is addressed. Matthew says, "Then Jesus said *to the crowds* and to his disciples . . ." (v. 1). The order is significant. Beginning with the Sermon on the Mount and then throughout Matthew's gospel, the scenario we see is that of Jesus teaching his disciples, with the crowds listening in. Here in Matthew 23 the reverse is true, and Jesus' primary audience is the Temple crowds, with the disciples secondary. Throughout Matthew the conflict between the Pharisees and Jesus has been the practical matter of whose concept of the Law will have greater influence over the people. Now the issue comes to a head, and Matthew's Jesus attacks his rivals in public and with polemical vehemence.

> [1]Then Jesus said to the crowds and to his disciples, [2]"The scribes and the Pharisees sit on Moses' seat; [3]therefore, do whatever they teach you and follow it; but do not do as they do, for they do not practice what they teach. [4]They tie up heavy burdens, hard to bear, and lay them on

the shoulders of others; but they themselves are unwilling to lift a finger to move them. [5]They do all their deeds to be seen by others; for
they make their phylacteries broad and their fringes long. [6]They love to
have the place of honor at banquets and the best seats in the synagogues, [7]and to be greeted with respect in the marketplaces, and to
have people call them rabbi. [8]But you are not to be called rabbi, for you
have one teacher, and you are all students. [9]And call no one your father
on earth, for you have one Father—the one in heaven. [10]Nor are you to
be called instructors, for you have one instructor, the Messiah. [11]The
greatest among you will be your servant. [12]All who exalt themselves will
be humbled, and all who humble themselves will be exalted.

These verses manifest a basic parallel with Mark 12:38-40 (cf. also
Luke 11:43, 46; 20:46). The entire discourse of Matthew 23 appears
to be a fuller, more developed version of the points expressed in Mark
12:38-40. A key difference is that the Markan text made no mention
of the Pharisees; Mark's Jesus warned the Temple crowd solely about
"the scribes." The fact that Matthew's Jesus addresses "the scribes
and the Pharisees" corresponds to the Matthean tendency to give
more attention to the Pharisees as Jesus' opponents than does Mark.
Despite this emphasis on the Pharisees, however, Matthew still places
the scribes first in order, so that throughout verses 1-12 and the
remainder of Matthew 23 we consistently read of "*the scribes* and the
Pharisees." This order is precisely what we saw in the Sermon on the
Mount (5:20). It is also the order of Matthew 12:38, another unique
Matthean pericope. In fact, whenever the evangelist records unique
material having to do with both scribes and Pharisees, he always
places the scribes first in order. The only time in Matthew when the
order is reversed is when the author records Markan material where
Mark placed the Pharisees before the scribes (cf. Matthew 15:1 =
Mark 7:1).

Given the evangelist's clear intention of seeking to highlight the
Pharisees as Jesus' chief opponents, this equally clear pattern of
placing the scribes before the Pharisees must be for a reason. It evidences the fact that, despite the evangelist's greater interest in the
Pharisees per se, he still recognizes that the scribes, rather than the
Pharisees, are the formal and primary teachers of the Law. As I noted
earlier, when discussing the people's source of formal knowledge
about the Law, Mark spoke of "the scribes" (alone) fulfilling that role.
The author of Matthew follows suit; when using those particular

Markan pericopes, he does not change Mark's scribes to "Pharisees" as he tends to do in pericopes where scribes confront Jesus over halakhic matters. Thus, the author of Matthew follows Mark in presenting the scribes as the formal, primary teachers of the Law, and he manifests this procedure again in his unique material by always listing scribes before Pharisees.

While recognizing this fact, we must still probe Matthew's purpose in inserting "the Pharisees" into an expansion of Mark 12:38-40, a Markan polemic against scribes. Contrary to what some scholars suggest, the reason is not because the author of Matthew was ignorant of the distinction between scribes and Pharisees. Nor is the reason likely to be that Matthew's Pharisees symbolize the Jewish opponents of the (late first-century) Matthean community, opponents whose leaders were known to be Pharisees.[85] (If that were the case, wouldn't the evangelist want to place the Pharisees first in order?) The Matthean phrase "the scribes and Pharisees" indicates that the author of Matthew recognized that the Pharisees served a highly influential, albeit secondary teaching role alongside the scribes. Underlying the phraseology is the evangelist's recognition of two factors: (1) the influence that the Pharisees had on the scribes, especially due to the fact that some scribes were members of the Pharisaic party. Thus, while scribes were the formal and primary teachers of the people, the Pharisees were an indirect source of halakhic instruction; (2) the respect with which the Jewish people viewed the Pharisees, and hence their informal influence on the people.

Looking now at verses 2-3 in detail, we are faced with a text that is key in any discussion of Matthew's Pharisees. Yet, the exegesis of these verses is laden with difficulty. Here Jesus affirms, "The scribes and the Pharisees sit on Moses' seat; therefore, do whatever they teach you and follow it; but do not do as they do, for they do not practice what they teach." There are two exegetical questions here. (1) What is the meaning of the words "Moses' seat"? (2) How can Jesus say that the people should do whatever the scribes and Pharisees teach them?

Scholars have offered several suggestions as to the meaning of "Moses' seat" (τῆς Μωϋσέως καθέδρας). Perhaps it refers to actual stone benches that may have been used in first-century synagogues as seats for those presiding over the assembly.[86] Perhaps it refers to the receptacle for the synagogue's Torah scroll.[87] Whether or not a literal item of furniture is intended, the phrase could be a statement of the religious authority—whether presumed or actual—that the scribes and Pharisees possessed. It is this latter idea that raises the possibility in the minds of many scholars that these verses reveal a late first-century *Sitz im Leben* for Matthew's gospel where the Pharisees have gained formal religious control of the Jewish community.[88]

Most scholars are agreed that the idea of sitting on Moses' seat at least indicates some kind of teaching role.[89] But is Jesus seriously suggesting that the people ought to follow the halakha of the scribes and Pharisees? Some scholars say, yes. Ellis Rivkin goes so far as to affirm that since Matthew presents the Pharisees as teachers of the oral traditions concerning the Law, then that is precisely what sitting on Moses' seat must mean. Therefore, Matthew's Jesus is affirming the authority of the Pharisees and their halakha.[90] But that idea is completely discordant with the thrust of Matthew's gospel as a whole.

One cannot derive any kind of coherent picture from Matthew's gospel by saying that in this text Jesus acknowledges the Pharisaic halakha, when that is the very thing Jesus has repeatedly challenged and condemned throughout the gospel. Nor can the difficulty be mitigated by appealing to the fact that in verse 3 Jesus charges the scribes and Pharisees with hypocrisy. Though "they do not practice what they teach," Jesus still says for the people to "do whatever they teach you and follow it." Nor does it work to think that Jesus is merely saying to follow the halakha of the scribes and Pharisees *in principle*, just not in every detail.[91] Again, the text specifically says to "do whatever they teach you" (πάντα ὅσα ἐὰν εἴπωσιν ὑμῖν).

Some interpreters suggest, therefore, that Jesus' words should be understood sarcastically; perhaps he is mocking the presumptuousness of the scribes and Pharisees for assuming such a teaching role.[92] One could even understand the reference to Moses' seat as an acknowledgement of the scribes and Pharisees' position as authoritative teachers, without actually endorsing it.[93] Mark Powell has suggested that the idea of sitting on Moses' seat indicates not so much a teaching role for the scribes and Pharisees, but rather that they are the ones in Jewish society who control access to the Scriptures and so the Jewish populace relies on them for a knowledge of the biblical text.[94] The difficulty with this suggestion is that Matthew's Jesus specifically refers in these verses to the *teaching* of the scribes and Pharisees. A strong indication of the consternation this passage causes interpreters is the further suggestion that verses 2-3 are a piece of pre-Matthean tradition that cannot be harmonized with Matthew's overall portrait of Jesus.[95]

Is it possible to understand Jesus to be saying that the people should follow the scribes and Pharisees' teaching of the Scriptures, but just not their behavior or the halakha of their oral traditions? I believe that it is, since this is exactly what we have seen throughout our analysis of Matthew's gospel. In the Sermon on the Mount, Jesus' objection to the teaching of the scribes and Pharisees was not that their teaching of Scripture per se was wrong, but that their application of it failed to adequately fulfill the principles of the Law.[96] Their level of righteousness (i.e., righteous behavior) was what was inadequate (5:20), not what the people heard from them regarding what Scripture said. Jesus objected to the actions of the scribes and Pharisees. Angry epithets, lustful looks at women, bills of divorcement, vows made in vain, acts of personal vengeance, and unloving behavior all failed to measure up to the moral principles of Scripture that the scribes and Pharisees themselves taught. Thus, Matthew's Jesus says in the present discourse, ". . . Do whatever they teach you and follow it; but do not do as they do, for they do not practice what they teach" (v. 3).

In the Markan material on the Pharisees—all of which Matthew utilizes—Jesus likewise criticized the actions of the Pharisees as they applied their halakhic traditions. In reality, their traditions regarding Sabbath-keeping, hand-washing, and Corban enforcement resulted in violations of the Torah's precepts rather than the fulfillment of them.[97] Matthew's Jesus gives great emphasis to the false appearance of righteousness that the scribes and Pharisees displayed (e.g., 6:1-6, 16-18; 7:15-23; 23:5-7). The chief way in which the people learned the oral tradition of the scribes and Pharisees was by observing them and seeing how they applied the Torah. And though they gave every appearance of righteousness, their observable application of the Torah was precisely what Jesus did not want the Jewish people to emulate.

Loosely paralleling Mark 12:38-39, Matthew's Jesus says of the scribes and Pharisees, "They do all their deeds to be seen by others; for they make their phylacteries broad and their fringes long. They love to have the place of honor at banquets and the best seats in the synagogues, and to be greeted with respect in the marketplaces, and to have people call them rabbi" (vv. 5-7). The wearing of phylacteries and fringes on one's garments was intended to remind one to obey the statutes of the Law. The text may be indicating that the phylacteries and fringes of the scribes and Pharisees were particularly prominent. But in their case these items of adornment failed to serve their scriptural function, because while they gave the scribes and Pharisees an outward appearance of righteousness, violation of the Torah still persisted.

The hypocrisy charge that Matthew's Jesus levels against the scribes and Pharisees is precisely of this nature, and it conforms to the hypocrisy charge that we observed in Mark's gospel. It is not that the scribes and Pharisees were hypocrites in the sense of being duplicitous frauds, saying one thing while intending to do another. Rather, Jesus' charge of hypocrisy—vehement and harsh, to be sure—pertained to the problem of appearing to be righteous while in reality failing to fulfill God's statutes.

The seven woes in the next section of the discourse (23:13-33) tie in perfectly with this explication of verses 1-12. Matthew's Jesus castigates the scribes and Pharisees for failing in their public life to offer an adequate example of how to live so as to fulfill the Torah. For our purposes here, there is no need to address the intricacies of each woe and their highly polemical language. But a few points should be noted. The woe condemning Pharisaic oaths (vv. 16-22) corresponds to the similar discussion in the Sermon on the Mount (5:33-37). The issue is that of swearing oaths that, due to technical form of expression, are not regarded as binding. The two woes of verses 23-26 are significant because of the information they provide and because they are paralleled in Luke 11.

> [23]Woe to you, scribes and Pharisees, hypocrites! For you tithe mint, dill, and cummin, and have neglected the weightier matters of the law: justice and mercy and faith. It is these you ought to have practiced without neglecting the others. [24]You blind guides! You strain out a gnat but swallow a camel!
>
> [25]Woe to you, scribes and Pharisees, hypocrites! For you clean the outside of the cup and of the plate, but inside they are full of greed and self-indulgence. [26]You blind Pharisee! First clean the inside of the cup, so that the outside also may become clean.

The woe of verses 23-24 parallels Luke 11:42, and the woe of verses 25-26 parallels Luke 11:39. Most scholars therefore regard this material as derived from Q and treat it as early testimony of a Pharisaic emphasis upon strict tithing and ritual purification.[98] The issue of tithing is never mentioned in Mark, but the issue of ritual purification is what receives such prominence in Mark 7 (= Matthew 15). In particular, the latter woe offers corroboration of the editorial insertion of Mark 7:3–4 regarding the Pharisaic purification of food vessels. It also ties in with Mark 7:15-23 where Jesus makes a distinction between inner and outer purification.[99]

Conclusions and Final Observations

As I bring this essay to a close, let me summarize my conclusions about Matthew's portrait of the Pharisees and then make some observations about the use of Matthew and Mark in historical research on the Pharisees.

Our analysis of Matthew's gospel shows that the author presents a picture of the Pharisees that highly resembles what we observe in Mark. Matthew follows Mark closely, using all of the Markan pericopes on the Pharisees and the scribes. He does add some new data to these Markan pericopes, and there are some notable alterations. Matthew sometimes changes Mark's references to Jewish leaders who interact with the Pharisees. He shows little of Mark's interest in the Herodians, and substitutes instead references to Sadducees. Matthew's most significant alteration of Mark is that of designating as Pharisees the Markan scribes who oppose Jesus on matters of the Torah. This tendency reveals a key Matthean goal: to present the Pharisees and their approach to the Torah as the major obstacle to Jesus and his teaching.

But despite these alterations of Markan material, the author of Matthew never subverts the Markan picture of the Pharisees, their role in society, or their teaching. Matthew's portrait of the Pharisees is a thoroughly coherent picture that is substantially just what we observe in Mark. The Pharisees have a prominent presence in Galilee. They are not political or religious officials, but they do have an ancillary relationship to those groups who are in power. Pharisaic scribes might belong to the group of scribes who function alongside the chief priests and elders, but the text does not explicitly indicate this. Though scribes are the nation's formal teachers of the Law, the Pharisees are experts in the Law, they have opinions that carry weight in the synagogue, and they are confident in their piety and their traditions. They are especially concerned with following "the tradition of the elders." Honoring God is a paramount concern of the Pharisees—so much so that, on occasion, it may even supplant humanitarian obligations. Chief among their halakhic concerns are the proper observance of Sabbath, ritual purity, and Corban. Matthew adds only one religious trait that Mark doesn't present: Pharisees are scrupulous in their tithing.

Like the Pharisees in Mark, Matthew's Pharisees do not have table fellowship with nonobservant Jews. But this does not seem to mean that they would be opposed to associating with non-Pharisees as long as ritual purity at table was maintained. Particularly notable is the strong influence that the Pharisees have upon the Jewish people in matters of Torah observance. Matthew's non-Markan material does not present anything about the Pharisees that substantively alters the picture derived from the Markan material, but it does vividly highlight how influential the Pharisees are with the common people and why they pose such an impediment to the people's acceptance of Jesus and his teaching.

Having now analyzed the pictures of the Pharisees that we find in Mark and Matthew, we must ask: Do these documents provide us with accurate historical information about the Pharisees? To what degree are the recorded encounters between Jesus and the Pharisees relating historical events? Are they merely "ideal scenes" that reflect the situation of the church at the time when Mark and Matthew are written? If so, to what extent might these "ideal scenes" still offer valid information about the Pharisees' role in Palestinian society and their religious beliefs and practices? These are the kinds of questions that arise. Obviously, these questions intersect with the broader issue of the historical reliability of the gospels in general, a matter that is beyond the scope of this essay. But my concern here is how the Gospels of Matthew and Mark are to be used by modern scholars who seek information about the historical Pharisees. Let me make a few observations that I believe should be kept in mind as we engage this pursuit.

First, any data drawn from a gospel document for purposes of performing historical reconstruction on the Pharisees must be interpreted with regard for the entire picture of the Pharisees that the document presents. If a gospel's data, viewed as a whole, do yield a coherent and consistent picture of the Pharisees, then a historian must be careful not to place an interpretation on a particular text that would be contrary to what that text would signify when viewed with respect to the gospel as a whole. I have argued in this essay that Mark and Matthew each offer a coherent and consistent portrait of the Pharisees. Therefore, their data must be interpreted accordingly. One cannot pluck out an item here or an item there and give it a construction that, while "supporting" one's own theory of the Pharisees, subverts the meaning it would yield when viewed within its documentary context as a whole. When this happens, statements like "Mark shows . . ." or "Matthew indicates . . ." become meaningless. We need to move beyond these methodological pitfalls. Perhaps readers will want to criticize the picture of the Pharisees that I have observed in my reading of Mark or Matthew, or disagree with me that a coherent and consistent picture is presented at all. But the point is that this must be the starting point of our inquiry and our debate.

Second, scholars must carefully examine whether the evidence supports the common speculation that Matthew's Pharisees are to be understood as symbols of the Jewish leadership of the late first century who were dominated by Pharisees. The evidence for this view of Matthew's Pharisees rests largely on two factors: the prominence that Matthew gives to the Pharisees (over against Mark) as the major opponents of Jesus; and the statement in Matthew 23:2 about the Pharisees sitting on "Moses' seat."[100]

It certainly appears that the evangelist alters his source material so as to highlight the Pharisees as Jesus' chief opponents. But he does not substantially alter the role of the Pharisees from that which Mark presents. In the evangelist's use of Markan material, Q material, and unique material, the Pharisees are differentiated from the scribes, and scribes (rather than the Pharisees) are consistently presented as the formal teachers of the nation and as the ones who are directly connected to the nation's leadership. Matthew does not put the Pharisees in that position. Furthermore, I must question whether there is sufficient reason to construe the statement about the scribes and Pharisees sitting on "Moses' seat" to be a depiction of Pharisaic authority and dominance that emerged in the post-70 period. That construction of the passage disconnects the Pharisees of this one verse from the over- all portrait of the Pharisees that we see throughout the rest of Matthew. The verse can best be understood as a statement about the scribes and Pharisees that comports with the picture we observe throughout Matthew and throughout Mark: they simply are the teachers of the Jewish people—the scribes in a formal capacity, and the Pharisees in an informal and secondary capacity.

Third, we must question the view that the encounters between Jesus and the Pharisees in Matthew and Mark are best understood as unhistorical "ideal scenes." It is easy to assert, as does E. P. Sanders, that the pericopes reporting Pharisaic accusations of Sabbath viola- tions (viz., plucking of grain and healing) and a failure to observe rit- ual hand-washing have virtually no historical basis and were contrived in order to address the church's current issues.[10] An assump- tion like this allows Sanders to disregard any of the gospels' data that conflict with his position about the Pharisees and "Common Judaism." But the matter cannot be dismissed so easily.

The material in Mark, which Matthew re-presents in a way that is substantially compatible, is normally dated to the general time period of 70 CE, and so most scholars concede that the Markan material gives us at least some reliable information about the historical Pharisees prior to 70. If Matthew 23:25 is regarded as coming from Q, we seem to have a measure of corroboration for the Markan explanation of Pharisaic cleansing rituals and Jesus' opposing view on inward defilement. Early corroboration for another item of the Markan material—namely, Jesus' teaching on divorce—comes from Paul's discussion of the matter in 1 Corinthians 7:10-11.

But more importantly, our analysis of the gospels' presentation of the debates between Jesus and the Pharisees reveals how particular were the halakhic issues under dispute, and these do not adequately correspond to the issues that we know of in the early church. There is no evidence to suggest that the early church had controversies over healing on the Sabbath, or plucking grain on the Sabbath, or hand-washing before meals, or matters pertaining to Corban. Nor can these halakhic disputes between Jesus and the Pharisees be treated as literary concoctions to depict the church's freedom from the Law. Matthew's and Mark's Jesus does not annul Mosaic food laws or abrogate Sabbath observance. The halakhic disputes between Jesus and the Pharisees are not addressing whether the Torah is binding, but how the Torah is to be applied. The evangelists' accounts of disputes between Jesus and the Pharisees could, of course, be used hortatively within the church; applications to current problems could be extrapolated. But it makes little sense to assert that these encounters between Jesus and the Pharisees were concocted out of whole cloth to address contemporary church issues, when in so many instances Jesus' disputes and the church's disputes do not coincide.[102]

CHAPTER 4

LUKE'S PHARISEES

Amy-Jill Levine

The third gospel's presentation of the Pharisees is "puzzling,"[1] lacking consistency,[2] "complex,"[3] and "disputed."[4] Whether approached primarily by literary or by historical questions, Luke's Pharisees elude clear answers.

The reasons for this confusion are several, of which the following four are major. First, the relationship between this gospel and the Acts of the Apostles, Luke's second volume, complicates assessment of figures that appear in both texts. Pharisees in Acts include Gamaliel, "a teacher of the Law, respected by all the people," Gamaliel's student Paul, "a Pharisee, the son of Pharisees" (5:34; 23:6), "believers who belonged to the sect of the Pharisees" (15:5), and "the scribes of the Pharisees' group" (23:9). However, the Pharisees in Acts similarly elude definitive assessment: is Gamaliel admirable because he cautions against persecuting Jesus' followers or the villainous mentor of the arch-persecutor Paul? Do Pharisees demonstrate Scriptural fidelity or do they block the Holy Spirit by insisting Gentile Christians follow the Mosaic Law? Moreover, their depictions impact any assessment of the Gospel of Luke if one seeks a consistent presentation.[5]

Second, source-critical questions remain uncertain. Most New Testament scholars propose that Luke relied on both Mark's gospel and a (hypothetical) source shared with Matthew, labeled Q. A minority of scholars argue that Luke directly depended on Matthew and that Mark is a conflation of Matthew and Luke. Assessment of Luke's sources impacts understanding of Luke's Pharisees. Assessed in terms of Markan priority, Luke *adds* references to Pharisees in 5:17; 7:30; 7:36; 11:53; 13:31; 14:1, 3; 16:14; 17:20; and 18:10-14. Compared to Mark and Matthew, Luke highlights the Pharisees' love of money and their rejection of Jesus' association with tax collectors and sinners. But

113

Luke lacks the odd Matthean (27:62) combination of "chief priests
and Pharisees," for Luke mentions no Pharisees in the Passion narrative. Absent is Mark's note that the chief priests, scribes, and elders
(Mark 11:27) sent "Pharisees and Herodians" (12:13) to trap Jesus;
Luke speaks only of "spies" who pretended to be righteous (δικαίους;
20:20). Did Luke suppress this information? Was Luke aware of it?

Third, Luke's historical and social contexts remain speculative.
The Pharisees may represent "Jewish Christians" of Luke's own day.[6]
Or, they may be ahistorical foils designed to teach the author's audience by negative example. The invectives may be conventional (hypocrites, lovers of money), with no basis in reality. Or, they may reflect
the redactor's use of sources, themselves of unclear historical worth.
Nor are these options mutually exclusive. Further complicating this
issue: scholars have yet to reach any firm agreement on the composition of the intended audience or the identity of the author: Gentile
(the most common identification), proselyte, God-fearer, Jew.

Finally, all readers bring to the text their own presuppositions and
values. Some interpreters find Pharisaic presence *implied* where Luke
mentions none and ascribe to Pharisees *implied* concerns that Luke
does not note. Some begin with the view that all Pharisees are the
same; others conclude that these figures should be assessed as individuals, like the Gentiles and the Twelve.[7]

In recognition of such considerations, this essay takes the following
steps. First, it looks at Luke's gospel apart from Acts. Second, it does
not emphasize possible redactional changes. Third, eschewing reconstruction of Luke's social context, it focuses on the narrative: what the
gospel's Pharisees do and how the narrator describes them. Finally, to
enable readers to assess the data themselves, it addresses each pericope in which the Pharisees appear rather than organizing the information into categories, such as "Sabbath observance," "economic
status," or "table fellowship."

LUKE 5:17-26 (MATT 9:1-8; MARK 2:1-12)

Luke's Pharisees are introduced in a narrative context that already
depicts the fulfillment of Simeon's prediction: "this child is destined
for the falling and the rising of many in Israel, and to be a sign that

will be opposed" (2:34). Falling are those in the Nazareth synagogue who, incensed by Jesus' remark that they would not receive the benefits he offers others, "drove him out of the town . . . so that they might hurl him off the cliff" (4:29). In terms of rising, Jesus has healed Peter's mother-in-law (4:38-39), all "sick with various kinds of diseases" (4:40), and a leper (5:12-14). Thus, the Pharisees cannot represent "all Jews"; what is undetermined is whether they will fall or rise, accept or oppose.

The introduction itself suggests their ubiquitous presence: "while he was teaching, Pharisees and teachers of the Law (νομοδιδάσκαλοι) were sitting nearby (they had come from every village of Galilee and Judea and from Jerusalem) . . ." (5:17). The Pharisees' last appearance occurs immediately outside Jerusalem (19:39); the gospel does not depict them in the city. Since geographic markers may serve narrative purposes, their historicity is questionable. Pharisaic presence can indicate a Christological focus: although not explicit, Luke suggests that the Pharisees have traveled to see Jesus. That is, Jesus is sufficiently important to draw their attention. Likewise, Luke sees the Pharisees as important: *their* presence enhances Jesus' role, and Luke, compared to Mark and Matthew, highlights their role. Whereas Luke mentions Pharisees twice (5:17, 21), Mark and Matthew mention only scribes and withhold reference to them until after Jesus forgives the paralytic.

Robert Brawley suggests that this introduction presents the Pharisees as "an organized body," that "the broad geographical base introduces [them] as representing all the territory of the Jewish people," and that the Jerusalem reference "may be added specifically to imply official status."[8] Then again, ubiquity need not indicate unanimity: not all in a synagogue share the same views of Sabbath healing (13:10-17); one sheep can stray from its flock (15:3-7); the Twelve do not share common cause once Jesus enters Jerusalem. Regarding ubiquity, the Pharisees are no more omnipresent than Jews who seek Jesus' healing power or who are curious about his teaching. Finally, the Jerusalem reference need not indicate any "official" connection; had Luke wished to make such a connection, the Passion narrative would have provided an opportunity.

The reference to the "teachers of the Law" both associates and distinguishes them from the Pharisees: they are separate groups with common interests. Luke may have employed this term rather than the more common "scribes" (γραμματεῖς; 5:21, 30; 6:7; 9:22; 11:53; 15:2; 19:47; 20:1, 19, 39, 46; 22:2, 66; 23:10) to emphasize the Pharisees' interest in Torah interpretation. Or, Luke could be associating the groups (the one other use of νομοδιδάσκαλος in Luke's corpus is Acts 5:34, a description of Gamaliel).

The Pharisees' presence itself creates interpretive problems, since Luke has not revealed their intent. Neutrally, they may have wanted to hear what Jesus was teaching. Then again, their description as "sitting" rather than "gathering to hear Jesus" or to seek healing may suggest nefarious motives, and the description of Jesus as "teaching" (διδάσκων; 5:17) may indicate a contrast between Jesus and the "teachers of the Law" along with their Pharisaic associates, just as Luke's note that the "power of the Lord was with [Jesus]" indicates that it was not with the Pharisees.

Jesus' statement to the paralytic, "Friend, your sins are forgiven you" (5:20), catalyzes the Pharisees who, now along with scribes, "began to question" and so issue their first words: "Who is this who is speaking blasphemies? Who is able to forgive sins but God alone?" From a narrative perspective, the question has three functions. First, it connects the Pharisees to the Nazareth congregation and to those who witnessed the healing of the demoniac in the Capernaum synagogue: in each setting, people question Jesus' identity (4:22, 36). Second, it establishes an association to Jesus' first words recorded in Luke's gospel, which are also a question. To his distraught mother, he asks, "Why were you searching for me? Did you not know that I must be in my Father's house?" (2:49). Structurally, the Pharisees occupy the same position as Mary. Third, it shifts the pericope from healing narrative to controversy story.

The controversy genre will continue to involve Pharisees (5:30; 6:1-5, 6-11). For this introduction, however, the controversy is itself disrupted: the Pharisees are neither angry nor desiring to silence Jesus. When the pericope ends with the notice that "Amazement (ἔκστασις) seized all of them, and they glorified God and were filled with awe, saying, 'We have seen strange things today'" (5:26), there is no reason to distinguish the Pharisees from "all of them."[9]

LUKE 5:27-32 (MATT 9:9-13; MARK 2:14-17)

The scene changes to the house of Levi the tax collector. Although described as having "left everything" (καταλιπὼν πάντα; 5:28) to follow Jesus, "everything" refers to his profession only. Levi gives a "great banquet" for Jesus; attending is a "large crowd of tax collectors and others" (5:29) along with, apparently, Jesus' disciples. Again the Pharisees raise a question, but this time with a grumbling tone (ἐγόγ-γυζον) and directed to Jesus' disciples: "Why do you eat and drink with tax collectors and sinners?" (5:30); they replace the narrator's "others" with the specific "sinners." Compared to Mark, Luke highlights the Pharisees' role by removing the reference to scribes (but see 15:2, where "Pharisees and scribes" grumble about Jesus' welcoming "sinners"). The issue is table fellowship.

Jerome Neyrey suggests that "Pharisees illustrate perfectly the principle that people basically eat with others with whom they share values (e.g., haburah meal). Hence, the Pharisees criticize Jesus, who claims to teach a way of holiness, for eating with tax collectors and sinners, because shared table-fellowship implies that Jesus shares *their* world, not God's world of holiness."[10] The issue is not clearly "holiness"; nor is it ritual purity (which the *haburah* reference implies). It is the impression Jesus gives that he approves of his dining companions qua tax collectors and sinners. The Pharisees' labeling of the "others" as "sinners" confirms this point. No mention has been made of Jesus' exhorting them to repent or providing them guidance on behavior (as John the Baptist did [3:8, 12]). Jesus thus insists: "I have come to call not the righteous but sinners to repentance" (5:31). The response seems to satisfy the Pharisees, who shift the question from table fellowship to fasting.

LUKE 5:33-39 (MATT 9:14-17; MARK 2:18-22)

The interlocutors remain Pharisees along with their scribes, despite the awkward third-person reference: "Then they said to him, 'John's disciples, like the disciples of the Pharisees, frequently fast and pray, but your disciples eat and drink'" (5:33). Mark (2:18) has the same

grammatical glitch; Matthew assigns the observation to John's disciples (9:14). The Pharisees, showing no hostility, question practices that
differ from their own: Jesus eats with sinners and tax collectors but
Pharisees do not; Jesus does not fast but Pharisees do (see also 18:12).
The pericope ends with Jesus' explication based on practical wisdom:
no one puts new wine into old wineskins. The Pharisees do not
respond.

LUKE 6:1-5 (MATT 12:1-8; MARK 2:23-28)

The next episode is set on "one Sabbath" and in a grainfield rather
than a house, but the subject remains eating. "*Some* of the Pharisees"
(τινὲς δὲ τῶν Φαρισαίων)—a delimiting compared to Mark 2:24 and
Matthew 12:2—inquire why the disciples are "doing what is not permitted (οὐκ ἔξεστιν) on the Sabbath," namely, rubbing grain in their
hands and thus winnowing. The issue is Torah *interpretation*: what
"work" is permitted on the Sabbath? Referring to 1 Samuel 21:1-6,
Jesus justifies their practice by exegetical precedent, and he concludes
by stating that "the Son of Man is lord of the Sabbath" (6:5). The
Pharisees have no response.

Explanations of the Pharisees' presence in the grainfield vary. The
more common view is that they are spying on Jesus. Alternatively,
"some" could have been following Jesus because his teaching
intrigued them. Claims that Jesus and the Pharisees both would have
been in violation of Sabbath law by traveling on the Sabbath[11] are
speculative; Luke makes no comment about the distance covered.

LUKE 6:6-11 (MATT 12:9-14; MARK 3:1-6)

The second Sabbath controversy suggests an unfriendly Pharisaic
presence. In a synagogue, "The scribes and the Pharisees watched to
see whether [Jesus] would cure on the sabbath, so that they might find
an accusation against him" (6:7). Jesus, aware of their agenda, first
questions them: "Is it permitted to do good or to do harm on the
Sabbath, to save life or to destroy it?" (6:9). The question presupposes
that the Pharisees have the halakhic knowledge. Jesus then heals a

man with a withered hand, but not by "work"; he orders the man to "stretch out" his hand, and the hand "was restored" (passive).

The Pharisees, "filled with fury" (ἀνοίας), discuss among themselves what "they might do to Jesus" (6:11). Compared to the reaction in the Nazareth synagogue, to Mark's notice (3:6) that following this incident the Pharisees plotted with the Herodians to kill Jesus, and to Matthew's notice (12:14) that the Pharisees sought to kill him, Luke's description is benign.

Johnson suggests that the Pharisees emerge as "arbiters of piety, particularly with regard to the Sabbath" and that they "claim to protect the integrity of Torah by placing all observances on an equal plane of obligation and seriousness" whereas Jesus "establishes a priority for moral activity above ritual."[12] "Arbiters" in the sense of having decision-making authority or even influence to sway opinion may be too strong. Luke does not depict Pharisees influencing or even teaching anyone. Instead, they tend to converse with each other, speak to Jesus or his disciples privately, or engage in interior monologue.

LUKE 7:29-30

Luke observes that "all the people" who heard Jesus' comments, "including the tax collectors, praised [literally, "justified"] God because they had been baptized with John's baptism. But by refusing to be baptized by him, the Pharisees and the lawyers rejected God's purpose for themselves" (7:29-30; see 3:7-18). Matthew 3:7 depicts "many Pharisees and Sadducees coming for baptism." The aside adds a negative element to Luke 3: readers might have initially concluded that those ubiquitous Pharisees were among the people baptized by John. Their absence also indicates that they were *not* among those "filled with expectation" about the Messiah (3:15).

LUKE 7:36-50 (MATT 26:6-13; MARK 14:3-9; JOHN 12:1-8)

Luke several times associates the Pharisees with *not* eating: not eating with sinners; fasting; not plucking grain. The gospel now presents the first of three banquets (7:36-50; 11:37-54; 14:1-24) hosted by a

Pharisee. Ironically, the scene falls immediately after Jesus complains to the crowd, "The Son of Man has come eating and drinking, and you say, 'Look, a glutton and a drunkard, a friend of tax collectors and sinners'" (7:34). That Pharisees share table fellowship with Jesus suggests that they do not consider his other associations to compromise their views or practices.

Only Luke depicts Jesus dining with Pharisees, and of the four versions of Jesus' anointing, only Luke specifies that host was a Pharisee. Malina and Neyrey assert: "Although we know the name of only one Pharisee ('Simon,' Luke 7:36, 40), we know him and all other Pharisees by the stereotypical label alone (e.g., Luke 11:38; 14:1-6; 15:1-2; 16:14)."[13] Supporting this view is Luke's repeated reference to Simon's Pharisaic connection: he is "one of the Pharisees" (v. 36) in "the Pharisee's house" (v. 36); Jesus is "eating in the Pharisee's house" (v. 37), and "the Pharisee who had invited" (v. 39) Jesus questions his knowledge. Other guests appear to be Pharisees or at least hold opinions Pharisees share, for they repeat the question voiced by Pharisees and scribes: "Who is this who even forgives sins?" (7:49; cf. 5:21). However, the stereotype is challenged by references to "some" Pharisees and depictions of others as individuals. The "group" focus may be less "Pharisaic" than a connection to Simon's role as host, a role that serves as the occasion for social commentary.[14] Thus, Jesus' comment to Simon that "you gave me no water for my feet . . . you gave me no kiss . . . you did not anoint my head with oil" (7:44-45) need not be seen as a slight.[15] Servants would have provided water and oil; the kiss was not mandatory. The point is the lavishness of the woman's response, not the host's failure (cf. 10:28-32).

The banquet setting not only connects the pericope with other meal scenes; it also suggests the symposium genre.[16] Fulfilling the convention, the Pharisee is of the urban elite,[17] a householder and patron. The convention anticipates a wise guest who stumps the host and an intruder who provides the occasion for conversation. The uninvited woman begins the action: she anoints Jesus' feet while he reclines at table. Although Jesus later describes the Pharisees as "lovers of money," no one at the banquet observes that the money she spent could have been used for the poor (Matt 26:8-9; Mark 14:4-5; John 12:5-6). Her actions rather prompt Simon's interior observation: "If this man were a prophet, he would have known who and what kind of woman this is who is touching him—that she is a sinner" (7:39).

Neyrey states that for Luke, "in no case and at no time was Jesus ever compromised by his contact with the unclean of Israel, despite the judgment of the Pharisee to the contrary." [18] Neither the narrator nor the Pharisee says anything about being "unclean." Were the woman unclean, and were Simon so concerned, then not only would her contact with Jesus have been immediately stopped, but the Pharisee's house would not be open to uninvited guests.

LUKE 10:25-37

Although no Pharisee appears in the setting for the parable of the good Samaritan or the parable itself, Ringe proposes: "One might surmise from the question [concerning eternal life] that the lawyer is a Pharisee whose theology included belief in the resurrection of the dead. . . . The exchange of questions and answers that ensues (10:26-37) fits what we know about the way various points of religious law were debated among the Pharisees, who were the principal forerunners of rabbinic Judaism." [19] The exchange is more comparable to the conversations Jesus has with the rich ruler (18:18-25), "chief priests and the scribes . . . with the elders" (20:1-8), and Sadducees (20:27-39). Conversely, Pharisees tend not to respond to Jesus' questions.

LUKE 11:37-54 (MATT 15:1-9; 23:1-36; MARK 7:1-9)

Again a Pharisee invites Jesus to dine; present are lawyers (11:45; cf. 5:17; 7:30) and, as the plural address in 11:39-44 suggests, other Pharisees. The host, like Simon, does not vocalize his concerns: "The Pharisee was amazed to see that [Jesus] did not first wash before dinner" (11:38; *m. Yad.* 4). The term "amazed," ἐθαύμασεν, describes Jesus' reaction to the faithful centurion (7:9) and so carries no negative judgment. "Wash," ἐβαπτίσθη, recollects the Baptist; whereas the Pharisees refused John's "washing," now the Pharisaic host queries Jesus' not "washing." [20]

Jesus, again demonstrating prophetic (or telepathic) ability, goes on the offensive.

> Then the Lord (ὁ κύριος) said to him, "Now you Pharisees clean (καθαρίζετε) the outside of the cup and of the dish, but inside you are full of greed and wickedness. You fools! Did not the one who made the outside make the inside also? So give for alms those things that are within; and see, everything will be clean (καθαρά) for you. But woe to you Pharisees! For you tithe mint and rue and herbs of all kinds, and neglect justice and the love of God. . . . Woe to you Pharisees! For you love to have the seat of honor in the synagogues and to be greeted with respect in the marketplaces. Woe to you! For you are like unmarked graves, and people walk over them without realizing it." (11:39-44)

The woes address purity (washing cup and dish; unmarked graves creating corpse contamination), tithing, and honor. The first charge (see *m. Kelim* 2:1–3:8) includes a theological interest. It does not, however, imply either an "exclusivist posture" [21] or the separation of Pharisees from "non-Jews and non-observant Jews." [22] Luke mentions no "non-observant" Jews; the discussions concern Torah *interpretation*. Further, Pharisees associate with those who do not observe their interpretations, including Jesus, whether in the synagogue, the market, or at table. The claim that Luke's Pharisees have a "militant concern for matters such as purity, tithing, and the Sabbath observance (see *m. Demai* 2:3), and were willing to harass those of whom they disapproved (cf. Josephus, *Life* 191, 198–203)" [23] also overstates: the Pharisees do not seek Jesus' life; they typically do not challenge him in public. They are no more "militant" regarding Torah observance than anyone else in the gospel; compared to the Baptist and Jesus, they are doves.

The charge of tithing herbs not required according to the Torah (Lev 27:30-33; Deut 14:22-29; 26:12-15; cf. Mal 3:8-10) reinforces Pharisaic expansion of *halakhah* and attention to food. Johnson proposes that Luke may have erred in listing rue, since *m. Shebith* 9:1 regards it as exempt. [24] However, the exemption may indicate that some believed that rue was to be tithed.

Regarding alms, Luke 18:12 suggests that Pharisees give alms, or at least tithe, although Luke accuses them of rapacity (16:14). The concern for public recognition, which locates the Pharisees amid the hoi polloi, resembles Jesus' charge made in the Temple against the scribes: "In the hearing of all the people he said to the disciples, 'Beware of the scribes, who like to walk around in long robes, and love to be greeted with respect in the marketplaces, and to have the seats of honor in the synagogues and places of honor at banquets. They devour widows' houses and for the sake of appearance say long prayers" (20:45-47a). A few commentators, perhaps seeing 20:45-47 as a gloss on 11:42, conclude that 11:42 sees Pharisees as "extortionists,"[25] despite Luke's distinguishing between lawyers/scribes and Pharisees.

When a lawyer responds to Jesus' invective with the remarkably civil line, "Teacher (διδάσκαλε), when you say these things, you insult us too" (11:45), Jesus charges that lawyers "load people with burdens hard to bear" without lifting a finger themselves, "build the tombs of the prophets" whom their ancestors had killed, and hinder others by taking away "the key of knowledge" (11:46-52). Lawyers, not Pharisees, appear to hold the public teaching function.

Only after Jesus exits do the Pharisees and "scribes" (replacing "lawyers") begin to become hostile; having been called "fools" (11:40), "unmarked graves" (11:44), and associates with murderers (11:48), their reaction is not unexpected. What is surprising is how long it took, that they plan no violence, and that the hostility does not clearly continue. They subsequently "began . . . to cross-examine him about many things, lying in wait for him, to catch him in something he might say" (11:53-54, literally "draw from [his] mouth" [ἀποστοματίζειν]). The focus is on teaching.

LUKE 12:1 (MATT 16:5-6; MARK 8:14-15)

Jesus immediately warns his disciples, in the earshot of a crowd of several thousand: "Beware of the yeast of the Pharisees, that is, their hypocrisy" (12:1). Both the metaphor of leaven and Jesus' following remark, "Nothing is covered up that will not be uncovered" (12:2), indicate that nothing in the Pharisees' actions would lead anyone to think ill of them. The other synoptics mention both "Pharisees and Sadducees"; neither mentions hypocrisy.

Luke 13:31

Readers who have concluded that Luke's Pharisees epitomize those who reject Jesus understand 13:31—"some Pharisees (τινὲς Φαρισαῖοι) said to [Jesus], 'Get out and go from here, for Herod wants to kill you'"—to be insincere, motivated by a desire to undermine Jesus' support, or designed to thwart Jesus from his mission. Johnson, for example, observes that "neither before this scene or after are we given any indication that Herod wants to kill Jesus. Just the opposite: he 'seeks to see him'" (see 9:9b).[26] Others, seeing *some* Pharisees as redeemable, assess the warning as a sincere attempt to aid Jesus and/or to thwart Herod. Sanders notes, "Jesus' criticism falls on Herod, not on the Pharisees."[27]

Instead of heeding their warning to go (πορεύου; v. 31), Jesus orders the Pharisees to go (πορευθέντες) to Herod. Both warning and response locate the Pharisees as politically connected. They can be seen as opposing Herod nonviolently. That Luke dissociates Pharisees from Herodians (cf. Mark 3:6) strengthens this impression.

Luke 14:1-24

For the third dinner, the host is "a leader of the Pharisees" (τινος τῶν ἀρχόντων [τῶν] Φαρισαίων). Luke does not explain how the man with dropsy came to be present. Given dropsy's association with wealth, indulgence, greed, and desire, readers may be expected to regard him as the ruler's associate.[28] Johnson proposes that if the edema were obvious, "he would be regarded as impure because of the Levitical strictures concerning 'swellings' that were associated with leprosy (Lev 13:2)."[29] The importing of purity concerns is unnecessary. Further, Leviticus 13:2 specifies the presence of leprosy: "When a person has on the skin of his body a swelling or an eruption or a spot, *and it turns into a leprous disease on the skin. . . .*"

The scene recapitulates the Sabbath healings of 6:6-11 and 13:10-17. "Lawers and Pharisees were watching [Jesus] closely" (see 6:7; 20:20), and Jesus issues the familiar challenge, "Is it permitted (ἔξεστιν) to heal on the Sabbath or not?" (14:3). The question is a rhetorical trap, since it cannot be answered with a simple "yes" or

"no" (e.g., "Yes, if to save a life"; "No, except in certain circumstances"). The guests are thus "silent," unable to answer (14:4).

Having healed the man, Jesus continues: "If one of you has a son or
an ox that has fallen into a well, will you not immediately pull him up
on a Sabbath day?" (14:5; see Matt 12:11-12). In 13:15, Jesus addresses
a similar question to the "*leader* of the synagogue" (ἀρχισυνάγωγος);
the emphasis falls on rulers, not Pharisees. The *qal v'homer* argument—
from the lesser to the greater—is that Pharisees and lawyers would rescue the victim. Commentators often cite CD 11:13–17, which permits
rescue of a person but not an animal, and *b. Shabbat* 117b, which gives
conflicting comment concerning the animal.

Talbert, among others, finds that "Jesus' behavior and words expose
[the Pharisees'] callous unconcern for the man even as they profess to
protect the rituals of religion."[30] However, no one had forbidden the
healing; no outraged interior monologue is recorded; none condemns
Jesus for the healing. That the Pharisees are hostile to Jesus may be
implied by the notice that they are "watching" (παρατηρούμενοι) him;
that they opposed his healing is a different question.

Following the healing, Jesus continues his instructions. Seeing how
the guests chose honorable places, he warns them to avoid the best
seat, lest the host elevate someone more worthy. To his host, Jesus
insists, "When you give a luncheon or a dinner, do not invite your
friends or your brothers or your relatives or rich neighbors" (14:12).
Rather, invite those who cannot reciprocate: "the poor, the crippled,
the lame, and the blind" (14:13). The exhortation, coupled with the
parable of the great dinner (14:16-24; Matt 22:1-10), presumes that
the Pharisees participate in this class-based system; Luke's readers
may be in the same situation. Commentators often mention that
Leviticus 21:17-21 excludes the lame, blind, and crippled from the
priesthood, that 1QM 7:4 extends these disqualifications to the eschatological war, and that 1QSa 2:5-6 extends them to the eschatological
banquet.[31] Their presumption is that Pharisees create outcasts of the
physically challenged. Ignored is the fact that most people are
excluded from the priesthood (an inherited role) and that Jesus' eschatological scenario finds no one physically challenged (they would have
been healed). Luke gives no indication that Pharisees would have
barred these individuals from the eschatological table, or from their
own. These individuals are mentioned not because of their physical

state as such, but because that state implies lack of funds (a point confirmed by the parable). Finally, commentators rarely mention that
Pharisees do open their guest list beyond the rich and related: they
invite Jesus.[32]

The ending of the pericope is prompted by a guest's remark,
"Blessed is anyone who will eat bread in the kingdom of God"
(14:15). The comment indicates a Pharisaic (or at least lawyerly)
expectation of an eschatological banquet, although no messiah is
mentioned.

LUKE 15:1-32

Repeating that "the Pharisees and the scribes" grumble about Jesus'
welcoming sinners and eating with them, Luke introduces the para-
bles of the lost sheep, lost coin, and prodigal son. Commentators
remind readers that the Pharisees object to "Jesus' relations with outcasts,"[33] despite the absence of anyone being "cast out." Although
Luke makes no explicit allegorical connection, many commentators
find the connection "irresistible"; Johnson, for example, speaks of
"the Pharisaic refusal out of envy and resentment to accept this good
news extended to the outcast. . . . They, like the elder son, had stayed
within the covenant. . . . They had never broken any of the commandments. But (the story suggests) they regarded themselves not as
sons so much as slaves. And they resented others being allowed into
the people without cost."[34] The Pharisees' other appearances in the
gospel do not suggest a slavish attitude; nor does Luke deny that
Pharisees would welcome *repentant* sinners. The distinction is that
while Jesus seeks out sinners, they do not. When the Pharisees question such association, Jesus either remarks on the sinner's change
(7:47–48, the woman's actions imply repentance) or notes that he
demands repentance (e.g., 5:32).

The parable of the prodigal son ends with the father's comment to
the older son: "you are always with me, and all that is mine is yours"
(15:31). If the father represents God and the elder son the Pharisees,
then Luke sees the Pharisees as charged with stewardship roles on
earth and as participating in the eschatological reward. However,
nothing requires that the allegory be either present or consistent.

LUKE 16:14-15 (16-18, 19-31)

Luke announces that the Pharisees are "lovers of money" (φιλάρ-γυροι) who ridicule Jesus for insisting, "You cannot serve God and wealth (lit. 'mammon']" (16:13; cf. Matt 6:24). Jesus responds by accusing them of self-righteousness (16:15). Money-loving (see 1 Tim 6:10), a conventional charge, again connects the Pharisees with wealth; Josephus (*Ant.* 13.171–173) states, "The Pharisees simplify their standard of living, making no concession to luxury."

Commentators, accepting Luke's stereotype as fact, sometimes provide a Pharisaic justification for serving God and "mammon." Craddock explains: "As Pharisees whose religion was of the Book, their love of wealth found its confirmation in the law and the prophets . . . Deut. 28:3-4." [35] Luke mentions nothing about how the Pharisees came to be "lovers of money" or if they "justified them-selves" by exegetical means. Luke does not have them cite Scripture.

Luke 16:17 (Matt 5:18) is Jesus' assertion of the Torah's perma-nence, a view Pharisees share. The next verse insists, "Anyone who divorces his wife and marries another commits adultery, and whoever marries a woman divorced from her husband commits adultery" (Matt 5:32; 19:9; Mark 10:11-12). The statement could indicate that, for Luke, Pharisees granted divorces and permitted divorced women to remarry, a view consistent with both biblical and rabbinic tradition.

The parable of the rich man and Lazarus (16:19-31), which men-tions no Pharisees explicitly, could nevertheless be read as implying such connections. If so, it yields several pieces of information about Luke's Pharisees. First is the reiteration of elite status: the rich man "dressed in purple and fine linen and . . . feasted sumptuously every day" (16:19). Second, ignoring Lazarus recollects Jesus' command that his Pharisaic host invite those who cannot reciprocate. Third, the parable presupposes Pharisaic belief in angels (16:22), heaven (a place where one dines with Abraham), and hell (where the damned are in agony because of the flames). Fourth, Abraham's comment that "Moses and the prophets" provide sufficient soteriological guidance suggests the canonical status of the Torah and the prophetic writings (*Nevi'im*). Finally, the rich man's insistence that "if someone goes to them from the dead, they will repent" (16:30) confirms Pharisaic belief in resurrection, albeit here decoupled from the eschaton.

Luke 17:20-21

Luke 17:20 reports, "Once Jesus was asked by the Pharisees when the kingdom of God was coming." This (nonhostile) query indicates belief in a future (i.e., eschatological) kingdom, in contrast to Luke's depiction of the kingdom as "among you" (v. 21). The question is neutral; the narrative context, especially given 11:53, can but need not suggest hostility.

Luke 18:9-14

Addressing a parable to "some who trusted in themselves that they were righteous and regarded others with contempt" (18:9), Jesus recollects 10:29, where the lawyer was "wanting to justify himself," and 16:15, where the charge of self-righteousness is laid against Pharisees. The contempt is, apparently, for the "tax collectors and sinners."

The parable depicts a Pharisee "standing by himself" in the Temple and praying thus, "God, I thank you that I am not like other people: thieves, rogues, adulterers, or even like this tax collector. I fast twice a week; I give a tenth of all my income" (18:11-12). While 5:23 identified Pharisees as fasting, no commandment recommends fasting twice weekly. Deuteronomy 14:22-29 mandates tithing, but only of agricultural products. The prayer itself is distinct from other prayers of the period, despite occasional associations with 1QH[a] 15:34, *t. Berakhot* 6.18 (the prayer in which the male Jew gives thanks for not having been made a Gentile, uneducated, or a woman), and *b. Berakhot* 28b.[36]

Luke 19:37-40

When Jesus, hailed by the "multitude of the disciples" with the acclamation "Blessed is the king who comes in the name of the Lord" (19:38), nears Jerusalem, "some of the Pharisees" say to him: "Teacher, order your disciples to stop" (19:39). This is their last explicit mention. As with 13:31, their intent remains ambiguous. They may have feared that the acclamation would bring a reprisal from the Romans (see 23:2); they may have sought to protect Jesus or to stop him from gaining more popularity; they may have rejected a kingly claim or even been "scandalized by the type of praise being given him." [37]

OBSERVATIONS

Concerning Pharisaic activities and practice, Luke provides the following details: Pharisees associate with lawyers (5:17) and scribes (5:21), come from every village of the Galilee and Judea and Jerusalem (5:17), find blasphemous the arrogation of the privilege to forgive sins (5:21; 7:49), complain about Jesus' associating with tax collectors and sinners (5:30; 7:39; 15:2), have disciples (5:33) and scribes (5:30), fast and pray (5:33; 18:10, 12), protect Sabbath sanctity (6:1; 14:3-6), would rescue a child or an ox from a well on the Sabbath (14:5), frequent synagogues (6:7), do not approve of Sabbath healings (for chronic conditions) (6:7), refuse John's baptism (7:29), are members of the urban elite (7:36; 11:37; 14:1, 7-11, 12-14) who dine with members of their own class (14:12), wash before eating (11:38), "clean the outside of the cup and of the dish" (11:39), "tithe mint and rue and herbs of all kinds" (11:42), love the first seats in synagogues and salutations in marketplaces (11:43), have access but not loyalty to Antipas (13:31), anticipate a future and/or heavenly kingdom that will include dining with the patriarchs (14:15; 16:22-31; 17:20), believe in angels (16:22), hold sacred the Law and the Prophets (16:29), find plausible the idea of a resurrection (16:30) not connected to the messianic age, and pray in the Temple (18:10). Luke implies that they are literate, accept Scriptural precedent (6:3-4) (although they do not cite it themselves) and conventional wisdom (14:5), permit divorce and remarriage (16:18), and are politically savvy (19:39). Among the criticisms, Luke describes the Pharisees as hypocrites (12:1), lovers of money (16:14), self-righteous (16:15; cf. 18:9), and having contempt for others (18:9).

Absent are several views readers typically import: Pharisees are not obsessed with ritual purity and not removed from the population: they open their table to Jesus and others; they are neither militant nor violent but appear to be excellent hosts who refuse to humiliate their guest.

They are lackeys neither of Rome nor of the Herodian household. They are not obsessed with messianic speculation, they do not cite Scripture themselves, and they did not participate in John's baptism.

Whether Luke sees the Pharisees as a group or as individuals, whether his gospel offers pictures of the Pharisees as neutral, benevolent, and evil incarnate . . . these questions will remain debated.

CHAPTER 5

JOHN'S PHARISEES

Raimo Hakola and Adele Reinhartz

The title of this volume asks two questions. The first—What do we really know about the Pharisees?—implies that while it is possible to know something about the historical Pharisees, our knowledge may be more meager than some might think. The second—How do we know it?—raises the tricky methodological issue of how to read history from texts and artifacts that do not have our historical interests in view. This methodological problem looms large in virtually all historical study that must perforce rely on ancient sources. In addressing the problem of the historical Pharisees, however, it emerges acutely with regard to the Gospel of John, in which the Pharisees are given a prominent, and largely negative, narrative role. We begin by considering the literary representation of the Pharisees, the passages in which they appear and the parts they play in the story. We then situate these literary Pharisees in the context of historical studies of the gospel and, finally, offer some comments on their role in the process by which the Johannine community developed and solidified its own group identity.

The Johannine Pharisees as Characters in the Gospel Narrative

The Pharisees are mentioned explicitly approximately twenty times in the Fourth Gospel.[1] These references are distributed among ten scenes; these scenes, in turn, present a fairly consistent picture of this group, including its association with other groups.

The first reference occurs in John 1:24.[2] In this passage, priests and Levites sent by the Pharisees subject John the Baptist to cross-examination about his baptizing activities, and his identity—is he the Messiah, Elijah, or "the prophet"? John assures his interlocutors that he is none of the above, merely the precursor to the "one whom you do not know," namely, Jesus. The passage establishes the Pharisees from the outset as a group that is extremely anxious about claimants to messiahship, and that has a cohort of priests and Levites ready to do its bidding.

Next we encounter an individual, Nicodemus, described as a Pharisee and leader of the Jews (3:1). Nicodemus comes by night— that is, secretly—to speak with Jesus and to inquire about his message. This Pharisaic leader is sympathetic to Jesus, though apparently he does not truly grasp Jesus' message as he takes his words far too literally. But Nicodemus is not typical of the Johannine Pharisees, who in the rest of their appearances in this gospel return to the aggressive, even hostile behavior attributed to them and their agents in John 1.

In John 4:1, the narrator informs us that Jesus decided to leave Judea because he heard that the Pharisees were aware that he or, rather, his disciples (4:2) were exceeding John in baptizing activity. This decision implies fear or, at least, anxiety on Jesus' part and a desire to escape the Pharisees' purview.

Jesus' anxiety is justified, at least according to John 7:32-49. In this pericope, Jesus' activities in Jerusalem during the Feast of Tabernacles arouse the Pharisees' concern. They, along with the chief priests, send Temple police to arrest Jesus, but the priests do not do so, explaining, "Never has anyone spoken like this!" To this the Pharisees respond: "Surely you have not been deceived too, have you? Has any one of the authorities or of the Pharisees believed in him? But this crowd, which does not know the law—they are accursed" (47-49). At this point Nicodemus steps in to defend Jesus without, however, confessing to his earlier nocturnal visit or expressing his personal interest in Jesus (cf. 7:50).

As the story proceeds, the Pharisees' antagonism toward Jesus grows. In John 8:13, they dismiss his claims to be the "light of the world" and to offer his followers respite from the darkness (8:12): "You are testifying on your own behalf; your testimony is not valid." The issue of false testimony is also at stake in 9:13-40. In this passage the Pharisees interrogate the man born blind, whose sight Jesus has newly restored.

> Then the Pharisees also began to ask him how he had received his
> sight. He said to them, "He put mud on my eyes. Then I washed, and
> now I see." Some of the Pharisees said, "This man is not from God,
> for he does not observe the sabbath." But others said, "How can a man
> who is a sinner perform such signs?" And they were divided. (9:15-16)

In John 9:39, John's Jesus divulges the metaphorical message of the
event to the man born blind: "I came into this world for judgment so
that those who do not see may see, and those who do see may become
blind." Some of the Pharisees who overheard confronted Jesus
directly: "Surely we are not blind, are we?" But Jesus does not back
down: "If you were blind, you would not have sin. But now that you
say, 'We see,' your sin remains" (9:40). The brief allusion to sympathetic Pharisees in 9:16 ("but others said . . .") is quickly forgotten in
the overall negative tone of the pericope as a whole.

The raising of Lazarus further heightens Pharisaic anxiety about
Jesus' activities. When some of the witnesses to Jesus' miracle tell the
Pharisees what Jesus had done (11:46), "the chief priests and the
Pharisees called a meeting of the council, and said, 'What are we to
do? This man is performing many signs'" (11:47). In response to this
question, Caiaphas the high priest expresses the view "that it is better
for you to have one man die for the people than to have the whole
nation destroyed" (11:50). This declaration establishes the agenda of
the Jewish leadership; henceforth they will actively seek his death.
The search for Jesus moves into high gear: "Now the chief priests and
the Pharisees had given orders that anyone who knew where Jesus
was should let them know, so that they might arrest him" (11:57).

The main concern is Jesus' widespread popularity. In John 12:19,
the Pharisees lament to one another, "You see, you can do nothing.
Look, the world has gone after him!" In 12:42, the narrator confirms
that Jesus appeals not only to the everyday crowds but also to the
Jewish authorities themselves, for "many, even of the authorities,
believed in him. But because of the Pharisees they did not confess it,
for fear that they would be put out of the synagogue." The narrator
may well have Nicodemus in mind here as an example, though this
Pharisee is not mentioned explicitly.

The Pharisees' plot seemingly comes to a successful conclusion in
John 18:3, when "Judas brought a detachment of soldiers together
with police from the chief priests and the Pharisees, and they came

there with lanterns and torches and weapons." Jesus is arrested, tried, and summarily executed. Of course, as we know, that is not the end of the story, and Jesus' death by no means diminished his influence, as the subsequent history of Christianity shows.

Based on these passages, the Johannine Pharisees can be described as a group that enjoys considerable power and authority, including access to enforcement agents (police) as well as a network of agents (including priests and Levites) who interrogate suspicious figures on their behalf. The Pharisees also have judicial power—that is, the power to investigate, interrogate, and judge and to expel Jews from the synagogue for believing Jesus to be the Messiah. Not surprisingly, they are feared by the general population. They participate in the council and apparently have the authority to call a meeting of that body (11:47). The Pharisees view Jesus, and his following, as a major threat. They are motivated by a strong desire to eliminate Jesus, and they are not above employing stealth and intrigue to achieve this end. As Nicodemus demonstrates, however, even some of the Pharisees themselves are attracted to Jesus and his message.

Yet, virtually none of these features is unique to the Pharisaic group. Indeed, John's Pharisees are frequently associated in an undifferentiated manner with another group, the chief priests. In 7:45, "the temple police went back to the chief priests and Pharisees, who asked them, 'Why did you not arrest him?'" In 11:47, "the chief priests and the Pharisees called a meeting of the council" to take a decision about what to do about Jesus. In 11:57, the narrator explains that "the chief priests and the Pharisees had given orders that anyone who knew where Jesus was should let them know, so that they might arrest him," and 18:3 refers to the "[Roman][3] soldiers together with police from the chief priests and the Pharisees" who were led to Jesus by Judas. These passages do not differentiate in any meaningful way between the chief priests and the Pharisees with regard to authority and function. Indeed, the effect is to link them closely together.[4]

A more ambiguous situation exists with regard to another, less specific, term: "the authorities." In 7:48, the Pharisees reply to the temple police, "Has any one of the authorities [ἐκ τῶν ἀρχόντων] or of the Pharisees believed in him?" And in 12:42 the narrator informs us, "Nevertheless many, even of the authorities [ἐκ τῶν ἀρχόντων], believed in him. But because of the Pharisees they did not confess it,

for fear that they would be put out of the synagogue." While it may
seem logical to view "the authorities" as the more general and inclusive term, of which "the Pharisees" as well as "the chief priests" are
a part, these two passages imply a distinction between "authorities"
and "Pharisees." The first passage holds open the possibility that the
authorities might respond either the same as or differently from the
Pharisees when it comes to belief in Jesus. The second shows that this
is indeed the case for at least some of the authorities, who, like the
populace, fear the wrath of the Pharisees despite their own presumed
positions of authority. Any distinction between these two groups
therefore pertains not to their role or function but to their potential
responses to Jesus.

In this regard, John does not differ greatly from Matthew, Mark
and Luke-Acts, in which the Pharisees are paired with a variety of
other groups.[5] Lawyers and Pharisees appear in Luke 14:1-3:

> On one occasion when Jesus was going to the house of a leader of the
> Pharisees to eat a meal on the sabbath, they were watching him closely.
> Just then, in front of him, there was a man who had dropsy. And Jesus
> asked the lawyers and Pharisees, "Is it lawful to cure people on the sab-
> bath, or not?"

Matthew 27:62 indicates that the Pharisees along with the chief
priests brought charges against Jesus before Pilate. Despite their
prominence during Jesus' ministry, the Pharisees do not have a major
role in the Passion accounts except, as we have already noted, in
John's account of Jesus' arrest. As Brown notes with some surprise,
"Despite the frequent references to Pharisees in the public ministry of
Jesus . . . they are noticeably absent from the three Synoptic passion
predictions, from the plotting with Judas, and indeed from almost the
whole Passion Narrative!"[6]

In the synoptics and Acts the Pharisees are frequently paired with
another group, the Sadducees. According to Matthew 16:1, "The
Pharisees and Sadducees came, and to test Jesus they asked him to
show them a sign from heaven." Later, in Matthew 16:11-12, Jesus
reprimands his disciples:

> "How could you fail to perceive that I was not speaking about bread?
> Beware of the yeast of the Pharisees and Sadducees!" Then they
> understood that he had not told them to beware of the yeast of bread,
> but of the teaching of the Pharisees and Sadducees.

(In the Markan parallel, Mark 8:15, the Pharisees are paired with the little-known Herodians: "And he cautioned them, saying, "Watch out—beware of the yeast of the Pharisees and the yeast of Herod," suggesting that even the early Christian traditions did not distinguish definitively among these various groups.) This pairing does not exist in John, which has no references to the Sadducees whatsoever.

In contrast to John, Luke-Acts occasionally describes Pharisaic predilections. Luke 16:14 disparages the Pharisees as lovers of money. The distinctions between the Pharisees and Sadducees with regard to theology and practice are reflected briefly in Acts 23:6-8:

> When Paul noticed that some were Sadducees and others were Pharisees, he called out in the council, "Brothers, I am a Pharisee, a son of Pharisees. I am on trial concerning the hope of the resurrection of the dead." When he said this, a dissension began between the Pharisees and the Sadducees, and the assembly was divided. (The Sadducees say that there is no resurrection, or angel, or spirit; but the Pharisees acknowledge all three.)

That these are distinct, often rivalrous, groups is implied in Matthew 22:23-36:

> The same day some Sadducees came to him, saying there is no resurrection; and they asked him a question, saying, "Teacher, Moses said, 'If a man dies childless, his brother shall marry the widow, and raise up children for his brother.' . . . Jesus answered them, "You are wrong, because you know neither the scriptures nor the power of God. For in the resurrection they neither marry nor are given in marriage, but are like angels in heaven. And as for the resurrection of the dead, have you not read what was said to you by God, 'I am the God of Abraham, the God of Isaac, and the God of Jacob'? He is God not of the dead, but of the living." And when the crowd heard it, they were astounded at his teaching. When the Pharisees heard that he had silenced the Sadducees, they gathered together, and one of them, a lawyer, asked him a question to test him. "Teacher, which commandment in the law is the greatest?" (22:23-25, 29-36)

John's Pharisees differ from their synoptic counterparts only with regard to specificity. Whereas in both sets of texts they are paired in an undifferentiated way with other groups, the synoptic accounts also attribute to them distinct features particularly in comparison with the Sadducees. This points up even more the flatness of their Johannine representation and raises the possibility that the Pharisees function almost exclusively as a collective literary character, the villain of the piece.[7]

The Johannine picture is made even murkier by several passages in which the term "the Jews" is used interchangeably with "the Pharisees." In the scene of the Baptist's interrogation, 1:19 states that the interlocutors were sent by "the Jews," whereas 1:24 specifies that they were sent by "the Pharisees." In the discourse of John 8:12-51, Jesus' partners in dialogue are called "the Pharisees" in 8:13 and "the Jews" in 8:22. Most significant is the narrative of the man born blind, in which representatives interrogate the man and his family about his newly gained sight. At the outset of the questioning the story names the interrogators as Pharisees, but in 9:18 they are simply called "the Jews."

Less clear is the discourse in 7:32-35:

> The Pharisees heard the crowd muttering such things about him, and the chief priests and Pharisees sent temple police to arrest him. Jesus then said, "I will be with you a little while longer, and then I am going to him who sent me. You will search for me, but you will not find me; and where I am, you cannot come." The Jews said to one another, "Where does this man intend to go that we will not find him?"

Here it is not certain whether "the Jews" of 7:35 are to be identified with "the Pharisees" of 7:32 or with "the crowd" in the same verse. The context implies the latter, as this sequence is part of a larger pattern in which the crowd takes Jesus' pronouncements literally and in doing so also adds a layer of irony to the narrative presentation. These passages support Alan Culpepper's observation that "the evangelist lays the blame for much of the Jews' opposition to Jesus at the Pharisees' feet. If the unbelief of the world is represented by the Jews, then in similar fashion the hostility of the Jews toward Jesus is concentrated in the Pharisees."[8]

The above observations suggest that John's Pharisees bear little if any resemblance to their historical, first-century counterparts. The Gospel of John therefore provides little historical information beyond the fact that a group existed called the Pharisees that had some sort of leadership position. What it does provide is a clear statement of the Pharisees' responsibility for Jesus' execution, this despite two facts: that it was the Roman governor Pilate who pronounced the death sentence and that the Pharisees are not present throughout the

Passion narrative except indirectly as being among those who sent police and possibly soldiers to arrest Jesus. What emerges most clearly is the evangelist's animosity toward the Pharisees. While they are not the only Jews that John blames for Jesus' death, they are the ones portrayed as seeking his destruction from the outset. In this context, only Nicodemus stands out, and even he does not openly express his convictions, apparently for fear of his fellow Pharisees.

JOHN AND THE PHARISEES IN HISTORICAL PERSPECTIVE

Why are the Pharisees portrayed in this villainous role? Scholars have generally sought answers not within the actual or supposed historical events of Jesus' life and death but within the history and experience of the Johannine community, that (hypothetical) group for whom and within which the gospel was written in the last decade or so of the first century CE. Since the publication of J. L. Martyn's book *History and Theology in the Fourth Gospel* (1968; references to the 3rd ed., 2003), it has become almost axiomatic among Johannine scholars to connect John's references to the Pharisees to an allegedly bitter and violent conflict between the Johannine group and the post-70 CE emergent rabbinic Judaism.[9] Martyn proposes that we read the Gospel of John as a two-level drama that tells not only of Jesus' life but also about the contemporary situation of the Johannine community at the end of the first century. At this time, says Martyn, "the reins of Jewish authority are held to a large extent by the Pharisaic Bet Din in Jamnia, and, on the local scene, by a Gerousia, the majority of whose members are (or appear to John to be) Pharisees."[10] Martyn connects the passages that tell of the exclusion from the synagogue (John 9:22; 12:42; 16:2) to the *Birkat ha-Minim*, a Jewish prayer against heretics, and maintains that this prayer played a crucial role in the process that led to the separation of the Johannine Christians from their fellow Jews. By using the term "the Pharisees" for Jesus' opponents, John actually refers to "the Jamnia Loyalists who enforce the Benediction Against Heretics" in his surroundings.[11] For Martyn, the expulsion from the synagogue was not a unique event but part of the larger scene where the early rabbinic movement under the guidance of

R. Gamaliel II became the main persecutors of the Johannine Christians, even to the extent that they executed many believers.[12]

The general outline of Martyn's model is still widely applied in discussions concerning John's portrayal of the Pharisees. This portrayal is commonly connected to the rise of the rabbinic movement after 70 CE,[13] which is often seen as a plausible explanation for the expanded role of the Pharisees in John, Matthew, and Luke in comparison to Mark. Both Matthew and Luke insert the Pharisees into more narrative situations than Mark does, and John continues this development.

Scholars have usually accepted Martyn's fundamental premise that John's portrayal of the Pharisees as a strict and authoritative body capable of expelling Jesus' followers from the synagogue does not correspond to the historical circumstances in Jesus' lifetime.[14] On this premise it is argued that John's portrayal must reflect the situation following the destruction of the Jerusalem Temple in 70 CE when the rabbis gained the power and coerced other Jews to follow their form of Jewish religion. It is claimed that John simply read the rabbinic leaders of his own post-70 era back into Jesus' life as Pharisees.

The portrayal of early rabbis as a dominant force among Jews has also provided an explanation for the eventual rupture between Christianity and Judaism. Today many scholars emphasize the Jewishness of all first-century followers of Jesus, including Johannine Christians. It is not exceptional to speak of "the thoroughgoing Jewishness" of John and its readers.[15] James Dunn shares the view of many when he says that "as we move into the second century not only certain Christian sects can be described as 'Jewish-Christian,' but Christianity as a whole can still properly be described as 'Jewish Christianity' in a justifiable sense."[16] Dunn also notes, however, that the letter of Pliny, dated to 112 CE, shows that "the issue was clear: Christians are not Jews. By then the perception from outside reinforces the impression that *the partings of the ways had already become effective*."[17] This sudden change in the status of early Christians stems, in Dunn's view, from the emergence of rabbinic Judaism as "the first real or really effective form of orthodox or normative Judaism" that began "to draw boundaries more tightly round 'Judaism.'"[18]

Similarly, scholars have rationalized those features in John that suggest a break with the tenets most often regarded as distinctive to Jewish identity by placing John in the context of a conflict with

Pharisaic/rabbinic Judaism. For example, the Johannine Jesus refers
to the Torah as "your law" (8:17; 10:34; cf. 7:19, 22; 15:25) and to
Abraham as "your ancestor" (8:56). Many Johannine scholars agree
with Urban C. von Wahlde who says that John's outsider position in
relation to Jewishness "is due to expulsion; it is an outsider position
which is not willingly outsider." Von Wahlde, states explicitly that the
Johannine community always wanted to stay within the synagogue,
but was forced outside; it is for this reason that John uses "outsider"
language in relationship to Judaism.[19]

The expulsion theory has also provided a rationale for those passages that were later used as a foundation for Christian anti-Judaism.
The view of early rabbinic Judaism as a monolithic, legalistic, and
authoritarian movement allows commentators to describe the
Johannine community as a Jewish minority group oppressed by a hostile majority headed by the Pharisees. In this construction such difficult passages as John 8:44 ("You are from your father the devil")
become, if not acceptable in our eyes, then at least understandable in
a first-century context as a response to the violent policy of the
Pharisaic synagogue.[20] For example, Jean Zumstein admits that John
"undoubtedly contributed" to the history of anti-Judaism in the history of the church but excuses John's anti-Judaism by saying that "it
is still necessary to recognise that at the time the Fourth Gospel was
edited it was the Christians who were victims and the synagogue that
was the persecutor."[21]

By taking John's portrayal of the Pharisees as a direct reflection of
the post-70 situation scholars have been able to give answers to some
of the most urgent historical and theological questions in the interpretation of the Fourth Gospel. But despite its usefulness, the expulsion theory is open to challenge, for it is based to a great extent on a
portrayal of the Pharisees and early rabbis that has been seriously
questioned in recent scholarship.[22] In particular, many scholars are
now revising their views concerning the influence and power of the
early rabbinic movement.[23] Far from being authoritative, the early
rabbinic movement may well have been a relatively powerless group.
This view emerges from the study of the earliest layers of Mishnaic
law as well as from the study of legal case stories connected to rabbis
of different eras.[24] As Jacob Neusner has concluded, the rabbis
"enjoyed no documented access to power of any kind" and were

"unable to coerce many people to do very much." Thus, rabbinic ideals never "attained realization in the structure of actual institutions and in the system of a working government and . . . never actually dictated how people would do things."[25]

Furthermore, problems connected to the dating, the original wording, and the purpose of the *Birkat ha-Minim* have made many scholars rethink John's alleged connection to this prayer. The prayer may have never functioned as a tool for excommunicating dissident groups— *minim*—from the Jewish community, nor do we know exactly who these *minim* were. In some rabbinic texts, the *minim* seem to be Jewish Christians or Christians in general (e.g. *t. Ḥul.* 2:24). But many passages attribute clearly non-Christian beliefs to the *minim*; it is said, for example, that the *minim* deny the resurrection of the dead (*b. Sanh.* 90b), believe only in one world (*m. Ber.* 9:5) or worship idols (*t. Ḥul.* 1:1). Hence the term does not refer exclusively to Christians of any kind or to any other specific group considered heretical by the rabbis.

In fact, it seems that the rabbis were not interested in defining exactly who the *minim* are. Nor did they give any definite list of those beliefs or practices that make a person a *min*. Stuart S. Miller has observed that occasionally actions attributed to a *min* in one text appear in another text as actions of an anonymous person who is not called *min*.[26] Miller also notes that texts referring to the contacts between the rabbis and the *minim* tell mostly of an individual *min* and an individual rabbi, not well-organized rabbinic reaction to clearly defined heretical groups.[27] As Richard Kalmin says, rabbinic sources "give us rough stereotypes and sketches drawn in extremely broad strokes rather than finely nuanced portraits or scientifically precise descriptions."[28]

The very vagueness of the term *minim* discloses the attitude of the rabbis to those outside their own circles. By blending different heresies together, the rabbis could protect themselves against views they considered potentially dangerous. They did not need to take a stand on different heretical groups in detail, but it was sufficient to add these groups to the list of *minim*.[29] The rabbis could maintain their view of an idyllic Israel devoted to rabbinic halakha only by regarding as nonexistent those groups that did not match their ideals.[30] Martin Goodman states that "rather than attack heretical Jews, the tannaim [rabbinic generations prior to the compilation of the Mishnah]

preached that heretics should be ignored."[31] Rabbinic polemics
against the minim should be understood as an attempt by the rabbinic
movement to consider its identity rather than as a basis for exclusion-
ary policies and behaviors.

In his recent article on heresy and apostasy in early rabbinic writings, William Scott Green concludes that

> early rabbis were preoccupied with fixing the boundaries of their own
> group and . . . devoted extensive linguistic energy to a remarkably
> detailed elaboration of their own periphery. . . In the semantic universe
> they created for themselves, early rabbis do not appear as leaders or
> devotees of "the Jewish people," religiously or ethnically construed, but
> rather as a wary and watchful group of Jewish textualists.[32]

Therefore, it is unlikely that early rabbis were the instigators of any
kind of systematic oppression of the *minim* in general, or early
Christians in particular.[33]

Scholars have generally responded to the challenge presented by
recent rabbinic studies in three ways.[34] One response is simply to
maintain the status quo—that is, to choose not to revise in any way
the commonplace reconstruction of the conflict between the
Johannine community and the early rabbinic movement.[35] Yet it
remains to be demonstrated how and in which locale the rabbis, who
presumably did not have complete control even over Aramaic-speak-
ing Jewish synagogue communities, could have intimidated the lives
of Greek-speaking Johannine Christians in a way presupposed by the
supporters of the expulsion theory.[36] This is true even when John's
conflict with Pharisees and/or early rabbis is understood only as a
local and limited phenomenon that is otherwise unattested in our
sources, as is often done today.[37]

The second way to respond to recent rabbinic studies is to maintain that the main points in the expulsion theory are still right, even
though it is unlikely that the historical group gathered around
Yohanan ben Zakkai would have been the main opponents of the
Johannine community. This is the course taken by Wayne Meeks, who
dismisses the Yavnean rabbis as John's opponents and suggests that
some other Jewish group had sufficient power in synagogues to "expel
persons from membership, even to threaten their lives." Meeks locates
the Johannine community somewhere in Galilee, Batanaea, or "some

small *polis*" in a "society dominated by the Jewish community."[38] In this case, John's portrayal of the Pharisees as Jesus' main opponents may stem from earlier traditions. The advantage of this solution is that it clears the reputation of the rabbis as the main oppressors of post-70 Christians. A clear shortcoming in Meeks's proposition, however, is that there is no external evidence at all for the kind of authoritative, non-rabbinic group postulated by the expulsion theory.

For this reason, we propose a third way to apply recent theories about early rabbinic Judaism to an understanding of John's portrayal of the Pharisees, namely, by revisiting the methodological basis of the expulsion theory. In our view, the theory is open to serious critique in addition to the lack of external evidence. Applying Martyn's two-level reading strategy to passages other than John 9 (the account of the man born blind that is the basis for Martyn's reading of the gospel) suggests other models for the interactions between Jesus' followers and the Jews. John 11 may point to speaks of ongoing and peaceful communication between Johannine believers and other Jews.[39] John 8:30-31 may point to Jewish Christians who, unlike the Johannine writer, did not see any clear contradiction between their faith and traditional Jewish identity.[40] If so, it is quite possible that some who believed in Jesus may have continued to interact with other Jews and to find Jewish practices attractive, hence arousing the ire of the evangelist or others within the Johannine community.[41] The Gospel of John may therefore reflect a social situation that is much more complex than is presupposed by the expulsion theory with its basis in the assumption that Jewish synagogue communities had strict boundaries defined by a strong leadership class.

It is also unlikely that John's outsider position in relation to Jewishness could be ascribed, on the whole, to the policy of his opponents. The attitude of the Johannine Jesus to the pillars of Jewish identity such as the Temple, worship, the Sabbath, circumcision, the revelation at Sinai, law, Moses, and Abraham is highly ambivalent, thereby implying a growing separation from the Jewish ethos.[42] It is preferable to see in John's portrayal of the Jews and Jewishness a more prolonged and gradual process of separation from what was regarded as distinctive to Jewishness than a traumatic expulsion from the synagogue.

THE SOCIAL IDENTITY APPROACH

How can the above proposition account for the treatment of the Pharisees in John as the main persecutors of Jesus and his followers? Many scholars recognize that the Pharisees are presented in an exaggerated and stereotyped way in the New Testament gospels. Nevertheless, these scholars maintain that there must be at least some kernel of truth behind even the most extreme early Christian stereotypes of the Pharisees. By contrast, we prefer to study the gospels' portrayal of the Pharisees first and foremost not as a direct reflection of historical realities but as an attempt by early Christians to construct their own identity. In this regard, the so-called social identity perspective that deals extensively with the formation of stereotypes proves fruitful. This approach has recently been applied also to early Jewish and Christian sources, and may help to explain why the Pharisees become Jesus' main enemies in Christian tradition.[43]

The social identity approach views stereotyping as being closely connected to social categorization, which in turn, is a fundamental aspect of group behavior.[44] When we define ourselves in relation to other people, we experience ourselves as similar to one clearly defined category of people and therefore as different from those in other categories. This process helps us to orientate ourselves in variable social environments by making those environments more predictable and meaningful. Social categorization, however, results in exaggeration and a polarization of perception whereby individuals belonging to different groups are viewed as being more different from each other than they really are, while individuals belonging to the same group are perceived as more similar.[45] For this reason, social categorization can be described as "a cognitive grouping process that transforms differences into similarities, and vice versa."[46]

Because categorization tends to amplify similarities within groups and differences between groups, it helps to define groups as distinct entities.[47] The process of social categorization thus often elevates what has been called the "entitativity" of a group. Entitativity is a somewhat clumsy term that refers to "the importance of the degree to which a collection of persons is perceived as a unified group."[48] The degree of entitativity is created by such things as "similarity among group members, proximity, the extent of interaction, the degree of common goals and common fate, the importance of the group to the members, group size, etc."[49]

The degree of perceived entitativity is important because it affects the ways that outsiders process the information related to different groups. A group generates different responses and expectations depending on whether it is perceived as a unified entity or not. First-century and rabbinic Jews, for example, perceived the Pharisees as a clearly identifiable group. Many details in the descriptions of the Pharisees are still open to discussion, but Josephus, New Testament, and early rabbinic sources agree that the Pharisees had their own beliefs and practices that, at least to a degree, marked their group off from other Jews, even if, as in the case of John, there is no obvious knowledge of what these beliefs and practices were.

In his three-volume study on the rabbinic traditions about the Pharisees, Jacob Neusner has made a strong case that the legal agenda of the Pharisees in rabbinic sources is virtually identical to the agenda of the Pharisees in the synoptic gospels: tithing, purity laws, Sabbath observance, and vows.[50] These discussions show that, if not the historical Jesus, then at least his followers, got caught up in a bitter dispute with the Pharisees who opposed positions taken by early Christians on various legal issues. On the basis of these discussions, early Christians may have had good reason to regard the Pharisees as their opponents. As we have already seen, however, early Christian sources do not only present the Pharisees as Jesus' rivals in various legal debates but also expand their threat by ascribing to them the will and power to persecute Jesus and his followers.

This negative portrayal is not surprising in light of the ways in which outsiders tend to process the information related to groups that are perceived both as rivals and as cohesive entities. It has been proposed that "the perception of high entitativity of an outgroup will lead to greater perceived potency of the group, where potency implies the capacity to do either good or bad things." It is predicted that those outgroups that are regarded as rivals "would be perceived as having greater potential for inflicting harm as perceived entitativity increases."[51] The information concerning these groups is processed in a highly schematic fashion, resulting in the emergence of extreme stereotypes related to these groups. This means that once such a group as the Pharisees was perceived as an enemy by early followers of Jesus, the door was open to exaggerating their threat to the point where they became the main source of persecution in the proto-Christian imagination.

Another concept that may be helpful in understanding these proto-Christian portrayals of the Pharisees is that of "illusory correlation." While we as human beings are certainly capable of logical and systematic mental processing, we frequently form our opinions of other individuals and groups based on little or no concrete evidence. The concept of illusory correlation tries to explain why people often believe that there is a correlation between a certain group and a certain action even though there is no clear evidence for such a correlation.[52] For example, if proto-Christians knew that some individual Pharisees like Paul (Gal 1:13, 23) engaged in sporadic actions against them, they may well have seen in these actions the very essence of Pharisaism. This kind of prior assessment may have colored all their subsequent encounters with the Pharisees. If so, they would not only present some individual Pharisees as their opponents but also view the entire group as being engaged in a purposeful and persistent campaign against their Lord and his followers.[53]

A similar development may have taken place in the formation of traditions about rival Pharisaic schools. Jacob Neusner has suggested that the stories referring to the use of violence or force by the House of Shammai against the House of Hillel are a late aspect of the anti-Shammaite polemic characteristic of the post-70 Hillelites. Neusner concludes that post-70 Hillelites created these stories to explain the common recollection of Shammaite predominance before the destruction of the Temple. Hillelites explained this predominance by claiming that Shammaites outnumbered their rivals by using force or even by murdering their opponents (e.g., *y. Šabb.* 1:4; *b. Šabb.* 17a).[54] The development of these legends and of proto-Christian traditions about the Pharisees demonstrate how natural it is to dramatize the threat of a group once it is perceived to be hostile. In both cases, a group originally regarded as a rival in various halakhic debates is later imagined as powerful enough to fulfill their hidden murderous agenda.

The above discussion should be understood only as a preliminary attempt to explain the growing role of the Pharisees in John in terms of the cognitive and motivational processes that lie behind the formation of stereotypes. This approach suggests that John's extreme and stereotyped portrayal of the Pharisees reflects the process of early Christian self-understanding rather than the real-life policy of the Pharisees or the early rabbis.

CONCLUSIONS

Our analysis of John's Pharisees strongly suggests that the Fourth Gospel contributes little if anything to our understanding of the historical Pharisees of the early decades of the first century—the time of Jesus—or of the relationship between them or their post-70 CE successors and the group within which and for which the gospel was likely written. Certainly the evangelist betrays no special knowledge of the Pharisees as a distinctive entity with a specific political role in the spectrum of Jewish leadership groups and particular beliefs and practices. Rather, the Pharisees play primarily literary and ideological roles. From a literary perspective, the Pharisees, alongside other Jewish groups, fulfill the narrative role of the villain, without which the story of Jesus would lack drama, tension, and emotional impact. But this literary role itself may also reflect the attempts of the Johannine community, as a proto-Christian group, to forge their own identity separate from and alongside the Jewish groups that did not accept Jesus as the Messiah and Son of God.

CHAPTER 6

PAUL AND THE PHARISEES

Bruce Chilton

Only one passage within the New Testament, Acts 15:1-5, puts Paul in direct confrontation with Pharisees. This single pericope is plausible within its own terms of reference and the evidence of other sources. Although Acts' agenda and Paul's are not the same, the passage enables us to appreciate why Paul in his letters refers to his opponents in the way that he does, and why he refers to Pharisaism only once, in order to describe his own orientation within Judaism.

Acts 15

Acts 15 deals with two disputed issues, circumcision and purity, as if they were the agenda of a single meeting of leaders in Jerusalem. Paul in Galatians 2 more accurately treats the meeting he had with the leaders as distinct from a later decision to return to the question of purity.[1] The first item on the agenda is settled by having Peter declare that, since God gave his Holy Spirit to Gentiles who believed, no attempt should be made to add the requirement of circumcision to them (Acts 15:6-11). Paul could scarcely have said it better himself; and that is consistent with the version of Paulinism represented in Acts.

The second item on the agenda is settled on James's authority, not Peter's, and the outcome is not in line with Paul's thought. James first confirms the position of Peter, but he states the position in a very different way: "Symeon has related how God first visited the Gentiles, to take a people in his name" (Acts 15:14). James's perspective here is not that all who believe are Israel (the Pauline definition), but that in addition to Israel God has established a people in his name. How the new people are to be regarded in relation to Israel is a question that is implicit in the statement, and James goes on to answer it.

James develops the relationship between those taken from the
Gentiles and Israel in two ways. The first method is the use of
Scripture, while the second is a requirement of purity. The logic of
both inevitably involves a rejection of Paul's position (along the lines
Paul himself lays out in Galatians 2).

The use of Scripture, like the argument itself, is quite unlike Paul's.
James claims that "with this [that is, his statement of Peter's position]
the words of the prophets agree, just as it is written" (Acts 15:15), and
he then cites the book of Amos. The passage cited will concern us in
a moment; the form of James's interpretation is an immediate indication of a substantial difference from Paul. As James has it, there is
actual agreement between Symeon and the words of the prophets, as
two people might agree: the use of the verb *sumphoneo* is nowhere else
in the New Testament used in respect of Scripture. The direct continuity of Christian experience with Scripture is marked as a greater
concern than within Paul's interpretation, and James expects that
continuity to be verbal, a matter of agreement with the prophets'
words, not merely with possible ways of looking at what they mean.

The citation from Amos (9:11-12, from the version of the
Septuagint, which was the Bible of Luke-Acts) comports well with
James's concern that the position of the Church agree with the prin-
cipal vocabulary of the prophets (Acts 15:16-17):

> After this I will come back and restore the tent of David which has
> fallen, and rebuild its ruins and set it up anew, that the rest of men may
> seek the Lord, and all the Gentiles upon whom my name is called.

In the argument of James as represented here, what the belief of
Gentiles achieves is, not the redefinition of Israel (as in Paul's
thought), but the restoration of the house of David. The argument is
possible because a Davidic genealogy of Jesus—and, therefore, of his
brother James—is assumed.

The account of James's preaching in the Temple given by
Hegesippus (as cited by Eusebius in *Ecclesiastical History* 2.23) represents Jesus as the Son of Man who is to come from heaven to judge
the world. Those who agree cry out, "Hosanna to the Son of David!"
Hegesippus shows that James's view of Jesus came to be that he was
related to David (as was the family generally) and was also a heavenly
figure who was coming to judge the world. When Acts and
Hegesippus are taken together, they indicate that James contended

Jesus was restoring the house of David because he was the agent of final judgment, and was being accepted as such by Gentiles with his Davidic pedigree.

But on James's view, Gentiles remain Gentiles; they are not to be identified with Israel. His position was not anti-Pauline, at least not at first. His focus was on Jesus' role as the ultimate arbiter within the Davidic line, and there was never any question within this position but that the Temple was the natural place to worship God and acknowledge Jesus. Embracing the Temple as central meant for James, as it meant for the generality of those associated with worship there, maintaining the purity that it was understood that God required in his house. Purity involved excluding Gentiles from the interior courts of the Temple, where Israel was involved in sacrifice. The line of demarcation between Israel and non-Israel was no invention within the circle of James, but a natural result of seeing Jesus as the triumphant branch of the house of David.

Gentile belief in Jesus was therefore in James's understanding a vindication of Davidic triumph, but it did not involve a fundamental change in the status of Gentiles vis-à-vis Israel. That characterization of the Gentiles, developed by means of the reference to Amos, enables James to proceed to his requirement of their recognition of purity. He first states that "I determine not to trouble those of the Gentiles who turn to God" (15:19) as if he were simply repeating the policy of Peter in regard to circumcision. (The implicit authority of that "I" [we might say, an episcopal "I"] contrasts sharply with the portrayal in Acts of apostolic decision as communal, and suggests the influence of a source derived from James's circle.) But he then continues that his determination is also "to write to them to abstain from the pollutions of the idols, and from fornication, and from what is strangled, and from blood" (15:20).

The rules set out by James tend naturally to separate believing Gentiles from their ambient environment. They are to refrain from feasts in honor of the gods and from foods sacrificed to idols in the course of being butchered and sold. (The notional devotion of animals in the market to one god or another was a common practice in the Hellenistic world.[2]) They are to observe stricter limits than usual on the type of sexual activity they might engage in, and with whom. (Gross promiscuity need not be the only issue here; marriage with

relations is also included within the likely area of concern. That was
fashionable in the Hellenistic world but proscribed in the book of
Leviticus [see chapters 18 and 20:17-21]). They are to avoid the flesh
of animals that had been strangled instead of bled, and they are not
to consume blood itself. The proscription of blood, of course, was
basic within Judaism; and strangling an animal (as distinct from cut-
ting its throat) increased the availability of blood in the meat. Such
strictures are consistent with James's initial observation, that God had
taken a people from the Gentiles (15:14); they were to be similar to
Israel and supportive of Israel in their distinction from the Hellenistic
world at large.

The motive behind the rules is not separation in itself, however.
James links them to the fact that the Mosaic legislation regarding
purity is well and widely known (15:21): "For Moses from early generations has had those preaching him city by city, being read in the
synagogues every Sabbath." Because the law is well known, James
insists that believers, even Gentile believers, are not to live in flagrant
violation of what Moses enjoined. In the words of Amos, they are to
behave as "all the Gentiles upon whom my name is called." As a
result of James's insistence, the meeting in Jerusalem decides to send
envoys and a letter to Antioch, in order to require Gentiles to honor
the prohibitions set out by James (Acts 15:22-35).

The same chapter of Leviticus that commands "love your neighbor as yourself" (19:18) also forbids blood to be eaten (19:26) and fornication (19:29; see also 18:6-30). The canonical (but secondhand)
Letter of James calls the commandment of love "the royal law"
(James 2:8), acknowledging that Jesus had accorded it privilege by citing it alongside the commandment to love God as the two greatest
commandments (see Mark 12:28-32). In Acts James himself, while
accepting that Gentiles cannot be required to keep the whole law,
insists that they should acknowledge it, by observing basic requirements concerning fornication and blood and idolatry.

It is of interest that Leviticus forbids the eating of blood by
sojourners as well as Israelites, and associates that prohibition with
how animals are to be killed for the purpose of eating (17:10-16).
Moreover, a principle of exclusivity in sacrifice is trenchantly maintained: anyone, whether of Israel or a sojourner dwelling among
them, who offers a sacrifice which is not brought to the LORD's

honor in the Temple is to be cut off from the people (17:8-9). In other words, the prohibitions of James, involving sacrifice, fornication, strangled meat produce, and blood, all derive easily from the very context in Leviticus from which the commandment to love is derived. They are elementary, and involve interest in what Gentiles as well as Israelites do. The position of James as reflected in Acts upholds the integrity of Scripture in the discipline of the church in a way that recalls both the *mebaqqer* from Qumran and the *episkopos* from the pastoral epistles.[3]

James's prohibitions as presented in Acts are designed to show that believing Gentiles honor the law that is commonly read, without in any way changing their status as Gentiles. Thereby, the tent of David is erected again, in the midst of Gentiles who show their awareness of the restoration by means of their respect for the Torah. The interpretation attributed to James involves an application of Davidic vocabulary to Jesus, as is consistent with the claim of Jesus' family to Davidic ancestry. The transfer of Davidic promises to Jesus is accomplished within an acceptance of the terms of reference of the Scripture generally: to embrace David is to embrace Moses. There is no trace in James's interpretation of the Pauline gambit, setting one biblical principle (justification in the manner of Abraham) against another (obedience in the manner of Moses). Where Paul divided the Scripture against itself in order to maintain the integrity of a single fellowship of Jews and Gentiles, James insisted upon the integrity of Scripture, even at the cost of separating Christians from one another. In both cases, the interpretation of Scripture was also—at the same moment as the sacred text was apprehended—a matter of social policy.

In a conference at Trinity Western University, John J. Collins referred to the two citations of Amos 9:11 that are attested at Qumran.[4] He relied on his findings in an earlier work that the two exegeses are quite different from one another, and from James's exegesis.[5] For reasons that will emerge shortly I would be inclined to describe the relationship among the interpretations as complementary. The more recently identified usage (in 4Q174 3:10–13, a florilegium) is the more straightforward, in that the image of the restoration of the hut of David is associated with the promise to David in 2 Samuel 7:13-14 and with the Davidic "branch" (cf. Isaiah 11:1-10), all taken in a messianic sense.[6] Given the expectation of a son of David as messianic king (see *Psalms of Solomon* 17:21–43), such an application of the passage in Amos, whether at Qumran or by James, is hardly strange. On the other hand, it is striking at first sight that the passage in Amos—particularly, "the fallen hut of David"—is applied in the Damascus Document (7:15-17), not to a messianic figure, but to the law which is restored. Now, the book of Amos itself makes Judah's contempt for the Torah a pivotal issue (Amos 2:4) and calls for a program of seeking the Lord and his ways (Amos 5:6-15), so it is perhaps not surprising that "the seeker of the law" is predicted to restore it in the Damascus Document. Still, Damascus Document 7:15–20 directly refers to the "books of the Torah" as "the huts of the king," interpreted by means of the "fallen hut of David." Evidently, there is a precise correspondence between the strength of the Messiah and the establishment of the Torah, as is further suggested by the association with the seeker of the law *not only here*, in the Damascus Document, but also in the Florilegium. A contextual reading of the two passages demonstrates a dual focus, on Messiah and Torah in each case, such that they stand in a complementary relationship. The possibility of Essene influence on James's interpretation of Amos as presented in Acts 15 may not be discounted.

The conditions of the church in Jerusalem, the most intense in its relations with other Jewish groups within the church as a whole prior to the great revolt that culminated in the destruction of the Temple, occasioned the emergence of a new institution. James, the brother of Jesus, whose devotion to the Temple brought him both respect and antagonism in Jerusalem, became the *mebaqqer*—as the overseer at Qumran was called—of a group whose teaching in regard to the Torah, whose practice of purity, and whose dedication to the sacrificial worship of Israel made for uniqueness. Transferred to a Hellenistic and Christian environment, the Jacobean institution became the episcopate, and saw Christianity through its formative period and beyond.

But the presentation in Acts permits us to see even more. Acts reflects (1) a particular context of consultation in which James's halakhic interpretation becomes normative, and (2) the establishment of a policy and style of argument that substantially contradicts Paul's, even as it embraces a view of circumcision that he can only have accepted. In both respects, Acts articulates what would become governing structures of Catholic, Orthodox Christianity, apart from which the evolution of the Church in late antiquity cannot be understood.

THE CONSEQUENCES OF THE POLICY OF JAMES

In Acts 15, James speaks within a specific context, not only in Jerusalem, but also within international Christianity (such as it then existed). A controversy erupts because "some had come down from Judea, who were teaching the brothers, If you do not circumcise by the custom of Moses, you are not able to be saved" (15:1). The result is a dispute with Paul and Barnabas, which is not surprising, since they have just returned to Antioch after a successful completion of the work which the prophets and teachers there, by the direction of the Holy Spirit, had sent them out to do (Acts 13:1–14:28; see 13:3 and 14:26 for the framing of the section in terms of the work they had completed). They announce that, by means of their ministry, God has "opened a door of faith for the Gentiles" (Acts 14:27).

That, of course, is the most positive way of relating their experience of preaching in Asia Minor. In the same section of Acts, a pattern is developed according to which Paul and Barnabas announce that they now "turn to the Gentiles" because they have been rejected, even persecuted, by Jews (see Acts 13:46, and the whole of vv. 42-51; 14:1-5, 19). Indeed, that is the providential pattern of the whole of Luke-Acts, in which even Jesus is rejected by his own—to the point of coming near to execution by stoning—and speaks of the extension of the work of the prophets to those outside of Israel as a consequence of that rejection (so Luke 4:14-30).[7] It is frequently and rightly maintained that the rejection of Jesus and his message by the Jews is a pivotal motif in Luke-Acts, in that it permits the transition in the narrative to the emphasis on the Gentiles that is a signature concern of the author.[8] But the relationship between Israel and the Gentiles in Acts is actually more than a matter of the apologetic explanation of how Gentiles came to predominate in the church. The mention of the issue of circumcision in Acts 15, and the emphasis that the Council in Jerusalem met to address that issue first of all, reflect an awareness that the identity of the church in respect of Israel is at stake.

Because the question of circumcision has already been dealt with in Acts 10 and 11, as a consequence of Peter's baptisms in the house of Cornelius, the mention of the issue in Acts 15 can only be read as a deliberate resumption of what was a genuinely contentious concern within primitive Christianity. The extensive narrative in Acts 10 has already confirmed—by vision and the coming of the Holy Spirit upon those in Cornelius's house—that non-Jews are indeed to be baptized, and Peter in Acts 11 personally rehearses those events for "the apostles and brothers who were in Judea" (11:1). Having heard his response to "those of the circumcision" in Jerusalem, who taxed Peter for visiting and eating with those who were foreskinned (11:2-3), Peter's hearers are reported to accept that "God has granted even the Gentiles repentance for life" (11:18).

In *Judaism in the New Testament*,[9] attention has already been called to the "romanticized" quality of Acts 15, in which the issues of both circumcision and the purity to be required of Gentiles are taken up in a single meeting. Paul's account of his relations with those in Jerusalem in Galatians 2 was cited in order to support that observation. But now we can observe that the account in Acts is not only romanticized, but self-consciously so. The Council will simply confirm the earlier finding in regard to circumcision, on the precedent of Peter's baptisms in the house of Cornelius, and then proceed to the question of the regulations of purity that baptized non-Jews are to uphold.

By dealing with these issues together, Acts conflates not only the particular topics but also the leaders who settle both questions. The representative function of Paul and Barnabas (along with others) for the church in Antioch is underlined, because they bring news of the conversion of the Gentiles to Phoenicia and Samaria on their way to Jerusalem, to the "great joy" of all (Acts 15:3). These *apostles* of Antioch (see Acts 14:4, 14) are then received by both *the apostles and the elders* of the church in Jerusalem (Acts 15:4). When the gathering gets down to business, apostles and elders are again named as the participants (Acts 15:6). So the usual reference to this meeting as "the Apostolic Council of Jerusalem" is amply warranted.[10] In fact, we can go further: it would be better to speak of the Council "in" Jerusalem, since apostles from other places are included. In addition, the "elders" are emphatically a part of proceedings, within a document in which elders and bishops together are understood to function within the apostolic succession (see especially Acts 14:23; 20:28). The Council is both apostolic and episcopal, and the latter aspect is especially reinforced by the later appearance of James, the *mebaqqer/episkopos*.

Thus, the two major strands of power—apostolic and episcopal (the latter in the shape of James, its generative authority)—are concentrated in the Council, and the first issue of concern is circumcision. Believers who are named as "Pharisees" insist, "it is necessary both to circumcise them and to command them to keep the law of Moses" (15:5). That sets the stage for conflict, not only with Paul and Barnabas but also with Peter. And it is Peter who, in the midst of great controversy, rehearses what happened in the house of Cornelius yet again (15:7-11). Peter comes to what is not only a Pauline expression, but more particularly an expression of the Pauline school, that "through the grace of the Lord Jesus we believe to be saved, in the manner they also shall be" (Acts 15:11; cf. Eph 2:8). For that reason, it seems natural for the reference to Barnabas and Paul to follow (15:12). That order of names is no coincidence: after all, Barnabas is much better known and appreciated in Jerusalem than Paul.

After this point, any version of Paulinism is difficult to discern in the decision of the Council. For the moment, it is pertinent simply to observe how the Petrine settlement regarding circumcision and baptism is accepted by James (15:13-18), and how the final disposition of the matter is under the signature of "the apostles and elders with the whole church," including Paul and Barnabas as emissaries with Judas Barsabbas and Silas (15:22). The Council explicitly declares that the Holy Spirit warrants the position of James, and that no other requirement as coming from Jerusalem is to be credited (15:24-29). The characterization of Judas and Silas remaining in Antioch in their role as prophets, together with Paul and Barnabas, reinforces that the letter was written unanimously (*homothumadon*, 15:25[11]), and by the authority of the Holy Spirit (15:28). Every charism of leadership in the church is involved in this decision, Paul's included, under the guidance of the Holy Spirit; how much more striking is it, then, that vital characteristics of Paul's position are rejected in their substance. In particular, although rejecting the first part of the position of the believing Pharisees (Acts 15:5), that circumcision is to be required, James sustains the second part, that the Torah is to be kept throughout the church (also cited in 15:5); therefore, he rejects the policy—specifically endorsed by Paul in 1 Corinthians 8 and Romans 14—that the question of food sacrificed to idols was a matter of relative indifference.

THE REFUTATION OF PAUL IN FAVOR OF THE TEMPLE

What is confirmed here of Paul's activity among Gentiles and his theological vocabulary of grace can hardly conceal what is implicitly denied: there is no assertion of Paul's characteristic claim that all believers become sons of Abraham—and therefore Israel—by baptism. Even in Paul's own speech in the synagogue in Pisidian Antioch, the showcase of his theology in the Lukan account, although he imagines that "everyone who believes in him is justified" from what one can not be justified from by Torah (13:39, a properly Pauline formulation), he addresses these words to "sons of the family of Abraham, and those who fear God" (13:26; see also 13:17[12]). In other words, Acts 13 has him make just the distinction he argues *against* in Galatians, much as in Acts 15 he delivers a letter whose policy about purity he rejects in 1 Corinthians 8 and Romans 14. Acts is very plain: whatever may be acceptable of Paul's theology, his claim that believers become Israel without remainder[13] is jettisoned in favor of James's conviction, that Gentile belief is meant to restore the fortunes of the family of David,[14] consonant with the prophecy of Amos (Acts 15:16-21).

To understand the position that is evolved in Acts, and that is woven into the fabric of apostolic-episcopal authority, we must again refer to James's position, in this case in regard to circumcision. Acts 15:14-15 is explicit: James accepts Peter's account of how "God first visited, to take a people from Gentiles for his name" (15:14). That "first" is notable, because it confirms the impression that the Pentecostal theology of the Petrine school occasioned a new understanding of the horizon of God's spirit. Moreover, James here acknowledges that Peter's experience amounts to a precedent, which he personally accepts. Gentiles who believe in Jesus are not to be required to circumcise.

Recently, that picture in Acts has been rigorously denied by Robert Eisenman:[15]

> Whenever Acts comes to issues relating to James or Jesus' brothers and family members generally, it equivocates and dissimulates, trailing off

finally into disinformation, sometimes even in the form of childish fan-
tasy. Though sometimes humorous, especially when one is aware of
what the parameters of the disputes in this period really were, this is
almost always with uncharitable intent.

Most scholars of the literature would agree that this is an exaggerated
finding.[16] One of the reasons for the freighted rhetoric is that
Eisenman is concerned to insist, in the face of good indications to the
contrary, that James required all believers to be circumcised.[17]

In his concern, he illustrates why there has been confusion in this
regard. Galatians reflects the obvious dispute between Paul and the
circle of James, and at one point Paul accuses Peter and Barnabas of
"fearing those of the circumcision" (Gal 2:12). Eisenman then links
that statement with the characterization of James in the Pseudo-
Clementine *Homilies*, where James warns Peter not to communicate
with those who are unworthy. Both of those alleged supports in fact
demonstrate the extraordinary weakness of his assertion (which may
explain why it is fitted out with so much rhetoric).

When Paul uses the noun "circumcision" (*peritome*), he does so as a
metonym for ancestral Judaism. So, for example, in the same chapter
of Galatians, he refers to himself as entrusted with the gospel of
uncircumcision and Peter as entrusted with the gospel of circumcision, one predominantly for Gentiles and the other predominantly for
Jews and God-fearers (2:7-8). Moreover, James and John are specifically included in this arrangement with Peter, on the side of circumcision, with Paul and Barnabas on the other side in mutually
recognized ministry of the gospel (2:9). To give the term a new sense,
the sense of those who compel circumcision, is unnatural within the
logic of Galatians 2. Within the logic of the letter as a whole, it is even
more unnatural: Paul makes a very clear distinction between his disagreement with the circle of James over the question of purity at
meals (2:11-21) and his open, crudely expressed contempt for those
who are attempting to circumcise converts to Christianity (5:1-12).
When Peter and Barnabas fall in with the policy of James in regard
to purity, Paul calls that hypocrisy (2:11-13); when unnamed teachers
urge circumcision on the Galatians, Paul tells them to cut their geni-
tals off (5:1-12). In substance and tone, his attitude is different,
because James—following Peter's lead—accepted that circumcision
could not be required, while the anonymous disturbers in Galatians

5:12 most emphatically did not. Acts itself recognizes the existence of such teachers and attests their implicit claim to represent the church in Jerusalem (15:24). The presence in Jerusalem of teachers whom Acts styles as believing Pharisees would suggest that they are the source of the simple conviction that the Torah, in this case Genesis 17:10-14, was to be upheld in the preaching of Jesus. Straightforward as that claim is, Acts attests just as emphatically that James is not its source: rather, he sees a place for Gentiles as Gentiles, in a role of support for an essentially Davidic revelation.

That picture of a place for the Gentiles within Christian preaching is actually confirmed by the Pseudo-Clementine literature that Eisenman cites in support of his argument. That literature is particularly pointed against Paul (whom it refers to as *homo inimicus*) and in favor of James. Indeed, the *Recognitions* (1.43–71) even relate that, prior to his conversion to Christianity, Saul assaulted James in the Temple. Martin Hengel refers to this presentation as an apostolic novel (*Apostelroman*), deeply influenced by the perspective of the Ebionites, and probably to be dated within the third and fourth centuries.[18] The ordering of Peter under James is clearly a part of that perspective, as Hengel shows, and much earlier Joseph Lightfoot found that the alleged correspondence between Clement and James was a later addition to the Pseudo-Clementine corpus.[19] But even if the Pseudo-Clementines are taken at face value, they undermine Eisenman's view:[20] they portray James as the standard for how Hellenistic Christians are to teach (see *Recognitions* 11.35.3).[21]

In a sense there is nothing surprising about that portrayal, in that Paul himself—writing in Galatians, where he has every interest in diminishing any sense that he is dependent upon his predecessors in Jerusalem—describes himself as laying out his gospel for the Gentiles for apostolic scrutiny, "lest I were running or had been running in vain" (2:1-2). He had earlier framed his gospel in discussion with Peter, and had also met James, whom he describes as an apostle at that point (around the year 35 CE; see Gal 1:18-19). Then, fourteen years after his conversion in 32 CE (or in 46 CE), it is before three "pillars" of the church—James and Peter and John, in that order—that Paul lays out his case, and receives authorization to continue among the Gentiles (Gal 2:3-10).

In his description of James's circle, Irenaeus (around 180 CE) refers to their permitting activity among the Gentiles, while they themselves preserve their proper customs (*pristinis observantionibus*; *Against Heresies* 3.12.15). As Hengel points out, most of the sources regarding James do not involve him in disputes concerning the law, and when the Pseudo-Clementines target such disputes, they do so by way of an attack on Paul.[22] Epiphanius reports the legend among the Ebionites that Paul accepted circumcision in the first place only to marry the daughter of the high priest, and then—disappointed in his design—attacked circumcision and the law (*Pancrion* 30.16). In other words: the Ebionite case against Paul is made, not by claiming James required circumcision, but by asserting that Paul accepted and then opposed circumcision for the worst of motives, whether theological or personal. Implicitly, the sources are in agreement that James did not require circumcision of Gentile converts to Christianity.

Where Eisenman and the Tübingen school of the nineteenth century, whose insights he pursues, have erred is not in imputing controversy to the Christian movement in its earliest stages, but in imputing the *same controversy* to every division. Paul disagreed with James, Peter, and sometimes with Barnabas, but not over the issue of whether circumcision should be required. Believing Pharisees did, on the other hand, disagree with all of those named apostles. Where James and Paul went their separate ways—ways between which Peter and Barnabas hesitated—was in the identification of non-Jewish believers. For Paul, they were Israel; for James, they were not.

The key to James's position in this regard was brilliantly provided by Kirsopp Lake in his study of the Council in Jerusalem. Scholarship since his time has provided a striking confirmation of his suggestion. Lake uses the proscriptions James insisted on—of food sacrificed to idols, blood, things strangled, and fornication—as a way of describing how James and the Council would identify believing Gentiles in relation to Israel. He observes the affinity with the rules in Leviticus 17 regarding non-Israelites who reside in the land: they are to desist from offerings to other gods, and from the usage of any altar but in the Temple (17:7-9), they are to abstain from blood (17:10-13), and to avoid the sexual relations described in Leviticus 18:24-30. By the time of the Talmud (Sanhedrin 56b), such prohibitions were elaborated into the so-called Noachic commandments, binding upon humanity generally, but Lake rightly observes they are formulated too late to have influenced Acts.[23]

The position of James in regard to the book of Leviticus, however, cannot be set aside simply by observing the date of the Talmud. We have already seen that just the section of Leviticus in which chapters 17 and 18 are included (i.e., chapters 16–19) were particularly resonant with James's view of how the Torah was to be upheld in respect of Gentiles. Lake is correct to point out that the regulations in Leviticus are for non-Israelite residents in the land, not abroad, and that fact needs to be taken into account. Nonetheless, there is nothing intrinsically improbable with the hypothesis that James's stipulations with regard to non-Jewish believers were framed with their compatibility with worship in the Temple in mind.

In any case, Lake also called attention to the requirements made of Gentiles within a work of Hellenistic Judaism, book 4 of the *Sibylline Oracles* (4:24-34):[24]

> Happy will be those of earthly men who will cherish the great God, blessing before eating, drinking and having confidence in piety. They will deny all temples and altars they see: purposeless transports of dumb stones, defiled by animates' blood and sacrifices of four-footed animals. But they will behold the great renown of the one God, neither breaking into reckless murder, nor transacting what is stolen for gain, which are cold happenings. They do not have shameful desire for another's bed, nor hateful and repulsive abuse of a male.

What is especially striking about this prophecy is that it is directed to the people of Asia and Europe (*Sib. Orac.* 4:1) through the mouth of the Sibyl (4:22–23), the legendary oracle of mantic counsel. Her utterance here is explicitly backed up by the threat of eschatological judgment for all (4:40–48).

A growing body of opinion has found that the emphasis upon prophecy in Luke-Acts accords with the perspectives of Hellenistic historians such as Diodorus Siculus and Dionysius of Halicarnassus.[25] The place of Sibylline prophesies, deriving from a prophetess whose origin "was already lost in the mist of legend by the fifth century" CE,[26] is prominent in both. But while Luke-Acts invokes the motif of prophecy (literary and contemporary), the Sibyl makes no appearance in a work that is, after all, the largest in the New Testament. That suggests that the way for the synthesis of Hellenistic oracles and

Hebrew prophecy had been prepared, especially by works such as the *Sibylline Oracles* of Hellenistic Judaism, but then that Luke-Acts insists on the attestation of Jesus' coming (directly or indirectly) as an indispensable criterion of true prophecy.[27]

The development of ethical requirements for Gentiles in view of eschatological judgment was therefore part of the ethos of Hellenistic Judaism at the time Luke-Acts was composed. The concerns cited by Lake in book 4 of the *Sibylline Oracles*[28] comport well with the requirements set out in Acts 15, except for the specific proscription of blood. Still, reciting a blessing prior to eating might suggest that what is eaten is to be pure, and immersion is mentioned later in the *Sibylline Oracles* (4:165), so the issue is scarcely outside the range of concerns of Hellenistic Judaism.

Indeed, that horizon of interest is inherent in book 3 of the *Sibylline Oracles*, which Collins dates within the period 163–145 BCE.[29] There, the Sibyl is portrayed as Noah's daughter-in-law (3:823–829), and it was Noah whom God instructed with the commandment not to consume blood or to shed human blood (Gen 9:4-6). Noah receives cognate treatment in books 1 and 2 of the *Sibylline Oracles*. The dates of that part of the corpus are uncertain, and Christian additions are evident, but Collins seems on secure ground in his argument that the Judaic redaction was completed before 70 CE in Phrygia.[30] Noah is here made an articulate preacher of repentance to all peoples (*Sib. Orac.* 1:128–129) in an elegant expansion of the biblical story (1:125–282) that has the ark make land in Phrygia (1:262). The persistence of such an association between Noah and Asia Minor is intimated by 1 Peter 3:20, where the number of those in the ark (eight) is stressed, as in the *Sibylline Oracles* 1:282, in comparison to those who were punished.

Within the context of Hellenistic Judaism as reflected in the Sibylline Oracles, then, a prohibition of blood to Gentiles seems quite natural. If it is anachronistic to speak at this point of Noachic commandments, we may at least refer to the motif of Noah's instruction of all humanity as well established by the first century CE. Unfortunately, the *Genesis Apocryphon* from Qumran is fragmentary just as it speaks of Noah, but it is notable that Noah is told there that he is to rule over the earth and the seas and that "you shall not eat any blood" (*Gen. Apoc.* 7.1; 11.17). Both those statements are more emphatic than what is said in the corresponding text of Genesis in Hebrew (Gen 9:2, 4).

The possible connection between the motif in the *Sibylline Oracles* and the treatment of Noah in the *Genesis Apocryphon* is intriguing. Book 3 of the *Sibylline Oracles* is associated with the priestly family of the Oniads that had been pushed out of Jerusalem prior to the Maccabean revolt.[31] They eventually settled in Egypt and enjoyed protection under the Ptolemies there, which is why Collins dates the *Sibylline Oracles* between 163 and 145 CE. They were responsible for building the Temple at Leontopolis, in evident protest against the settlement in Jerusalem (Josephus, *Jewish War* 1.33; 7.420–432). Prior to settling in Egypt, however, Syria had been the Oniads' base.[32] The cultic protest of the Oniads, their chronology, and their association with Syria have all led to the inference that they were connected with the rise of the Essenes, and Philo's reference to Essenes in Egypt would support that inference.[33] To this we may add Josephus's observation that the Essenes were noted for their prophecy (for example, in *Jewish War* 2.159):[34] prophecy is a connecting link among the Essenes, the *Sibylline Oracles*, the emissaries of James and the Council who were prophets, and the ethos of Luke-Acts.

James's interpretation of Scripture, as we have seen, shows similarities to the interpretation instanced at Qumran. His halakhic approach comports with an emphasis on the necessity for all people, even Gentiles, to keep a degree of purity out of regard for the Torah. The evidence of the *Sibylline Oracles* reinforces the impression of James's Essene orientation, and shows how that perspective could be developed within a field well prepared by Hellenistic Judaism.

But what James's circle prepared on that field was a particular devotion to the Temple in Jerusalem. The ideal of Christian devotion that James has in mind is represented in Acts 21. There, Paul and his companion arrive in Jerusalem and are met by James and the elders, who report to them that Paul's reputation in Jerusalem is that he is telling Jews in the Diaspora to forsake Moses, and especially to stop circumcising their children (Acts 21:17-21). Paul is then told to take on the expense of four men who had taken a vow, and to enter the Temple with them to offer sacrifice (Acts 21:22-26).

The nature of the vow seems quite clear. It will be fulfilled when the men shave their heads (so Acts 21:24). We are evidently dealing with a Nazirite vow.[35] As set out in Numbers 6, a Nazirite was to let his hair and beard grow for the time of his vow, abstain completely from grapes, and avoid approaching any dead body. At the close of the period of the vow, he was to shave his head, and offer his hair in proximity to the altar (so Num 6:18). The end of this time of being holy, the LORD's property, is marked by the Nazirites' being able to drink wine again (6:20).

These very practices of holiness are attributed by Hegesippus (as cited by Eusebius, *Eccl. Hist.* 2.23) to James. The additional notice, that he avoided oil and use of a traditional bath, is consistent with the especial concern for purity among Nazirites. They were to avoid any contact with death (Num 6:6-12), and the avoidance of all uncleanness, which is incompatible with sanctity, follows naturally. The avoidance of oil is also attributed by Josephus to the Essenes (*Jewish War* 2.123), and the reason seems plain: oil, as a fluid pressed from fruit, was considered to absorb impurity to such an extent that extreme care in its preparation was vital.[36] Absent complete assurance, abstinence was a wise policy. James's vegetarianism also comports with a concern to avoid contact with any kind of corpse. Finally, although Hegesippus's assertion that James could actually enter the sanctuary seems exaggerated, the latter's acceptance of a Nazirite regime, such as Acts 21 explicitly associates him with, would account for such a remembrance of him, in that Nazirites were to be presented in the vicinity of the sanctuary.

As it turned out, James's advice proved disastrous for Paul. Paul's entry into the Temple caused a riot, because it was supposed he was bringing non-Jews in. As a result, he was arrested by a Roman officer (Acts 21:27–28:21), and so began the long legal contention that resulted ultimately in his death. The extent to which James might have anticipated such a result cannot be known, but it does seem obvious that his commitment to a Nazirite ideology blinded him to the political dangers that threatened the movement of which he was the nearest thing to the head.

The particular concern of James for practice in the Temple has left its mark on teaching attributed to Jesus. In Mark 7:15, Jesus set down a radical principle of purity: there is nothing outside a person, entering in that can defile, but what comes out of a person is what defiles a person. That principle establishes that those in Israel were to be

accepted as pure, so that fellowship at meals with them, as was characteristic in Jesus' movement from the beginning, was possible. Their
usual customs of purity, together with their generosity in sharing and
their willingness to receive and accept forgiveness, readied them to
celebrate the fellowship of the kingdom of God.[37] His program was
not as suited to Nazirites as it was to those his opponents called "tax
agents and sinners"; to these opponents Jesus seemed a drunk and a
glutton (see Matt 11:19; Luke 7:34).

But within this same chapter of Mark in which Jesus' principle is
clearly stated, a syllogism is developed to attack a particular practice
in the Temple (Mark 7:6-13). Two features of this argument are striking. It assumes familiarity with the vow of *qorbana*, which does indeed
mean "gift" in Aramaic. One could, in effect, shelter one's use of
property to dedicating it to the Temple at one's death, continuing to
use it during one's life.[38] The Mishnah envisages a man saying,
"Qorban be any benefit my wife gets from me, for she stole my purse"
(Nedarim 3:2). The simple complaint about the practice in Mark
7:11-12 may indeed reflect Jesus' position, since his objection to commercial arrangements involving worship is well attested. But that only
focuses our attention all the more on the syllogistic nature of the argument, which is unlike what we elsewhere find attributed to Jesus.

The argument as a whole is framed in Mark 7:6-7 by means of a
reference to the book of Isaiah (29:13): the people claim to honor God,
but their heart is as far from him as their vain worship, rooted in
human commandments. That statement is then related to the custom
of *qorban*, which is said to invalidate the plain sense of Moses' prescrip-
tion to honor parents.[39] The simple and inevitable conclusion is that
the tradition violates the command of God (see Mark 7:8-9, 13).

The logic of the syllogism is not complicated, and it can easily be
structured in a different way.[40] The association of similar Scriptures is
reminiscent of the rabbinic rule of interpretation, that a principle
expressed in a text may be related to another text, without identity of
wording between the two passages.[41] But the scriptural syllogism by no
means requires the invocation of any such formal principle. The fundamental argument is that the Law and the Prophets are antithetical
to the practice of authorities in the Temple.

The rhetoric of the syllogism turns on the necessity of honoring
Moses, as in the interpretation attributed to James in Acts 15 (see

v. 21). Moreover, the principle inherent here is that Scripture is that which is actually implemented in the case of Jesus' movement. Finally, the centrality of the Temple is manifest throughout.

The stance of James as concerns purity and the Temple, as well as his interpretation of Scripture, comports well with Hegesippus's description of his particular practices. The evidence in aggregate suggests that James understood his brother as offering an access to God through the Temple, such that Israel could and should offer God the Nazirites with their vows, such as Moses provided for. It has been argued that Jesus himself adhered to such a position,[42] but that seems to put a strain on his usual practice of fellowship at meals.[43]

Indeed, our suggestion that James was a Nazirite, and saw Jesus' movement as focused on producing more Nazirites, enables us to address an old and as yet unsolved problem of research. Jesus, bearing a common name, is sometimes referred to as "of Nazareth" in the gospels, and that reflects how he was specified in his own time. There is no doubt but that a geographic reference is involved (see John 1:45-46).[44] But more is going on here. Actually, Jesus is rarely called "of Nazareth" or "from Nazareth," although he was probably known to come from there. He is usually called "Nazoraean" or "Nazarene." Why the adjective, and why the uncertainty in spelling? The Septuagint shows us that there were many different transliterations of "Nazirite," reflecting uncertainty as to how to convey the term in Greek. (That uncertainty is not in the least surprising, since even the Mishnah refers to differing pronunciations [see Nazir 1:1].) Some of the variants are in fact very close to what we find used to describe Jesus in the gospels.

In the Gospel according to Mark, the first usage is in the mouth of a demon, who says to Jesus (1:24):

> We have nothing for you, Nazarene Jesus!
> Have you come to destroy us?
> I know who you are—the holy one of God!

In this usage, "Nazarene" in the first line clearly parallels "the holy one of God" in the last line. The demon knows Jesus' true identity, but those in the synagogue where the exorcism occurs do not. And they do not hear the demons, because Jesus silences them (see Mark 1:25). This is part of the well-known theme of the "Messianic secret" in Mark.[45]

For James and those who were associated with him, Jesus' true
identity was his status as a Nazirite. The demons saw what others did
not, and after the resurrection the knowledge of the holy one of God
could be openly acknowledged and practiced. That practice could
include men, women, and slaves, in accordance with the Mishnah
(Nazir 9:1). In the Christian movement, the custom was apparently
widespread. In Acts 18:18, it is said that even Paul "had his head
shorn in Kenkhraea, because he had a vow." Such vows in regard to
hair alone were held in Mishnah to equate to a Nazirite vow (Nazir
1:1), so that whatever Paul thought of his vow from his own perspective, many would have seen him as falling in with the program of
James, the brother of Jesus. Under the influence of James, they might
have said, even Paul was concerned with getting it right.

Where Paul got it precisely wrong, from the point of view of the
Council in Jerusalem, was in his assertion that food sacrificed to idols
could be consumed, provided only it did not mislead anyone into a
belief in the actuality of any god behind the idol. His mature articulation of his principle in this regard would involve at most grudging
respect for the letter sent from the Council to Antioch (see Rom
14:14-15):

> I know and I am convinced in the Lord Jesus that nothing is impure in
> itself, but to one who considers something to be impure, it is impure for
> him. If your brother is aggrieved on account of food, you are no longer
> walking by love: do not ruin with food that one for whom Christ died.

The whole of Romans 14 is devoted to this issue, so that it is plain that
the controversy is significant in Rome, as it had been in Corinth (see
1 Cor 8).

At the end of the day, it might be argued that the application of
Paul's principle would lead to acquiescence with the ruling of the
Council, but his stance is hardly a ringing endorsement. For that reason, it is a bit difficult to imagine Paul—as Acts 15 clearly portrays
him—delivering the Council's letter with Barnabas and Judas and
Silas (Acts 15:22). After all, for the Council and for James there is
something intrinsically impure in what is specified, and believing
Gentiles are to avoid it, as a matter of loyalty to the Torah. Paul is not
in complete opposition to the policy, and he shows that in matters of
sexuality there are impure relations that are to be avoided at the peril
of one's eschatological judgment (see 1 Cor 5).[46] But to imagine him

as complicit in the letter and delivering it in Antioch strains credulity. It is more likely that the meeting in respect of circumcision and the meeting in respect of impurity were distinct events.[47] For that reason, Christians continued to be divided over the question of whether the meat of animals notionally sacrificed to gods could be eaten.[48]

The Council of Luke-Acts of Acts 15 controverts Pauline principle not only in substance but also in style. Gone are the dialectics of discovering one element in Scripture in opposition to another, in order to discover which of them accords with the gospel of Jesus. Gone are the long arguments that explain how the triumphant element in Scripture can have been obscured by others, and how the unity of divine revelation may be maintained nonetheless. Gone is the elevation of that method to the point it offers a way of understanding all human relations with God. Indeed, Paul himself, in Romans 14 and 1 Corinthians 8, is providing an example of how different from the Lukan James's is his own take on what to do with a principle under active discussion within Christianity. Whether or not Paul knows James articulated the principle that food sacrificed to idols is not to be eaten, he obviously knows it is a serious principle, ardently maintained by some Christians. But instead of simply finding for or against the policy, Paul measures each and every act of eating against one's evaluation of the conscience of the person with whom one is eating. Pauline dialectics are deployed as much in ethics as they are in Scripture.

All of that is set aside by the Council. The food not to be eaten and the behavior not to be indulged are stated, on the assertion that the Holy Spirit and the Council, in accordance with the words of the prophet Amos as cited by James, making that the rule to be followed. Argument is beside the point. Once the consensus of the Council agrees with Scripture, that conciliar interpretation becomes normative. Because the Council in question is both apostolic and episcopal, Luke-Acts here provides a normative model of ecclesiastical authority, as well as a normative ruling.

THE CHRISTIAN PHARISEES

The very force of that ruling, of course, necessarily implied a breach with the believing Pharisees, for whom circumcision could not be treated as optional. In a forthcoming article, Paul Flesher shows how axiomatic the practice of circumcision was within the understanding of conversion. Indeed, he describes the scholarly discussion concerning "proselyte baptism" as an artifact of imposing a Christian paradigm on the sources of rabbinic Judaism.[49] But that artifact pales in comparison to the dominant portrayal in the gospels of Jesus and the Pharisees in persistent antipathy. In his influential book, *Jesus and Judaism*, E. P. Sanders has demonstrated how deeply anachronistic that portrayal is.[50] Sanders himself develops the thesis, which has not been widely accepted, that Jesus did not require repentance of sinners, which would in fact explain the gospels' anachronism as being accurate.[51] Herbert Basser's position, that Jesus' debates with the Pharisees represent dispute within a shared religious vocabulary, is far more plausible.[52] In this regard, the friendly warning Pharisees give Jesus about Herod Antipas (see Luke 13:31) stands in telling opposition to the claim that the Pharisees plotted to kill Jesus from the moment they disagreed about healing on the Sabbath (see Matt 12:14; Mark 3:6; Luke 6:11).

How could dispute with the Pharisees have been elevated to mortal enmity in the portrayal of the gospels? Jesus' actual disputes with Pharisees might be described as a necessary condition of that portrayal, but they hardly provide the sufficient condition. The growing influence of the Pharisees after 70 CE did clearly result in mounting tension with Christian communities (as Matthew 23 reflects), just as it resulted in Josephus's attempt to portray the Pharisees in a somewhat more favorable light in his *Antiquities* than he had in his *Jewish War*.[53] But does that really explain why, for example, the Gospel of John should speak of believers being expelled from the synagogue (*aposynagogos genesthai*) by Pharisees as a result of belief in Christ (9:22; 12:42; 16:2)? The specificity of the antagonism with those named as Pharisees invites us to discover a focused issue of contention.

The attempt in Acts to kill Paul in the Temple is occasioned by the charge that he would introduce the uncircumcised into the Temple (Acts 21:27-36). Shortly after that time (in 62 CE), James himself was killed by stoning, also in the Temple. No doubt, the enmity of the high priesthood was a determinative factor,[54] and it was a principal factor in the execution of Jesus. But by the time of Paul and James, the issue of circumcision had also produced a common front between the high priesthood and the Pharisees that had not existed in the case of Jesus.

Paul was the precipitating cause of the new alliance. After all, he had been "according to the Torah, a Pharisee" as he himself put it (see Phil 3:5). But that is exactly what he had come to see as "forfeit on account of Christ" (Phil 3:7). He who had been a convert to Pharisaism became a convert against it, and both conversions had to with the evaluation of the Torah.[55] That it was "Jews from Asia," his own native area, who objected to Paul's presence in the Temple (Acts 21:27) comports with the reading that Paul the double convert offended just the constituency he had once tried to please.

James' stance in regard to circumcision was not as obviously offensive as Paul's. Yet once Paul had radicalized the situation, by his appearance in the Temple, James had to answer a single question, "What is the gate of Jesus?" (Eusebius, *Eccl. Hist.* 2.23). In other words: was there a way into the covenant apart from by the practice of circumcision? James replied to that question by his insistence on Jesus' status as the Son of Man, who offered a way for both Israel and non-Jews, and the result was his death in Jerusalem.

In both disputes, what was the role of the Christian Pharisees of Acts 15? Insofar as they understood the covenant with Abraham to have been confirmed by Jesus, even as it might be extended to others, there is no reason to doubt the claim that they insisted on the practice of circumcision. That put them at odds—and at odds which proved to be mortal—with the positions of Paul and of James, and that made Pharisaism a rhetorical category of enmity *within* Christianity, a category that was then retrojected into the gospels, to describe the opposition to Jesus.

PAUL, THE CHRISTIAN PHARISEES, AND THE LANGUAGE OF OPPOSITION

Paul, far from compromising with the Christian Pharisees as he did with James, rejects their position with contempt. In fact, he does not even refer to their views as Pharisaic. Instead, they are "the circumcision." The term "Pharisee" is too good for them, in Paul's mind: the only time in his entire corpus that he speaks of a Pharisee, it is to describe himself as developing "according to the law, a Pharisee" (Phil

3:5). The believing Pharisees that Acts 15 mentions, to whom Paul also refers in Galatians 2, are "false brethren" (Gal 2:4), who continued to militate for "circumcision" long after (2:12). From Galatians onward, of course, "the circumcision"—when it means imposing that requirement on Gentile believers—becomes metonymic for opposition to Christ, as far as Paul was concerned. That was why, even late in life, he can dismiss them as "the mutilation" (Phil 3:2).[56]

Global though the implicit rejection of these opponents in Galatians is, it is even more sweeping in Paul's earlier language. The first letter to the church in Thessaloniki, which Paul wrote with Silas (a key figure in connection with the church in Jerusalem) and Timothy, represents the earliest example of Paul's preserved correspondence. Paul takes the lead in 1 Thessalonians, because it was addressed principally to Gentile Christians there.[57] In the way of first efforts, there is a tentative quality here compared to Paul's later letters. Nonetheless, the three teachers say that their message comes from God's own Spirit (1:5) and focuses on Jesus as divine Son, who alone can deliver humanity from the rapidly approaching end of the ages (1:10).

This eschatological tenor is typical of primitive Christianity, and characterizes Paul's letters as a whole. Time is truly short, because the day of the Lord comes as a thief in the night (5:2), at a time that cannot be reckoned. In view of this impending judgment, the Thessalonian Gentiles had put their idols aside (1:9), and that also meant (as Paul is never slow to point out) that sexual sanctification had to follow. Lust was a reflex of idolatry: now was the time for "every one of you to keep one's own vessel in sanctification and honor, and not in the passion of lust just like the Gentiles who do not know God" (4:4-5). The three teachers agreed that turning from idolatry and perversion to serve the living God was the only means of human salvation in the short time before the Day of Judgment.

Paul, Silas, and Timothy also fiercely stated that the Pharisaic teachers from Judea who had tried to prevent contact with Gentiles formed an obstacle to the gospel (1 Thess 2:14): "For you, brothers, became imitators of the churches of God that are in Judea in Jesus Christ, because you also suffered the same things from your kinspeople as they did from the Jews." This refers back to deep contention in Jerusalem. They are using the word "Jews" (*Ioudaioi* in Greek) to mean the people back in Judea who wished to "forbid us to speak to the Gentiles" (2:16). But the same term could also be used during the first century (and later, of course) to mean any practitioners of Judaism anywhere, and that is the sense of the term "Jew" in common usage. So the three companions, writing to Thessalonica and dealing with local issues and recent history, spoke in a way that has encouraged anti-Semitism. Had they known they were writing for something called the New Testament, and how their words would be used to justify the persecution of Jews, they obviously would have spoken differently. But whether the term for the opposition to Paul's teaching, with Peter's and James' early Christianity's moment of greatest interior contention, rather than from a conscious confrontation with Judaism.

CHAPTER 7

PAUL AND GAMALIEL

Bruce Chilton and Jacob Neusner

DID PAUL LEARN FROM GAMALIEL? THE PROBLEM

Acts 22:3 claims regarding Paul that, as a Pharisee, he studied "at the feet of Gamaliel"; that is, with the patriarch of the Pharisaic party of the Land of Israel in the succession from Hillel, thence, via the chain of tradition, from Sinai. What can he have learned from Gamaliel? Here we identify a program of topics that Paul can have taken up in his discipleship or indeed in any association or familiarity with Gamaliel—specifically, subjects and in some cases even halakhic principles important in certain formal constructions of the Mishnah plausibly identified with the patriarchate in general, and with Gamaliel (or at least a Gamaliel) in particular.[1] We propose to outline subjects treated in such constructions that are covered, also, in Paul's letters— a limited proposal but one that, in context, carries implications at once historical and theological.

Formulating the problem in a minimalist framework conveys our critical judgment that we cannot immediately reconstruct the teachings of the Mishnah's named authorities, including Gamaliel. Why should we not take whatever the Rabbinic sources—early, late, and medieval—attribute to (a) Gamaliel at face value? The answer to that question hardly requires elaborate statement, but perhaps it does bear repeating in outline. No critical scholar today expects to open a rabbinic document, whether the Mishnah of ca. 200 CE or the Talmud of Babylonia (Bavli) of ca. 600 CE, and to find there what particular sages on a determinate occasion really said or did. Such an expectation is credulous.[2] There is a second problem, separate from the critical one. Even if we were to accept at face value everything Gamaliel is supposed to have said and done, we should still not have anything remotely yielding a coherent biography, or a cogent theology, or even a legendary narrative of more than a generic and sparse order. We have only episodic and anecdotal data, bits and pieces of this and that, which scarcely cohere to form a recognizable whole.

Although the person of Gamaliel is not accessible, we do have a corpus of compositions that portray convictions characteristic of the institution of which in his time he was head,[3] and which is represented by passages in the Mishnah that exhibit a distinctive form and *Sitz im Leben*. We refer to what became the patriarchate. Gamaliel, as we shall see, is identified as part of the patriarchal chain of tradition that begins at Sinai and culminates in the Mishnah. What became the patriarchate is embodied in Hillel, Gamaliel I, Simeon his son, Gamaliel II (after 70), Simeon b. Gamaliel II (of the mid-second century), and the Mishnah's own sponsor, Judah the Patriarch (ca. 170–210). Whatever its standing and form prior to 70, its theological tradition is situated by tractate Abot chapters 1 and 2 squarely within that traditional continuum. Form-analysis of traditions formally particular to Gamaliel and Simeon b. Gamaliel affords episodic access to a number of theological convictions and topics important to the continuing tradition of the patriarchate preserved, on its own terms, in the Mishnah. These, then, in our view will suggest the topical program and perspective to which Paul would have been exposed in any association with the patriarch Gamaliel—a program characteristic of the patriarchate throughout its history, as we shall show.[4]

THE PATRIARCHATE AND THE COLLEGIUM OF SAGES

Our account of the theologies of the patriarchate and sages' collegium begins not with the Mishnah but with Abot, its first apologia, which reached closure ca. 250 CE, a generation or so after the completion of the Mishnah. There we begin, as the passage cited indicates, with a chain of tradition extending from Sinai to Hillel, and that links the figures of the patriarchal house—Gamaliel, Simeon, Gamaliel, Simeon, and Judah—to Sinai through Hillel. An abbreviated citation suffices:

TRACTATE ABOT 1:1–18

1:1   A.   Moses received Torah at Sinai and handed it on to Joshua, Joshua to elders, and elders to prophets.
      B.   And prophets handed it on to the men of the great assembly.
1:2   A.   Simeon the Righteous was one of the last survivors of the great assembly.
1:3   A.   Antigonos of Sokho received [the Torah] from Simeon the Righteous.
1:4   A.   Yosé b. Yoezer of Seredah and Yosé b. Yohanan of Jerusalem received [it] from them.
1:6   A.   Joshua b. Perahiah and Nittai the Arbelite received [it] from them.
1:8   A.   Judah b. Tabbai and Simeon b. Shatah received [it] from them.
1:10 A.   Shemaiah and Abtalion received [it] from them.
1:12 A.   Hillel and Shammai received [it] from them.
1:16 A.   Rabban Gamaliel says,
1:17 A.   Simeon his son says,
1:18 A.   Rabban Simeon b. Gamaliel says . . .

The following chapter carries the list forward with the names of Judah the Patriarch, sponsor of the Mishnah, and his sons: then breaks off and reverts to Yohanan ben Zakkai—as heir of Hillel and Shammai.

The pivotal names here are:

2:1   A.   Rabbi
2:2   A.   Rabban Gamaliel, son of R. Judah the Patriarch
2:4   C.   Hillel

The stem of the tradition of Sinai that encompasses sages (not the patriarchate) begins with the explicit intrusion of an authority who received the tradition not from Simeon b. Gamaliel via Gamaliel but directly from Hillel and Shammai, a stunning shift possible only as part of an accommodation of the authority of the sages with that of the patriarchate; both derive from Sinai, both pass through Hillel.

2:8   A.   Rabban Yohanan b. Zakkai received [it] from Hillel and Shammai.
      C.   He had five disciples, and these are they: R. Eliezer b. Hyrcanus, R. Joshua b. Hananiah, R. Yosé the priest, R. Simeon b. Netanel, and R. Eleazar b. Arakh.
2:15 A.   R. Tarfon says . . .

What is important here is that the chain of tradition is picked up by Rabbi (Judah the Patriarch) and his two sons, named for the first-century figures Gamaliel and Hillel. Then, as we said, comes a new and comparable institutional continuator to receive the Torah from Hillel and Shammai, namely, the sages' collegium. That is embodied in the figure of the founder of the Yavnean academy after 68 CE, Yohanan ben Zakkai, and his disciples, including the two principal masters of the generation of Yavneh, Joshua and Eliezer, masters of 'Aqiba.

The critical language therefore presents itself in the duplicated genealogy of the dual Torah: Hillel to Gamaliel and Simeon his son, Hillel and Shammai to Yohanan ben Zakkai and his disciples, principals of the period after 70. The Mishnah, sponsored by the patriarchate, and embodying the normative law of the rabbinic sages, joins two distinct institutional partners. The upshot may be simply stated: (1) the chain of tradition runs from Sinai to the masters of the Mishnah through the patriarchate—Hillel, Shammai, and Hillel's heirs and successors, Gamaliel, Simeon, Gamaliel, Simeon—and (2) it is also taken up by the collegium of the sages, represented by Yohanan ben Zakkai and his disciples.

The pertinence of that fact to our problem will become clear when we ask, how do the two foci of authority, patriarch and sage, relate? In the portrait of the Mishnah, the following anecdote, famous in the study of rabbinic Judaism, captures the conflict and how it is resolved—that is, the conflict between institutional authority vested in the patriarch, here, Gamaliel, and the juridical authority vested in qualified sages. This is how the sages, who dominated in the formation of the Mishnah, represent matters, with the obvious acquiescence of the patriarchate.

MISHNAH-TRACTATE ROSH HASHANAH 2:7

2:7 C. Whether it appears in the expected time or does not appear in the expected time, they sanctify it.

D. R. Eleazar b. R. Sadoq says, "If it did not appear in its expected time, they do not sanctify it, for Heaven has already declared it sanctified."

MISHNAH-TRACTATE ROSH HASHANAH 2:8–9

2:8 A. A picture of the shapes of the moon did Rabban Gamaliel have on a tablet and on the wall of his upper room, which he would show ordinary folk, saying, "Did you see it like this or like that?"

B.   M'SH S: Two witnesses came and said, "We saw it at dawn on the morning [of the twenty-ninth] in the east and at eve in the west."

C.   Said R. Yohanan b. Nuri, "They are false witnesses."

D.   Now when they came to Yavneh, Rabban Gamaliel accepted their testimony [assuming they erred at dawn].

E.   And furthermore two came along and said, "We saw it at its proper time, but on the night of the added day it did not appear [to the court]."

F.   Then Rabban Gamaliel accepted their testimony.

G.   Said R. Dosa b. Harkinas, "They are false witnesses."

H.   "How can they testify that a woman has given birth, when, on the very next day, her stomach is still up there between her teeth [for there was no new moon!]?"

I.   Said to him [Dosa] R. Joshua, "I can see your position [and affirm it over Gamaliel's]."

2:9 A.   Said to him [Joshua] Rabban Gamaliel, "I decree that you come to me with your staff and purse on the Day of Atonement which is determined in accord with your reckoning [so publicly renouncing his ruling in favor of Gamaliel's]."

B.   R. 'Aqiba went and found him [Joshua] troubled.

C.   He said to him, "I can provide grounds for showing that everything that Rabban Gamaliel has done is validly done, since it says, 'These are the set feasts of the Lord, even holy convocations, which you shall proclaim' (Lev 23:4). Whether they are in their proper time or not in their proper time, I have no set feasts but these ["which you shall proclaim"] [vs. m. 2:7D]."

D.   He came along to R. Dosa b. Harkinas.

E.   He [Dosa] said to him, "Now if we're going to take issue with the court of Rabban Gamaliel, we have to take issue with every single court which has come into being from the time of Moses to the present day, since it says, 'Then went up Moses and Aaron, Nadab and Abihu, and seventy of the elders of Israel' (Exod 24:9). Now why have the names of the elders not been given? To teach that every group of three [elders] who came into being as a court of Israel—lo, they are equivalent to the court of Moses himself."

F.   [Joshua] took his staff with his purse in his hand and went along to Yavneh, to Rabban Gamaliel, on the Day of Atonement that is determined in accord with his [Gamaliel's] reckoning.

G.   Rabban Gamaliel stood up and kissed him on his head and said to him, "Come in peace, my master and my disciple—

> My master in wisdom, and my disciple in accepting my rul-
> ings."

The key language is "My master in wisdom," which concedes to the collegium of sages superior knowledge of the Torah. But the patriarchate gets its share too: "My disciple in accepting my rulings." The obvious bias in favor of the sages' claim need not detain us. How the patriarchate will have represented matters institutionally remains to be seen. The Gamaliel stories we shall consider signal the answer to that question. 'Aqiba holds that the action of the sages' court in sanctifying the new month is decisive; Eleazar b. R. Sadoq maintains that the decision is settled in Heaven, whatever the state of sightings of the new moon on earth. 'Aqiba supports Gamaliel's ruling — not because it is the patriarchal decision but because it is the decision of the Torah authorities on earth (including the patriarch, to be sure). Dosa still more strongly invokes the authority of sages in support of the patriarch. So both affirm Gamaliel's authority, by reason of his acting in behalf of the sages' collegium. That theme recurs in the Mishnah, which both acknowledges the patriarchal authority and insists on its subordination to that of the collegium of sages: the normative halakha as defined by them. How the contrary position, that of the patriarchate, is represented remains to be seen.

What reliable historical information do we claim to derive from this story? It concerns not the historical patriarch, Gamaliel II, nor the historical Joshua, 'Aqiba, and Dosa; and we do not allege that we know what happened in determining the advent of Tishré and the date of the Day of Atonement in some specific year after 70. What we claim is that the institutional arrangements upon which the Mishnah rests come to the surface in the narrative at hand. There the sages' perspective on matters governs: the patriarchate has the power, but the sages have the learning, and the patriarch concedes that fact in so many words.

Within that perspective, we may ask how representations of incidents involving Gamaliel yield an account of a man within the institutional framework. The answer now is clear: what we allege to define is a reliable picture of enduring attitudes and institutionally supported teachings of, if not a particular patriarch, then the patriarchate over time, including the earlier times—from the third century back to the first. But then the formally distinct composites and compositions concerning an individual patriarch, Gamaliel, embedded within the Mishnah but distinct from its normal media of discourse, will lead us from the institutional figure to the representations of a particular individual within the institution. Thus, everything rests on the identification of individuated compositions and composites: formally distinct writings that in form and content stand for a particular patriarch within the larger patriarchal view of matters.

THE PATRIARCHAL AUTHORITY AS PORTRAYED BY THE COLLEGIUM OF SAGES

The governing criterion for identifying stories and sayings that portray Gamaliel within the patriarchal framework requires definition. First comes a negative indicator. The sages' ideology of the patriarchate, paramount in the Mishnah and explicit in the famous story of Gamaliel and Joshua cited earlier, represents the patriarch as subject to the same principles of legitimacy as govern all (other) sages, but as possessed of authority by reason of position: "My master in wisdom, and my disciple in accepting my rulings." A story at Yerushalmi Horayot 3:1 fills in the obvious gap: Why, apart from the patriarch's superior power represented as Roman in origin (inclusive of a platoon of Gothic troops assigned to his service), should sages submit to him? In the translation, boldface represents the Mishnah; italics, the use of Aramaic; and plain type, the use of Hebrew. Indentations signal secondary developments of the primary composition:

YERUSHALMI HORAYOT 3:1
[A] **An anointed [high] priest who sinned and afterward passed from his office as anointed high priest,**
[B] **and so too, a ruler who sinned and afterward passed from his position of greatness—**
[C] **the anointed [high] priest brings a bullock,**
[D] **and the patriarch brings a goat [m. 2:6].**
[E] **An anointed [high] priest who passed from his office as anointed high priest and then sinned,**
[F] **and so a ruler who passed from his position of greatness and then sinned —**
[G] **a high priest brings a bullock.**
[H] **But a ruler is like any ordinary person.**

[I:1.A] Said R. Eleazar, "A high priest who sinned—they administer lashes to him, but they do not remove him from his high office."

[B] Said R. Mana, "It is written, 'For the consecration of the anointing oil of his God is upon him: I am the Lord' (Lev 21:12).

[C] "That is as if to say: 'Just as I [stand firm] in my high office, so Aaron [stands firm] in his high office.'"

[D] Said R. Abun, "'He shall be holy to you [for I the Lord who sanctify you am holy]' (Lev. 21:8). "That is as if to say: 'Just as I [stand firm] in my consecration, so Aaron [stands firm] in his consecration.'"

[E] R. Haninah Ketobah, R. Aha in the name of R. Simeon b. Laqish: "An anointed priest who sinned—they administer lashes to him by the judgment of a court of three judges.

[F] "*If you rule that* it is by the decision of a court of twenty-three judges [that the lashes are administered], it turns out that his ascension [to high office] is descent [to public humiliation, since if he sins, he is publicly humiliated by a sizable court]."

[G] R. Simeon b. Laqish said, "A ruler who sinned—they administer lashes to him by the decision of a court of three judges."

[H] What is the law as to restoring him to office?

[I] *Said R. Haggai, "By Moses! If we put him back into office, he will kill us!"*

[J] R. Judah the Patriarch heard this ruling [of Simeon b. Laqish's] and was outraged. *He sent a troop of Goths to arrest R. Simeon b. Laqish. [R. Simeon b. Laqish] fled to the Tower, and some say, it was to Kefar Hittayya.*

[K] *The next day R. Yohanan went up to the meeting house, and R. Judah the Patriarch went up to the meeting house. He said to him, "Why does my master not state a teaching of Torah?"*

[L] *[Yohanan] began to clap with one hand [only].*

[M] *[Judah the Patriarch] said to him, "Now do people clap with only one hand?"*

[N] *He said to him, "No, nor is Ben Laqish here [and just as one cannot clap with one hand only, so I cannot teach Torah if my colleague, Simeon b. Laqish, is absent]."*

[O] *[Judah] said to him, "Then where is he hidden?"*

[P] *He said to him, "In the Tower."*

[Q] *He said to him, "You and I shall go out to greet him."*

[R] *R. Yohanan sent word to R. Simeon b. Laqish, "Get a teaching of Torah ready, because the patriarch is coming over to see you."*

[S] *[Simeon b. Laqish] came forth to receive them and said, "The example that you [Judah] set is to be compared to the paradigm of your Creator. For when the All-Merciful came forth to redeem Israel from Egypt, he did not send a messenger or an angel, but the Holy One,* blessed be he, himself came forth, as it is said, 'For I will pass through the land of Egypt that night' (Exod 12:12)—*and not only so, but he and his entire retinue.*

[T] "[What other people on earth is like thy people Israel, whom God went to redeem to be his people (2 Sam 7:23).] 'Whom God went' [sing.] is not written here, but 'Whom God went' [plural—meaning, he and all his retinue]."

[U] *[Judah the Patriarch] said to him, "Now why in the world did you see fit to teach this particular statement [that a ruler who sinned is subject to lashes]?"*

[V] *He said to him, "Now did you really think that because I was afraid of you, I would hold back the teaching of the All-Merciful?* [And lo, citing 1 Sam 2:23,] R. Samuel b. R. Isaac said, '["Why do you do such things? For I hear of your evil dealings from all the people.] No, my sons, it is no good report that I hear the people of the Lord spreading abroad. [If a man sins against a man, God will mediate for him; but if a man sins against the Lord, who can intercede for him?" But they would not listen to the voice of their father, for it was the will of the Lord to slay them (1 Sam 2:23-25).] [When] the people of the Lord spread about [an evil report about a man], they remove him [even though he is the patriarch]."

When the sage stands up to the patriarch, both parties subject to the same Torah, it is the sage who knows the meaning of a matter—that construction conveys the sages' view of things. The patriarch is given no counterpart statement. But in due course we shall see elements of one. The ideology of this Talmudic account of the patriarch's authority does not greatly differ from that of the story at *m. R.H.* 3:8-9. So much for the negative account supplied by the collegium of sages. What positive evidence do we find in the Mishnah to afford access to the theological and legal agenda of the patriarchate?

THE GAMALIEL-CORPUS IN THE MISHNAH'S *MA'ASIM*: FORM-ANALYSIS

We find within the Mishnah a distinct strand of materials particular to the patriarchate in a Mishnah form that is linked in particular to the patriarchate via the names of two patriarchs, Gamaliel and Simeon b. Gamaliel. To understand this strand, we need to recall that, in addition to its apodictic statements of law, the Mishnah occasionally sets forth a kind of narrative that it marks with the label, *Ma'aseh*, which stands for a case or a precedent.

Usually the Mishnah's *Ma'aseh* follows a simple, fixed form: statement of a situation in court or school-session or a transaction, a sage's ruling, thus:

> MISHNAH-TRACTATE SUKKAH 3:8
>
> A.   "They bind up the lulab [now: palm branch, willow branch, and myrtle branch] only with [strands of] its own species," the words of R. Judah.
> B.   R. Meir says, "Even with a rope [it is permitted to bind up the lulab]."
> C.   Said R. Meir, "M'SH B: The townsfolk of Jerusalem bound up their palm branches with gold threads."
> D.   They said to him, "But underneath they [in fact had] tied it up with [strands of] its own species."

The precedent that is adduced is rejected in the transaction, the *Sitz im Leben* of which clearly is the court or school session. The Mishnah contains numerous such cases or precedents, all situated in the same life situation, and these include Gamaliel in the status of a sage among sages.

But there is another kind of *Ma'aseh*, the domestic *Ma'aseh*, characteristic only of the patriarchal figures Gamaliel and Simeon b. Gamaliel, exceedingly rare for prominent sages. We now turn to the complete Gamaliel corpus among the Mishnah's *Ma'asim*. Through the use of differing margins—broad for the narrative, indented for the context—we preserve the narrative in its larger halakhic setting while signaling its particular limits. We cannot point to any narrative that stands autonomous of its context. We present in detail the *Ma'asim* that speak of Gamaliel or other patriarchal figures (Simeon b. Gamaliel, and occasionally, Hillel). To place the Gamaliel-*Ma'asim* into their larger form-analytical context, the entire corpus of *Ma'asim*, division by division, is summarized at the end of the presentation of each of the Mishnah's six divisions.

Seder Zeraim

MISHNAH-TRACTATE BERAKHOT 1:1

- A. From what time do they recite the Shema in the evening?
- B. From the hour that the priests [who had immersed after uncleanness and awaited sunset to complete the process of purification] enter [a state of cleanness, the sun having set, so as] to eat their heave offering—
- C. "until the end of the first watch," the words of R. Eliezer.
- D. And sages say, "Until midnight."
- E. Rabban Gamaliel says, "Until the rise of dawn."
- F. *Ma'aseh*: His sons came from the banquet hall.
- G. They said to him, "We have not recited the Shema"
- H. He said to them, "If the morning star has not yet risen, you are obligated to recite [the Shema]."
- I. And not only [in] this [case], rather, all [commandments] which sages said [may be performed] until midnight, their religious duty to do them applies until the rise of the morning star.
- J. [For example], as to the offering of the fats and entrails—the religious duty to do them applies until the rise of the morning star.
- K. All [sacrifices] which are eaten for one day, their religious .duty to do them applies until the rise of the morning star.
- L. If so why did sages say [that these actions may be performed only] until midnight?
- M. In order to keep a man far from sin.

This ruling concerns the household, not the court, and treats Gamaliel's conduct as exemplary. Gamaliel's domestic rulings are then treated as normative law. The narrative, *m. Ber.* 1:1F–H, consists of an incident: (1) the sons come home late, (2) consult their father on whether it is still appropriate to recite the Shema, and (3) he gives them his ruling that it is. The ruling repeats his abstract opinion, E, that the time for reciting the Shema extends to dawn. The case stands on its own. The narrative is ignored at I–M, which carries forward the ruling of Gamaliel at E and at the end bears a mediating explanation of the positions of sages and Gamaliel.

The form of the Mishnah's *Ma'aseh* is captured here: (1) statement of the case and (2) the sage's ruling, unadorned and stripped down to its simplest elements. Rarely do we find analysis of the problem, secondary development of the ruling, or other marks of revision in

context. But, as we shall see, focus on domestic conduct is characteristic of Gamaliel's and the patriarchs' *Ma'asim*. That bears an implication: the patriarchs' household represents the model for normative
conduct within the community of Israel, and his rulings in private
bear public, halakhic weight. What is important, as we shall see in
due course, is that domestic rulings in the *Ma'aseh* form are common
for the patriarchal names and rare for other names.

MISHNAH-TRACTATE BERAKHOT 2:5

2:5 A. A bridegroom is exempt from the recitation of the
       Shema' on the first night
       [after the wedding] until after the Sabbath [following
       the wedding],

B. if he did not consummate [the marriage].

C. Ma'aseh S: Rabban Gamaliel recited [the Shema] on the
    first night of his marriage.

D. Said to him [his students], "Did our master not teach us that
    a bridegroom is exempt from the recitation of the Shema on
    the first night?"

E. He said to them, "I cannot heed you to suspend from myself
    the kingdom of heaven [even] for one hour."

2:6 A. [Gamaliel] washed on the first night after the death of his
       wife.

B. Said to him [his students], "Did not [our master] teach us
    that it is forbidden for a mourner to wash?"

C. He said to them, "I am not like other men, I am frail."

2:7 A. And when Tabi, his servant, died, [Gamaliel] received con-
       dolences on his account.

B. Said to him [his students], "Did not [our master] teach us
    that one does not receive condolences for [the loss of]
    slaves?"

C. He said to them, "Tabi my slave was not like other slaves. He
    was exacting."

The formal pattern, repeated three times, involves a report of
what Gamaliel did (*m.* 2:5C, *m.* 2:6A, and *m.* 2:7A), the question
raised by the disciples, and his response thereto. The set involves
diverse classifications of the halakha—reciting the Shema, washing in
the mourning period, receiving condolences for a slave—and what
holds the stories together as a composite is the formal pattern, including the name of Gamaliel. In each case, the point of the narrative is
reached only at the end: Tabi is different. That answers the question
of the students and explains the data of the case. Without the climax

of 2:5C/2:6C/2:7C, the three cases have no context, and the students' question, at B, only articulates the context and focuses attention on what is to come. The patriarch is represented as unique and still exemplary.

The halakhic context serves only *m.* 2:5A–B, but *m.* 2:6 and 2:7 encompass the halakhic context within the narrative discourse, using formulaic language portrayed as the master's own words. The topical principle of category formation dominant in the Mishnah is set aside in favor of the selection of teachings about the named patriarch, whose household is regarded as at the one time exemplary and unique. He is a model of piety, unwilling to relinquish the performance of religious obligations even beyond the measure of the law; so, too, his slave was exceptional; and he was frail, a mark of piety within the rabbinic framework.

LAMENTATIONS RABBAH LXXIV.12.

A.   A member of the household in the establishment of Rabban Gamaliel had the habit of taking a basket carrying forty *seahs* of grain and bringing it to the baker.

B.   He said to him, "All this wonderful strength is in you, and you are not engaged in the Torah?"

C.   When he got involved in the Torah, he would begin to take thirty, then twenty, then twelve, then eight *seahs*, and when he had completed a book, even a basket of only a single *seah* he could not carry.

D.   And some say that he could not even carry his own hat, but others had to take it off him, for he could not do it.

E.   That is in line with this verse: "encrusted with sapphires" [for study of the Torah drains the strength of people].

Stories such as the foregoing attest to the attitude that finds virtue in physical weakness, a mark of prowess in Torah learning.

MISHNAH-TRACTATE PEAH 2:5-6

2:5 A.   One who sows his field with [only] one type [of seed], even if he harvests [the produce] in two lots

B.   designates one [portion of produce as] peah [from the entire crop].

C.   If he sowed [his field] with two types [of seeds], even if he harvests [the produce] in only one lot,

D.   he designates two [separate portions of produce as] peah [one from each type of produce].

E.   He who sows his field with two types of wheat—

F.   [if] he harvests [the wheat] in one lot, [he] designates
one [portion of produce as] peah.

G.   [But if he harvests the wheat in] two lots, [he] designates
two [portions of produce as] peah.

2:6   A.   Ma'aseh: R. Simeon of Mispah sowed [his field with two
types of wheat].

B.   [The matter came] before Rabban Gamaliel. So they went
up to the Chamber of Hewn Stone, and asked [about the
law regarding sowing two types of wheat in one field].

C.   Said Nahum the Scribe, "I have received [the following
ruling] from R. Miasha, who received [it] from his
father, who received [it] from the Pairs, who received [it]
from the Prophets, [who received] the law [given] to
Moses on Sinai, regarding one who sows his field with
two types of wheat:

D.   "If he harvests [the wheat] in one lot, he designates one
[portion of produce as] peah.

E.   "If he harvests [the wheat] in two lots, he designates two
[portions of produce as] peah."

A–B serve C–E. Without A–B, C–E stand on their own. Read as a
unitary construction, the narrative is: (1) Case, (2) Gamaliel was asked
to rule and referred it to the higher court. Referring cases to the
higher court is rare among the *Ma'asim* of the Mishnah.

Let us now consider the Gamaliel compositions with the other
Ma'asim of Mishnah Seder Zeraim. These follow the same form in
that they uniformly describe a situation and specify the halakhic ruling that governs.

1. *m. Ber.* 2:5: Gamaliel/bridegroom/Shema
2. *m. Ber.* 2:6: Gamaliel/mourning/washing
3. *m. Ber.* 2:7: Gamaliel/mourning/condolences for slave
4. *m. Ber.* 5:5: Hanina b. Dosa/how he knows when prayer will be
answered
5. *m. Shebi'it* 10:3: Hillel/access to loans/prosbol
6. *m. Hal.* 4:10-11: priests' decision in cases of priestly gifts, dough-
offering, firstfruits, firstborn, from wrong place or at wrong time

The narratives of Mishnah Seder Zeraim are few, uniform, and
subordinate to the purposes of the Mishnaic composition in which
they are situated. That is, the halakhic context frames the narratives,
and in most instances is required to make sense of them. The sages'
halakhic *Ma'asim* follow a single form: *described incident* + *ruling*. The
exposition of the described incident is simple and never complex; the

presentation is one-dimensional, limited to a laconic, economical account of the action a person took that requires classification or the situation that requires resolution. There is no character differentiation, let alone development, no consideration of motive, no picture of details that amplify the incident or action, no sequence of action and response, only the stripped-down sequence: X did so and so with the following consequence. The context supplies the remainder of the information required for comprehension and meaning: the rules of narrative respond to and take for granted the documentary setting. Outside that setting none of the halakhic narratives is fully comprehensible; none exemplifies much beyond itself. Thus, the narratives of the *Ma'aseh* classification take for granted the Mishnaic-halakhic context as much as the expository prose that defines their setting.

The patriarchal names Gamaliel and Hillel are represented as halakhic models, and in the narratives and pseudonarratives no one sage corresponds. The patriarchate can have its principals represented as halakhic models and sources, through their very deeds, of authoritative law. But that explanation for the phenomenon competes with others. We do not know what to make of the omission of the signal, *Ma'aseh*, from the priests' cases, which otherwise conform to the precedent form. Provisionally, we may conceive that *Ma'aseh* signals a sage's precedent only.

At no point do we leave the limits of the halakhic setting in which the narrative is situated. The principal purposes of the narrative is to show how an anomaly is resolved, or to illustrate how the halakha functions in everyday life, or to provide a precedent for a ruling. None of these entries carries us to some viewpoint outside of the halakhic framework. In the narratives as authentic stories that we meet at *m. R.H.* 2:8-9 (and *m. Ta.* 3:9–10, not cited here), we see how a narrative finds its focus outside the limits of the halakhic context altogether.

Seder Moed

MISHNAH-TRACTATE SHABBAT 16:8

16:8A.   A gentile who lit a candle—

B.   an Israelite may make use of its light.

C.   But [if he did so] for an Israelite, it is prohibited [to do so on the Sabbath].

D. [If a gentile] drew water to give water to his beast, an
   Israelite gives water to his beast after him.

E. But [if he did so] for an Israelite, it is prohibited [to use
   it on the Sabbath].

F. [If] a gentile made a gangway by which to come down
   from a ship, an Israelite goes down after him.

G. But [if he did so] for an Israelite, it is prohibited [to use
   it on the Sabbath].

H. Ma'aseh B: Rabban Gamaliel and elders were traveling by
   boat, and a gentile made a gangway by which to come down
   off the ship, and Rabban Gamaliel and sages went down by
   it.

The incident, H, forms a precedent and an illustration of the law,
not a narrative in which the order of events or sequence of actions
registers. The action of the patriarch is deemed authoritative for "elders," and they are not represented as ruling in concurrence, only as
replicating his action and accepting his ruling. The sages clearly
acknowledge his authority and subordinate themselves to it.

MISHNAH-TRACTATE ERUBIN 4:1–2

4:1 A. He whom gentiles took forth [beyond the Sabbath
       limit],

B. or an evil spirit,

C. has only four cubits [in which to move about].

D. [If] they brought him back, it is as if he never went out.

E. [If] they carried him to another town,

F. or put him into a cattle pen or a cattle-fold,

G. Rabban Gamaliel and R. Eleazar b. Azariah say, "He
   may walk about the entire area."

H. R. Joshua and R. 'Aqiba say, "He has only four cubits [in
   which to move about]."

I. Ma'aseh S: They came from Brindisi [Brundisium] and their
   ship was sailing at sea.

J. Rabban Gamaliel and R. Eleazar b. Azariah walked about
   the whole ship.

K. R. Joshua and R. 'Aqiba did not move beyond four cubits.

L. For they wanted to impose a strict ruling on themselves.

4:2 A. On one occasion [P 'M 'HT] they did not enter the
       harbor until it had gotten dark [on Friday night]—

B. They said to Rabban Gamaliel, "Is it all right for us to
   disembark?"

C. He said to them, "It is all right, for beforehand I was
   watching, and we were within the Sabbath limit before
   it got dark."

The two *Ma'asim*, each in sequence bearing its conventional marker ([1] Ma'aseh, [2] P'M 'HT), hardly qualify as narratives. The first of the two, *m.* 4:1I–L, illustrates the rulings of *m.* 4:1G, H; there is no progression toward a conclusion that makes the rest cohere. *m.* 4:1E–H, *m.* 4:1I–L are out of context. The second of the two, *m.* 4:2, is tacked on and does not connect to the abstract halakha of *m.* 4:1A–H. Here is no domestic *Ma'aseh*; rather, the patriarch is deemed no more authoritative than any other sage.

MISHNAH-TRACTATE ERUBIN 6:1–2

m. 6:1   A.   "He who dwells in the same courtyard with a gentile,

        B.   "or with [an Israelite] who does not concede the validity of the fictive fusion meal—

        C.   "lo, this one [the gentile or nonbeliever] restricts him [from using the courtyard]," the words of R. Meir.

        D.   R. Eliezer b. Jacob says, "Under no circumstances does anyone prohibit [the believer in the fictive fusion meal to make use of the courtyard] unless two Israelites prohibit one another."

m. 6:2   A.   Said Rabban Gamaliel, *Ma'aseh* B: "A Sadducean lived with us in the same alleyway in Jerusalem.

        B.   "And father said to us, 'Make haste and bring all sorts of utensils into the alleyway before he brings out his and prohibits you [from carrying about in it].'"

Once more, the function of the *Ma'aseh* is to provide a setting for the ruling. Without the ruling, *m.* 6:1–2 is wholly out of context. Of greater interest here: the ruling involves the domestic practice of the patriarch's household, not the public decision of a sages' court.

MISHNAH-TRACTATE ERUBIN 10:10

        A.   A bolt with a knob on its end—

        B.   R. Eleazar prohibits.

        C.   And R. Yosé permits.

D.   Said R. Eleazar, *Ma'aseh* B: "In the synagogue in Tiberias they permitted [using it on the Sabbath],

E.   "until Rabban Gamaliel and elders came and prohibited it for them."

E   R. Yosé says, "They treated it as prohibited. Rabban Gamaliel and the elders came and permitted it for them."

A situation is described, with the sages' decision recorded, following the pattern of the *Ma'aseh* as precedent. This remains wholly within the halakhic framework. The form persists in singling out Gamaliel from the collegium of elders.

MISHNAH-TRACTATE PESAHIM 7:2

A.   They do not roast the Passover offering either on a [metal] spit or on a grill.

B.   Said R. Sadoq, "Rabban Gamaliel said to Tabi his servant, 'Go and roast the Passover offering for us on a grill.'"

C.   [If] it touched the earthenware part of an oven, one should scale off that place [which has been roasted by the heat of the oven side].

D.   [If] some of its gravy dripped on the earthenware and went back onto it, he must take some [of the meat] away from that place [and burn it].

E.   [If] some of its gravy dripped on the flour, he must take a handful away from that place.

Gamaliel's action is recorded in a domestic framework. His action is treated as equivalent to an abstract ruling. It is not "They do not roast . . . and R. Sadoq said Rabban Gamaliel said, They do roast . . ." Rather, the formal ruling is set aside and left implicit in the exemplary, authoritative deed of the patriarch in instructing his slave.

MISHNAH-TRACTATE SUKKAH 2:1

A.   He who sleeps under a bed in a Sukkah has not fulfilled his obligation.

B.   Said R. Judah, "We had the practice of sleeping under the bed before the elders, and they said nothing at all to us."

C.   Said R. Simeon, "Ma'aseh B: Tabi, Rabban Gamaliel's slave, slept under the bed.

D.   "And Rabban Gamaliel said to the elders, 'Do you see Tabi, my slave—he is a disciple of a sage, so he knows that slaves are exempt from keeping the commandment of dwelling in the Sukkah. That is why he is sleeping under the bed' [rather than directly beneath the Sukkah-covering, which is what defines the Sukkah and renders it effective in fulfilling the commandment of dwelling in the Sukkah, that is, under its shade, during the festival].'

E.   "Thus we learned that he who sleeps under bed has not fulfilled his obligation."

As in the triplet of cases in Mishnah-tractate Berakhot 2:5–7, what marks the *Ma'aseh* as a narrative is E, which imparts cogency and significance to the record of action and speech of C–D. The conflict is between halakhic rulings, A vs. B. Then the *Ma'aseh*, C–D, realizes the same conflict in the narrative, which is resolved at E. The narrative qualifies as a halakhic precedent, pure and simple. What is required to fulfil the formal requirement is a report of an action and a comment on that action. The correspondence of *m.* 2:1A and E underscores that the domestic arrangement of the patriarch qualifies as a valid ruling, no different in standing from an explicit halakhic ruling of a sage or of sages as a collegium.

MISHNAH-TRACTATE SUKKAH 2:4–5

2:4 A. He who makes his Sukkah among trees, and the trees are its sides—it is valid.

B. Agents engaged in a religious duty are exempt from the requirement of dwelling in a Sukkah.

C. Sick folk and those who serve them are exempt from the requirement of dwelling in a Sukkah.

D. [People] eat and drink in a random manner outside of a Sukkah.

2:5 A. *Ma'aseh* W: They brought Rabban Yohanan b. Zakkai some cooked food to taste, and to Rabban Gamaliel two dates and a dipper of water.

B. And they said, "Bring them up to the Sukkah."

C. And when they gave to R. Sadoq food less than an egg's bulk, he took it in a cloth and ate it outside of the Sukkah and said no blessing after it.

The halakhic ruling, *m.* 2:4D, is illustrated by *m.* 2:5A–B vs. C. That is, eating in a random manner outside of a Sukkah during the festival is illustrated by Sadoq, who consumed less than the amount of food required to constitute a meal, while Yohanan b. Zakkai and Gamaliel reject the rule of *m.* 2:4D and eat even a random meal in the Sukkah. The described action does not rise to the status of a narrative, because there is no point at which the logic of teleology imposes coherence on the components. What illustrates the halakha does not qualify. That point distinguishes *m.* 2:4–5 from *m.* 2:1.

The *Ma'aseh, m.* 2:8C, takes on meaning only in the halakhic context. There is no teleological logic that holds the details together otherwise.

MISHNAH-TRACTATE BESAH 3:2

3:2 A. Nets for trapping a wild beast, fowl, or fish, which one set on the eve of the festival day—

B. one should not take [what is caught therein] out of them on the festival day,

      C.   unless one knows for sure that [creatures caught in them] were trapped on the eve of the festival day.

      D.   Ma'aseh B: A gentile brought fish to Rabban Gamaliel, and he said, "They are permitted. But I do not want to accept them from him."

The *Ma'aseh* supplies an illustrative case in the halakhic framework. Here again the patriarch shows himself distinguished in piety, not taking advantage of lenient rulings that are commonly accepted.

MISHNAH-TRACTATE ROSH HASHANAH 1:5–6

1:5 A.   Whether [the new moon] appeared clearly or did not appear clearly,

      B.   they violate the [prohibitions of] the Sabbath on its account.

      C.   R. Yosé says, "If it appeared clearly, they do not violate the prohibitions of the Sabbath on its account."

1:6 A.   Ma'aseh S: More than forty pairs of witnesses came forward.

      B.   But R. 'Aqiba kept them back at Lud.

      C.   Rabban Gamaliel said to him, "If you keep back the people, you will turn out to make them err in the future."

The *Ma'aseh* coheres only in line with *m.* 1:5, with the conflicting positions, *m.* 1:5A vs. B, C, replicated at *m.* 1:6C versus 1:6A–B. This is another halakhic illustration, lacking the indicative qualities of a narrative.

The foregoing corpus of *Ma'asim* in Mishnah Seder Moed are part of the larger population as follows:

1.   Mishnah-tractate Shabbat 1:4 These are some of the laws which they stated in the upper room of Hananiah b. Hezekiah b. Gurion when they went up to visit him. They took a vote, and the House of Shammai outnumbered the House of Hillel.

2.   Mishnah-tractate Shabbat 3:3–4 The people of Tiberias brought a pipe of cold water through a spring of hot water.

3.   Mishnah-tractate Shabbat 16:8 Rabban Gamaliel and elders were traveling by boat, and a gentile made a gangway by which to come down off the ship, and Rabban Gamaliel and sages went down by it.

4.   Mishnah-tractate Shabbat 24:5 In the time of the father of R. Sadoq and of Abba Saul b. Botnit, they stopped up the light hole with a pitcher and tied a pot with reed grass [to a stick] to know whether or not there was in the roofing an opening of a handbreadth square.

5.   Mishnah-tractate Erubin 4:1–2 They came from Brindisi [Brundisium] and their ship was sailing at sea. Rabban Gamaliel and R. Eleazar b.

Azariah walked about the whole ship. R. Joshua and R. 'Aqiba did not move beyond four cubits.

6. Mishnah-tractate Erubin 6:1–2 Said Rabban Gamaliel, Ma'aseh B: "A Sadducean lived with us in the same alleyway in Jerusalem. And father said to us, 'Make haste and bring all sorts of utensils into the alleyway before he brings out his and prohibits you [from carrying about in it].'"

7. Mishnah-tractate Erubin 8:7 From the water channel of Abel did they draw water at the instruction of the elders on the Sabbath.

8. Mishnah-tractate Erubin 10:9 In the poulterers' market in Jerusalem they used to shut up their shops and leave the key in the window above the door."

9. Mishnah-tractate Erubin 10:10 In the synagogue in Tiberias they permitted [using it on the Sabbath], until Rabban Gamaliel and elders came and prohibited it for them.

10. Mishnah-tractate Pesahim 7:2 "Rabban Gamaliel said to Tabi his servant, 'Go and roast the Passover offering for us on a grill.'"

11. Mishnah-tractate Yoma 6:3 "Arsela led it out, and he was an Israelite."

12. Mishnah-tractate Sukkah 2:4–5 They brought Rabban Yohanan b. Zakkai some cooked food to taste, and to Rabban Gamaliel two dates and a dipper of water. And they said, "Bring them up to the Sukkah."

13. Mishnah-tractate Sukkah 2:7 Was not the precedent so, that the elders of the House of Shammai and the elders of the House of Hillel went along to pay a sick call on R. Yohanan b. Hahorani, and they found him sitting with his head and the greater part of his body in the Sukkah, and his table in the house, and they said nothing at all to him.

14. Mishnah-tractate Sukkah 2:8 Shammai the Elder's daughter-in-law gave birth, and he broke away some of the plaster and covered the hole with Sukkah roofing over her bed, on account of the infant.

15. Mishnah-tractate Sukkah 3:8 The townsfolk of Jerusalem bound up their palm branches with gold threads.

16. Mishnah-tractate Besah 3:2 A gentile brought fish to Rabban Gamaliel, and he said, "They are permitted. But I do not want to accept them from him."

17. Mishnah-tractate Besah 3:8 Abba Saul b. Botnit would fill up his measuring cups on the eve of a festival and hand them over to purchasers on the festival itself.

18. Mishnah-tractate Rosh Hashanah 1:5–6 More than forty pairs of witnesses came forward. But R. 'Aqiba kept them back at Lud.

19. Mishnah-tractate Rosh Hashanah 1:7 Tobiah, the physician, saw the new moon in Jerusalem—he, his son, and his freed slave. And the priests accepted him and his son [as witnesses to the new moon], but they invalidated the testimony of his slave.

20. Mishnah-tractate Ta'anit 2:5 In the time of R. Halapta and R. Hananiah b. Teradion someone passed before the ark and completed the entire blessing, and they did not answer after him "Amen."

This list shows the singularity of the items in which Gamaliel figures; the domestic *Ma'asim* in which he is principal have few counterparts or parallels. We cannot ignore the special interest of *m. R.H.* 2:8–9, concerning Gamaliel and Joshua, cited above, and the famous story of Honi the Circle-Drawer and Simeon *b. Shatah, m. Ta'anit* 3:8–9, which in this context requires no discussion. The complex stories of Gamaliel and the sages, on the one side, and Honi and the sages, concern the power relationships within the institutional frameworks of rabbis in relationship to others, the patriarch, and the wonder-worker, respectively. But they attest to the rabbinic viewpoint on Honi, and we are inclined to think, on Gamaliel as well, whose authority prevails even though his decision errs. In both cases the message is: greater force prevails, sometimes, over rabbinic wisdom and learning. In both cases it is Heaven's right to override sages' knowledge. So the remarkable narratives of *m. R.H.* 2:8–9 and *m. Ta.* 3:9–10, about Honi and the sages, Gamaliel and the sages, respectively, set forth the perspective of the rabbinic narrator and his politics. They attest to rabbinic thought, which has coalesced and been realized in an other than conventional way.

Seder Nashim

We find no domestic case reports. Here is the repertoire of *Ma'asim* in this division:

1. Mishnah-tractate Yebamot 16:4 A certain person fell into a large cistern, and came up [alive] after three days. A blind man went down to immerse in a cave, and his guide went down after him, and they stayed [in the water] long enough to drown. A certain man in Asya was let down by a rope into the sea, and they drew back up only his leg.

2. Mishnah-tractate Yebamot 16:6 A certain person stood on top of a mountain and said, "Mr. So-and-so, the son of So-and-so, of such-

and-such a place, has died." And they went but did not find anyone there. And they [nonetheless] permitted his wife to remarry. In Salmon, a certain person said, "I am Mr. So-and-so, the son of Mr. So-and-so. A snake has bitten me, and lo, I am dying." And they went, and while they did not recognize him, they permitted his wife to remarry.

3. Mishnah-tractate Yebamot 16:7 Said R. 'Aqiba, "When I went down to Nehardea to intercalate the year, Nehemiah of Bet Deli came upon me. He said to me, 'I heard that only R. Judah b. Baba permits a wife in the Land of Israel to remarry on the evidence of a single witness [to her husband's death].' The Levites went to Soar, the date town, and one of them got sick on the road, and they left him in an inn. And upon their return, they said to the inn hostess, 'Where is our good buddy?' She said to them, 'He died, and I buried him.' And they permitted his wife to remarry [on the strength of her evidence]."

4. Mishnah-tractate Ketubot 1:10 Said R. Yosé, M'SH B: "A girl went down to draw water from the well and was raped."

5. Mishnah-tractate Ketubot 7:10 In Sidon there was a tanner who died, and he had a brother who was a tanner. Sages ruled, "She can claim, 'Your brother I could take, but I can't take you [as my levir].'"

6. Mishnah-tractate Nedarim 6:6 "R. Tarfon prohibited me from eating eggs which were roasted with it [meat]."

7. Mishnah-tractate Nazir 2:3 A woman was drunk, and they filled a cup for her, and she said, "Lo, I am a Nazirite from it.' Sages ruled, "She intended only to say, 'Lo, it is unto me as a Corban.'"

8. Mishnah-tractate Nazir 3:6 Helene the Queen—her son went off to war, and she said, "If my son comes home from war whole and in one piece, I shall be a Nazirite for seven years." Indeed her son did come home from war, and she was a Nazirite for seven years.

9. Mishnah-tractate Nazir 6:11 In behalf of Miriam of Tadmor [Palmyra] one of the drops of blood was properly tossed, and they came and told her that her daughter was dying, and she found her dead.

10. Mishnah-tractate Gittin 1:5 They brought before Rabban Gamaliel in Kepar Otenai the writ of divorce of a woman, and the witnesses thereon were Samaritan witnesses, and he did declare it valid.

11. Mishnah-tractate Gittin 4:7 In Sidon a man said to his wife, "Qonam if I do not divorce you," and he divorced her. But sages permitted him to take her back, for the good order of the world.

12. Mishnah-tractate Gittin 6:6 A healthy man said, "Write a writ of divorce for my wife," and then went up to the rooftop and fell over and died.

13. Mishnah-tractate Gittin 7:5 In Sidon there was a man who said to his wife, 'Lo, this is your writ of divorce, on condition that you give me my cloak,' but the cloak got lost. Sages ruled, 'Let her pay him its value.'"

14. Mishnah-tractate Qiddushin 2:7 Five women, including two sisters, and one gathered figs, and they were theirs, but it was Seventh-Year produce. And [someone] said, "Lo, all of you are betrothed to me in virtue of this basket of fruit," and one of them accepted the proposal in behalf of all of them.

We do not see how these items qualify as a narrative focused on conduct in the household as halakhically exemplary.

Seder Neziqin

MISHNAH-TRACTATE EDUYYOT 7:7

A. They gave testimony concerning the boards of bakers, that they are susceptible to uncleanness.

B. For R. Eliezer declares [them] insusceptible.

C. They gave testimony concerning an oven which one cut up into rings, between each ring of which one put sand,

D. that it is susceptible to receive uncleanness.

E. For R. Eliezer declares it insusceptible.

E They gave testimony that they intercalate the year at any time in Adar.

G. For they had said, "Only up to Purim."

H. They gave testimony that they intercalate the year conditionally.

I. *Ma'aseh* B: Rabban Gamaliel went to ask for permission from the government in Syria and he did not come back right away, so they intercalated the year on the condition that Rabban Gamaliel concur.

J. And when he came back, he said, "I concur."

K. So the year turned out to be deemed to have been intercalated.

The sages' explicit subordination to the patriarch's ruling is illustrated, but this is clearly not a domestic *Ma'aseh*.

MISHNAH-TRACTATE ABODAH ZARAH 3:4

A. Peroqlos b. Pelosepos asked Rabban Gamaliel in Akko, when he was washing in Aphrodite's bathhouse, saying to him, "It is written in your Torah, And there shall cleave nothing of a devoted thing to your hand (Deut 13:18). How is it that you're taking a bath in Aphrodite's bathhouse?"

B.   He said to him, "They do not give answers in a bathhouse."

C.   When he went out, he said to him, "I never came into her domain. She came into mine. They don't say, 'Let's make a bathhouse as an ornament for Aphrodite.' But they say, 'Let's make Aphrodite as an ornament for the bathhouse.'

D.   "Another matter: Even if someone gave you a lot of money, you would never walk into your temple of idolatry naked or suffering a flux, nor would you piss in its presence.

E.   "Yet this thing is standing there at the head of the gutter and everybody pisses right in front of her."

F.   It is said only, ". . . their gods" (Deut 12:3)—that which one treats as a god is prohibited, but that which one treats not as a god is permitted.

Not correctly labeled as a *Ma'aseh*, this composition establishes a narrative setting to dramatize the exchange of opinions; it does not fall into the halakhic framework at all, and Gamaliel is not represented as a singular authority in the halakha.

These are the only items that include Gamaliel within a composition bearing the marker *Ma'aseh*. The pertinent *Ma'asim* of Seder Neziqin are as follows:

1.   Mishnah-tractate Baba Mesia 7:1 Ma'aseh B: R. Yohanan b. Matya said to his son, "Go, hire workers for us."

2.   Mishnah-tractate Baba Mesia 8:8 In Sepphoris a person hired a bathhouse from his fellow for twelve golden [denars] per year, at the rate of one golden denar per month [and the year was intercalated].

3.   Mishnah-tractate Baba Batra 9:7 The mother of the sons of Rokhel was sick and said, "Give my veil to my daughter," and it was worth twelve maneh. And she died, and they carried out her statement.

4.   Mishnah-tractate Sanhedrin 5:2 Ben Zakkai examined a witness as to the character of the stems of figs [under which the incident took place].

5.   Mishnah-tractate Sanhedrin 7:2 The daughter of a priest committed adultery. And they put bundles of twigs around her and burned her.

6.   *m. Eduyyot* 5:7K Karkemit, a freed slave girl, was in Jerusalem, and Shemaiah and Abtalion administered the bitter water to her.

7.   Mishnah-tractate Eduyyot 7:7 Rabban Gamaliel went to ask for permission from the government in Syria and he did not come back right away, so they intercalated the year on the condition that Rabban Gamaliel concur.

8. Mishnah-tractate Abodah Zarah 3:7 In Sidon there was a tree which people worshipped, and they found a pile of stones underneath it. Said to them R. Simeon, "Investigate the character of this pile of stones."

9. Mishnah-tractate Abodah Zarah 5:2 Boethus b. Zonen brought dried figs by ship, and a jar of libation wine broke open and dripped on them, and he asked sages, who permitted [the figs, once they had been rinsed].

10. Mishnah-tractate Abodah Zarah 3:4 Peroqlos b. Pelosepos asked Rabban Gamaliel in Akko, when he was washing in Aphrodite's bathhouse, saying to him, "It is written in your Torah, And there shall cleave nothing of a devoted thing to your hand (Deut 13:18). How is it that you're taking a bath in Aphrodite's bathhouse?"

Nos. 1 and 3 enter the category of a domestic *Ma'aseh*. They do not conform to the domestic *Ma'aseh* form in that they contain no ruling, just an anecdote from which a ruling may be adduced.

Seder Qodoshim

MISHNAH-TRACTATE KERITOT 1:7

    A. The woman who is subject to a doubt concerning [the appearance of] five fluxes,

    B. or the one who is subject to a doubt concerning five miscarriages

    C. brings a single offering.

    D. And she [then is deemed clean so that she] eats animal sacrifices.

    E. And the remainder [of the offerings, A, B] are not an obligation for her.

    F. [If she is subject to] five confirmed miscarriages,

    G. or five confirmed fluxes,

    H. she brings a single offering.

    I. And she eats animal sacrifices.

    J. But the rest [of the offerings, the other four] remain as an obligation for her [to bring at some later time]—

  K. *Ma'aseh* S: A pair of birds in Jerusalem went up in price to a golden denar.

  L. Said Rabban Simeon b. Gamaliel, "By this sanctuary! I shall not rest tonight until they shall be at [silver] denars."

  M. He entered the court and taught [the following law]:

  N. "The woman who is subject to five confirmed miscarriages [or] five confirmed fluxes brings a single offering.

O.   "And she eats animal sacrifices.

P.   "And the rest [of the offerings] do not remain as an obligation for her."

Q.   And pairs of birds stood on that very day at a quarter-denar each [one one-hundredth of the former price].

While not a domestic *Ma'aseh*, this item belongs among *Ma'asim* because the patriarch's ruling is represented as absolute. The *Ma'aseh* at K would ordinarily carry in its wake a description of sages' response, e.g., "sages' ruled" + N–Q, and that would serve the purpose.

All the *Ma'asim* of the fifth division are halakhic, some of them formally more conventional than others.

1.   *m. Menahot* 10:2 Ma'aseh S: It was brought from Gaggot Serifin, and [the grain for] the two loaves [Lev 23:17] from the valley of En Sokher.

2.   *m. Bekhorot* 4:4 The womb of a cow was removed. And R. Tarfon had it [the cow] fed to the dogs. The case came before sages, and they declared it permitted.

3.   Mishnah-tractate Bekhorot 5:3 An old ram, with its hair dangling— quaestor saw it. He said, "What sort of thing is this?" They said to him, "It is a firstling. And it is slaughtered only if there is a blemish on it." He took a dagger and slit its ear. And the case came before sages, and they declared it permitted.

4.   Mishnah-tractate Bekhorot 6:6 One squeezed and it did not descend. And it was slaughtered. And it [the testicle] was found cleaving to the groin.

5.   Mishnah-tractate Bekhorot 6:9 Ma'aseh S: The lower jaw stretched beyond the upper one.

6.   Mishnah-tractate Arakhin 5:1 Ma'aseh B: The mother of Yirmatyah said, "The weight of my daughter is incumbent on me." And she went up to Jerusalem, and weighed her [Yirmatyah], and paid her weight in gold.

7.   Mishnah-tractate Arakhin 8:1 Ma'aseh B: One man sanctified his field because of its poor quality. They said to him, "You declare first." He said, "Lo, it is mine for an issar." They said to him, "It's yours!"

8.   Mishnah-tractate Keritot 1:7 A pair of birds in Jerusalem went up in price to a golden denar. Said Rabban Simeon b. Gamaliel, "By this sanctuary! I shall not rest tonight until they shall be at [silver] denars." He entered the court and taught [the following law] . . ."

We see no domestic *Ma'aseh* comparable to those involving Gamaliel.

Seder Tohorot

MISHNAH-TRACTATE KELIM 5:4

A.   An oven which was heated from its outer sides, or which was heated without his [the owner's] knowledge, or which was heated in the craftsman's house, is susceptible to uncleanness.

B.   Ma'aseh S: Fire broke out among the ovens of Kefar Signa, and the matter came to Yavneh, and Rabban Gamaliel declared them unclean.

This is a standard *Ma'aseh*, following the established form. It does not qualify as domestic, and the deed of the patriarch is not represented as authoritative, only his ruling in the manner of the sages. We do not log it in the list of authoritative rulings based on narratives of domestic arrangements of the patriarch.

MISHNAH-TRACTATE YADAYIM 3:1

A.   He who pokes his hands into a house afflicted with a Nega—

B.   "his hands are in the first remove of uncleanness," the words of R. 'Aqiba.

C.   And sages say, "His hands are in the second remove of uncleanness."

D.   Whoever imparts uncleanness to clothing, when in contact [with them], imparts uncleanness to the hands—

E.   "So that they are in the first remove of uncleanness," the words of R. 'Aqiba.

F.   And sages say, "So that they are in the second remove of uncleanness."

G.   Said they to R. 'Aqiba, "When do we find that the hands are in the first remove of uncleanness under any circumstances whatsoever?"

H.   He said to them, "And how is it possible for them to be in the first remove of uncleanness without his body's [being] made unclean, outside of the present case?"

I.   "Food and utensils which have been made unclean by liquids impart uncleanness to the hands so that they are in the second remove of uncleanness," the words of R. Joshua.

J.   And sages say, "That which is made unclean by a Father of Uncleanness imparts uncleanness to the hands. [That which has been made unclean] by an Offspring of Uncleanness does not impart uncleanness to the hands."

K.   Said Rabban Simeon b. Gamaliel, "Ma'aseh B: A certain woman came before Father.

L.   "She said to him, 'My hands entered the contained airspace of a clay utensil.'

M.   "He said to her, 'My daughter, By what had it been made unclean?' [He thus wished to ascertain the remove of uncleanness that had affected the contained airspace of the clay utensil.]

N.   "But I did not hear what she said to him."

O.   Said sages, "The matter is clear. That which has been made unclean by a Father of Uncleanness imparts uncleanness to the hands. [That which has been made unclean] by an Offspring of Uncleanness does not impart uncleanness to the hands."

Here is a standard *Ma'aseh*, not based on the domestic arrangements of the patriarch or sage. But the patriarch, Gamaliel, is represented as a legal authority certainly as learned as any other, contrary to the claim of *m. R.H.* 3:8–9.

The *Ma'asim* are as follows:

1.   Mishnah-tractate Kelim 5:4 Ma'aseh S: Fire broke out among the ovens of Kefar Signa, and the matter came to Yavneh, and Rabban Gamaliel declared them unclean.

2.   Mishnah-tractate Ohalot 17:5 Letters were coming from abroad to the sons of the high priests, and there was on them a seah or two seahs of seals, and sages were not scrupulous about them on account of uncleanness.

3.   Mishnah-tractate Miqvaot 4:5 Ma'aseh B: "A trough of Jehu was in Jerusalem, and it was perforated with a hole as large as the spout of a water-skin.

4.   Mishnah-tractate Niddah 8:2 One woman came before R. 'Aqiba. She said to him, "I have seen a bloodstain."

5.   Mishnah-tractate Makhshirin 1:6 People in Jerusalem hid away their fig cakes in water because of the usurpers.

6.   Mishnah-tractate Makhshirin 3:4 The people of Mahoz were dampening [wheat] in sand.

7.   Mishnah-tractate Yadayim 3:1 Said Rabban Simeon b. Gamaliel, *Ma'aseh* B: "A certain woman came before Father. She said to him, 'My hands entered the contained airspace of a clay utensil.' He said to her, 'My daughter, By what had it been made unclean?'"

*Domestic Precedents in the Mishnah: Practice in the Household of a Named
Authority, by Authority*

One can make a case for a *Sitz im Leben* in the patriarchal setting
(inclusive of Hillel). The domestic conduct of the named authority in
a specific incident is represented as equivalent to a sage's ruling in the
following cases involving *household practice*, not in a sages' court, as a
precedent or exemplary case:

Domestic *Ma'asim* Assigned to Patriarchs, Gamaliel, Simeon

Gamaliel/Simeon b. Gamaliel: *m. Ber.* 1:1, 2:5, 6, 7 (triplet focused on
Gamaliel's unique actions); *m. Peah* 2:5–6; *m. Shab.* 16:8 (Gamaliel's
action is deemed ample precedent, sages concur and follow suit); *m. Er.*
4:1–2 (Gamaliel rules for Joshua, 'Aqiba, Eleazar b. Azariah); *m. Er.* 6:2
(Gamaliel reports his father's ruling); *m. Pes.* 7:2; *m. Suk.* 2:1
(Gamaliel/Tabi); *m. Suk.* 2:5; *m. Bes.* 3:2; *m. Yad.* 3:1 (ruling attributed
to Gamaliel I)

Domestic Ma'asim Assigned to Members of the Collegium of Sages

Abba Saul b. Botnit: *m. Bes.* 3:8—1
'Aqiba:—
Daughter of Shammai the Elder: *m. Suk.* 2:8:—1
Eleazar b. Azariah:—
Eliezer:—
Hillel:—
Ishmael:—
Joshua:—
Judah:—
Meir:—
Sadoq: *m. Suk.* 2—1
Shammai:—
Simeon:—
Tarfon: *m. Ned.* 6:6—1
Yohanan b. Zakkai: *m. Suk.* 2:5—1
Yohanan b. Matya: *m. B.M.* 7:1—1
Yohanan Hahorani: *m. Suk.* 2:7— 1
Yosé:—

By our estimate the Mishnah contains twenty domestic *Ma'asim*,
and 65 percent of them involve patriarchal names. While in the corpus of Gamaliel (father and son) the domestic precedent plays a considerable role, no other authority is represented as setting forth his

halakhic rulings on the foundations of comestic arrangements and conduct. What is characteristic of the presentation of the rulings of patriarchs is rare in the report of sages, and even there, at least occasionally (Yohanan b. Zakkai) sages' domestic conduct is reported along with that of the patriarch. What the sages could do only in the context of the collegium of sages, the patriarchal figures could do within their households. And the form of the domestic *Ma'aseh* should register: a deed described, not a ruling set forth in abstract terms. The specific actions of the patriarchal figure weighed as heavily as the general ruling of a sages' court. The patriarchal theology implicit in that contrast, its bearing on the definition and standing of the Torah of Sinai in its acutely contemporary realization—these matters are now blatant and hardly require comment.·

THE INSTITUTIONAL PERSPECTIVE IN THE GAMALIEL-*MA'ASEH*-CORPUS

What do we think we learn about the historical Gamaliel, whichever Gamaliel we contemplate? Nothing at all. What we learn about the institution of the patriarchate and its theology, by contrast, is considerable.

1. *Logic of Coherent Discourse and Organization*. We learn that the patriarchate, represented by the Mishnah's domestic Ma'aseh, had its own theory of how the Mishnah should be composed. It preferred organizing data by the name of an authority, rather than by a topic, as shown in the Gamaliel stories that cross topical boundaries. The very name of the patriarchal authority on its own imposed coherence on data that, organized topically, would not cohere.

2. *Rhetorical Preference*. The patriarchate rejected the notion of preserving disputes but focused on the rulings of a single unchallenged authority, as shown in the utter absence of contrary opinions in the domestic *Ma'asim*. Disputes represented exchanges between equals, and the special standing accorded to the patriarch in the halakhic exposition could not be conveyed if his opinion were balanced against other equally authoritative rulings.

3. *Topical Preference and Propositions*. Above all, the patriarchate regarded the record of the patriarch's deeds as sufficient to illustrate the normative law. Not only so, but the patriarchate did not concede the characterization of the patriarch as less in knowledge of the Torah than the

body of sages, let alone as bereft of moral authority and dependant
on Gothic troops. On the contrary, the patriarch demanded of himself a more rigorous observance of the law than applied to ordinary
people, and claimed for himself the markers of mastery of the Torah,
physical weakness commensurate with his intellectual power. The
patriarch need not apologize for his mastery of the Torah, but he distinguishes himself from other masters of the Torah by reason of his
ancestry, and with that, the ancestry of the Torah in Israel: a chain of
oral tradition from Sinai, in which the patriarchs form the links of the
chain.

What was at stake for the patriarchate clearly concerns who carries
forward the tradition of Sinai embodied in the Torah. These components of a theological system sustaining the authority and centrality
of the patriarchate in the disposition of the Torah's power point to
the heart of the matter, which defined our starting point. At issue is
the theology of the patriarchate: the patriarch, deriving from Judah
the Patriarch back to Hillel, in his own right possesses the Torah of
Sinai and stands in a chain of tradition to Sinai. Then tractate Abot
forms the patriarchal apologia for the Mishnah, as much as the patriarchal institutional theology. The Mishnah stands on the integrity of
the claim of its sponsor, the patriarchate, to possess a free-standing
oral tradition of Sinai.

A further formal peculiarity of the Mishnah underscores the specificity of that claim. In the aggregate, the Mishnah only occasionally
adduces proof-texts in behalf of its legal rulings. The contrary view—
"whence this ruling . . . as it is said . . ."—embodies the apologia for
the Mishnah that would represent the sages, possessed, as they constantly allege, of superior knowledge of the Torah, with special reference to its exegesis. The Tosefta frequently, and the two Talmuds very
commonly, adduce scriptural foundations for laws that the Mishnah
sets forth without proof-texts, rather, as free-standing traditions. In
that context, Hillel's confrontation with the sons of Beterah on the
matter of the Paschal Lamb and the Sabbath, *t. Pisha* 4:13ff., resolves
itself precisely where the patriarchate would have wished. After logical arguments by analogy, by arguments based on shared language,
and by arguments *a fortiori*, Hillel triumphs, at *t.* 4:14C, with the argument that the patriarchate deemed decisive: "And furthermore: I have
received a tradition from my masters that the Passover sacrifice over-
rides [the prohibitions of the Sabbath]—and not [solely] the first

Passover but the second Passover sacrifice, and not [solely] the Passover sacrifice of the community but the Passover sacrifice of an individual." Then, and only then, the opposition gave way.

The claim of tradition governs, and the chain of tradition continues from Sinai to Judah the Patriarch through Hillel, Gamaliel, Simeon b. Gamaliel, Gamaliel, and Simeon b. Gamaliel, father of Rabbi. Domestic doings then form links in that chain, and the successive patriarchs embody the Torah in exemplary realizations through their household activities. No wonder then that, in representing the Mishnah, the two Talmuds' sages would preserve domestic *Ma'asim* about sages' and not only patriarchs' or exilarchs' deeds in the household. But that is another story. But the story that we cannot recover at the end we should recall: the biography of the historical Gamaliel.

These are topics on which traditions reliably assigned to patriarchal authorities ruled:

1. *m. Ber.* 2:5 Gamaliel/bridegroom/Shema'

2. *m. Ber.* 2:6 Gamaliel/mourning/washing

3. *m. Ber.* 2:7 Gamaliel/mourning/condolences for slave

4. Mishnah-tractate Shabbat 16:8 Rabban Gamaliel and elders were traveling by boat, and a gentile made a gangway by which to come down off the ship, and Rabban Gamaliel and sages went down by it.

5. Mishnah-tractate Erubin 4:1–2 They came from Brindisi [Brundisium] and their ship was sailing at sea. Rabban Gamaliel and R. Eleazar b. Azariah walked about the whole ship. R. Joshua and R. 'Aqiba did not move beyond four cubits.

6. Mishnah-tractate Erubin 6:1–2 Said Rabban Gamaliel, Ma'aseh B: "A Sadducean lived with us in the same alleyway in Jerusalem. And father said to us, 'Make haste and bring all sorts of utensils into the alleyway before he brings out his and prohibits you [from carrying about in it].'"

7. Mishnah-tractate Erubin 10:10 In the synagogue in Tiberias they permitted [using it on the Sabbath], until Rabban Gamaliel and elders came and prohibited it for them.

8. Mishnah-tractate Pesahim 7:2 "Rabban Gamaliel said to Tabi his servant, 'Go and roast the Passover offering for us on a grill.'"

9. Mishnah-tractate Besah 3:2 A gentile brought fish to Rabban Gamaliel, and he said, "They are permitted. But I do not want to accept them from him."

10. Mishnah-tractate Eduyyot 7:7 Rabban Gamaliel went to ask for permission from the government in Syria and he did not come back right away, so they intercalated the year on the condition that Rabban Gamaliel concur.

11. Mishnah-tractate Yadayim 3:1 Said Rabban Simeon b. Gamaliel, Maʿaseh B: "A certain woman came before Father. She said to him, 'My hands entered the contained airspace of a clay utensil.' He said to her, 'My daughter, by what had it been made unclean?'"

If we had to construct components of the curriculum of studies that Paul would have followed at the feet of Gamaliel, that is, under the auspices of the patriarch, it would include questions of liturgy, mourning, treatment of slaves, observance of the Sabbath (travel on the Sabbath, carrying objects from one domain to another on that day), preparation of the Passover offering, preparation of food on the festival, intercalation of the calendar, matters of uncleanness—nearly the whole of the Pharisaic program involving Sabbath and festival observance and cultic cleanness that is well attested to first-century venue.

Our way forward from the topical program that Paul can have followed in his studies with Gamaliel to the topics important in Paul's corpus begins, then, with these highly likely areas of halakhic learning. But it cannot end there.

PAUL: THE NARRATIVE OF ACTS

Those who programmatically maintain the historicity of Acts express confidence about Paul's study with Gamaliel,[6] but caution is appropriate.[7] Paul himself proudly asserts he was a Pharisee (Phil 3:5) but nowhere identifies his principal teacher. A recent school of thought holds that Paul remained a Pharisee during this activity as an apostle of Jesus Christ (both in Acts and in his own mind).[8] But although his Pharisaic status prior to his conversion is evident—and his standing as such in some regards conceivable—his own letters never mention Gamaliel in any connection.

Acts may be said to be apologetic in purpose, but Paul's silence in this regard is also tendentious: his theme when he speaks of his conversion in Galatians is that his gospel came from heaven by apocalypse and that human contacts in that connection are beside the point

(Gal 1:11-12). Who actually immersed Paul in Jesus' name? Acts might be wrong in saying it was Ananias (Acts 9:17-18; 22:12-16), but someone evidently did (so Gal 4:3-7), despite Paul's reticence to say whom. Where was he baptized? Galatians 1:16-17 gives the appearance of an immediate departure for "Arabia" after God "was pleased to reveal his Son to" Paul, but he admits in the same breath that after an Arabian sojourn of three years, he "returned" to Damascus. In this case, he lets a circumstantial detail slip, rather than giving anything out. Although Paul speaks of his mastery of patriarchal tradition (Gal 1:14), the only source of the Torah he studied that he mentions is Moses and the angels (Gal 3:19). Even that mention is ultimately designed to show that he, Paul, confronts the divine glory more directly than Moses ever did (2 Cor 3:12-18). (How such assertions can be squared with the thesis that Paul remained a Pharisee after his conversion is beyond the scope of this consideration.) Paul wrote in the bold strokes of an eternal paradigm, where the details that mattered were how salvation could be won and sanctification effected; the little matter of his Pharisaic and Christian teachers was lost in the shuffle of his conversion from Moses' covenant to Jesus' fulfillment of the covenant with Abraham.

The principle of John Knox—that Paul's letters are to be accorded precedence over Acts in writing about Paul—has been broadly accepted in the present phase of Pauline scholarship, although it has also been refined, to allow for the place of Acts as a resource for the study of earliest Christianity.[9] But absent confirmation from Paul's letters, the reference to Gamaliel in Acts is often dismissed as a legend. When accepted, it is usually on the *a priori* grounds of Acts' alleged reliability.

It has been asserted that the debate must be resolved on the basis of such global considerations as the balance between legend and reliability in the book of Acts. Jerome Murphy-O'Connor has observed, "The details of Gamaliel's teaching are not relevant" to this consideration. Yet in the same study he does cite Gamaliel's teaching in regard to the two Torahs in a relatively late source (Sifré 351),[10] in order to support the contention of Acts that Gamaliel was a prominent Pharisee.[11] We wish to demur both from excluding reference to Gamaliel's teaching in relation to Paul's thought and from adducing the position of Gamaliel on the basis of its latest attested forms.

Although the identity of Paul's teacher can not be established on purely literary grounds, we will suggest in our analysis below that there are affinities between Paul's teaching in his letters to views of Gamaliel as articulated in the Mishnah, Tosefta, and Talmud. These affinities are the only interest here; in that sense, the concern is literary. The "historical" Paul and Gamaliel are not the issue, but the textual figures that the New Testament and rabbinic documents refer to as such. In the case of Paul, letters sometimes called "authentic," whose priority to the others has been well established, are privileged, because they set the standard within any literary comparison. For Gamaliel, we will make a start with passages of the form-critical category of the *Ma'aseh*—the "deed" form—because they have been shown to constitute a genre that was established prior to the redaction of the Mishnah ca 200 CE. Other passages will be cited in their increasing distance from the Mishnah. In this way, we do not compare historical figures, but Paul and Gamaliel as literary references at key moments within the evolution of the relevant literature. One might take a further step of inference from literary history to history as such, but that is a separate project.

Following our analysis we infer that within some topics Paul's argumentation was analogous to Gamaliel's; we leave open the identity of the Pharisee who personally instructed Paul.

ANALYSIS: PATRIARCHAL NARRATIVES OF (A) GAMALIEL AND THE PAULINE CORPUS

In that the present purpose is comparison with the Pauline corpus, the material attributed to Gamaliel will be reviewed heuristically, by topic: (a) calendar, travel, and contact with idols in the Diaspora; (b) keeping house, marriage, work, and slaves; and (c) rules for festivals and the Temple. These are appropriate rubrics in line with our findings on the domestic and nondomestic *Ma'asim*, their topics and their tendencies. Once the topic registers, we are able to take up other details besides those covered by the domestic *Ma'aseh*. At some few points we recapitulate sources already set forth. Unless otherwise signified, all passages derive from the Mishnah.

Calendar, Travel, and Contact with Idols in the Diaspora

Gamaliel's authority in establishing the calendar, his contacts with the government, and his influence in the Diaspora are attested in what has been shown to be an early form of tradition in the Mishnah, called the *Ma'aseh*. In this form, what a sage did is shown to establish halakha (Eduyyot 7:7):

> Rabban Gamaliel went to ask for permission from the government in Syria and he did not come back right away, so they intercalated the year on the condition that Rabban Gamaliel concur. And when he came back, he said, I concur. So the year turned out to be deemed to have been intercalated.

What kind of permission did Gamaliel seek in Damascus (the seat of government in all Syria, and therefore the center of government for Jerusalem and Judea as well)? The Mishnah provides no direct answer. The sages who produced that work were much more interested in getting the year right than in the politics of the empire.

Rome nonetheless had an interest in when great feasts were held and arrangements for security during those feasts. Festal celebrations could and sometimes did tip into riot or revolt, and the governor in Damascus and the prefect in Judea jealously guarded the emperor's arrangement to have the sacrifices he provided offered by Israelite priests in the Temple.[12] This vignette reflects a time when Gamaliel was a go-between who negotiated the interests of the Temple with the government, demonstrating his role in international Judaism as well as in Jerusalem proper.

As in the case of Christian texts, Roman histories, Greek philosophical discourses, and gnostic speculations, the Mishnah and other rabbinic sources sometimes speak from the context of a cultural environment and people that we can identify. In the case of Gamaliel, the form of *Ma'aseh* is often used in a way that refers clearly to the period prior to the destruction of the Temple. Guided by his observation of that form, we can discern Gamaliel's location in the society of Jerusalem.

The Tosefta (Sanhedrin 2:6)[13] depicts Rabban Gamaliel and elders writing by means of a scribe named Yohanan to Galilee and the Diaspora:

A. M'SH B: Rabban Gamaliel and sages were in session on the steps to the Temple.
B. And Yohanan the scribe was before them.
C. He said to him, "Write:
D. "[In Aramaic]: 'To our brethren, residents of Upper Galilee and residents of Lower Galilee, May your peace increase! I inform you that the time for the removal has come, to separate the tithes from the olive vats.'
E. "'To our brethren, residents of the Upper South and residents of the Lower South, may your peace increase! We inform you that the time for the removal has come, to separate the tithes from the sheaves of grain.'
F. "'To our brethren, residents of the Exile of Babylonia, and residents of the Exile of Media, and of all the other Exiles of Israel, may your peace increase! We inform you that the pigeons are still tender, the lambs are thin, and the spring tide has not yet come. So it is proper in my view and in the view of my colleagues, and we have added thirty days to this year.'"

Setting the calendar—in this case by introducing an intercalated month to coordinate Passover with springtime—obviously impinged directly on the cycle of sacrifice in the Temple, and this tradition no doubt makes Gamaliel more autonomous in relation to the priesthood than he really was. Still, Gamaliel clearly emerges from the sources as a force to be reckoned with in Jerusalem and beyond, although that influence is also something of a puzzle.

The "brethren" are most unlikely to be Pharisaic colleagues, since the evidence for Pharisees in the Diaspora is thin at best. But it does seem reasonable that the Pharisees would attempt to influence practices such as tithing far outside their own immediate circle (see the charge in Matt 23:15).[14] For this reason, the existence of "some sort of archive for the preservation and transmission of written materials" has plausibly been suggested.[15]

Gamaliel's influence in this field was such that his son Simeon also was involved in such correspondence according to a later source, Midrash Tannaim to Deuteronomy 26:13.[16] The issue here, of course, is not the fact of that correspondence, but Simeon's reputation for engaging in such correspondence. That reputation is consistent with the Mishnaic statement that people appealed to him to adjudicate how to charge rent during a year in which there was an extra month (Baba Mesia 8:8). The case concerned derives from Sepphoris, so the presence of Pharisees or Pharisaic sympathizers is presupposed. The recent evidence concerning first-century buildings suitable for synagogues and *miqvaot* in Galilee would tend to provide context for that finding.[17]

The memory of Gamaliel's contacts with the Diaspora is persistent. The Talmud recollects that he had five hundred young men in his "house" (meaning his quarter of the city) who studied the Torah and five hundred who studied Greek wisdom (Bavli Baba Qamma 83a). Even allowing for hyperbole, that attests an influence far beyond Jerusalem proper. In fact, the text goes on to relate that Gamaliel was exceptional because he had close contacts with the Roman administration.

Contacts with the Diaspora, we have seen, are said to be both physical (in the case of the Syrian journey) and textual (in the case of the encyclical letter). Gamaliel's practices when at sea also became legal precedents, because he defined how to maintain the prohibitions of work and extensive travel on the seventh day under those conditions (Shabbat 16:8):[18] "Rabban Gamaliel and elders were traveling by boat, and a gentile made a gangway by which to come down off the ship, and Rabban Gamaliel and sages went down by it." He exemplified a practice in which an Israelite can avail himself of the results of what a Gentile does, although such work would be prohibited to an Israelite. Still, this was a permissive teaching, not a requirement. When a Gentile brought fish to Rabban Gamaliel under similar circumstances, he said, "They are permitted. But I do not want to accept them from him" (Besah 3:2). Another deed story (Erubin 4:2) portrays Gamaliel as permitting his colleagues to disembark from a ship on the Sabbath, because he observed, before the Sabbath had begun at sundown, that their boat was so near to port it did not go beyond the limit permitted as a Sabbath journey.

Living among Gentiles as he often did, Gamaliel could be called on to justify his behavior. An elaborate story (not a simple *Ma'aseh* albeit still in the Mishnah) conveys that kind of defense (Abodah Zarah 3:4):

> Peroqlos b. Pelosepos asked Rabban Gamaliel in Akko, when he was washing in Aphrodite's bathhouse, saying to him, It is written in your Torah, And there shall cleave nothing of a devoted thing to your hand

(Deut 13:18). How is it that you're taking a bath in Aphrodite's bath-house? He said to him, They do not give answers in a bathhouse. When he went out, he said to him, I never came into her domain. She came into mine. They don't say, Let's make a bathhouse as an orna-ment for Aphrodite. But they say, Let's make Aphrodite as an orna-ment for the bathhouse. Another matter: Even if someone gave you a lot of money, you would never walk into your temple of idolatry naked or suffering a flux, nor would you piss in its presence. Yet this thing is standing there at the head of the gutter and everybody pisses right in front of her . . . that which one treats as a god is prohibited, but that which one treats not as a god is permitted.

Gamaliel's principle is simple, and its application would permit any Jew to pass as a participant in Greco-Roman culture: provided an Israelite realizes that what is treated as a god is no such thing, the lit-tle matter of an idol in a bathhouse was neither here nor there.

The assumption behind this story, of course, is that it is pleasant to bathe, and that was a feeling Gamaliel shared with his predecessor (according to Aboth 1.18, cf. 13–16; 2.5), Hillel. Hillel once remarked (according to a late tradition in Leviticus Rabbah 34.3, which nonetheless accords with the perspective of Gamaliel in the Mishnah) that if idolaters think it an honor to wash the images of their gods, so an Israelite should embrace the honor of bathing his body, which is made in the image of God.

Keeping House, Marriage, Work, and Slaves

Erubin 6:2 is embedded in a consideration of what to do when there is objection to the construction of an *erub*. Gamaliel taught his family that if they had to share an alleyway with priests, they should awaken early to put any vessels outside the house. That way the priests would have no opportunity to set out their own vessels and insist that only their receptacles could be in the alleyway that day. Staking a claim to an *erub* may have been the point of the teaching prior to its incorpo-ration here, but it is notable that there is no direct reference to the *erub* in what Simeon reports in his father Gamaliel's name. The issue might initially have been a more routine question of how to deal with nearby Sadducean families who claimed that the presence of their vessels in an alleyway precluded others, on grounds of priestly purity.

In either case, however, the assumption of this story is that there was a Sadducean neighborhood in proximity to a Pharisaic neighborhood (in Jerusalem, presumably), and that they disputed about who could use the alleyway. That supports both the assertion that the father in the story is Gamaliel and the plausibility of the attribution to Simeon ben Gamaliel.[19]

The extent of Gamaliel's influence is shown by his capacity to establish that a single witnesses could establish a man's death, and therefore the freedom for the wife to marry again (Yebamot 16:7).[20] That discussion unfolds in a consideration of the calendar, because the Israelite calendar also involved the taking of testimony (in relation to phases of the moon, especially). Just as the application of Gamaliel's principle allowed the testimony of slaves and female slaves in the case of a man's death, Samaritans could witness a writ of divorce in his view (Gittin 1:5). Indeed, the testimony of a man who commanded a writ of divorce and then committed suicide was in Simeon ben Gamaliel's opinion to be accepted (Gittin 6:6). He was familiar with cases as far away as Sidon (Gittin 7:5). But although the influence of Gamaliel's house was felt widely, there was no question of its exerting central authority. In the matter of conditions of work, for example (Baba Mesia 7:1), Simeon ben Gamaliel insisted that "the practice of the province" should be honored.

Gamaliel was so attached to Tabi, his slave, he allegedly broke his own rule that a man should not receive condolences for the death of a slave (berakhot 2:7). His justification? "Tabi my slave was not like other slaves. He was exacting." By contrast, when his wife died, Gamaliel washed on the first night after the death of his wife (Berakhot 2:6). His disciples remonstrated: "Did not our master teach us that it is forbidden for a mourner to wash?" He said to them, "I am not like other men, I am frail."

Rules for Festivals and the Temple

Influence such as Gamaliel's did not come just from acting wisely and speaking to the point. His house could also, by means of devoted *disciples*, enforce his teachings, even in the Temple. A deed story in the Mishnah-tractate Sheqalim (3:3) demonstrates that. When he gave in the annual shekel tax, he had a member of his household throw it right in front of the collector, to make sure his money went for public sacrifices. If the collector needed prompting, a little gang of Pharisees gathered, yelling out, "Take up the offering, take up the offering." Gamaliel's crowd was learned, but also resourceful. The result was that they defended their own way of determining when an animal should be excluded from sacrifice (Bekh. 6:9), cooking the lamb of Passover (Pes. 7:2), sleeping in a sukkah (Suk. 2:1), determining how much of a field should be left unharvested for the poor to glean in (Peah 2:5–6), and adjudicating when an unclean oven might convey impurity to a woman's hand (Yad. 3:1). In the cases of Passover preparation and bedtime in a sukkah, Gamaliel's Gentile slave Tabi features prominently.

Simeon ben Gamaliel's resourcefulness and influence in Temple praxis is implicit in a case in which he was angered by how much a pair of sacrificial birds cost for any woman who wished to purify herself after a miscarriage or an irregular period (Ker. 1:7). He reacted by teaching that a woman in that position could wait until five such cases had passed, before bringing the birds. The priests and the merchants they authorized to sell on the Mount of Olives got the message, and the price of birds in Jerusalem plummeted.

Ad hoc interventions are instanced in several deed stories. When his sons returned late from a banquet with the embarrassing news that they had failed to recite the Shema that evening, Gamaliel ruled that they could do so until the appearance of Venus, the morning star (Ber. 1:1). But this attitude was not simply one of leniency. He himself agreed (Ber. 2:5) that a bridegroom is exempt from the recitation of the Shema on the first night of his marriage. But his disciples heard him recite it on his own wedding night. When they reminded him of his teaching the next morning, he said, "I cannot heed you to suspend from myself the kingdom of heaven [even] for one hour."

Gamaliel, finally, is associated with particular devotion to the remembered place of the ark in the Temple (Sheq. 6:1–2):

> A. (1) Thirteen shofar chests, (2) thirteen tables, [and] (3) thirteen acts of prostration were in the sanctuary.
> B. The members of the household of Rabban Gamaliel and the members of the household of R. Hananiah, Prefect of the Priests, would do fourteen prostrations.

    C. And where was the additional one?
    D. Toward the woodshed,
    E. for so did they have a tradition from their forebears that there the ark was stored away.

6:2 A. M'SH B: A priest was going about his business and saw that a block of the pavement was slightly different from the rest.
    B. He came and told his fellow.
    C. He did not finish telling [him] before he dropped dead.
    D. Then they knew without doubt that there the ark had been stored away.

B–E clearly establishes Gamaliel's association with Hananiah, which is consistent with our analysis of the traditions regarding the calendar. Moreover, 6:2 A–D underscores their common practice as having an esoteric and potentially dangerous dimension. Perhaps we should associate with this aspect of Gamaliel's teaching the claim that he "saw directly by the holy spirit" (*t. Pes.* 1.27[21]) and preserved his separateness (*Sot.* 9.15) and that his son deliberately guarded his silence (*Abot* 1.17).

INFERENCE

Placing Gamaliel in Jerusalem in the period 20–50 CE[22] makes his overlap with Paul possible, and his influence in the diaspora enhances any such overlap. The Temple-oriented material in several of the stories attributed to Gamaliel makes Acts 5:34 seem more plausible than might otherwise be the case.[23]

But for all those incidental considerations, what stands out unmistakably is that there is nothing like a quotation from Paul of Gamaliel's teaching (or vice versa), nor a common reference to a specific exegetical tradition, nor a comparable stance to an institution (for example, the Temple). These three types of analogy, which have been instanced in the study of the gospels in relation to rabbinic literature,[24] simply do not apply to the case of Gamaliel and Paul.

But a fourth type of analogy does apply: an analogy of logic or argumentation. If we review Paul's concerns through the lens of Gamaliel's halakha, we discover a resonance between the two that, at the level of thought, is as striking as the shared traditions that the gospels sometimes evince with rabbinic documents.

Calendar, Travel, and Contact with Idols in the Diaspora

Paul's reasons for being upset with his readership in Galatia include the complaint that they observe days and months and seasons and years (Gal 4:10); it makes him despair that he had labored for nothing (Gal 4:11). In that Paul had called his readers from the planetary worship of the local elementary substances, the abuse he has in mind is likely of Galatian (that is, Celtic) origin. Yet at the same time, he makes a transition through the section in which he elaborates on his despair (vv. 12-20) to speak in the most derogatory terms he ever uses of the Law and Covenant given on Sinai (vv. 21-31): the correspondence he posits with Hagar, rather than Sarah, and slavery as distinct from freedom would make him—if he were still a Pharisee—the oddest member of the class imaginable.

Here contrast with Gamaliel totally dominates any glimmer of similarity. In the same letter, Paul does evince interest in a "season" (*kairos*), but of a different sort: the eschatological harvest (Gal 6:9). This trumping of calendrical time with the eschatological moment is also instanced in the effective sarcasm of 1 Thessalonians, where Paul, Silvanus, and Timothy remark that they have no need of writing concerning times and season, because their readers know accurately that "the day of the Lord will come like a thief in the night" (1 Thess 5:1-2). In the foreshortened time in which Paul lived, feasting and fasting were as irrelevant as mourning and rejoicing, because the very structure of this world was passing away (1 Cor 7:29-31).

Where contrast with Gamaliel is blatant in the case of calendar, the instrument of the divergent teaching is interesting: in Paul's case, the use of letters as means to influence communities is manifest. Indeed, he even attempts to convene a court of judgment in Corinth at a distance, demanding that the Corinthians gather with his own spirit and the power of Jesus to condemn a case of fornication (1 Cor 5:1-13), and he insists that such courts should be routine in the settlement of less drastic cases (1 Cor 6:1-11).

The issues of travel and Sabbath do not consume Paul's attention, but that of fellowship at meals does. The events of Galatians 2 need not be rehearsed here,[25] but it is worth noting that they are crucial events in Paul's recitation. That is, Paul uses Peter's *deeds* to contradict his behavior. Because Peter once ate together with Gentiles, and then withdrew when people from James arrived, Paul accuses him of hypocrisy (Gal 2:11-21). The form of *Ma'aseh* is here used to devastating effect. But that does not prevent Paul from specifying elsewhere the people one is not to eat with (so 1 Cor 5:11) and foods to be avoided the eating of which might promote idolatry (1 Cor 8:1-13; Rom 14:13-23).

The issue of idolatry brings us to an argumentative analogy between Gamaliel and Paul, rather than a contrast. Paul's principle is simple: "we know that 'no idol in the world really exists,' and that 'there is no God but one'" (1 Cor 8:4). Therefore, the notional sacrifice of food to idols (contrary to the position of James as cited in Acts 15:19-21) must be beside the point. Yet if the freedom of action this principle implies were to lead a brother to falter, he says he would prefer not to eat meat at all (v. 13, cf. Rom 14:13, 20).

As Paul's statement of the principle is much less colorful than Gamaliel's vivid depreciation of Aphrodite, his application is also more cautious. After all, he is dealing with some people who had actively served idols. For all that, it is striking that Paul simply asserts the view that idols are nonentities, as if a position along the lines of Gamaliel's had been widely accepted.

Keeping House, Marriage, Work, and Slaves

Paul's conception of an eschatologically foreshortened time did not prevent him from setting out famous advice in regard to marrying and not marrying, divorcing, and virginity in the same discussion in which he speaks of time's shortness (1 Cor 7). A particular point where he and Gamaliel agree was that death freed a wife from the bonds of marriage so as to marry without any suspicion of adultery (see Rom 7:1-3).

Although he does not address the issue of purity in a household as such, Paul does in two ways speak of domestic matters in terms of the related issue of sanctification. First, he turns out in 1 Corinthians to be much less sanguine about idols than 1 Corinthians 8 alone might suggest. In the run-up to his discussion of Eucharistic practice, he sets out a very tough analysis in the course of demanding that his readers flee idolatry (10:14-22). Referring to food sacrificed to idols, he says, "what pagans sacrifice, they sacrifice to demons and not to God. I do not want you to be partners with demons" (v. 20). Further, he insists that "You cannot drink the cup of the Lord and the cup of demons. You cannot partake of the table of the Lord and the table of demons" (v. 21). These demons and their offerings might be nothing (as he repeats in v. 19), but they are to be avoided absolutely, because the sacred meal of Christ is directly compared with the sacrifices in the Temple (vv. 16-18). That sanctification in Eucharistic practice obliges a complete removal of idolatry at home.

Second, this same principle of sanctification adheres to the physical bodies of those baptized into Christ. The idea of the body of Christ is fully worked out in 1 Corinthians 12:12-31), but already here, in chapter 10, Paul refers to baptism (vv. 1-13) as well as the Eucharist, and speaks of belonging to a single body (v. 17). Just as the body of the faithful forms the body of Christ, so individual believers form the body of the faithful. The individual, too, is "a temple of Holy Spirit within you, which you have from God" (1 Cor 6:19). This sanctification cuts two ways: *against* making your flesh one with that of a prostitute (1 Cor 6:15-20), and *for* the corollary that a man or a woman sanctifies an unbelieving spouse, so that their children are "holy" (1 Cor 7:14).

The issue of work as such does not appear to have disturbed Paul, except as a necessity (see 1 Thess 2:9; 1 Cor 4:12; 9:19; 2 Cor 11:7). But just as he argued for remaining married if one were married, and remaining single if that were one's state, he also—and in this same discussion—advised against epispasm as well as circumcision, against seeking manumission as well as against putting oneself into artificial submission (1 Cor 7:17-24).

But if this is intended as a global imperative, the letter to Philemon is a startling exception. There Paul pleads the case of Onesimus: as a servant he was taken from Philemon for a while, but Philemon should now accept him back as a "brother" (v. 16). Like Tabi before him, Onesimus could hope for a better deal than most in his station.

Rules for Festivals and the Temple

Given our findings concerning calendar, travel, and contact with idols, we might expect this section to be extremely thin. Once the body of a believer has been made into the Temple, and the Eucharist is the altar of sacrifice, interest in the Jerusalem Temple would seem to be precluded. But famously that is not the case. Even omitting Acts from consideration, which mentions Paul's vow (18:18) and his under-writing of Nazirites' offerings in the Temple (21:17-26), Paul mani-fests a cultic interest.

Paul was unquestionably capable of using cultic language as metaphor. Romans 12:1 provides the example of the addressees being called to present their bodies as "a living sacrifice, holy and acceptable to God." Indeed, Romans 15:16 itself can only refer to Paul's priestly service metaphorically, as the means by which the offering of the nations might be completed. But is "the offering of the Gentiles" itself to be taken only as a metaphor? Two standard commentaries suggest that should be the understanding as a matter of course. C. E. B. Cranfield reads the metaphor explicitly within the context of a cultic theology of the significance of Jesus' death:[26] "The sacrifice offered to God by Christ, which Paul has here in mind, con-sists of the Gentile Christians who have been sanctified by the gift of the Holy Spirit." Otto Michel links the passage more strictly with 12:1, and takes it that, in both cases, the cult is transcended eschato-logically:[27] "Das Besondere an dieser Bildsprache des Paulus besteht darin, dass der Begriff auf den eschatologischen Vollzug der Heilsgeschichte hinweist. *Was der Kultus besagen will, erfüllt sich in der Endgeschichte*." Both of these exegeses rely on the invocation of con-texts that may indeed be recovered from Paul's theology, but that are not explicit here. It is, of course, impossible to exclude the meanings that Cranfield and Michel suggest, but it is striking that neither com-mentator considers the possibility that Paul might speak of an actual offering, provided by Gentile Christians for sacrifice in Jerusalem. That meaning should not be excluded, unless the straightforward sense of the words is found to be implausible.[28]

In that Paul refers to the collection just ten verses after he speaks of the offering of the nations (cf. Rom 15:16, 26), it seems only pru-dent to associate the two. In Corinthians 16:8, Paul even refers to his decision to stay where he is until the feast of Pentecost: it has been suggested that he intends at that time to take the collection he refers to in 16:1, 2.[29] Whether or not that is the case, Paul clearly keeps the calendar of Judaism in his own mind (even though he did not commend it to Gentile Christians, as we have seen) when the issue of the collection is in play.

A final contrast with Gamaliel completes this picture. While Gamaliel's prostrations suppose knowledge of where the ark had been in the Temple, Paul refers to Christ as a *hilasterion*. Because sacrifice in the Temple still proceeds, Paul's assertion in Romans 3:25 is not to be understood as positing a formal replacement of the cult by Jesus' death. The standard references to similar usages in 2 Maccabees (3:33) and 4 Maccabees (6:28, 29; 17:20-22) ought long ago to have warned commentators against any reading that involves such notions, whether in the key of Hebrews (as in Cranfield's reading) or in the key of a transcendent eschatology (as in Michel's reading).

2 Maccabees 3:33, after all, simply speaks of a high priest "making appeasement" by cultic means. That usage is an extension of the Septuagintal language of hilasmos, where the emphasis falls on the divine affect involved in forgiveness. Even 4 Maccabees, which is probably too late a composition to be used as representing the milieu that was the matrix of Paul's letters, maintains a distinction between God's pleasure in sacrifice and the means of that sacrifice. In 6:28, 29, God is asked to be pleased (*hileos*) with his people by Eleazar, and to make his blood their purification and his life their ransom. The plea is that heroic martyrdom be accepted in an unusual way in the light of a radical challenge to the usual means of sacrifice. 4 Maccabees envisages the restoration of cultic sacrifice in the Temple as a result of the sort of heroic sacrifice that is praised.

The usage of the Septuagint, and particularly of 2 Maccabees and 4 Maccabees, militates against the conflation of *hilasterion* in Romans 3:25 with the "mercy seat" of Leviticus 16, as—of course—does the absence of the definite article in Paul's usage. There is a natural relationship between the two, because the *hilasterion* of Leviticus 16 (vv. 2, 13, 14, 15) is where the high priest makes appeasement (*exilasetai*, v. 16, cf. vv. 17, 18, 20). Jesus for Paul is a *hilasterion* because he provides the occasion on which God may be appeased, and for that reason an opportunity for the correct offering of sacrifice in Jerusalem.

CONCLUSION

What we have shown are points of congruence, intersections of topics set forth in the two traditions, Paul's and the Mishnah's for the
patriarchate. Our intent has been not only to move from the particular, Gamaliel, to the general, the patriarchate, to the global, the topical program, and back via the global and the topical and the general
to the particular, Paul, as we have done. It is also to identify the fundamental principles that animated the theological systems of Paul
and of the patriarchate. The particulars and the consequent topical
interests attain cogency precisely where, in Judaism, they should,
which is, in the theology of the Torah and its contemporary realization that animated the Mishnah and that in the counterpart to the
Torah, Christ, formed the foundation of Paul's system as well.

CHAPTER 8

THE PHARISEES AND THE DEAD SEA SCROLLS

James C. VanderKam

The Dead Sea Scrolls are rightly celebrated as firsthand witnesses to the ways and thoughts of a Second Temple Jewish group, as pristine texts not overlaid with editorial accretions from later ages. Among the invaluable disclosures of the Qumran texts has been information about the controversies waged by the group and their attitudes toward opponents who disputed their understanding of God's revelations. Modern readers are naturally interested in knowing more about these controversies and those involved in them, but when they turn to the texts with such questions in mind they are typically frustrated. The writers of the scrolls rarely divulge specific data about an opponent, preferring to label them with insulting names rather than historically recognizable ones. This problem has been at the heart of the debate whether the scrolls deal with the Pharisees. The name *Pharisee* does not occur in the scrolls. Nevertheless, there is good reason to expect they are present in them: not only were Pharisees prominent contemporaries of the Qumran community, they were also interested in the sorts of issues that engaged the covenanters. Do the Dead Sea Scrolls tell us about the Pharisees? If so, what do they tell us about them?

This chapter falls into two parts. The first surveys and discusses the evidence that allows us to say the Pharisees do play a role in the scrolls; the second assembles passages that give a broader picture of the Pharisees as the writers of the scrolls saw them.

"THOSE WHO SEEK SMOOTH THINGS" AS PHARISEES

There is a venerable tradition among scholars of the scrolls that "those who seek smooth things [דורשי החלקות]" are Pharisees and that the word חלקות is a play on הלכות, which is supposed to be a Pharisaic term for legal positions.[1] Although the hypothesis was stated before John Allegro published Pesher Nahum (4Q169), the occurrences of the expression in the commentary on the prophecy provide, according to many scholars, the decisive data for the conclusion.[2] The next paragraphs review the occurrences of the epithet "those who seek smooth things," ending with those in Pesher Nahum. The data from these texts will then be compared with Josephus's narratives about Alexander Jannaeus, Alexandra, and the Pharisees. The review will show that "those who seek smooth things" are indeed Pharisees.

Occurrences

The first word in the construct phrase דורשי החלקות designates individuals who search; the searching could be studying or investigating the Scriptures. The second word means "smooth," and it can have a negative connotation when describing words or speech (see Prov 26:28; Dan 11:32).[3] The epithet may refer to people who are trying to flatter, but also to someone looking for easy interpretations, rather than the full and perhaps more rigorous meaning of a law.[4]

The phrase *those who seek smooth things* appears (with slight variations) in five texts found at Qumran.

Damascus Document

After God raised up the Teacher for the community, an opponent of the new group and its leader came on the scene:

> [T]he Scoffer [איש הלצון] arose who shed over Israel the waters of lies. He caused them to wander in a pathless wilderness, laying low the everlasting heights, abolishing the ways of righteousness and removing the boundary with which the forefathers had marked out their inheritance, that he might call down on them the curses of His Covenant and deliver them up to the avenging sword of His Covenant. For they sought smooth things [דרשו בחלקות] and preferred illusions (Isa. xxx, 10) and they watched for breaks (Isa. xxx, 13) and chose the fair neck; and they justified the wicked and condemned the just, and they transgressed the Covenant and violated the Precept. They banded together against the life of the righteous (Ps. xciv, 21) and loathed all who

walked in perfection; they pursued them with the sword and exulted in the strife of the people. And the anger of God was kindled against their congregation [בעדתם] so that He ravaged all their multitude; and their deeds were defilement before Him. (CD 1.14–2.1)[5]

The author of the Damascus Document accused the Scoffer of misleading a congregation into violating the covenant. Their pursuit of "smooth things" is just one in a catalog of charges against these early opponents.

Hodayot

In 1QHᵃ X, 31–38 (Sukenik, col. II) the poet thanks the Lord for saving him "from the zeal of lying interpreters [מליצי כזב], and from the congregation of those who seek smooth things [ומעדת דורשי חלקות]" (X, 31–32). He claims they tried to murder him and calls them "seekers of falsehood" (line 34). In the hymn that begins at XII, 5 (Sukenik, col. IV), the poet says, "they, teachers of lies and seers of falsehood, have schemed against me a devilish scheme, to exchange the Law engraved on my heart by Thee for the smooth things [להמיר תורתכה אשר שננתה בלבבי בחלקות] (which they speak) to Thy People" (XII, 9–11). The opponents are condemned for their lying language, which entailed rejecting the revealed Torah for something else and for inducing others to do likewise. Both of these passages occur in poems that may come from the Teacher himself.

Two other references appear in broken contexts.

4Q163 (4QpIsaᶜ) 23 ii 10–12

This passage identifies them as a community and locates them in Jerusalem. The word תורה also appears in the context.

4Q177 (Catena A) frg. 9 4–5

This passage calls them a community and speaks of their hostility.

These scattered references permit some conclusions about "those who seek smooth things": (1) they followed the Scoffer so that they broke the covenant; (2) they rejected the Torah of the Teacher; (3) they were a community with members in Jerusalem. But these bits of information are too vague to allow one to infer who these people were. As a result, much of the case for identifying them has depended on what is said about them in 4Q169.

4Q169 (Pesher Nahum)

"Those who look for smooth things" appear first in the comment on Nahum 2:11b: "where the lion goes, and the lion's cubs, with no one to disturb them." About the passage the commentator writes:

> [Interpreted, this concerns Deme]trius, king of Greece who sought, on the counsel of those who seek smooth things, to enter Jerusalem. [But God did not permit the city to be delivered] into the hands of the kings of Greece, from the time of Antiochus until the coming of the rulers of the Kittim. But then she shall be trampled under their feet. (3–4 i 2–3)

The passage refers to two Seleucid kings by name (Demetrius and Antiochus), and the context makes it highly likely that Demetrius is Demetrius III Eukerus (95–88 BCE),[6] whom Alexander Jannaeus's enemies invited to invade Judea in ca. 88 BCE. The passage pictures the seekers as active in national affairs in the early first century BCE. The comment on Nahum 2:12b ("he has filled his caves with prey and his dens with torn flesh") is even more helpful because it mentions a distinctively horrific event in this historical context: "Interpreted, this concerns the furious young lion [who executes revenge] on those who seek smooth things and hangs men alive . . . formerly in Israel. Because of a man hanged alive on [the] tree, He proclaims, 'Behold, I am against [you, says the Lord of Hosts']" (3–4 i 6–9).[7] The pesher also places *Ephraim* and "those who seek smooth things" in apposition (3–4 ii 2; see also 3–4 ii 4–5, 8–10); the two therefore appear to be synonymous.[8]

Josephus on Alexander and the Pharisees

The comments in Pesher Nahum have, of course, been compared with accounts about Alexander Jannaeus and the Pharisees in Josephus's histories. Even scholars who do not accept the דורשי החלקות = Pharisees equation agree that the pesher echoes events in the reign of Jannaeus, the angry young lion of the Hebrew text.[9] The point that has aroused debate is whether Josephus's versions of the story about Jannaeus and his opponents are specific enough to identify those enemies as Pharisees.

Josephus's storyline in the two histories is similar, although he provides more detail in *Antiquities*. In *War*, the relevant passages are 1.4, 3–6 (88–98) and 1.5, 2–3 (110–114); in *Antiquities* the parallels are 13.13, 5–13.14, 2 (372–83) and 13.15, 5–13.16, 2 (398–415). In both works the historical sequence under discussion begins with a notice that after a number of battles against external foes,[10] the Jewish populace revolted against Alexander, taking the opportunity afforded by a festival when many of them had congregated at the temple. In *Ant.* 13.13, 5 (372), where the Latin text names the holy day as the festival of tabernacles,[11] the historian fills out the sparse givens of *War* by relating the incident of the citrons with which the crowd pelted the high priest Jannaeus as he was about to officiate at the altar. Neither source names the opponents; they are simply Jewish subjects of the king. He was able to crush the uprising only through the use of his mercenary forces, an exercise that cost some six thousand Jews their lives.

Jannaeus's troubles continued as his incessant wars depleted human and financial resources.[12] He met internal opposition so vigorously that over a six-year period more than fifty thousand Jews are said to have fallen victim to him (*War* 1.4, 4 [91]; *Ant.* 13.13, 5 [376]). Later he tried more conciliatory tactics, without success:

> But his change of policy and inconsistency of character only aggravated their hatred; and when he inquired what he could do to pacify them, they replied, "Die; even death would hardly reconcile us to one guilty of your enormities." They simultaneously appealed for aid to Demetrius, surnamed the Unready. Hopes of aggrandizement brought from him a prompt response. Demetrius arrived with an army, and the Jews joined their allies in the neighborhood of Sichem. (*War* 1.4, 4 [92]; cf. *Ant.* 13.13, 5 [376])

Again the opponents are not assigned a specific name; they are simply "the Jews."

Although Demetrius defeated Jannaeus in the ensuing battle, Josephus says that the Jewish allies of the Seleucid monarch soon abandoned him and that Alexander, who had fled the battlefield, was joined by six thousand Jews who felt sorry for him. Josephus does not

230 JAMES C. VANDERKAM

say whether these six thousand were the soldiers who had joined Demetrius and then deserted him. Demetrius left Judea, but relations between Jannaeus and sizable parts of the Jewish population did not improve. Josephus tells of continued strife, with Alexander killing large numbers of his enemies and cornering the rest of them inside a city:

> [H]aving subdued this town, he brought them up to Jerusalem as prisoners. So furious was he that his savagery went to the length of impiety. He had eight hundred of his captives crucified in the midst of the city, and their wives and children butchered before their eyes, while he looked on, drinking, with his concubines reclining beside him. Such was the consternation of the people that, on the following night, eight thousand of the hostile faction fled beyond the pale of Judaea; their exile was terminated only by Alexander's death. (*War* 1.4, 6 [97–98]; see *Ant.* 13.14, 2 [380])[13]

In neither book does Josephus name the foes,[14] although in *Antiquities* he says they were among the most powerful of the rebels. He does, however, associate them specifically with the invitation to Demetrius:

> This was the revenge he took for the injuries he had suffered; but the penalty he exacted was inhuman for all that, even though he had, as was natural, gone through very great hardships in the wars he had fought against them, and had finally found himself in danger of losing both his life and his throne, for they were not satisfied to carry on the struggle by themselves but brought foreigners as well, and at last reduced him to the necessity of surrendering to the king of the Arabs the territory which he had conquered in Moab and Galaaditis and the strongholds therein, in order that he might not aid the Jews in the war against him; and they committed countless other insulting and abusive acts against him. (*Ant.* 13.14, 2 [381–382])[15]

If the above exhausted the evidence, we would have to admit that Josephus does not supply enough information to identify as Pharisees the eight hundred whom Alexander had crucified. They were sworn enemies of Jannaeus, with little specific being said about them. From this it would also follow that we would lack sufficient warrant for saying that the seekers of smooth things in the Qumran texts are Pharisees, since the inference is largely based on identifying the eight hundred crucified men as Pharisees. But there is more in the sequel to Josephus's story.

Josephus on Alexander, Alexandra, and the Pharisees

The relevant material figures in the section regarding the succession to Alexander. In the shorter version in *War*, Josephus chides Alexandra, Jannaeus's wife and successor, for her excessive reliance on the Pharisees who rose to great power during her reign (1.5, 2 [110–112]). As an example of the Pharisees' authority while she ruled, Josephus mentions the case of Diogenes whom they executed. He was "a distinguished man who had been a friend of Alexander"; this man they accused

> of having advised the king to crucify his eight hundred victims. They further urged Alexandra to make away with the others who had instigated Alexander to punish those men; and as she from superstitious motives always gave way, they proceeded to kill whomsoever they would. The most eminent of the citizens thus imperiled sought refuge with Aristobulus. (1.5, 3 [113–114]).

The section claims that Pharisees were the ones concerned to punish those who had advised Jannaeus to kill the eight hundred. This is not the same as saying the eight hundred were Pharisees, but the Pharisees won them some belated revenge.[16]

Antiquities adds a deathbed discussion between Alexander and Alexandra, during which the king urged her to allow the Pharisees greater power in her administration.[17] Since the hostility of so many to Jannaeus endangered her and her sons' hold on royal power, she should, Alexander advised, capture some fortresses and

> she should yield a certain amount of power to the Pharisees, for if they praised her in return for this sign of regard, they would dispose the nation favorably toward her. These men, he assured her, had so much influence with their fellow-Jews that they could injure those whom they hated and help those to whom they were friendly; for they had the complete confidence of the masses when they spoke harshly of any person, even when they did so out of envy; and he himself, he added, had come into conflict with the nation because these men had been badly treated by him. (13.15, 5 [401–402])

Here Jannaeus confesses that he had mistreated the Pharisees and that his miscalculation had led to the troubles he had experienced with his own people. For him, the Pharisees were the cause of the revolts and unrest.

To this advice King Alexander added a suggestion about his body.

> "And so," he said, "when you come to Jerusalem, send for their [i.e.,
> the Pharisees'] partisans [text: soldiers],[18] and showing them my dead
> body, permit them, with every sign of sincerity, to treat me as they
> please, whether they wish to dishonour my corpse by leaving it
> unburied because of the many injuries they have suffered at my hands,
> or in their anger wish to offer my dead body any other form of indig-
> nity." (13.15, 5 [403])

Alexandra turned his body over to the Pharisees (we do not learn
what they did with it), they became her allies, and they even praised
her departed husband (13.16, 1 [405–406]).

The story about Alexander's body supplies the missing link for
identifying as Pharisees the eight hundred men whom he had crucified. Alexander had mistreated the bodies of the crucified men; here
we find the most specific confession about abusing the bodies of his
enemies, whereas regarding all the others we learn only of their
deaths, not how they died. Now he was allowing their fellow Pharisees
to avenge his brutality against their colleagues by turning over his
corpse to them, to be treated as they wished. The gesture seems to be
a case of *quid pro quo*: he invited surviving Pharisees to mistreat his
body as he had abused the bodies of the eight hundred Pharisees
whom he hanged alive.

The factuality of the conversation between Alexandra and Alexander can, of course, be questioned. After all, speeches in ancient histories were open invitations to editorial mischief. Also, this one figures
in *Antiquities*, not in *War*, and in the former, on one view, Josephus
handles the Pharisees in a more tendentious manner. Some experts
believe his opinion of them is consistent throughout his histories,[19]
while others detect a change from one work to the other. Some of
those experts who perceive a more positive view of the Pharisees in
Antiquities than in *War* have interpreted the change as Josephus's way
of commending the Pharisees (or people like them) to the Romans as
the ones best suited to lead Jewish society in the post-70 CE period.[20]
The issue cannot be entirely avoided here because it impinges on the
historicity of the data in Josephus, but the focus in this chapter is only
on whether the eight hundred men whom Jannaeus crucified were
Pharisees. Although one cannot prove the conversation between
Alexander and Alexandra took place, it is reasonable to think some-

thing of the sort occurred. The Pharisees according to both histories, became the effective power in Alexandra's administration and took steps to punish the ones responsible for crucifying the eight hundred victims. The drastic switch of allegiance by the Pharisees—from armed resistance to Jannaeus to enthusiastic support of his wife and successor—must have been caused by something. If the men who avenged the eight hundred were Pharisees, as Josephus says, then there is reason for thinking the executed group were also Pharisees. If the story about the corpse of Alexander is true, the case is stronger yet. If the eight hundred whom Jannaeus crucified were Pharisees and Pesher Nahum calls them דורשי החלקות, the דורשי החלקות are Pharisees.

FURTHER CHARACTERIZATIONS OF PHARISEES IN THE SCROLLS

There is another line of argument that supports this conclusion and broadens what may be inferred from it. The Qumran texts associate the ones who look for smooth things with a leader and charge both with embracing incorrect legal positions and sinning through speech.

Leader and Followers

The leader is called at least several unflattering names, all tied together by a set of disreputable characteristics like לצון and כזב.

The Scoffer (איש הלצון)

We have already seen that the first column of the Damascus Document associated the Scoffer with "those who seek smooth things." The Scoffer is credited with dripping lies over Israel (מטיף לישראל מימי כוב) and is associated with misleading (ויתעם) many. Not surprisingly, we meet his followers called scoffers in several passages. These people, who are said to be in Jerusalem, have rejected the Law and will be judged (CD XX, 11; 4Q162 II, 6, 10; cf. 4Q525 23, 8).

The Liar (איש הכזב)

This title probably applies to the same man but highlights a slightly different character fault. The two may be identified because the writers charge them with the same sins. The Liar also rejected the Law of the Teacher and formed a group around himself: "those who were unfaithful together with the Liar, in that they did not listen to the word received by the Teacher of Righteousness from the mouth of God." (1QpHab II, 1–3) The same text (V, 11–12), speaking about the disloyal house of Absalom, says of those who were with them that "they gave him [i.e., the Teacher] no help against the Liar who flouted [מאס] the Law in the midst of their whole [congregation]." The desertion by the scoffers who despised the new covenant precedes mention of another abandonment: "From the day of the gathering in of the Teacher of the Community until the end of all the men of war who deserted to the Liar there shall pass about forty years (Deut. ii, 14)" (CD XX, 13–15). 4Q171 charges the Liar with leading many astray (התעה) "by his lying words so that they chose frivolous things and heeded not the interpreter of knowledge [מליץ דעת]" (1–2 i 26–27).[21]

The Spouter/Preacher of Lies (מטיף הכזב)

This, too, is likely the same individual who corrupts others with falsehood. His misleading many is noted in 1QpHab X, 9–10, as is the fact that he formed a congregation. The Spouter also figures in CD VIII, where he is associated with a group: "But all these things the builders of the wall and those who daub it with plaster (Ezekiel xiii, 10) have not understood because a follower [שוקל] of the wind, one who raised storms, and rained down lies [ומטיף כזב], had preached to them (Mic. ii, 11), against all whose assembly [עדתו] the anger of God was kindled" (VIII, 12–13).[22]

Pharisaic Terms and Views

The epithets are linked with some beliefs and terms that may well have been particular to the Pharisees in this period.

Builders of the Wall

These "builders of the wall [בוני החיץ]," who obeyed the Spouter of Lies and "followed after 'Precept [צו]'—'Precept' was a spouter [מטיף] of whom it is written, *They shall surely spout* (Mic. ii, 6)—shall be caught in fornication" (IV, 19–20). As Vermes's translation indicates, the spouting language echoes Micah 2:6, but the Damascus Document borrows "Precept" from Hosea 5:11: "Ephraim is oppressed, crushed in judgment, because he was determined to go after vanity [הלך אחרי צו]." It is very tempting to think that צו here was understood to be the individual called the Scoffer, with the two letters echoing לצון[23] and the verb הלך also intended as a play on הלכה. The builders also figure in CD VIII, 12, 18 (with parallels in XIX, 25, 31) where the divine wrath is kindled against them for judgment, as they have not understood the message of God. The epithet "builders of the wall" has of course been related to the familiar "hedge around the law" in *m. Avot* 1.1.[24]

Niece Marriages

The author says that the builders of the wall were caught in fornication, one of the three nets of Belial. As he goes on to explain the double way in which they were guilty of sexual misconduct, he raises the subject of niece marriages (V, 7–11). Niece marriage was something permitted later by the rabbis and could, therefore, have been a position advocated by the Pharisees whom the sages considered their predecessors.[25]

Talmud

Another possible extension by association involves the title "those who seek smooth things." We have seen that they are Pharisees and that "Ephraim" appears in apposition to this title in 4Q169. This is evident in 3–4 ii 1–2: "*Woe to the city of blood; it is full of lies and rapine* (iii, 1a–b). Interpreted, this is the city of Ephraim, those who seek smooth things during the last days, who walk in lies and falsehood." If we may regard the two titles as referring to the same people, 3–4 ii 8 becomes interesting: "Interpreted, this concerns those who lead Ephraim astray, who lead many astray through their false teaching [בתלמוד שקרם], their lying tongue, and deceitful lips." Since we are very likely dealing with Pharisees here, the word תלמוד is worth noting. B. Z. Wacholder calls attention to the three parallel expressions (לשון כוזביהם, תלמוד שקרם, שפת מרמה) placed between two phrases regarding misleading (מתעי אפרים and יתעו רבים). Because of the parallels, both לשון and שפה should clarify the meaning of תלמוד. According to Wacholder:

> Since neither the biblical nor Qumran texts supply any examples, we may *provisionally* interpret the phrase as if it were part of rabbinic terminology. It was shown that "betalmud" is to "tongue" and "lip" what "false" is to "lie" and "deceit." It follows that the *Pesher of Nahum* was denouncing something oral when using the term "betalmud."

He suggests the meaning "those who by their false oral teaching (or oral interpretation)."[26]

Orality

The expressions in the scrolls regarding the Pharisees and some of their views have been surveyed above, but an aspect of the negative vocabulary used for them deserves underscoring: much of it has to do with speech: scoffing, lies, smooth things, preaching or spouting, and talmud. The Pharisees, as described by Josephus and the New Testament, were noted for their oral tradition, their unwritten laws. The scrolls do not verify that the Pharisees had an oral tradition, but they do consistently deride them for their abuse of speech through which they misled others.[27]

In summary, we may say that the Dead Sea Scrolls do refer to the Pharisees and their leader under a variety of abusive names, and they do reflect some of the traits of the Pharisees as known from other sources.

CHAPTER 9

ARCHAEOLOGY AND THE PHARISEES

James F. Strange

It is a challenge to address the topic of the archaeology of the Pharisees for at least four reasons. First, modern scholarship exhibits a wide range of constructions of the place of the Pharisees in Judean society. Were they a nationalistic-political movement, a separated religious elite, a religious reform movement within Judaism, an influential movement stressing their understanding of the Torah (but not withdrawing, unlike the Essenes), a small philosophical school with no real influence, a traditional religious group that was or was not apocalyptic, or something other? Second, there is a rather narrow literary base for understanding the Pharisees' religious and political activities in the first century, even though it is spread over three sources: Josephus, the gospels, and the Mishnah. However, the limitation these documents impose lies not simply in the fact that so few sources exist, but the nature of the sources themselves. The authors rarely felt the need to describe at length matters that participants (in the authors' world) knew well. Third, there is not yet an agreement about the origins of the Pharisees, their political power in the first century CE, their relation to the Second Temple, or their relation to the synagogue. Fourth, though we have broad agreement that Pharisaic interests included tithing, purity laws, agriculture, Sabbath and Festival observance, and vows,[1] the hermeneutical move from these concerns to archaeological materials is not immediately transparent. That is, what parts of the material culture correlate uniquely with these concerns?

The above list is not unique to the Pharisees, however, or to any other group in early Judaism, so far as we know. Therefore, the attempt to detect these concerns in the archaeological record may disclose details of observance that characterized many groups besides Pharisees.

However, rather than remain silent, it seems worthwhile to learn from the archaeological record those items that correlate with Pharisaic interests. In other words, though we will not always be treating archaeological matters that are unique to the Pharisees, we may still learn a great deal about their interests, broadly understood. Besides, we may detect trends in the material culture that do not necessarily appear in the texts.

THEORETICAL AND METHODOLOGICAL CONSIDERATIONS

We reason that specific Pharisaic interests result in stereotypical behaviors or rituals. We reason by analogy with other components of the culture that these behaviors or rituals probably have a corresponding component in the material culture. That is, certain artifacts, equipment, and architecture facilitate and even embody these rituals.

For example, Josephus, the New Testament, and the Mishnah yield evidence of Pharisaic ritual washings (stereotypical behaviors). We conclude that the material culture should show a corresponding concern for purity, even if we cannot prove that every instance of purity in the material culture is an example of Pharisaic purity. Yet, analysis of the items of material culture may illuminate what ritual purity means concretely and in general, even though we have not unearthed any Pharisees.

Tithing is another Pharisaic concern. However, it is not yet clear to anyone which rituals are required for tithing, if any. Without a ritual or stereotypical behavior it is impossible to identify artifacts, equipment, or architecture that illuminate the Pharisaic concern.

Consequently, even though the sources are few and scant on the details of the Pharisees and their rituals, and even though the level of agreement among scholars is low, it is possible to call attention to certain archaeological evidences that seem to correlate with so-called Pharisaical interests. In other words, the archaeologist may be able to throw some light on the actual imprint in the archaeological record that was formed from certain ritual behaviors. If more than one group is engaged in ritual washings, then analysis of the behaviors implied by ritual pools and immersion vessels can at least allow one to form some understanding of what transpired in ritual washing, whether by the Pharisees or by other groups.

The assertion about "analysis of the behaviors implied by [certain archaeological remains]" rests on a social model of human ritual (or habituated) behavior. Simply articulated, the model asserts that human beings tend to act in specific stereotypical behaviors in religious rituals. Human beings therefore fashion ritual objects, equipment, and space (architecture) in order to facilitate and represent the behaviors, beliefs, and values appropriate to the ritual environment. "Fashioning" and "representing" show intentionality, but not necessarily conscious intentionality. In the ancient world, therefore, a temple with its enclosure is a human accommodation to the need for ritual space of a specific type. Ritual space contextualizes ritual behaviors, beliefs, and values and provides us with their imprint. An altar is also a ritual object and is an accommodation to the requirement for a ritual action or complex of actions called "sacrifice," as in Temple Judaism. A priestly garment is a ritual object unique to the priesthood. The garment correlates with the role of the priest in ritual sacrifice. To move to the nonpriestly world, a room in a house or public building that was set aside for ritual is now a human accommodation to the need for ritual space of a different type. The ritual pool permanently installed in the ritual space of the house or public building is a ritual object and is an accommodation to ritual bathing and the ideas associated with ritual bathing. A white garment that is donned after ritual bathing, like the priestly robe, is a ritual object that correlates with the "purity" of any Israelite engaged in ritual bathing. Such objects embody or stand for the ritual action, the beliefs associated with the action, and the values held in association with the action.

All of these objects just named operate as metaphors for the ritual system under consideration. For participants in this religious system, any or all of these objects can be understood to be "solid metaphors" for the ritual component of the system.[2] Whether they were recognized by everyone in the ancient context or only by a few is another matter.

Archaeologists typically interpret ritual artifacts, equipment, and architecture by resorting to the religious literature of the religion in question. (a) In this case we would consult Josephus, the gospels, or the Mishnah in search of statements that reveal ritual behaviors, beliefs, and values of the Pharisees. (b) We would also search the same literature for artifacts, equipment, and architecture mentioned in the text and also in association with the Pharisees and their concerns. (c) With a catalog of artifacts, equipment, and architecture in hand we then might search the secondary archaeological literature for description and interpretation of items identified as those mentioned in the texts and as found here and there in excavation.[3] The result of such analyses for the fairly narrowly defined idea of "pure table vessels" is not a simple presence/absence counting system but reveals that there was an extensive and nuanced reliance on numerous types of soft stone or chalk vessels, all of which we know from *m. Kel.* 4:4 would not be subject to impurity. The vessels enter the archaeological record in numbers in the first century BCE and begin to disappear from that record precipitously after two revolts against Rome. Excavations to this date show a wide variety and broad distribution of chalk-stone vessels from the Galilee and the Golan Heights to Samaria to Judea, coterminus with Jewish occupation or the political entity of ancient Judea.[4]

Of course, what often limits such an investigation is that the ancient sources may not describe a ritual sufficiently (or at all) so that the proper correlation can be made. For example, it has been a matter of scholarly puzzlement for some time that Matthew 3:6 reports that people were immersed (ἐβαπτίζοντο) in the Jordan "by him" (the Baptist). What precisely did John do? We have no such report of an agent of immersion in the tractate *Miqvaot* of the Mishnah. On the other hand, when John 2:6 reports that the stone vessels in the house at Cana stood there "according to the Jewish [rites] of purification" (κατὰ τὸν καθαρισμὸν τῶν Ἰουδαίων), one word ("purification") describes an entire complex of ritual behaviors, beliefs, and values that we can only partially flesh out by reference to Matthew and Luke.

There is a second, more important limitation in this mode of deduction. Although it is often a joke that anything archaeologists cannot understand they designate as "cultic" (ritualistic), there is an important principle buried in the joke. The principle is that an artifact fashioned for a specific culture not our own or for a set of behaviors we do not know (or only partially know) is not a metaphor for us. The artifact cannot "stand for" a set of ritual behaviors, if we do not know them. The object is beyond our analytical understanding, no matter how much we examine it. In this case, we see through a glass darkly or not at all.

AN ANALYSIS OF SIX PHARISAIC CONCERNS

From the list of Pharisaic concerns enumerated above it is possible to deduce a list of more narrowly defined ideas that probably have counterparts in the material culture. To mention the same example, from concerns about purity and from certain texts in the Mishnah and the gospels, it is possible to deduce that ritual washing of vessels was indeed practiced by the Pharisees. For example, we read in Mark 7:3-4 about "the Pharisees, and all the Jews . . . immersing cups, pitchers, and bronze vessels" (βαπτισμοὺς ποτηρίων καὶ ξεστῶν καὶ χαλκίων) and in John 2:6 about "six stone water jars were there," (see above). What is the vessel that Mark and John presupposed for ritual immersion of these smaller vessels? The usual answer is the lathe-turned stone vessel that stands about 0.55 to 0.80 m high and features a pedestal or footed base.⁵ A second possibility is any large, chalk-stone basin.

Below is a chart of proposed Pharisaic concerns or ideas matched with items from the material culture that appear to yield a correlation with the ideas.

Proposed Pharisaic Idea	*Material Culture*
1. Serving food at table	Small stone vessels
2. Immersion of tableware (dishes)	Large stone vessels
3. Immersion of the person	Ritual pools, or *miqvaot*
4. Washing hands	"Measuring cups" of stone, i.e., "lavers"
5. Resurrection and afterlife	Tombs and ossuaries
6. Synagogue activity	Synagogue plans and architecture

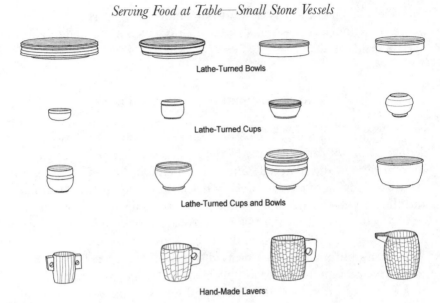

Figure 1: Small Stone Vessels and Lavers

The archaeological record is replete with stone vessels of a type that is most easily interpreted as more or less ordinary serving vessels. Y. Magen, following Rahmani,[6] interpreted the use of the chalk-stone vessel for a century and a half (ca. 50 BCE to 150 CE) as following from the Pharisaic idea of ritual purity. He explains that the great variety of vessels is due to artisans' copying other vessels in pottery, wood, and metal.[7] Since these vessels were found at Qumran, they are not unique to Pharisees.[8]

These small vessels are of the Early Roman period and are lathe turned. There is no real consistency in naming the types, but I suggest the following classifications: bowls, cups,[9] lavers, footed goblets, stoppers, jars, and basins. In addition Cahill presents one lamp and one possible inkwell, but from an earlier period, namely the "Persian/Hellenistic."[10]

The lathe-turned bowls range in diameter from 18 to 26 cm and stand about 4 cm high. There are a few larger bowls. Their form resembles imported ceramic luxury wares. They comprise the first row in figure 1.

Lathe-turned cups appear to range from about 6 to 12 cm in diameter at the rim. These stand about 8 to 10 cm high with walls that slope inward and are rounded. They comprise the second row in figure 1.

The footed goblet appears to be a cup standing on a column upon a flat base. It resembles the goblet or footed water glass in Europe and the Americas, though not so finely cut in stone. The goblets apparently stood about 7 to 10 cm in height and are rare in excavations. They are not illustrated in figure 1.

The stoppers have round heads and a projecting central plug that appears to be designed for juglets and jugs with necks of inside diameter about 4 cm. No stone vessels with this size neck were found in Jerusalem or even elsewhere, so Cahill concludes that they are for ceramic vessels. They do not appear in figure 1.

Since these vessels appear to be modeled after existing ceramic (and perhaps metal) vessels, they are only distinguished by their material. The chalk stone is very soft and breaks easily, but it is therefore very easy to work.

Immersion of Tableware (Dishes)—Large Stone Vessels

0   50 cm

Figure 2: Large Standing Stone Vessels

The best candidates for the immersion of small vessels are the large stone vessels found throughout the Land of Israel. These vessels stood about 0.55 to 0.80 m high on a pedestal or footed base. They have been found from Jerusalem to Samaria to Galilee, and some are known from the Golan Heights.[11] The two in figure 2 are from Jerusalem.

One notices a certain constancy in design and presentation of these vessels, wherever they are found. This suggests that they were manufactured according to a certain mental template on the part of the artisan.

The height of the vessel seems to be about the height of the hips or waist of a standing adult. This suggests that the vessel is used by standing over it and immersing dishes by hand.

Another possibility for the immersion of small vessels is basins. If Cahill's basins are published at the same scale as the other figures, then no. 1 is about 44 cm in diameter and no. 2 would be about 38.5 cm in diameter. They are of indeterminate depth.[12] These would sit on a table or on the ground for use.

Immersion of the Person—Ritual Pools, or Miqvaot

Ritual pools, or *miqvaot*, are well known and well published in archaeological reports that range from Judea to Galilee and the Golan Heights. They are a main feature of Qumran.[13] Again one cannot help but notice constancy in design and presentation. Typically the ritual bath or pool is large enough for at least one person and is built underground. A flight of steps leads down into the water. The entire cavity including the steps is plastered with hydraulic plaster or at least a very fine plaster. The steps may be narrow, presupposing usage by one person, or the flight is much wider. The builders may have installed a low, narrow parapet or divider on the wide steps. We infer that one descended one side and ascended on the other. This division is described in *m. Sheq.* 8.2, though the text assumes two separate paths.[14] Some excavated ritual baths not only have a divider on the steps but also have two entrances, or either side of the entrance/exit is separated by a column of stone in the middle.

Some ritual pools are filled from another collecting pool that is called an *otsar*. Sanders took the position that those ritual pools with an *otsar* are Pharisaic, while others without the *otsar* are not Pharisaic, relying on *m. Miq.* 6:8.[15] This remains an interesting hypothesis until we develop a method of testing the hypothesis against new texts or archaeological materials.

These ritual baths serve Pharisaic interests and were surely frequented by Pharisees. We cannot prove that this is a distinctive Pharisaic institution imprinted into the archaeological record, but it is arresting that they are so well represented in the material culture throughout the country.

Washing Hands—"Measuring Cups" (Lavers) of Chalk Stone

The "measuring cups" or "mugs" found by the hundreds in Early Roman contexts are not for measuring at all, but were so named because they resembled modern measuring cups. They are shaped like small barrels with the diameter at the center of the body greater than the diameter of the rim and base (see the bottom row of figure 1). They usually have one or two handles, though some have no handles at all or simply lug handles. Some of them feature long pouring lips. They seem to serve the purpose of washing hands better than that of serving food, therefore the suggestion that they are actually "lavers."

The ritual of washing the hands (*nitilat yadayim*) is well attested, mostly in late texts such as the Bavli.[16] Explanation of the ritual appears in Mark 7:3-4: "For the Pharisees, and all the Jews, do not eat unless they vigilantly wash their hands, thus observing the tradition of the elders." The text does not describe the ritual in detail (nor do the rabbis), evidently assuming that the readership knows already.

Those vessels carved with spouts or pouring lips give away their purpose as pouring vessels or lavers. They are unique in that they are not finished like the lathe turned vessels. They retain the marks of chiseling and shaving. The display of the chiseling and shaving in effect shows that no other change has been forced on the stone than carving, perhaps thus preserving its purity. Yet it seems appropriate to hypothesize that these cups seem specifically adapted to the washing of hands. Those cups with two handles would serve well to pour water with one hand while holding one handle with the other, then switching hands to pour water on the other hand.[17]

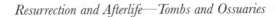

Resurrection and Afterlife—Tombs and Ossuaries

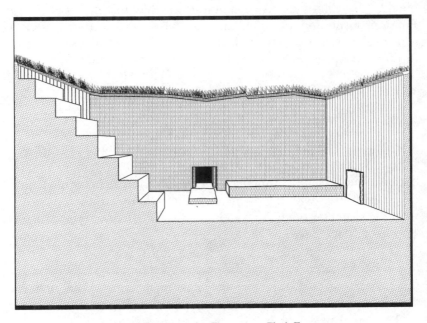

Figure 3: Cut-Away of a First-century Tomb Forecourt

It is well known that Josephus and the New Testament authors agree that the Pharisees and Sadducees differed on the afterlife.[18] However, afterlife or not, one must bury the dead. Therefore, there are extensive cemeteries in every major site of the Early Roman period in ancient Judea. There is also an extensive literature on these tombs, ossuaries, and burial customs.[19]

Tombs or burial caves were in continual use for generations by the same family. Such a custom emphasizes family ties. Tombs had a narrow opening (not usually a door as tall as a human being), sealed with a square stone, or occasionally a rolling stone.[20] Some tombs are known with very artistic facades, decorated with floral motifs, grapes,

Figure 4: Cut-Away Perspective of First-century Tomb

and other bas-relief. In primary burial, bodies were placed in niches or slots (*kokhim*) or on benches with arches cut out of the bedrock above them (*arcosolia*). Stone boxes or ossuaries with rounded or gabled lids of stone are commonly found in these tombs. Some bear inscriptions (mostly names) in Greek, Hebrew, or Aramaic.

One of the most common interpretations of ossuary use is that the custom of *ossolegium*, or secondary burial in ossuaries, derives from the classic belief in the resurrection of the dead.[21] Since this is explicitly a Pharisaic belief, then it follows that ossolegium is more likely to be Pharisaic than not.

Ossuaries are hand carved from blocks of soft chalk limestone.[22] The lids are custom fitted to each box, and sometimes the craftsman placed an X on the lid and box at the same point to indicate proper fit. In many cases ossuaries bear the names of those interred within them. Rachmani interprets such simple markings as serving the needs of grieving family members.[23]

Often the artisans who carved the ossuaries decorated them with many different artistic motifs. One of the most common motifs is two side-by-side rosettes. Although the debate about the meaning of this ornamentation has gone on since Goodenough, the debates do not seem to yield a single outcome as yet.[24] It is probably best to agree with Rachmani that the symbol of the resurrection is the ritual of ossolegium itself, not the receptacle. After all, the ossuary stood in the dark of the tomb.[25] In any case, the archaeology of the ossuary stands a good chance of elucidating the Pharisaic belief in the resurrection. The ritual of ossolegium yields its imprint in the ossuary. Or, to express it another way, the ossuary is a solid metaphor for the belief in resurrection.

Synagogue Activity—Synagogue Plans and Architecture

There seems to be a recurring debate whether the Pharisees had any controlling interest in the synagogue. Martin Hengel is usually credited with the argument that the Pharisees originated the synagogue in Palestine.[26] E. P. Sanders has not followed Hengel, based on the Theodotus inscription, in which Theodotus is a priest and *archisynagogos*.[27] Lee I. Levine says that the synagogue was not ruled by the Pharisees, but by the priests.[28]

The archaeology of the earliest synagogues reveals a certain constancy in plan. These are the synagogues of Gamla, earliest Capernaum,[29] Qiryat Sepher, Modi'in, Herodian Jericho, Herodium, and Masada.[30] The constant element is a pattern of nesting. The builders nested benches inside the walls around two, three, or all four walls. They nested a walkway all around inside the benches. Next they nested a rectangle of columns inside the walkway. Finally the builders nested a central space inside the columns, presumably for declamation of the Torah and other elements of ritual. The result is cumbersome for vision but good for audition.

I have pointed out elsewhere that this architectural space is foreshadowed in the series of colonnades comprising the exterior courts of the Second Temple. That is, the space from wall to columns is in effect a porch or stoa arrangement.[31] Two porches running parallel with a roof on top is a basilica, as is usually reconstructed on the south side of the Temple court in Jerusalem, following Josephus.

At the moment there is no way to prove that the synagogue building was modeled on the courts of the Temple Mount. On the other

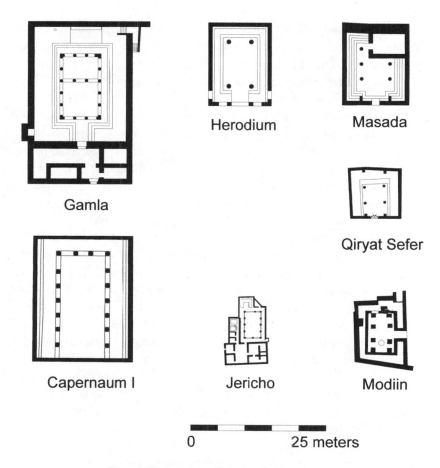

Figure 5: Plans of Seven First-Century CE Synagogues

hand, a circumstantial case can be made: (1) The courts are where the Torah was read aloud to the people, which seems to be the primary purpose of the synagogue. (2) The courts were roofed from wall to the line of columns. (3) From a few texts about Jesus "sitting" on the Temple Mount to teach the people, we infer benches against the walls, as benches in antiquity were ordinarily so constructed (Matt 26:55; Mark 12:41). (4) The basilica was already available in Judea as a part of Roman culture. The basilica, as pointed out above, seems to combine architectural elements of the colonnaded porch. (5) So far the only first-century-CE synagogue with decoration is that of

Gamla. This decoration is formed of meanders in bas-relief on capitals and with palm fronds incised on two lintels. These specific decorations are not found in the Second Temple, but the Second Temple bore geometric decorations in bas-relief, the same method of carving of the meanders at Gamla.

With this many connections between the Temple courts and the plan of the synagogue, one wonders if this does not establish that the synagogue was founded by the priests (see note 28). If the synagogue were a priestly institution, then we should expect a strong priestly role in the synagogue post 70 CE. This is not the case, however. Our sole witness to such a role is the Theodotus inscription. If the synagogue owes its form and function to the priests, then we would expect that excavations will find late first-century-BCE or early first-century CE synagogues in Galilee in the places where the priestly courses settled. So far the archaeology or accidental finds and systematic archaeology of early remains in these twenty-four localities in Galilee have not turned up first-century synagogues.[32] Of course, this may change. However, it is the rabbis, the heirs to the Pharisees, and not the priests, who continued to legislate about the Temple rituals and sacrifices post 70—as far as we know (no priestly literature has been preserved). It is the rabbis as descendants of the Pharisees who have revealed a vested interest in the institution of the synagogue (*m. Meg.*). It appears that the links between the plans of synagogues and the plans of the Temple courts tend to confirm the hypothesis that the Pharisees had an interest or concern in the institution of the synagogue. This interest parallels their desire that all Israel would eat their food in ritual purity, like priests serving in the Temple. This interest would also help us understand why Matthew does not hesitate to indicate that Pharisees were in attendance in the synagogue (12:9-14). In other words, the authorship of Matthew does not find it incongruous that Pharisees would be found in that village institution.

CONCLUSIONS

We have examined six concerns or interests of the Pharisees that we believe had left an imprint in the archaeological record. These concerns and their proposed counterparts in the material culture were (1) serving food at table—small stone vessels; (2) immersion of tableware (dishes)—large stone vessels; (3) immersion of the person—ritual pools or *miqvaot*; (4) washing hands—"measuring cups" (lavers) of chalk stone; (5) resurrection and afterlife—tombs and ossuaries; and (6) synagogue activity—synagogue plans and architecture. The results were threefold: (1) There was sufficiently strong interest in purity as a broad category in antiquity that a stoneware industry was founded with centers near Jerusalem, in lower Galilee, and probably elsewhere. The Jerusalem center was apparently also the locus of manufacture of ossuaries, an artifact that reflects another concern with afterlife and resurrection. (2) There was also a matching industry, though usually not called that, of constructing ritual baths (and collecting pools to fill them) from south to north in the country and extending into the Golan Heights. (3) There are seven buildings understood to be synagogues that reveal a striking similarity of plan using nested elements. This is a small sample compared to the thousands of stone vessels, but the geographic distribution of these few structures virtually "from Dan to Beersheba" itself agues that synagogues did not appear solely because of local interests, but because of the interests of a class or body of people who saw to it that they were constant in plan for the sake of the declamation of the Torah.

Although there were probably others who were interested in public purity in much the same way as the Pharisees—notably at Qumran—there is no catenae of texts that make it clear that the bulk of Israelites during the period of the Second Temple observed purity laws strictly. Yet the broad distribution of artifacts associated with purity and considered here suggests that some major group led the way in preserving the traditions of purity outside the Temple. Furthermore, this group may well have legislated about the form and function of the items of material culture so that they achieved a kind of standardization. The group that appears to have sufficient status in Second Temple Judaism to be responsible for this state of affairs— especially after 70 CE— is the Pharisees. This testable hypothesis is the major result of the above analysis.

PART TWO

THE PHARISEES IN RABBINIC JUDAISM

CHAPTER 10

THE PHARISEES AND THE SADDUCEES
IN THE EARLIEST RABBINIC DOCUMENTS

Jack N. Lightstone

INTRODUCTORY REMARKS: THE LARGER QUESTION
AND THE FOCUS OF THIS CHAPTER

One underlying problematic informing this volume's subject is that
the ancient evidence about the Pharisees is variegated. More impor-
tant still, these different, sometimes divergent, portrayals of the
Pharisees in the ancient sources stem, to a significant degree, from the
variety of the *types* of sources from which the evidence comes—from
Hellenistic-historiographical and Hellenistic-autobiographical texts
(Josephus), through aretalogical-evangelical documents (the gospels),
to rabbinic-legal treatises (the Mishnah and the Tosefta), and so on.
Of course, the various ancient authors or "authorships" (to use
Neusner's term for early rabbinic documents, which have a more
"collective" provenance) will bring their own idiomatic perspectives
and tendentious agendas to bear on their portrayal of the Pharisees.
But in addition, the literary and rhetorical conventions that govern
the *types* of writing, genre, or expression within which each author or
"authorship" works affects how matters are portrayed. Finally, not
only must modern historians of religion cope with a variety of
idiomatic perspectives, agendas, and literary-rhetorical conventions
in the sources, they must also consider the question: Which author or
"authorship" was in a position to know what about whom, and how?

The upshot of the above is that over the course of the last thirty
years of historical scholarship on the ancient Pharisees, the problem
of how to read and assess the historical value of the ensemble of witnesses in an either integrated or composite fashion has been at the
forefront. Much, if not most, of the scholarly debate has in effect

revolved around whether such an integrated or composite reading is methodologically possible. What may be glossed over or lost of the idiomatic nature of the various bodies of evidence in their respective portrayals of the Pharisees, if scholars rush to propound some composite picture, impelled by the desire to "discover" the "historical" Pharisees?

With these considerations in mind, this chapter considers one particular type of evidence about the Pharisees, from a specific swath of early rabbinic literature. I analyze those passages in which the term "Pharisee(s)" is juxtaposed with "Sadducee(s)" (or "Boethusian[s]"). Moreover, I restrict my attention to those passages meeting these criteria in the Mishnah and Tosefta.[1]

SOME CONCEPTUAL AND METHODOLOGICAL CONSIDERATIONS

The Primacy of Mishnaic and Toseftan Evidence

Why I focus on passages in which "Pharisees" are juxtaposed with "Sadducees" will be made clearer in subsequent sections of this chapter. Why I concentrate on Mishnaic and Toseftan passages is simple. The Mishnah is the earliest document produced and promulgated as authoritative in the early rabbinic movement. The Tosefta is arguably the first attempt within the early rabbinic movement to compose (or compile, as some would prefer to state) a sustained commentary of sorts on the Mishnah; hence, the Tosefta is more likely than other ancient rabbinic texts to contain materials that date to a period and provenance close to the Mishnah's.[2] While it is *possible* that later rabbinic documents, like the Babylonian Talmud, contain information (for example, in its *beraitot*) of so-called "tannaitic" provenance and contemporaneous with the Mishnah and its sources, it is *less probable* that an allegedly ancient "tradition" that first appears in the Babylonian Talmud stems from the same era as evidence in the Mishnah and Tosefta.

Therefore, what the authorships of the Mishnah and Tosefta "know," believe they "know," or wish us to "know" about the Pharisees and Sadducees is not likely to be improved on by the search for more reliable evidence in later rabbinic writings. Moreover, the primacy and authority of the Mishnah and the passages of the Tosefta for later rabbinic authorships means that parallel passages in later rabbinic documents most often reinterpret and recontextualize these earlier (so-called) tannaitic witnesses.[3] It is less likely and, in my own scholarly experience, less frequently the case that the parallel in the later rabbinic document can be shown to have preserved the earlier version. Hence, limiting this study to passages in the Mishnah and Tosefta is a methodologically cautious stance. It is one I favor in full recognition that some allegedly "tannaitic" traditions in later rabbinic texts might proffer evidence contemporaneous with that in the Mishnah or Tosefta.[4]

All this being said, while the passages in the Mishnah and Tosefta concerning both Pharisees and Sadducees are more likely to be earlier than passages in later rabbinic documents, one cannot thereby maintain that they are historically accurate witnesses to the Pharisaic and Sadducean groups. Nor can one say that these passages preserve traditions that date significantly before the Mishnah and the Tosefta (turn of the third century CE and latter half of the third century CE, respectively). And one certainly cannot conclude *ab initio* that these traditions are likely to date to the era before 70 CE, the alleged heyday of the Pharisaic and Sadducean groups in the Land of Israel. These are matters that must be considered on a passage by passage basis, *if* there is any evidentiary basis for addressing these questions at all.

About Religious Rivalries and Group Self-Definition

Why now do I concentrate on passages in which both Pharisees and Sadducees are mentioned—treating these passages as a distinctive body of evidence worthy of study apart from and alongside other rabbinic evidence concerning the Pharisees? I have two reasons in mind. One stems from some general claims about religious groups' inter- and intrareligious rivalries and such groups' struggles for success. The second reason has to do with certain sustained idiomatic literary traits of earliest rabbinic literature, specifically the Mishnah and correlative passages in the Tosefta. Let me first deal with the former issue.

Since the mid-1990s, I have participated in an ongoing seminar of the Canadian Society of Biblical Studies examining religious rivalries and the "struggle for success" among Jews, Christians, and Gentiles in the Late Roman Mediterranean world. By rivalry and the "struggle for success" the seminar means, among other things, groups' competition for adherents, sympathizers, social and physical space, and resources, all the while addressing issues of social formation and self-definition.[5] Among the conclusions that I have drawn from my own participation in, and contributions to, this seminar, several stand out as relevant to the case at hand. "Rival" religious groups lived cheek by jowl in relatively confined, shared social contexts. This was especially the case in urban environments. Such social environments required rival groups to share substantial sets of common social norms and patterns. Were this not the case, the social stability of the communities in which these people lived, and on which they depended, would have been undermined.

Yet, it was what set these groups apart (in their own eyes), not the many and substantial matters that they had in common, that provided the foundation of their respective senses of distinctiveness and self-definition. A group's social identity was socially constructed on the foundation of the perception of these differences and their perceived importance. And this was the case, even if what "rivals" shared by way of common social perceptions and norms far exceeded what they perceived set them apart.

Consequently, constructing socially differentiated identities within the larger context of their shared norms and common social worlds required each rival group to foster a kind of context-appropriate social myopia. In these moments of group myopia, social perception is limited to a select set of binary opposites with respect to which members of the group could say vis-à-vis their "competitors": "*We* do (or believe) *x, but they* do (or believe) *not x.*"

It bears repeating, however, that these heightened and delimited perceptions of opposing differences must necessarily be restricted to specific, relevant social moments, else members of these competing groups could not share social space, a requisite of their social existence. In sum, in the eastern Mediterranean Roman world, religious rivalry and group self-definition over against some important other(s) usually reposed on its necessary social corollary, namely, a "critical mass" of intergroup cooperation and shared perceptions and norms. The chief exceptions to this generalization are historical moments of rampant persecution or "(civil) war"; and real as these moments are, they are the exceptions that prove the rule in Roman Mediterranean society.)[6]

How does the above bear on the case at hand? Within a distinctive group constructing and maintaining its social formation, the specification of a clear set of "binary opposites" that serve to distinguish themselves from some important other(s) played an inordinately important role in identity and group formation. And this will be the case even when much, if not most, of their socially constructed world and shared perceptions of that world were also shared by their "significant" rivals. This is not only true of inter-religious competition and rivalry, the subject of the seminar, but also of intrareligious rivalry and competition, the case at hand in this chapter on Pharisees and Sadducees. Indeed, in intrareligious group formation, where that which is shared is all the more vast, I would posit that the putative binary opposites that establish the basis for group differentiation become exaggerated in importance.

The consequence of the foregoing is that one potentially cogent body of early rabbinic evidence for who and what the Pharisees were, or were portrayed as being by the early rabbinic movement (their alleged heirs), will be those passages of the sort: "*We* do (or believe) *x, but they* do (or believe) *not x.*" Here Pharisees would be juxtaposed with Sadducees as "rivals," at least in the literary realm; and those binary opposites that, in the minds of the authors of the Mishnah and Tosefta, constituted the foundation for Pharisaic group self-definition and social formation over against the Sadducees would be evident.

Having argued that from a conceptual-theoretical viewpoint those passages in earliest rabbinic literature that juxtapose Pharisees and Sadducees potentially offer better "purchase" on understanding the self-identity and self-definition of these two groups, permit me to say that there is also a lexical-philological reason for focusing on this set of passages. As E. Rivkin points out, it is clear that not all instances of the *perushi/perushim* in rabbinic literature ought properly to be translated "Pharisee(s)." At times, the context demands that *perushi* be rendered "separatist" or "abstainer" (as Neusner sometimes does in his own translations of the term at various junctures). In other instances, either "separatist/abstainer" or "Pharisee" might be legitimate renderings, with little or no basis for making a definitive choice.

Only when *perushi(m)* are juxtaposed with Sadducees or Boethusians (or with some other named group or movement) can we be certain that "Pharisees" are the intended meaning.[7]

Mishnaic and Toseftan Literary Forms and Traits

Thirty years ago, J. Neusner, in his groundbreaking work *Rabbinic Traditions about the Pharisees before 70 CE*, discovered that the constituent traditions of early rabbinic documents were cast in accordance with definitive rules for literary formulation—in other words, what Rudolf Bultmann had decades earlier described as "forms" in the gospel traditions. Among the first forms identified by Neusner in rabbinic literature was the dispute form in the Mishnah and in the Tosefta, arguably the earliest strata of rabbinic literature. Another was the "debate" form. The dispute form was liberally replicated in still later, allegedly tannaitic, rabbinic traditions, specifically in the *beraitot* of the Palestinian and Babylonian Talmuds. Later, Neusner[8] and others uncovered other early rabbinic literary forms and demonstrated that discrete rabbinic documents, as opposed to the early rabbinic corpus as a whole, each evinced distinctive formal traits that distinguished the work of one "authorship" from another, this despite the strong inter- and intra-textual relationships across these documents.

Given my remarks in the previous section, it is both fortuitous and problematic that two of the literary forms that pervade the Mishnah and the Tosefta are the "dispute" and the "debate" forms. The former juxtaposes opposing legal rulings to a single legal case. In its simplest version, the "dispute" is structured thusly:

> State of affairs comprising case;
> X says A;
> Y says opposite of A.

The "debate," more common in Toseftan passages than Mishnaic ones, appends to the dispute:

> He (X) said to him (Y): laconic argument against opposite of A;
> He (Y) said to him (X): laconic counterargument.

For our purposes, I need not elaborate on the variations of these forms. But disputes in particular are characterized by laconic language and tightly balanced lemmas attributed to the disputants. The "case" that is the subject of the opposing rulings of the "disputants" typically is equally laconic in language, and that language often repeats, or is some variation of, phrases and terms of immediately preceding cases in the larger literary unit of which the "dispute" is one part. Thus, one might see:

A. state of affairs a plus b
B. unattributed ruling x
C. state of affairs a plus c
D. unattributed ruling x
E. state of affairs a plus not b
F. unattributed ruling x
G. state of affairs a plus not c
H. named authority y rules x
I. named authority z rules opposite of x

The very language of A, C, E, and G would be constructed by means of the simple repetition or permutation of very few and the same tightly formulated phrases and clauses: the clean fish that swallowed an unclean fish . . .; the unclean that swallowed the clean . . . Indeed, it is via the repetition, concatenation, inversion, and permutation of a limited set of phrases, clauses, or terms that the Mishnah, in particular, will spin out those cases that define a Mishnah "chapter." As a result, the "case" addressed in a dispute often derives its language and form largely from the language and form of the "chapter" as a literary unit, rather than the dispute (or the pericope in which the dispute is situated) as some independent literary formulation.[9] It further follows that in such instances the language and form of the case addressed by the disputants comes from the formulators of the "chapters" rather than from any putative tradent of the alleged dispute between the legal authorities "cited."

The Mishnah and Tosefta, therefore, use the dispute form (and the debate form) to place in apposition opposing views attributed to two parties (rarely more) on a single problem. Consequently, the Mishnah and Tosefta will by formal convention tend to characterize the Pharisees' (or the Sadducees') policies and beliefs by casting them in some variation of this form. *Prima facie*, this is fortuitous, because, as stated, group formation and identity in a social context of intrareligious rivalry tend to be defined in terms of "*We* do (or believe) x, *but they* do (or believe) *not x*." That is, the Mishnah and Tosefta will have a formal literary tendency to give us the type of evidence we want to consider.

By the same token, the pervasiveness of the dispute form in the Mishnah (and of the dispute and debate forms in the Tosefta) is highly problematic; the rules for casting the language of both. the legal case and the disputants' opposing rules are so tightly defined and determined by the formal requirements of the dispute form itself and the literary conventions for formulating the larger literary units ("chapters"), of which any one dispute is an element, that some significant percentage of the very substance of the passage may be driven by formal and literary requirements and conventions of the formulator of the chapter (let alone of the dispute), rather than by some putative underlying historical traditions about the "real" Pharisees or "real" Sadducees. Classical form criticism differentiated form from the idiomatic content at any one instance of the form's use, and this is valid. Nevertheless, the analysis of Mishnaic language clearly shows that formal requirements significantly prejudice what can and cannot be said—that is, content.[10] We shall have to be sensitive to this fact as we review the passages analyzed in the remainder of this chapter. We will want, in particular, to pay attention to the literary and formal traits of "cases" addressed by the disputant "Pharisees" and "Sadducees" and these traits relation to the "chapter" of which they form a part. If the former is highly driven by the latter, the probability increases that some significant amount of the content of the "case" under dispute derives from the formulator of the chapter, the Mishnah's ultimate or penultimate authors.

THE EVIDENCE

With the foregoing conceptual and methodological concerns in mind, let us first consider in turn each of the sources at hand: those pericopes in the Mishnah and Tosefta in which "Pharisees" are juxtaposed with "Sadducees" or "Boethusians." Later, in the final section of the chapter I discuss what may be concluded from the ensemble of passages, of which there are six (plus two questionable passages).[11]

Sources in Mishnah and Tosefta Tractate Yadayim

Three of the most often cited passages juxtaposing "Pharisees" and "Sadducees" appear at *m. Yadayim* 4:6, 4:7a, and 4:7b as a sort of "triptych." A pericope fragment at *t. Yadayim* 1:19 (2:19) complements or comments on *m.* 4:6. Finally, *t. Yadayim* 1:20 (2:20) proffers a fourth element to M.'s triptych. In all, then, five passages in the Mishnah and Tosefta Yadayim (*m.* 4:6, 7a, 7b and *t.* 1:19[2:19], and 1:20 [2:20]) juxtapose "Pharisees" and "Sadducees" [or "Boethusians"]. These comprise almost all such evidence in the Mishnah and Tosefta. Hence, they have figured heavily in scholarly treatment of the early rabbinic evidence concerning the Pharisees.[12] In light of this chapter's discussion of conceptual and methodological issues, I begin with an examination of the literary, formal, and rhetorical traits and interrelationships of these five passages.

Literary Context

The immediate literary context for the three similarly formulated Mishnah passages at *m. Yadayim* 4:6 through 7b—our triptych—begins at *m. Yadayim* 4:5. In turn (and quite uncharacteristically of the Mishnah), the latter's literary and logical antecedent appears considerably earlier, at *m. Yadayim* 3:5b—separated from one another by an extensive section, *m.* 4:1–4:4. Therefore, to understand the place of our triptych in its context, I present *m.* 3:5b, engage in very brief discussion of the interposing sections of *m.* 4:1 through 4:4, and recommence at *m.* 4:5 and our triptych, *m.* 4:6, 7a, and 7b.[13]

A. All holy Scriptures render the hands unclean.
B. [Among them] the Song of Songs and Ecclesiastes [which therefore also] render the hands unclean.
C. Rabbi Judah says: the Song of Songs renders the hands unclean, and [concerning] Ecclesiastes [there is] dispute.
D. Rabbi Yosé says: Ecclesiastes does not render the hands unclean, and [concerning] the Song of Songs [there is] dispute.
E. Rabbi Simeon says: Ecclesiastes is [the subject of] a lenient [ruling] of the House of Shammai, and is [the subject of] a stringent [ruling] of the House of Hillel.
F. Said Rabbi Simeon ben Azzai: I have a tradition directly from the seventy-two elders on that day that they seated Rabbi Eleazar ben Azariah in the Academy [as its president]—

G. that [both] the Song of Songs and Ecclesiastes render the hands unclean.

H. Said Rabbi ʿAqiba: Heaven forfend! No one in Israel disputes that

I. the Song of Songs renders the hands unclean,

J. for the whole world is not equal [in value] to the day that the Song of Songs was delivered to Israel,

K. for all of the Scriptures is [like] the Sanctuary, and the Song of Songs is [like] the Holy of Holies,

L. and if they disputed, they disputed only regarding Ecclesiastes.

M. Said Rabbi Yohanan ben Joshua, the son of the father-in-law of Rabbi ʿAqiba: In accordance with [the teaching of] Ben Azzai—so they voted and so they taught.

(*m. Yad.* 3:5b)

Immediately following the above, chapter 4 of *m. Yadayim* commences with an extended quasi- or pseudonarrative composition from 4:1 to 4:4, each larger element of which commences with the formulaic phrase "On that [self-same] day, (בו ביום). In the current literary context, the formulaic phrase functions to link the elements of *m.* 4:1 through 4:4 to *m.* 3:5b F ("on that day [ביום] that they seated Rabbi Eleazar ben Azariah in the Academy [as its president]"), making the latter become an "umbrella" narrative context for the former.[14] In this manner, *m.* 3:5b F and *m.* 4:1 through 4:4 are transformed editorially into a loosely constructed (and quite contrived, in my view) extended narrative. The legal content of this "narrative," constructed via liberal use of the dispute form within a "thin" (contrived), narrative shell, has nothing to do with the legal topic of 3:5b, the uncleanness of Holy Scriptures.[15] Treatment of the uncleanness of Holy Scriptures resumes at *m. Yad.* 4:5, followed thereafter by the triptych of passages dealing with Sadducees and Pharisees.

A. Aramaic [passages] (תרגום) that are in [the book of] Ezra[-Nehemiah] and that are in the [the book of] Daniel render the hands unclean.

B. Aramaic [passages] written in Hebrew,

C. And Hebrew [passages] written in Aramaic,

D. And [Scriptures written in] Hebrew script, do no render the hands unclean.

E. They [Scriptures] do not ever render [the hands] unclean, unless they shall be written in Assyrian script [i.e., the "square" Hebrew script in use since the Greco-Roman period], on parchment and in ink.

(*m. Yad.* 4:5)

A. Say the Sadducees: We cry out against you Pharisees, for you say:
   The Holy Scriptures render the hands unclean, and the books of
   Homer (המרס) do not render the hands unclean.

B. Said R. Yohanan b. Zakkai: And have we not more against the
   Pharisees but this alone? Lo, they say: The bones of an ass are clean,
   and the bones of Yohanan the High Priest are unclean.

C. [The Sadducees] said to him: As is their belovedness so is their
   uncleanness, so that a man will not make of the bones of his mother
   and father spoons.

D. [R. Yohanan b. Zakkai] said to them: Even so [are] the Holy
   Scriptures. As is their belovedness so is their uncleanness. And the
   books of Homer which are not beloved—they do not render the
   hands unclean.

                                                            (m. Yad. 4:6)

A. Say the Sadducees: We cry out against you Pharisees, for you declare
   clean the uninterrupted flow of liquid [flowing from a clean to an
   unclean vessel].

B. Say the Pharisees: We cry out against you Sadducees, for you declare
   clean the spring of water which comes from a cemetery.

                                                           (m. Yad. 4:7a)

A. Say the Sadducees: We cry out against you Pharisees! [שאתם אומרים
   to פטורין missing in the Kaufman, Parma, and Naples MSS; [שורי to
   פטורין missing in Lowe,] If [in the case of] my ox and my ass, concerning which no commandments are imposed upon me, lo, I am
   accountable for damage done by them, then [in the case of] my
   manservant and my maidservant, concerning whom commandments are imposed upon me, how much more so [must it be the case]
   that I be accountable for damage done by them.

B. [The Pharisees] said to them: No! If you say [thus] concerning my
   ox and my ass which do not possess understanding, will you say
   [thus] concerning my manservant and my maidservant who possess
   understanding? For if I anger them, they will go and set fire to the
   stack of grain of another, and I will be responsible to pay [for the
   damages].

                                                           (m. Yad. 4:7b)

As noted, two passages in t. Yadayim (1[2]:19 and 1[2]:20) serve to
complete or complement m. Yadayim 4:6 through 4:7b. The former
provides additional language (rendered in italics below) meant conceptually either to be interpolated between the two statements attributed to Yohanan at 4:6D or to replace altogether the second
statement at m. 4:6D.

> Said to them [the Sadducees] R. Yohanan b. Zakkai: [Concerning] the
> Holy Scriptures—as is their belovedness so is their uncleanness. *So that
> one will not make of them mats for [one's] animal.*
>
> (*t. Yad.* 1(2):19, ed. Zuckermandel)

The latter, t. Yadayim 1(2):20, adds a fourth element to the triptych in
M., imitating, albeit imperfectly, the literary-rhetorical patterns of the
latter, and using "Boethusians" as the lexical equivalent to the
Mishnah's "Sadducees."

> A. Say the Boethusians: We cry out against you Pharisees! If the daugh-
> ter of my son, who came from the strength of my son, who [in turn]
> came from my strength, lo, inherits me, then [is it not the case that]
> my daughter, who came [directly] from my strength should, all the
> more so, inherit me?
> B. Say the Pharisees: No! If you say [thus] in the case of a daughter of
> a [deceased] son who shares with the brothers [i.e., her paternal
> uncles in the inheritance of her paternal grandfather], then will you
> say [thus] in the case of a daughter, who does not share with the [i.e.,
> her own] brothers [in the inheritance of their father]?
>
> (*t. Yad.* 1(2):20, ed. Zuckermandel)

All of the sources from Mishnah and Tosefta Yadayim are now at
hand. I initially discuss their literary-rhetorical and formal traits, in
context. Subsequently, I comment on their substance.

First, let me point out that *m. Yadayim* chapters 3 and 4 do not faith-
fully represent in several important ways the literary-rhetorical characteristics of more "normative" Mishnah chapters. (In this respect,
these chapters join several Mishnah-tractates, like Edduyot.) What is
the "norm" from which chapters 3 and 4 depart? Briefly stated, the
usual Mishnaic mode of constructing substantial compositions that
constitute a "chapter" (or a large element thereof) is to "spin out" various cases that together treat a defined topic. Normally, such a "chapter" or larger subdivision of a "chapter" continues to the point that
the underlying legal principles relevant to the topic emerge "induc-
tively," that is, via their application to a set of highly differentiated
hypothetical circumstances.[16] How does the extended composition in
m. Yadayim 3 and 4 differ? In *m. Yadayim* 3 and 4, that which unifies
larger subcompositions of the "chapter" is not topical coherence, but
that which was allegedly decided "on that [self-same] day" at *m.* 4:1
to 4:4 and the reported confrontations at 4:6 though 4:7b between

"Sadducees" and "Pharisees" over specific laws on quite disparate topics. Thus, while *m.* 4:6 through 4:7b (and *m.* 4:1–4:4, for that matter) is a kind of list (a typically Mishnaic enterprise), it is not organized in the manner more typically evident in Mishnaic list making, since the latter is generally organized topically.[17] (Moreover, *t. Yadayim* 1(2):20 simply serves to augment the Sadducees-versus-Pharisees triptych by one element, while *t.* 1(2):19 proffers an alternate text for part of the first triptych).

To emphasize further the foregoing points, let us excise 4:1–4 (the "on that [self same] day" passages) and 4:6–7b (the Sadducees-versus-Pharisees passages), as well as 4:8 (the "Galilean heretic" pericope) from the whole. What remains would be a more typically formulated, rather elegant, Mishnaic composition:

A. All holy Scriptures render the hands unclean.

B. [Among them] the Song of Songs and Ecclesiastes [which therefore also] render the hands unclean.

C. Rabbi Judah says: the Song of Songs renders the hands unclean, and [concerning] Ecclesiastes [there is] dispute.

D. Rabbi Yosé says: Ecclesiastes does not render the hands unclean, and [concerning] the Song of Songs [there is] dispute.

E. Rabbi Simeon says: Ecclesiastes is [the subject of] a lenient [ruling] of the House of Shammai, and is [the subject of] a stringent [ruling] of the House of Hillel.

F. Said Rabbi Simeon ben Azzai: I have a tradition directly from the seventy-two elders on that day that they seated Rabbi Eleazar ben Azariah in the Academy [as its president]—

G. that [both] the Song of Songs and Ecclesiastes render the hands unclean.

H. Said Rabbi 'Aqiba: Heaven forfend! No one in Israel disputes that

I. the Song of Songs renders the hands unclean,

J. for the whole world is not equal [in value] to the day that the Song of Songs was delivered to Israel,

K. for all of the Scriptures is [like] the Sanctuary, and the Song of Songs is [like] the Holy of Holies,

L. and if they disputed, they disputed only regarding Ecclesiastes.

M. Said Rabbi Yohanan ben Joshua, the son of the father-in-law of Rabbi 'Aqiba: In accordance with [the teaching of] Ben Azzai—so they voted and so they taught.

(*m. Yad.* 3:5b)

A. Aramaic [passages] (תרגום) that are in [the book of] Ezra [-Nehemiah] and that are in the [the book of] Daniel render the hands unclean.

B. Aramaic [passages] written in Hebrew,

C. And Hebrew [passages] written in Aramaic,

D. And [Scriptures written in] Hebrew script, do not render the hands unclean.

E. They [Scriptures] do not ever render [the hands] unclean, unless they shall be written in Assyrian script [i.e., the "square" Hebrew script in use since the Greco-Roman period], on parchment and in ink.

(m. Yad. 4:5)

With *m.* 4:1–4 and 4:6–8 gone, *m.* 3:5b–4:5 makes a reasonably well formulated Mishnaic composition. It begins with a general ruling, followed by an *on-topic* dispute and other attributed sayings (m. 3:5b Aff.) concerning the status of Ecclesiastes and Song of Songs. The series of attributed sayings at *m.* 3:5b E–M is perhaps more characteristic of Toseftan commentary on, or complement of, the Mishnah; however, they cohere well ad locum in Mishnah and are certainly dependent on *m.* 3:5b A–D. In our reconstructed version of the extended unit, the ruling of *m.* 3:5b A is again taken up and further explored at *m.* 4:5, which considers factors that might condition the application of the general ruling at *m.* 3:5b A. The whole ends with a second general ruling at *m.* 4:5E, which serves to make explicit the principle at work implicitly in the immediately preceding rulings (m. 4:5A–D) and which provides a complement to the general ruling that opened our reconstructed extended unit at *m.* 3:5b A.

The topical coherence and unity of this reconstructed "larger unit" is reinforced by the repetition of the same language in the legal apodases throughout: "render/do not render the hands unclean"—in all, a rather normal Mishnaic formulation. Moreover, the patterning at *m.* 3:5b B–C—

> Song of Songs, yes; Ecclesiastes, yes;
> Song of Songs, yes; Ecclestiastes, dispute;
> Ecclesiastes, no; Song of Songs, dispute—

is typical, even elegant, Mishnaic rhetorical patterning. So, too, is the patterning at 4:5:

> Aramaic in . . ., yes
> Aramaic in Hebrew, and
> Hebrew in Aramaic, and
> . . . in Hebrew Script, no.

All this being the case, it appears likely that *m.* 4:1–4 (the "on that self same day" section) was formulated independently of its current context and inserted between *m.* 3:5b plus 4:5 (our reconstructed larger unit); *m.* 4:1–4 breaks the unity and coherence of the latter and shows little dependency in substance or form on *m.* 3:5b plus 4:5.[18] Aside from the term "on . . . the day" (ביים), which, as previously noted, appears at several junctures in *m.* 4:1–4, only the language "and [so] they taught" (יגמרו) at the beginning of *m.* 4:1 reflects language in the preceding pericope—גמרו at the very end of *m.* 3:5b M. Hence, וגמרו probably constitutes an editorial effort to supply joining language for the otherwise disconnected collection of *m.* 4:1–4.

What now of our triptych, *m.* 4:6 through *m.* 4:7b, involving the Pharisees and the Sadducees? Was it too probably formulated elsewhere independently and merged with *m.* 3:5b plus *m.* 4:5? The evidence is more complex here than is the case with the "on that self same day" collection. The matter requires some extensive analysis of the formal, literary, and rhetorical characteristics of the three passages in the Mishnah, together with the two related passages in the Tosefta. To that analysis I now proceed.

Literary, Formal, and Rhetorical Traits

Certainly the first passage of the triptych (*m.* 4:6), presenting Yohanan's defense of the Pharisaic position on the uncleanness of the Scriptures against his Sadducean protagonists, appears on topic; the passage deals with the uncleanness of Holy Scriptures, the theme of *m.* 3:1b–4:5. Whether it was formulated for its current place with, and at the end of, *m.* 3:5b plus *m.* 4:5 is another matter, to which I will return after considering the second and third elements of the triptych.

Neither *m.* 4:7a nor *m.* 4:7b (nor, for that matter, the fourth element supplied by *t.* 1[2]:20) bear on the subject matter of *m.* 3:5b–4:5 (that which we deemed the coherent, typically Mishnaic larger unit). These second and third elements of the triptych (and the two related Tosefta passages) depend *solely* on *m.* 4:6 for some substantive, redactional, and literary context. The salient literary elements of *m.* 4:6 that provide that context are: (a) verbal confrontation between the Sadducees (or Boethusians) and Pharisees over law; (b) formulation as a kind of stylized debate; and (c) the language, "we cry out against you. . . ." In all, it seems reasonable that either the second and third elements of the triptych were formulated *with* the first element, or the second and third elements were *spun out* of the first, after which someone further spun out a fourth (provided at *t.* 1[2]:20). If the former is the case, all three elements, roughly as currently formulated, probably circulated independently, apart from (and maybe prior to the formulation of) the larger unit comprising *m.* 3:5b + 4:5. If the latter is the case, the triptych may or may not have circulated independently in its present formulation; one must withhold judgment until one considers whether the first element, *m.* 4:6 was expressly formulated for or with *m.* 3:5b + 4:5, on which subject matter *m.* 4:6 (and only *m.* 4:6 of the three elements of the triptych) bears. Therefore, let us examine more closely *m.* 4:6—Yohanan, on behalf of the Pharisees, *versus* the Sadducees.

First, in what typically Mishnaic (or early rabbinic) literary form, if any, is *m.* 4:6 cast? At first glance, *m.* 4:6 is a "debate":

> Say x to y, attack on y's position;
> Said y to x, attack on x's position;
> [x] said to him [y] plus reason for x's position;
> [y] said to them [x] plus reason for y's position.

But by Mishnaic (or Toseftan) standards, *m.* 4:6 is a very peculiar debate, both in form and content.

First, in the Mishnah, debates follow disputes and depend on them in literary and substantive ways. In the Tosefta, the same is true, although often Toseftan debates depend on disputes in the Mishnah. *Where is* the formalized dispute for which *m.* 4:6 supplies the formalized debate? Nowhere in the Mishnah (or in the Tosefta)! *What is* the substance of the missing formalized dispute that the debating parties at *m.* 4:6 attack and defend in turn? It is not certain! Is it that the Pharisees and Sadducees disagree about whether Holy Scriptures render the hands unclean, or is it that they disagree about whether the pagan books about pagan gods (like the books of Homer) should render the hands unclean (like an artifact of a pagan cult)? In light of the context of *m.* 3:5b + 4:1, the entire interpretive tradition of rabbinic literature assumes the inferred existence of a dispute about the former; and this is, of course, the most reasonable choice. But the fact remains that the debate itself has no clear dispute as its referent, leaving the issue of the dispute somewhat undefined. Indeed, one could read *t.* 1(2):19's provision of alternative language for *m.* 4:6D, as someone's attempt to conclude the debate in a manner that more clearly makes the uncleanness of Scriptures the topic of the missing dispute. How so? By eliminating any reference to the books of Homer in Yohanan's culminating argument, intended to be the *coup de grâce* of the debate, matters are focused solely on the uncleanness of Scriptures.

Second, the opening attributional formula, "say" (a present particle), is not typical of debates in the Mishnah or Tosefta. Typically it should be "said" (in the perfect), as it is in the rest of the pericope from B through D. Why the present participle in A (as well as in *m.* 4:7a A and B and *m.* 4:7b A)? Because there is no dispute for which *m.* 4:6 is the debate (and *mutatis mutandis* for *m.* 4:7a and *m.* 4:7b). The present particle, however, is used in disputes. Some formulator or redactor, then, has used the present participle rather than the perfect to make literary allowance for the missing dispute(s); *m.* 4:6A thus is transformed into a poor second-rate substitute for a dispute (which it is not), so that the remainder of the "debate" can follow. And the same may be said for the use of "say" in the present particle at *m.* 4:7a A and B and *m.* 4:7b A. (However *m.* 4:7a, as will be discussed below, is neither a dispute nor a debate, but some poor hybrid form between the two.)

Third, the content of the "debate" at *m.* 4:6 is quite atypical for debates in Mishnah or Tosefta. Typically in debates, formulators attribute to the named authorities in an antecedent dispute a truncated *reasoned argument* in support of their own position or against the view of the opposing authority, producing a debate of two lemmas in length. In addition, longer debates may be formulated by attributing additionally a reasoned rebuttal to each named authority's initial reasoned argument—adding two more lemmas to the stylized debate. What tends to count as reasoned arguments may include: appeals to scriptural law; appeals to analogy; or arguments as to why an analogy is inappropriate; arguments *a fortiori*; or *a miniori.* *m.* 4:6 proffers very poor arguments by Mishnaic or Toseftan conventions; indeed, by these conventions, these are not valid forms of argument at all. Rather they are rhetorical jibes more than arguments. For example, Yohanan's retort at B, challenging the Sadducees for not further criticizing what "they say" about the bones of human dead in contrast to the bones of unclean animals, is neither a rebuttal of the adversaries' view nor a defense of the Pharisaic one. And since it is scriptural law that human bones are unclean, C's response to B is equally bizarre. Rather, C simply "sets the stage" for D's rebuttal, itself a poor legal argument by early rabbinic standards.

Because the content of *m.* 4:6 accords with the formal requisites of neither a dispute nor a debate in the Mishnah or Tosefta, it is important to note that the Qumran fragments designated 4QMMT expressly deal with the issues raised at *m.* 4:6B, the "setting of the stage" attributed to Yohanan. For example, lines 24–35 of the composite text of 4QMMT from Strugnell and Qimron read: "And also concerning the hid[es and the bones of unclean animals; they shall not make] [from their bones] and from their hides, handles of ves[sels]." The context is the maintenance of purity; such handles would render the vessels unclean. Similarly, the issue of human bones being brought into the Temple appears at lines 43–44. Clearly, these topics were matters of concern in Qumran legal texts, and this well before the authorship of the Mishnah or the Tosefta.

Fourth, the language at the beginning of A ("We cry out against you . . ., for you say") is not part of the repertory of formularies in either disputes or debates in Mishnah or Tosefta. So, too, B's "And have we not more against . . . but this alone?" Again, these are rhetorical jibes and are atypical of Mishnaic rhetorical formulations.

Turning briefly now to the literary-formal traits of *m.* 4:7a, it has the look of neither a dispute nor a debate, although it tries "to pass" as something of both. B is clearly meant as some sort of counter to A (another poorly conceived debate lemma), not just the statement of the opposing legal view (as one would find in a dispute). And the attributional formulas (x say[s], y say[s]) in the present participial form gives it the flavor of a dispute, which it is not, because two opposing legal views are not juxtaposed. Again, we have the use of the nonstandard rhetorical harangue "we cry out against you," language that now provides much of the literary coherence and unity of *m. Yadayim* 4:6 through 4:7b (plus the complementary element provided by *t.* 1[2]:20). Finally these, too, are not bona fide arguments by the early rabbinic standards of formalized legal rhetoric, either in form or substance. As before, 4QMMT (lines 57–61 of the composite text) offers a parallel, articulating precisely the view that opposes the position attributed by 4.7a A to the Pharisees. Once more, we are confronted with matters seemingly at issue in Qumran legal texts produced considerably before the Mishnah and Tosefta.

As to the literary and formal characteristics of *m.* 4:7b, again we have a "debate" without a dispute as in *m.* 4:6, with the attributional formula at A in the present participial form compensating for the dispute's absence. And again, we have the rhetorical harangue, "we cry out against you," at A, providing the link to the preceding pericopes. However, *m.* 4:7b is to be distinguished from the preceding passage in one important respect: the reasoned arguments from analogy and *a fortiori* at A and B fall well within the norm of what is standard and typical rhetorical form for debates in the Mishnah and Tosefta.

In formal-literary terms, *t.* 1(2):20, the complementary fourth element proffered in the Tosefta, seems closely modeled on *m.* 4:7b. However, the legal content is bizarre, since the legal position being "argued" by the Boethusians (Sadducees) is counter to the biblical law, and the "argument" by analogy and *a fortiori* in B essentially restates biblical law. Surely, all that would be required in B is to appeal to Scripture, a trump card that far outweighs any such arguments. Hence, the Boethusians (Sadducees) at A are provided with a straw-man position that the Pharisees at B knock down with a contrived, superfluous argument (since reference to scriptural law would suffice). Thus it is clear that the pericope is expressly constructed in order to model *m.* 4:7b, because the modes of argument in *m.* 4:7b are entirely inappropriate to the case at hand in *t.* 1(2):20. Indeed, the case itself, as presented in the saying attributed to the Boethusians, is trite, as it has no legal weight; the saying simply serves the rhetorical purposes of the formulator of the pericope.

In light of the above, what may be said of the literary and redactional history of the elements of the Mishnah's triptych on Pharisees and Sadducees and of the two related Toseftan passages?

First, *t.* 1(2):19 is an attempt to redirect or focus *m.* 4:6 on the issue of the uncleanness of Scriptures. By so doing, it clarifies ambiguities around the topic of the inferred (but missing) "dispute" logically underlying *m.* 4:6, and it helps cement *m.* 4:6 to the topical theme of the larger and more coherent and unified unit comprising *m.* 3:5b + 4:5. Consequently, the formulator of *t.* 1(2):19 probably cast this Toseftan passage with *m.* 4:6 in hand and in all likelihood with *m.* 4:6 in its current locus, appended to *m.* 3:5b + 4:5. Since 3:5b + 4:5 exhibits literary and rhetorical traits fairly typical of those who created the Mishnah's "chapters," and since these "chapters" have been demonstrated by Neusner to be the work of the penultimate redactors/formulators of Mishnah,[19] *t.* 1(2):19 likely postdates the latter's work.

Second, *t.* 1(2):20 seems expressly modeled on *m.* 4:7b. The Toseftan passage mimics literary-rhetorical traits of the latter to a tee, using precisely the same form of argumentation, which, while poorly conceived in substance, is in rhetorical form an excellent example of what would be found in a typical Mishnaic or Toseftan debate—except for the lack of a dispute and the language "we cry out against you. . . ." Whoever formulated *m.* 4:7b likely did not formulate or know *t.* 1(2):20, since they otherwise could have circulated as a matched pair, and it appears that they did not. In that instance, both would have been placed in *m. Yadayim* 4. In sum, *t.* 1(2):20 was probably formulated later than *m.* 4:7b, and was likely unknown to whatever redactor placed *m.* 4:7b in its current locus. Finally, the formulator of *t.* 1(2):20 was intimately familiar with proper rhetorical-formal conventions for arguments in Mishnaic or Toseftan debates. For these reasons, I believe, again, that we are dealing with a source formulated no earlier than the end of the second century CE or the first few decades of the third century, and in any case later than *m.* 4:7b's formulation and placement in its current redactional context in *m. Yadayim* 4.

Third, as noted, the formulator of *m.* 4:7b was well versed in the standard rhetorical forms for lemmas in debates in the Mishnah and (especially) the Tosefta. In this particular respect, *m.* 4:7b differs distinctively from *m.* 4:7a and *m.* 4:6, on which it depends ad locum for an intelligible context. Consequently, it is unlikely that the formulator of 4:7b, so knowledgeable of proper Mishnaic-Toseftan rhetorical form for debate lemmas, was the formulator of 4:6 or 4:7a, both of which exhibit little concern (or knowledge) of proper form. Hence, I lean heavily toward *m.* 4:7b having been formulated later than, and having been spun out of, *m.* 4:6 and *m.* 4:7a. Since it is difficult to say when "standard" rhetorical forms for debate lemmas took hold in early rabbinic literary circles, the formulation of *m.* 4:7b is hard to date. While I believe that a date no earlier than near the end of the second century is preferable, I must admit that this is because I believe

that the use of "standardized" or normative literary-rhetorical conventions for the formulation of early rabbinic materials took hold
during and as a result of the penultimate stages of the Mishnah's
redaction. In any case, the polemical-rhetorical refrain "we cry out
against you . . ." and the juxtaposition of Sadducees and Pharisees
from *m.* 4:6 and 4:7a have been blended by the formulator of *m.* 4:7b
with otherwise good Mishnaic-Toseftan debate form at *m.* 4:7b A and
B to produce the spun-out, third element of the triptych and to unify
the resulting pericope with the first two, *m.* 4:6 and 4:7a.

Fourth, *m.* 4:7a either is spun out of *m.* 4:6 or has been formulated
with it. In either case, the formulator of *m.* 4:7a does not use standard
rhetorical form or modes of argument in this debate of sorts. As in *m.*
4:6, on which *m.* 4:7b depends both for context and literary-rhetorical
traits, the polemical-rhetorical refrain "we cry out against you," and
the juxtaposition of attributions to Sadducees and Pharisees form the
structural edifice of the pericope. I am particularly struck by the fact
that *m.* 4:7b's mode of argument, which as noted is quite atypical of
both the Mishnah and Tosefta, is identical to that in *m.* 4:6 A and B.
Indeed, without C and D of *m.* 4:6, *m.* 4:6 and 4:7b would form a reasonably matched doublet. And I am inclined, therefore, to see some
version of such a doublet as having circulated apart from the larger
extended, typically-Mishnaic composition comprising *m.* 3:5b + 4:5.
Assuming that the first element of the doublet (now *m.* 4:6) had anything at all to do with the uncleanness of Holy Scriptures, only a light
touch-up of language would have been required to join *m.* 4:6 to the
extended unit *m.* 3:5b + 4:5: "Holy Scriptures" and "render the hands
unclean" would have had to be substituted for any other similar terms,
if other language was present in the first place. (Indeed, at other junctures in *m.* 4:6, simply "is/are unclean" and "is/are clean" appear,
rather than "render the hands unclean.") Finally, the fact the modes
of argument and the literary-rhetorical traits exhibited in these so-
called "debates" are atypical of either the Mishnah or Tosefta may
mean one of several things: the pericopes may have been formulated
prior to the emergence of standard Mishnaic and Toseftan literary and
rhetorical conventions in those early rabbinic circles which ultimately
produced and promulgated Mishnah and Toseftan materials; or the
pericopes may have origins in literary circles outside of those specifically responsible for the penultimate formulation of Mishnah and

Tosefta. Whether one or the other, some of the literary circles involved seem to have been "cousins" of those responsible for the Mishnah and Toseftan materials, given that *m.* 4:6 and 4:7a come at some point in the processes of transmission and formulation to exhibit literary-rhetorical traits at least comparable to those of more-standard passages in the Mishnah and Tosefta.

Substance

Over the course of discussing the literary context and traits of the five passages in *m.* and *t. Yadayim* in which Pharisees and Sadducees are juxtaposed, I have already had occasion to remark on the legal substance of these sources. Now I concentrate specifically on these passages' content.[20] What, if anything, do they portray, or seek to project on the protagonists, of the substantive issues by which the Sadducees and the Pharisees constructed in apposition to one another their respective group identities?

M. 4:6, in its current context, portrays a divide on the matter of the uncleanness of Holy Scriptures; Yohanan ben Zakkai, acting for the Pharisees, defends the position that, as we know from *m.* 3:5b + 4:1, is Mishnaic-rabbinic law. (Perhaps in some other context the passage could be read as a disagreement about the uncleanness of books referring to pagan gods, that is, as documentary artifacts of foreign worship. But this is highly speculative and not worth further discussion.) Presumably, the retort at B is effective, because the formulators understand that both parties agree that the bones of an ass are clean, while those of a human corpse are unclean—basically the position of scriptural law.[21] 4QMMT agrees with this position, as one would expect, but takes the view that the bones of an unclean animal are also unclean, which is the contrary position of Yohanan's "they." Moreover, the Pharisaic (rabbinic) position on the uncleanness of Holy Writ has no basis in biblical legislation and cannot be grounded in any of the legal principles of Mishnaic purity law.[22] More to the point, I cannot discern *any* grand and defining legal, philosophical, theological, or programmatic principles that may lie at the heart of the alleged divide between the Pharisees and Sadducees at *m.* 4:6.[23] The parties disagree on a point of law—no more no less—and, as already noted, the "arguments" are weak in bona fide legal reasoning.

In light of the foregoing, it is clear that the heart and substance of *m.* 4:6 is simply the portrayal of Yohanan's rhetorical (as opposed to legal) prowess at besting the Sadducees in the latter's challenges of Pharisaic law. Moreover, this is about the clearest and most explicit expression in early rabbinic literature of the early rabbinic claim to be allied with Pharisaic legal positions over against Sadducean ones; after all, it is Rabban Yohanan ben Zakkai, not some anonymous Pharisee, who is depicted as defending the Pharisees. Indeed, for all intents and purposes *m.* 4:6 identifies Yohanan himself as a Pharisee.

Much of what has been said of *m.* 4:6 holds for *m.* 4:7a. Each group is portrayed as simply haranguing the other for what is viewed by the other as a patently ridiculous legal stance, again on the topic of uncleanness. What is attributed to the Sadducees at A is a statement of alleged Pharisaic law that to the Sadducees is seemingly counter-intuitive. Again, 4QMMT sides with the Mishnah's Sadducees. *M.* 4:7a B's Pharisees counter in kind. Again, what is portrayed as Pharisaic law at A is found elsewhere in Mishnah law at *m. Makhshirin* 5:9 (see also *m. Parah* 3:7): "Any uninterrupted flow of liquid [flowing from a clean to an unclean vessel] is clean, except. . . ." Thus, the link between Pharisaic law and early rabbinic law is not as explicitly made in *m.* 4:7a as it was in *m.* 4:6, for which the correlative rabbinic position appears in immediately antecedent passages.

The legal position represented as Pharisaic in *m.* 4:7a A and reflected in Mishnaic law at *m. Makhshirin* 5:9 is that the stream of liquid flowing from the top (clean) vessel to the lower (unclean) one does not serve as a connection for the transmission of uncleanness to the top vessel. The rejoinder attributed to the Pharisees at B is, as in *m.* 4:6 B, a legal position supposedly shared by *both* the Pharisees and Sadducees. More to the point, it is a legal position that is as equally counterintuitive as the Pharisees' position decried by the Sadducees at A. Again as in *m.* 4:6 B, the legal position at *m.* 4:7a B is scriptural law.[24] Consequently, the force of the retort is that the seemingly counterintuitive Pharisaic legal position (A) is no more or less counterintuitive than scriptural law shared by both groups—a rhetorical parry that once more is a rather weak legal defense of the position attributed to the Pharisees at A. Finally, as in *m.* 4:6, no grand, overarching legal, theological, philosophical, or programmatic differences between the Sadducees and Pharisees seem at play. Rather, the groups disagree on a point of law, period.

With *m.* 4:7b, as noted earlier, we have bona fide Mishnaic-Toseftan debate argument, from which we must reconstruct the assumed legal positions of the groups. *M.* 4:7b A assumes that the Pharisees do not hold a master responsible for damage done by servants to another's property; presumably the position of the Sadducees of *m.* 4:7b is that the master is liable. As to the analogy to damage done to another's property by one's livestock, A's Sadducees promote the analogy, on the grounds that a master is responsible for ensuring that certain Israelite laws are observed by his servants; for example, one must see to the circumcision of one's male servants (Gen 17:12) and ensure that servants observe the rites of Passover (Exod 12:44). This "greater" responsibility for one's servants as members of an Israelite household is the basis for the argument *a fortiori*. Pharisees argue that the analogy is inappropriate based on practical considerations: you hand over to disgruntled servants an effective means of seeking fiscal revenge on their master. (The last sentence of B makes this explicit. But without the last sentence, B makes a nice formal match for A, and provides sufficient formal reasoning in itself by Mishnaic and Toseftan standards of formal rhetoric and argument.)

Once again, it is difficult to discern distinct and opposing grand, overarching legal or theological programs that underlie the Pharisaic and Sadducean positions. Scripture is clear on one's responsibility for damage done to another's property or person by one's livestock (see Exod 21:28ff.) but is silent concerning damage done to another's property by one's servants. If anything, it is the position attributed here to the Sadducees that ramifies biblical law,[25] and the alleged Pharisaic position that remains with the scriptural position proper. However, once more there is insufficient warrant for interpreting the debate before us as having to do with distinct and differing principles concerning the nature and use of scriptural law versus extrabiblical extensions or complements of biblical legislation. The parties are portrayed as differing on a point of law; they are presumed to share biblical legislation; and the Pharisees rhetorically best the Sadducees in debate, this time both parties proffering "proper" modes of Mishnaic-Toseftan argument.

As stated, *t.* 1(2):20 is a literary-rhetorical match for *m.* 4:7b, from which it was probably spun out. As to substance, the position attributed to the Pharisees appears to accord with biblical law, while that attributed to the Sadducees would seem to contravene scriptural legislation. Moreover, the allegedly Pharisaic position here accords with the early rabbinic position as given in *m. B.B.* 8:2. Numbers 27:8 states: "If a man dies, and has no son, then you shall pass his inheritance to his daughter." In other words, sons have prior right of inheritance, and daughters inherit nothing unless the deceased has no sons. *m. B.B.* 8:2 extrapolates: "the son precedes the daughter, and all of the son's offspring precede the daughter." As one can readily see, the seemingly *a fortiori* argument at *t.* 1(2):20 B is no such thing; it is really a restatement in *a fortiori* language of the ruling in *m. B.B.* Again, no grand principles are in evidence differentiating the Sadducees and Pharisees. The Tosefta represents them as differing on a point of law, and here the Pharisees, not the Sadducees, appear to adhere more closely to biblical legislation.

Finally, as to *t.* 1(2):19, there is no discussion to be had about its legal content; it is, as already noted, simply a redirected version of the "argument" at *m.* 4:6 D.

Tosefta-Tractate Hagigah 3:35

In the Mishnah and Tosefta, one other passage juxtaposes "Pharisees" and "Sadducees," *t. Hag.* 3:35b; consequently, we turn to it next, in context.

Literary Context

The immediate literary context of *t. Hag.* 3:35b seems not to be *t.* 3:35a (as implied by the versification in the Erfurt and Vienna MSS.), but *m. Hag.* 3:8:

    A. How do they move[26] [the Temple paraphernalia for immersion] with respect to (*'l*) [maintaining] the cleanness of the [Temple] court?

    B. They immerse the vessels that were in the Sanctuary,

    C. and they say to them [i.e., those who move the vessels suspected of being unclean]: Be warned, [so] that you do not (*šl'*) touch the Table

[of the show bread] and the menorah [the seven branched cande-
labra, and so make them suspect of being unclean in the process of
removing other vessels for immersion.]

D. All of the vessels that were in the Sanctuary had second and third
    [standby copies],
E. so that if the first [set] were rendered unclean, they would bring the
    seconds.
F. All of the vessels that were in the Sanctuary are subject to immer-
    sion,
G. except the Altar of Gold and the Altar of Bronze,
H. because they are affixed to the ground, the words of R. Eliezer.
I. But (w) the sages say: Because they are plated [in gold and bronze]

                                                            (m. Hag. 3:8)

t. Hag. 3:35b complements m. 3:8 with the following text:

A. (m'śh w, wm'śh š in Erfurt) They [the Pharisees] immersed the meno-
    rah [on a festival day: missing in Erfurt, London, and Genizah frgs.].
B. And the Sadducees used to say: Come and see the Pharisees, who are
    immersing the 'light of the moon' [the menorah].

                                                        (t. Hag. 3:35b)[27]

Logically speaking, t. Hag. 3:35b glosses m. 3:8 by providing a supporting "precedent narrative." The Mishnah at 3:8 C has Temple workers warned not to render unclean other vessels in the Sanctuary, when
removing those requiring immersion, and m. 3:8F–G maintains that
all utensils and vessels in the Temple, with the exceptions of the altars
of bronze and of gold, are susceptible to uncleanness and consequently require immersion, if they are suspected of having become
unclean. t. Hag 3:35b A proffers that the anonymous "they" (paralleling, in a sense, the anonymous "them" of m. 3:8 C) immersed the
menorah on a particular occasion, supporting m. 3:8.[28] Section B of t.
Hag. 3:35b makes the focus of the pericope a confrontation of sorts
between the Pharisees and the Sadducees; the Sadducees take issue
with, indeed ridicule, Pharisaic practice (which itself is consonant
with Mishnaic law as given in m. 3:8).

Literary, Formal, and Rhetorical Traits

It is precisely the literary relation of sections A and B of t. Hag. 3:35b
that require further discussion. Section A, and section A alone, introduced by the stock formulary m'śh w (wm'śh š in the Erfurt MS), pro-

vides the "precedent narrative" for the Mishnaic ruling at *m.* 3:8. In light of the normal literary, formal, and rhetorical traits for precedent narratives in earliest rabbinic literature, section B of *t. Hag.* 3:35b adds little or nothing to the narrative's force as legal precedent. (In fact, it detracts.) In order better to assess the source at hand, permit me some remarks about the more typically structured precedent narrative in earliest rabbinic literature.

Short precedent narratives appear from time to time in both the Mishnah and the Tosefta. However, they are more frequent in Tosefta. Typically, the force of the precedent presented in a narrative derives from the authority of the rabbinic figure or figures who appear in the narrative as validating, or acting in a manner that corroborates, a particular legal ruling given in the Tosefta or the Mishnah passage for which the Toseftan passage provides some comment or complement. Thus, in a typical precedent story we would find:[29]

> A. *m'sh w, wm'sh s̆:* such and such happened (or such and such circumstances arose),
> B. and Rabbi x (or the sages) ruled (or acted) in such and such a way;
> or
> A. *m'sh b:* rabbi(s) x(y and z),
> B. who (s̆) were in such and such circumstances,
> C. did/ruled in such and such a way.

Viewed in light of these more typically formulated early rabbinic precedent stories, *t. Hag.* 3:35b is an oddity. Section A has no named rabbinic figure(s) or even the anonymous "sages" as the required authoritative *dramatis personae*. Instead, we have a "precedent story" the force of which is borne by a third-person plural verb, giving us the anonymous "they" as the actors. It is, then, section B that identifies A's "they" as, or turns A's "they" into, Pharisees. Again, in section B, no named rabbinic figure or the anonymous "sages" validate the state of affairs in A. While the Mishnah (and Tosefta) periodically represent rabbinic law as in continuity with Pharisaic teaching and practice (our pericope being perhaps such a case), *t. Hag.* 3:35b appears an oddity in formal literary-rhetorical terms as an early rabbinic precedent story. Moreover, it is difficult to see in the language before us such a typically formulated early rabbinic precedent story that has been "doctored." In fact, the opposite seems the case; it is the introductory formulary, *m'sh w/wmˤsh ̌s*, at the outset of A, that the pericope into a (poorly conceived) precedent story.

If *t. Ḥag.* 3:35b is not a (typical) precedent story by early rabbinic literary-rhetorical standards, what is (or was) it? The verb forms in sections A and B may provide some limited indication. Section A uses the perfect tense (they immersed), bespeaking of a particular instance. Section B uses a perfect progressive form (and the Sadducees used to say), conveying the sense of a commonly repeated event. These two verb forms do not fit well together in the current pericope. Either sections A and B were not formulated as one unit or one of the verb tenses has been modified. The former option is difficult to defend, since B is meaningless on its own. B has to be a response to something and there is no evidence in hand suggesting that it might originally have been a response to something other than A. As to the verb form of A having been modified, this seems more likely since the perfect tense more easily follows the formulary *mˤsh w*. Perhaps, then, section A has been modified—the language having been "picked up" from *m.* 3:8B *(mtbylyn)*— when the pericope (A + B) was adapted to serve as an early rabbinic precedent story.

Under this last-mentioned scenario, section A of *t. Ḥag.* 3:35b would have originally had other language, language more suitable to the current formulation of section B. Section B's "Pharisees" might not have appeared from seemingly nowhere, as they do in the current formulation. Alas, no parallel provides any basis for reconstructing the language of such a story. We are left with the remains of a doctored story, modified to function as Mishnaic-Toseftan precedent narrative, of which it remains a shabby example by the literary-rhetorical norms for such precedent narratives.

Substance

It is difficult to ascertain from *t. Ḥag.* 3:35b what legally is at issue between the Pharisees and Sadducees in the narrative at hand. Presumably both Pharisees and Sadducees had rules about maintaining Temple purity in general and maintaining the Temple's paraphernalia in the requisite state of cleanness. The "precedent story" plays on the notion that their rules differed in specific respects. Since rabbinic law as reflected in *m. Ḥag.* 3:8 posits that some Temple objects were not susceptible to uncleanness—in the Mishnah pericope at hand, the altars of gold and of bronze, either because they are permanently affixed to the earth (which dissipates uncleanness) or because they are plated—it is understandable that Pharisees and Sadducees may well have differed about which classes of objects could or could not contract uncleanness and about the principles that determined these matters. However, what we have in *t. Hag.* 3:35b provides no basis for surmising what differing principles were at play in the *portrayed* distinction between the Pharisees and Sadducees on the uncleanness of the menorah. The story in its current formulation is based in the recognition that what was obvious for the Pharisees with respect to the menorah in particular was obviously ridiculous for the Sadducees. We are left completely in the dark about underlying legal matters.[30]

Even more curious about *t. Hag.* 3:35b's substance is that the Sadducees seem to get the last say, the last laugh, as it were. Nothing rebuts their ridiculing of the Pharisaic practice of immersing the menorah. Who in rabbinic circles would formulate or circulate such a story as is? Again, I am left with the impression that an earlier (perhaps more complete) version has been lost and that what we have in hand is some doctored snippet of it modified to function as a short "precedent narrative" for *m. Hag.* 3:8. What in the end seems important is that the Toseftan authors/editors exploited an opportunity to support a Mishnaic ruling by appealing to Pharisaic tradition, thus portraying rabbinic law in this instance as having a Pharisaic heritage. In this respect, *t. Hag.* 3:35b resembles in motive *m. Yadayim*'s appending of the Pharisees/Yohanan vs. Sadducees "debate" about the uncleanness of Scriptures to the antecedent Mishnaic rulings about the same. What we do not see in *t. Hag.* 3:35b is any concern to give the Pharisees that last definitive say or act in their confrontation with the Sadducees.

Two Questionable Passages in Tosefta-Tractates Yoma 1:8 and Niddah 5:3

Two other passages in the Tosefta, *t. Yoma* 1:8 and *t. Nid.* 5:3, have usually been included among those sources which portray Sadducees (or Boethusians) in juxtaposition with Pharisees, despite the fact that *in neither of these two passages (nor in t. Yoma 1:8's parallel passage in the Yerushalmi, y. Yoma 1:5) do Pharisees appear.* Why? Their parallels in the Babylonian Talmud (at *b. Yoma* 19b and *b. Nid.* 33b respectively) refer to Pharisees and Sadducees, where the Toseftan texts (and *y. Yoma* 1:5) juxtapose "[the] sages" and the Sadducees. However, there is no warrant for claiming that the parallels in the Babylonian Talmud (ca. late sixth century) preserve the "original" language of the Toseftan passages. Consequently, I do not undertake in this chapter the presentation and detailed analyses of *t. Yoma* 1:8 or *t. Nid.* 5:3.[31] Rather, I restrict myself to some summary remarks, which follow.

All the passages concerned are prefaced by the formularies that introduce "precedent stories—that is, some version or another of *m'śh b* (itself preceded in B. by *tnw rbnn*). The authors/editors of both *t. Yoma* 1:8 and *t. Nid.* 5:3 wish to portray the Sadducees as subject to the rulings of the (pre-70 CE) anonymous "sages" with respect to the conduct of the Temple service and the laws of menstrual uncleanness as they pertain to the wives of Temple priests, some of whom they portray as Sadducees. Moreover, these same "sages" stand in continuity with those authorities from whom Mishnaic law stems. Indeed, in neither *m. Nid.* nor *m. Yoma ad locum* do "Pharisees" appear. In general, the Mishnah projects a view of Temple and priestly practice in which pre-70 proto-rabbinic "sages" tell priests what to do. Our two Toseftan passages, in fact, reflect the Mishnah's *tendenz* in this regard. The editors/authors of the two *beraitot* in B., by contrast, wish to portray Pharisees as the specific group acting as protagonists with respect to Saducean practice among the Temple priesthood. The *beraitot* serve as well to identify the Mishnah's pre-70 proto-rabbinic "sages" with the Pharisees.

As to the legal content of the two Toseftan passages, *t. Yoma* 1:8 portrays the Sadducees as having a different version than the "sages" ("Pharisees" in *b. Yoma* 19b) of the rite for purifying the Holy of Holies on the Day of Atonement. The distinction is founded on different exegeses of the same biblical verse (Lev 16:13). *T. Nid.* 5:3 assumes that the Sadducees' manner of determining when a woman is free of menstrual uncleanness differs from the norms of the "sages" ("Pharisees" in *b. Nid.* 33b) for the same. Again the topical context is priestly practice. *t. Yoma* 1:8, finally, adduces the death of the Sadducean high priest as divine indication of the falsity of their position. In this, the author of the story merely follows Scripture for a conclusion to the story, since Leviticus 16:13 states explicitly that if and only if the rite in question is done properly by the high priest, ". . . he will not die."

DISCUSSION AND CONCLUSIONS

What now may be said of the body of evidence at hand?[32] First, I begin with legal content. Passages in the Mishnah and Tosefta in which Sadducees and Pharisees appear in juxtaposition portray these groups as differing on specific laws. Topically, the passages deal with purity, Temple practice, inheritance, and damages. While purity predominates, the fact that we have so few sources makes such an observation insignificant. Perhaps, given the paucity of the sources, it is the range of topics that is the more significant observation.

Second, one cannot induce from these passages any overarching general principles or programs with respect to law or the interpretation of Scripture that help define the Sadducees or Pharisees as groups and that inform their specific legal positions.[33] Nothing that we have seen bespeaks of some general, principled disagreement over "oral law" (= Pharisees) versus "predominantly or exclusively written scriptural law" (= Sadducees) or over more literal/plain sense (= Sadducees) versus less literal (= Pharisees) approaches to scriptural interpretation. Indeed, in *t. Yad.* 2:20 it is the Pharisaic position that represents scriptural law (Num 27:8) and the Sadducean position that departs from the plain sense of Scripture. H. Albeck[34] notes that the Sadducean position portrayed in *t. Yad.* 2:20 more closely reflects Hellenistic legal practice, but this does not provide sufficient evidence to say that Sadducees are understood in the Mishnah and Tosefta as Hellenizers and Pharisees as leaders of the resistance to Hellenization. (Indeed, if consistency with or outright dependency on Hellenistic or Roman law in individual legal rulings were an indicator of advocating Hellenization, the authors of the Mishnah could be deemed a pro-Hellenization party, since the Mishnah often reflects the influence of Greco-Roman law.)

Third, the portrayed Pharisaic legal position in every instance examined coincides with early rabbinic law as attested to *ad locum* or elsewhere in the Mishnah or Tosefta. However, one must be cautious in drawing inferences from this observation. Does the evidence at hand reflect rabbinic dependence in these particular instances on Pharisaic law? This we cannot say, even if we cannot rule it out. Why? Because we do not have a body of Pharisaic law—that is, from the Pharisees themselves—to which we can compare Mishnaic law. Consequently, in evidence such as that before us, we cannot distinguish instances when Mishnaic law may reflect antecedent pharisaic positions from occasions when early rabbinic authors/editors have projected Mishnaic law on the Pharisees so as to represent the latter as their legal predecessors. If one posits that the early rabbinic movement either had a particular historical affinity with the pre-70 Pharisees or wished to lay claim to such an affinity, then both reliance on Pharisaic law and projection of rabbinic law on Pharisees is to be equally expected. Moreover, it is in the specific interests of the authors/editors of early rabbinic literature to mask whether one or the other process has occurred. We can only hope that sometimes they will clearly fail, and we will discern it. Such is not the case, however, with the particular body of evidence under consideration.

Therefore, in the end, we can say only that the authors/editors of the Mishnah and in particular the Tosefta exhibit a strong tendency to represent Mishnaic law as consistent with (allegedly earlier) Pharisaic positions. Indeed, when early rabbinic authors/editors use the introductory formulary for a "precedent story" (*m'śh b* or any of its variants), they are making explicit the claim that Pharisaic practice or rulings proffer authoritative warrant for rabbinic practice or rulings. Finally, in these regards, the representation of Rabban Yohanan ben Zakkai as a chief protagonist on behalf of the Pharisees in debate with the Sadducees makes this claim of especial affinity between the early rabbis and the Pharisees with particular dramatic force.

Fourth, near the outset of this chapter, I stressed the degree to which the authors\editors of the Mishnah (in particular) and the Tosefta formulated their materials in accordance with well-defined formal, literary, and rhetorical conventions. Throughout my analyses of the passages under discussion, I have systematically commented on their formal, literary and rhetorical traits, measuring them against these well-defined conventions. In almost all cases, the passages analyzed have proven to be quite poor exemplars of these conventions.

For example, we have seen debates that are not really debates by the standards of the Mishnah and Tosefta. Our evidence includes "precedent stories" that are not well constructed or well conceived in comparison with the norms for the same. And, in the case of the passages in *m. Yadayim* (the bulk of our evidence), we have seen a poorly constructed Mishnah "chapter," which without our materials (and without the "on that self-same day" materials), would have otherwise been a typical and elegant exemplar of such a chapter.

The modes of argument in evidence in many of our passages look superficially like conventional modes of argument in the Mishnah and Tosefta. In reality, they depart significantly from convention and have virtually no persuasive power by early rabbinic conventions for argument. Rather, many of the passages are fraught with argument that amounts to rhetoric (in the common sense of the term) and polemic, again not the literary and formal norms for the Mishnah and Tosefta.

It is difficult, therefore, to see how those authorship circles responsible for the formulation of the language of the Mishnah and of so much of the Tosefta could also have formulated the language of those passages analyzed in this chapter. I am left with the strong impression that the language formulated in other circles (perhaps also early rabbinic circles) has been touched up by those responsible for the penultimate editing of the Mishnah and Tosefta for inclusion in these latter works. Thus, we have poor exemplars of debate form or of precedent stories, rather than materials which make no pretence at being a Mishnaic or Toseftan debate or precedent story. Another way of putting matters is that our passages seem to be only partially "digested" by the authorship processes responsible for the lion's share of the language, formulations, and compositions of the Mishnah and Tosefta in comparison with other antecedent traditions that these authors may have had in hand.

Since we have no well-substantiated model for, or historical reconstruction of, *how* the authors of the Mishnah and Tosefta *generally* worked and with *what* antecedent source materials, it is difficult to interpret the significance of the foregoing observations. We have no such models because (a) generally speaking these authors'/editors' (re)formulation of language in accordance with their conventions is so thorough that we cannot discern what they possessed,[35] and (b) no independent body of their source materials exists.[36] All we can say with respect to the passages analyzed here is that something different has happened. Perhaps our materials arrived in the hands of the authors/editors of the Mishnah and Tosefta at a different stage in their work, and/or in a different literary state exhibiting other formal and literary conventions, and/or from different tradent circles than was generally the case. To say much more would amount to heaping conjecture on top of speculation. Nevertheless, the "odd" formal, rhetorical and literary traits of our materials bespeak some specific provenance outside the more conventional for the Mishnah and Tosefta. That provenance seems to have had a penchant for polemic, or at least a different form of polemic than that typical of the Mishnah and Tosefta, in their literary formulations for self-justification and self-definition. In those circles, the portrayal of *confrontations* between Pharisees and Sadducees, and the besting of the latter by the former, seems to have played a more significant role.

Fifth, in the end, the foregoing conclusions are a disappointment. At the outset, we stated that groups tend to define themselves over against a salient other—*we* do/teach/believe *x*, while *they* do/teach/believe *not x*. We had hoped that if programmatic and overarching *x*s and not *x*s were to be uncovered with respect to the Pharisees, they would be in sources portraying their confrontations with their important others, the Sadducees. We have seen a number of very discrete legal *x*s and not *x*s but, as noted, nothing that adds up to programmatic, overarching, principled differences that would provide some of the foundations for the social formation and identity of the Pharisees (or the Sadducees). Nonetheless, our evidence does confirm an important claim; early rabbinic authors/editors see the Sadducees as the undisputed important other, over against whom the Pharisees defined themselves and with respect to whom the Pharisees justified their own existence.

How do we know this? Early rabbinic authors/editors consistently and invariably portray Pharisees *in conflict* and *in confrontation with Sadducees—and only with Sadducees*. One might state that this claim is an instance of circular reasoning; after all, I have chosen to limit my data set to those passages in which Pharisees are juxtaposed with Sadducees. However, as a quick glance at concordances and indexes of the Mishnah and of Tosefta will show, there is no other group who are portrayed in these sources as disputants of the Pharisees (with only one exception).[37] To say that the early rabbinic portrayal of matters—that Pharisees defined themselves primarily with respect to Saducean positions that they opposed—reflects pre-70 historical reality is another step. It is a step that rabbinic evidence on its own may not permit us to make, but about which evidence discussed in other chapters of this volume is more relevant. Finally, by portraying Sadducees as the principal important other over against which Pharisaic identity is formed, the early rabbis are in essence saying the same about their own identity vis-à-vis the Sadducees. As stated, the authors/editors of the Mishnah and Tosefta consistently portray Pharisaic rulings in dispute with Saducean law as precedent for their own.

Sixth, in a related vein, the passages analyzed assume that the Pharisees and Sadducees share for the most part a common socially constructed world in which they both act and interact. It is assumed that, for both, this world is constructed largely through the practice of Torah law. That the foundation of the latter is scriptural is also portrayed by the passages as a foundational principle for both groups. Moreover, that Torah law includes considerable ramification of and complement to scriptural law is depicted as equally the case for Pharisees and Sadducees. Neither group is portrayed as a "Scripture-alone" party or as a "plain-sense-of-Scripture-alone" movement. However, the passages analyzed also convey that the differences on specific points of law that separate Sadducees and Pharisees are of critical saliency, and that these differences can be resolved only by one group (the Sadducees) abandoning their positions in favor of those of the other (the Pharisees).

Seventh, and finally, the pericopes discussed not only assume that Pharisees and Sadducees share a socially constructed world in a conceptual or "ideal" sense (conceptually differing on and debating about points of law within what they maintain is or ought to be a common Torah-legal framework); the sources analyzed also portray Pharisees and Sadducees as living together cheek by jowl in shared social settings. These settings occasion confrontation, as depicted stylistically and in a formalized manner by rabbinic literary circles. Moreover, in these portrayals Sadducees and Pharisees have or attempt to exercise common or like authoritative roles in their socially shared world. In sum, in our sources, the Sadducees are for the Pharisees that "close-cousin other" with respect to which the basis for a distinctively Pharisaic social formation and identity is grounded.

I conclude this chapter by posing one final question, and venturing a preliminary answer. Why would late second- and third-century rabbinic authors/editors feel impelled not only to lay claim to pre-70 Pharisaic roots for discrete rulings but also, by so doing, to construct their own group identity, in part, over against a Sadducean "other"? The answer may lie in the (implicit) claim of the early rabbinic movement to have inherited or superceded the authority of the pre-70 Temple priesthood. This claim is at the foundation of the topical agenda of the Mishnah, the first rabbinic magnum opus, so much of which is a legal study of an ideal, Temple-centered world. Strictly speaking, the biblical law identifies priests as the ruling authority of that world. And for centuries leading up to that Temple's demise in 70 CE, those claiming origins in the Saddokite priestly clan were generally at the top of the Temple's hierarchy.[38] The very name "Sadducee" lays claim to the authority of the Saddokite priestly clan. The early rabbis' own claim to mastery over the Temple-centered Israelite "world" as expressed in the Mishnah's agenda, their appeal to Pharisaic paternity as represented in our evidence, and their own self-representation as being in opposition to the pre-70 Sadducees, again as expressed in the passages analyzed above—all this seems part and parcel of the same self-defining and self-justifying myth-making for the social foundation of the early rabbinic movement.

APPENDIX

t. Yoma 1:8	*b. Yoma* 19b
1. (שקבר היה מעשה ב) A certain Boethusian [High Priest] prepared the incense while he was outside [the Holy of Holies] and the cloud of the incense went forth and shook the Temple.	1. (תנו רבנן מעשה ב) A certain Sadducee who prepared [the incense] outside [the Holy of Holies] and [then] entered [the Holy of Holies] in coming out was exceedingly happy.
2. For the Boethusians say: He shall prepare the incense while he is outside [the Holy of Holies], as it is said: *and the cloud of the incense shall cover the ark cover* (Lev 16:13).	2.
3. Said to them the sages: Has it not already been said: *and he shall put he incense upon the fire before the Lord* (Lev 16:13)? If so, why is it said: and the cloud of the incense shall cover? It teaches that he puts in them [i.e., the ingredients of the incense] a smoke-producing substance. Lo, if he did not put in them a smoke-producing substance, he is deserving of death.	3.
4. When he emerged, he said to his father: All of your days you interpreted [the scriptural injunction in accordance with my behavior] and you did not do [thus], until I came and did [so] myself.	4. [see below, #5]
5. [His father] said to him: Although we interpret [the Scripture thus], we do not do [thus]. We obey the words of the sages. You will astonish me if you do not last [more than a few] days.	5. His father met him and said to him: My son, although we are Sadducees, we fear the Pharisees.

6. [see above, # 4]

6. [His son] said to him: All my days I was troubled over this scriptural verse: For I appear in the cloud above the ark cover (Lev 16:2). I said: When will it be in my power to fulfill it? Now that it has come into my power, shall I not fulfill it?

7. It was not [but] three days until they placed him in his grave.

7. They said: It was not [but] a few days until he died and was thrown on a dungheap, and worms were coming out of his nose.

8.

8. And some say: [Immediately] upon his emerging [from the Holy of Holies] he was stricken.

[*t. Yoma* 1:8, ed. Lieberman (*y. Yoma* 1:5), trans. based on my own previously published; see above, note 1]

[*b. Yoma* 19b, translation based on my own previously published; see above, note 1]

---

t. Nid. 5:3

b. Nid. 33b

1. (ב מעשׂה) A certain Sadducee (fem. [*sic*]) was conversing with the High Priest, and some spittle squirted from his [*sic*] mouth and fell upon the garments of the High Priest; and the face of the High Priest turned greenish;

1. (ב מעשׂה רבנן תנו) A certain Sadducee was conversing with the High Priest in the market place, and some spittle from his mouth fell upon the garments of the High Priest; and the face of the High Priest turned greenish;

2. and they came and asked his [the Sadducee's] wife and she said: Sir High Priest, although we are Sadducean women, they all inquire of a sage.

2. and he [the High Priest] came to his [own] wife, and she said to him: Although they are the wives of Sadducees, they fear the Pharisees, and they show [their vaginal] blood to the sages [for a ruling with respect to uncleanness].

3. Said R. Yosé: We are more familiar with the Sadducean women than

3. Said R. Yosé: We are more familiar with them [the wives of

[with] all [others], for they all inquire of a sage, except for one who was among them, and she died.	Sadduccees] than [with] all [others], and they show their [vaginal] blood to the sages, except for one woman who was in our neighborhood, she did not show [her vaginal] blood to the sages, and she died.
[*t. Nid.* 5:3, ed. Zuckermandel, translation based on my own previously published; see above, note 1]	[*b. Nid.* 33b, translation based on my own previously published, see above, note 1]

In my earlier article of nearly three decades ago (see above, note 1), *t. Yoma* 1:8 and *t. Nid.* 5:3 were discussed in full as part of the corpus of what I then called the tannaitic evidence. The term "tannaitic" now seems more problematic than it did then, if one means by "tannaitic" having a historical provenance in rabbinic circles contemporaneous with or earlier than Rabbi Judah the Patriarch (late second and early third century). One simply cannot ignore the fact that *beraitot* in the Babylonian Talmud, despite their attribution to second-century rabbinic circles and authorities, appear in a document produced and promulgated in the sixth century, notwithstanding the truism that those who produced the Babylonian Talmud had antecedent written sources in hand. It is possible that a beraita in the Babylonian Talmud may preserve an earlier version than its parallel in the Tosefta (ca. mid to late third century), but the burden of proof in any one case lies with whoever would make such a claim.

However, even though the burden of proof lies in the direction just mentioned, what might I say to dissuade one from attempting to make the proof in this case? As mentioned, *in neither of these two Toseftan passages do Pharisees appear*; nor in the case of *t. Yoma* 1:8 do Pharisees appear in the parallel passage in the Yerushalmi at *y. Yoma* 1:5. Rather, it is only their parallel *beraitot* in the Babylonian Talmud—at *b. Yoma* 19b and *b. Nid.* 33b, respectively—that mention Pharisees. Indeed, *b. Nid.* 33b mentions both Pharisees and sages. The Toseftan passages (and Y.) refer to "[the] sages" only. Moreover, the very same language is used in the two *beraitot* with respect to the Pharisees: "although we/they are . . . Sadducees, we/they fear the Pharisees."

In all likelihood, then, the language of one of the *beraitot* has been modeled on that of the other; hence the identical language in referring to Pharisaic dominance over Sadducees in the Temple and over its priesthood. That is to say, reference to anonymous "sages," as is the case in both of the Toseftan versions, seems the earlier reading in at least one of the two beraitot, if not in both. In which one we cannot say. Consequently, the question of whether the Toseftan passage (in which the language "we/they fear the Pharisees" does not appear) or its parallel beraita in the Babylonian Talmud (in which it does) preserves the early version is a moot issue with respect to one of the parallel pairs. With respect to the other pair, the question at least still stands. However, we do not know with respect to which of the two the issue is moot. Finally, there is a tendency among *beraitot* in the Babylonian Talmud to modify source materials so that traditional disputants are juxtaposed; this might account for the appearance of Pharisees in *b. Yoma* 19b and *b. Nid.* 33b despite their absence from *t. Yoma* 1:8 and *t. Nid.* 5:3.

The last-mentioned point raises the question of generalization. I cannot in this context address the issue of whether in *general* Toseftan passages tend to preserve versions of traditions earlier than their parallel *beraitot*—which view, incidentally, I do endorse. Nor would appealing to such a general observation be necessarily probative in all cases, since general trends always admit of exceptions. Are the *beraitot* at hand such exceptions? It would seem not, since what we do know, in the end, is that the language of *at least* one of the *beraitot* seems to have been modified, and this based on the evidence at hand for these specific passages; specifically, "we fear the Pharisees" seems to have migrated from one of the B's texts to the other. Moreover, the parallel at *y. Yoma* 1:5 of *t. Yoma* 1:8 reflects the Toseftan version of the passage. Finally, whereas at *t. Nid.* 5:3 the saying attributed to Yosé is independent of what precedes it, the parallel in *b. Nid.* 33b has interpolated into Yosé's saying language from the antecedent stiche of the pericope, better integrating the saying attributed to Yosé with the rest of the passage. (See my previous analyses [referenced above at note 1] of these passages in "Sadducees versus Pharisees.")

Are, then, B's versions actually based on T's? That, too, is difficult to say. The exegetical debate that occurs at sections 2 and 3 of *t. Yoma* 1:8 (a) interrupts the story and (b) is absent from the *b. Yoma* 19b. More likely, *t.* and *b.* each depend on some common source (in which, in my view, "Pharisees" did not appear).

As to the term "tannaitic," I now avoid the term as a historical descriptor whenever possible (as discussed above at note 3). Used as a historical qualifier, it is more confusing than edifying. I much prefer to talk of texts "in the Mishnah" or "in the Tosefta" or of beraitot in the Yerushalmi or Babylonian Talmud. Indeed, "tannaitic" seems more appropriately a qualifier associated with certain literary traits. One of these traits (only) is the tendency to attribute rulings, when attributed at all, to rabbinic figures whom the authors believed lived in the time of Rabbi Judah the Patriarch or earlier. And one could specify a number of other quite discrete literary traits characteristic of these materials.

CHAPTER 11

THE RABBINIC TRADITIONS ABOUT THE PHARISEES BEFORE 70 CE: AN OVERVIEW

Jacob Neusner

We begin our account of the rabbinic traditions about the pre-70 CE Pharisees with an overview of the entire corpus as it is set forth in the earliest rabbinic compilations, those of the third century CE. Then, in chapter 12, we survey the topical program in detail. In chapter 13 we consider the formative history of those same traditions, from 70 to 140 and from 140 to 170 CE.

THE SHAPE OF THE RABBINIC TRADITIONS
ABOUT THE PRE-70 PHARISEES

The rabbinic traditions about the Pharisees before 70 CE are those compositions in the Mishnah (ca. 200) or the Tosefta (ca. 300) in which we find the names of rabbinic sages presumed to have lived before 70, or the Houses of Shammai and Hillel, two such masters.[1] Why Pharisaic in particular? The indicated pre-70 authorities are sages named in the chains of authorities down to and including Gamaliel (Paul's teacher, per Acts 22:3)[2] and Simeon b. Gamaliel (labeled by Josephus as a Pharisee in *Life* 38) and masters referred to in pericopes of those same authorities. Those lists include Mishnah-tractate *Hagigah* 2:2 and tractate *Abot* 1:1–18.

Because Gamaliel and Simeon b. Gamaliel, who appear on the list in *Abot* 1:1–18, are identified as Pharisees, I assume that all others on the list formed part of that same chain of tradition that Gamaliel and Simeon received, in the mythic narrative, from Sinai—a single ongoing tradition deriving from Pharisees. The topical congruence we shall review in this chapter and chapter 12 between the gospels' indictment of Pharisaism and the rabbinic traditions in the names of figures on the lists of masters in Hagigah and Abot reinforces that judgment.

Clearly, this account of the matter depends on the reliability of the attributions of sayings to named authorities and the accuracy of what is attributed—neither of which has been demonstrated. But we have good reason to regard what is attributed as representative of Pharisaic topics and opinion on those topics. For, as we shall see, the topics of the rabbinic traditions attributed to pre-70 Pharisees correspond closely with the agenda of Matthew 23:1-33 and Luke 11:37-52 in the woe sayings that pertain to the Pharisees, and we shall see that the later rabbinic traditions and the earlier gospel traditions concur in their portrait of the topical program of those traditions. The rabbinic traditions about the pre-70 Pharisees address the same topics as take a prominent position in the gospels' traditions about the pre-70 Pharisees. As to the details—the legal issues—there is in general no way to correlate the two bodies of data, since only rarely do the gospels' Pharisaic references go into details of the law.

PROGRAMMATIC TRAITS OF THE RABBINIC TRADITIONS ABOUT THE PRE-70 PHARISEES

The rabbinic traditions in the Mishnah and the Tosefta about the Pharisees before 70 CE consist of approximately 371 separate items—stories or sayings or allusions—which occur in approximately 655 different pericopes. Of these traditions, 280, in 456 pericopes, pertain to Menahem, Shammai, Hillel, and the Houses of Hillel and Shammai—that is, the generation from about 25 BCE to 25 CE In all, these make up approximately 75 percent. A roughly even division of the materials would give 23 traditions in 40 pericopes to each name or category, so the disparity is enormous. Exact figures cannot be given, for much depends on how one counts the components of composite pericopes or reckons with other imponderables.

The following approximate figures suffice to indicate that the disproportionately greater part of the rabbinic traditions of the Pharisees pertains to Hillel and people involved with him.

Master	Number of	
	Traditions	*Pericopes*
Simeon the Just	10	30
Antigonus of Sokho	2	2
Yosé b. Yoezer	4	10
Yosé b. Yohanan	6	13
Joshua b. Perahiah	3	6
Nittai the Arbelite	2	2
Judah b. Tabbai	7	26
Simeon b. Shetah	13	38

Hillel and people involved with him:

Master	Number of	
	Traditions	*Pericopes*
Shemaiah/Abtalion	11	18
Shammai	15)	25)
Menahem	2)	3)
Hillel	33) 61	89) 156
Shammai/Hillel	11)	39)
Gamaliel	26	41
Simeon b. Gamaliel	7	13
Houses of Shammai and Hillel	219	300
	371	655

An overview of the topics yields a simple result: approximately 67 percent of all legal pericopes deal with dietary laws: ritual purity for meals and agricultural rules governing the fitness of food for Pharisaic consumption. Observance of Sabbaths and festivals is a distant third. The named masters normally have legal traditions of the same sort; only Gamaliel greatly diverges from the pattern, Simeon b. Shetah somewhat less so. Of the latter we can say nothing. The wider range of legal topics covered by Gamaliel's legal lemmas and stories only confirms the tradition that he had an important position in the civil government.

What We Do Not Find in the Rabbinic Traditions about the Pre-70 Pharisees

The rabbinic traditions about the Pharisees as a whole may be characterized as self-centered, the internal records of a party concerning its own life, its own laws, and its own partisan conflicts. The omission of records of what happened outside the party is not only puzzling, but nearly inexplicable. Almost nothing in Josephus's picture of the Pharisees seems closely related to much, if anything, in the rabbis' portrait of the Pharisees, except the rather general allegation that the Pharisees had traditions from the fathers, a point made also by the synoptic storytellers. The rabbis' Pharisaic conflict stories moreover do not tell of Pharisees opposing Essenes, Christians, or Sadducees, but of Hillelites opposing Shammaites. Pharisaic laws deal not with the governance of the country but with the party's rules for table fellowship. The political issues are not whether one should pay taxes to Rome or how one should know the Messiah, but whether in the Temple the rule of Shammai or that of Hillel should be followed in a minor festal sacrifice.

From the rabbinic traditions about the Pharisees we could not have reconstructed a single significant public event of the period before 70—not the rise, success, and fall of the Hasmoneans, nor the Roman conquest of Palestine, nor the rule of Herod, nor the reign of the procurators, nor the growth of opposition to Rome, nor the proliferation of social violence and unrest in the last decades before 66 CE, nor the outbreak of the war with Rome. We do not gain a picture of the Pharisees' philosophy of history or theology of politics. We should not even know how Palestine was governed, for the Pharisees' traditions according to the rabbis do not refer to how the Pharisees governed the country—the rabbis never claim the Pharisees did run pre-70 Palestine, at least not in stories told either about named masters or about the Houses—nor do they tell us how the Romans ran it. Furthermore, sectarian issues are barely mentioned, and other sects not at all.

THE RABBIS' PHARISEES: FIGURES OF THE LATE HERODIAN AND ROMAN PERIODS

The rabbis' Pharisees are mostly figures of the Late Herodian and Roman periods. They were a nonpolitical group, whose chief religious concerns were for the proper preservation of ritual purity in connection with eating secular food (not deriving from God's altar in the Jerusalem Temple or eaten in the Temple courtyard), and for the observance of the dietary laws of the day, especially those pertaining to the proper nurture and harvest of agricultural crops. Their secondary religious concern was with the proper governance of the party itself. By contrast, as Professor Mason's chapters have shown us, Josephus's Pharisaic records pertain mostly to the years from the rise of the Hasmoneans to their fall. They were a political party that tried to get control of the government of Jewish Palestine, not a little sect drawn apart from the common society by observance of laws of table fellowship. Josephus's Pharisees are important in the reigns of John Hyrcanus and Alexander Jannaeus, but drop from the picture after Alexandra Salome. By contrast, as we saw in the chapters by Professors Levine, Hakola and Reinhartz, and Pickup, the gospels' Pharisees appropriately are much like those of the rabbis; they belong to the Roman period, and their legal agendas are virtually identical: tithing, purity laws, Sabbath observance, vows, and the like.

How do we account for the shift in the program of the traditions from pre-Herodian times to post-Herodian times? The rabbinic tradition thus begins where Josephus's narrative leaves off, and the difference between them leads us to suspect that the change in the character of Pharisaism from a political party to a sect comes with Hillel. If Hillel was responsible for directing the party out of its political concerns and into more passive, quietist paths, then we should understand why he dominates the subsequent rabbinic tradition. If Hillel was a contemporary of Herod, then we may commend his wisdom, for had the Pharisees persisted as a political force, they would have come into conflict with Herod, who could have wiped them out. Hillel's policy may have been shaped by remembrance of the consequences to the party of its conflict with Alexander Jannaeus.

The extreme rarity of materials of masters before Simeon b. Shetah, except those of Yohanan the High Priest (John Hyrcanus), suggests that few survived Jannaeus's massacres, and that those few did not perpetuate the policies, nor, therefore, the decisions of their predecessors. Hillel and his followers chose to remember Simeon b. Shetah, who was on good terms with Alexandra, but not his followers, who were almost certainly on bad terms with Aristobulus and his descendants, the leaders of the national resistance to Rome and to Antipater's family (see Josephus's story of Aristobulus's protection of the Pharisees' victims). As Herod's characteristics became clear, therefore, the Pharisees must have found themselves out of sympathy with the government and the opposition alike. And at this moment Hillel arose to change what had been a political party into a table-fellowship sect, not unlike other, publicly harmless and politically neutral groups, whatever their private eschatological aspirations.

All this is more than mere conjecture, but less than established fact. What is fact is that the vast majority of rabbinic traditions about the Pharisees relate to the circle of Hillel and certainly the best attested and most reliable corpus, the opinions of the Houses, reaches us from that circle's later adherents. The pre-Hillel Pharisees are not known to us primarily from the rabbinic traditions, and when we begin to have a substantial rabbinic record, it is the record of a group very different from Josephus's pre-Hillelite, pre-Herodian party.

THE CHAINS OF TRADITION

This brings us back to the chains of tradition. We have three chains of Pharisaic tradition—that is, lists of names of authorities in succession, to each of which names is given an opinion. The first (*m. Hag.* 2:2) is a list of six pairs: Yosé b. Yoezer and Yosé b. Yohanan, Joshua b. Perahiah and Nittai the Arbelite, Judah b. Tabbai and Simeon b. Shetah, Shemaiah and Abtalion, Hillel and Menahem, Shammai and Hillel; the opinions are *to lay* or *not to lay* hands on the festival offering before slaughter on the Sabbath. The subscription assigns to the first the office of patriarch, to the second the office of "father of the court." The latter office is never elsewhere referred to in the rabbinic traditions about the pre-70 Pharisees. The former occurs only with regard to Hillel's rise to power in the Temple.

The second lists, on uncleanness, have only six names, in three pairs: Yosé b. Yoezer and Yosé b. Yohanan, Simeon b. Shetah and Judah b. Tabbai, Shammai and Hillel. The form calls for *decreed uncleanness* plus objects: land of the peoples, metal utensils, uncleanness on hands, respectively.

The moral sayings of *m. Abot* 1:1–18 are explicit in linking Yohanan b. Zakkai, or Gamaliel and Simeon b. Gamaliel, to Hillel. They take for granted that the latter two were his heirs and successors, although nothing in any of the early traditions links him to Hillel through either stories or citations of regal teachings. Simeon b. Gamaliel was represented by his son, Gamaliel II, as a Shammaite. It looks to me as if the predominance of Hillelites later on called for the establishment of a relationship between Hillel and the authorities who came between him and the Yavnean Hillelites, so Gamaliel I was made his son, Simeon b. Gamaliel his grandson, and—in a different circle—Yohanan b. Zakkai into his successor (still later, his outstanding disciple).

FORMAL TRAITS OF THE RABBINIC TRADITIONS ABOUT THE PRE-70 PHARISEES

In the Mishnah and the Tosefta and the continuation documents, the two Talmuds, clear-cut and well-defined forms were used for the transmission of the Houses materials, Hillel pericopes, and related data. The single striking formal characteristic of the whole corpus is, of course, attribution to named authorities; this applies throughout—by definition. The form developed for such attributions, namely, *X says*, produces the dispute form (*Statement of problem, X says . . . Y says . . .*), the debate form (*They said to them . . . They said to them . . .*), and related forms. All are well attested at early Yavneh—commented on by authorities who lived after 70 and are identified with the rabbinic institution in the town of Yavneh or Jamnia—and are used primarily for Houses materials, secondarily for the masters standing behind the Houses, finally for later first-century authorities. The Houses form (*The House of Shammai say . . . The House of Hillel say . . .*) comes when the Houses are of roughly equal strength, so that the form used for the transmission of their opinions will give parity to both sides. The dispute form is standard in the Mishnah and the Tosefta and is not particular to the Houses of Shammai and Hillel. But when the participants in the dispute are the Houses, the form is rigid and produces mnemonic patterns easily mastered.

The smallest whole unit of discourse is made up of fixed, recurrent formulas, clichés, patterns, or little phrases, out of which whole pericopes, or large elements in pericopes (e.g., complete sayings), are constructed. An example of part of a pericope composed primarily of recurrent formulas is as follows:

> *A basket of fruit intended for the Sabbath*
> House of Shammai declare exempt
> And the House of Hillel declare liable.

The italicized words are not fixed formulas. "And" is redactional; the formulation of the statement of the problem does not follow a pattern. The Houses sentences, by contrast, are formed of fixed, recurrent phrases, which occur in numerous pericopes. Similarly:

> House of Shammai say . . . House of Hillel say . . .

are fixed small units, whether or not the predicate matches; when it balances, we have a larger unit of tradition composed of two small units:

> 1. House of Shammai say,   2. BKY YTN
> 3. House of Hillel say,   4. Not BKY YTN.

In this pericope, only the statement of the problem or protasis, not given, would constitute other than a fixed unit; "House of Shammai/ Hillel" + "say" are complete units, and the opinions in the apodosis are others—thus, as I said, a pericope, the apodosis of which is composed entirely of fixed, small units of tradition. By definition these small formulas cannot be random, or they would not constitute formulas. Such small units are whole words, not syntactical or grammatical particles.

This form seems on the basis of attributions to derive from early Yavneh, because it is attested in the earliest Yavnean stratum—the corpus of sayings attributed to authorities who flourished after the destruction of the Temple in 70 CE. Whatever forms were used by the respective Houses of Shammai and Hillel for the preservation of their in-house traditions were abandoned. Only the form that unites the two Houses' opinions in a single coherent statement on a single shared topical agenda persists. Then the whole corpus of earlier materials characteristic of the respective Houses was transmuted into the joint Houses form, with the Houses' opinions given on a mutually determined agenda of legal problems, and with an antithetical relationship preserved throughout.

Forms for the citation of Scripture seem primarily redactional in origin; they differ from one document to the next and are consistent within the respective compilations. Where we do have a well-defined form for Scriptural pericopes, it appears primarily in Hillel materials. Thirty-three of thirty-five exegeses for legal purposes are attributed to Hillel, Shammai, or the Houses.

Not only do most of the forms we are able to isolate derive from Yavneh, specifically from the circles responsible for the redaction of the Houses' antithetical pericopes, but evidence of mnemonic techniques first occurs in precisely the materials produced by those same circles. First, as I said, the form of the apodoses of Houses pericopes invariably is: *House of X say* . . . , *House of Y say.* . . . Furthermore, the actual opinions of the Houses normally are balanced opposites, or other mnemonic devices are used to set up the same balance. Some of the patterns derive from a balanced number of syllables. Others are conventional syzygies, such as unclean/clean. Still others involve fixed changes in morphological or syntactical elements. Approximately 105 pericopes do not exhibit any sort of mnemonic formula or pattern; approximately 82 exhibit some sort of pattern, generally external to the substance; and 314 pericopes contain small units of tradition or other highly disciplined mnemonic forms.

In all, Houses pericopes and Hillel/Shammai pericopes normally exhibit mnemonic patterns or are balanced in some way or other. Pericopes of other named masters are apt not to be balanced or to exhibit other mnemonic patterns. Thus, the evidence indicates that, although these forms and patterns were used in compositions produced by later masters, the Yavnean tradents were the first who shaped and fixed traditions in clear-cut literary forms and who created the common lemmas in such a way as to facilitate memorization and transmission.

An Oral Tradition?
The Oral Torah Revealed by God to Moses at Sinai

This does not prove that the Yavnean materials originally were orally formulated and orally transmitted. The only allegation we find about pre-70 Pharisees is that they had traditions. Nothing is said about whether these traditions came from Moses, nor about whether they were in oral form. They generally are ascribed to the fathers, and their form is not specified. No mention of an Oral Torah or a dual Torah occurs in pre-70 pericopes, except for the Hillel-and-the-convert story, certainly not weighty evidence. The text is bilingual, in Hebrew and in Aramaic. What is in Hebrew is in plain type; in Aramaic, in italics.

> BAVLI SHABBAT 2:5 I.11/31a
>
> A. *Our rabbis have taught on Tannaïte authority:*
> B. There was the incident of a certain gentile who came before Shammai. He said to him, "How many Torahs do you have?"
> C. He said to him, "Two, one in writing, one memorized."
> D. He said to him, "As to the one in writing, I believe you. As to the memorized one, I do not believe you. Convert me on condition that you will teach me only the Torah that is in writing."
> E. He rebuked him and threw him out.
> F. He came before Hillel. He said to him, "Convert me." [ARN: My lord, how many Torahs were given?" He said to him, "Two, one in writing, one memorized." He said to him, "As to the one in writing, I believe you. As to the memorized one, I do not believe you."]
> G. On the first day he said to him, "Alef, bet, gimel, dalet." The next day he reversed the order on him.
> H. He said to him, "Well, yesterday, didn't you say it differently?"
> I. He said to him, "Didn't you depend on me then? Then depend on me when it comes to the fact of the memorized Torah too." [ARN: He said to him, "My son, sit." He wrote for him, Alef, bet. He said to him, "What is this?" He said to him, "An alef." He said to him, "This is not an alef but a bet." He said to him, "What is this?" He said to him, "Bet." He said to him, "This is not a bet but a gimel." He said to him, "How do you know that this is an alef and this a bet and this a gimel? But that is what our ancestors have handed

over to us—the tradition that this is an alef, this a bet, this a gimel. Just as you have accepted this teaching in good faith, so accept the other in good faith" [The Fathers according to Rabbi Nathan XV:V.1].

I.12 A. There was another case of a gentile who came before Shammai. He said to him, "Convert me on the stipulation that you teach me the entire Torah while I am standing on one foot." He drove him off with the building cubit that he had in his hand.

B. He came before Hillel: "Convert me."

C. He said to him, "'*What is hateful to you, to your fellow don't do.*' That's the entirety of the Torah; *everything else is elaboration. So go, study.*"

This famous story is frequently reduced to proof of the Pharisees' doctrine of the Oral Torah with the simple reference, "see Bavli Shabbat 31A." It first surfaces, however, in the Babylonian Talmud, ca. 600 CE; and without corroboration, which is lacking, it cannot tell us the state of the tradition in the first century BCE, six hundred years earlier.

Moreover, the Pharisaic laws contain no instructions on how materials are to be handed on, nor references to how this actually was done. Allegations that Moses dictated an Oral Torah to Aaron in much the same way as rabbis taught the Mishnah first occur with 'Aqiba, who in fact undertook exactly that process in the formulation of his traditions. The myth of oral formulation and oral transmission is first attested by Judah b. Ilai, although a dispute between Eliezer and 'Aqiba presupposes oral formulation and transmission in Yavnean circles.

So much for the period at which Yavneh formed the center of the tradition, that is, ca. 70–120 CE. Later authorities, of the mid-second century, after the Bar Kokhba War, assembled at Usha, a Galilean town, and in ca. 135–170 continued work on the rabbinic traditions. We are able to verify the existence of the larger part of the Houses corpus both at Yavneh and Usha. The verifications exhibit a uniform pattern: types of laws attributed to the Houses at Yavneh are the same types attributed to them at Usha. The Houses form was not used as a mere mnemonic device, to facilitate the memorization of traditions of any sort, but was reserved for the redaction of materials on a few themes on which the Yavneans and Ushans evidently believed the

Houses actually legislated. This further justifies our attribution of the forms and mnemonic patterns to Yavnean tradents.

WHAT DO WE HAVE IN A PRE-70 FORMULATION?

But we cannot suppose that a great part of the rabbinic tradition has been left in its pre-70 form. On the contrary, I take it for granted that the individual Houses preserved records of their own opinions not in juxtaposition to the opinions of the opposing House, just as did Qumranians. The model would be the uncleanness saying of Yosé b. Yoezer, perhaps also the three abrogations of Yohanan the High Priest. But the Shammai-Hillel-Houses corpus of laws follows a single form, and that is, the *dispute*—even using it where the opinions of the Houses do not differ. It follows that the people responsible for the Houses dispute form and the mnemonic small units inserted in it also recast the whole of the antecedent tradition in this form, obliterating the earlier forms of whatever materials they had. This makes it all the more striking that the earliest and most substantial verifications come from the disciples of Yohanan b. Zakkai and their contemporaries, at the very outset of the Yavnean tradition.

If Yavneans and Ushans were meticulous in reporting the Houses' disputes, they were not equally careful to preserve a balanced picture of the period from Hillel to the destruction of the Temple. The picture they produced is the work of Yavneans more than of Ushans. It reflects intense competition between Yavnean Hillelites and the Shammaite opposition. Evidently the Hillelites predominated at Yavneh but had to overcome the common recollection of Shammaite predominance before the destruction. This they accounted for through a number of vicious stories about Shammaites' use of force and even murdering their Hillelite opponents. It is striking that the generation (if not the same tradents) responsible for the carefully balanced disputes also produced entirely unbalanced stories. The thematic authenticity of the laws seems to me beyond doubt. The historical accuracy of the stories is similarly to be affirmed, for their picture of pre-70 politics seems to me plausible, albeit prejudiced. Along with the latter, however, goes the body of anti-Shammaite polemic, much of it Yavnean, and most of it probably grossly exaggerated if not wholly false. We may conjecture that the legal material with its fixed forms is the official product of the Yavnean academy in which the parties, under Yohanan b. Zakkai's leadership and the pressure of necessity, cooperated, and that the stories and propaganda, in less fixed forms, represent what was then the private gossip of the Hillelite party, and which only later, with the triumph of that party, got into the official tradition. But this is only conjecture

THE SHAPE OF THE RABBINIC TRADITIONS
ABOUT THE PRE-70 PHARISEES

The rabbinic traditions about the Pharisees pertain chiefly to the last half-century or so before the destruction of the Temple—at most, seventy or eighty years. Then the Pharisees were primarily a society for table fellowship, the high point of their life as a group. That is, the laws that concerned them had to do with the cultic cleanness of food and the proper tithing of agricultural produce—dietary laws in both instances. The laws of table fellowship predominate in the Houses disputes, as they ought to—three fourths of all pericopes—and correspond to the legal agenda of the Pharisees according to the synoptic gospel stories. A few mostly narrative traditions about masters before Shammai-Hillel persisted, but these do not amount to much and in several cases consist merely of the name of a master, plus whatever opinion is given to him in the chain in which be appears. The interest of the nonlegal materials concentrates on the relationships of Shammai and Hillel, on the career of Hillel, and related matters. Materials on their successors at best are perfunctory, until we come to men who themselves survived to work at Yavneh, such as Hananiah Prefect of the Priests and, of course, Yohanan b. Zakkai.

So, in all, we have from the rabbis a very sketchy account of the life of Pharisaism during less than the last century of its existence before 70 CE, with at most random and episodic materials pertaining to the period before Hillel. We have this account, so far as it is early, primarily through the medium of forms and mnemonic patterns used at Yavneh and later on at Usha. What we know is what the rabbis of Yavneh and Usha regarded as the important and desirable account of the Pharisaic traditions: almost entirely the internal record of the life

of the party and its laws—the party being no more than the two fac-
tions that predominated after 70, the laws being mainly rules of how
and what people might eat with one another.

THE RABBINIC PICTURE OF THE PRE-70 PHARISEES COMPARED TO THE ACCOUNTS OF THE GOSPELS AND JOSEPHUS

There is a striking discontinuity among the three principal sources
that speak of the Pharisees before 70: the gospels and the rabbinic
writings of a later period, on the one side, and Josephus, on the other.
What Josephus thinks characteristic of the Pharisees are matters that
play little or no role in what Mark and Matthew regard as significant,
and what the later rabbis think the Pharisees said scarcely intersects
with the topics and themes important to Josephus. But, as we see in
these pages, the picture drawn by Matthew and Mark and that drawn
by the later rabbis are essentially congruent, and together differ from
the portrait left to us by Josephus. The traits of Pharisaism emphasized by Josephus, their principal beliefs and practices, nowhere occur
in the rabbinic traditions of the Pharisees. When we compare what
Josephus says about the Pharisees to what the later rabbinic traditions
have to say, there is scarcely a point of contact, let alone intersection.
Josephus says next to nothing about the predominant issues in the
rabbinic traditions about the Pharisees. Shammai and Hillel are not
explicitly mentioned, let alone their Houses. Above all, we find not
the slightest allusion to laws of ritual purity, agricultural taboos,
Sabbath and festivals, and the like, which predominate in the traditions of the Houses. In the detailed account of the reign of Alexander
Jannaeus, Simeon b. Shetah does not occur. Apart from the banquet
of John Hyrcanus, we could not, relying on Josephus, recover a single
significant detail of the rabbinic traditions about the Pharisees, let
alone the main outlines of the whole.

As to the topical program of the Pharisees, Josephus's agenda of
Pharisaic doctrine hardly coincide with those of the rabbis. For example, while Josephus seems to paraphrase 'Aqiba's saying, that all is in
the hands of heaven yet man has free choice, that saying is nowhere
attributed to pre-70 Pharisees, certainly not to the Pharisees who
would have flourished in the period in which Josephus places such

beliefs. We find no references to the soul's imperishability, all the more so to the transmigration of souls. The Houses' debate on the intermediate group comes closest to Josephus's report. As to Josephus's allegation that the Pharisees are affectionate to one another, we may observe that is not how the Hillelites report matters. Josephus knows nothing of the Shammaites' slaughter of Hillelites, their mob action against Hillel in the Temple, and other stories that suggest a less than affectionate relationship within the Pharisaic group. So, for Josephus, the three chief issues of sectarian consequence are belief in Fate, belief in traditions outside the Mosaic Law, and influence over political life. The Pharisees believe in Fate, have traditions from the fathers, and exercise significant influence in public affairs. The Sadducees do not believe in Fate, do not accept other than Mosaic laws, and have no consequence in public life. For the rabbinic traditions about the Pharisees, the three chief issues of sectarian consequence are ritual purity, agricultural taboos, and Sabbath and festival behavior.

The relationship between the rabbinic traditions about the Pharisees and the gospels' accounts of the Pharisees by contrast is symmetrical. There is one topic on which these sources are apt to be essentially sound, namely, the themes of the laws they impute to the figures before 70 who we believe were Pharisees. The congruity in the themes of the laws attributed to the Pharisees by both the gospels and the later rabbinic sources is striking. What it means is that, from speaking of traditions about the Pharisees, we are apt to address the historical Pharisees themselves in the decades before the destruction of the Temple in 70 CE. The historical Pharisees in the decades before the destruction of Jerusalem are portrayed by legal traditions that are judged in these pages to be fundamentally sound in topic, perhaps also in detailed substance, and attested by references of masters who may reasonably be supposed to have known what they were talking about.

CHAPTER 12

THE PHARISAIC AGENDA: LAWS ATTRIBUTED IN THE MISHNAH AND THE TOSEFTA TO PRE-70 PHARISEES

Jacob Neusner

THE COINCIDENCE OF THE RABBINIC PHARISEES AND THE GOSPELS' PHARISEES: CULTIC CLEANNESS, TITHING FOOD

When we examine the topical program of the laws attributed in the Mishnah and the Tosefta, we find that the rabbinic traditions about the pre-70 Pharisees and the gospels' accounts of Jesus' encounter with Pharisees coincide. Both bodies of writings stress three topics: tithing, cultic cleanness at domestic meals, and Sabbath observance.[1]

Before proceeding, let me give a single example of a pericope that sets forth a dispute between the House of Shammai and the House of Hillel on a matter of uncleanness having to do with eating ordinary food (not deriving from the Temple offerings or altar) in the home (not in the Temple or in Jerusalem)—yet in a state of cleanness akin to that required for the Temple. What we shall see is that details of the law originating in Scripture express in concrete terms abstract issues of natural philosophy. The message derives from Leviticus 11:34, 37. The rabbinic exegetes read those verses to mean that what is dry is insusceptible to uncleanness, while what has been wet down deliberately is susceptible. Consequently, the message concerns the status of liquid: wanted or unwanted, subject to the desire of a person or not subject to that desire. The method in the exposition to follow addresses the matter of intentionality, which carries with it ongoing reflection on when action is required to confirm intention. The medium is a dispute on the status of honey in honeycombs: when does it become susceptible to uncleanness?

The triangulation of message, method, and medium occurs in the form of a dispute at Mishnah-tractate Uqsin 3:12. Here are the contending views:

313

A. Honeycombs—from what point are they [is the honey-liquid] susceptible to uncleanness as liquid?
B. The House of Shammai say, "When one will smoke out [the bees therefrom]."
C. And the House of Hillel say, "When one will have broken [the honeycombs to remove the honey]."

The message is now self-evident. Liquid is susceptible to uncleanness when it is wanted (per Lev 11:34, 37, as the sages read those verses), that is, when it serves human purposes, and it is not susceptible to uncleanness when humans do not regard it as bearing consequence.

What is the method that defines what is at stake here? The important distinction is, is liquid deliberately applied to produce? If dry produce, insusceptible to uncleanness, has been deliberately wet down, then because of human action it has been brought into the system of uncleanness and rendered susceptible. But how does the case frame the issue of intentionality?

That brings us to the medium, the particular case. When the beekeeper smokes out the bees from the honeycombs, he exhibits his intention to take and use the honey some time in the future. That is the point at which susceptibility to receive uncleanness affects the liquid honey, or in the correct context, it is the point at which the honey if applied to dry produce imparts to the produce that puissant moisture that imparts susceptibility—that is to say, liquid deliberately put onto the produce. So far as the House of Shammai are concerned, therefore, a secondary cause (smoking out the bees) serves as readily as a primary cause (actually breaking the honeycombs). But the House of Hillel insist, and the halakha with it, that one actually must have carried out an action that directly confirms the intentionality. Secondary causation does not suffice; primary causation is required. It is clear that what is at issue is a matter of philosophical importance—the relationship between intention and action—but that issue is framed in very concrete and trivial terms. No wonder people outside of Pharisaic circles thought they were preoccupied with minor matters of the law or the Torah. But as we see, the differences concerned profound principles.

LAWS TO DIFFERENTIATE A SECT FROM THE LARGER COMMUNITY OF ISRAEL, THE HOLY PEOPLE

Which laws pertained primarily to Pharisaism, and which were part of the law common to all of Palestinian Jewry? Most of the laws affect primarily the sectarian life of the party. The laws that made a sect sectarian were those that either were interpreted and obeyed by the group in a way different from other groups or from common society at large, on the one hand, or were to begin with observed only by the group, on the other. In the latter category are the purity laws, which take so large a place in the Pharisaic corpus. One primary mark of Pharisaic commitment was the observance of the laws of ritual purity outside the Temple, where everyone kept them. Eating one's secular, that is, unconsecrated, food in a state of ritual purity as if one were a Temple priest in the cult was one of the two signifiers of party membership. The manifold circumstances of everyday life required the multiplication of concrete rules. Representative of the other category may be the laws of tithing and other agricultural taboos. Here we are less certain. Pharisees clearly regarded keeping the agricultural rules as a primary religious duty. But whether, to what degree, and how other Jews did so is not clear. And the agricultural laws, just like the purity rules, in the end affected table fellowship, namely, what and with whom one might eat.

The early Christian traditions on both points represent the Pharisees as reproaching Jesus because his followers did not keep these two kinds of laws at all. That is, why were they not Pharisees? The answer was that the primary concern was for ethics. Both the question and the answer are disingenuous. The questioners are represented as rebuking the Christians for not being Pharisees—which begs the question, for everyone presumably knew Christians were not Pharisees. The answer takes advantage of the polemical opening: Pharisees are not concerned with ethics, a point repeatedly made in the anti-Pharisaic pericopes, depending on a supposed conflict between rules of table fellowship on the one hand and ethical behavior on the other. The obvious underlying claim is that Christian table fellowship does not depend on the sorts of rules important in the table fellowship of other groups.

As to the Sabbath laws, the issue was narrower. All Jews kept the Sabbath. It was part of the culture of their country. The same applies to the festivals. Here the Pharisaic materials are not so broad in interest as with regard to agricultural rules and ritual purity. They pertain primarily to Gentiles' working on the Sabbath for Jews and to the preparation of the *'erub* or fusion meal to join private domains into a common area for Sabbath use. Like the levirate rule, the *'erub* laws must be regarded as solely of sectarian interest. The Mishnaic references to the unobservant Sadducee make this virtually certain. Since the tithes and offerings either went to the Levites and priests or had to be consumed in Jerusalem, and since the purity rules were to begin with Temple matters, we note that the Pharisees claimed laymen are better informed as to purity and Temple laws than the Temple priesthood. That is not to suggest that the historical Pharisees were only or principally a table fellowship commune. It is only to say that, whatever else they were, they surely identified themselves as Pharisees by the dietary rules, involving cultic cleanness, and certain other sectarian practices as to marital relationships, which they observed. More than this we do not know on the basis of the rabbinic evidence, as correlated with the gospels' accounts.

Josephus's picture of the group is asymmetrical to this picture, and a simple hypothesis is to assign his account to the period of which he speaks when he mentions the Pharisees as a political party, which is the second and first centuries BCE, and the rabbis' and gospels' account to the period of which they speak, which is the first century CE.

Most of the laws we have before us, verified early or late, therefore affect primarily the sectarian life of the party. Other laws, not in the materials attributed to the pre-70 Pharisees but referred to, or taken for granted, by Yavneans and later masters may derive from, or reflect, antecedent common law. Of this we cannot be certain. But since laws of marriage, divorce, transfer of real property, litigation of torts, damages, criminal law, court testimony, and the like equally pertained to everyone, it is consequential that the Houses materials contain remarkably few, if any, rulings on such subjects. Of these, levirate marriage, because of conflicting verses of Scripture, was bound to produce sectarian controversy. The paucity of laws pertaining to the Temple is not without reason. Since the Pharisees did not run the

Temple, they had no occasion to develop a substantial corpus of laws about the cult and how it should be carried on. Morton Smith observes:

> Differences as to the interpretation of the purity laws and especially as to the consequent question of table fellowship were among the principal causes of the separation of Christianity from the rest of Judaism and the early fragmentation of Christianity itself. The same thing holds for the Qumran community, and, within Pharisaic tradition, the *haburah*. They are essentially groups whose members observe the same interpretation of the purity rules and therefore can have table fellowship with each other. It is no accident that the essential act of communion in all these groups is participation in common meals.[2]

Since food that had not been properly grown or tithed could not be eaten, and since the staple of the diet was agricultural products and not meat, the centrality of the agricultural rules in no small degree is on account of precisely the same consideration: What may one eat, and under what circumstances? Smith states, "The obligation to eat only tithed food was made the basis of elaborate regulations limiting table fellowship in a way comparable even to the effect of the purity laws" in the reforms of Nehemiah.[3] Nehemiah's third reform, in addition to purifying the Temple and enforcing the giving of tithes to Levites, was the enforcement of the Sabbath, also represented in a more than random way in the Pharisaic laws.

"The normative religion of the country," Smith observes, "is that compromise of which the three principal elements are the Pentateuch, the Temple, and the *'ammé ha'ares*, the ordinary Jews who were not members of any sect."[4] The Pharisaic laws virtually ignore the second element, treat the third as an outsider, and are strangely silent concerning the first. They supply no rules either about synagogue life or about reading the Torah and preaching in synagogues. It would be difficult to maintain that the sect claimed to exercise influence in the life of synagogues not controlled by its own members or that they preached widely in synagogues.

The fact is, therefore, that the laws we have are the laws we should have: the rules of a sect concerning its own sectarian affairs, matters of importance primarily to its own members. That seems to me further evidence of the essential accuracy of the representation of the Houses in the rabbinic traditions. To be sure, not all laws before us portray with equal authenticity the life of pre-70 Pharisaism. But the themes of the laws, perhaps also their substance in detail, are precisely what they ought to have been according to our theory of sectarianism.

THE TOPICAL AGENDA OF THE HOUSES COMPOSITIONS IN THE MISHNAH AND THE TOSEFTA

I now briefly categorize Houses materials in detail, with reference to the Mishnah (m.) and the Tosefta (t.). Here are the topics and rulings.

A. Agricultural Laws

1. Corner of field and other agricultural gifts to the poor
   m. Pe'ah 3:1, 6:1, 2, 3, 5

2. Agricultural taboos (fourth-year fruit, mixed seeds, untithed foods, disposal of food to insure tithing, purity, seventh-year tithes, second tithes, removal of old produce at Passover)
   m. Pe'ah 7:6; *m. Demai* 1:3, 3:1, 6:6; *t. Demai* 1:26–27; *m. Kil.* 2:6, 4:1, 5, 6:1; *t. Kil.* 3:17, 4:11; *m. Shebi'it* 1:1, 4:2, 4, 10, 5:4, 8, 8:3; *t. Shebi'it* 1:5, 2:6, 4:5B, 4:21, 6:19; *m. Ma.* 4:2; *m. M.S.* 2:7–9, 3:6–7, 9, 13, 4:8, 5:6–7; *t. M.S.* 2:11; *t. M.S.* 2:12; *t. M.S.* 5:17–20; *m. Suk.* 3:5; *m. R.H.* 1:1; *m. Hul.* 1:3

3. Priestly and Levitical gifts from agricultural produce (challah, heave offering and its rules, including cleanness)
   y. Demai 5:1; *m. Terumot* 1:4, 4:3, 5:4: *t. Terumot* 3:12, 3:14, 3:16, 5:4; *t. Ma.* 3:13: *t. M.S.* 2:18, 3:14–15; *m. Hal.* 1:6, 11:2; *m. Bekh.* 5:2; *t. Bekh.* 3:15–16

4. Ritual slaughter of animals
   m. Hul. 1:2

5. Milk/meat taboo
   m. Hul. 8:1; *t. Hul.* 8:2–3

B. Ritual Uncleanness

1. Uncleanness of animals
   m. Kil. 8:5 (weasel)

2. Uncleanness in agricultural products
   t. Terumot 3:2 (vat); *t. Terumot* 6:4 = *m. Terumot* 5:4 (unclean heave offering); *b. Pes.* 20b; *y. Pes.* 3:6; *m. M.S.* 2:3, 4, 3:9; *t. M.S.* 2:1, 2:16; *m. 'Orl.* 2:4–5, *m. Oh.* 18:1, 4, 8; *t. Ah.* 16:6, 17:9, 13; *m. Toh.* 9:1, 5, 7, 10:4; *t. Toh.* 8:9–10, 10:1–2; *m. 'Uqs.* 3:6–11

3. Invisible uncleanness and how it comes and goes, e.g., tent, stoppers, split in roof (re woman baking); connectors; causes; etc.

t. Shab. 1:18; m. Kel. 9:2; m. Oh. 2:3, 5:1–4, 7:3, 11:1–8, 13:1, 4, 15:8; t. Ah. 3:4, 5:11, 8:7, 12:1, 14:4, 15:9; m. 'Ed. 1:14; m. Par. 12:10; t. Par. 12:18; m. T.Y. 1:1; t. T.Y. 2:3; m. Yad. 3:5

4. Capacities of objects to receive and produce uncleanness

m. Kel. 11:3, 14:2, 18:1, 20:2, 20:6, 22:4, 26:6, 28:4, 29:8; t. Kel. B.Q. 2:1, 6:18; t. Kel. B.M. 3:8, 4:5, 16, 8:1, 11:3, 7; t. Kel. B.B. 1:12, 4:9, 5:7–8, 7:4; m. Makh. 1:2–4, 4:4–5, 5:9; t. Makh. 1:1–4, 2:6

5. The ritual pool

m. Miq. 1:5, 4:1, 5, 5:6, 10:6; t. Mcq. 1:7, 10, 5:2 (m. 'Ed. 1:3: Shammai + Hillel)

6. Ritual cleanness of women (re sexual relations or preparation of "purities" [food])

m. Nid. 2:4, 6 (sex), 4:3 (food, sex), 10:1, 4, 6, 7, 8 (food); t. Nid. 5:5–7, 9:19 (sex)

7. Ritual cleanness of those who suffer a flow

m. Zab. 1:1–2; t. Zab. 1:1–8

C. Sabbath and Festival Laws

1. Preparing and keeping food on festival, Sabbath (and other table rules in connection with festivals and Sabbath), also 'erub for cooking, search for leaven on Passover, Passover Seder

t. Ma. 3:10; m. Shab. 3:1, 21:3; t. Shab. 1:14, 1:20, 2:13, 16:7; m. 'Erub. 6:6; m. Pes. 1:1, 10:2, 6; t. Pisha 1:6; 7:2; t. Pis. 10:2–3, 9; m. Bes. 1:1–9, 2:1–7; t. Y.T. 1:4, 8, 10, 11, 12–14, 15–17, 21, 2:4

2. Work started before Sabbath and finished on Sabbath, also Gentile work on Sabbath, work on Sabbath and on festivals

m. Shab. 1:4–9; t. Shab. 1:22, 14:1, 16:21–22; m. Pes. 4:15; t. Y.T. 2:10

3. 'Erub to permit carrying on Sabbath

m. 'Erub. 1:2, 6:2, 4A, 8:6

4. Laws of Sukkah

m. Suk. 1:1, 7, 2:7, 3:9

5. Pilgrimage laws

m. Hag. 1:1–3, 2:3–4; t. Hag. 1:4, 2:10

D. Family Laws

1. Levirate marriage

m. Yebam. 1:4, 3:1, 5; t. Yebam. 1:7–13, 5:1

2. Disposition of wife's property

m. Yebam. 4:3; m. Ket. 8:1, 6; m. B.B. 9:8–9; t. B.B. 10:13

3. Sexual duties
   m. Yebam. 6:6; *t. Yebam.* 8:14; *m. Ket.* 5:6; *t. Ket.* 5:6

4. Minor's right of refusal
   m. Yebam. 13:1; *t. Yebam.* 13:1

5. Remarriage of widow
   m. Yebam. 15:2–3; *t. Nid.* 2:12

6. Vows of wife
   t. Ned. 6:3–4

7. Marriage of half-slave
   m. Git. 4:5

8. Divorce
   m. Git. 8:4, 8–9, 9:10; *t. 'Arak.* 4:5; *t. Git.* 8:8

9. Betrothal
   m. Qid. 1:1; *t. Qid.* 4:1

10. Coming of age
    m. Nid. 5:9, 10:1; *t. Nid.* 9:7–9

E. *Temple Oaths and Vows*

1. Shekel offering
   m. Sheq. 2:3

2. Disposal of unclean offerings
   m. Sheq. 8:6; *t. Sheq.* 3:16

3. Sotah-rite
   m. Sotah. 4:2

4. Sprinkling blood
   m. Zebah. 4:1; *t. Zebah.* 4:9

5. Offering of woman who miscarries etc.
   m. Ker. 1:6; *t. Ker.* 1:9

6. Corban vows
   m. Ned. 3:2; *t. Nez.* 1:1

7. Nazirite vows
   m. Naz. 2:1–2, 3:6–7; *t. Nez.* 2:10, 3:1, 17, 19

8. Dedications
   m. Naz. 5:1–5

9. Also D. 6

F *Liturgical and Ritual Matters*

1. How to recite *Shema'*
   m. Ber. 1:3

2. Blessings and conduct at meals
   m. Ber. 6:5, 8:1–8

3. Liturgy on New Year that coincides with Sabbath
   t. Ber. 3:13

4. Tefillin
   b. Ber. 23a

5. Circumcision
   t. Shab. 15:9; *m. Pes.* 8:8; *t. Pis.* 7:4

G. *Civil Law, Torts, Damages*

1. Thievery: recompense
   t. B.Q. 9:5

2. Misappropriation of bailment: Recompense
   m. B.M. 3:12, *t. B.M.* 3:12

H. *House of Study*

1. Blessing in house of study
   t. Ber. 5:30; *b. Ket.* 53a

DIETARY LAWS OF AN EATING CLUB

Of the 341 individual pericopes, no fewer than 229 directly or indirectly pertain to table fellowship, approximately 67 percent of the whole. The rest are scattered through all other areas of legal concern, a striking disproportion.

Houses rulings pertaining either immediately or ultimately to table fellowship involve preparation of food, ritual purity, either purity rules directly relating to food, or purity rules indirectly important on account of the need to keep food ritually clean, and agricultural rules pertaining to the proper growing, tithing, and preparation of agricultural produce for use at table. All agricultural laws concern producing or preparing food for consumption, assuring either that tithes and offerings have been set aside as the Law requires or that the conditions for the nurture of the crops have conformed to the biblical taboos. Ritual slaughter, appropriately, occurs in only one minor matter; likewise, the milk/meat taboo is applied to chicken and cheese.

The laws of ritual cleanness apply in the main to the preservation of the ritual cleanness of food, of people involved in preparing it, and of objects used in its preparation. Secondary considerations include the ritual pool. These matters became practically important in the lives of Pharisees in regard to the daily preparation of food, in the lives of all Jews only in connection with visiting the Temple, and of the priests in the cult itself. Laws regarding Sabbath and festivals furthermore pertain in large measure to the preparation and preservation of food on festivals and the Sabbath. The ritual of table fellowship also included blessings and rules of conduct at meals.

We find no such concentration of interest in any other aspects of everyday life. To be sure, ritual considerations in respect to sexual relations, apart from the preparation of food, do figure; but these are a minor part of the matter, and the ritual uncleanness that prevents sexual relations also makes a woman unclean for the preparation of food. One aspect of Sabbath law, as I have said, is surely sectarian—that is, the 'erub to permit carrying. It was supplied to alleyways, not to whole towns, which means that Pharisees never considered the possibility that they might control a larger domain.

The problem of work that was begun before the Sabbath and finished on the Sabbath and related matters looks to be of theoretical more than practical interest. People presumably kept such laws, but once a routine was established, they would not have had to receive admonition in the mat Terumot. The laws of the sukkah are tangential to the festival. Like the Sabbath and other festivals, Sukkot was part of the culture of the country. The Pharisees do not allude to building a sukkah different from that of other folk; the rulings in the matter are minor and of no great consequence.

Miscellaneous Laws

Pilgrimage laws and Temple rules are not all of the same sort. The former theoretically pertain to all Jews and concern offerings for various purposes and their cost, the liability of children to make the pilgrimage, and similar matters. But Pharisees could well have obeyed these laws without appearing to be much different from other people. The expenditure of funds, for instance, for the various pilgrim offerings was not a matter subject to the close supervision of Temple authorities. Other Temple rules seem sectarian. The references to various rites and offerings, to the way in which blood was sprinkled, to the disposal of unclean offerings, and the like are all of theoretical interest, and some of these pericopes seem to have been shaped in Yavnean times.

We should have expected more laws pertaining to family matters. Levirate marriage, the disposition of the wife's property, annulling the vows of a wife, the remarriage of a widow, exercising a minor's right of refusal, and similar topics are represented only in one or two rulings. These affect strikingly fundamental matters. One can hardly suppose that for many centuries Jews had not known what to do in these aspects of family life. In some cases, especially Gamaliel's rulings about divorce documents, we may imagine that the Pharisees have taken over and made their own the rulings of the civil authority, perhaps of Gamaliel himself, just as the form of *m. Ket.* 13:1ff. looks like a Pharisaic record of approved decrees of municipal authorities. Levirate marriage, on the other hand, apparently involved considerations internal to the sect itself. Of other items we can be less certain. Perhaps some of the rulings were primarily for the members of the group; others may represent ratification by the group of laws pertaining to everyone and issued by other authorities.

Oaths and vows, which figure in the Christian indictment of Pharisaism, play a smaller role in the traditions than their place in that indictment would have led one to anticipate. I take it for granted that the Houses did debate the theory of erroneous consecrations, or perhaps later masters discovered that specific Houses disputes revolved around that general theory. It looks as though Nazirite vows indeed were made and carried out. I should suppose party members would have been governed by party rules, while Jews not in the Pharisaic group who made Nazirite vows would have turned to Temple priests for instruction.

Ritual and liturgical matters not involving table fellowship are episodic: reciting the *Shema'*, a liturgy for the New Year that coincides with the Sabbath, the unlikely need to rule on the circumcision of a child born circumcised.

The two matters of civil law and torts both relate to how to assess damages. Whether these rules derive from Temple times or not, they do not leave the impression that Pharisees bore heavy responsibilities in the administration of justice.

GATHERINGS OF THE PHARISAIC GROUP?

If the Pharisees were, as has been taken for granted, primarily a group for Torah study (as the Qumranian writers describe themselves), then we should have expected to see more rules about the school, perhaps also scribal matters, than we actually find. Indeed, we have only one, and that, while attested at early Yavneh, merely involves sneezing in the schoolhouse. Surely other, more fundamental problems presented themselves. Nor do we find much interest in defining the master-disciple relationship, the duties of the master and the responsibilities and rights of the disciple, the way in which the disciple should learn his lessons, and similar matters of importance in later times.

This brings us to a puzzling fact: nowhere in the rabbinic traditions about the Pharisees do we find a reference to ritual gatherings of the Pharisaic party, as a whole or in small groups, for table fellowship, apart from the allusions to the question of the *'erub* for several *havurot* in the same hall. This surely supplies a slender basis on which to prove the Pharisaic party did conduct communion meals, especially so since no sectarian ritual meal is ever mentioned. By contrast, the Qumranian laws, which make much of purity, also refer to communion meals and the right, or denial of the right, of access to them for members of the commune.

Why do we find no stories of how the haberim gathered to eat and so-and-so happened or was said? Why is not the communion meal a redactional or formulary cliché, alongside *testified before Gamaliel*, or *the Elders of the Houses assembled and*? The editorial and redactional framework is silent about table fellowship. The narrative materials say nothing on the mat Terumot. And yet the laws concentrate attention on rules and regulations covering most aspects of a ritual meal, which then is never described or alluded to as such.

CHRISTIANS, PHARISEES, ESSENES

It seems to me these facts point to one conclusion: the Pharisaic groups did not conduct their table-fellowship meals as rituals. The table-fellowship laws pertained not to group life, but to ordinary, daily life lived quite apart from heightened, ritual occasions. The rules applied to the home, not merely to the cultic center, be it synagogue, Temple, or sectarian rite house (if such existed). While the early Christians gathered for ritual meals and made of these ritual meals the high point of their group life, the Pharisees apparently did not.

The very character of the sectarianism of the Pharisees therefore seems to differ from that of the sectarianism of the Christians in this important detail. What embodied and actualized group or sectarian life for the Christians and came as the climax of the group's existence was the communion meal. What expressed the Pharisees' sense of self-awareness as a group apparently was not a similar ritual meal. Eating together was a less ritualized occasion, even though the Pharisees had rituals in connection with the meal. No communion ceremony, no rites centered on meals, no specification of meals on holy occasions seem uniquely to characterize Pharisaic table fellowship. The one communion meal about which we do find legislation characterized all sects, along with the rest of the Jews: the Passover Seder. Eating in the sukkah is not of the same order. For the Seder, as for the observance of Sukkoth, the Pharisees may have had rules separate from, and additional to, those observed by everyone else. But that is not the same thing as a sectarian communion meal.

Pharisaic table fellowship thus exhibits a different quality from that of the Christians: it was of a quite ordinary, everyday character. The various fellowship rules had to be observed in a wholly routine circumstance, daily, for every meal, but without accompanying rites other than a benediction for the food. Unlike the Pharisees the Christians had a meal myth through which ritual rendered table fellowship into heightened spiritual experience: *Do this in remembrance of me.* The Pharisees told no stories about purity laws, except (in later times) to account for their historical development (e.g., who had decreed which purity rule). When they came to table, so far as we know, they told no stories about how Moses had done what they now do, and they did not do these things in memory of Moses "our Rabbi."

Qumranian table fellowship was open on much the same basis as the Pharisaic: appropriate undertakings to keep ritual purity and consume properly grown and tithed food. Priests, not laymen, said the blessings. Indeed, table fellowship depended on the presence of a priest ("Let there not lack among them a man who is a priest, and let them sit before him, each according to his rank" [1 QS vi 2–3]; "And then when they set the table to eat or prepare the wine to drink, the priest shall first stretch out his hand to pronounce a blessing on the first-fruits of bread and wine" [1 QSa ii 11–22]. Only those who knew the secret doctrine of the sect were fully accepted in table fellowship. Sinners were excluded, whether the sins pertained to the rituals of the table or otherwise. The "Messiah of Israel," after the priests, blessed the bread, then each blessed according to his rank. The blessing of the meal is an important rite, but the Qumranian table-meal references do not seem to have included a ceremony equivalent to the Eucharist. In this respect they appear to be somewhat similar to the Pharisaic meal.

Both Christians and Pharisees lived among ordinary folk, while the Qumranians did not. In this respect the commonplace character of Pharisaic table fellowship seems all the more striking. The group's ordinary gatherings were not as a group at all, but in the private home, with all participating in an ordinary meal. *All* meals required ritual purity. Pharisaic table fellowship took place in the same circumstance in which all *nonritual* table fellowship occurred: common folk, eating everyday meals, in an everyday way, amid neighbors who were not members of the sect and who engaged in workaday pursuits like everyone else. This made the actual purity rules and food restrictions all the more important, for only they set the Pharisee apart from the people among whom he constantly lived. Not on festivals nor on Sabbaths alone, but on weekdays, in the towns, without the telling of myths or the reading of holy books (Torah talk at table is attested only later), or the reenactment of first or last things, Pharisaic table fellowship depended solely on observance of the law.

That observance, apart from the meal itself, was not marked off by benedictions or other rites. No stories were told during the meal or about it. Keeping the laws included few articulate statements, such as blessings. The setting for observance was the field and the kitchen, the bed, and the street. The occasion for observance was set every time a person picked up a common nail or purchased a *seah* of wheat, by himself, without priests to bless his deed or sages to tell him what to do. So keeping the Pharisaic rule required neither an occasional, exceptional rite at, but external to, the meal, as in the Christian community, nor taking up residence in a monastic commune, as among the Qumranians, but perpetual ritualization of daily life as well as constant inner awareness of the communal order of being.

CHAPTER 13

THE PRE-70 PHARISEES AFTER 70 AND AFTER 140

Jacob Neusner

THE UNFOLDING HISTORY, IN THE LATE FIRST AND SECOND CENTURIES, OF THE RABBINIC TRADITIONS ABOUT THE PHARISEES BEFORE 70

The rabbinic traditions are attributed by the Mishnah and the Tosefta to named authorities, and the names do not circulate in random combinations but are grouped. For example, the names of Yohanan ben Zakkai, Eliezer b. Hyrcanus, and Joshua b. Hananiah commonly intersect, as do Eliezer, Joshua, Tarfon, and 'Aqiba. These figures are assumed to have flourished in Yavneh, the town to which Yohanan ben Zakkai escaped before the fall of Jerusalem, from 70 CE, when the Temple was destroyed, and for about a generation. But those names rarely or never intersect with such names as Meir, Judah bar Ilai, Yosé, or Simeon, who also form a distinct grouping. They are alleged to have gathered in the Galilean town of Usha, and they figure from the end of the Bar Kokhba War, 132–135.

Using the place-names to stand for the period, Yavneh refers to the period from 70 to ca. 130, and Usha from 140 to 170. The pericopes in which the former authorities figure are classed as the Yavnean stratum; the latter, the Ushan one. How each set of authorities dealt with the traditions attributed to the Pharisaic authorities before 70—the Houses, for example—portrays the unfolding history of the traditions about the Pharisees.

THE YAVNEAN STRATUM

References by authorities after 70 to Houses disputes alleged to have taken place prior to 70 are by far the most important in helping us to estimate the condition, by ca. 100 CE, of the traditions concerning the Pharisees. Pericopes are verified by references in the name of authorities who flourished later on. Some lack verification; these may occasionally derive from the period before 70. But materials known to Yavneans—that is to say, on which authorities from 70 comment or in which they figure—are claimed by the attributions of sayings to Yavnean authorities to have come into being and formed part of the normative tradition before, or by the time of, authorities that refer to them.

Thus, for example, such pericopes as *m. Ber.* 1:3 and *m. Yebamot* 1:4, subjected to repeated verifications by Yavnean masters (e.g., Tarfon for *m. Ber.* 1:3) must have been in something like their present form before the masters referred to them.

MISHNAH-TRACTATE BERAKHOT 1:3

A.   The House of Shammai say, "In the evening everyone should recline to recite the Shema', and in the morning they should stand.

B.   "As it says, 'When you lie down and when you rise up' (Deut 6:7)."

C.   And the House of Hillel say, "Everyone recites according to his usual manner.

D.   "As it says, 'And as you walk by the way' (ibid.)."

E.   "If so why does [the verse] say, 'When you lie down and when you rise up'?

F.   "[It means, recite the Shema] at the hour that people lie down [at night] and at the hour that people rise [in the morning]."

G.   Said R. Tarfon, "I was coming on the road and I reclined, so as to recite the Shema', according to the words of the House of Shammai. And I placed myself in danger of [being attacked by] thugs."

H.   They said to him, "You have only yourself to blame [for what might have befallen you], for you violated the ruling of the House of Hillel."

MISHNAH-TRACTATE YEBAMOT 1:4

A.   The House of Shammai declare the co-wives permitted [to enter into levirate marriage with] the other brothers.

B.   And the House of Hillel declare [them] prohibited.

C.   [If] they have performed the rite of removing the shoe,

D.   the House of Shammai declare [them] invalid [for marriage with] the priesthood.

E.   And the House of Hillel declare [them] valid.

F.   [If] they have entered into levirate marriage,

G.   the House of Shammai declare them valid [for marriage with the priesthood].

H.   And the House of Hillel declare them invalid.

I.   Even though these declare prohibited and those permit, these declare invalid and those declare valid. the House of Shammai did not refrain from taking wives from the women of the House of Hillel, nor [did] the House of Hillel [refrain from taking wives from the women] of the House of Shammai.

J.   [And despite] all those decisions regarding matters of cleanness or uncleanness in which these did declare clean and those unclean,

K.   they did not refrain from preparing things requiring preparation in a state of cleanness in dependence on one another.

TOSEFTA YEBAMOT 1:9–10

1:9   A.   [If] they entered into levirate marriage,

.   B.   the House of Shammai say, "They are valid and the off-spring is valid."

      C.   And the House of Hillel say, "They are invalid, and the off-spring is a *mamzer*" [m. Yeb. 1:4F–H].

      D.   Said R.Yohanan b. Nuri, "Come and observe how this [version of the] law is prevalent among the Israelites: to act indeed in accord with the opinion of the House of Shammai [so entering into levirate marriage], [but to treat the offspring as] a mamzer in accord with the opinion of the House of Hillel.

      E.   "If it is to act in deed in accord with the opinion of the House of Hillel, the offspring is blemished in accord with the opinion of the House of Shammai.

      F.   "But: Come and let us impose the ordinance that the cowives should perform the rite of *halisah* and not enter into levirate marriage."

      G.   But they did not have a moment in which to complete the matter, before the times prevented it.

1:10 A.   Said Rabban Simeon b. Gamaliel, "What shall we do with the former cowives?"

      B.   They asked R. Joshua, "What is the status of the children of the cowives?"

      C.   He said to them, "On what account do you push my head between two high mountains, between the House of Shammai and the House of Hillel, who can remove my head!

      D.   "But, I hereby give testimony concerning the family of the House of 'Aluba'i of Bet Seba'im and concerning the family of the House of Qipa'i of Bet Meqoshesh,

E.   "that they are children of cowives, and from them have
     been chosen high priests, and they did offer up sacrifices on
     the Temple altar."
F.   Said R. Tarfon, "I crave that the cowife of the daughter
     should come my way, and I should [so rule as to] marry her
     into the priesthood."
G.   Said R. Eleazar, "Even though the House of Shammai dis-
     puted with the House of Hillel regarding the cowives, they
     concur that the offspring is not a *mamzer*.
H.   "For the status of a *mamzer* is imposed only on the offspring
     of a woman who has entered into a marriage prohibited on
     account of licentiousness [one of those listed at Lev 18],
     and on account of which they [who enter into such a mar-
     riage] are liable to the penalty of extirpation."
I.   Even though the House of Shammai and the House of
     Hillel disputed concerning the cowives, concerning sisters,
     concerning the married woman, concerning a superannu-
     ated writ of divorce, concerning the one who betroths a
     woman with something of the value of a *perutah*, and con-
     cerning the one who divorces his wife and spends a night
     with her in an inn,
J.   the House of Shammai did not refrain from taking wives
     among the women of the House of Hillel, and the House of
     Hillel from the House of Shammai [*m. Yeb.* 1:41].
K.   But they behaved toward one another truthfully, and there
     was peace between them,
L.   since it is said, "*They loved truth and peace*" (Zech 8:19).

M. Yebamot 1:4 preserves a Houses dispute on basic levirate rules. The
Tosefta citation and gloss contain verifications from a variety of
Yavnean authorities. Similarly, *m. Ber.* 1:3, which contains the Houses'
dispute on the proper way of reciting the *Shema‘*, generates stories
involving Tarfon, Eleazar b. Azariah, and Ishmael. In these instances,
the fact that the Houses disputed such a point of law is satisfactorily
attested. To be sure, the actual form of the present pericope is not
necessarily attested. Tarfon does not say, "The House of Shammai
say . . . The House of Hillel say . . ." Joshua likewise does not cite *m.
Yebamot* 1:4 verbatim, but he does make clear reference to its substance, so that anyone familiar with the standard form might easily
reconstruct the dispute as we now have it. And the existence of the
Houses form seems to be adequately attested in earliest Yavnean
times. So while we cannot claim that the exact words of the pericopes

in the Mishnah before us derive from early Yavneh, we may aver that both the substance and the form of the pericopes are attested at that early period, and that both, surely the former, are quite likely to come from that time. It comes down to much the same thing.

HOUSES COMPOSITIONS
VERIFIED BY SAYINGS ATTRIBUTED TO YAVNEH AUTHORITIES

Let us now review the Yavnean verifications. We shall attempt to reconstruct the Houses traditions that were known by ca. 100–120 CE. We shall next add laws for the first time attested in the Ushan stratum.

A. History

1. Names—*m. Hagigah* 2:2 (Possibly Yavnean, certainly fixed by Usha)
2. Simeon b. Shetah hung eighty women in Ashqelon (Eliezer b. Hyrcanus)
3. Baba b. Buta, Shammaite disciple, offered daily suspensive guilt offering (Eliezer b. Hyrcanus)
4. Yohanan b. Zakkai and Simeon b. Gamaliel wrote epistles to outlying regions re agricultural taboos (Joshua)
5. Name: Yosé b. Yoezer of Seredah (Eliezer b. Hyrcanus + ʿAqiba)

B. Temple Law, Jerusalem, Pilgrimage, and Priestly Dues

1. Burning unclean with clean meat of Temple altar (Eliezer + ʿAqiba)
2. Laying on of hands (*m. Hag.* 2:2) (Abba Saul)
3. Bitter-water ritual (ʿAqiba)
4. Israelites eat first-born with priests (ʿAqiba)
5. Children make pilgrimage (ʿAqiba)

C. Agricultural Tithes, Offerings, and Taboos

1. Unclean heave offering mixed with clean (Eliezer b. Hyrcanus)
2. Giving heave offering of grapes and the remainder is eventually made into raisins (Eliezer b. Hyrcanus)
3. Removing old produce at Nisan (Joshua b. Hananiah)
4. *Peʾah* from olives, carobs—how given (Gamaliel II)
5. Forgotten sheaf rules (Eleazar b. Azariah, Joshua b. Hananiah)
6. Seventh-year produce rules (Tarfon)

7. Second-tithe money in Jerusalem (Tarfon, Ben Zoma, Ben Azzai, 'Aqiba)

8. Heave offering vetches ('Aqiba)

9. Fleece offering ('Aqiba)

10. Date of New Year for trees ('Aqiba)

11. Olive presses in walls of Jerusalem ('Aqiba)

12. Fourth-year fruit rules ('Aqiba)

13. Mixed seeds in vineyard ('Aqiba)

14. Heave offering from black and white figs (Ilai)

D. Sabbath Law

1. *'Erub* in public domain (Hananiah nephew of Joshua)

2. *'Erub* for separate kinds of food (Hananiah nephew of Joshua)

3. *'Erub* for alley (Eliezer b. Hyrcanus + 'Aqiba + Disciple of Ishmael)

4. Gentile/Sadducee in alley re *'erub* (Gamaliel II = Meir + Judah)

5. Work started before Sabbath ('Aqiba)

E. Festival Law

1. How much does one drink to be liable on the Day of Atonement (Eliezer b. Hyrcanus)

2. Large cakes re Passover (Gamaliel II)

3. Pick pulse on festival (Gamaliel II)

4. Other festival rules (Gamaliel II)

5. Size of sukkah (Eleazar b. R. Sadoq)

F. Liturgy

1. Order of blessing: oil vs. myrtle (Gamaliel II)

2. Proper position for saying *Shema'* (Eleazar b. Azariah, Ishmael, Tarfon)

3. How far recite Hallel at Seder (Tarfon, 'Aqiba)

4. Tefillin in privy ('Aqiba)

5. Where to shake *lulab* ('Aqiba, re Gamaliel, Joshua)

6. Limit re *Sisit* (Jonathan b. Bathyra)

7. Circumcision of child born circumcised (Eleazar b. R. Sadoq)

G. Uncleanness Laws

1. Quarter-*qab* of bones in "tent" (Joshua b. Hananiah)

2. Woman kneading in "tent" ('Aqiba, Joshua b. Hananiah)

3. If man shook tree—preparation for uncleanness by reason of water (Joshua b. Hananiah)

4. Uncleanness of liquids—Yosé b. Yoezer (Eliezer b. Hyrcanus + 'Aqiba)

5. Uncleanness of scroll wrappers (Gamaliel II)

6. When do olives receive uncleanness in harvest (Gamaliel II)

7. Mustard strainer (Eleazar b. R. Sadoq)

8. Itch inside itch (cleanness rite) ('Aqiba)

9. Insusceptibility of sheet ('Aqiba)

10. Searching grave area ('Aqiba)

11. Issue of semen in third day ('Aqiba)

12. Uncleanness of fish ('Aqiba)

H. Civil Law, Torts, and Damages

1. Damaged bailment ('Aqiba)

I. Family Law and Inheritances

1. Vow not to have intercourse (Eliezer b. Hyrcanus)

2. Husband's inheritance when wife dies as a minor (Eliezer b. Hyrcanus)

3. Signs of adulthood (Eliezer b. Hyrcanus)

4. Levirate rules re brothers married to sisters (Eliezer b. Hyrcanus, Eleazar b. Azariah, Abba Saul)

5. Levirate rules re cowives (Tarfon, Eleazar b. Azariah, 'Aqiba, Joshua b. Hananiah)

6. Test rags for each act of intercourse (Joshua b. Hananiah)

7. Sanctifies property and intends to divorce wife (Joshua b. Hananiah)

Larger issue, erroneous consecrations, verified also by Tarfon.

8. Wife remarries on testimony of one witness ('Aqiba, Gamaliel II)

9. Grounds for divorce ('Aqiba)

10. Dividing estate where order of deaths is unclear ('Aqiba)

11. Blood of woman who has given birth and not immersed (Eliezer b. Hyrcanus)

J. Miscellany

1. Taboo against drinking gentile wine (Gamaliel II)

2. Eliezer b. Hyrcanus re overturning couch before festival, *b. M.Q.* 20a, is given by Eleazar b. R. Simeon as Houses dispute, *t. M.Q.* 2:9

The bulk of the Houses disputes relate to three major sorts of law: agricultural tithes, offerings, and taboos; uncleanness laws; and Sabbath and festival laws. A fourth, somewhat less important area of law pertains to family life and estates. Now we see that roughly the same proportions apply to the Yavnean verifications.

THE RABBINIC TRADITIONS ABOUT THE PHARISEES BEFORE 70: THE SHAPE OF THE TRADITION BY 130

We may reliably allege that by the end of Yavnean times the names of the pre-70 Pharisees were fairly well established in the lists represented in *m. Hagigah* 2:2. We have additional verification of the names of Yosé b. Yoezer, Simeon b. Shetah, Baba b. Buta, and Simeon b. Gamaliel. Simeon b. Shetah's hangings at Ashqelon are attested very early. So are the epistles of Yohanan b. Zakkai and Simeon b. Gamaliel as well as Yosé b. Yoezer's uncleanness rulings. That constitutes the whole of the historical record indubitably known at Yavneh.

Clearly, the earliest Yavneans had only a modest interest in Pharisaic history. They exhibit no claim to begin something new, but rather they take for granted their continuity with the antecedent Pharisees. It simply cannot be maintained that early Yavneans were aware of a fundamental break between themselves and earlier generations.[1] Further, since no one makes a point of denying any sort of break with the past, we assume that it was unnecessary to do so. The continuity between Temple and post-Temple times evidently was a fixed element in the self-understanding of Yavneans. There is no evidence that the work of writing the history of what had gone before was undertaken at Yavneh. That seems to have been an Ushan project, after the end of the Bar Kokhba debacle and the clear evidence that the Temple and Jerusalem were gone for the foreseeable future. A new age had begun and had made its mark.

We have no considerable evidence of special interest in Temple laws, the Jerusalem pilgrimage, priestly dues, and the like. While it is alleged that some of the earliest tractates were formed for the purpose of preserving records of the Temple rites, the evidence before us would not seem to contribute much support for that thesis. Neither, however, does it refute it, since Temple practices before 70 were pre-

sumably settled by priestly law and were not matters about which disputes between the Houses were likely to arise, or, if they arose, to be
either important or remembered. The absence of any considerable
record of such disputes implicitly contradicts the later rabbinic claim
that before 70 the Pharisees settled questions of Temple procedures.
Apart from the laying-on-of-hands dispute, which is surely old and
pertinent primarily to the party's inner life, the laws of none of the
verified Temple pericopes required Pharisaic adjudication at just this
time. Clearly the rule on burning unclean with clean meat, the question of whether Israelites join with priests in eating the firstborn animal, the law concerning children's making pilgrimages, and the
bitter-water ritual—all these were matters of fact. Asking any Temple
priest should have produced an authoritative answer. They are random and do not exhibit a single pattern of relationships or common
underlying themes.

The considerable list of laws about agricultural tithes, offerings,
and taboos points toward a more extensive corpus of law than is actually attested. It is taken for granted that the tithes and offerings are
given and the agricultural taboos observed. The particular problems
under discussion in the very earliest period do not leave the impression that early Yavneans had to settle fundamental issues about such
matters. On the contrary, only minor details remained to be worked
out. For example, the rule that one gives a heave offering only for the
same species—for example, grapes for grapes, but not wine for
grapes—must lie far in the background, if the question now is asked,
What about grapes that *eventually* are made into raisins? Some of the
other issues evidently are brought up by legal logic, rather than by the
exigencies of daily life; the olive press in the walls of Jerusalem is one
obvious case.

Sabbath and festival laws are not sufficiently numerous to justify an
equivalent opinion. Clearly, the 'erub was accepted in Pharisaic law
and may have formed a point in sectarian debate before 70. The rule
about making an 'erub for an alleyway seems to be a genuine Houses
dispute of pre-70 times; the masters debate whether the Houses had
said one had to do both, or either, of the required procedures.

Some of the liturgical laws, however, form a striking contrast
because of their elementary character. Is it possible that it was only in
early Yavneh that rabbinic Jews recited the Shema'? To be sure, the

problem of where to shake the *lulab* now first faced Jews who had formerly observed the pilgrim festivals primarily in Jerusalem. So the inquiries on such matters seem to pertain to fundamental liturgical problems. But the number of verified laws is small, and we cannot draw significant conclusions from them. Similarly, Jews, including Pharisees, presumably had observed the Passover Seder for generations before Tarfon and 'Aqiba referred to the Houses dispute on how far one recites the Hallel. From the content of such laws we cannot derive reliable conclusions. It is only the contrast between the elementary problems of liturgy and the far-fetched issues faced by the Houses with reference to agricultural and uncleanness laws that is suggestive.

The uncleanness pericopes likewise take for granted a very considerable corpus of antecedent rulings. For example, the rule about conveying uncleanness by a "tent" underlies many Houses disputes with early verifications; the uncleanness of liquids, the rule "If water be put on," the question of when various objects cease, or begin, to receive uncleanness—these rules are secondary and peripheral to the pericopes in which they stand. One does not receive the impression that the early Yavneans were engaged in the process of shaping a considerable corpus of new laws concerning ritual cleanness.

By contrast, we have only one verified pericope concerning civil law, torts, and damages—that about the compensation for a damaged bailment. On that basis, one can hardly imagine the later Pharisees had left a considerable corpus of laws dealing with civil affairs. Further, there is the remarkable paucity of pericopes, with or without verification, in the whole of the division of Damages (*Seder Neziqin*). Later rabbis presumably took over and refined and developed whatever civil laws survived the destruction, but they did *not* attribute them to the Houses of Shammai and Hillel. This seems to me to suggest two things. First, the pre-70 Houses did not hand over a substantial corpus of laws concerning civil matters, torts, and damages. They did not do so probably because they did not have much occasion to develop such a corpus of laws. The civil courts were in the hands of Temple priests, not sectaries, and the Pharisees concentrated their attention on those sorts of law of immediate sectarian interest, specifically agricultural, cleanness, Sabbath and festival, and to a smaller degree, family laws. Second, the attributions of laws and disputes to the pre-70 Pharisees are apt in the main to be reliable, for the later rabbis evidently did not assign to pre-70 Pharisees, or to the Houses, disputes or laws on subjects about which the pre-70 Pharisees in fact did not hand on traditions.

Family and inheritance law is of several kinds. Part of family law pertains to the division of property—for example, the sanctification of property in connection with a divorce, dividing estates, and the like. The other part deals with sexual taboos, such as the laws of menstrual purity, the prohibition of marriage among various relationships, and so on. The former leaves the impression of the development of relatively new types of rules. Thus, Gamaliel's saying that "we are having difficulty in rationalizing one rule, so do not raise a problem in connection with another" suggests that the early Yavneans took over a considerable corpus of law—partly from the Pharisaic party, partly from common law—and had to work out and rationalize the whole. And while the Houses dispute about levirate marriage rules seems to me firmly attested, that the pre-70 Houses debated the matter appears beyond reasonable doubt.

To summarize: the work of Yavneh consisted, first, in establishing viable forms for the organization and transmission of the Houses material. These forms obliterated whatever antecedent materials were available, for, as I have said, we may assume the respective Houses shaped autonomous materials, not merely in antithetical relationship to the opposition, and handed down those materials in coherent units. Second, the Yavneans made considerable progress in redacting antecedent materials in the forms they created. We have already listed the areas of law to which they gave most attention. The Yavnean stratum is virtually exhausted by those materials. It also is possible that much of the anti-Shammaite polemic of the Hillelites may derive from Yavnean times, when the issues separating the parties still were hotly debated.

THE PRE-70 PHARISEES AT USHA

The Ushan verifications require specification in terms of the sorts of law and traditions pertaining to pre-70 Pharisees that were attested within less than a century after the destruction of the Temple.

A. History

1. Echo to Simeon the Just and Yohanan the High Priest (Judah b. Baba)
2. Echo to Hillel, Samuel the Small, etc. (Judah b. Baba)
3. Hillel came up at forty (Post-Aqibans?)
4. Rise of Hillel (*t. Pisha* 4:13 version)
5. Hillel expounded language of common folk (Meir + Judah?)
6. Disputes come from poor (Yosé)
7. End of grapeclusters (Judah b. Baba)
8. Trough of Jehu (Judah b. Ilai)
9. Hillel: Scatter/gather (Simeon b. Yohai)
10. Who prepared heifer sacrifices (Meir)
11. Lay/not lay (Meir + Judah)
12. Temple of Onias (Meir + Judah)
13. Simeon b. Shetah vs. Judah b. Tabbai as Nasi (Meir + Judah)
14. Letter of Gamaliel to the Diaspora (Judah)
15. Yohanan b. Gudgada's sons (Judah)

B. Temple Law, Jerusalem, Pilgrimage, and Priestly Dues

1. Two sprinklings of sacrificial blood (Eliezer b. Jacob)
2. Coins for shekel (Simeon b. Yohai)
3. Burn flesh inside/outside (Meir + Judah)

C. Agricultural Tithes, Offerings, and Taboos

1. Watering plants until New Year of seventh year (Yosé b. Kifar, or Eleazar b. R. Sadoq)
2. Israelite woman eats Terumah (Yosé)
3. Dough for challah (Yosé)
4. Heave offering of oil for crushed olives (Yosé)
5. Produce not fully harvested passed through Jerusalem (Yosé)
6. Olive presses in walls of Jerusalem (Yosé)
7. *Demai* re '*omer* (Simeon b. Yohai)
8. *Demai* re challah (Simeon b. Yohai)
9. Change silver and produce (Meir)
10. Heave offering of fenugreek (Meir + Judah)
11. Fruit of prepared field in seventh year (Judah)

12. Vineyard patch (Judah)

13. Burn doubtful heave offering (Judah)

14. Young shoot over stone (Simeon b. Gamaliel, Yosé + Meir)

15. Assigning produce to past/coming year (Simeon b. Gamaliel)

16. Fruit of fourth-year vineyard re fifth removal (Simeon b. Gamaliel)

17. *Demai* re sweet oil (Nathan)

D. *Sabbath Law*

1. Clearing table on Sabbath (Yosé)

2. Work started before Sabbath, completed on Sabbath (Yosé)

3. *'Erub* with Sadducee (Meir + Judah)

4. Put back on stove (Meir + Judah)

5. Food for Sabbath (Judah)

6. Work to gentile launderers before Sabbath (Simeon b. Gamaliel)

7. Charity on Sabbath (Simeon b. Gamaliel)

8. *'Erub* for cistern (Simeon b. Gamaliel)

E. *Festival Law*

1. Proselyte on day before Passover (Yosé)

2. Gifts on festival (Yosé + Judah)

3. Return *pesah* whole (Simeon b. Yohai)

4. Tying pigeon (Simeon b. Yohai)

5. Egg laid on festival (Meir)

6. Prepare spices, salt on festival (Meir)

7. Timber roofing of sukkah (Meir + Judah)

8. Pick pulse on festival (Judah)

9. More vessels on account of need (Simeon b. Gamaliel)

F. *Liturgy*

1. Order of Habdalah (Meir + Judah)

G. *Uncleanness Laws*

1. · Vessels before *am ha'aretz* (Dosetai b. K. Yannai)

2. Uncleanness of weasel (Yosé)

3. Burn clean and unclean meat together (Yosé)

4. Measure chest (Yosé)

5. Split in roof (Yosé)

6.   Gather grapes in grave area (Yosé)

7.   Lid chain connector (Yosé)

8.   Place water (*m. Makh.* 1:4) (Yosé + Judah)

9.   Vessel under waterspout (Yosé + Meir)

10.   Water from roof leaked into jar (Yosé + Meir)

11.   Uncleanness of *Qohelet* (Yosé + Simeon)

12.   Uncleanness of girdle (Simeon b. Yohai)

13.   Removing pot for heave offering (Simeon b. Yohai)

14.   Uncleanness of her who has difficulty giving birth (Simeon b. Yohai)

15.   Sin-offering water that has fulfilled its purpose (Simeon b. Yohai)

16.   How much lacking in skull (tent) (Meir)

17.   When is tube clean (Meir + Judah)

18.   When is sheet clean (Meir + Judah)

19.   Stool on baking trough (Meir + Judah)

20.   Menstrual blood of gentile woman (Meir + Judah)

21.   Quarter-*qab* of bones in tent (Judah)

22.   When is vat made unclean (Judah)

23.   Open hole to let out uncleanness (Judah)

24.   Anoint self with clean oil (Judah)

25.   Blood of carcass (Judah)

26.   Water-skin (Judah)

27.   Sell food to *haber* (Simeon b. Gamaliel)

28.   When is ritual pool deemed clean (Simeon b. Gamaliel)

H. *Civil Law, Torts, and Damages*

1.   Hillel and futures (usury) (Meir, Judah, Simeon)

2.   Restore beam or value (Simeon b. Gamaliel)

I. *Family Law and Inheritances*

1.   Lewdness with minor son (Yosé)

2.   Cohabitation with mother-in-law (Yosé + Judah)

3.   Girl married before flow (Meir, Simeon b. Gamaliel, Judah)

4.   Nursing mother remarries (Meir + Judah)

5.   Betrothed woman disposes of goods (Judah)

6. How many children before desisting from marital life (Nathan)

7. Annulling daughter's vows (Nathan)

8. Three betroth woman-witness/agent (Nathan)

J. Miscellany

1. Targum of Job (Yosé)

2. Nazir: Erroneous vow (Yosé. Judah)

3. Chicken and cheese (Yosé)

4. Nazirite vow for longer period (Judah)

THE RABBINIC TRADITIONS ABOUT THE PHARISEES BEFORE 70:
THE SHAPE OF THE TRADITION BY 170

The work of the Ushan period lasted for a generation, 140–170. In general, the pattern discerned in Yavnean attestations persists, but with one important change. Ushans clearly were involved in the development of a history of pre-70 Pharisaism. Nearly all historical pericopes for which we could suggest verification derive from Ushans—in particular, Judah b. Baba, Meir, and Judah. Clearly, important elements of the rabbinic history of Pharisaism were given approximately fixed form in Ushan times. Otherwise, the earlier proportions are not greatly revised. We find no important increase in Temple, Jerusalem, pilgrimage, and priestly laws. Agricultural tithes and related matters and uncleanness rules continue to constitute by far the largest part of Ushan attestations. Those sorts of law concerning which we found few rules remain the same; we observe no tendency to shape, in the names of the Houses, laws on civil and family affairs.

We cannot hypothesize that the Houses serve as a mere literary convenience for the formation of laws in easily remembered patterns. Had there been such a convenience, it should have served for civil laws no less than cleanness ones. Since it does not, I suppose that the tradents of Yavneh and Usha did not invent, in the names of the Houses, pericopes dealing with laws on which they had no traditions from the Houses. They clearly reworked both protases and apodoses of various sorts of Houses materials. But, as I have said, they apparently did not fabricate laws according to the Houses pattern concerning matters about which the historical Houses had left them no traditions whatsoever. This seems to me very persuasive evidence of the fundamental authenticity of the rabbinic traditions about the pre-70 Pharisees. It was not likely that later tradents invented out of whole cloth something without any foundation at all in earlier traditions.

It may now be suggested that the pre-70 Houses handed on traditions concerning three areas of law: agricultural tithes, offerings, and taboos; Sabbath and festival law; and cleanness rules. It is entirely possible that a few family laws were formulated, in particular with relationship to levirate marriage. Whether the details of the laws attributed to the Houses actually derive from the pre-70 masters is of course a more difficult question. Our earlier studies have shown a tendency to revise both protases and apodoses, though never in the same pericope. So it would seem that the *thematic* substance, but not the details, of the pre-70 traditions, particularly those deriving from the Houses, in considerable measure lies before us.

From a legal standpoint, the Ushan verifications do not significantly alter the picture yielded by the Yavnean ones. The areas of law on which the Houses legislated do not appreciably expand. What becomes commonplace is the revision of earlier Houses materials. We find in some later Yavnean pericopes a few items in which a master alleges the Houses did not really differ about the matter on which it is alleged they differed. But rather, on that matter they were in complete agreement, very often on the Hillelite side. They really differed concerning a much finer point of law. In Ushan pericopes this mode of interpretation of Houses pericopes becomes commonplace, and in the circles of Judah the Patriarch it predominates to the near exclusion of all other sorts of commentary. This means that in the study of the Houses materials, the Ushans were prepared both to revise what they had, and to investigate the legal principles underlying the antecedent materials, extending actual disputes to the most ambiguous possible matters. This mode of study signifies that the Ushans and the circle of Judah the Patriarch found the Houses materials especially interesting as sources for legal theory, no longer attending to the actualities of the earliest disputes, if they had access to such information to begin with. And this further implies that the historical Houses lay sufficiently far in the background such that legal theory, rather than practical politics, might become the focus of inquiry.

At the same time Ushans gave considerable effort to the working out and redaction of historical materials. Indeed, most verifiable historical materials in the rabbinic traditions about the Pharisees are attested for the first time at Usha. It seems that the Ushans, aware of the need to reconstruct out of the remnants of pre-140 rabbinic traditions a viable legal and political structure, at the same time sought to establish historical continuities between themselves and the earlier masters. This was done in part by telling about the pre-70 masters and attempting to systematize and organize their history, not merely their legal traditions. While redacting 'Aqiban materials, the Ushans included in the normative tradition as much as they could about ancients, back to Moses. So the Mosaic origins of the Oral Torah and the history of the Oral Torah from Moses down to Usha itself supplied the primary theme of Ushan historians. That seems to me to signify awareness of a lack of continuity with the past, just as the Yavneans' apparent indifference to historical questions tends to suggest a strong sense that nothing much had changed. It is still another mark of the abyss separating pre- from post-Bar Kokhban times. It suggests that the real break in the history of the Pharisaic-rabbinic movement comes not at 70, with the destruction of the Temple, but at 140, with the devastation of southern Palestine and the reconstitution of the rabbinic movement and the patriarchal government in the north.

The Ushans evidently are responsible for introducing into the normative tradition various historical themes. Simeon the Just and Yohanan the High Priest and their heavenly messages first occur in pericopes apparently redacted at Usha. Hillel becomes a central figure. His migration from Babylonia is taken for granted; his rise to power is the subject of serious historical efforts; his sayings about futures, his ordinances about the redemption of property, his expounding the language of common people, some of his moral sayings—these are materials first attested at Usha. Part of the reason may be, as I have suggested, the renewed interest of the patriarchate, now under Simeon b. Gamaliel, in discovering for itself more agreeable ancestors than the discredited Gamaliel II. And part of the reason (for it was not a patriarchal venture alone) must be the interest in recovering usable heroes from within Pharisaism itself, in place of Bar Kokhba and other messianic types. A further—though, I think, minor—subtheme of Hillel materials was to stress that masters came to Palestine from Babylonia, not the reverse; at this time important masters had located themselves in Babylonia and others tended to leave Palestine for foreign parts.

The Houses disputes, now well known, had to be explained. This was attributed to the failure of disciples. The same theme recurs in the grapecluster pericope, certainly an Ushan invention. Since, as Gary G. Porton has shown, Bar Kokhba had made extensive use of the symbol of the grapecluster on his coins and was the first to do so (the symbol occurs only once, on a coin of Archelaus, before his time), it stands to reason that the characterization of Pharisaic masters as grapeclusters, bearers of the abiding blessing, was neither accidental nor irrelevant to the Ushan situation. The claim seems to be that sages, not messiahs, are the source of blessing. This theme then is tied into the issue of the disputes of the former generations. Disputes are traced to the end of the grapeclusters, with the concomitant warning that new disputes will call into disrepute the work of the Ushans as well. Therefore, people had better learn their lessons well and avoid controversy. And to this theme is tied still another: Hillel, Samuel the Small, and Judah b. Baba all would have received the Holy Spirit, but the generation was unworthy. At Usha this has obvious implications: those who now claim to receive the Holy Spirit are charlatans. No one, not even the great Hillel, had received it. Furthermore, the unworthiness of the generation prevented it then, and if the generation now does not conform to the Torah, it, too, cannot hope to receive divine communications.

The grapecluster pericope is only one effort to periodize the history of ancient times. Another is represented by the Meir-Judah discussion on the Pharisaic chains; *to lay/not to lay* is verified at Usha. Just as the supernatural history was divided into periods, so, too, was the history of the Pharisaic party itself worked out in terms of the names of the presiding authorities in each stage of the party's history. The dispute about the relative places of Judah b. Tabbai and Simeon b. Shetah is closely related to this matter. Meir and Judah seem primarily responsible for the provision of a history for Pharisaism, with Judah b. Baba responsible for the account of the supernatural history. Yosé b. Halafta did not know the uncleanness chain, and this may mean either that it comes later than Usha or that it was made up in a different circle and not transmitted to Sepphoris, where he conducted his school, during his lifetime. Meir and Judah likewise debate the circumstances of the founding of the Temple of Onias in Alexandria. Judah supplies the letter of Gamaliel and the Elders to the Diaspora, here following the model of Joshua's letter of Simeon and Yohanan, assuming the latter is validly attributed and, indeed, is prior because of that attribution. Judah is responsible for the precedent about the Helene story, which shows an interest in first-century Pharisaic history. Likewise, *who prepared the heifer ceremony* is discussed at Usha. Thus, the five central issues of sacred history—the history of the supernatural, the history of the messianic blessing, the history of the Pharisaic party and of the Oral Torah, and the history of the cult—all were worked out at Usha.

THE RABBINIC (USHAN) HISTORY OF PHARISAISM

If we now review the Ushan history of Pharisaism, we arrive at the following picture: from the time of Moses onward, the divine blessing inhered in the grapeclusters. These were men who bore the special grace of God. They lasted to the time of the Yosé's, after which dissension split the Oral Torah into many parts, and the blessing was lost. But it was restored by Judah b. Baba, who had ordained the surviving students of 'Aqiba. Those very students now dominate at Usha. So the grapecluster-blessing of ancient times has been restored. If the disciples at Usha learn their lessons and satisfactorily serve their masters, the blessing will persist. And the grapecluster, everyone knew, was the sign of the Messiah. Therefore, on the unity of the rabbinic group at Usha depended the hope of Israel for the coming of the Messiah—on that unity and *not* on the pretensions of messianic generals. Meanwhile, none should suppose that the chain has been broken that extends from Usha back to Sinai. On the contrary, the list of the masters from Sinai onward demonstrates the perfect continuity of the tradition. What began at Sinai endures to this very day.

Heavenly messages came to worthy men in the past—Simeon the Just and Yohanan the High Priest were even able to tell what was happening at distant places. Hillel himself alleged that the Holy Spirit was upon Israel. So those who today want to rely on the echo and on the Holy Spirit may take comfort. However, Hillel himself did not receive the Holy Spirit, and the reason was the unworthiness of his contemporaries. Just as the decline of generations and the rise of disputes had withdrawn the blessing of the grapecluster, and with it the messianic hope, from Israel, so the unworthiness of the generation has deprived Israel of its spiritual gift of receiving revelation.

The stress on sin as the cause for the thwarting both of the messianic hope and of the capacity to receive the marks of divine concern corresponds to the message of Yohanan b. Zakkai's circle after the destruction of the Temple: Take comfort, for he who punished you for your sins can be relied on to recognize your penitence and to respond to and reward your regeneration. Here, too, the comfort is that Israel's own sin, and not the might of a foreign conqueror, accounts for Israel's present condition. These primary spiritual concerns for the Messiah and for receiving direct divine communications suggest that people claimed to have heavenly messages in Bar Kokhban times. But they certainly point toward the messianic claim of Bar Kokhba himself. 'Aqiba's students could not affirm the master's view that Bar Kokhba had been the Messiah. What they could and did allege was that the messianic blessing remained intact, enduring within the rabbinical group itself. This accomplished two important purposes. First, it saved from the debacle of Bar Kokhba the remnant of the messianic hope. Second, it made certain that anyone who was subject to the influence of the rabbis would reject the notion that someone who was not a rabbi might again enjoy the sponsorship of rabbis in asserting a messianic claim.

The Temple lay in ruins, and now prospects of rebuilding it were hardly encouraging. The founding of a Temple not in Jerusalem was attributed to disreputable persons. Anyone who proposed to build a Temple in some place safer than Jerusalem, as did Onias in Leontopolis, could not hope to enjoy the support of Palestinians or the approval of the rabbis. This message was brought by Ushans to Hananiah, Joshua's nephew, in Babylonia.[2]

The patriarch descended from the Babylonian, Hillel, not from those discredited in the tumult of the approach of the Bar Kokhba War. Hillel had been a Babylonian, but had had to endure poverty in order to study in Palestine, and all his power depended on that study. Therefore, the rabbis going abroad should know it is better to remain in Palestine and to study even though in poverty than to emigrate to a more abundant but spiritually deprived land.

These, I think, are some of the contemporary motifs emerging from the Ushan pericopes on the history of Pharisaism. Of course, we cannot claim that Ushan storytellers invented the stories in order to make these very points. That is something we do not know. It is clear, however, that in telling such stories, they conveyed a message peculiarly pertinent to their own situation—point by point.

PART THREE

THE PHARISEES IN MODERN THEOLOGY

CHAPTER 14

THE GERMAN THEOLOGICAL TRADITION

Susannah Heschel

The Pharisees have long served as a metonymy for Judaism in Christian scholarship, so that studies of their history and beliefs have presented the Pharisees as the Jews par excellence, an essence of what Judaism, especially rabbinic Judaism, proclaims and practices. As a result, scholarship on the Pharisees by Christians in pre-World War II Germany was often infused with political and cultural biases toward Judaism, just as Jewish scholarship on the Pharisees often functioned apologetically.

Interest in the Pharisees on the part of German Protestant scholars[1] was prompted in particular by issues related to the gospels and the origins of Christianity, especially the question of Jesus' relationship to the rabbis of his day. Did Christianity arise as a Jewish—even Pharisaic—religion, taught by Jesus, or as a movement in opposition to it? Jesus' relation to the Pharisees was the pivotal point in arguing not only for the nature of Jesus' own religiosity, but also for the relationship between his faith and the Christianity that subsequently developed concerning him. For Jews, Pharisee scholarship constituted a defense of rabbinic Judaism against Christian hostility, but the scholarship also was intricately bound to the newly arising reforms of Judaism, especially Jewish law. Whether Jews advocated Orthodoxy or Reform, Pharisaism was claimed as the justification and inspiration for their theological position.

Abraham Geiger, whose work on the Pharisees "set the terms for the debate in the nineteenth and twentieth centuries,"[2] inaugurated modern scholarship in the field not only because of his radically new conceptualization of the nature of Pharisaism, but because he introduced a new set of primary sources, the Mishnah and the Targumim, and claimed to find references to Pharisee-Sadducee

debates in apocryphal and pseudepigraphical literature. His redefinition of Pharisaic Judaism as a liberalizing, progressive movement
and of Jesus as a representative of that movement combined both to
undermine claims to Jesus' originality and to assert a Pharisaic spirit
of liberalization as guiding contemporary reforms of Jewish law.
Although his conclusions were accepted by most subsequent Jewish
scholars, they won almost universal dismissal by German Protestants,
including Wellhausen, Schürer, Bousset, and Meyer, who presented
the Pharisees as legalistic and religious materialists against whom
Jesus protested. Rejecting rabbinic literature as a basis of information about the Pharisees, Protestants adhered to Josephus and the
gospels as the primary reliable sources and used those texts to
describe what they claimed was the negative and often degenerate
nature of Pharisaism.

Few nineteenth- and twentieth-century Christian scholars in
Germany applied the rigorous historical-critical methods common to
scholarship in other fields to their analysis of sources regarding the
Pharisees. The testimonies of Josephus concerning the Pharisees were
accepted without skepticism, and the gospel texts, despite their
polemical and theological nature, were allowed to define the nature of
early first-century Pharisaism, despite problems with dating those
texts. For example, the Pharisees were assumed to be identical to the
rabbis; no historical development within Pharisaic Judaism was
described; Pharisaism was presented as identical with postrabbinic
Judaism; and the Pharisees were described using adjectives drawn
from modern anti-Jewish literature. Little suspicion was brought to
the later rabbinic texts or to the Christian literature that claimed to
reveal the origins and nature of Pharisaic concerns. Few Christian
scholars cited rabbinic texts or constructively engaged the work of
contemporary Jewish scholars. Most Christian scholarship made
Pharisaism representative of Judaism and characterized it as superfi-
cial, legalistic, materialistic, and religiously degenerate. A typical
example is the comment of Gustav Volkmar, one of the leading figures in the Tübingen school of the nineteenth century, who wrote in
1857, "The Pharisees represent a wish to deceive oneself and, on top
of it, God, [a wish] which turned out to be no more than an ever-
growing despair, the tighter and more hardened the shackles of the
idolatrous power, which one hoped to evade through hypocrisy."[3]

Given the sharply historicist commitments of the Tübingen school, which dated the gospels' composition very late and viewed their claims not as historical but as theologically tendentious evidence, Volkmar's comments are particularly disturbing.

Most important among the issues debated in pre-World War II Pharisee scholarship was whether Mishnaic texts constituted a usable source for first-century Pharisaism, and how to weigh evidence that conflicted with the gospels and Josephus. Given the importance of studies of the Pharisees not only for the reconstruction of Second Temple Judaism, but also for Christian origins, the influence of scholarly conclusions was broad. The many histories of the New Testament era that began to be published in the 1860s included chapters on Pharisaic religion, as did gospel commentaries, so that even the more rarified scholarship trickled down to pastors and their congregants.

The hostile appellations given to the Pharisees in certain gospel passages and repeated in Christian classics were generally accepted without question by modern Christian scholars. Pharisaic religion was described as rigid, petrified, degraded, cankered, disfigured, wrathful, violent, and even as a cadaver; Pharisaism was alleged to be a religion of materialism, deception, hypocrisy, abomination, and shackles; it murders the conscience, gentleness, and the true religious spirit and, in the end, persecutes Jesus with enraged frenzy, to cite just a few of the adjectives used in modern Christian scholarship.[4] There was little deviation in Christian and even in some early Jewish historiography from the view that the Pharisees were the bitter opponents of Jesus who were ultimately responsible for his trial and death, and that as a religious group they typified insincerity.

One example is an early book-length German Protestant study of the Pharisees, published in 1824 by Michael Wirth, which spoke of the Pharisees' hidden inveterate evil (*Krebsschaden*)[5] and warns: "These shadows, which exalt the glory of our Lord, are the Pharisees. In them, however, and through us a repellent picture is set up, which strongly warns against hypocrisy, which is an abomination in the eyes of God."[6] In 1848 the theological encyclopedia edited by Georg Winer, the *Biblisches Realwörterbuch*, a standard reference work, defined the Pharisees as hypocritical, ambitious, and zealously legalistic. Arising after the return to Palestine from Babylonian exile, the Pharisees, according to Winer, took shape during the Maccabean era and had the support of the masses and, particularly, Jewish women. Winer cited Christoph Friedrich von Ammon (1766–1850), professor at Erlangen and court preacher of Saxony, in blaming the Pharisees' opposition to Jesus on their character traits of "hypocrisy" and "ambition."[7]

Similar conclusions are found in the 1846 *Encyclopedia* of Ersch and Gruber, a nontheological academic publication, which defined the Pharisees as a theological-political faction, not a religious sect, whose fiery nationalist zeal encouraged their heated resistance to the Romans and whose religious views placed them in bitter opposition to Jesus.[8]

Such views recapitulated the views promoted by eighteenth-century scholars, such as Buxtorf, Cappellus, and Hottinger, as well as those of early nineteenth-century scholars, including August Neander, Matthias Schneckenburger, and August Gfrörer.[9] Neander, himself a Jewish convert to Christianity, presented the Pharisees without reference to any Hebrew-language sources, and described them as persecuting the early Christians because of their "hostile tendencies." They taught a syncretistic religion that combined Mosaism with speculative mysticism, yet were unable, according to Neander, to accept anything new beyond the law.[10] The New Testament scholar Matthias Schneckenburger viewed the Pharisees as narrow-minded, legalistic ascetics who sought political power, and he emphasized the bitterness, fanaticism, and murderous hatred of the Pharisees toward Jesus, the apostles, and Paul.[11] Gfrörer (1803–1861), a librarian in Stuttgart who had studied with F. C. Baur in Tübingen, changed the terms of the discussion, presenting the Pharisees not as a sect, but as a theological-political faction that originated with the return from Babylonian exile. Pharisaic ideas not found in the Hebrew Bible were assumed to have been developed under Babylonian or Persian influence, and because the ideas were foreign, the Sadducees objected to them and set themselves in opposition to the Pharisees.[12]

One early Jewish historian, Isaac Jost, spoke in the 1820s of the Pharisees' legalism and narrow-mindedness (*Spitzfindigkeit*) and blamed their hostility toward Rome for kindling the revolt, holding them responsible for its failure.[13] Jost writes of the Pharisees' blind rage and its destructive consequences: "If the accusation falls to the Jews, that they destroyed themselves, then the Pharisees carry the greatest blame. History will show us their conduct."[14] Levi Herzfeld, whose three-volume political history of the Jews appeared between 1847 and 1857, used milder language but still spoke of Pharisaism as a routinized religion.[15]

Scholarly depictions of the Pharisees were inflected by a range of theological and political concerns and were also affected by changing standards of historical investigation during the nineteenth century. Gfrörer was hailed by G. F. Moore as marking the advent of modern Christian studies of Judaism.[16] Yet, although Gfrörer considered the emancipation of the Jews a "duty of humanity,"[17] he also expected Jews to bring an end to Judaism, a point Moore fails to note. Presumably, his often harsh description of the Pharisees was intended to discourage Jews from continued attachment to Judaism. Despite Gfrörer's extensive use of rabbinic literature and contemporary Jewish scholarship, his depiction of Judaism, elaborated at length in his two-volume work, *Das Jahrhundert des Heils*, published in 1838, remained consistent with the stereotypes of Christian theological polemics.[18] For example, he writes, "That our Lord healed the sick on the Sabbath, that his disciples plucked branches on these days, the Pharisees needed as the reason for furious persecution. They hated with all their hearts a teacher who lifted up substance over form, love and true convictions over outward appearances."[19] In Gfrörer's view, the Pharisees are worse than the Catholics: "The Pharisees closed the gate of the tradition much more eagerly than did the papacy; they plugged the fountains from which any kind of renewal in their church circles might flow."[20] By contrast, the Sadducees are described, by Gfrörer and others, as proto-Protestants.[21] Throughout, Gfrörer cites rabbinic sources and warmly commends the recent work of Jewish scholars, including Geiger, but his work, in turn, was generally ignored by Jewish historians, including Geiger, whose own scholarship soon rendered Gfrörer's work outmoded.

Serious German scholarship on the Pharisees began with the publication of Geiger's *Urschrift und Übersetzungen der Bibel* in 1857. Prior to that time, the Pharisees were discussed, but without the critical methods that mark historical scholarship. The *Urschrift*, one of the seminal works of the Wissenschaft des Judentums, drew a complex portrait of the Pharisees and their antagonists, the Sadducees, based on a wide range of textual sources and on a theory of religion that integrated political, cultural, and cultic elements in its history of Judaism during

the years between 200 BCE and 200 CE. Geiger drew as sources for
his history on redactions and translations of the biblical text, including the Samaritan, Septuagintal, Masoretic, and Targumic, arguing
that what determines the nature of a religion is political and social
context, not ahistorical points of dogma.[22]

Prior to Geiger, historians generally had accepted without question
the gospels' depiction of the Pharisees and Josephus's reconstruction
of the differences between the Pharisees and Sadducees, despite the
lack of external corroboration by other sources from the same period.
Josephus's claims were assumed to be accurate by modern historians
as much as by the church fathers. Josephus's claim that the Sadducees
accepted only the written law, while rejecting the oral law of the
Pharisees, led Geiger to one of his central and most significant arguments: that the Sadducees as well as the Pharisees developed an oral
law.[23] Priestly service in the Temple required interpretation and
expansion of biblical law, leading to what Geiger called a Sadducean
halakha. The Sadducees' halakha and that of the Pharisees operated
on comparable principles; Geiger rejected the suggestion that the
Sadducees were biblical literalists while the Pharisees were open to
interpretation of the Bible. However, he argued that Sadducean
halakha sought to preserve the prerogatives of the priests and to
establish a hierarchy within Jewish religious practice, and was generally conservative and reluctant to implement change. Among the
examples Geiger presented was levirate marriage; he argued that
debates over it illustrated Sadducean and Pharisaic positions. Geiger
argued that the Sadducees limited levirate marriage to cases of a vir-
gin woman whose betrothed husband had died, whereas the Pharisees
liberalized the circumstances to include cases in which the marriage
had been sexually consummated.[24]

In early articles of the 1830s, Geiger portrayed the Pharisees,
Sadducees, and Essenes phenomenologically, as representing religious
tendencies of rationalism, supernaturalism, and mysticism, respectively.[25] The Pharisees and Sadducees were not sects, according to
Geiger, but national religious parties that expressed two basic tendencies within Judaism that had taken shape in ancient Israelite religion,
and which represent conflicting tendencies existing within most religions. During the Babylonian exile, according to Geiger, the limita-
tions of movement and distance from the Land of Israel brought

about a stagnation of religious life, and elements of both kingdoms, Israel and Judah, were united in the religious traditions that were consolidated there. Following the return from Babylonian exile, leadership was centralized in the Davidic kingly house and in the priestly family of Zadok. The Davidic dynasty declined with the loss of political autonomy, while the Zadokite priestly house rose and developed into priestly kings, suppressing the religious heritage of Judah. The spirit of Judah, however, remained alive among the common people, and eventually took shape in the Pharisaic movement, which Geiger describes as a liberalizing, democratizing effort that sought an equality of religious leadership and practice: "Pharisaism is therefore no term worthy of disgrace, it is a name of honor, in its circles it describes the principle that the entire history of the world moves as a progressive development."[26]

By contrast, Geiger's later studies of the Pharisees and Sadducees introduce sociological categories of analysis. Political interests and social position determine religious doctrines, he argued. According to the *Urschrift*, modern scholarship had relied too heavily on Josephus, the gospels, and the church fathers; Geiger gave priority to rabbinic texts, including the Mishnah, selected midrashim, and the Targumim, and also interpreted 1 and 2 Maccabees as Sadducean and Pharisaic texts, respectively. 2 Maccabees, he argued, was a Pharisaic text written during the middle of the first century BCE as an effort to undermine the legitimacy accorded the Sadducees, and in opposition to Roman rule. The priests are portrayed as neglecting their Temple duties in order to watch the Greek games, in violation of the divine commandments and the sensibilities of the people. In sharp contrast to the priests, the text stresses the sincere religiosity of the general populace, who are identified by Geiger as representing Pharisaic interests. The motto of the Pharisees, Geiger wrote, is proclaimed in 2 Maccabees 2:17: "To all is given the inheritance, the kingdom, the priesthood and its power of sanctification [*Allen ist gegeben das Erbe, das Königreich, das Priestertum und die Heiligung*]."[27] The distinctive attributes of Pharisaic belief identified by Josephus appear in 2 Maccabees, including reference to angels, miracles, a coming redeemer, devout observance of the Sabbath commandments even during times of warfare, strict adherence to the law, and what Geiger described as a polemical repetition of belief in resurrection of the dead. Belief in resurrection of the dead is emphatic, as is strict adherence to Sabbath observance even in battle.

Geiger's definition of the Pharisees as liberalizers of Jewish law, influenced by cultural and social interests, became a definition promoted in subsequent years by most Jewish scholars with surprisingly little deviation, particularly those supporting reform of Judaism. By contrast, it became the object of unrelenting mockery by Christian scholars, who repudiated in particular Geiger's claim that rabbinic texts could serve as reliable historical evidence for the nature of Pharisaic religion. Their hostility was undoubtedly strengthened by their outrage at Geiger's subsequent claims, in his publications of the 1860s and 1870s, that Jesus was himself a Pharisee and that Pharisaic and Sadducean influences could be identified within the New Testament itself. Orthodox Jews, opposed to Geiger's advocacy of reforms of synagogue liturgy, accused Geiger of manipulating his scholarship to justify those reforms. In hindsight, the depiction of the Pharisees presented by Geiger, and by subsequent Jewish thinkers, such as Leo Baeck and Ismar Elbogen, reflect the influence of liberal Protestantism: the Pharisees are modeled after the images of the liberal Jesus. Indeed, Geiger stated the issue quite baldly: "Protestantism is the full mirror of Pharisaism, whereas Catholicism [mirrors] Sadduceism."[28]

In the several studies of first-century Judaism that were published by German Protestant scholars in the 1860s and 1870s, Geiger's work was invariably cited, occasionally with approval, but his conclusions were virtually always rejected. For example, while footnoting Geiger's work throughout, Theodor Keim (1825–1878), professor of theology at the University of Zürich and a student of both Heinrich Ewald and F. C. Baur, termed the Pharisees "pious Democrats" and cited Matthew 23 as reliable evidence for their character: "All these heavy burdens, an infinity of legal ordinances which not only occupied and diverted from higher moral pursuits every moment of life, but also filled life with a continual fear of omission, were imposed by the Pharisees upon themselves and upon the nation."[29] While citing Geiger's work in his footnotes, Daniel Schenkel (1818–1885), professor of theology at the University of Heidelberg, defined the Pharisees not in terms of their actions or beliefs, and rarely with reference to primary sources: "Thus Pharisaism undermined the conscience, killed religion and morality at their roots. Under its influence all moral earnestness died away, and the marrow of the life and strength of the people perished. It was the religion of appearances and had the morality of a specious superficiality. It was the lean and Jesuitical pietism of the world before Christ."[30] By contrast, according to Schenkel, Jesus recognized that the Mosaic Law was irreconcilable with the conscience.[31]

Jesus' singularity was demonstrated for Schenkel not by his teachings, but by his triumph over Pharisaic religion. The Pharisees were Jesus' "dangerous and determined opponents," and because Jesus' exposure of their hypocrisy aroused the Pharisees' animosity, he was forced to flee to the Galilee.[32] As the ones ultimately responsible for the death of Jesus, the Pharisees, according to Schenkel, are "murderers of the new life which God sought to communicate to his people . . . enemies of God."[33]

A more complicated case was that of Adolf Hausrath (1837–1909), professor of theology at the University of Heidelberg, who frequently praised Geiger's publications in the pages of the journal, *Protestantische Kirchenzeitung für das evangelische Deutschland*.[34] Hausrath wrote that he agreed with Geiger that, though Josephus was unreliable and the gospels were distorted, Christian scholars had granted "citizenship" to those sources, shaping an image of the Pharisees as politically reactionary religious hypocrites, "the crusaders of Jerusalem." The Sadducees, Hausrath continued, are then constructed as the polar opposite: if the Pharisees are represented as "a distinguished bunch of sanctimonious parsons," then the Sadducees of necessity become an "unprincipled party of education and freedom." Not only does this image contradict the reports of Josephus, it ignores the accomplishment of Jewish scholars, Hausrath writes, who "made headway to a better understanding of the tendencies and positions of both parties in detail." Geiger's work is presented by Hausrath as the most reliable study of rabbinic Judaism.

In his own synthetic histories of the New Testament period, however, Hausrath relied heavily on Josephus, Philo, and the gospels and reverted to old clichés and misinterpretations of rabbinic sources. Hausrath retained the old caricatures, describing the Pharisees as "religiously degenerate," the Sadducees as "ethically wild."[35] Geiger, in his review of the first volume of Hausrath's book, concluded that the weaknesses of Hausrath's book resulted from the state of contemporary Christian theology. Christian theologians, Geiger wrote, cannot accept that historical investigation demonstrates that Christianity is "the fruit of a natural historical development," making it "simply a new phase of Judaism, not a new religion."[36] By 1872, with the appearance of Hausrath's second volume, Geiger's tone became enraged. In a letter to Joseph Derenbourg, he wrote, "What is now to be done? One can, from our side, still protest so much, [but] they do not listen, and since they are more numerous and have the power, they shout louder than us. And yet! Truth and genuine research still prevail."[37] That Hausrath ignored the very arguments by Geiger that he had been praising for the previous decade was clearly disappointing, but the larger frustration for Geiger was the absence of an unbiased Christian scholarship; the reigning conviction was that "Judaism must be bad, Christianity full of holiness, even if the historical facts announce the opposite just as loudly and decisively."[38]

Geiger's contemporary, Heinrich Graetz, did not engage contemporary scholarly debates and presented the Pharisees and rabbis primarily in hagiographical terms in his eleven-volume *History of the Jews*.[39] Graetz idealized rabbinic leadership and differentiated between the Pharisees as religious and the Sadducees as political. The former could not have been hypocrites, given the wide support they received from the Jewish populace of their day, he argued. Controversies between them arose primarily due to the Sadducees' literalistic interpretation of Scripture, though he did not explain the reasons for that. Graetz saw the emergence of the Pharisees as a quietistic, halakhically loyal group who, he claimed, began during the era of Ezra the scribe and took formal shape during the reign of John Hyrcanus. Their primary goal was strict adherence to the "oral law," and their major opponents were the "Hellenizers" within the Jewish community, specifically the Sadducees, who were identified by Graetz in Josephan terms. By the second half of the first century BCE, according to Graetz, the Pharisees turned away from political interests and increasingly toward halakhic study and interpretation, an argument subsequently reiterated by Bousset and Neusner.[40] By the time of Hillel, the Pharisees had shaped the Judaism that was to prevail in subsequent generations until the present, Graetz concluded, and that also resolved the conflicts between Pharisaism and Sadduceism.[41]

In a highly critical review, Graetz claimed that Geiger's *Urschrift* was without foundation,[42] and Geiger replied that Graetz's scholarship was corrupted by his conservative religious commitments.[43] Ultimately, Graetz's discussion of the Pharisees exerted little influence on subsequent historical scholarship regarding the Jewish background of Christian origins, particularly the Pharisees, and did not hinder the perpetuation of negative stereotypes. Geiger's work, however, was widely discussed.

Apart from Wellhausen and Schürer, most contemporary Christian scholars focused their discussions of Geiger not on historical questions, but on his challenges to traditional Christian stereotypes of the Pharisees and his identification of Jesus as a Pharisee. For example, Geiger's disavowal that the Pharisees were hypocrites was vehemently rejected by by Heinrich Ewald, one of the most prominent and liberal biblical scholars of his day: "this is only too true and proven through the entire true history." In his own discussion of the Pharisees in the revised and expanded edition of his *Geschichte Israels*, published in 1864, Ewald writes in a footnote, "The views of Jewish writers of the present day [*heutigen Juden*], Geiger and Grätz (and also Jost), on the origin and value of the Pharisees and Sadducees are wholly unhistorical and baseless, because they are themselves nothing but Pharisees and do not intend to be anything else."[44] Privately, Ewald accused Geiger of formulating his defense of the Pharisees out of hatred of Christianity.[45] Franz Delitzsch opposed Geiger's depiction of Pharisaism because it called into question, in his view, the veracity of gospel descriptions of the Pharisees.[46]

Geiger's arguments, however, were carried beyond Germany by students and colleagues. Joseph Derenbourg (France), Kaufmann Kohler (United States), and Daniel Chwolsohn (Russia) expanded Geiger's views of the Pharisees in their work, particularly in defining Jesus as a Pharisee and the Pharisees as liberalizers of halakha, even as German Protestant scholars reiterated the negative stereotypes.[47]

The most significant critique of Geiger's work came from Julius Wellhausen, whose reading of the *Urschrift* had inspired his study of 1 and 2 Samuel, published in 1871.[48] Soon after, he devoted a series of lectures at the University of Greifswald to a refutation of the *Urschrift*,[49] subsequently published as a book, *Pharisäer und Sadducäer: Eine Untersuchung zu inneren jüdischen Geschichte*, in 1874 and reprinted in

1924 and 1967.[50] The significance of Wellhausen's critique of Geiger's work stems from the detail with which he examined Geiger's arguments and from Wellhausen's reputation as a scholar, which lent prominence to his claims.[51] That he would devote an entire volume to a detailed refutation of Geiger's work is revealing of Geiger's significance. At the same time, Wellhausen did not acknowledge his debt to Geiger in placing both Pharisees and Sadducees in a sociological/political context. He did, however, make it clear that his underlying purpose was a general evaluation of the nature and worth of Judaism, writing that the Pharisees were "the Jews in superlative, the true Israel"[52] and that they were characterized by a blind, absolute obedience to the law.[53] Their conflicts with the Sadducees exemplified, according to Wellhausen, an inner contradiction within Judaism: the conflict between the political and the religious.[54]

Wellhausen's criticisms extend in two directions: a disagreement over the general portrait of the nature of Sadducean and Pharisaic Judaism and a negative evaluation of Geiger's reading of primary sources, particularly of rabbinic literature. He rejected out of hand Geiger's claim that Pharisaism constituted a liberalization of Jewish religious practice and disallowed Geiger's readings of political and religious tendencies in Mishnaic disputes. Wellhausen also dismissed Geiger's claim of an older and newer halakha.

There is little indication that Wellhausen had any independent knowledge of rabbinic sources; he cites only what was presented by Geiger. Indeed, in a letter to Theodor Nöldeke, written in 1915, Wellhausen acknowledged as much: "You are exaggerating my knowledge absurdly, I know the extra-biblical Jewish literature only insofar as it is written in Greek, and even that only partially."[55] It is not surprising that Wellhausen favored the Greek texts, but it is striking that he did not bring the same skepticism regarding historical reliability to bear on Josephus, the Apocrypha, and the Gospels that he did to the Mishnah. The third-century redaction of the Mishnah indicates to Wellhausen that it cannot be reliably used as a historical source for first-century controversies between Pharisees and Sadducees; he does not indicate any historical unreliability of the gospels as evidence for the nature of first-century Judaism nor challenge the varied and sometimes conflicting reports in the writings of Josephus.

According to Wellhausen, the Sadducees were not a party of priests, but a national political aristocracy that stood in opposition to the Pharisees, a religious party that did not believe in political action. The relationship between the Pharisees and Sadducees is better understood, according to Wellhausen, by analogy to the relationship between prophets and kings. Their differences on religious matters were of minor consequence, which explains the relatively few references to the Sadducees in rabbinic texts, in contrast to their more extensive presence in Greek sources, which are more concerned with political issues.[56]

The emphasis is placed by Wellhausen on defining the nature of Pharisaic religion, and in so doing, he is defining the nature of Judaism: "the Pharisees are the Jews in superlative, the true Israel. The goal of the people and that of the Pharisees are the same."[57] Thus, when Wellhausen speaks of the Pharisees, he is also commenting on Judaism: "the Pharisees killed nature through the commandments. There were 613 written commandments and 1000 other laws, and they leave no room for conscience. One forgot God and the way to him in the Torah."[58] What characterizes the Pharisees is their "religious materialism."[59] Ultimately, in Wellhausen's 1894 *Israelitische und jüdische Geschichte*, the Pharisees come to be termed idolaters of the law.[60] The difference between the Pharisees and the common people lies only in the former's zealousness and acerbity.[61]

Wellhausen was repeating older Christian traditions and did not attempt to provide source evidence to justify them. He did, however, defend as a legitimate historical source, Jesus' notorious accusations that the Pharisees are "hypocrites," in Matthew 23. Its very exaggeration, he writes, signifies that the passage is a "candid" expression and therefore most probably more authentic than the "smarmy picture" of the Pharisees as first-century "preachers"; moreover, it is confirmed by the prophets' criticisms and by Paul's fight against the law.[62] The New Testament epistles are also good sources for defining Pharisaism, he writes, because Paul was the "great pathologist of Judaism."[63] What Wellhausen concludes is that the Pharisees can claim the merit of having crushed the Hasmonean state and having saved Judaism—a dubious honor, given Wellhausen's judgment of Judaism.[64]

In his critique of Geiger's reading of primary sources, Wellhausen states that Geiger's importance is in developing a method of critical interpretation of rabbinic texts; that is Geiger's contribution.[65] In reviewing the Mishnaic texts that Geiger presents, however, Wellhausen argues that they do not support a conclusion that the Sadducees "treat their prerogatives as an exploitative monopoly, while the Pharisees, by contrast, represent the principles of the community."[66] The texts are too few to support Geiger's conclusions, and in some cases contradict Geiger's thesis explicitly. Wellhausen points to *m. Yadayim* 4:7, in which the Sadducees argue that owners are responsible for damages caused by their slaves, while the Pharisees hold the owners exempt. He asks, "If the Sadducees represented the slave-owning aristocracy, as Geiger claimed, why would they make owners liable for damages caused by their slaves?" That the Sadducees might have deviated in this particular example from their own self-interest is not considered by Wellhausen, whose purpose is to argue against the use of Mishnaic texts as a historical source. He writes, "This controversy [in *m. Yadayim* 4:7] requires no further elucidation; it teaches us nothing in particular, except perhaps that in some respects the Sadducees were more intelligent than their opponents."[67] In general, rabbinic texts cannot be used, because they are an ex post facto effort to legitimate Pharisaic rule, and are therefore not unbiased sources.[68] Moreover, he argues, if rabbinic literature is concerned to legitimate the rule of the Pharisees, it cannot be read as an autonomous, objective source.

That the Pharisees were characterized by their democratization of the exclusivity of Saducean religion—Geiger's central thesis—is rejected absolutely by Wellhausen. He notes that the table fellowship characterizing the Pharisees was also found among the Essenes, who were undeniably not interested in democratizing or liberalizing priestly religion. Similarly, he questions why, if Geiger's thesis is correct, it had been concealed for two thousand years in obscure legalistic jargon. If rabbinic law should be understood as an internal debate between Pharisaic and Saducean positions, why did the Talmud and halakhic midrashim preserve the positions of the Pharisees while ignoring or concealing the Sadducees' views? The scanty traces of an older halakha were ferreted out by Geiger through complex interpretive maneuvers, which led Wellhausen to demand why such allegedly significant aspects of Jewish thought would be concealed in the literature and nearly lost over the centuries. Yet for Geiger, it is precisely the obscurity of Sadducean halakhic positions that proves the success of the Pharisees in wiping out even a memory of the ideology of the Sadducees. In cases in which Wellhausen accepts Geiger's reading of Mishnaic sources, he rejects his interpretations; drawing a principle linking the sources is *blöd* (foolish), he writes.[69] There is simply too little in rabbinic literature on the Pharisees and Sadducees to draw general conclusions.

Wellhausen also rejected Geiger's thesis regarding the derivation of the name "Pharisee." The name cannot be derived from the *nivdalim* mentioned in the biblical book of Ezra, Wellhausen argues, because in Ezra the term refers to the Jewish separation from pagans, not an inner-Jewish separation. The Sadducees were not a party of priests, but aristocratic followers of the Hasmoneans who viewed the priesthood as a means to maintain their political rule. By contrast, the Pharisees wanted foreign rule, not a Hasmonean state. Some of Geiger's interpretations are treated by Wellhausen with a tone of astonishment, without further discussion. For example, Geiger's identification of Second Isaiah, chapters 40–66, as an example of Pharisaic opposition to the Sadducees and the suffering servant in Isaiah 53 as a metaphor for the Pharisees is rejected out of hand by Wellhausen.[70] Even when Wellhausen agrees with Geiger's conclusions, as in the origins of the name Sadducee, he attacks Geiger's methods: "seldom [has] a groundless point of view been established in a worse fashion."[71]

Like Geiger, Wellhausen presents Judaism as a religion emerging within its own world, without major influences from outside, whether Persian, Greek, or Christian. Unlike Geiger, however, Wellhausen finds no positive influence of Judaism on Christianity or on any other elements within Western culture. Numerous critics in recent years have charged Wellhausen with a bias against Judaism in his scholarship.[72] His defenders, notably Rudolf Smend, have claimed that Wellhausen was as anti-Christian as he was anti-Jewish.[73] Wellhausen's identification of Jesus as a Jew has also come under reevaluation recently by New Testament scholars; Hans Dieter Betz, for example, interprets Wellhausen as arguing that Jesus was the last Jew because Judaism as a historical religion had come to an end with Jesus.[74] Ultimately, Wellhausen's critique overshadowed Geiger's work on rabbinic sources, and it is his depiction of the Pharisees, not

Geiger's, that triumphed in the end within German New Testament scholarship.[75]

The same year that Wellhausen's study appeared also saw the publication of Emil Schürer's *Lehrbuch der neutestamentlichen Zeitgeschichte*.[76] In the chapters on the Jewish sects, Schürer acknowledged Geiger's work as inaugurating the scholarship in the field, even while he disagreed with most of Geiger's conclusions concerning the Pharisees and labeled all Jewish-authored scholarship with an asterisk in his bibliography. Pharisaism represented the essence of Judaism, Schürer wrote, "that those who do not follow the law are cursed" and not a principle of progressive development and liberalization.[77] Schürer rejected Geiger's distinction between a Sadducean and Pharisaic halakha, denying any religious interests on the part of the Sadducees, who solely represented, he wrote, the political interests of the aristocracy, even as he accepted, without acknowledgment, Geiger's sociological distinction between the Pharisees as a party of the people and the Sadducees as a party of the priestly aristocracy. The Pharisees, he claimed, constituted the party of the people, marked by a zealous legalism that began with Ezra and Nehemiah, continuing in the Maccabean era with the Hasidim, and emerging during that era as Pharisees, "separatists," those opposing the impurity of non-Jews. The Pharisees, for Schürer, represented Judaism's ideal Jew, whereas the Sadducees were a smaller, marginal groups of aristocrats.

At the time Schürer published the *Lehrbuch* he was just thirty years old and a lecturer in theology at the University of Leipzig. His book was very well received, viewed as a more scholarly survey of the material than that of Adolf Hausrath, though criticized for ignoring political conditions within the Roman Empire.[78] Schürer made extensive use of rabbinic literature, more than any other Christian scholar of the era, but his citations are all intended to demonstrate the "legalism" of Judaism. Schürer's chapter "Life Under the Law," describing the alleged misery of rabbinic Judaism, became notorious as an anti-Jewish polemic,[79] yet its claims were neither new nor unique within German Christian scholarship; virtually all prior descriptions of rabbinic Judaism were comparably negative. The distinction, however, came from Schürer's amassing of rabbinic "proofs," which lent the chapter an aura of scholarly invincibility and seemed to defeat Jewish claims that Christian scholars could not understand early Judaism because they made no use of rabbinic literature. Surprisingly, Schürer's work was perceived at the time of its publication by some Christian scholars as adhering too closely to the Jewish scholarship of Geiger, with the focus on Palestinian rabbinic Judaism as the setting for the New Testament and omitting discussion of Hellenistic religions and their influence on the New Testament.[80]

The existence of a split between Hellenistic and Palestinian (i.e., rabbinic) Judaism in antiquity became a dogma of scholarship that has been challenged only in recent decades. Emphasis on the Hellenistic context for early Christianity was a technique for excluding or downplaying Jewish influence and reflected the broader preoccupations in German intellectual and academic societies with classical Hellenic culture as the opposite of Hebraic and biblical culture. The opposition between Hellenic and Hebraic came to be challenged in the last decades of the nineteenth century with the rise of Orientalism, as Suzanne Marchand has delineated, which emphasized the ancient Near East, especially Babylonia and Persia, as the original religious context for both the Hebrew Bible and early Christianity.[81] The exploration of the Near East, which gave rise to new archaeological and textual discoveries, provided a broader context for analyzing biblical literature, and became a focus of fascination for German scholars and the general populace at the turn of the century. However, the "Furor Orientalis" encompassed all religions of the Near East and Asia with the exception of Judaism. Indeed, Orientalism became a tool for the exclusion of Judaism from the scholarly investigation of religions of antiquity. It also influenced the rise of the history of religions school, which renounced theological commitments in the interest of an objective historiography of early Christianity, yet which arrived at equally negative conclusions regarding Judaism and the Pharisees.

The prime example of the history of religions approach is the work of Wilhelm Bousset (1865–1920), professor at Göttingen and, later, Giessen. His widely read study *Die Religion des Judenthums im neutestamentlichen Zeitalter* first appeared in 1903, presenting itself as a new approach that used the methods of the history of religions school to identify and describe what he termed "late Judaism," the Judaism of the Second Temple period.[82] The Pharisees, according to Bousset, had initially (under the Hasmoneans) been a progressive movement, urging a democratic control of religious issues by the Jewish populace, but after achieving power in the Hasmonean era they were were quickly transformed into rigid, aristocratic conservatives: "piety in their hands became stiff and lifeless . . . within their ranks arose the new ideas of the later Jewish religion."[83] Like Wellhausen, Bousset dismissed the Mishnah as a viable historical source; while recognizing that the gospels present a polemic against Pharisaism, they nonetheless provide, he wrote, the best illustration of the character of the Pharisees and Sadducees.[84] Bousset also did not cite the work of any Jewish scholars.

Bousset concluded his depiction by writing that Judaism is a religion of external observance lacking sincerity. The Pharisees were agents of hypocrisy and legalism: observance of Jewish law would bring reward but lacked spiritual or ethical meaning. With regard to Torah piety, Bousset stated that, although the "law" was the "pride and joy of Jewish life," fulfilling the commandments, for the Pharisees, was purely external and aimed at a reward either in this or the next world.[85] In general, he traced all ethical and religious deficiencies he glimpsed in "late Judaism" back to the fact that "the law had poisoned the religion of Judaism in its core." His characterization was based entirely on the "basic tendency in which the morality of the Pharisees moved"—pure negativity, insincerity, hypocrisy—that was diagnosed "correctly by Jesus."[86] Ultimately, for all of Bousset's claims to be developing new historiographical methods, his depiction of the Pharisees was taken straight out of the gospels.

Bousset's work brought an outcry among Jewish scholars, who condemned his characterization of Pharisaism and his failure to engage seriously the work of Jewish scholars, and it sparked the publication of several studies of Pharisaism by Jewish authors. Felix Perles was among several Jewish scholars who published heated responses to the work, accusing Bousset of ignoring Jewish scholarship, lacking training in rabbinic sources, and engaging in anti-Jewish polemics under the guise of objective scholarship.[87]

Despite the dismay with which most Jewish scholars reacted to the depictions of rabbinic religion by Wellhausen, Schürer, and Bousset and the continued negative stereotyping of the Pharisees by modern Christian scholars, there were no Jewish academic institutions nor unified scholarly consensus to allow an organized response. Given that Jewish scholars of early Judaism were not affiliated as professors at German universities, nor invited, as Jews, to contribute to the major university journals of the field, most of which were controlled by Protestant theological faculties, they were kept disaffiliated, structurally and institutionally, from academic forums.

By the 1920s and 1930s, increasing numbers of German Protestants established themselves as scholars of rabbinic literature and began publishing critical editions of Mishnah-tractates, although the context in which those texts were presented was at times highly biased and designed to undermine comparisons of Jesus with the Pharisees. Most egregious was the edition of Mishnah Pesachim, published by Georg Beer, professor at the University of Heidelberg, who dismissed connections between the Last Supper and the Passover Seder, arguing that the latter was an expression of Jewish hope for world domination.[88] With the rise of Protestant scholarship on rabbinics, Jewish scholars were sometimes marginalized. Hugo Gressmann, for example, dismissed the work of Jewish scholars as biased by their commitment to the Talmud. Emerging instead was a wider consensus that Hellenistic Judaism, which was sharply distinguished from the rabbinic Judaism of the Pharisees, was a more important context for understanding the emergence of Christianity. Rabbinic Judaism was characterized even by a scholar as sympathetic to Judaism as Gressmann as "dead or gradually dying."[89] In his article in the standard reference work, *Religion in Geschichte und Gegenwart*, published in 1930, Paul Volz blamed the Pharisees for having created the "spirit" that led to Jesus' crucifixion, even though they are not mentioned in the gospels' accounts of the death of Jesus.[90] That the narrow-minded, materialistic Pharisees were so popular among Jews in antiquity, Volz explained, is proof that they represented a widespread legalistic mentality among Jews, reinforced by the popularity of their miracles and healings. Publication of the Damascus Document in 1910, a scroll fragment discovered in 1896 in the Cairo Genizah by Solomon Schechter, led to speculations regarding its evidence for Pharisaism. Joachim Jeremias interpreted it as a Pharisaic text indicating that the Pharisees were not simply the party of the Jewish masses, but rather members of closed religious conventicles, for whom the laws of tithing and purity were of particular concern.[91] While they exerted a strong influence on the general populace, as well as the Temple and the Sanhedrin, Jeremias distinguished the intensity of their religious practice from that of ordinary Jews of the day.[92]

An even more problematic direction for Pharisee scholarship developed during the 1930s among German Protestants influenced by history of religions methods and the racial politics that infiltrated the universities. Carl Schneider, a student of Johannes Leipoldt, published a textbook of New Testament history in 1934, dedicated to Leipoldt, to prove that the New Testament was an authentically Hellenistic work. Filled with anti-Jewish clichés, Schneider presents the Pharisees as calling for the establishment of a theocracy and describes a "piety of legalism" (*Gesetzesfrömmigkeit*) as characteristic of the Pharisees and in contrast to Hellenism. However much Christianity was rooted in Palestine, it was a product of Hellenism, according to Schneider. A second example came from Herbert Preisker, professor of New Testament at the University of Breslau, whose 1937 study of New Testament history argued that the Pharisees, abandoning their identification with the Jewish people, turned into rigid Talmudists who brought about the defeat of the Jews. Both Schneider and Preisker were active members of an anti-Semitic propaganda institute formed in 1939, the Institute for the Study and Eradication of Jewish Influence on German Religious Life, contributing to its production of a de-Judaized version of the New Testament.[93]

Scholars of the Pharisees face two central issues: determining which sources they will use as historically reliable evidence, and deciding which methods to use in interpreting those sources. On both points, Geiger's decisions have generally prevailed over subsequent scholarship. It was Geiger who expanded the number of primary sources to be used for evidence of the nature of Pharisaism to include early rabbinic and Targumic texts, apocryphal and pseudepigraphical texts, as well as the conventional sources—Josephus and the gospels. Similarly, it was Geiger who introduced sociological categories that interpreted religious positions in relation to the political commitments and social structures of Jewish society in Palestine.

Nonetheless, despite claims of being guided by strict principles of historicism—and for some, of following the even more historicist methods of the history of religions school—German Protestant scholars remained embroiled in theological presuppositions. The gospels' negative passages regarding the Pharisees served to override other sources of evidence and to reject the alternative interpretations of the Pharisees developed by Jewish scholars. Ultimately, the conclusions of a Wellhausen or Schürer or Bousset are not much different from the depiction of the Pharisees of a village pastor. The emergence of new centers of scholarship on the New Testament and early Judaism after World War II, both in the United States and Great Britain, brought a fresh approach far less bound to Christian theological commitments and far more congenial to Jewish historiography.

CHAPTER 15

THE ANGLO-AMERICAN THEOLOGICAL TRADITION TO 1970

Jacob Neusner

APOLOGETICS AND GULLIBILITY

Defining principal parts of Pharisaic theology proves difficult. First, we do not know whether pre-70 authorities whom we assume to have been Pharisees really said what is assigned to them in the rabbinic documents. Second, the theological side to Pharisaic Judaism before 70 CE is not easily accessible, for in the case of the rabbinic traditions about the pre-70 Pharisees the pre-70 beliefs, ideas, and values have been taken over and revised by the rabbinic masters. We cannot reliably claim that an idea first known to us in a later rabbinic document, from the third century and afterward, was originally both known and understood in the same way. But critical considerations have not prevented facile use of the rabbinic sources, taken at face value as facts not concerning the period in which they surfaced—for example, ideas held in the time of the Mishnah or the Talmud of Babylonia (200, 600, respectively)—but concerning the time of which they speak. Not only uncritical but also anachronistic, the program of scholarship focused on issues of apologetics, with special interest in the first-century Christian indictment of Pharisaic Judaism and its Christian continuators later on, through the Reformation and into the Roman Catholic-Protestant debates of the nineteenth and twentieth centuries. These two traits of mind—gullibility toward what was said and theological apologetics for the meanings imputed to what was said—characterized most, though not all, writing on the Pharisees.

Accordingly, scholarship on the Pharisees conducted under Anglo-American auspices to 1970, when my *Rabbinic Traditions about the Pharisees before 70* appeared, pursued a program of apologetics for Judaism, deemed to descend from Pharisaism, with historical narrative as the medium for apologetics. The narrative was constructed on the foundations of a literal and gullible reading of the narratives and attributed sayings of the rabbinic documents, from the Mishnah of ca. 200 into the later Middle Ages. Everything was deemed historically factual, and the task of the scholar was to form the facts into a favorable picture of the Pharisees, who were assumed to have founded rabbinic or normative Judaism. My *Rabbinic Traditions* introduced the critical agenda of the academy to the study of the rabbinic traditions about the Pharisees, and it was rapidly followed by approaches, associated with the names Steve Mason and the late Anthony J. Saldarini by way of example, that moved beyond my work and carried it forward. But my contribution was to render obsolete nearly all historical scholarship on the Pharisees of the preceding two hundred years

The Quest for Hiddushim: The Yeshiva Métier

Uncritical and credulous reading of the sources defined all else. The study of Talmudic and related literature for historical purposes stands conceptually and methodologically a century and a half behind biblical studies. While biblical literature has for that long been subjected to the criticism of scholars who did not take for granted the presuppositions and allegations of the text, Talmudic literature was studied chiefly in *Yeshivot*, whose primary interests were not historical to begin with, and whose students credulously took at face value both the historical and the legal sayings and stories of the Talmudic sages. Here the influences of literary and historical criticism emanating from universities were absent. The circle of masters and disciples was unbroken by the presence of nonbelievers; those who lost the faith left the schools. When Talmudic literature was studied in universities, it was mainly for philological, not historical, purposes.

Those Talmudists, such as Abraham Geiger and Louis Ginzberg, moreover, who did acquire a university training, including an interest in history, and who also continued to study Talmudic materials, never fully overcame the intellectual habits ingrained from their beginnings in *Yeshivot*. Characteristic of Talmudic scholarship is the search, first, for underlying principles to make sense of discrete, apparently unrelated cases; second, for distinctions to overcome contradictions between apparently contradictory texts; and third, for *hiddushim*, or new interpretations of particular texts. That exegetical approach to historical problems which stresses deductive thought, while perhaps appropriate for legal studies, produces egregious results for history, for it too often overlooks the problem of evidence: How do we know what we assert? What are the bases in actual data to justify *hiddushim* in small matters, or in large ones the postulation of comprehensive principles (*shitot*) of historical importance?

Ginzberg's famous theory that the disputes of the Houses of Shammai and Hillel and the decrees of the earlier masters reflect economic and social conflict in Palestine is not supported by reference to archaeological or even extra-Talmudic literary evidence. Having postulated that economic issues were everywhere present, Ginzberg proceeded to use this postulate to "explain" a whole series of cases. The "explanations" are supposed to demonstrate the validity of the postulate, but in fact merely repeat and illustrate it. What is lacking in each particular case is the demonstration that the data could not be explained equally well—or even better—by some other postulate or postulates. At best we are left with "this *could have been* the reason," but with no concrete evidence that this was the reason. Masses of material perhaps originally irrelevant are built into pseudohistorical structures that rest on nothing more solid than "We might suppose that . . ." The deductive approach to the study of law ill serves the historian. One of the most common phrases in the historical literature before us is "If this supposition is sound, then . . ." I found it in nearly every historian who wrote in Hebrew. It is Talmudics extended to the study of history.

I do not unreservedly condemn Talmudics, except in connection with historical studies. It is a great tradition, interesting and important as a phenomenon of intellectual history, beautiful and fascinating as an intellectual exercise, and a powerful instrument for apologetics and for the reinterpretation necessary to make ancient laws and doctrines apply to modern problems. I should not even deny that it may be a valuable instrument for philosophical research. For instance, Morton Smith comments on the work of Harry A. Wolfson, "Wolfson's achievements by his 'hypothetico-deductive method' are justly famous. But when Wolfson uses the method, the hypotheses are made from a minute study of the primary sources, and the deductions are checked at every point by careful consideration of the historical evidence, and those which cannot be confirmed are clearly indicated as conjectural."[1] My objection is that when used by scholars without Wolfson's historical training, mastery, and conscience, the method lends itself easily to abuse, to the invention of imaginary principles and distinctions for which there is no historical evidence whatsoever, and to the deduction of consequences that never appear in the texts. It can too easily be used to obscure real differences of opinion or practice, to explain away the evidences of historical change, and to produce a picture of antiquity that has no more similarity to the facts than the Judaism of contemporary New York does to that of ancient Palestine.

APOLOGETICS IN PLACE OF HISTORICAL CRITICISM

A further, even more serious impediment to the development of the historical study of Talmudic literature was the need for apologetics. Talmudists with university training encountered the anti-Pharisaic, anti-Judaic, and frequently anti-Semitic attitudes of Christian scholars, who carried out polemical tasks of Christian theology in the guise of writing history. The Jewish historians undertook the defense. Two polemical themes recur. First, the Christians' account of the Pharisees ignores rabbinic sources and is therefore incomplete. The reason is that the Christian scholars do not know the rabbinic literature; thus, whatever they say may be discounted because of their "ignorance." Second, the Pharisees were the very opposite of what Christians say about them. The former polemic produced the Christian response that the rabbinical materials are not reliable, because they are "late" or "tendentious." Many Christian scholars drew back from using rabbinic materials, or relied on secondary accounts of them that they presumed to be accurate, because they were thoroughly intimidated by the claims of the Jewish opposition as to the difficulty of properly understanding the materials, and because they had slight opportunity to study the materials with knowledgeable scholars of Judaism.

The latter polemic—to prove the Pharisees the opposite of what had been said of them—was all too successful. When Christian scholars became persuaded that the earlier Christian view had been incorrect, they took up the polemic in favor of the Pharisees. In doing so, they of course relied on Jewish scholarship and took over uncritically its uncritical attitude toward the material. Consequently, on both sides, sources were more often cited as facts than analyzed as problems. We commonly find a source cited without attention to how the citation is supposed to prove the "fact" it purportedly contains. Systematic analysis of texts is rare; allusion to unexamined texts is commonplace. Thus, studies of the rabbinic traditions about the Pharisees prove to be seriously inadequate, because, in general, the historical question has been asked too quickly and answered uncritically. The inadequacy results from the false presumption that nearly all sources—appearing in any sort of document, early, late, or medieval—contain accurate historical information about the people and events of which they speak.

The historians are further to be blamed for allowing the theologians to set the issue: Were the Pharisees really hypocrites? On the part of the Jewish scholars, the issues were: What shall we say in response to the Christian theological critique of Pharisaism? How shall we disprove the allegations of the Christians' holy books? On the Christian side, there were few "historians" worthy of the name, for most served the church and not the cause of accurate and unbiased historical knowledge. Since the Christian theological scholars set the agenda, the Jewish ones can hardly be condemned for responding to it, especially since contemporary anti-Semitism was both expressed and aided by the Christian scholarly assessment of Pharisaism. In fact, the European Jewish scholars turn out to have been fighting for the lives of the Jews of their own day and place. They lost that fight. It was a worthy effort, but it was not primarily an exercise of critical scholarship, and it seriously impeded the development of scholarly criticism.

Although originating in the Central European intellectual milieu, Leo Baeck exercised considerable influence in the Anglo-Saxon theological world. His work *The Pharisees and Other Essays* is the best representative of Judaic apologetics. For Baeck, the Pharisees were "a movement within the Jewish people," not a party or a sect (manifestly false).[2] They were ascetics, Essenes (certainly not), and separatists. They were committed to the "search for the exact meaning and the ultimate [?] law," and were primarily a movement of exegetes of Scriptures: "The Pharisaic trend found its leaders in the scribes." The Pharisees were "prominent figures, especially in the spiritual life." We have "hardly any names of Sadducean scribes." The Pharisees were also "the men of the synagogue," against the Sadducees, "the men of the Temple." Baeck concludes: "Pharisaism represents a great attempt to achieve the full domination of religion over life, both over the life of the individual and the life of the collectivity. It took the idea of saintliness in earnest. Pharisaism was a heroic effort to prepare the ground for the kingdom of God." One could make an equally good case for the proposition that the Pharisees were concerned to limit as precisely as possible the claims of religion upon life. Various Tannaim—whom Baeck would have considered Pharisees, though they were not—were notoriously hostile to preparations for the coming of the kingdom, for one thing. Baeck had a romantic view of the Pharisees and treated as fact a variety of unlikely propositions.

ANGLO-SAXON APOLOGETICS

Two examples of the Anglo-Saxon tradition of apologetic literature suffice. R. Travers Herford, *The Pharisees*,[3] and George Foot Moore, *Judaism in the First Centuries of the Christian Era*,[4] mark the high point of the apologetic movement.

Herford observes that the German and other non-Jewish scholars "all seem to have the contrast with Christianity more or less consciously present in their minds, not realizing that two things cannot be rightly compared until it has first been ascertained what each of them is in itself . . . to call the New Testament as the chief witness upon the question who the Pharisees really were is false in logic and unsound in history." He further contends that the Jewish scholars "know what Pharisaism is like from the inside"—as if the rationalistic Judaism of the nineteenth century were still Pharisaism! Lauterbach is Herford's guide: the Pharisees stood for the Oral Tradition. For his historical account, Herford turns to Josephus (a prejudiced and unreliable source), whose story he embellishes with some Talmudic stories (from mostly the late second and third century CE). The descriptions of "Pharisaic religion" then draw upon the whole corpus of rabbinic literature.

Moore's apologetic work is less homiletical in form and is far superior in method. His treatment of the Pharisees (1:56ff.) is accompanied by excellent notes (3:17ff.) in which he carefully explains

(3:17–22) his approach and method, furthermore specifying his differences from the earlier scholars. Moore's account of the "rise of the Pharisees" follows Josephus's narrative. Moore summarizes Josephus's stories about the Pharisees and Alexander Jannaeus; Simeon b. Shetah comes in at the end: "According to the Rabbinical sources, this restoration took place under the superintendence of Simeon b. Shetah, a brother of the queen." The Pharisees murdered their opposition. The historical account ends here. The Pharisaic beliefs then are summarized. They believed in traditional law; "they were the zealous partisans of the unwritten law." The Sadducees believed only in the written law and were more literal in interpreting it. The Sadducees saw Scripture as the only authority, whereas Scripture and tradition were the authority for the Pharisees. The Sadducees were rich; the Pharisees had the masses on their side. These are all standard generalizations for their time.

Moore resumes the historical narrative in the next chapter, giving a paraphrase of Josephus, *Antiquities* 14. Then Shammai and Hillel are introduced, as the last of the pairs and "the beginning of the Tannaite school tradition." Hillel's hermeneutical rules "came from the Babylonian schools [about which we know nothing before CE]." In Jerusalem "the doctors of the Law sat at the fountainhead of tradition and were able to draw directly upon that source for answer to the questions that arose in practice. . . . In remoter lands this appeal to tradition must often have been unavailable, and the necessity of arriving at an authoritative conclusion from the biblical text itself must have been correspondingly more strongly felt." Moore then follows the story of the rise of Hillel, paraphrasing it just as he does Josephus's stories, and refers to anecdotes about Shammai and Hillel. He then returns to the Babylonian origin of the exegetical principles. In Babylonia much of the law had only an academic interest: "It was natural under these circumstances that the unwritten law should be more largely deducted from the text itself by certain exegetical principles. When he came to be head of a school in Jerusalem, Hillel recognized that the laws must take account of actual conditions." This accounts for his devising the *prosbul*, "which left the law unchanged [!] but by a legal fiction secured the creditor against the loss of his loan through the coming of the year of release." Hillel and Shammai produced two schools. The Shammaites predominated until after the fall of Jerusalem. What Moore supplies, then, is a paraphrase of the stories told by Josephus and the later rabbinic sages.

JUDAIC THEOLOGICAL POLEMICS

G. H. Box seems to me to have been among the first to call attention to the Jewish counter-attack on Christian scholarship about the Pharisees. His "Survey of Recent Literature on the Pharisees and Sadducees"[5] discusses fourteen items published between 1900 and 1908, including encyclopedia articles, brief monographs, and major studies. What impressed Box was that "Jewish scholarship is beginning to assert itself in the domain of New Testament historical science." The issues defined by that scholarship centered on the evaluation of the Pharisees: Were they all really hypocritical, or merely some of them? Was their legalism merely stiff and lifeless, dry and trivial, or was it sincere and inward?

The Jewish critique of Christian writings about the Pharisees began with the assertion that the non-Jewish scholars simply did not understand Pharisaic Judaism, because they did not control its sources. Had they understood rabbinic literature, they would have seen the Pharisees were "men of cultivated character and of piety true and deep." Only when Jewish scholars touched on New Testament materials did the Christians meet the attack. For reasons integral to his thesis about the extent of the purity laws, Büchler alleged that Mark 7:1ff. is "not authentic as an incident in the life of Jesus." Box then found it necessary to differ. One might say whatever he liked about the Pharisees, but in the spirit of the early twentieth-century Anglo-American scholarship on the subject, favorable judgments on the Pharisees would be more readily accepted than unfavorable ones.

A second Jewish polemic had to do with the "guilt" for the trial and death of Jesus. Since Jesus had said and done nothing "which would render him liable to the death penalty according to the criminal law of the Pharisees (of which we have exact knowledge) [!], his death was the work of "the Sadducean High Priesthood." No one now claimed to inherit "Sadducean Judaism," and on the Jewish side everyone purported to be true heirs of the Pharisees, so it seemed safe to blame the

Sadducees. Box phrases the now-predominant issue: "One of the most difficult problems that confronts the New Testament student who wishes to take account of the Jewish background and to be just to the Palestinian Judaism of the first Christian century is concerned with the classification and estimate of the great Jewish parties, especially the Pharisees and Sadducees" (132).

More pretentious but less satisfactory is Ralph Marcus's "The Pharisees in the Light of Modern Scholarship."[6] Marcus gives a brief résumé of suggestions on the meaning of the word Pharisee and on the historical Pharisees. His paper marks the high tide of the "sociological interpretation," which, to be sure, began with Josephus's characterization of the Sadducees as rich and nasty and the Pharisees as poor, humble, and kindly. Marcus takes for granted the accuracy of the picture of Geiger, Ginzberg, and Finkelstein, who portrayed the Pharisees as liberal, proletarian city-dwellers and their enemies as the reactionary, rich, landed aristocracy. He traces the beginning of "scientific discussion" of the Pharisees to Abraham Geiger, then alludes to Derenbourg, Wellhausen, Graetz, and Schürer. In all, for Marcus the primary issue remains whether the Pharisees were good or bad, legalistic or not legalistic, sincere or hypocritical, universalistic or particularistic. Marcus concludes that today most people agree with Geiger and "are prepared to vindicate the Pharisees of the age-old charge that they were narrow legalists and hypocrites." He further holds that there was no irreconcilable difference between Jesus and the Pharisees. Marcus's paper at best is reportorial. He brings no new ideas to the history of scholarship and makes no effort to relate the backgrounds of the several scholars to the judgments they have reached. The "sociological interpretation' is limited to the Pharisees, not extended to the study of scholarship about the Pharisees.

SOLOMON ZEITLIN

Not all historical and religions-historical and theological work produced before 1970 is worthless except as a curiosity. Some of the work of law and philology retains interest. Certainly the most formidable scholar of Pharisaic Judaism working in the first half of the twentieth century, and the most influential albeit today nearly forgotten,

Solomon Zeitlin of Dropsie College in Philadelphia, produced excellent work of halakhic analysis, joined with gullible use of narratives as collections of historical facts.

In his "Studies in Tannaitic Jurisprudence,"[7] Zeitlin states, "Intention as a factor in Jewish law was first recognized and given a status by Hillel, who insisted that we ought to take into consideration not only the primary act of a man, but also his intention. This innovation was strenuously opposed by his colleague Shammai." Numerous Houses disputes are explained in terms of this disagreement (e.g., *m. Makh.* 1:1, 6; 4:3; *t. Makh.* 2:16; *m. Kel.* 26:5–8). Intention in laws of the Sabbath explains the Houses' differences. Work is forbidden "in which a man intends a particular result; any ML'KH-act in the doing of which the man contemplated no particular result is not forbidden."

In "Les principles des controverses halachiques entre les écoles de Schammai et de Hillel,"[8] Zeitlin refers to four principles on which the Houses differed: (1) rabbis have the right to interpret and emend the law through legal fictions; (2) rabbis may interpret the law according to its spirit, rather than its letter; (3) one should build a fence around the law; (4) intention is taken into account in the application of the law. In all four the Shammaites took a negative position; the Hillelites a positive one. As to *m. Peah* 6:1, the difference of opinion pertains to the law of *res nullius*: if a person renounces his property rights, expressly stipulating that certain persons may not acquire that property, the object is regarded by Meir (a Shammaite) as *res nullius*, for at the moment that the rights are abandoned the object becomes ownerless. Yosé (a Hillelite) does not consider the object as *res nullius*, for in abandoning his rights the owner has not lost his title or his responsibility for the object. The disputes in *m. Ed.* 1:2 pertain to the same issue. Zeitlin assembles a number of other disputes in which the same principle recurs. What impresses me in these and related papers of Zeitlin is his careful and judicious use of the legal materials for essentially legal purposes, that is, the elucidation of the underlying principles of various discrete cases. Zeitlin here makes no historical claims (if we discount his assumption that attributions invariably are correct, and that assumption plays no significant role in his argument). He shows that concrete issues of specific cases reflect underlying disputes on important legal issues.

While I find much to admire in Zeitlin's legal-historical studies, I regret to observe that the more narrowly historical articles and books uniformly exhibit unparalleled dogmatism, joined with the allegation that no one else understands Talmudic literature. Zeitlin's papers confidently and repeatedly present as fact a wide range of quite dubious notions.

For example, in "Prosbol: A Study in Tannaitic Jurisprudence,"[9] Zeitlin takes for granted the literal, historical accuracy of the prozbol stories. He does not analyze the literary traits of the stories and sees no historical problems in them. The primary issue is legal, but what the law describes is taken for granted as social and historical fact. Here that assumption is central to the argument. Zeitlin claims:

> Before his [Hillel's] time, the creditor in order not to lose the money which he had loaned to his fellow men on account of the sabbatical year, deposited with the court a promissory note given to him by the debtor. Such a promissory note had a clause to the effect that the real property of the debtor was mortgaged to the creditor. In such a case, the creditor had the right to collect the debt even after the sabbatical year. . . . According to the opinion of the school of Shammai, anything which ultimately has to be collected is considered as already collected [his entire footnote: "*b. Git.* 37a"—which contains an Amoraic *interpretation*]. However, that was only a custom and had not as yet been sanctioned: Hillel introduced the takkanah that the creditor may write a *Prosbol*, even without the knowledge of the debtor, in which he declares that he will collect all the debts people owe him. The *Prosbol* is valid, whether or not the creditor has a promissory note, and whether or not the note was deposited with the court. This takkanah Hillel made a law by supporting it by a verse in the Pentateuch. A *takkanah* must always be based on the Pentateuch.

Zeitlin thus takes for granted that the sabbatical laws were everywhere enforced. It was moreover possible for the Pharisees to effect changes in the administration of commercial (and real estate) law.

Further, Zeitlin claims that the *Prosbol* was in existence before Hillel's time, which is not what the story says. He claims this was merely a "custom," but the story says Hillel introduced that custom. Zeitlin has imposed a theory on stories that in their present form contradict his theory. It hardly serves to argue that Hillel "really" did introduce the *Prosbol* as the stories say, against the view that all he did was to find a scriptural basis for a rather minor alteration of existing practice. Indeed, one can hardly argue with this sort of allegation, without being drawn into the conceptually primitive framework of discussion. What Hillel "really" did or did not do is not a suitable subject for analysis, given the condition of the sources.

In "Hillel and the Hermeneutic Rules," [10] Zeitlin again discusses the several stories of Hillel's rise to power. "Hillel introduced the term kal wa-homer, but not the principle of logic." This was well known. Hillel did not introduce the term *gezerah shavah*, nor the principle of analogy. Judah b. Tabbai and Simeon b. Shetah knew it. Zeitlin refers to the story of the people's bringing knives in the wool of lambs: "This story reveals that the ordinary people, the farmers . . . knew that if the eve of Passover fell . . . " and so on. Why did not the Bathyrans know it too? According to Zeitlin, they were newcomers and did not know the Oral Torah (!).

The Bene Bathyra who rejected Hillel's view to make the custom of the slaughtering of the paschal lamb a statutory law, accepted Hillel's statement that it was permissible to do so on the authorization of Shemaiah and Abtalion. The Bene Bathyra relinquished their leadership and Hillel became the nasi of the Bet Din. This occurred in the year 31 B.C.E. . . . It corresponds to another statement in the Talmud that Hillel and his descendents headed the Sanhedrin for a hundred years. From 31 B.C.E. to 69 C.E., when Simeon ben Gamaliel was assassinated, makes one hundred chronological years.

In "The Pharisees and the Gospels," [11] Zeitlin regards as "historically accurate" only the controversies between the Pharisees and the Sadducees. "The Halakhot of the Schools of Hillel and Shammai, Akiba and Eliezer, etc., belong to the history and the development of the halakhah, but have nothing to do with the Pharisees." So the Houses and presumably their founders were not Pharisees! The Sadducees ended at 70, "and thus the Pharisees likewise disappeared as opponents." But the Pharisees "had great influence on the Halakhot of the Schools of Hillel and Shammai." There was "no such sect as the 'Pharisees.'" All this is very confusing. The difference between the teachings of Jesus and the teachings of the Pharisees is accounted for as follows: "The Pharisees, leaders of the Jewish people, although maintaining that ethical teachings are important for the development of human nature, insisted on the fulfillment of the law. . . . A state cannot exist unless it is maintained by law and order. On the other hand, Jesus, not being interested in the State, appealed to his fellow men to refrain from doing evil."

Zeitlin's work thus intuits various sorts of *novellae*, offering his own certainty of the truth of his allegation in place of evidence or careful argumentation. Perhaps the most striking example of his quite arbitrary definitions is found in "The Semikhah Controversy between the Zugoth."[12] Here Zeitlin proposes that the "lay on hands" of *m. Hag.* 2:2 has *nothing* to do with performing the ceremony of laying of hands upon the head of the sacrificial animal in the Temple court on holy days. While the Houses did dispute that question, the pairs did not. Since the Tosefta asks, "Over which *semikhah* were the schools of Shammai and Hillel divided?" and *not* "Over which *semikhah* were the *Zugoth* divided?" Zeitlin claims that this clearly (!) shows "that the two controversies were not considered identical." It is his contention that "according to *y. Hag.* 2:2 the *semikhah* was the only subject of contention debated during the administration of all the Zugoth." The words *LSMK* and *L' LSMK* do *not* denote here "to lay on the hands on an object, but express the derivative meaning of the verb . . . i.e. to depend, to rely, to accept the authority of, and the question discussed by the *Zugoth* was whether we could depend upon the authority of the hakhamim." Zeitlin asserts that those who held the negative said that "we ought not to rely on the sages in their innovations upon the Torah; the colleagues say we rely entirely upon the sages even in their innovations in the Torah." The entire basis for this "insight" is that Zeitlin announces it.

Zeitlin then analyzes the legal materials attributed to the pairs and distinguishes the opinion depending on "the sages" from that depending on the Scripture. The Shammai-Hillel disputes concern four issues: (1) "a fence for the Torah," vs. "let the strict law prevail" (*m. Nid.* 1:1; *m. Ed.* 5:2); (2) the challah offering, in which Shammai rules that the strict law must prevail; (3) the *semikhah* controversy, which in *m. Ed.* 1:3 pertains to the tradition of Hillel on the drawn water; and (4) *intention* in respect to grapes for the winepress (*b. Shab.* 17a).

Tacking on to stories his own improvements, Zeitlin interprets the language of Shammai to Hillel in *b. Shab.* 17a, "If you anger me," as follows: "If you will bring the principle of intention to prevail, I shall decree that olives are also made susceptible to Levitical uncleanness by their own liquid though no one desires this superfluity."

Another characteristic of Zeitlin's pseudocriticism is his resort to facile emendations to solve historical problems. Since the facticity of the historical stories is taken for granted, emending the sources supplies the answer to any difficulty and forthwith creates a new fact. For example, in "Sameias and Pollion,"[13] Zeitlin reviews the references of Josephus and then asks, "Who are the two men . . . ?" He forthwith reviews various suggestions and possibilities, rejecting each in turn. In the end he concludes the references of Josephus are not always to the same men. In one passage Sameias is Shammai; in two others, he is Shemaiah. The consequences of this theory are then spelled out. The passages are treated as literally true and accurate accounts of what was really said and done. Zeitlin then turns to Pollion the Pharisee, who must be Hillel. Josephus's Pollion is represented as the teacher of Sameias. "But Hillel was not the teacher of Shemaiah— he was his pupil. This reversing of relations can be explained as due to a scribal error."

Zeitlin's most ambitious work is *The Rise and Fall of the Judaean State: A Political, Social and Religious History of the Second Commonwealth.*[14] He holds that the Pharisees "stressed the principle of the universality of God" while the Sadducees held "that Yahweh is an ethnic God." He does not cite the Sadducean documents on this matter; there are no evidences on their views. Zeitlin sees the Talmudic account of Hyrcanus's split with the Pharisees as older than Josephus's "as the language makes clear. The conversive *Waw* . . . was used here—this usage is frequently employed in the Bible but this is the only instance of its occurrence in the Talmud."

The Pharisees go back to earliest Second Temple times: "The original Pharisees supported Zerubbabel" (!). They were the "main factor in the revolt against the domination of the Syrians." The Sadducees demanded rigid observance of the Pentateuchal law. "The Pharisees, however, strove to amend the Pentateuchal law in order to bring religion into consonance with life. They were ready to modify the Pentateuchal law in order to enable it to accord with the requirements and demands of ever-changing life." The Pharisees disapproved of class distinctions. The *haberim* and Pharisees "were not identical. Although many of the *haberim* undoubtedly were Pharisees, not all the Pharisees were *haberim*. The *haberim* had no theories of life. They only stressed the observance of the Pentateuchal laws of Levitical purity and tithes. [This seems to me plausible.] The Pharisees on the other hand had well developed beliefs with regard to both the individual and the Judaean community as a whole."

Much of Zeitlin's account simply paraphrases the rabbinic fables, with his embellishments to add color:

> In the spring of 31, Hillel became head of the Bet Din. Josephus calls him Pollion—"the hoary or venerable." Hillel was a man of peace. His brother "named Shabneh was a business man." Hillel migrated "presumably to find solutions for three contradictions he found in Pentateuchal laws." Hillel wanted to "verify whether his interpretations were in fact Judaean law. . . . When Hillel arrived in Judea . . . he learned that his independent interpretations were all correct, well-established halakoth." His rise to power vindicated the oral Torah. All his hermeneutic principles "had been used by Judaean before Hillel. . . . What was novel in Hillel's approach was the application of these principles to actual cases of statutory law . . . Hillel's method was too radical for the Bene Bathyra and they rejected it.

The House of Shammai and the House of Hillel represented conservative and liberal viewpoints, respectively. Zeitlin does not try to prove his view, he simply imputes it and cites stories and rulings that in his mind illustrate it. There is no rigorous argument, just a lot of invective. Shammai followed the established law, while Hillel was the innovator. He introduced another new concept, the principle of intention. He made a legal distinction "between happenings which stem from volition and those which do not." "Four controversies are recorded between Shammai and Hillel. In all Tannaitic controversies recorded in the Talmud, the name of the person who adhered to the conservative point of view is given first. Shammai's name, however, is given first in three of the disputes . . . while in the controversy on Semikhah, that is, the transmittal of authority to introduce new laws, Hillel's name is given first. This is due to the fact that this principle had already been accepted. Shemaiah and Abtalion had already debated this issue, and the name of Shemaiah, who adhered to this principle, was recorded first." The debates between the Houses "actually took place."

The Hillelites insisted that people should lay hands on the sacrifice. They realized that "if people were not allowed to lay their hands on the sacrifices, they would not bring them and would not make pilgrimages." They therefore took a positive view "so as to encourage pilgrimages. . . . The contention of the Hillelites that the Shammaite view would deter pilgrimages was proved correct: the Temple became deserted on the holidays [!]. The view of the Hillelites then became the law." So much for Baba b. Buta! "Many citations in the Mishne (sic] are Pharisaic formulations from the period of the Second Commonwealth. This is evident not only in their content, but also in their wording and style."

So much for Zeitlin, who spent the last two decades of his active career trying to prove that the Dead Sea Scrolls were medieval forgeries.

JACOB Z. LAUTERBACH

Like Louis Ginzberg, Jacob Z. Lauterbach, a professor at Hebrew Union College in Cincinnati, enjoyed wide influence for several decades. His ideas were part of the repertoire carried by his students, who were Reform rabbis, to American Jewry. Herford says that he revised his own views of the Pharisees after reading Lauterbach. Lauterbach posits his own set of theories to account for various disputes. In general, he falls in line with the opinion of Reform Jewish scholars, beginning with Geiger, that the Sadducees were reactionaries, while the Pharisees were liberals. The whole is then embellished with sermons of various kinds.

Lauterbach, in "The Sadducees and Pharisees," "A Significant Controversy between the Sadducees and the Pharisees," and "The Pharisees and Their Teachings" (all found in his *Rabbinic Essays*[15]), postulates that the Sadducees were the older, more conservative party; the Pharisees the younger, "broader and more liberal in their views, of progressive tendencies and not averse to innovations." Lauterbach treats the division of the two parties, which he assigns to *early* (!) in Second Temple times. Pharisees emerge from lay teachers; the Sadducees were formed by the priestly aristocracy. Like Moore, Lauterbach draws upon the whole corpus of rabbinic literature for his description of the Pharisees (called "sages of Israel").

The significant difference between the parties was the "identification of the Law with the ever growing and changing ideas of the teachers." The Pharisees claimed the right to make laws necessary for their time. The Sadducees denied that right. "Sadducaism, because of its rigid conservatism in following the letter of the Law, gradually lost all influence upon the life of the main body of the Jewish people."

The "significant controversy" between the parties concerned the manner in which the high priest should bring in the incense into the Holy of Holies on the Day of Atonement. "The Sadducees said it must be prepared outside of the Holy of Holies. The Pharisees said it should not be put into the censer outside, but the high priest should enter the Holy of Holies carrying the censer with the fiery coals in his right hand and the spoon full of incense in his left hand. Only inside the curtain should he put the incense upon the fiery coals on the censer and thus offer it there." Lauterbach asks how the Pharisees could have known the law, when the Sadducees were in control of the Temple. The Pharisees, he claims to prove, introduced "a radical reform." The Sadducees retained "many of the primitive notions both about God and the purpose of the service offered to Him in the Temple."

The Pharisees had a "purer God conception and less regard for the sacrificial cult. . . . They tried . . . to democratize and spiritualize the service in the Temple and to remove from it . . . the elements of crude superstition and primitive outworn conceptions." Preparing the incense outside was a measure of precaution; the smoke would pro-tect the priest from "the danger of Satan's accusations." Further, the smoke would prevent the high priest from "involuntarily looking the Deity in the face." These "primitive" theological views were rejected by the Pharisees.

"The Pharisees and their Teachings" makes the same point, that the Pharisees offered a "more spiritual" conception of religion than did their opposition. Their victory "had to result in a broad liberal universalism." Christianity sprang from Pharisaic Judaism. "Jesus and his disciples did not belong to the priestly aristocratic party of the Sadducees. They were of the plain humble people who followed the Pharisees." Each of the ancient sources—the Talmud, Josephus, and the New Testament—preserves "some accurate information about these two parties." The Pharisees were the newer party; the Sadducees the older; the latter were conservative, strict interpreters of the Torah. The Pharisees were "the younger, progressive party com-posed originally of democratic laymen who outgrew some of the older notions, cherished modern and liberal ideas, and therefore became separated from the older group and formed a distinct party. They were the liberal separatists, the dissenters who rejected some of the ancient traditional conceptions of religion and who broke away the primitive traditional attitude toward the Torah." "The Pharisees were heirs of the prophets and disciples of the priests" (even though elsewhere Lauterbach sees the Sadducees as the priests!).

LESSER FIGURES: SALO W. BARON AND GEORGE BUCHANAN

Zeitlin and Lauterbach were intellectually vigorous and ambitious figures who mastered the sources and scholarly literature and produced an important oeuvre. What of lesser lights? Two figures suffice to show the character of work on the Pharisees produced by inferior scholars.

Salo Wittmayer Baron, in *A Social and Religious History of the Jews: Ancient Times* II, rapidly summarizes the views of various scholars (something he excelled at).[16] The Pharisees "enjoyed great popularity and may be said to have represented the large majority of the nation . . . in fact every one of the Babylonian leaders known to us was a Pharisee, as were in essence also Philo in Alexandria, Paul's father in Tarsus, and Theudas in Rome." The Sadducees were wealthy, educated, and nationalistic and insisted "on the rigid application of Jewish law." But they had "lost contact with the living currents of their faith." The Pharisees represented "the living ethnic body" and insisted on the validity of the oral law. "As late as the days of Hillel, we are told, leaders of the Sanhedrin, puzzled by a legal problem, invited this relatively unknown foreign student to communicate to them some traditions which he had learned from their own predecessors in office." "In short, by synthesizing traditions with the revealed words of Scripture, the Pharisees acknowledged the supremacy of the time element, of national evolution, of history. The Sadducees, however, adhering to the basis of their political power, had to attach more importance to the space element, to the unchanging and permanent, to the revealed word of God in its most literal sense." These are standard positions for their day, not Baron's brew.

In *The Consequences of the Covenant*,[17] George Wesley Buchanan says, "The Pharisees did not necessarily write all of the Rabbinic literature, and may not therefore be adequately represented there. Some of the Rabbis may have been Pharisees but not necessarily all. Because some of the doctrines in Rabbinic literature were similar to those of the Pharisees it has been supposed that they were responsible for the entire body of literature."

He further comments,

> It is very difficult, if not impossible, to learn the character of the Pharisees in the first century of the Christian Era in Palestine from Rabbinic literature, which was mostly edited or originally composed in the diaspora sometime between the third and the seventh century A.D., and which seldom mentioned the Pharisees by name. Some early tradition may be preserved in this literature, but it must be demonstrated point by point by comparison with Josephus, Philo, or some other earlier writer. A statement attributed to an early Rabbi may have been composed, as well as attributed to him, by a later Rabbi. Literature written and preserved by the Rabbis may or may not have been written by Pharisaic Rabbis, and the date of its composition must still be established by some other criterion than the date at which the Rabbi in question lived.

"These discussions relating Hillel, Shammai, and R. Joshua to the Pharisees do not prove that these Rabbis were themselves Pharisees. . . . The quarrels between the Pharisees and Sadducees were reported neither from a pro-Pharisaic nor anti-Pharisaic point of view, so there is little direct evidence that the Pharisees wrote either the Mishnah or the Tosefta." All of this represents the future, not the past. But what went wrong is that Buchanan did not do the work to make his points register; he announced them with great certainty but did not produce the text-analysis to establish the facts.

What does not ring true in Buchanan's account is, first, his allegation that rabbinic literature "was mostly edited . . . in the diaspora," for he cites no evidence whatsoever that Mishnah-Tosefta were not Palestinian documents. Most scholars think they were. I do not know why Buchanan supposes otherwise.

Further, he seems not to take seriously the fact that later masters do refer to earlier sayings and stories. This would seem to mean those sayings and stories are not to be dated at the very end of the Talmudic period—600 CE —but, with some reservations, may be assigned to the period before the time of the masters who evidently knew them. To be sure, attributions are not always reliable. But we are no better off in deciding they *never* are reliable and in rejecting out of hand the reliability of the rabbinic process of transmission, in particular after 140 CE, when it appears to be sound and under excellent control.

The real problem in Buchanan's account, however, is not his thesis that the Pharisees do not stand behind elements of the Mishnah and Tosefta, but his failure to do more than to enunciate that theory. In this respect he can hardly be differentiated from the various Talmudic historians already considered, who announce "revolutionary" theories and then take them for granted, without subjecting their theories either to close examination or to the test of evidence. What is pseudocritical here, therefore, is the display of the form of the critical approach without the substance of the critical process. In other chapters of the same book, moreover, Buchanan takes for granted the accuracy not only of attributions to various masters but also of what is attributed to them.

CONCLUSION

Admittedly, historians of the Pharisees face a very knotty problem. Information on the Pharisees derives from difficult and diverse sources. These sources are quite different from one another and in some measure entirely discrete. Schürer and the other Germans were baffled by the evidences of Talmudic literature; the New Testament materials have not been critically examined by the Talmudists, who read the New Testament in exactly the same literal way in which they read the Talmud; and as of 1970 rigorous work on Josephus, represented by Professor Mason, had not yet begun. The generality of scholarship in European languages now affirms the critical program that, before 1970, seldom governed. Debates have shifted to new problems, as the exchange with Professor Sanders in the next chapter shows.

CHAPTER 16

THE DEBATE WITH E. P. SANDERS SINCE 1970

Jacob Neusner

Despite the risible misnomer of his book of miscellaneous essays,[1] claiming to speak of "Jewish law . . . to the Mishnah" while discussing mere anecdotes and episodes in Jewish law in the first century with special reference to the gospels, Professor Edward P. Sanders's current account of his views should not be dismissed as the merely random thoughts of one who wanders aimlessly beyond the fence of his field of firsthand knowledge. Holding Sanders to his claim that he knows something about what he calls "Jewish law," let us take seriously his conception of the Pharisees of the first century. Since Sanders— intending to persuade colleagues that his picture of, and apologia for, the Pharisees, not mine, accurately portray how things really were in the first century—devotes two of his five chapters to that subject, we turn forthwith to the contrasting results contained in his current book.

WHAT DO WE KNOW ABOUT THE PHARISEES AND HOW DO WE KNOW IT?

Since the announced purpose of the pertinent chapters is to criticize my position and set forth a different one, to begin with let me briefly summarize my views. Viewed as a historical problem, identifying the Pharisees begins with attention to the sources that refer to them. No historical knowledge reaches us out of an *a priori* corpus of principles, and what we cannot show, we simply do not know. A principal problem in arguing with Sanders is his rich capacity to make up distinctions and definitions as he goes along,[2] then to impose these distinctions and definitions on sources that, on the face of it, scarcely sustain them. Sanders proceeds to form out of a priori distinctions and definitions a deductive argument, which makes it exceedingly difficult to compose an argument with him. For how are those of us who appeal to evidence and the results of the analysis of evidence to compose an argument against fabricated definitions and distinctions, which to begin with derive not from evidence and analysis thereof? The fundamental difficulty in dealing with Sanders, therefore, begins with the basic problem of reading scholarship that is accessible only within its own framework of premises and even language. Looking at the evidence in its own terms, by contrast, requires us to classify our documents and analyze them, only afterward turning to the issues of special concern to us.

Now to Sanders's critique and his concomitant reconstruction of the matter. He deals with two consequential matters: first, Did the Pharisees have oral law? and second, Did the Pharisees eat ordinary food in purity? To these questions I state my answer up front. So far as Sanders claims to argue with me in particular, I have not called into question the proposition that, in addition to Scriptures, Pharisees, like pretty much every other group, had some further law or tradition, and that that additional material can have been formulated and transmitted orally, in memory. But, as a matter of fact, no evidence pertaining in particular to the Pharisees permits us to impute to them the fully exposed myth of the dual Torah—part in writing, part oral— that comes to complete expression only in the later documents of the Judaism of the dual Torah, in particular, in the Talmud of Babylonia. As to whether Pharisees ate ordinary food in a state of cultic cleanness, I of course do not know what they actually did. I claim to know only how the earlier strata of the Mishnah's law represent matters in sayings attributed to authorities before 70. And the answer is, the earlier strata of Mishnaic law take for granted that the laws of cultic cleanness, applicable to priests' eating their Temple food, are assumed to apply outside of the Temple, and also to persons who were not members of the priestly caste.

DID THE PHARISEES HAVE ORAL LAW?

While announcing that he agrees with me, Sanders claims to find confusing my treatments of this matter. But the source of his confusion is that he imputes to me that same confusion between history and theology that characterizes his work. I am consistently explicit on that distinction, for example, "*viewed from the perspective of Judaic faith*, the teachings of the named sages of late antiquity . . . preserve principles . . . handed on by tradition from Sinai."[3] I am equally clear that, *described historically*, the conception that "Moses received the Torah at Sinai in two media" emerges at a given point, fairly late in the formative history of the Judaism of the dual Torah. Obviously, a critical historical account presents information of one kind; a theological statement, information of another. Sanders states: "He continues to publish things whose [*sic*] fundamentalism would embarrass the most conservative talmudists."[4] What Sanders means by "fundamentalism" is not clear to me, since, in Judaism, there is no "fundamentalism" in the Protestant sense. I have never misrepresented myself. I am a believing and practicing Jew, without apology. I affirm with all my heart that God revealed the one whole Torah, oral and written, to Moses, our rabbi, on Mount Sinai. I have produced historical results that impart to that statement of faith and theology a set of meanings that are not historical at all. This I have shown in many passages (which as a Christian Sanders evidently finds offensive) of my writing, but especially in *Uniting the Dual Torah: Sifra and the Problem of the Mishnah.* The closing lines of that book form a statement of what we can mean by "Moses received Torah at Sinai," when that is taken to refer to not historical but other matters altogether—matters of eternity, sanctification, and salvation, for example. I have not confused history with theology, nor have I followed the model of those biblical theologians whose historical work leads them to modify theological truth in light of facts of a different order altogether.

In point of fact, however, Sanders concurs with everything that I have maintained on this topic. Explicitly concurring with my results, Sanders proceeds to give a survey of matters on the Oral Torah that he finds in various rabbinic documents. Some of these passages attribute views to pre-70 authorities we assume were Pharisees; most do not, and therefore his account draws on evidence not pertinent to the Pharisees in particular. Since Sanders himself admits that "we have come to a view proposed by Neusner on the basis of a partially different body of evidence," it hardly seems interesting to spell out all of the mistakes Sanders makes in selecting and interpreting the evidence he deems pertinent, nor is time devoted to pointing out the confusion of distinct bodies of evidence well spent.[5] In this chapter Sanders affirms precisely the results that I have set forth.

DID THE PHARISEES EAT ORDINARY FOOD IN PURITY?

Here again, Sanders's conclusion is "Neusner's standards for collective evidence mark a distinct advance." He concurs with much that I say, tinkering with nuance and emphasis, rather than with fact and substance. But there can be an argument, since he also maintains, "He misinterpreted his own material. Use of his analytical work leads to other conclusions about the Pharisees than the ones which he drew."[6] On method Sanders and I differ in one fundamental way. He takes as generally reliable attributions of sayings to named authorities. Since in historical study what we cannot show, we do not know, I am inclined to a more reserved position, asking for evidence that permits us to assign to a period in which a named authority is assumed to have lived a saying attributed to that authority. Beyond that point, the evidence in hand does not permit us to go, since we do not have books written by specific, named authorities, or even collections of sayings formed prior to, and demonstrably utilized by, the compilers and editors of the late, anonymous documents that we do have. Sanders concedes that materials attributed to the Houses in fact were formulated after 70. But that does not prevent him from using those materials he chooses for evidence on the *topics* under discussion.[7] If, however, the attributions are not reliable, then how can we know for sure that people at that time talked about the topics?

Sanders accuses me of not noting "the importance of the distinctions which the Houses made between the priests' food and their own with regard to harvesting, handling, and processing it." The locus classicus for those distinctions between food prepared in conditions of cultic cleanness for use in the Temple by the priests and food prepared in conditions of cultic cleanness for use other than in the Temple by the priests must be Mishnah-tractate Hagigah 2:5–3:3. Because it is fundamental, let me place it into the hands of the reader, and only then specify why I think it is important.[8]

2:5   A.   They wash the hands for eating unconsecrated food, tithe, and heave offering;

      B.   and for eating food in the status of Holy Things they immerse;

      C.   and as to [the preparation of] purification water through the burning of the red cow, if one's hands are made unclean, his entire body is deemed to be unclean as well.

2:6   A.   He who immerses for the eating of unconsecrated food and is thereby confirmed as suitable for eating unconsecrated food is prohibited from eating tithe.

      B.   [If] he immersed for eating tithe and is thereby confirmed as suitable for eating tithe, he is prohibited from eating heave offering.

      C.   [If] he immersed for eating heave offering and is thereby confirmed as suitable for eating heave offering, he is prohibited from eating food in the status of Holy Things.

      D.   [If] he immersed for eating food in the status of Holy Things and is thereby confirmed as suitable for eating food in the status of Holy Things, he is prohibited from engaging in the preparation of purification water.

      E.   [If, however,] one immersed for the matter requiring the more stringent rule, he is permitted to engage in the matter requiring the less stringent rule.

      F.   [If] he immersed but was not confirmed, it is as though he did not immerse.

2:7   A.   The clothing of ordinary folk is in the status of Midras uncleanness for abstainers [= *Perushim*, Pharisees].

      B.   The clothing of abstainers is in the status of Midras uncleanness for those who eat heave offering [priests].

      C.   The clothing of those who eat heave offering is in the status of Midras uncleanness for those who eat Holy Things [officiating priests].

      D.   The clothing of those who eat Holy Things is in the status of Midras uncleanness for those engaged in the preparation of purification water.

      E.   Yosé b. Yoezer was the most pious man in the priesthood, but his handkerchief was in the status of Midras uncleanness so far as eating Holy Things was concerned.

      F.   For his whole life Yohanan b. Gudgada ate his food in accord with the requirements of cleanness applying to Holy Things, but his handkerchief was in the status of Midras uncleanness so far as those engaged in the preparation of purification water were concerned.

3:1   A.   A more stringent rule applies to Holy Things than applies to heave offering,

I   B.   for: They immerse utensils inside of other utensils for purifi-
           cation for use with [food in the status of] heave offering,

     C.   but not for purification for use with [food in the status of
           Holy Things].

II   D.   [They make a distinction among] outer parts, inside, and
           holding place in the case of use for heave offering,

     E.   but not in the case of use for Holy Things.

III F.   He who carries something affected by Midras uncleanness
           [may also] carry heave offering,

     G.   but [he may] not [also carry food in the status of] Holy
           Things.

IV   H.   The clothing of those who are so clean as to be able to eat
           heave offering

     I.   is deemed unclean in the status of Midras uncleanness for
           the purposes of Holy Things.

     J.   The rule for Holy Things is not like the rule for heave
           offering.

V   K.   For in the case of [immersion for use of] Holy Things one
           unties a knot and dries it off, immerses and afterward ties it
           up again.

     L.   And in the case of heave offering one ties it and then one
           immerses.

3:2 VI

     A.   Utensils that are completely processed in a state of insuscep-
           tibility to uncleanness [and so when completed are clean]
           require immersion for use in connection with Holy Things,

     B.   but not for use in connection with heave offering.

VII C.   A utensil unites everything contained therein for the pur-
           poses of Holy Things,

     D.   but not for the purposes of heave offering.

VIII E.   [That which is made unclean in] the fourth remove from the
           original source of uncleanness in the case of Holy Things is
           invalid,

     F.   but only [that which is made unclean in] the third in the case
           of heave offering.

IX   G.   And in the case of heave offering, if one of one's hands is
           made unclean, the other is clean.

     H.   But in the case of Holy Things one has to immerse both of
           them.

X   I.   For one hand imparts uncleanness to the other for the pur-
           poses of Holy Things,

     J.   but not for the purposes of heave offering.

3:3 XI

     A.   With unclean hands they eat food that has not been wet
           down in the case of heave offering,

B.   but not in the case of Holy Things.

XII C.   He who [prior to interment of the deceased] mourns his next of kin [without having contracted corpse uncleanness] and one whose atonement rite is not complete [because an offering is yet required] require immersion for the purposes of Holy Things,

D.   but not for the purposes of heave offering.

The passage distinguishes between the cleanness required for eating unconsecrated food, food that has been designated as tithe or priestly rations ("heave offering"), and food that is in the status of Holy Things. "Holy Things" are the share of the officiating (or other) priests in what has been offered on the altar—for example, the priests' share of the sin offering. Priestly rations comprise the share of a crop that the farmer designates for transfer to the priesthood. Scripture certainly takes for granted that Holy Things will be eaten in the Temple, therefore in a state of cultic cleanness, and priestly rations are supposed likewise to be eaten in a condition of cultic cleanness; since the family of the priest likewise eats priestly rations, it is assumed that women and children not located in the Temple at the time of their meal likewise will be concerned about cultic cleanness when it comes to eating this food as well. The nub of the matter is the classification of food called "unconsecrated." Unconsecrated food is food that has no relationship to the cult or the Temple. If one eats it with considerations of cultic cleanness in mind at all, then, there can be only one reason, and that is, that someone proposes to eat unconsecrated food in a state of cultic cleanness. That seems to me the simple fact of the matter, and Sanders's ingenious distinctions and definitions notwithstanding, that remains the plain sense of the numerous passages that distinguish among unconsecrated food, priestly rations, and Holy Things.

We see that there are diverse standards of cultic cleanness that pertain to food that is unconsecrated, priestly rations, and Holy Things, and these standards are of course hierarchical,[9] with the most stringent rules (the details of which we may bypass) required for Holy Things, less stringent ones for priestly rations, and least stringent for unconsecrated food. Now to my way of thinking, when at *m. Hagigah* 2:7A–C we are told that the clothing of ordinary folk is in the status of Midras uncleanness for Pharisees, and that of Pharisees in the same state for those who eat heave offering, in the present context it

seems to me that a single conclusion must be drawn. Pharisees, at
2:7A, are concerned with cultic cleanness; they are not the same as
priests, who are dealt with at 2:7B, but are of a lesser standing in the
hierarchy of cultic cleanness. Then priests eating priestly rations or
heave offering are hierarchically situated as well, now at a lesser status than priests who are going to eat Holy Things deriving from the
altar. The context throughout is preparation for eating food, as the
language that is used demonstrates. The explicit reference to
Pharisees certainly yields the thesis that Pharisees are not classified as
priests, that is, as persons who eat priestly rations or heave offering.
But they are persons who are placed within the hierarchy of cultic
cleanness in eating food. The food that they eat is not food that is
reserved for priests, so it can only be food that is not reserved for
priests, which is to say, secular or unconsecrated food. That passage
on the face of it therefore sustains the view that Pharisees are persons
who eat unconsecrated food in a state of cultic cleanness, or, more
accurately, within the hierarchy of states of cultic cleanness that the
Mishnah's paragraph's framer proposes to spell out.

Now let us turn directly to Sanders's own thesis. It is best to turn
directly to the passage I have cited, since where and how Sanders's
Pharisees differ from mine is best discerned on the common ground
of shared evidence. He states the following:

> Hagigah 2.7 fits Pharisees into a hierarchy . . . it indicates that
> Pharisees were more scrupulous with regard to one (minor) form of
> impurity than were other lay people.
>
> How important were these rules to the Pharisees? Purity was cer-
> tainly important to them, and protecting the priesthood and the tem-
> ple from impurity was a very substantial concern. The purity of their
> own food seems to have been of less importance. . . .
>
> . . . since Pharisees did not observe the purity laws of the priesthood
> with regard to their own food, why did they have so many rules about
> corpse-impurity and Midras-impurity? I propose, To make minor ges-
> tures towards extra purity. I call them minor gestures in comparison
> with what they are thought to have done: expelled their wives, done all
> the domestic work one week in four, and so on. The word 'minor,' how-
> ever, probably misleads us with regard to their own intention. It sounds
> as if they made the comparison which I have made, and found their
> own efforts trivial. This is most unlikely. We cannot assign precise
> motives, but I think we can safely assign a general one: to be pure,
> because purity is good.[10]

Apart from the rather subjective judgment at the end, I could not have said it better myself. That is precisely what my reading of this, and various other, passages tells me. When Sanders proceeds to announce that the Pharisees also did other things, for example, "they worked from dawn to dusk . . . and they had to study," he cannot imagine anyone is going to be surprised. But he proceeds, "The legal discussions attributed to Pharisees never take study as their topic, and thus mechanical counting failed to reveal to Neusner that it is a main theme. It is the basis of the entirety of the material, and every discussion rests on it."

Here, alas, Sanders confuses an activity with the mythology attached to the activity. No one doubts people acquired information, that is, studied. What I have called into question is whether Torah study as the principal mode for the imitation of God, which the later rabbinic Torah-myth set forth as a critical and central proposition, is attested in the rabbinic traditions about the Pharisees. I did not find it there, and Sanders's reminder that people learned things is, like much else that he says, monumentally irrelevant to the issue. In the successor system, first attested by writings that reached closure long after the first century, knowledge more than merely informs, it saves. What happens to me in Torah study in the theory of the religious successor-system that does not happen to me in Torah study in the theory of the Mishnah—itself no Pharisaic writing—is that I am changed in my very being. This transformation of the one who knows is not alone as to knowledge and understanding (let alone mere information), nor even as to virtue and taxic status, but as to what the knower is. The one who knows the Torah is changed and saved by Torah knowledge, becomes something different from, better and more holy than, what he was before he knew, and whether the complement is "the mysteries" or "the Torah [as taught by sages]" makes no material difference.[11]

When Sanders tells me that people learned things and so alleges that Torah study was a "main theme" of Pharisaism, he shows that he does not grasp the point of the myth of Torah study within the Judaism of the dual Torah. Scarcely a single passage that is supposed to pertain to the pre-70 Pharisees imagines such a gnostic Torah.

SECTARIANISM, EXCLUSIVISM, AND SANDERS'S PROTESTANT THEOLOGICAL APOLOGETIC FOR A JUDAISM IN THE PROTESTANT MODEL

What is at stake? My reading of the evidence leads me to treat the Pharisees as ordinary people eating meals at home in conditions that are analogous to the conditions required of priests in the Temple or in their homes. Sanders treats Pharisees as people who were "more scrupulous with regard to one (minor) form of impurity than were other lay people." I see here a distinction that yields no difference at all. Anyone who can tell me how this difference—scarcely in degree, but not at all in kind—has persuaded Sanders to spend so much time on details of the law of the Mishnah and the Tosefta, which he time and again either reads out of context or simply does not understand at all, will win my thanks. Sanders minimizes purity laws, it would seem, because he wants to argue against the notion of Pharisaic "exclusivism." [12] Sanders wishes to deny that the category "sect" applies to the Pharisees:

> [W]e should reserve the word "sect" for a group which was to an appreciable degree *cut off* from mainline society. It should *reject* some important part of the rest of society, or it should *create* an alternative structure. Neusner frequently compared the Pharisees to the Dead Sea Sect, finding basic agreements and minor differences. But the differences are large and clear, and they show that one was a sect and the other not. [13]

Of course, a group that did not set up a commune off all by itself is different from a group that by all evidence remained within the common society, and if the former is a sect, then the latter is something else. We need not quibble; I think my definition functions well: a group of people who interpreted and obeyed law "in a way different from other groups or from society at large." [14] But if he means that while the Essene community was exclusivist but the Pharisees were not, then we really do differ in a fundamental way. In my judgment every Judaism, including the Pharisees' Judaic system, by definition is exclusivist, in that it identifies who is saved and who is not. That the authors of the gospels saw the Pharisees as a distinct "group," whether that group be classified as a sect, a party, a club, or something else, seems to me to underline that the group was exclusivist, as indeed were the various Christian or other Judaic communities of the same time and place—by nature, by definition. Why not?

Sanders responds to a long tradition of anti-Judaism and even anti-Semitism in New Testament scholarship. He denies that Judaism was what its academic and theological enemies maintain. His book in the context of contemporary Protestant theological debate makes a point important in its setting:

> The Pharisees had a positive concern for purity; it was better to be pure than not. They were not alone. The same was true of a lot of Jews and of a lot of pagans. . . . "Ritual purity". . . now has to many people an unfavorable connotation, and it is thought that what is wrong with the Pharisees is that they favored it. But this would only mean that what is wrong with them is that they lived in the ancient world—where most people favored it. Most Christian scholars . . . think that it was precisely "ritual" which Jesus and Paul attacked. Since the major point of the Jewish law which is treated negatively in both the synoptic gospels and Paul is the Sabbath, the assumption that they attacked "ritual" implies that rest on the Sabbath should be considered "ritual." It was instead commemorative (of God's rest) and ethical (not only men, but also women, servants, animals, and the land itself were allowed to rest). The Pharisees' concern to be pure went beyond the requirements of the law—as did that of others. . . . People thought that purity was a good thing, and they tried to avoid impurity, even though it had no practical consequence. There were many who wanted to be able to "distinguish between the holy and the common. . . ." The Pharisees fully participated in this spirit. They differed from others in many particulars, they defined certain impurities very carefully, they probably extended corpse-impurity more than did most, and they may have tried harder than did most to avoid the new sources of this impurity. The desire to be pure, however, they shared with the populace in general.[15]

I cite the passage at length, because it seems to me to point toward the benevolent intent of Sander's scholarship. He takes up an important position in the tradition of Christian apologetics for Judaism graced by the names of Herford, Danby, Moore, and his teacher W. D. Davies.

PART FOUR

CONCLUSION

and Paul's real letters both were produced before the destruction of the second Temple in 70 CE, so they have pride of place in this list. In addition, because the Dead Sea Scrolls were preserved but not transmitted, they have some of the "accidental" quality and character of archaeological remains. Taken together, all these five earliest sources suggest that the Pharisees (and perhaps the Sadducees as well) were active in the Land of Israel from the period of the Hasmonean dynasty until the time of the destruction of the Jerusalem Temple—a span of nearly two centuries. Broad interest in the Pharisees, however, stems not from their antiquity longevity but rather from their depiction in the gospels as principal opponents of Jesus and/or his disciples. In popular imagination, the Pharisees emerge as perhaps the primary "not-Jesus" over and against whom Jesus and his religious teachings are defined. The picture of the Pharisees as formalists and hypocrites derives from this conception. Not surprisingly, as Susannah Heschel and Jacob Neusner demonstrate, the gospels' picture has dominated most scholarly descriptions of the Pharisees. In general, scholars have used the gospels' image as the standard either according to or against which historical descriptions of the Pharisees should be drawn. In recent decades, scholarship has worked to break the gospels' grip on the historical reconstruction of the Pharisees. This book aims to contribute to that effort.

The articles collected in this volume suggest that earliest sources for the Pharisees of history neither entail nor generate one another. It seems impossible, for instance, to deduce from Josephus or the Mishnah the specific teachings and traits assigned to the Pharisees in the New Testament, or the reverse. Each of these early sources and collections must be seen primarily as independent and unconfirmed historical witnesses. The papers in this book follow this approach by treating each source about the Pharisees discretely, in terms of its own traits and aims.[3] Since the time of Herodotus and Thucydides, however, it has been an axiom of critical history that isolated, singular testimony constitutes weaker evidence about the past than do multiple accounts from different sources. Corroboration enhances credibility. If so, then examining the sources chronologically for mutually reinforcing testimony can help to establish a firm evidentiary foundation for a controlled description of the historical Pharisees.[4] In the best case, that testimony would be both descriptive and substantive. It would cover the traits and characteristics assigned to the group as well as its beliefs and practices. For example, it is one thing to claim that the Pharisees were "lenient." It is another thing to know precisely and concretely in what "leniency" consisted and how it was justified.

THE DEAD SEA SCROLLS

Contemporary scholarship has established two basic areas of overlap for the Dead Sea Scrolls: one with the writings of Josephus and one with some traditions in rabbinic literature. As James VanderKam indicates, although the Pharisees do not appear by name in the writings preserved at Qumran, there is widespread and longstanding scholarly agreement that a group called "Those Who Seek Smooth Things" mentioned in the Damascus Document, the Thanksgiving Scroll, and the commentaries to Isaiah and Nahum are Pharisees. Martin Jaffee's summary description is helpful.

It is likely that the phrase "Expounders of Smooth Things" [= "Those Who Seek Smooth Things"] is indeed a reference to the Pharisaic group that came into conflict with the Yahad [Qumran community] over political affairs during the reign of Alexander Jannaeus. It also seems clear that, from the Yahad's point of view, Pharisaic faults included not only political treason, but a more fundamental rejection of the legal prescriptions revealed to Israel in the study vigils at Qumran. Pharisaic life—as the Yahad perceived it, at least—was, by contrast, governed by reference to "easy expositions" of the Torah and a penchant for finding "loopholes."[5]

James VanderKam reaches similar conclusions. He supplies reasons for specifically identifying "Those Who Seek Smooth Things" with the Pharisees described by Josephus as opponents executed by Alexander Jannaeus. The Qumran texts he reviews depict "Those Who Seek Smooth Things" as follows: "(1) They followed the Scoffer so that they broke the covenant. (2) They rejected the Torah of the Teacher [of Righteousness]. (3) They were a community with members in Jerusalem." Further, the scrolls polemicize against them for their lax interpretation of the Torah and, in VanderKam's terms, for "rejecting the revealed Torah for something else." These texts are long on name-calling but short on substance. They indicate that the

Yahad likely opposed the Pharisees, but they are silent on the content of the conflict. We cannot learn from these sources the precise substance of Pharisaic teaching.

Some recent scholarship has sought to derive that content from the religious behaviors mandated in the Qumran texts. The Dead Sea Scrolls contain halakhic positions that conflict with teachings in rabbinic texts[6] or that rabbinic literature assigns to Sadducees.[7] For example, three specific rulings in 4QMMT (*Miqsat Ma'aseh ha-Torah*) are attributed to Sadducees in the Mishnah: "the red heifer could be burned only by priests who were in a state of complete ritual purity [4QMMT B:13–17/*m. Parah* 3:7]; non-kosher animals' bones were considered impure [4QMMT B:21–23/*m. Yadayim* 4:6]; and liquid poured from a pure vessel into an impure one rendered the former impure [4QMMT B:55–58/*m. Yad.* 4:7/*m. Toh.* 8:9]."[8] In *m. Yadayim* 4:6 and 4:7, the contrary positions are assigned to Pharisees. In *m. Parah* 3:7, the contrary position is attributed to the "elders of Israel." On the basis of this kind of evidence, some scholars have concluded "that Qumranic halakhah was essentially Sadducean halakhah"[9] and have associated with the Pharisees halakhic positions in rabbinic literature that contradict those in the Dead Sea Scrolls, even if the rabbinic positions are not explicitly assigned to Pharisees.[10] It is suggested that the allegedly "Pharisaic" positions are more lenient than those at Qumran. The thinking behind this approach appears to be that if it is possible to demonstrate the prerabbinic antiquity of positions ascribed to Sadducees in rabbinic literature, it is reasonable to suppose in general that the anti-Sadducean positions in rabbinic writings have similar antiquity and derive from the Pharisees.[11] Both Yaakov Elman[12] and Eyal Regev urge caution about this position. Elman warns against the comparison of discrete *halakhot* from Qumran and rabbinic literature and emphasizes "the importance of *systemic* examination in the comparative study of Qumranic and rabbinic Halakhic texts."[13] His analysis displays the complexity of the interpretation of *m. Yadayim* 4:7 and shows how the comparison of isolated halakhic passages from the two literatures can result in false similarities. He also demonstrates that from a systemic perspective the claim that rabbinic *halakhot* are always more lenient than those at Qumran is doubtful at best. Regev echoes Elman's conviction about the importance of systemic analysis, the comparison of "Halakhic systems."[14] He shows that halakhic agreement between positions in the scrolls and those assigned to Sadducees in the rabbinic corpus is hardly comprehensive and that "although there are undoubtedly several similarities, the differences are much more significant than the points of agreement."[15] Indeed, there are points on which the views at Qumran and those assigned to rabbis also agree. Regev's comparison between *halakhot* at Qumran and his reconstructed Sadducean halakha suggests that in some areas the Pharisees may have developed "innovations of greater lenience" than either the positions at Qumran or those assigned to Sadducees:

> The Pharisees introduced the concept of *'erua haserot*; they introduced a new level of purity/impurity, *tevul yom*, not mentioned in the Torah, ruling that the priest who burnt the red heifer need reach only that level and did not have to wait for sunset; they instituted complex definitions of pure and impure blood, including the principle of the monthly cycle (to the extent that this principle was known in antiquity, it is not documented in pre-Rabbinic literature).[16]

The evidence supplied by Elman and Regev challenges the view that the halakha at Qumran is pervasively Sadducean and that, as a consequence, halakhic views that oppose it are, by definition, Pharisaic. They also show how the larger meaning of discrete rulings depends on understanding their place in a comprehensive halakhic system. Thus, even if all of Regev's suggested "innovations" could be assigned to Pharisees with certainty, absent knowledge of the Pharisees' halakhic system, their religious positions or principles are difficult to discern.

THE LETTERS OF PAUL

Paul's letters offer a single explicit reference to the Pharisees: Paul's claim in Philippians 3:5 to have been a Pharisee (or like a Pharisee) with respect to "the law." Martin Jaffee rightly observes that the claim "offers nothing . . . by way of an explanation of the specific content" of Pharisaic "norms, their authority, or their relation to the revealed prescriptions of Scripture."[17] In this volume, Jacob Neusner and Bruce Chilton probe the assertion in Acts 22:3 that Paul studied in Jerusalem with the Pharisee Gamaliel. They explore the range of substantive overlap between teachings presented in a literary form, the "domestic *ma'aseh*," that seems distinctive to Gamaliel and the patriarchal house. The patriarchal agenda in the "domestic *ma'aseh*" includes the following topics: "(a) calendar, travel, and contact with idols in the Diaspora; (b) keeping house, marriage, work, and slaves; and (c) rules for festivals and the Temple." Substantive overlap between Paul and these traditions is meager:

> [W]hat stands out unmistakably is that there is nothing like a quotation from Paul of Gamaliel's teaching (or vice versa), nor a common reference to a specific exegetical tradition, nor a comparable stance to an institution (for example, the Temple). These three types of analogy . . . simply do not apply to the case of Gamaliel and Paul.

Neusner and Chilton do suggest that there is "an analogy of logic and argumentation" between Paul and the traditions of Gamaliel on the issues of idolatry (common judgment of the unreality of idols), and possibly on the matter of the treatment of slaves (a possible analogy between Gamaliel's slave, Tabi, and Philemon's former slave, Onesimus). All of this falls far short of a substantive religious agenda. If Paul really was a Pharisee and studied with Pharisaic masters, extremely little of concrete, identifiable Pharisaic teaching is evident in his letters.

THE GOSPELS AND ACTS

For the gospels and Acts, there appear to be two possible instances of overlap with another source. First, both the book of Acts (23:6-10) and Josephus (*War* 2:163, *Ant.* 18:14–17) claim that the Pharisees believe in the resurrection of the dead and an afterlife, but the Sadducees disagree. Second, the assertion in the Gospel of Mark (7:1-13; cf. Matt 15:3-9) that the "Pharisees and the scribes" follow a "tradition of the elders" may reinforce a comparable claim by Josephus that Pharisees, as Steve Mason puts it, "follow a special set of legal prescriptions . . . 'from a succession of fathers . . . *in addition to the laws of Moses*.*" Mason makes clear that Josephus does not claim that the Pharisees possessed an oral tradition. Paul also claims (Gal 1:14) to have been "zealous for the traditions of my ancestors." If he was a Pharisee, this would constitute another, independent testimony of a

Pharisaic teaching. Albert I. Baumgarten has studied this issue in some detail. After a review of a range of sources, he concludes that "the terms *paradosis* of the elders and of the fathers were deliberate attempts by the Pharisees to give their tradition a pedigree that it might have seemed to lack."[18] That is, the use of the term *paradosis* may suggest "how the Pharisees wanted to appear and were seen by their contemporaries in Palestine prior to the destruction of the Temple."[19] Even if the claim to possess an ancestral tradition derives from the Pharisees, it is only a justification. It does not describe the content of that tradition or delimit the range, scope, or theology of the Pharisees' religious practices.

In contrast to these two instances of overlap, all of the gospels' other claims about the Pharisees are either singletons or repetitions of a singleton with slight modification. It is useful here to remind ourselves that the repetition of a discrete tradition from one gospel to another does not enhance the tradition's credibility as a historical witness. Repetition is not multiple attestation. The Gospel of Mark contains six substantive traditions about the Pharisees: (1) They do not eat with sinners and tax collectors (Mark 2:15-17/Matt 9:10-13/Luke 5:29-32); (2) They fast (Mark 2:18-22/Matt 9:14-17/Luke 5:33-39); 3) They do not pick grain on the Sabbath (Mark 2:23-28/Matt 12:1-8/Luke 6:1-5); 4) They disapprove of healing on the Sabbath[20] (Mark 3:1-6/Matt 12:9-14/Lk 6:6-11/Luke 14:1-6); 5) They wash their hands before eating (Mark 7:1-13/Matt 15:1-9); 6) They practice divorce (Mark 10:2-12/Matt 19:3-9). Other Markan traditions, such as the Pharisees asking for a "sign" (Mark 8:11-13/Matt 16:1-4) or whether or not it is legitimate to pay taxes to Caesar (Mark 12:13-17/Matt 22:15-22/Luke 20:20-26) use the Pharisees as a narrative foil for Jesus, but contribute virtually nothing to a picture of their ideas and behaviors. Matthew 23:1-36/Luke 11:39-52, which is assigned to the hypothetical Q source of New Testament materials, ascribes the following to the Pharisees: (1) They wear phylacteries, (2) attend synagogue, (3) are called "rabbi," (4) proselytize, (5) make vows, (6) tithe, (7) wash the outside of their dishes, and (8) have knowledge of the "greatest commandment." If we take the synoptic materials and the Q materials to derive from different sources, there appears to be no substantive overlap between them about the Pharisees. Martin Pickup and Amy-Jill Levine demonstrate the differ-

ent ways these materials are used in different gospels. As to the discrete materials about the Pharisees in the Gospel of John, Raimo
Hakola and Adele Reinhartz observe that these exhibit "no obvious
knowledge" of the Pharisees' "beliefs and practices."

In his discussion of the Q materials on the Pharisees, Martin
Jaffee correctly points out that the "references to such practices as
cleansing cups or tithing herbs" do not "necessarily distinguish these
practices as central to or distinctive of Pharisaic tradition."[21] The
force of this observation extends to the all other views and practices
attributed to the Pharisees in the gospels. It surely is reasonable to
suppose that these particular teachings were important to the framers
of those gospel traditions. But there is no way with certainty to move
directly from the gospels to the historical Pharisees. That a teaching
mattered to the framers of the gospels does not mean it was equally
important—or important at all—to the Pharisees, if, in fact, it derives
from the Pharisees in the first place. Jaffee's observation underscores
yet again the importance of seeing particular behavioral and theological teachings in their systemic context.

In his discussion of Paul and the Pharisees, Bruce Chilton raises
yet another caveat. Scholarship on the Pharisees nearly uniformly
supposes that "Pharisees" refers to a Jewish, that is, a non-Christian,
group. On the basis of Acts 15:1-5, however, Chilton proposes that
the Christian Pharisees "insisted on the practice of circumcision that
put them at odds . . . with the positions of Paul and of James, and that
made Pharisaism a rhetorical category of enmity *within* Christianity,
a category that was then retrojected into the gospels, to describe the
opposition to Jesus." He suggests, in other words, that in the gospels
the Pharisees (who, in the words of Acts, were actually believers who
belonged to the sect of the Pharisees) came to represent and symbolize "not-Jesus," the category over and against which Jesus and his religious teachings were constructed, because of a religious struggle
inside the early Christian community. He explains that

> whether the term for the opposition to Paul's teaching, with Peter's and
> James's, happens to be "the Pharisees" (as in the gospels and Acts) or
> "Jews" or "the circumcision" (as in Paul's letters), the originating heat
> of the argument came from early Christianity's moment of greatest
> interior contention, rather than from a conscious confrontation with
> Judaism.

This approach requires the assumption that Acts 15 presents at least some historically plausible—if not authentic—description of religious divisions among the earliest Christians as they sought to develop their collective theological self-understanding and behavioral regimen. Such an assumption hardly represents methodological radicalism within New Testament studies, and the passage from Acts 15 is no more or less useful than any other discrete and uncorroborated testimony about the Pharisees from the gospels and Acts. It therefore deserves thoughtful and probing consideration. Chilton's suggestive proposal significantly would reshape the framework for any critical scholarly reading of the depiction of the Pharisees in the gospels and Acts. It also might help to explain the intensity of some exchanges between Jesus (and/or his disciples) and the Pharisees, and to clarify the urgency of the stakes in the disagreements between them. At the very least, Chilton has opened up an additional interpretive option that must be considered in future scholarship on the Pharisees in the New Testament.

THE WRITINGS OF JOSEPHUS

Steve Mason offers a succinct statement of the limited areas in which Josephus and other sources confirm one another:

> Josephus's handling of the three Judaean philosophical schools should make us wary about using his descriptions of the Pharisees in these sketches for historical purposes. Some aspects of Sadducean and Essene thought and life can be confirmed by the New Testament and Philo (also Pliny): we may conclude from such independent witnesses that Sadducees rejected the afterlife and that Essenes lived in highly regimented "philosophical" communities that stressed simplicity of life (Philo, *Prob.* 75–91; Pliny, *Nat.* 5.73). Of the Pharisees, the New Testament confirms that they observed a special legal tradition "from the fathers" and that they believed in the afterlife; Josephus's language permits the notion of resurrection, even though he does not spell it out. Rabbinic literature on *Perushim* and *Tzadukim* presents considerable difficulties, both internally and in relation to the Pharisees and Sadducees of Josephus and the New Testament. For the finer details of life and practice among these groups, however, we are frustrated partly by the general dearth of evidence, partly by an author who uses them as set pieces to be manipulated along with the rest of his material.

Mason also reminds us that the Pharisees figure "only incidentally" in the writings of Josephus and that their role in Josephus's "narrative world" limits the value of Josephus's writing for reconstructing the Pharisees of history.

> Pharisees appear as an occasional aggravation to the elite. They are a nonaristocratic group with enormous popular support and a perverse willingness to use that support demagogically, even on a whim, to stir up the masses against duly constituted authority—Hasmonean, Herodian, or Josephan. In *War*, the moment of Pharisaic ascendancy is the reign of Queen Alexandra, though Josephus says as little as possible about the group after that. In *Antiquities*, Alexandra's reign is again a watershed, but now Josephus offers a backstory, the preceding interval from Hyrcanus I to Alexandra, as a failed experiment in governance *without* the popular Pharisaic jurisprudence. Ever since Alexandra's reign, therefore—under Herod's government and through the first century until Josephus's time—the Pharisaic program has again been in place: one who accepts office must listen to "what the Pharisee says." We do not know, because Josephus does not explain, how his audience should have understood the mechanisms of Pharisaic influence, let alone the content of the Pharisees' jurisprudence or how it was implemented. He seems uninterested in moving from complaint to clarification.

Josephus's apparent hostility toward the Pharisees may constitute an instance of a text testifying against itself and thus may lend some credibility to Josephus's claim about the Pharisees' popular influence over an extended period of time. But Daniel Schwartz points out that the "critique [of the Pharisees in Josephus] does not necessarily make the claims true. . . . Josephus could complain about Pharisaic control even if the Pharisees were not dominant, just as whoever wants to can always claim that Jews control all the banks and newspapers."[22] He also demonstrates that 4QMMT does not support the view that the majority of the Jews were Pharisees. Without supporting evidence, most of the materials from Josephus constitute an elaborate but singular testimony.

EARLY RABBINIC LITERATURE

Of the early materials about the Pharisees, rabbinic literature is by far the latest. The earliest rabbinic document is the Mishnah, typically dated to 200 CE, and the materials it contains, as Jack Lightstone demonstrates, result from an elaborate and intricate reformulation and redaction that virtually prevent them from offering direct testimony about anything other than their own formulation. Rabbinic literature also does not claim that its teachings and ideas derive from the Pharisees. Indeed, as we have seen, the Mishnah contains teachings assigned to Sadducees as well as to Pharisees. The claim that early rabbinic documents contain teachings of pre-70 Pharisees derives from two instances of overlap among the early sources: first, the appearance in Paul, Acts, and the Mishnah of a first-century figure named Gamaliel—identified as a Pharisee only in Acts 5:34—and second, the appearance of the name of Simeon b. Gamaliel in the Mishnah and in Josephus, who alone identifies him as a Pharisee. As Jacob Neusner explains, the justification for assuming that the Mishnah presents a Pharisaic chain of tradition derives from these two uncorroborated nonrabbinic identifications of Gamaliel and his son as Pharisees.

> The rabbinic traditions about the Pharisees before 70 CE are those compositions in the Mishnah (ca. 200) or the Tosefta (ca. 300) in which we find the names of rabbinic sages presumed to have lived before 70, or the Houses of Shammai and Hillel, two such masters. Why Pharisaic in particular? The indicated pre-70 authorities are sages named in the chains of authorities down to and including Gamaliel (Paul's teacher, per Acts 22:3) and Simeon b. Gamaliel (labeled by Josephus as a Pharisee in *Life* 38) and masters referred to in pericopes of those same authorities. Those lists include Mishnah-tractate Hagigah 2:2 and tractate Abot 1:1–18.
>   Because Gamaliel and Simeon b. Gamaliel, who appear on the list in Abot 1:1–18, are identified as Pharisees, I assume that all others on the list formed part of that same chain of tradition that Gamaliel and Simeon received, in the mythic narrative, from Sinai—a single ongoing tradition deriving from Pharisees.

Neusner's analyses demonstrate that, in comparison to the other early sources, the rabbinic materials about the pre-70 Pharisees are massive and not uniformly distributed across generations or among individual sages.

> The rabbinic traditions in the Mishnah and the Tosefta about the Pharisees before 70 CE consist of approximately 371 separate items—stories or sayings or allusions—which occur in approximately 655 different pericopes. Of these traditions, 280, in 456 pericopes, pertain to

Menahem, Shammai, Hillel, and the Houses of Hillel and Shammai—
that is, the generation from about 25 BCE to 25 CE. In all, these make
up approximately 75 percent. A roughly even division of the materials
would give 23 traditions in 40 pericopes to each name or category, so
the disparity is enormous.

Neusner further explains that the rabbinic traditions about the pre-
70 Pharisees offer virtually no testimony about life outside their own
circle:

They supply no rules either about synagogue life or about reading the
Torah and preaching in synagogues. It would be difficult to maintain
that the sect claimed to exercise influence in the life of synagogues
not controlled by its own members or that they preached widely in
synagogues.

From the rabbinic traditions about the Pharisees we could not have
reconstructed a single significant public event of the period before
70—not the rise, success, and fall of the Hasmoneans, nor the Roman
conquest of Palestine, nor the rule of Herod, nor the reign of the
procurators, nor the growth of opposition to Rome, nor the proliferation of social violence and unrest in the last decades before 66 CE, nor
the outbreak of the war with Rome. We do not gain a picture of the
Pharisees' philosophy of history or theology of politics. We should not
even know how Palestine was governed, for the Pharisees' traditions
according to the rabbis do not refer to how the Pharisees governed the
country—the rabbis never claim the Pharisees did run pre-70
Palestine, at least not in stories told either about named masters or
about the Houses—nor do they tell us how the Romans ran it.
Furthermore, sectarian issues are barely mentioned, and other sects
not at all.

Rather, the focus of these early rabbinic materials is largely internal to the life and thought of the group: "The fact is, therefore, that
the laws we have are the laws we should have: the rules of a sect concerning its own sectarian affairs, matters of importance primarily to
its own members." In these traditions, Neusner identifies "ritual
purity, agricultural taboos, and Sabbath and festival behavior" as the
"three chief issues of sectarian consequence." He points out that
there is a thematic congruence between these passages and some
teachings assigned to the Pharisees in the gospels. It is helpful here to
keep the nature of the gospels' materials in perspective. The materials about the Pharisees in the synoptic gospels and Q offer perhaps a
dozen traditions on what charitably could be called halakhic matters,

each discrete and uncorroborated. In Neusner's counting, for example, there are more than ten traditions about the Houses of Hillel and Shammai on matters of tithing. In the synoptic gospels, by contrast, there is one tradition about the Pharisees tithing, and its focus is not tithing per se, but the importance of tithing relative to other religious obligations. The thematic overlap between the two sets of source material remains close to the surface.

ARCHAEOLOGICAL EVIDENCE

A distinctive contribution of this collection on the Pharisees in history is the inclusion of archaeological evidence that may help illuminate them. James Strange offers one of the very few attempts to consider the literary material about the Pharisees against the archaeological background of the Land of Israel. His conclusion therefore merits citation in full.

> We have examined six concerns or interests of the Pharisees that we believe had left an imprint in the archaeological record. These concerns and their proposed counterparts in the material culture were (1) serving food at table—small stone vessels; (2) immersion of tableware (dishes)—large stone vessels; (3) immersion of the person—ritual pools or *miqva'oth*; (4) washing hands—"measuring cups" (lavers) of chalk stone; (5) resurrection and afterlife—tombs and ossuaries; (6) synagogue activity—synagogue plans and architecture. The results were threefold: (1) There was sufficiently strong interest in purity as a broad category in antiquity that a stoneware industry was founded with centers near Jerusalem, in lower Galilee, and probably elsewhere. The Jerusalem center was apparently also the locus of manufacture of ossuaries, an artifact that reflects another concern with afterlife and resurrection. (2) There was also a matching industry, though usually not called that, of constructing ritual baths (and collecting pools to fill them) from south to north in the country and extending into the Golan Heights. (3) There are seven buildings understood to be synagogues that reveal a striking similarity of plan using nested elements. This is a small sample compared to the thousands of stone vessels, but the geographic distribution of these few structures virtually "from Dan to Beersheba" itself agues that synagogues did not appear solely because of local interests, but because of the interests of a class or body of people who saw to it that they were constant in plan for the sake of the declamation of the Torah.

Although there were probably others who were interested in public purity in much the same way as the Pharisees—notably at Qumran—there is no catenae of texts that make it clear that the bulk of Israelites during the period of the Second Temple observed purity laws strictly. Yet the broad distribution of artifacts associated with purity and considered here suggests that some major group led the way in preserving the traditions of purity outside the Temple. Furthermore, this group may well have legislated about the form and function of the items of material culture so that they achieved a kind of standardization. The group that appears to have sufficient status in Second Temple Judaism to be responsible for this state of affairs—especially after 70 CE—is the Pharisees. This testable hypothesis is the major result of the above analysis.

The archaeological record that Strange reviews demonstrates "broad distribution of artifacts associated with purity" throughout the Land of Israel. This suggests that Judaic purity practices were widely observed across a range of locations and social groups. The issue is how to relate these data to the Pharisees. Strange argues that because these remains exhibit "a kind of standardization" they are the result of the work of a single group in ancient Judaism that advocated their use and may have "legislated" about their "form and function." He suggests that the Pharisees were this group. This certainly is a reasonable and plausible interpretation of the evidence.[23]

But the nature of the archaeological record Strange presents does not foreclose an alternative reading of the same evidence. Strange observes that there is no textual record that the "bulk of the Israelites during the period of the Second Temple observed purity laws strictly." This observation raises two issues. First, in the nature of things, the "bulk" of the ancient Jews did not produce a textual record. Second, as we have seen, terms such as "strict" or "lenient" are relative. For the writer of 4QMMT, some Pharisaic teachings may have seemed lenient. For the framers of gospel traditions, the Pharisees seemed strict. That Jews in the Land of Israel did not uniformly observe purity practices "strictly" does not mean that they observed none at all. From this perspective, the archaeological record supplies evidence of widespread Judaic purity practice that the texts, produced by and largely for elites, do not. Different Judaic religious groups disputed with one another about the nature of purity regulations, and those disputes mattered because they presupposed a popular practice of Judaic purity rather than a narrow sectarian one. This scenario, which is no less faithful to the evidence than the one proposed by Strange, depicts the Pharisees as one group among several working against a backdrop of the popular practice of a Levitical religion.

CONCLUSION

The materials reviewed in this volume about the Pharisees in history produce a remarkably small core of hard historical evidence. We possess testimonies from at least two sources that the Pharisees had an independent tradition, that they affirmed resurrection of the dead and an afterlife, that they opposed Alexander Jannaeus, that they differed from and sometimes disputed with Sadducees, and that they practiced a Levitical piety outside the Temple. Beyond that, the sources about them reinforce one another, when they do at all, only at the most general level. This means that our historical description of the Pharisees must come from discrete, uncorroborated materials, which, by their very nature, do not constrain speculation. As Jacob Neusner observed, no source describes the nature of Pharisaic group life or the content of their beliefs. Although some specific halakhic opinions reasonably can be ascribed to Pharisees, these do not constitute a system. This makes it difficult to discern the larger meaning of particular rulings and opinions. The principles behind the rulings and opinions remain necessarily conjectural. We cannot limn the contours of Pharisaic religious belief and behavior. Even the established picture of the Pharisees as the primary Judaic opponents of Jesus is now open to question.

In his discussion of Josephus, Steve Mason draws an instructive "distinction between interpretation—focused on the text as medium of communication—and reconstruction of realities behind the text." The materials about the Pharisees assessed in this volume are far better suited to interpretation than to reconstruction. This guarantees that the study of the Pharisees will remain an important "cottage industry" in scholarship on ancient Judaism and Christianity.

JOURNAL AND SERIES ABBREVIATIONS

ACS	American Classical Studies
ABRL	Anchor Bible Reference Library
AUSS	*Andrews University Seminary Studies*
AGJU	Arbeiten zur Geschichte des antiken Judentums und Urchristentums
BHWJ	*Bericht der Hochschule für die Wissenschaft des Judentums*
Bib	*Biblica*
BA	*Biblical Archeologist*
BAR	*Biblical Archaeology Review*
BibSem	The Biblical Seminar
BETL	Bibliotheca ephemeridum theologicarum lovaniensium
BJS	Brown Judaic Studies
CGTSC	*Cambridge Greek Testament for Schools and Colleges*
CBQ	*Catholic Biblical Quarterly*
CBQMS	Catholic Biblical Quarterly Monograph Series
CA	*Classical Antiquity*
CQ	*Classical Quarterly*
CSCT	Columbia Studies in the Classical Tradition
DSD	*Dead Sea Discoveries*
DJD	Discoveries in the Judaean Desert
ETL	*Ephemerides theologicae lovaniensis*
HTR	*Harvard Theological Review*
HUCA	*Hebrew Union College Annual*
ICC	International Critical Commentary
IBC	Interpretation: A Bible Commentary for Teaching and Preaching
IEJ	*Israel Exploration Journal*
JQR	*Jewish Quarterly Review*
JSJ	*Journal for the Study of Judaism*
JSJSup	Journal for the Study of Judaism Supplements

JSNTSup	Journal for the Study of the New Testament: Supplement Series
JSPSup	Journal for the Study of Pseudepigrapha: Supplement Series
JAAR	*Journal of the American Academy of Religion*
JAOS	*Journal of the American Oriental Society*
JANES	*Journal of Ancient Near Eastern Studies*
JBL	*Journal of Biblical Literature*
JETS	*Journal of the Evangelical Theological Society*
JHC	*Journal of Higher Criticism*
JJLP	*Journal of Jewish Lore and Philosophy*
JJS	*Journal of Jewish Studies*
JR	*Journal of Religion*
JSS	*Journal of Semitic Studies*
JTS	*Journal of Theological Studies*
JZWL	*Jüdische Zeitschrift für Wissenschaft und Leben*
NAC	New American Commentary
NIB	*The New Interpreter's Bible*
NTL	New Testament Library
NTS	*New Testament Studies*
NTTS	New Testament Tools and Studies
NovT	*Novum Testamentum*
OEANE	*The Oxford Encyclopedia of Archaeology in the Near East,* ed. E. M. Meyers
OTP	*Old Testament Pseudepigrapha*
PEQ	*Palestine Exploration Quarterly*
PW	Paulys Realencyklopädie der classischen Altertumswissenschaft
PKZ	*Protestantische Kirchenzeitung für das evangelische Deutschland*
RST	Regensburger Studien zur Theologie
RGG	*Religion in Geschichte und Gegenwart,* ed. K. Galling. 7 vols. 3rd ed. Tübingen, 1957–1965
RevExp	*Review and Expositor*
RRJ	*Review of Rabbinic Judaism*
RTP	*Review of Theology and Philosophy*
RevQ	*Revue de Qumran*
REJ	*Revue des Études Juives*
RM	*Rheinesche Museum*
SP	Sacra Pagina
SNTSMS	Society for New Testament Studies Monograph Series
SBLMS	Society of Biblical Literature Monograph Series
SBLSP	*Society of Biblical Literature Seminar Papers*

SBLSymS	Society of Biblical Literature Symposium Series
StPB	Studia post-biblica
SNTSU	Studien zum Neuen Testament und seiner Umwelt
SUNT	Studien zur Umwelt des Neuen Testaments
SR	*Studies in Religion*
SNTW	Studies of the New Testament and Its World
NovTSup	Supplements to Novum Testamentum
TSAJ	Texte und Studien zum antiken Judentum
TLZ	*Theologische Literaturzeitung*
TRu	*Theologische Rundschau*
TSK	*Theologische Studien und Kritiken*
ThTo	*Theology Today*
TynBul	*Tyndale Bulletin*
VTSup	Vetus Testamentum Supplements
WUNT	Wissenschaftliche Untersuchungen zum Neuen Testament
WZJT	*Wissenschaftliche Zeitschrift für jüdische Theologie*
ZDMG	*Zeitschrift der deutschen morgenländischen Gesellschaft*
ZNW	*Zeitschrift für die neutestamentliche Wissenschaft und die Kunde der älteren Kirche*
ZRGG	*Zeitschrift für Religions- und Geistesgeschichte*
ZTK	*Zeitschrift für Theologie und Kirche*
ZWT	*Zeitschrift für wissenschaftliche Theologie*

NOTES

CHAPTER 1

1 J. Neusner, *From Politics to Piety: The Emergence of Pharisaic Judaism* (Englewood Cliffs, N.J.: Prentice Hall, 1973), 13.

2 Examples in S. Mason, *Flavius Josephus on the Pharisees: A Composition-Critical Study*, StPB 39 (Leiden: Brill, 1991), 1–10 and related notes.

3 On the problem of historical method and the use of Josephus, see S. Mason, "Contradiction or Counterpoint? Josephus and Historical Method," *RRJ* 6 (2003): 145–88.

4 Essene positions, however, are now ascribed to the whole nation, as Porphyry seems to have realized (*Abst.* 4.11.1–2).

5 Josephus's intricate handling of the biblical narrative is the best-documented analysis of his narrative methods: H. R. Moehring, "Novelistic Elements in the Writings of Flavius Josephus" (PhD diss., University of Chicago, 1957); L. H. Feldman, *Josephus's Interpretation of the Bible* (Berkeley: University of California Press, 1998); L. H. Feldman, *Studies in Josephus' Rewritten Bible* (Leiden: Brill, 1998); L. H. Feldman, *Flavius Josephus: Translation and Commen-tary*, vol. 3 of *Judean Antiquities 1–4*, ed. S. Mason (Leiden: Brill, 2000); C. Begg, *Flavius Josephus: Translation and Commentary*. vol. 4 of *Judean Antiquities 5–7*, ed. S. Mason (Leiden: Brill, 2004). For the historical implications, see H. R. Moehring, "Joseph ben Matthia and Flavius Josephus," in *Aufstieg und Niedergang der Römischen Welt*, ed. H. Temporini and W. Haase (Berlin: Walter de Gruyter, 1984), 2.21.2, 864–917; Mason, "Contradiction or Counterpoint?"

6 See F. Millar, "Last Year in Jerusalem: Monuments of the Jewish War in Rome," in *Flavius Josephus and Flavian Rome*, ed. J. Edmondson, S. Mason, and J. Rives (Oxford: Oxford University Press, 2005), 101–28.

7 See, e.g., Aristotle, *Rhet.* 1.2.1–15.1356a; 2.1.2–3.1377b; Cicero, *De or.* 2.182; Quintilian, *Inst.* 5.12.10; Aulus Gellius, *Noct. att.* 4.18.3–5; J. M. May, *Trials of Character: The Eloquence of Ciceronian Ethos* (Chapel Hill: University of North Carolina Press, 1988), 6–8; G. A. Kennedy, *A New History of Classical Rhetoric* (Princeton: Princeton University Press, 1994), 102–27.

8 Along with known works by Herodotus, Hecataeus, and Strabo (among many), note Plutarch (*Mor.* 3.799b–800a) on the distinctive character of each *polis*, and Quintus Curtius (8.9.20) on the environment and character

429

of India and its inhabitants. For the classical grounding of this conception see Plato, *Resp.* 544d–591; W. Jaeger, *Paideia: The Ideals of Greek Culture* (Oxford: Oxford University Press, 1973), 2.320–47; B. Isaac, *The Invention of Racism in Classical Antiquity* (Princeton: Princeton University Press, 2004), 56–74.

9   W. R. Farmer, *Maccabees, Zealots, and Josephus: An Inquiry into Jewish Nationalism in the Greco-Roman Period* (New York: Columbia University Press, 1956); M. Hengel, *The Zealots: Investigations into the Jewish Freedom Movement in the Period from Herod I until 70 A.D.* (Edinburgh: T&T Clark, 1989), 149–55, 171–73 (a history of scholarship on the question), 377.

10   D. Daube, "Typology in Josephus," *JJS* 31 (1980): 18–36; S. J. D. Cohen, "Josephus, Jeremiah, and Polybius," *History and Theory* 21 (1982): 366–81; S. Mason, "Josephus, Daniel, and the Flavian House," in *Josephus and the History of the Greco-Roman Period*, ed. F. Parente and J. Sievers (Leiden: Brill, 1994), 161–91.

11   G. W. Bowersock, *Greek Sophists in the Roman Empire* (Oxford: Clarendon Press, 1969); E. L. Bowie, "The Greeks and Their Past in the Second Sophistic," *Past and Present* 46 (1974): 3–41; A. M. Eckstein, "Josephus and Polybius: A Reconsideration," *CA* 9 (1990): 175–208; A. M. Eckstein, *Moral Vision in the Histories of Polybius* (Berkeley: University of California Press, 1995); S. Swain, *Hellenism and Empire: Language, Classicism, and Power in the Greek World, AD 50–250* (Oxford: Oxford University Press, 1996); S. Goldhill, ed., *Being Greek under Rome: Cultural Identity, the Second Sophistic, and the Development of Empire* (Cambridge: Cambridge University Press, 2001).

12   R. Syme, *The Roman Revolution* (Oxford: Oxford University Press, 1939), 415, 419–39; W. Eck, *The Age of Augustus*, trans. D. L. Schneider (Oxford: Blackwell, 2003), 113–25.

13   S. Mason, "Flavius Josephus in Flavian Rome: Reading on and between the Lines," in *Flavian Rome: Culture, Text, Image*, ed. A. J. Boyle and W. J. Dominik (Leiden: Brill, 2002), 559–89.

14   S. Mason, "Figured Speech and Irony in T. Flavius Josephus," in Edmonson, et al., *Flavius Josephus and Flavian Rome*, 243–88.

15   See, e.g., *War* 2.443, 264; 4.177–178, 273–279, 397; 5.18–19, 363; 6.102.

16   Cf. Plato's programmatic distinction between the world of appearances, sense perception, and opinion, on the one hand, and knowledge and the real, on the other (*Resp.* 514a–517c). In Josephus's *War*, Hyrcanus II's mischievous courtiers complain that he has only the title (ὄνομα) and not the authority (ἐξουσία) of king (1.209). Later (1.561), Antipater pleads with his father not to leave him the mere title of king while others hold the real power. At 2.208, *princeps*-designate Claudius promises through Agrippa I that he will rest content with honor of the title or address (προσηγορία) while governing in fact through senatorial consultation. More generally on reputations or seeming in contrast to being: *War* 1.648; *Ant.* 17.41; 19; 332; *Apion* 1.18, 67; Cassius Dio 36.11.

17   V. Rudich, *Political Dissidence under Nero: The Price of Dissimulation* (London: Routledge, 1993); V. Rudich, *Dissidence and Literature under Nero: The Price of Rhetoricization* (London: Routledge, 1997); S. Bartsch, *Actors in the Audience:*

Theatricality and Doublespeak from Nero to Hadrian (Cambridge, Mass.: Harvard University Press, 1994).

18 *War* 2.162; *Ant.* 17.41; *Life* 191; cf. Mason, *Flavius Josephus on the Pharisees*, 89–113.

19 G. Hölscher, "Josephus," *PW* 18:1934–2000 (Munich: A. Druckenmüller, 1916); D. R. Schwartz, "Josephus and Nicolaus on the Pharisees," *JSJ* 14 (1983): 157–71; E. P. Sanders, *Judaism: Practice and Belief, 63 BCE–66 CE* (Philadelphia: Trinity International Press, 1992), 390.

20 D. C. Braund, "Cohors: The Governor and His Entourage in the Self-Image of the Roman Republic," in *Cultural Identity in the Roman Empire*, ed. R. Laurence and J. Berry (London: Routledge, 1998), 10–24; E. Meyer-Zwiffelhoffer, Πολιτικῶς ἄρχειν: *Zum Regierungsstil der senatorischen Statthalter in den kaiserzeitlichen griechischen Provinzen* (Stuttgart: F. Steiner, 2002).

21 See, e.g., Sanders, *Judaism: Practice and Belief*, 385.

22 This is favorite, formulaic language in Josephus.

23 Note the prominence of constitution language in strategic places: *Ant.* 3.84, 213; 4.45, 184, 191, 193–195, 196–198, 302, 310, 312; 5.98, 179; 15.254, 281; 18.9; 20.229, 251, 261; *Apion* 2.188, 222, 226, 272–273. At *Apion* 2.287 Josephus recalls that he wrote the *Antiquities* in order to give "an exact account of our laws and constitution."

24 Plato, *Resp.* 544d–591; Jaeger, *Paedeia*, 2.320–47.

25 Famously, the sixth book of Polybius's *History*.

26 R. Syme, *Tacitus* (Oxford: Clarendon, 1958), 408–34; B. Otis, "The Uniqueness of Latin Literature," *Arion* 6 (1967): 199; R. Mellor, *Tacitus* (London: Routledge, 1993), 87–112.

27 See note 11 above.

28 See, e.g., Feldman, *Flavius Josephus*—both his detailed commentary on *Ant.* 1–4 and my introductory essay.

29 *Ant.* 4.223; 5.135; cf. Mason, "Flavius Josephus in Flavian Rome."

30 *Ant.* 4.186, 218, 220, 255, 256, 325; 5.15, 43, 55. For the priestly core of this senatorial aristocracy, see *Ant.* 3.188; 4.304; *Life* 1; *Apion* 1.29–37; 2.184–186.

31 See, e.g., Cicero, *Rep.* 2.12.23; Livy 1.17.3.

32 T. P. Wiseman, *Death of an Emperor: Flavius Josephus* (Exeter: University of Exeter Press, 1991).

33 Mason, "Flavius Josephus in Flavian Rome," and Mason, "Figured Speech and Irony in T. Flavius Josephus."

34 These parallels are explored in great detail by R. Laqueur (*Der jüdische Historiker Flavius Josephus: Ein biographischer Versuch auf neuer quellenkritischer Grundlage* [1920; repr., Darmstadt: Wissenschaftliche Buchgesellschaft, 1970]) and S. J. D. Cohen, *Josephus in Galilee and Rome: His Vita and Development as a Historian.* CSCT 8 [Leiden: Brilll, 1979]). For a comparative table illustrating the degree of difference between *War* and *Life*, see Appendix C in S. Mason, ed., *Flavius Josephus: Translation and Commentary*, vol. 9 of *Life of Josephus* (Leiden: Brill, 2001).

35 See, e.g., C. Pelling, *Plutarch and History* (Swansea: Classical Press of Wales, 2000).

36 Programmatically, Laqueur (*Der jüdische Historiker Flavius Josephus*); H. Rasp, "Flavius Josephus und die jüdischen Religionsparteien," *ZNW* 23 (1924): 27–47.

37 Further, Mason, *Flavius Josephus*, xxxvii–xli.

38 J. M. Baumgarten, "The Unwritten Law in the Pre-Rabbinic Period," *JSJ* 3 (1972): 12–14; E. Rivkin, *A Hidden Revolution: The Pharisees' Search for the Kingdom Within* (Nashville: Abingdon, 1978), 41–42.

39 So J. Neusner, *The Rabbinic Traditions about the Pharisees before 70* (Leiden: Brill, 1971), 2:163; Mason, *Flavius Josephus on the Pharisees*, 240–43.

40 Mason, *Flavius Josephus on the Pharisees*, 96–106.

41 The Bible requires execution by an "avenger of blood" not only for murder, idolatry, and blasphemy but also for cursing parents (Exod 21:17; Lev 20:9), owning an animal that gores a person to death (if the animal has also harmed others, Exod 21:29), being a medium or wizard (Lev 20:27), violating the sabbath (Exod 31:14-15; 35:2), kidnapping (Exod 21:16), and adultery (Lev 20:10). On corporal punishment (for unspecified offenses), see Deut 25:2-3.

42 See, e.g., *m. RH* 2.5; *Yeb.* 16.7.

43 For a thorough examination of the humane character of Pharisaic jurisprudence, argued on the basis of rabbinic halakha, see, famously, L. Finkelstein, *The Pharisees: The Sociological Background of Their Faith* (Philadelphia: Jewish Publication Society of America, 1938).

44 On the need for *everyone* who wished to live by the Bible to fill its "gaps," and for a fascinating exposition of Pharisaic and other tradition in the context of rapidly growing literacy from the Hasmonean period, see A. I. Baumgarten, *The Flourishing of Jewish Sects in the Maccabean Era: An Interpretation* (Leiden: Brill, 1997), 114–36.

45 Eck, *Age of Augustus*, 79. From the early third century CE, Roman law would formalize the long evident legal distinction between the mass of free citizens (*humiliores*) and the privileged (*honestiores*).

46 See, e.g., *War* 2.234, 259–260, 321–332, 399, 406, 411–417, 427, 523–526; 5.527–528; *Ant.* 1.115; 3.24–27, 68–69, 295–315; 4.37; 19.202; cf. Polybius 6.9.8–9; 44.9; Cicero, *De re pub.* 1.42.65; Tacitus, *Hist.* 1.4, 32.

47 Mason, *Flavius Josephus on the Pharisees*, 219; cf. the similar story told of Jannaeus in *b. Kadd.* 66a.

48 Although some MSS have Samaias here as the Pharisee, with a student also named (a form of) Samaias, this would only postpone the problem until 15.370, where the text clearly gives the relationship above. It seems clear that some copyists adjusted the names at 15.3 to remove the contradiction with 14.172–176; they either did not notice 15.370 or could not bring themselves to "correct" the text a second time.

49 Rasp, "Flavius Josephus," 39, 44, 47; M. Black, "Judas of Galilee and Josephus's Fourth Philosophy," *Josephus-Studien: Untersuchungen zu Josephus, der antiken Judentum und dem Neuen Testament* (Göttingen: Vandenhoeck & Ruprecht, 1974), 50; G. Alon, *Jews, Judaism, and the Classical World* (Jerusalem: Magnes Press, 1977), 44–47.

50 Greek: ἐπιτηδεύσει τοῦ ἐπὶ πᾶσι κρείσσονος ἔι τε τῇ διαίτῃ τοῦ βίου καὶ λόγοις. Although Feldman in the Loeb edition renders the former phrase "by practicing the highest ideals," presumably in view of the preceding ἀρετή αὐτοῖς (Feldman, "the excellence of the Pharisees"), in *Ant.* 17–19 ἀρετή need not mean moral virtue or excellence, but often retains its older sense of morally neutral strength or force (e.g., 17.44, 49, 171, 238, 277, 279).

51 Greek: ἀνεκτός. Seven of its eleven occurrences in Josephus are in *Ant.* 18, one of many features embedding this passage in the surrounding narrative.

52 See note 19 above.

53 For a full examination of the passage, see S. Mason, "Was Josephus a Pharisee? A Reconsideration of *Life* 10–12," *JJS* 40 (1989): 31–45.

54 *Ant.* 4.13; 13.432; 14.91; 15.263; 18.44; 20.251; *Life* 258, 262.

55 See, e.g., *Ant.* 3.188; 4.186, 218, 222, 224, 304, 325; 5.15, 23, 55, 57, 103, 353; 10.12, 62; 11.8, 11, 17, 62, 139–140; 12.142, 13.166; 14.211; . . . 20.6, 180–181.

56 Although I am trying to interpret the narrative, one can imagine that such dynamics might have been in play historically. Whereas scholars like to pass judgment on whether certain chief priests, Josephus himself, or leading Pharisees were "pro- or anti-Roman," as if this were a fixed trait, Josephus's narrative resonates with our common experience of places caught up in unrest. Native leaders are often faced with conflicting allegiances: sharing popular resentment of intrusive great powers and wanting to express that outrage, yet trying to manage dissent in safe ways, while preserving their own lives (e.g., not being tarred as collaborators) and social stability; seeing the futility of reckless or implacable revolt and yet possibly agreeing at certain moments to guerrilla strikes for the sake of honor.

57 See, e.g., Eckstein, *Moral Vision in the Histories of Polybius*; Swain, *Hellenism and Empire*.

58 Among relatively recent works, see L. L. Grabbe, *Judaism from Cyrus to Hadrian* (Minneapolis: Augsburg Fortress, 1992), 2:470–76; Sanders, *Judaism*, 386.

59 Whereas in historical reconstruction each reconstructed phenomenon must be argued separately, when interpreting a narrative we are entitled to accept conditions of Judean life painstakingly established by the author at one place (*Ant.* 13) and assumed again later (*Ant.* 18) as holding in the intervening narrative as well: he need not pause every few pages, especially when speaking of Roman or Babylonian affairs, to remind us that Pharisees are still influential with the Judean masses.

60 Grabbe, *Judaism from Cyrus to Hadrian*, 474.

CHAPTER 2

1 E.g., Hölscher, "Josephus," n.*; G. F. Moore, "Fate and Free Will in the Jewish Philosophies according to Josephus," *HTR* 22 (1929): 371–89; M. Black, "The Account of the Essenes in Hippolytus and Josephus," in *The Background of the New Testament and Its Eschatology*, ed. W. D. Davies and D. Daube, 172–82 (Cambridge: Cambridge University Press, 1956); M. Smith,

"The Description of the Essenes in Josephus and the Philosophoumena," *HUCA* 35 (1958): 273–93; Schwartz, "Josephus and Nicolaus on the Pharisees"; R. Bergmeier, *Die Essener-Berichte des Flavius Josephus: Quellenstudien zu den Essenertexten im Werk des jüdischen Historiographen* (Kampen: Kok Pharos, 1993).

2 For criticism of source theories, see C. Burchard, "Die Essener bei Hippolyt: Hippolyt, REF. IX 18, 2–28, 2 und Josephus, Bell. 2, 119–161." *JSS* 8 (1977): 1–41; A. I. Baumgarten, "Josephus and Hippolytus on the Pharisees," *HUCA* 55 (1984): 1–25; Mason, *Flavius Josephus on the Pharisees*, 176–77, 306–8, 384–98; D. S. Williams, "Josephus and the Authorship of *War* 2.119–161 (on the Essenes)," *JSJ* 25 (1994): 207–21.

3 Plato's *Republic*, a dialogue on the meaning of justice, is only the most famous example. See Jaeger, *Paedeia*, 2.198–208.

4 Greek: αἱρέσεις. In earlier Greek, the noun αἵρεσις indicated one's "choosing" or "taking"—in any field (Plato, *Phaed.* 99b; Soph. 245b; *Phaedr.* 249b; Aristotle, *Ath. pol.* 3.6; *Eth. eud.* 1249b; Lucian, *Phal.* 1.9). Perhaps because the term came to be employed so frequently in philosophical-ethical discussion, concerning one's choice of a way to live (Lucian, *Hermot.* 21, 28), it had by Josephus's time become also a technical term for a philosophical school or sect (cf. Galen, *De ord. libr.* 19.50; Lucian, *Demon.* 13; *Hermot.* 48; Diogenes Laertius 1.18–21; cf. 2.47). Diogenes notes that several others before him had written books "On the Schools" (περὶ αἱρέσεων; 1.19; 2.65, 87). Although Josephus can use αἵρεσις in its broader senses—the "taking" or "capture" of a town (*Ant.* 7.160; 10.79, 133, 247; 12.363, etc.); another sort of "choice" or "option" (*War* 1.99; 6.352; *Ant.* 1.69; 6.71, etc.)—in thirteen of its thirty-one occurrences it means for him "philosophical school" (*War* 2.118, 122, 137, 142, 162; *Ant.* 13.171–173; *Life* 191, 197). He freely interchanges φιλοσοφία and cognates (*War* 2.119, 166; *Ant.* 18.11, 23, 25). He thus presents Judean culture as wholly comparable to Greek: it even has its own philosophies.

5 On happiness as goal, see Plato, *Resp.* 421b, and especially Aristotle, *Eth. eud.* 1214a, 1217a, 1219a–b; *Eth. nic.* 1095–1097, 1099a, 1102a, 1153b, 1177a–b, etc.; Seneca, *Ep.* 15.1; Plutarch, *Lyc.* 13.1; 29.2–4; 31.1; *Comp. Dem. Cic.* 1.1; *Mor.* 5c, 24b–25a, 97d. The second- and third-century commentaries on Aristotle by Aspasias and Alexander feature εὐδαιμονία conspicuously.

6 Dionysius of Halicarnassus, *Ant. rom.* 2.21.1, 68.2; 5.12.3; 11.1.4; *Ant. or.* 1.13; 4.13; *Isoc.* 1.9, 43; 4.21; 7.28; Dio Chrysostom, *Or.* 1.9; 2.24, 26; 7.128; 12.9; 18.7; 20.11; 27.7, etc.; Epictetus, *Diatr.* 1.8.13, 15.t, 2, 4, 25.33; 2.11.1, 13, 14, 17.30, 24.15; 3.13.23, 31.22, etc.; Justin, *Apol.* 3.2.5; 4.8.2; 7.3.3; 12.5.4; 26.6.4; *Dial.* 1.3.7, 11; 6.3; 2.1.2, 4–5.

7 Epictetus, *Diatr.* 3.21.20, 23.37; Lucian, *Nigr.* 1, 33-38; Diogenes Laertius, *Lives* 4.16; 5.22.12; Augustine, *Conf.* 3.4.7; cf. A. D. Nock, *Conversion: The Old and the New in Religion from Alexander the Great to Augustine* (London: Oxford University Press, 1933), e.g., 185; H. I. Marrou, *A History of Education in Antiquity* (Madison: University of Wisconsin Press, 1956), 206–7. It is no coincidence that second-century Christians, such as Justin Martyr, the

author of the *Epistle to Diognetus*, Clement of Alexandria, and Augustine understood philosophy as the category best suited to explain their way of life—and conversion to that life.

8   E. N. Tigerstedt, *The Legend of Sparta in Classical Antiquity* (Stockhold: Almquist and Wiksell, 1974), 1:228–2:30–48.

9   A. Wardman, *Rome's Debt to Greece* (Bristol: Bristol Classical Press, 1976), 90–93.

10   M. L. Clarke, *Higher Education in the Ancient World* (London: Routledge and Kegan Paul, 1971), 93.

11   Cf. A. Momigliano, *Quarto Contributo alla Storia degli Studi Classici e del Mondo Antico* (Rome: Edizioni di Storia e Letteratura, 1969), 240; A. Meredith, "Later Philosophy," in *The Roman World*, ed. John Boardman, Jasper Green, and Oswyn Murray (Oxford: Oxford University Press, 1988), 290.

12   G. B. Conte, *Latin Literature: A History* (Baltimore: The Johns Hopkins University Press, 1994), 177.

13   R. MacMullen, *Enemies of the Roman Order: Treason, Unrest, and Alienation in the Empire* (London: Routledge, 1966), 47.

14   Cf., on Josephus, T. Rajak, *Josephus: The Historian and His Society* (London: Duckworth, 1983), 34–38.

15   E.g., in Aristotle's famous three-volume *Rhetoric*.

16   See Marrou, *A History of Education*; and now R. Cribiore, *Gymnastics of the Mind: Greek Education in Hellenistic and Roman Egypt* (Princeton: Princeton University Press, 2001) for a vivid introduction to the world of elite education.

17   J. Marincola (*Authority and Tradition in Ancient Historiography* [Cambridge: Cambridge University Press, 1997]) illustrates the point thoroughly.

18   Hellenistic philosophers such as Chrysippus and Poseidonius often compare Stoics and Epicureans (according to extant fragments) while working out their own views, but they are in a different category from the aristocratic amateurs I am discussing here.

19   I owe this reference to Richard Wenghofer, doctoral student at York University researching Greco-Roman ethnography.

20   Similar youthful enthusiasm, appropriately abandoned for serious public life, is reported by Seneca, of himself (*Ep.* 108.22), and by Tacitus, of his father-in-law Agricola (*Agr.* 4.3).

21   Nock, *Conversion*, 62.

22   As I shall show more fully in a forthcoming *JSJ* article, Greek *-ismos* nouns are a false friend to English *-isms* that indicate a system of belief and practice.

23   Cf. Cicero, *Fam.* 3.9; 9.25; 13.1, 38; *Red. sen.* 6.14; Epictetus, *Diatr.* 3.24; Suetonius, *Lucr.* 1.

24   On *pronoia* in the *Antiquities*, see H. W. Attridge, *The Interpretation of Biblical History in the Antiquitates Judaicae of Flavius Josephus* (Missoula, Mont.: Scholars Press [for HTR], 1976), 67–70.

25   At least, these are executive aspects of the divine (*Ant.* 10.277–280; 16.395–404; cf. *Apion* 2.180–181).

26   D. Satran, "Daniel: Seer, Prophet, Holy Man," in *Ideal Figures in Ancient Judaism: Profiles and Paradigms*, ed. J. J. Collins and G. W. E. Nickelsburg (Chico, Calif.: Scholars Press, 1980), 33–48.

27 Cf. M. Luz, "Eleazar's Second Speech on Masada and Its Literary
    Precedents," *Rheinisches Museum* 126 (1983): 25–43; D. J. Ladouceur,
    "Josephus and Masada," in *Josephus, Judaism, and Christianity*, ed. L. H.
    Feldman and G. Hata (Detroit: Wayne State University Press, 1987), 95–113.

28 *Apion* 2.145–46, 293–94, pieces of panegyric on the Judean laws, can be
    matched phrase for phrase with earlier descriptions of the Essenes. See also
    Apion 1.225; 2.193–196, 199–202, 205, 223.

29 For this and other verbal parallels with Cicero's Chrysippus, see Moore,
    "Fate and Free Will," 384.

30 S. Schechter, *Aspects of Rabbinic Theology: Major Concepts of the Talmud* (New
    York: Schocken, 1961), 285.

31 "That which lies in one's power": *War* 3.389, 396; 5.59; *Ant.* 1.178; 5.110;
    13.355; 18.215; 19.167. Souls are imperishable: *War* 3.372. Souls go into
    new bodies: *War* 3.375; *Apion* 2.218. On language concerning the soul and
    afterlife throughout Josephus, see especially J. Sievers, "Josephus and the
    Afterlife," in *Understanding Josephus: Seven Perspectives*, ed. S. Mason, 20–31
    (Sheffield: Sheffield Academic, 1998).

32 It is an intriguing question, why Josephus located the passage here. From a
    narrative point of view the opening chronological tag "at about this time"
    seems to date the appearance of the schools, though he does not spell this
    out. Certainly, the passage gives him a base from which to describe
    Pharisees and Sadducees at 13.297–98, and it is a device of his to plant a
    seed to which he will later return. For other proposals, see J. Sievers,
    "Josephus, First Maccabees, Sparta, the Three Haireseis—and Cicero," *JSJ*
    32 (2001): 241–51.

33 *War* 2.50, 60, 152–153; 3.229–230, 472–488; 5.71–97, 277–278, 305–306,
    315–316; 6.13–14, 33–53.

34 H. S. J. Thackeray, *Josephus: The Man and the Historian* (1929; repr., New York:
    Ktav, 1967), 107–15.

35 G. C. Richards, "The Composition of Josephus' Antiquities," *CQ* 33 (1939):
    36–40; R. J. H. Shutt, *Studies in Josephus* (London: SPCK, 1961), 59–75;
    Rajak, *Josephus*, 47–63, 233–36.

36 L. R. Palmer, *The Greek Language* (London: Faber, 1980), 159.

37 Greek Σαδδουκαίοις δὲ τὰς ψυχὰς ὁ λόγος συναφανίζει τοῖς
    σώμασι—a statement worth investigating. The verb is sparsely attested
    before Josephus (Strabo, *Geogr.* 6.1.6; 8.6.23; 12.8.17; 17.3.12; Dionysius of
    Halicarnassus, *Ant. rom.* 1.1.2; Philo, *Leg.* 194; a fragment attributed to
    Pythagoras), and in these authors it is always in the middle or passive voice.
    Josephus uses it only here, and in the active voice. An intriguing possibility:
    the only writer in this group to speak of souls disappearing with bodies is
    the historian Dionysius, who in the prologue to his magnum opus speaks of
    historians not wanting their souls to disappear along with their bodies
    (hence they write memorials in the form of histories). Since Dionysius's
    twenty-volume *Roman Antiquities* was not only famous in Rome, but also a
    principal model for Josephus's twenty-volume *Judean Antiquities*, it is quite
    plausible (the means of proof elude us) that he intends a witty allusion to
    Dionysius's prologue here.

38 Some important efforts to reach the historical reality of these three schools
    are: L. Wächter, "Die unterschiedliche Haltung der Pharisaeer, Sadduzaeer
    und Essener zur Heimarmene nach dem Bericht des Josephus," *ZRGG* 21
    (1969): 97–114; G. Maier, *Mensch und freier Wille: Nach den Juedischen Religions-
    parteien zwischen Ben Sira und Paulus* (Tübingen: Mohr-Siebeck, 1981); A. J.
    Saldarini, *Pharisees, Scribes, and Sadducees in Palestinian Society: A Sociological
    Approach* (Wilmington, Del.: Michael Glazier, 1988); Sanders, *Judaism:
    Practice and Belief*; Grabbe, 2.463–554; G. Stemberger, *Jewish Contemporaries of
    Jesus: Pharisees, Sadducees, Essenes*, trans. Allan W. Mahnke (Minneapolis:
    Fortress Press, 1995); and Baumgarten, *Flourishing of Jewish Sects in the
    Maccabean Era.*
39 In particular, A. I. Baumgarten, "The Pharisaic Paradosis," *HTR* 80, no. 1
    (1987): 63–77.
40 E. Rivkin, "Defining the Pharisees: The Tannaitic Sources," *HUCA* 40
    (1969): 205–49; Neusner, *Rabbinic Traditions about the Pharisees*, 3:304; also,
    Saldarini, *Pharisees, Scribes, and Sadducees.*

CHAPTER 3

1   These pericopes may be seen as part of a larger unit of material, Mark
    2:1–3:6, consisting of five controversy stories. See J. Dewey, "The Literary
    Structure of the Controversy Stories in Mark 2:1–3:6," in *The Interpretation
    of Mark*, ed. W. Telford (Edinburgh: T&T Clark, 1995), 141–51.
2   In Mark the identity of the questioners is left vague, with no expressed sub-
    ject for the words καὶ ἔρχονται καὶ λέγουσιν αὐτῷ. Matthew (9:14) spec-
    ifies John's disciples as the questioners.
3   The Pharisees of the previous pericope must be the understood subject of
    the verb παρετήρουν ("they watched") in 3:2. These last two pericopes of
    the grouping, both of which address a dispute over Sabbath observance, go
    together. The point is confirmed by the specific reference to the Pharisees
    again in 3:6.
4   C. S. Mann, *Mark* (Garden City: Doubleday, 1986), 243.
5   The Greek could be understood as saying that only the scribes came from
    Jerusalem, implying that the Pharisees were in Galilee to begin with.
    Matthew's version of the pericope (15:1) clearly portrays both groups as
    coming from Jerusalem.
6   The controversy between Rabbis Hillel and Shammai over the proper inter-
    pretation of the case law in Deuteronomy 24:1-4 (*m. Gittin* 9:10) provides a
    plausible background for why Pharisees might test Jesus with this question,
    particularly since Mark's Pharisees allude to the Deuteronomy passage in
    verse 4. But Mark does not bring out any particulars of the rabbinic debate.
7   The ambiguous "they" who send the Pharisees and Herodians would seem
    to be "the chief priests, the scribes, and the elders" of 11:27. These appear
    to be the ones in 12:12 who want to have Jesus arrested but cannot do so at
    that moment for fear of the crowds.
8   Cf. Josephus's reference to Pharisaic tradition in *Ant.* 13.10.6; 18.1.3–4.

9 On the identity of the Herodians, see R. Guelich, *Mark 1–8:26* (Dallas: Word, 1989), 138–39. The Herodians are not presented as opponents of Jesus on religious grounds. Rather, they are political figures whose assistance the Pharisees need if they are to put an end to Jesus' teaching ministry.

10 Anthony Saldarini, in his sociological analysis of the Pharisees, classifies them as part of the "retainer" class in Palestine; see *Pharisees, Scribes and Sadducees*. This particular classification has been criticized; see S. Mason, "Revisiting Josephus' Pharisees," in *Judaism in Late Antiquity: Where We Stand* 2, ed. J. Neusner and A. J. Avery-Peck (Leiden: Brill, 1999), 33–37. Still, recent researchers agree that, overall, the Pharisees' role in society was not inherently political, but tangential to those power bases and possessing the ability to exert strong influence on them. (Some sources do place individual Pharisees on the Sanhedrin [e.g., Acts 5:34], and the data in the Gospel of John regarding the Pharisees' connection with the Sanhedrin needs to be accounted for.)

11 The contrast may center on the fact that Jesus appealed to his own authority rather than just the teaching of Scripture (Mark 2:28), or it may (also) allude to Jesus' rejection of the "tradition of the elders" to which the scribes adhered (Mark 7:5). Mark Powell suggests that the point of the contrast is not that of teaching style as observed by the crowds (i.e., Jesus teaches authoritatively and the scribes do not), but rather that, from the point of view of the narrator, Jesus has authority and the scribes do not; see "Do and Keep What Moses Says (Matthew 23:2-7)," *JBL* 114, no. 3 (1995): 422.

12 This phraseology is found only here in Mark's gospel. Cf. that of Luke 5:30, "the Pharisees and their scribes" (οἱ Φαρισαῖοι καὶ οἱ γραμματεῖς αὐτῶν), and that of Acts 23:9, "certain scribes of the Pharisees' group" (τινὲς τῶν γραμματέων τους μέρους τῶν Φαρισαίων).

13 Ellis Rivkin argues that scribes and Pharisees are basically synonymous; see "Who Were the Pharisees?" in *Judaism in Late Antiquity: Where We Stand* 3, ed. A. J. Avery-Peck and J. Neusner (Leiden: Brill, 2000), 2, 14. But the data in Mark do not yield this conclusion.

14 Raymond Brown, *The Death of the Messiah: From Gethsemane to the Grave. A Commentary on the Passion Narratives in the Four Gospels* ABRL (Garden City, N.Y.: Doubleday, 1994), 2:1426–28.

15 Mann, *Mark*, 229–30.

16 The same coupling of terms appears also in Matthew and Luke, not only in the parallel passages, but in Matthew 11:19 and Luke 7:34; 15:1.

17 Guelich, *Mark*, 102.

18 See E. P. Sanders, *Jesus and Judaism* (Philadelphia: Fortress, 1985), 177–82. The word ἁμαρτωλός was sometimes used as a virtual synonym for ἔθνη (Gentile).

19 See Sanders (*Jesus and Judaism*, 187). There is no warrant in Mark, however, for Sanders's arbitrary contention (206–11) that Jesus may not have required repentance from the tax collectors and sinners. Jesus' statement about these people being "sick" and in need of a "physician" implies that Jesus' goal was that of correcting their aberrant behavior (cf. Mark 1:15; 6:12).

20 W. Lane, *The Gospel according to Mark* (Grand Rapids: Eerdmans, 1974), 103–4; R. Gundry, *Mark: A Commentary on His Apology for the Cross* (Grand Rapids: Eerdmans, 1993), 128; C. Keener, *Matthew* (Grand Rapids: Eerdmans, 1999), 296.

21 Some scholars have understood Neusner's description of the Pharisees as "a table-fellowship sect" (e.g., *From Politics to Piety*, 80) to imply a degree of exclusivity in terms of societal interaction that Neusner perhaps did not intend. See Neusner's response to the criticisms of E. P. Sanders along this line in *Judaic Law from Jesus to the Mishnah* (Atlanta: Scholars Press, 1993), 270–72.

22 R. Banks, *Jesus and the Law in the Synoptic Tradition* (Cambridge: Cambridge University Press, 1975), 113–23; E. Schweizer, *The Good News according to Matthew*, trans. D. Green (Atlanta: John Knox, 1975), 276–79.

23 I do not mean that Jesus was emulating the kind of formal halakhic methodology that we find in rabbinic literature. In that corpus an aggadic incident (such as the incident with David and the showbread) could never carry halakhic weight. One should be careful about critiquing or analyzing the gospels' argumentation by the standards of the (later) rabbis.

24 First Samuel 21:1 identifies the priest as Ahimelech, but Mark 2:26 calls him Abiathar.

25 W. Davies and D. Allison Jr., *A Critical and Exegetical Commentary on the Gospel according to Saint Matthew*, ICC, 3 vols. (Edinburgh: T&T Clark, 1991), 2:304–5. Thus, Marn (along with many commentators) misses the point when he says, "The difficulty in all this is that in the case of David the Law is acknowledged, but special circumstances are pleaded as a reason for setting the Law aside. But in the narrative before us there are apparently no special circumstances: hunger could not be pleaded as a reason for setting aside the rule. Perhaps there was no emergency of any kind at all, and Jesus' disciples were simply being lax in observance. Something far more was involved, but the compressed style of the narrative hardly allows us to do more than guess" (*Mark*, 239–40).

26 The scholarly discussion on these two aphorisms in verses 27-28 is vast. Opinions as to their meaning will vary based on whether or not the sayings are considered to have originated independently of the present narrative context, and then how that narrative context is itself understood. For overviews of various positions, see Guelich, *Mark*, 123–30 and Lane, *Mark*, 117–20.

27 The Leviticus passage ("P" material) is classified by many Pentateuchal scholars as a late text, written long after the Deuteronomistic history (though the traditional order of these documents has recently been reversed; see R. E. Friedman, *The Bible with Sources Revealed* [San Francisco: HarperSanFrancisco, 2003], 4–5). But this matter has no bearing on my point here, since there is no question that first-century Jews would have believed in the Mosaic origin of the Leviticus passage.

28 See Davies and Allison, *Matthew*, 2:308–9.

29 The Sabbath law not only commemorated God's rest; it stressed an ethical concept, for not only men, but also women, servants, and animals were allowed to rest on the Sabbath day.

30 Mark's gospel presents the very opposite picture of what E. P. Sanders contends when he says that Jesus' actual disputes with the Pharisees were relatively mild debates on trivial matters and that "there was no substantial conflict between Jesus and the Pharisees with regard to Sabbath, food, and purity laws" (*Jesus and Judaism*, 265).

31 Davies and Allison, *Matthew*, 2:518.

32 Albert Baumgarten's contrary assessment of this matter may be somewhat anachronistic. See "Pharisees," in *Encyclopedia of the Dead Sea Scrolls*, ed. L. Schiffman and J. VanderKam (Oxford: Oxford University Press, 2000), 2:659. Cf. J. Neusner, "Mr. Maccoby's Red Cow, Mr. Sanders's Pharisees— and Mine," *JSJ* 23, no. 1 (1992): 91–92.

33 The initial phrase in verse 4 (καὶ ἀπ᾽ ἀγορᾶς ἐὰν μὴ βαπτίσωνται οὐκ ἐσθίουσιν) could be rendered, "and they do not eat [anything] from the market unless they wash [it]," as in the NRSV quoted above. But βαπτίσωνται is in the middle voice, which would suggest a reflexive sense, and this could give the meaning, "And when they come from the market place, they do not eat unless they purify themselves," as in the RSV et al. Reflecting the latter sense, some witnesses read ἀγορᾶς ὅταν ἔλθωσιν. For a further discussion of this issue and other textual critical matters associated with this verse, see Gundry, *Mark*, 360.

34 Sanders, *Jesus and Judaism*, 186. There may be some kind of connection between the haberim and the Pharisees, but we cannot completely equate the two groups. See J. Neusner, "The Fellowship (חבורה) in the Second Jewish Commonwealth," *HTR* 53 (1960): 125–42.

35 E. P. Sanders, *Jewish Law from Jesus to the Mishnah: Five Studies* (London and Philadelphia: SCM Press and Trinity Press International, 1990), 39–40, 261–62. Cf. the washing rituals indicated in *Judith* 12:7; *Sib. Or.* 3:591–592; 4:165–166; *Ep. Arist.* 305–306; Luke 11:38; *m. Yad* 1:1–2:4; *m. Hag* 2:5–6.

36 See H. Harrington, "Did the Pharisees Eat Ordinary Food in a State of Ritual Purity?" *JSJ* 26 (1995): 53; Gundry, *Mark*, 358–59.

37 Sanders, *Judaism: Practice and Belief*, 437–38; *Jewish Law*, 39–40.

38 Sanders would also have to deal with Matthew 23:25, where Jesus speaks of the Pharisees washing the outside of cups and plates while neglecting the problem of inward, moral purity. Jesus' contrast between outward and inward purity makes no sense unless the washing of these eating vessels was a real practice. Davies and Allison (*Matthew*, 3:298) argue that Jesus' language in 23:25 has nothing to do with ritual cleansing of cups, but only ordinary cleaning of dirty vessels. But it is hard to think of Jesus' language in anything but a ritual sense in view of the close parallel that exists between the wording of verse 26 and Mark 7:15-23 (= Matt 15:10-20). Cf. also Luke 11:39-41.

39 See J. Poirier, "Why Did the Pharisees Wash Their Hands?" *JJS* 47 (1996): 226–27. He argues properly that hand-washing was done so that uncleanness on one's hands did not defile one's food. Poirier's further claim that the

ultimate purpose was to prepare one for prayer and Torah study seems, if mildly plausible, at least unnecessary.

40 This idea seems to me to be in harmony with Jacob Neusner's theory regarding the ultimate purpose of Pharisaic ablutions. Neusner argues that the Pharisees stressed ritual purity with regard to meals because they were trying to live in holiness as if they were priests, thus fulfilling the principle of Exodus 19 that stated Israel was to be a kingdom of priests. See Neusner, *From Politics to Piety*, 83.

41 See note 33.

42 Sanders believes that Pharisees would not have been motivated by a concern over contracting uncleanness from defiled food (*Jesus and Judaism*, 265–67). Sanders is motivated by his rejection of Neusner's theory that the Pharisees were trying to live in a state of holiness as if they were priests.

43 If that is not the case, then one is forced to regard the record of Jesus' response to the Pharisees' criticism in verses 14-23 as a hopelessly misplaced section of material.

44 Those who say that Jesus' discussion about what defiles the inner part of the body (vv. 14-23) has no connection to verses 1-5 fail to see any connection between Jesus' response about eating food and the initial issue of hand-washing.

45 It should be noted that the earlier charge against Jesus' disciples in Mark 2:23-24 only had to do with an alleged Sabbath violation due to plucking grain while walking through a field on the Sabbath. Nothing was said about the need to wash one's hands on such an occasion.

46 See, e.g., C. Carlston. "The Things That Defile (Mark VII.14) and the Law in Matthew and Mark," *NTS* 15 (1968–1969): 92–94.

47 See S. Westerholm, "Pharisees," in *Dictionary of Jesus and the Gospels*, ed. J. Green and S. McKnight (Downers Grove, Ill.: InterVarsity, 1992), 609–14; Davies and Allison, *Matthew*, 2:529–31; J. Donahue and D. Harrington, *The Gospel of Mark* (Collegeville, Minn.: Liturgical Press, 2002), 228–29.

48 Davies and Allison, *Matthew*, 2:531.

49 If so, the evangelist parallels the teaching of Paul in Romans 14:1-4, 17-21. See N. T. Wright, *Romans*, NIB 10 (Nashville: Abingdon, 2002), 730–43.

50 For a discussion of Jesus' "hypocrisy" charge, see Powell, "Do and Keep What Moses Says," 423.

51 See *m. Nedarim* (esp.) 4.7–8; 9.1; cf. *m. Hagigah* 1:8.

52 Sanders, *Jewish Law*, 56–57.

53 A parallel exists in *m. Nedarim* 9.1 where the sages were willing to release one from a vow in a matter between him and his father or mother because of the honor due to his father and mother. Cf. Matthew 5:33-37; 23:16-22.

54 This religious concept is seen throughout Mark's presentation of Jesus' teaching, but it perhaps reaches a climax in 12:28-34 when Jesus has a discussion with a scribe in the Temple about the two greatest commandments.

55 See Powell, "Do and Keep What Moses Says," 423.

56 In accordance with Sanders' distinction of these terms (*Jewish Law*, 240–42). But see Neusner's response in "Sanders's Pharisees and Mine," *Judaic Law from Jesus to the Mishnah*, 270–71.

57   M. Hengel and R. Deines, "E. P. Sanders' 'Common Judaism,' Jesus, and the Pharisees," *JTS* n.s., 46, no. 1 (1995): 44.

58   U. Luz presents an intriguing interpretation of Jesus' statement that "something greater than the Temple is here." He suggests that the statement sets up the subsequent quotation of Hosea 6:6 and that an act of "mercy" is what was greater than the Temple. See Luz, *Matthew 8–20*, trans. J. Crouch (Minneapolis: Fortress, 2001), 181–82.

59   Interestingly, the Essenes would not have made this exception, according to *CD* 11.13–14, 16–17.

60   In contrast to Mark, Matthew appears to have no significant interest in the Herodians and their combined efforts with the Pharisees to combat Jesus. The author of Matthew is much more concerned about the Sadducees and their efforts, along with the Pharisees, to oppose Jesus.

61   The significance of the omission of these words by Matthew depends on how they are interpreted and how the words of Mark 7:15 (= Matt 15:11) are interpreted. Those who understand Mark's insertion to be an effectual annulment of Mosaic food laws regard Matthew's omission as an indication of the author's opposition to Mark's interpretation of Jesus' teaching on impurity. On the other hand, if, as suggested earlier, Jesus' maxim was not abrogating Mosaic food laws per se, but only relativizing them, and if Mark inserted this statement for the benefit of a Gentile audience who needed to know that Jewish purity rituals were not binding on Gentiles, then the insertion would have been superfluous for Matthew's Jewish audience.

62   Matthew 12:38-42, a pericope unique to Matthew but quite similar in content to Matthew 16:1-4 (= Mark 8:11-13), records an occasion where "some of the scribes and Pharisees" ask Jesus to perform a sign.

63   Some scholars have suggested that Matthew's grammatical coupling of the Pharisees and Sadducees (οἱ Φαρισαῖοι καὶ Σαδδουκαῖοι), with one article governing both nouns, indicates (particularly in 16:11-12) that the author was ignorant of the distinctions between these two Jewish groups; see, e.g., J. Meier, *The Vision of Matthew: Christ, Church, and Morality in the First Gospel* (New York: Paulist Press, 1979), 20–23. It seems more reasonable to think that the author was speaking about the similar false teaching of the Pharisees and Sadducees, particularly in regard to their mutual opposition to Jesus (see Davies and Allison, *Matthew*, 1:32). Matthew's phraseology might be intended to indicate the solidarity of these two Jewish parties when it came to the matter of opposing Jesus. That idea is thought by many to be historically problematic, given the hostility that is known to have existed between the two parties (Josephus, *Ant.* 13.10.6; Acts 23:7-9). Yet, history is replete with examples of oppositional parties who unite to defeat a common enemy. (A similar issue arises with respect to Mark's portrayal of the Pharisees and Herodians in 3:6.)

64   Matthew's account only considers the scenario of a man divorcing his wife. But Mark 10:11 considers the additional scenario of a woman divorcing her husband.

65   Cf. Matthew 5:32, where the same exception clause is included.

66   The strictness of Jesus' prohibition of divorce comports with what Mark

and Matthew present concerning Jesus' fundamental halakhic principle that the proper treatment of a fellow human being takes precedence over legal formalities.

67 Matthew 12:14 does not include Mark's reference (3:6) to the Herodians joining forces with the Pharisees against Jesus. Also, Jesus' warning in Mark about "the yeast of the Pharisees and the yeast of Herod" (8:15) is presented in Matthew as a warning about "the yeast of the Pharisees and Sadducees," or "the teaching of the Pharisees and Sadducees" (16:6, 11-12).

68 Where Mark refers to the Jerusalem leadership—the chief priests, elders, and scribes—Matthew sometimes omits scribes from the list.

69 Matthew 9:34, a text unique to Matthew, records a similar incident and also attributes the accusation to Pharisees. I see no basis for G. Twelftree's conclusion regarding Matthew 12:24 that the attribution of the accusation to "Pharisees" rather than retaining Mark's original "scribes" indicates a Matthean "desire to rehabilitate [the scribes]," that is, to portray them in a more positive light than did Mark (see "Scribes," in *Dictionary of New Testament Background*, ed. C. Evans and S. Porter [Downers Grove, Ill.: InterVarsity, 2000], 1088). That conclusion does not square with the fact that, later, Matthew 22:34-40 alters the form of Mark 12:28-34, a pericope in which Mark presents a scribe in a positive light. I agree with Twelftree that Matthew saw the scribes associated with the Pharisees, rather than scribes in general, as the problem. But that idea is not absent in Mark.

70 Cf. Mark 7:3.

71 The word νομικός is used nowhere else in Matthew, and its manuscript support is questionable. It is a common Lukan term, however, and it may be that copyists introduced the term into Matthew 22:34 because of influence from Lukan usage.

72 In Mark this scribe does not come across as antagonistic, and he even receives a compliment from Jesus. Matthew's version is quite matter-of-fact, contains no positive statements about the man, and even says that he approached Jesus "to test him" (πειράζων αὐτόν).

73 Note, however, that Luke 5:21 (which parallels the pericope of Mark 2:6-7) identifies Jesus' opponents on this occasion as "the scribes and the Pharisees."

74 The Griesbach theory of gospel composition (i.e., that Mark summarized Matthew and Luke) is not supported by the above data. One can see a clear purpose underlying the Matthean material on the Pharisees if indeed Matthew is dependent on Mark: in order to highlight the Pharisaic opposition to Christianity, the author of Matthew changed Mark's "scribes" to "Pharisees" whenever there was reason to believe that the scribes in a given Markan pericope were Pharisaic scribes. But no satisfactory explanation exists for why the author of Mark's gospel would do the reverse and change Matthew's "Pharisees" into "scribes" (as, e.g., in Mark 3:22 [= Matt 12:24]). Clearly, the author of Mark did not believe that all Pharisees were scribes.

75 As we have seen, Matthew often joins these two Jewish parties together.

76 If Matthew is indicating that the Pharisees and Sadducees come to John for the purpose of submitting to baptism, this suggests that the evangelist does

not regard the Pharisees or the Sadducees to have been as inherently opposed to John the Baptist's ministry as they were the ministry of Jesus. We already have seen that, unlike Jesus' disciples, John's disciples fasted regularly, as did the Pharisees (Mark 2:18; Matt 9:14).The synoptic gospels indicate a degree of similarity between the Pharisees and John's disciples. Jesus likens both to an "old garment" and "old wineskins," incompatible with Jesus' new ministry of the Kingdom (Mark 2:18-22; Matt. 9:14-17).

77 Davies and Allison, *Matthew*, 1:304.

78 But perhaps we are to understand John's speech as a formulaic homily delivered to anyone and everyone who would come to John's baptismal site.

79 In Matthew 13:52 Jesus speaks of his disciples as scribes: "Therefore every scribe who has been trained for the kingdom of heaven is like the master of a household who brings out of his treasure what is new and what is old." Jesus probably uses this terminology because, like the Jewish scribes of Palestine, his disciples will be teachers of the Law, but the Law as Jesus unfolds it for the kingdom (cf. Matt 23:34).

80 R. Bultmann, *Jesus and the Word*, trans. L. Smith and E. Lantero (New York: Charles Scribner's Sons, 1958), 75–76, 89–90; M. Powell, *Fortress Introduction to the Gospels* (Minneapolis: Fortress, 1998), 69.

81 Matthew's portrayal of Jesus is one thing; whether the full break between the church and Judaism had or had not occurred by the time of the writing of Matthew is another matter.

82 Davies and Allison, *Matthew*, 1:481–82.

83 See F. Kermode, "Matthew," in *The Literary Guide to the Bible*, ed. R. Alter and F. Kermode (Cambridge: Harvard University Press, 1987), 388–94.

84 Jesus' subsequent examples of outward religiosity that fail to please God (6:1-6) may be intended as a specific reference to the ostentation of the scribes and Pharisees. Note the similar criticisms in 23:5-12.

85 Davies and Allison, *Matthew*, 3:267–68.

86 D. Hagner, *Matthew*, 2 vols. (Dallas: Word, 1993), 2:659.

87 C. Roth, "The 'Chair of Moses' and Its Survivals," *PEQ* 81 (1949): 100–101.

88 Davies and Allison, *Matthew*, 3:261.

89 Keener, *Matthew*, 541.

90 Rivkin, "Who Were the Pharisees?" 14.

91 N. S. Rabbinowitz, "Matthew 23:2-4: Does Jesus Recognize the Authority of the Pharisees and Does He Endorse Their Halakhah?" *JETS* 46, no. 3 (2003): 434–35.

92 D. A. Carson, *Matthew 13–28* (Grand Rapids: Zondervan, 1995), 473.

93 A. Saldarini, *Matthew's Christian-Jewish Community* (Chicago: University of Chicago Press, 1994), 47–48.

94 Powell, "Do and Keep What Moses Says," 431–35.

95 F. Beare, *The Gospel according to Matthew* (Peabody, Mass.: Hendrickson, 1981), 447–48; S. Mason, "Pharisees," in *Dictionary of New Testament Background*, ed. C. Evans and S. Porter (Downers Grove, Ill.: InterVarsity, 2000), 782–87.

96 Hagner, *Matthew*, 2:659.

97 D. Hagner, "The *Sitz im Leben* of the Gospel of Matthew," in *Treasures New and Old: Recent Contributions to Matthean Studies*, ed. D. Bauer and M. Powell (Atlanta: Scholars Press, 1996), 55–56. Rabbinowitz ("Matthew 23:2-4," 435), arguing against this view, asks whether such a bifurcation between Scripture and halakha is possible: "Can exegesis be so neatly separated from application and practice?" Yes, it can, and that is exactly what Matthew's Jesus has been doing in his confrontations with the Pharisees throughout the gospel.

98 G. Stemberger, *Jewish Contemporaries of Jesus: Pharisees, Sadducees, Essenes*, trans. Allan W. Mahnke (Minneapolis: Fortress, 1995), 23–24.

99 Davies and Allison, *Matthew*, 3:293; see note 38.

100 Davies and Allison, *Matthew*, 3:261.

101 Sanders, *Jewish Law*, 1–42.

102 Hengel and Deines, "'Sanders' 'Common Judaism,'" 4–7. Furthermore, issues that we know were problems within the mid-first-century church (e.g., circumcision, eating idol meat) clearly have no connection to anything we find in the gospels.

CHAPTER 4

1 J. T. Carroll, "Luke's Portrayal of the Pharisees," *CBQ* 50, no. 4 (1988): 604–21, esp. 604.

2 R. L. Brawley, *Luke-Acts and the Jews: Conflict, Apology, and Conciliation*, SBLMS 33 (Atlanta: Society of Biblical Literature, 1987), 84.

3 Saldarini, *Pharisees, Scribes, and Sadducees*, 179.

4 J. Darr, "Irenic or Ironic? Another Look at Gamaliel before the Sanhedrin (Acts 5:33-42)," in *Literary Studies in Luke-Acts: Essays in Honor of Joseph B. Tyson*, ed. R. P. Thompson and T. E. Philips (Macon, Ga.: Mercer University Press, 1998), 131.

5 Mikeal Parsons and Richard Pervo (*Rethinking the Unity of Luke-Acts* [Minneapolis: Fortress, 1993]) argue that the singular authorship of the two volumes need not imply narrative consistency or thematic unity.

6 See J. T. Sanders, "The Pharisees in Luke-Acts," in *The Living Text: Essays in Honor of Ernest W. Saunders*, ed. D. Groh and R. Jewett (Lanham, Md., New York: University Press of America, 1985), 141–88, and *The Jews in Luke-Acts* (Philadelphia: Fortress, 1987).

7 Sanders, "The Pharisees in Luke-Acts" and *Jews in Luke-Acts*; see also J. A. Ziesler, "Luke and the Pharisees," *NTS* 25 (1978–1979): 146–57.

8 Brawley, *Luke-Acts and the Jews*, 100.

9 Sanders, *Jews in Luke-Acts*, 92; contra L. T. Johnson, *The Gospel of Luke*, SP 3 (Collegeville, Minn.: Liturgical Press, 1991), 96.

10 J. Neyrey, "Ceremonies in Luke-Acts: The Case of Meals and Table-Fellowship," in *The Social World of Luke-Acts: Models for Interpretation*, ed. Neyrey (Peabody, Mass.: Hendrickson, 1991), 364.

11 S. Ringe, *Luke*, Westminster Bible Companion (Louisville, Ky.: Westminster John Knox, 1995), 86.

12 Johnson, *Gospel of Luke*, 103, 104.

13   B. Malina and J. Neyrey, "First-Century Personality: Dyadic, Not Individualistic," in Neyrey, *Social World of Luke-Acts*, 88.
14   See W. Carter, "Getting Martha Out of the Kitchen: Luke 10.38-42 Again," in *A Feminist Companion to Luke*, ed. A.-J. Levine, Feminist Companion to the New Testament and Early Christian Writings 3 (London and New York: Sheffield Academic Press and Continuum, 2002), 214–31.
15   See Sanders, *Jews in Luke-Acts*, 373 n. 70.
16   See inter alia E. S. Steele, "Luke 11:37-54—a Modified Hellenistic Symposium?" *JBL* 103 (1984): 379–94.
17   R. L. Rohrbaugh, "The Pre-industrial City in Luke-Acts: Urban Social Relations," in Neyrey, *Social World of Luke-Acts*, 140.
18   J. Neyrey, "The Symbolic Universe of Luke-Acts: 'They Turn the World Upside Down'," in Neyrey, *Social World of Luke-Acts*, 292.
19   Ringe, *Luke*, 156.
20   J. P. Heil, *The Meal Scenes in Luke-Acts: An Audience-Oriented Approach*, SBLMS 52 (Atlanta: Society of Biblical Literature, 1999), 84.
21   Carroll, "Luke's Portrayal of the Pharisees," 613.
22   So Neyrey, "Ceremonies in Luke-Acts," 384.
23   Johnson, *Gospel of Luke*, 104
24   Johnson, *Gospel of Luke*, 189 (see *m. Demai* 2).
25   J. H. Elliott, "Temple versus Household in Luke-Acts: A Contrast in Social Institutions," in Neyrey, *Social World of Luke-Acts*, 220; H. Moxnes, "Patron-Client Relations and the New Community in Luke-Acts," in Neyrey, *Social World of Luke-Acts*, 256.
26   Johnson, *Gospel of Luke*, 221.
27   Sanders, *Jews in Luke-Acts*, 86.
28   See Heil, *Meal Scenes in Luke-Acts*, 100.
29   Johnson, *Gospel of Luke*, 226.
30   C. H. Talbert, *Reading Luke: A Literary and Theological Commentary on the Third Gospel* (New York: Crossroad, 1992), 197.
31   See, e.g., Johnson, *Gospel of Luke*, 225.
32   Exceptional is Brawley, *Luke-Acts and the Jews*, 103.
33   Brawley, *Luke-Acts and the Jews*, 88.
34   Johnson, *Gospel of Luke*, 242.
35   F. B. Craddock, *Luke*, IBC (Louisville, Ky.: Westminster John Knox, 1990), 196, cf. 192; see also Talbert, *Reading Luke*, 156.
36   R. Doran, "The Pharisee and the Tax Collector: An Agonistic Story" (forthcoming).
37   Saldarini, *Pharisees, Scribes, and Sadducees*, 178.

CHAPTER 5

1   One of the twenty references occurs in 8:3, which is part of a passage (7:53–8:11, the story of the adulterous woman) that is not generally considered to be part of the original gospel. For the textual history of this passage and the reasons for considering it not to be Johannine, see R. E. Brown, *The Gospel according to John* (Garden City, N.Y.: Doubleday, 1966, 1970), 1:332–38.

2   The Greek text in 1:24 is disputed. The words ἀπεσταλμένοι ἦσαν ἐκ τῶν Φαρισαίων have sometimes been understood to refer to some Pharisees belonging to the delegation mentioned in 1:19 ("the Jews sent priests and Levites from Jerusalem") or to a separate delegation. The present narrative context and the gospel as a whole, however, support the view that 1:24 refers to a delegation that comprised priests and Levites and was sent by the Pharisees. See Brown, *John*, 1:43–44.

3   "Soldiers" likely refers to Roman soldiers, as distinct from and in addition to the forces under the authority of Jewish groups. Cf. Brown, *John*, 2:807–8.

4   A similar usage is apparent in 8:3, which links the scribes and Pharisees: "The scribes and the Pharisees brought a woman who had been caught in adultery; and making her stand before all of them. . . ."

5   In most cases, the various Jewish groups appear in combinations of two or three. Chief priests and scribes appear in Jesus' Passion prediction in Mark 10:33: "See, we are going up to Jerusalem, and the Son of Man will be handed over to the chief priests and the scribes, and they will condemn him to death; then they will hand him over to the Gentiles." Matthew 16:21 mentions elders, chief priests, and scribes: "From that time on, Jesus began to show his disciples that he must go to Jerusalem and undergo great suffering at the hands of the elders and chief priests and scribes, and be killed, and on the third day be raised." Mark 15:1 adds to this combination the whole council: "As soon as it was morning, the chief priests held a consultation with the elders and scribes and the whole council. They bound Jesus, led him away, and handed him over to Pilate."

6   Brown, *Death of the Messiah*, 2:1431.

7   According to François Tolmie, groups such as the Jews, the Pharisees, or the crowd are not really characterized in depth in John because, from John's point of view, it is not important who these groups really are but how they respond to Jesus. In the case of the Pharisees, the most important thing is their almost completely negative response, hence the small number of differentiating details. Cf. D. F. Tolmie, "The Ioudaioi in the Fourth Gospel: A Narratological Perspective," in *Theology and Christology in the Fourth Gospel: Essays by the Members of the SNTS Johannine Writings Seminar*, ed. G. van Belle, J. G. van der Watl and P. Maritz. BETL 184 (Leuven: Leuven University Press, 2005), 377–97, esp. 395.

8   R. A. Culpepper, *The Anatomy of the Fourth Gospel: A Study in Literary Design* (Philadelphia: Fortress, 1983), 131.

9   For more complete presentations and reassessments of Martyn's model, see A. Reinhartz, *Befriending the Beloved Disciple: A Jewish Reading of the Gospel of John* (New York: Continuum, 2001), 37–53; R. Hakola, *Identity Matters: John, the Jews and Jewishness*, NovTSup 118 (Leiden: Brill, 2005), 16–22, 41–86.

10   J. L. Martyn, *History and Theology in the Fourth Gospel*, NTL, 3rd ed. (Louisville, Ky.: Westminster John Knox, 2003), 86.

11   Martyn, *History and Theology*, 87–88.

12   Martyn, *History and Theology*, 69–83.

13   For Martyn's contribution to Johannine studies, see D. M. Smith, "The
     Contribution of J. Louis Martyn to the Understanding of the Gospel of
     John," in Martyn, *History and Theology*, 1–19. Concerning John's portrait of
     the Pharisees, Smith says that "if one asks for evidence of sharp conflict
     between early Christians and specifically Pharisaic Jews, the weightiest wit-
     ness would be the Gospel of John, understood along the lines that Martyn
     suggests." Furthermore, "the Johannine church's struggle with its Pharisaic
     Jewish opponents toward the end of the first century is, in the evangelist's
     view, the same struggle as Jesus' struggle with Pharisees in the first half of
     the same century" (18). Smith originally made this evaluation in 1990. In his
     recent postscript for the third edition of Martyn's *History and Theology in the
     Fourth Gospel*, Smith admits that Martyn's construal "is subject to question at
     a number of points" but he Smith regards its general outline as valid. See
     D. M. Smith, postscript for Martyn, 3rd ed., *History and Theology in the Fourth
     Gospel*, 21.
14   For a significant exception, see U. C. von Wahlde, "The Relationship
     between Pharisees and Chief Priests: Some Observations on the Texts in
     Matthew, John, and Josephus," *NTS* 42 (1996): 506–22. Von Wahlde argues
     that the combination of Pharisees and chief priests in John 7:45-52 and
     11:47-57 is by no means an anachronistic usage and a reflection of the
     influential role of post-70 rabbis, as is often claimed (e.g., Martyn, *History
     and Theology*, 86). While certain passages in Josephus support this aspect of
     von Wahlde's argument, his conclusion concerning the historical value of
     John's portrayal of the Pharisees is open to challenge. Von Wahlde argues
     that "both the combination [of the Pharisees and chief priests] and the
     larger role of the Pharisees in John is, as far as we can tell, historically accu-
     rate. As such it provides a further indication of the historical accuracy of the
     language and thought of the earliest stratum of material in John's gospel"
     (522). This conclusion immediately raises the question about the relation-
     ship between John and the synoptic gospels. If "the larger role of the
     Pharisees" in John is historically accurate, how are we to explain the fact
     that the Pharisees are far less prominent in the synoptics and are coupled
     with the chief priests only in passing (Matt 26:62)?
15   M. C. de Boer, "The Depiction of the 'Jews' in John's Gospel: Matters of
     Behavior and Identity," in *Anti-Judaism and the Fourth Gospel: Papers of the
     Leuven Colloquium, 2000*, ed. R. Bieringer, D. Pollefeyt and F. Vandercasteele-
     Vanneuville, Jewish and Christian Heritage Series 1 (Assen: Royal van
     Gorcum, 2001), 260–80, esp. 264.
16   J. D. G. Dunn, *The Partings of the Ways between Christianity and Judaism and Their
     Significance for the Character of Christianity* (London and Philadelphia: SCM
     Press and Trinity Press International, 1991), 234.
17   Dunn, *Partings of the Ways*, 241 (italics in original).
18   Dunn, *Partings of the Ways*, 221–22, 238.
19   U. C. von Wahlde, "'The Jews' in the Gospel of John: Fifteen Years of
     Research (1983–1998)," *ETL* 76 (2000): 30–55, esp. 53–55.
20   Many scholars say that Jesus' words in John 8:44 concern only a particular
     group of Jewish authorities who killed Jesus or persecuted the Johannine

Christians. For example, S. M. Schneiders, *The Revelatory Text: Interpreting the New Testament as Sacred Scripture*, 2nd ed. (Collegeville, Minn.: Liturgical Press, 1999), 164; C. K. Barrett, "John and Judaism," in Bieringer et al., *Anti-Judaism and the Fourth Gospel*, 401–17, esp. 405–6; de Boer, "Depiction of the 'Jews,'" 268–69. For the criticism of this view, see Hakola, *Identity Matters*, 180–83.

21　J. Zumstein, "The Farewell Discourse (John 13:31–16:33) and the Problem of Anti-Judaism," in Bieringer et al., *Anti-Judaism and the Fourth Gospel*, 461–78, esp. 470.

22　For the criticism of the expulsion theory, see also T. Nicklas, *Ablösung und Verstrickung: "Juden" und Jüngergestalten als Charaktere der erzählten Welt des Johannesevangeliums und ihre Wirkung ouf den impliziten Leser*, RST 60 (Frankfurt am Main: Peter Lang, 2001), 49–72.

23　For the full discussion with references, see Hakola, *Identity Matters*, 55–65.

24　J. Neusner, *Judaism: The Evidence of the Mishnah* (Chicago: The University of Chicago Press, 1981), 76–121; C. Hezser, *The Social Structure of the Rabbinic Movement in Roman Palestine*, TSAJ 66 (Tübingen: Mohr-Siebeck, 1997), 360–68; S. J. D. Cohen, "The Rabbi in Second-Century Jewish Society," in *The Cambridge History of Judaism: The Early Roman Period*, ed. W. Horbury, W. D. Davies and J. Sturdy (Cambridge: Cambridge University Press, 1999), 3:922–90, esp. 961–71. Many other rabbinic scholars (e.g., Martin Goodman, Lee I. Levine, Hayim Lapin, Günter Stemberger) have also made observations pointing in the same direction.

25　J. Neusner, *The Mishnah: Social Perspectives* (Leiden: Brill, 1999), 265–66.

26　S. S. Miller, "The Minim of Sepphoris Reconsidered," *HTR* 86 (1993): 377–402, esp. 396–97.

27　Miller, "The Minim," 400; "New Perspectives on the History of Sepphoris," in *Galilee through the Centuries: Confluence of Cultures*, ed. E. M. Meyers, Duke Judaic Studies Series 1 (Winona Lake, Ind.: Eisenbrauns, 1999), 145–59, esp. 151.

28　R. Kalmin, "Christians and Heretics in Rabbinic Literature of Late Antiquity," *HTR* 87 (1994): 155–69, esp. 169; *The Sage in Jewish Society of Late Antiquity* (London and New York: Routledge, 1999), 72.

29　A. F. Segal, "Judaism, Christianity, and Gnosticism," in *Anti-Judaism in Early Christianity: Separation and Polemic*, ed. S. G. Wilson, Studies in Christianity and Judaism 2 (Waterloo, Ont.: Wilfrid Laurier University Press, 1986), 133–61, esp. 141.

30　S. Stern, *Jewish Identity in Early Rabbinic Writings*, AGJU 23 (Leiden: Brill, 1994), 132–35.

32　M. Goodman, "The Function of Minim in Early Rabbinic Judaism," in *Geschichte-Tradition-Reflexion: Festschrift für Martin Hengel zum 70. Geburtstag. Band I: Judentum*, ed. H. Cancik, H. Lichtenberger, and P. Schäfer (Tübingen: Mohr-Siebeck, 1996), 501–10, esp. 507.

32　W. S. Green, "Heresy, Apostasy in Judaism," in *The Encyclopedia of Judaism*, ed. J. Neusner, A. J. Avery-Peck, and W. S. Green (Leiden: Brill, 2000), 1:366–80, esp. 372–73.

33 S. J. D. Cohen, "The Significance of Yavneh: Pharisees, Rabbis, and the End of Jewish Sectarianism," *HUCA* 55 (1984), 27–53, esp. 50; C. Setzer, *Jewish Responses to Early Christians: History and Polemics, 30–150 C.E.* (Minneapolis: Fortress, 1994), 161; Goodman, "Function," 506.

34 The above conclusions have sometimes been explained away by referring to a hidden political agenda among scholars, but the changes in rabbinic studies are so overwhelming that they cannot be ignored. Cf. R. Deines, *Die Pharisäer: Ihr Verständnis im Spiegel der christlichen und jüdischen Forschung seit Wellhausen und Graetz*, WUNT 101 (Tübingen: Mohr-Siebeck, 1997), 11. Deines has suggested that recent emphasis on the pluralistic and diverse nature of the first century Judaism is the result of a contemporary social and political ideology reflecting the needs of religious communities in modern, pluralistic societies. Deines claims that this ideology has replaced earlier confessional approach, which likewise resulted in a selective interpretation of the sources.

35 See J. D. G. Dunn, "The Embarrassment of History: Reflections on the Problem of 'Anti-Judaism' in the Fourth Gospel," in Bieringer et al., *Anti-Judaism and the Fourth Gospel*, 47–67, esp. 52–53. Dunn's way of reacting to recent changes in the study of rabbinic Judaism is typical of many scholars. As discussing of John's relationship to Pharisaic/early rabbinic movement after 70 CE, Dunn admits that "it took decades and even centuries for the rabbis to establish their interpretation of Judaism as the only authentic form of Judaism, to establish, that is to say, rabbinic Judaism as 'Judaism.'" But still Dunn notes that "the successors to the Pharisees were evidently able to establish themselves as the chief custodians of the Pharisaic heritage and, more important, as the only effective political force in the land." Dunn also describes Yohanan ben Zakkai as the one "who played the leading role in establishing the rabbis as the main power brokers within Israel and began the process of reconstituting Second Temple Judaism as rabbinic Judaism."

36 Cf. K. Wengst, *Bedrängte Gemeinde und verherrlichter Christus: ein Versuch über das Johannesevangelium*, 4th ed. (Munich: Kaiser Verlag, 1992), 155–56. Wengst says that the exclusion from the synagogue could have been a serious problem only for a Jewish-Christian community that lived in a Greek-speaking environment governed by the Pharisees or the early rabbis. For this reason, Ephesus or some other major city in the Diaspora is not a likely candidate for the home of the Johannine community (158). Wengst locates the Gospel to the regions of Batanaea and Gaulanitis where Jewish self-government in the time of Agrippa II would have made the Johannine situation understandable (157–79). For the problems of this proposal, see M. Hengel, *Die johanneische Frage: Ein Lösungsversuch*, WUNT 67 (Tübingen: Mohr-Siebeck, 1993), 290–91.

37 Thus, for example, F. J. Moloney, "Israel, the People and the Jews in the Fourth Gospel," in *Israel und seine Heilstraditionen im Johannesevangelium: Festgabe für Johannes Beutler SJ zum 70. Geburtstag*, ed. M. Labahn, K. Scholtissek and A. Strotmann (Paderborn: Ferdinand Schöningh, 2004), 351–64, esp. 362.

38 W. A. Meeks, "Breaking Away: Three New Testament Pictures of Christianity's Separation from the Jewish Communities," in *"To See Ourselves*

as Others See Us": Christians, Jews, "Others" in Late Antiquity, ed. J. Neusner and E. S. Frerichs, Studies in the Humanities 9 (Chico, Calif.: Scholars Press; 1985), 94–115, esp. 102–3.

39   Reinhartz, *Befriending the Beloved Disciple*, 40–48.

40   See M. Theobald, "Abraham – (Isaak –) Jakob: Israels Väter im Johannes-evangelium," in *Israel und seine Heilstraditionen im Johannesevangelium: Festgabe für Johannes Beutler SJ zum 70. Geburtstag*, ed. M. Labahn, K. Scholtissek, and A. Strotmann (Paderborn: Ferdinand Schöningh, 2004), 158–83, esp. 175–77; Hakola, *Identity Matters*, 180–87, and more fully, Hakola, "The Johannine Community as Jewish Christians? Some Problems in Current Scholarly Consensus," in *Reconsidering Jewish Christianity*, ed. M. Jackson-McCabe (Minneapolis: Fortress, forthcoming).

41   R. Kimelman, "*Birkat Ha-Minim* and the Lack of Evidence for an Anti-Christian Jewish Prayer in Late Antiquity," in *Aspects of Judaism in the Greco-Roman Period*, vol. 2 of *Jewish and Christian Self-Definition*, ed. E. P. Sanders, A. I. Baumgarten and A. Mendelson (Philadelphia: Fortress, 1981), 226–44, esp. 234–35. A. Reinhartz, "The Johannine Community and Its Jewish Neighbors: A Reappraisal," in *"What is John?": Literary and Social Readings of the Fourth Gospel*, ed. F. F. Segovia, SBLSymS 7 (Atlanta: Scholars Press, 1998), 2:111–38, esp. 136–37.

42   Hakola, *Identity Matters*, 215–21. See also W. R. G. Loader, "Jesus and the Law in John," in *Theology and Christology in the Fourth Gospel: Essays by the Members of the SNTS Johannine Writings Seminar*, ed. G. van Belle, J. G. van der Watt and P. Maritz, BETL 184 (Leuven: Leuven University Press, 2005), 135–54, esp. 153. Loader considers it probable that the Johannine Christians had already abandoned the circumcision and the observance of the Sabbath and the food laws.

43   For applications of the social identity approach to ancient Jewish and Christian writings, see P. Esler, *Galatians* (London and New York: Routledge, 1998) 40-57; *Conflict and Identity in Romans: The Social Setting of Paul's Letter* (Minneapolis: Fortress, 2003), 19–39; J. Jokiranta, "Social Identity Approach: Identity-Constructing Elements in the Psalms of Pesher," in *Defining Identities: Who is the Other? We, You, and the Others in the Dead Sea Scrolls. Congress Proceedings of 10QS. July 25–28, 2004, Groningen*, ed. F. G. Martínez (Leiden: Brill, forthcoming 2006); R. Hakola, "Being the Same and Different at the Same Time: Social Identities and Group Phenomena in the Second Temple Period," in *Explaining Early Judaism and Christianity: Contributions From Cognitive and Social Science*, ed. P Luomanen, I. Pyysiäinen and R. Uro (forthcoming).

44   For general introductions to the social identity approach, see J. C. Turner, "Some Current Issues in Research on Social Identity and Self-Categorization Theories," in *Social Identity: Context, Commitment, Content*, ed. N. Ellemers, R. Spears, and B. Doosje (Oxford: Blackwell, 1999), 6–34; M. A. Hogg, "Social Categorization, Depersonalization, and Group Behavior," in *Blackwell Handbook of Social Psychology: Group Processes*, ed. M. A. Hogg and R. S. Tindale (Oxford: Blackwell, 2001), 56–85.

45   P. J. Oakes, S. A. Haslam, and J. C. Turner, *Stereotyping and Social Reality* (Oxford: Blackwell, 1994), 95–96; P. J. Oakes, S. A. Haslam, and K. J. Reynolds, "Social Categorization and Social Context: Is Stereotype Change a Matter of Information or of Meaning?" in *Social Identity and Social Cognition*, ed. D. M. Abrams and M. A. Hogg (Oxford: Blackwell, 1999), 55–79, esp. 57–61.

46   Oakes, Haslam, and Reynolds, "Social Categorization," 60.

47   Hogg, "Social Categorization," 60.

48   S. J. Sherman, D. L. Hamilton and A. C. Lewis, "Perceived Entitativity and the Social Identity Value of Group Membership," in Abrams and Hogg, *Social Identity and Social Cognition*, 80–110, esp. 81.

49   Sherman, Hamilton, and Lewis, "Perceived Entitativity," 85.

50   For the summary, see Neusner, *Rabbinic Traditions about the Pharisees*, 3:301–19.

51   Sherman, Hamilton, and Lewis, "Perceived Entitativity," 100.

52   D. L. Hamilton and R. K. Gilford, "Illusory Correlation in Interpersonal Perception: A Cognitive Basis of Stereotypic Judgments," *Journal of Experimental Social Psychology* 12 (1976): 392–407; P. R. Hinton, *Stereotypes, Cognition and Culture*, Psychology Focus Series (Philadelphia: Taylor & Francis, 2000), 64–79.

53   Cf. J. Cooper and R. H. Fazio, "The Formation and Persistence of Attitudes That Support Intergroup Conflict," in *The Social Psychology of Intergroup Relations*, ed. W. G. Austin and S. Worchel (Monterey, Calif.: Brooks/Cole, 1979), 149–59, esp. 157. They remark that when a group is the object of social perception, the information concerning the group is processed in an exaggerated way which leads to the confirmation of one's initial judgment of the group. Because groups "represent a distribution of individuals with regard to certain characteristics, it becomes more probable that evidence can be found to support one's prior assessments. . . . Once such confirming evidence is found—either by active searching for or, more subtly, by selective attention—group members become still more confident of the attributions they have made to the outgroup."

54   Neusner, *Rabbinic Traditions about the Pharisees*, 3:266–68, 318.

CHAPTER 6

1   I deal with the distinction between the two meetings, one of which occurred with Paul as a participant in 46 CE and another in his absence in 52 CE, in *Rabbi Paul: An Intellectual Biography* (New York: Doubleday, 2004), 133, 141–46, 165–70.

2   See V. J. Rosivach, *The System of Public Sacrifice in Fourth-Century Athens*, ACS 34 (Atlanta: Scholars Press, 1994).

3   See Bruce Chilton, "James in Relation to Peter, Paul, and the Remembrance of Jesus," in *The Brother of Jesus: James the Just and His Mission*, ed. with J. Neusner (Louisville, Ky.: Westminster John Knox, 2001), 138–60.

4   See C. A. Evans and P. W. Flint, eds., *Eschatology, Messianism, and the Dead Sea Scrolls* (Grand Rapids: Eerdmans, 1997), 151. For an accessible and interesting presentation of the texts in English, see M. Wise, M. Abegg, and E. Cook, ed. *The Dead Sea Scrolls: A New Translation* (San Franscisco: Harper, 1996).

5   See J. J. Collins, *The Scepter and the Star: The Messiahs of the Dead Sea Scrolls and Other Ancient Literature*, ABRL (New York: Doubleday, 1995). He develops his reading of the difference between this interpretation and that contained in the Damascus Document on pages 64–65, following the lead of J. A. Fitzmyer.

6   Collins, *Scepter and the Star*, 61.

7   See Bruce Chilton, *God in Strength: Jesus' Announcement of the Kingdom*, SNTSU 1 (Freistadt: Plöchl, 1979), repr. BibSem 8 (Sheffield: JSOT Press, 1987): 136–43, 147–51.

8   See R. Maddox, *The Purpose of Luke-Acts*, SNTW (Edinburgh: Clark, 1982), 183; J. T. Squires, *The Plan of God in Luke-Acts*, SNTSMS 76 (Cambridge: Cambridge University Press, 1993), 187–89.

9   B. Chilton and J. Neusner, *Judaism in the New Testament: Practices and Beliefs* (London: Routledge, 1995), 104–5.

10 See K. Lake, "The Apostolic Council of Jerusalem," in *The Beginnings of Christianity* 5, ed. F. J. F. Jackson and K. Lake (Grand Rapids: Baker, 1979), 195–212.

11 The rendering of the RSV here ("in assembly") seems a bit weak; see J. R. Lumby, *The Acts of the Apostles*, CGTSC (Cambridge: Cambridge University Press, 1904), 282.

12 Of course, these are just the people, and just the recognition of categories of people, one should expect to find in a synagogue. See M. C. de Boer, "God-Fearers in Luke Acts," in *Luke's Literary Achievement: Collected Essays*, ed. C. M. Tuckett, JSNTSup 116 (Sheffield: Sheffield Academic, 1995): 50–71. In the presentation of Luke-Acts, Paul is careful to observe the traditional distinction and is persecuted by "the Jews" for his Christology. It is much more likely that his profound challenge of the very definition of Israel brought about discord. But because Luke-Acts does not share Paul's definition, it is silent in that respect.

13 See Chilton and Neusner, *Judaism in the New Testament*, 98–104; B. Chilton and J. Neusner, *The Intellectual Foundations of Christian and Jewish Discourse: The Philosophy of Religious Argument* (London: Routledge, 1997), 26–31.

14 That is the general position reached by D. Ravens in *Luke and the Restoration of Israel*, JSNTSup 119 (Sheffield: Sheffield Academic, 1995): 247–57.

15 See R. Eisenman, *James the Brother of Jesus: The Key to Unlocking the Secrets of Early Christianity and the Dead Sea Scrolls* (New York: Viking, 1996), 601.

16 See A. J. Saldarini's treatment of Eisenman's position in *The New York Times Book Review* (April 27, 1997), 41.

17 Eisenman, *James the Brother of Jesus*, 159, 600.

18 See M. Hengel, "Jakobus der Herrenbruder—der erste 'Papst'?" in *Glaube und Eschatologie. Festschrift für Werner Georg Kümmel zum 80. Geburtstag*, ed. E. Grässer and O. Merk (Tübingen: Mohr-Siebeck, 1985), 71–104, esp. 81.

19 See J. B. Lightfoot, *The Apostolic Fathers* (London: Macmillan, 1890), 1:414–20.

20 Or the view of the Tübingen school of the nineteenth century, as Hengel ("Jakobus der Herrenbruder," 92) points out, is the source of such contentions.

21 Cited by Hengel, "Jakobus der Herrenbruder," 89.
22 Hengel, "Jakobus der Herrenbruder," 90, citing the Pseudo-Clementine letter of Peter, 2.3ff.
23 Lake, "Apostolic Council of Jerusalem," 208. The attempt by Harvey Falk to attribute that program to Jesus is anachronistic, but his contribution does call attention to a genuine perspective within primitive Christianity; see *Jesus the Pharisee: A New Look at the Jewishness of Jesus* (New York: Paulist Press, 1985), and my review of the same in *ThTo* 42 (1986): 563–64.
24 Lake, "Apostolic Council of Jerusalem," 208–9, with a citation of the Greek text. For an English rendering and fine introductions and explanations, see John J. Collins, "Sibylline Oracles: A New Translation and Introduction," in *OTP* 1, ed. J. Charlesworth (Garden City, N.Y.: Doubleday, 1983). Collins dates this work within the first century, but after the eruption of Vesuvius in 79 CE (381–82). With due caution, he assigns book 4 a Syrian provenience.
25 See Squires, *Plan of God in Luke-Acts*, 121–54.
26 See Collins, *Scepter and the Star*, 317.
27 See B. Chilton and J. Neusner, *Types of Authority in Formative Christianity and Judaism* (London and New York: Routledge, 1999).
28 He also cites 4:162–170.
29 Collins, *Scepter and the Star*, 355.
30 Collins, *Scepter and the Star*, 331.
31 See Otto Mørkholm, "Antiochus IV," in *The Cambridge History of Judaism: The Hellenistic Age*, ed. W. D. Davies and L. Finkelstein (Cambridge: Cambridge University Press, 1989), 2:278–91; in the same volume, H. Hegermann, "The Diaspora in the Hellenistic Age," 115–66.
32 Onias III, deposed as high priest by his brother Jason, lived in Antioch for three years until his assassination by Menelaus in 172 BCE. His son, Onias IV, is reported by Josephus to have fled to Ptolemy in 162 BCE, when Alcimus assumed the high priesthood (so *Ant.* 12.387). Josephus also cites a purported letter from Onias IV to Ptolemy and Cleopatra (*Ant.* 13.65–68), in which he asks for permission to purify and rebuild an old temple in Leontopolis for the cultic usage of Jews there. As part of his case, he cites his service to them in Syria and Phoenicia (*Ant.* 13.65). During that time, he probably resided in Damascus, a crucial city within the history of the Essenes. See Uriel Rappaport, "Onias," in *ABD* 5:23–24 (Garden City, N.Y.: Doubleday, 1992).
33 See Stemberger, *Jewish Contemporaries of Jesus*, 125; L. R. Deeds, *Cultic Metaphors: Sacrificial Ideology and Origins in Selected Scrolls from the Dead Sea* (Annandale, N.Y.: Bard College, 1996), 94–101.
34 See M. Smith, "The Occult in Josephus," in Feldman and Hata, *Josephus, Judaism, and Christianity*, 236–56, esp. 248–50.
35 See R. Tomes, "Why Did Paul Get His Hair Cut? (Acts 18.18; 21.23-24)," in Tuckett, *Luke's Literary Achievement*, 188–97. Tomes rightly points out that there is considerable deviation from the prescriptions of Numbers 6 here, but the Mishnah (see below) amply attests such flexibility within the practice of the vow.

36 See Josephus, *Jewish War* 2.590–594; *m. Menahoth* 8:3–5; and the whole of *m. Makhshirin*. The point of departure for the concern is Leviticus 11:34.

37 For further discussion, see my: *The Temple of Jesus: His Sacrificial Program within a Cultural History of Sacrifice* (University Park: Pennsylvania State University Press, 1992); "A Generative Exegesis of Mark 7:1-23," *JHC* 3, no. 1 (1996): 18–37; *Pure Kingdom: Jesus' Vision of God*, Studying the Historical Jesus 1 (Grand Rapids, Eerdmans, 1996).

38 See *m. Nedarim*; Z. W. Falk, "Notes and Observations on Talmudic Vows," *HTR* 59 (1966): 309–12.

39 Compare Exodus 20:2; 21:17; Leviticus 20:9; Deuteronomy 5:16.

40 As happens in Matthew 15:3-9.

41 See B. Chilton and C. A. Evans, "Jesus and Israel's Scriptures," in *Studying the Historical Jesus: Evaluations of the State of Current Research*, ed. B. Chilton and C. A. Evans. NTTS 19 (Leiden: Brill, 1994), 281–335, esp. 294–95.

42 So M. Bockmuehl, "'Let the Dead Bury Their Dead': Jesus and the Law Revisited," in *Jewish Law in Gentile Churches: Halakhah and the Beginning of Christian Public Ethics* (Edinburgh: T&T Clark, 2000), 23–48. Of all the arguments adduced, the most attractive is that Jesus' statement concerning wine and the kingdom involves his accepting Nazirite vows. See P. Lebeau, *Le vin nouveau du Royaume: Etude exégétique et patristique sur la Parole eschatologique de Jésus à la Cène* (Paris: Desclée, 1966); M. Wojciechowski, "Le naziréat et la Passion (Mc 14,25a; 15:23)," *Bib* 65 (1984): 94–96. But the form of Jesus' statement has not been rightly understood, owing to its Semitic syntax. He is not promising never to drink wine, but to drink wine only in association with his celebration of the kingdom. See B. Chilton, *A Feast of Meanings: Eucharistic Theologies from Jesus through Johannine Circles*, NovTSup 72 (Leiden: Brill, 1994), 169–71.

43 It is for this reason that the circle of James also sought to restrict the definition of who might participate in the full celebration of the Eucharist. Mark 14:12-15 turns that meals into a Seder, in which only the circumcised could participate; see Chilton, *Feast of Meanings*, 93–108.

44 Indeed, there was even a place called Bethlehem of Nazareth, according to the Talmud; see Chilton, *God in Strength*, 311–13.

45 See B. Chilton, "Exorcism and History: Mark 1:21-23," *Gospel Perspectives* 6 (1986): 253–71. I have now pursued the origin of the usage in respect to exorcism to *Mary Magdalene* in *Mary Magdalene: A Biography* (New York: Doubleday, 2005), putting her source together with James's involved conflicting conceptions of Jesus' purity, which I am in the process of tracing through the synoptic gospels.

46 See B. Chilton, "Purity and Impurity," in *The Dictionary of the Later New Testament and Its Developments*, ed. R. P. Martin and P. Davids (Downers Grove, Ill.: InterVarsity, 1997), 988–96.

47 See D. Catchpole, "Paul, James, and the Apostolic Decree," *NTS* 23 (1977): 428–44. Catchpole even suggests that Paul's antagonists in Galatians 2 were delivering the ruling of the Council. Criticism of Catchpole has tended to run along the lines that he "discounts the historical value of Acts"; so T. George, *Galatians*, NAC 30 (Nashville: Broadman & Holman, 1994), 169

n. 138. What is more to the point is that the people described as "from James" in Galatians 2:12 prompt separation from believing Gentiles, not their maintenance of purity. They more likely correspond to those who claim the support of Jerusalem, but who are then denied support by the Council (see Acts 15:24).

48 In *Pagan Rome and the Early Christians* (Bloomington: Indiana University Press, 1986), Stephen Benko suggests that Peregrinus was excommunicated during the second century for eating "meat that was consecrated to pagan gods . . ." (32).

49 As he puts it, "the Mishnah neither provides usable first-century evidence regarding the immersion of proselytes nor indicates that Jews practiced an unrepeated, one-time-only immersion as part of their conversion rites" (P. Flesher, "The Fiction of Proselyte Baptism," in *Traversing Land and Sea: Proselytism in Judaism and Early Christianity*, ed. A.-J. Levine and R. Pervo [forthcoming; p. 2 of the MS]).

50 E. P. Sanders, *Jesus and Judaism* (Philadelphia: Fortress, 1985), 270–93.

51 See B. Chilton, "Jesus and the Repentance of E. P. Sanders," *TynBul* 39 (1988): 1–18.

52 See H. Basser, "The Gospels and Rabbinic Halakah," in *The Missing Jesus: Rabbinic Judaism and the New Testament*, ed. B. Chilton, C. A. Evans, and J. Neusner (Leiden: Brill, 2002), 77–99. This chapter was originally a paper delivered at the conference from which the volume is named, which took place at Bard College in October 1997.

53 See Cohen, *Josephus in Galilee and Rome*, 144–51, 236–38; and Chilton, *Temple of Jesus*, 69–87.

54 The fact that James was clubbed invites comparison with Sanhedrin 81b–82b, where clubbing is inflicted as a punishment on an unclean priest. Epiphanius, Panarion 78.13.3–5 makes the connection between Mark 14:51 and James's linen garment.

55 Again, this is an issue I detail further in *Rabbi Paul*, 28–71.

56 Chilton, *Rabbi Paul*, 186–90, 242–44.

57 Chilton, *Rabbi Paul*, 163–64.

CHAPTER 7

1 Which Gamaliel is meant by Acts and which by the counterpart rabbinic sayings attributed to a Gamaliel? Two Gamaliels flourished in the first century—the one, Hillel's heir; the other, the grandson of Hillel's heir. The chain of tradition set forth in tractate Abot, chapter 1 knows from Shammai and Hillel forward, the following:
    1:16 A. Rabban Gamaliel says,
    1:17 A. Simeon his son says,
    1:18 A. Rabban Simeon b. Gamaliel says
It is generally assumed that "Simeon his son" is duplicated by "Rabban Simeon b. Gamaliel." Thus, Gamaliel I is represented as Hillel's successor in the chain of tradition, followed by Simeon b. Gamaliel I. Elsewhere, a statement attributed to Judah the Patriarch claims Hillel as Judah's ancestor.

The patriarchal links are explicit. There is, moreover, a second Gamaliel in the first century, who flourished after the destruction of the Second Temple. And that Gamaliel II produced a second Simeon b. Gamaliel, the one who flourished in the second century and fathered Judah the Patriarch, sponsor of the Mishnah. The two Gamaliels and the two Simeon b. Gamaliels, continuing the Hillelite line, are further identified as patriarchs in their generation, a convention of the documents that will play a role presently. How does this fit together with Paul's having studied with (a) Gamaliel? The first Gamaliel was Hillel's son, so would have flourished in the first third of the first century, when Paul was getting his education. Then Simeon b. Gamaliel ("Simeon his son . . . Rabban Simeon b. Gamaliel") would figure in the second third of the century, active in the time of the First War against Rome. Now, since Josephus claims him as a worthy adversary (*Life* 191f.), Simeon b. Gamaliel would have thrived down to the destruction. Then comes his son, Gamaliel (II), after 70. What of the Gamaliels of whom the Mishnah speaks? It must follow that the Mishnah's Gamaliel can be either the first, with whom Paul in Acts is alleged to have studied, or his grandson. When a Gamaliel is mentioned in the company of Eliezer, Joshua, and 'Aqiba, that is the second. So the problem of the historical Gamaliel proves complicated by the question, which Gamaliel, and to whom do otherwise indeterminate Gamaliel sayings and stories belong? And the answer we give is, a particular corpus of Gamaliel sayings represent the patriarchate. But which ones? We answer that question in detail.

2   A choice example of false premises within a scholarly program is supplied by Cohen, "The Significance of Yavneh." To formulate and prove his theory, he has exhibited that gullibility that characterizes some scholarship even now in the encounter with the rabbinic sources for historical purposes. Except for arbitrary reasons of his own, Cohen consistently takes at face value the historical allegation of a source that a given rabbi made the statement attributed to him. That is his starting point throughout. This critique is spelled out in J. Neusner, *Reading and Believing: Ancient Judaism and Contemporary Gullibility*, BJS (Atlanta: Scholars Press, 1986). The argument there is that only on the premises of believing pretty much everything as historical fact can a variety of scholars have built their constructions.

3   We hasten to add: this "institution" in the pre-70 period was most unlike the political-religious authority of the early third-century patriarchate, with its Roman sponsorship. Clearly, the transformation of a sect, the Pharisees, into the administrative arm of the Roman government in the Land of Israel (meaning: for the ethnic community of the Jews), such as unfolded in the later first through the early third century, deserves study in its own terms. What is important is that the fully articulated patriarchate, represented by Judah the Patriarch, sponsor of the Mishnah, traced itself back to Hillel via Gamaliel I and II and Simeon b. Gamaliel I and II and, as we shall show, in the Mishnah preserved their traditions in a privileged literary formation, the domestic *Ma'aseh*, as distinct in its formal traits from the juridical *Ma'aseh*. The former reports personal practice as exemplary virtue; the latter reports court rulings not validated by the person of the sage who made

the ruling but by the consensus of sages. We maintain, then, that the topical program characteristic of the domestic Ma'aseh forms an ongoing tradition, preserved in its own literary construction, by the family represented in the tradition as Hillel–Gamaliel–Simeon b. Gamaliel–Gamaliel–Simeon b. Gamaliel–Judah the Patriarch (see note 1).

4   Obviously, we claim no more than that. We do not allege that it was only from the patriarchate (or its earlier, Pharisaic formation of the pre-70 age) that Paul could have derived that portion of his topical program represented in this study.

5   Whom Paul would have identified as the Christian counterpart, the patriarch, or Nasi of the Pharisees is not an issue at this point. But he clearly conceived of a hierarchical church order, and outside of the genealogy of Jesus (unlike James) and not possessed of living traditions received in the lifetime of Jesus (unlike Simon Peter), he will have had to frame a useful theory of authority on other grounds than the conventional ones.

6   For an informative defense of this view, see B. Rapske, *The Book of Acts and Paul in Roman Custody*, vol. 3 of *The Book of Acts in Its First-Century Setting* (Grand Rapids: Eerdmans, 1994), 94–99.

7   See the strictures of D. H. Akenson, *Saint Saul: A Skeleton Key to the Historical Jesus* (Oxford: Oxford University Press, 2000), 246–47.

8   See J. Jervell, *The Unknown Paul: Essays on Luke-Acts and Early Christian History* (Minneapolis: Augsburg, 1984), 71; Jervell's characterization of "the Pharisee Paul who remains a Pharisee after his conversion and never becomes an ex-Pharisee" is taken up by Rapske, *Paul in Roman Custody*, 94. A similar analysis is arrived at independently by Akenson, *Saint Saul*, 248–53, esp. 251, who describes Jesus and Paul as Pharisees "of a slightly off-brand sort."

9   For a fine consideration, see J. Murphy-O'Connor, *Paul: A Critical Life* (Oxford: Clarendon, 1996), v–vii.

10   Cf. Neusner, *Rabbinic Traditions about the Pharisees*, 1:343.

11   Murphy-O'Connor, *A Critical Life*, 54–56, esp. 56.

12   See Chilton, *Temple of Jesus*, 69–111.

13   See Neusner, *Rabbinic Traditions about the Pharisees*, 1:356–57, 360–61, 368, 372–73 (cf. Yerushalmi Ma'aser Sheni 5.4 and San 1.2; San 11b).

14   Cf. S. McKnight, *A Light among the Gentiles: Jewish Missionary Activity in the Second Temple Period* (Minneapolis: Fortress, 1991).

15   Neusner, *Rabbinic Traditions about the Pharisees*, 1:358.

16   Neusner, *Rabbinic Traditions about the Pharisees*, 1:378–79.

17   See J. L. Reed, *Archaeology and the Galilean Jesus: A Re-examination of the Evidence* (Harrisburg, Pa.: Trinity Press International, 2000).

18   There is another Gamaliel-at-sea story in Erubin 4:1, but that seems to refer to a later member of Gamaliel's family, judging by the other rabbis named.

19   Neusner, *Rabbinic Traditions about the Pharisees*, 1:379–80.

20   Neusner, *Rabbinic Traditions about the Pharisees*, 1:348–50.

21   See W. D. Davies, *Paul and Rabbinic Judaism: Some Rabbinic Elements in Pauline Theology* (London: SPCK, 1958), 331.

22   Neusner, *Rabbinic Traditions about the Pharisees*, 1:294, 3:306.

23   Neusner, *Rabbinic Traditions about the Pharisees*, 3:314.

24   See B. Chilton, "Reference to the Targumim in the Exegesis of the New Testament," in *SBLSP* 1995, ed. L. H. Lovering (Atlanta: Scholars Press, 1995), 77–82.

25   See B. D. Chilton and C. A. Evans, eds. *James the Just and Christian Origins*, NovTSup 98 (Leiden: Brill, 1999).

26   See C. E. B. Cranfield, *Epistle to the Romans*, vol. 2, ICC (Edinburgh: T&T Clark, 1986), 757.

27   O. Michel, *Der Brief an die Römer* (Göttingen: Vandenhoeck & Ruprecht, 1966), 458.

28   For a further defense of this point of view, see Chilton, *Feast of Meanings*, 182–93.

29   See H. Conzelmann, *1 Corinthians: A Commentary on the First Epistle to the Corinthians*, trans J. P. Leitch, Hermeneia (Philadelphia: Fortress, 1975), 294–97.

CHAPTER 8

This essay draws on, updates, and revises two of my earlier studies: "Those Who Look for Smooth Things, Pharisees, and Oral Law," in *Emanuel: Studies in Hebrew Bible, Septuagint, and Dead Sea Scrolls in Honor of Emanuel Tov*, ed. S. Paul et al., VTSup 94 (Leiden and Boston: Brill, 2003), 465–77; and "Pesher Nahum and Josephus," in *When Christianity and Judaism Began: Essays in Memory of Anthony J. Saldarini*, vol. 1, ed. A. J. Avery-Peck, D. Harrington, and J. Neusner, JSJSup 2 (Leiden: Brill, 2003), 299–311.

1   See W. Brownlee, "Biblical Interpretation among the Sectaries of the Dead Sea Scrolls," *BA* 14 (1951): 59; J. M. Allegro, "Further Light on the History of the Qumran Sect," *JBL* 75 (1956): 92. If the pun was intended, instances of חלקות would be the only places in the Qumran literature where הלכה by implication would be used in the sense of legal positions. See J. P. Meier, "Is There *Halaka* (the Noun) at Qumran?" *JBL* 122 (2003): 150–55.

2   Allegro first published parts of Pesher Nahum in the article noted above ("Further Light"); the official edition is in his *Qumrân Cave 4 I (4Q158–4Q186)*, DJD 5 (Oxford: Clarendon, 1968), 37–42, with pls. XII–XIV.

3   For references, see David J. A. Clines, ed. *Dictionary of Classical Hebrew*, 5 vols. (Sheffield: Sheffield Academic, 1993–1998), 3:242–43; H. Bengtsson, *What's in a Name? A Study of Sobriquets in the Pesharim* (Uppsala, Sweden: Uppsala University, 2000), 110–35.

4   A. I. Baumgarten, "The Name of the Pharisees," *JBL* 102, no. 3 (1983): 421 n. 42.

5   Quotations of the Qumran texts are from G. Vermes, *The Complete Dead Sea Scrolls in English* (New York and London: Penguin, 1997).

6   See M. Horgan, *Pesharim: Qumran Interpretations of Biblical Books*, CBQMS 8 (Washington, D.C.: Catholic Bible Association of America, 1979), 161, 173. The Antiochus who is mentioned may be Antiochus IV (r. 175–164 BCE; see Horgan, 173–74), although Antiochus VII (r. 138–129) is also possible, as he, too, could be said to have taken Jerusalem. The Kittim are the Romans in virtually all references to them in the scrolls (see T. H. Lim, "Kittim," in *Encyclopedia of the Dead Sea Scrolls* 1:469–71).

7   The most detailed study of the passage is G. L. Doudna, *4Q Pesher Nahum: A Critical Edition*, JSPSup 35/Copenhagen International Series 8 (Sheffield: Sheffield Academic, 2001), 389–433.

8   This is a widely accepted understanding that seems to be correct. For another approach see Doudna, *4Q Pesher Nahum*, 589–99.

9   For Alexander Jannaeus as כפיר החרון, see Horgan, *Pesharim*, 161, 175; H. Eshel, "Alexander Jannaeus," in *Encyclopedia of the Dead Sea Scrolls* 2:16–17. For a summary of the passages and arguments, see E. Schürer, *The History of the Jewish People in the Age of Jesus Christ (175 B.C.–A.D. 135)*, rev. and ed. G. Vermes, F. Millar, and M. Black (Edinburgh: T&T Clark, 1973–1987), 1:224–25 n. 22. For two scholars who suggested long ago that the events belong in Jannaeus's reign but denied "those who seek smooth things" were Pharisees, see C. Rabin, "Alexander Jannaeus and the Pharisees," *JJS* 7 (1956): 3–11; and F. Cross, *The Ancient Library of Qumran and Modern Biblical Studies* (Garden City: Doubleday, 1958), 91–95.

10   See Schürer, *History of the Jewish People*, 1:220–21.

11   R. Marcus, *Josephus*, vol. 7: *Jewish Antiquities, Books XII–XIV*, LCL (Cambridge, Mass.: Harvard University Press; London: Heinemann, 1966), 413. Citations from *Antiquities* are from this volume, while those from *War* are from H. Thackeray, *Josephus*, vol. 2: *The Jewish War, Books I–III*, LCL (Cambridge, Mass: Harvard University Press, 1976).

12   As Schürer commented, Jannaeus "was almost continuously involved in foreign and internal wars for the most part deliberately provoked by him" (*History of the Jewish People*, 1:220).

13   On this section in *War*, see Neusner, *From Politics to Piety*, 51–52.

14   Lee Levine argues that Josephus, with an eye toward his Roman readers, purposely did not identify Jannaeus's opponents as Pharisees so as not to mention them specifically in connection with rebels and people who undermine the national order ("The Political Struggle between Pharisees and Sadducees in the Hasmonean Period," in *Jerusalem in the Second Temple Period: Abraham Schalit Memorial Volume*, ed. A. Oppenheimer, U. Rappaport, and M. Stern [Jerusalem: Izhak ben-Zvi, 1980], 69 [Hebrew]).

15   On this addition to the *War* account and its significance, see Mason, *Flavius Josephus on the Pharisees*, 247–48. He thinks the passage comes from Josephus, not a source, and that it expresses the idea that what Jannaeus "did was wrong but, to some degree, understandable in the circumstances" (248).

16   See A. I. Baumgarten, "Seekers after Smooth Things," in *Encyclopedia of the Dead Sea Scrolls*, 2:858. E. P. Sanders shows from various details in the stories from the time of John Hyrcanus to that of Alexandra that the opponents of Jannaeus "included the Pharisees, probably as their leaders" (*Judaism: Practice and Belief*, 382). In the same place he adds that the seekers of smooth things in Pesher Nahum are Pharisees.

17   On the deathbed plan, see Mason, *Flavius Josephus on the Pharisees*, 248–54. He thinks the language of Jannaeus's speech is anti-Pharisaic and pro-Hasmonean and hence probably comes from Josephus, not Nicolaus of Damascus (250). Or, as he puts it: "Josephus must have formulated (or freely invented) Alexander's deathbed speech." This is hardly the only way of

reading the scene. Neusner writes: "The version in *Antiquities* of the Pharisees-in-power story is strikingly revised in favor of the Pharisees" (*From Politics to Piety*, 60; see also his comments on p. 63).

18 On the textual problem see Marcus, *Josephus VII*, 431 n. a.

19 See, e.g., Rivkin. *A Hidden Revolution*; Saldarini, *Pharisees, Scribes and Sadducees*, 83, 85–133. For an extended argument that Josephus is consistently negative about them. see Mason. *Flavius Josephus on the Pharisees.*

20 Leading exponents of this hypothesis are M. Smith, "Palestinian Judaism in the First Century," in *Israel: Its Role in Civilization*, ed. M. Davis (New York: Harper, 1956), 67–81; and J. Neusner in several publications. Examples are *From Politics to Piety*, 60–63 (specifically on our story); and "Josephus' Pharisees: A Complete Repertoire." in Feldman and Hata, *Josephus, Judaism, and Christianity*, 274–92. For a somewhat different understanding, see S. Schwartz, *Josephus and Judaean Politics*, CSCT 18 (Leiden: Brill, 1990). He finds that *Antiquities* "does not consistently propagandize for the Pharisees. Yet, despite the work's sloppiness and episodic character, it clearly is propagandistic, and its tendencies can be demonstrated with certainty because much of the work can be compared with its sources" (215). For Schwartz, the new leadership group supported by Josephus has much in common with the Pharisees though they are not called Pharisees; they appear to be the early rabbis (216). Another angle on the issue of the Pharisees in *War* and *Antiquities* has been expressed by D. Schwartz, who thinks that "[*Bellum Judaicum*] reflects Josephus' attempt to portray the Pharisees, incorrectly but safely, as uninvolved in politics and certainly as uninvolved in rebellion." In *Antiquities* and *Life*, which have the same viewpoint and were written after the revolt against Rome had receded farther into the past, "Josephus was less cautious and therefore much source material, which indicated Pharisaic involvement in politics and even in rebellion, found its way into these books" (Schwartz, "Josephus and Nicolaus on the Pharisees," 169).

21 The title reminds one of another epithet for the followers of the Scoffer: מליצי כזב (1QHᵃ X, 31; XII, 9–10).

22 Vermes's translation incorporates variants from the parallel material in CD XIX, 24–26. For an excellent study of these various titles for the same leader, see G. Jeremias, *Der Lehrer der Gerechtigkeit*, SUNT 2 (Göttingen: Vandenhoeck & Ruprecht, 1963), 79–126.

23 For Precept as an individual, see Jeremias, *Der Lehrer der Gerechtigkeit*, 97. L. Ginzberg understood him to be the Scoffer of CD I, 14 (*An Unknown Jewish Sect*, Moreshet Series 1 [New York: Ktav, 1970], 18).

24 For this view see, most recently, L. Schiffman, "The Pharisees and Their Legal Traditions according to the Dead Sea Scrolls," *DSD* 8 (2001): 268–69. Ginzberg (*An Unknown Jewish Sect*, 36) did not think this was an allusion to the hedge around the law, nor did he think the builders were Pharisees.

25 Obviously much care must be taken before drawing this conclusion, but it may be correct. Ginzberg (*An Unknown Jewish Sect*, 23–24) thought the teaching here was directed against the Pharisees.

26 B. Z. Wacholder, "A Qumran Attack on the Oral Exegesis? The Phrase 'šr btlmwd šqrm in 4 Q Pesher Nahum," *RevQ* 5 (1966): 576–77. See also Schiffman, "Pharisees and Their Legal Traditions," 266, 269.

28   For more detail see VanderKam, "Those Who Look for Smooth Things, Pharisees, and Oral Law," 469–77.

CHAPTER 9

1   For a summary of Pharisaic concerns before 70 CE, see chapter 11 in this volume.
2   For a full presentation of artifact as "solid metaphor," see C. Y. Tilley, *Metaphor and Material Culture* (Oxford: Blackwell, 1999).
3   This was the method of Samuel Krauss in *Talmudische Archäologie: Grundriss der Gesamtwissenschaft des Judentums*, 3 vols. (Leipzig, 1910–1912; repr., Hildesheim: G. Olms, 1966).
4   See the distribution map in J. Cahill, "Chalk Vessel Assemblages of the Persian/Hellenistic and Early Roman Periods," in *City of David Excavations, Final Report III*, ed. A. De Groot and D. T. Ariel, *Qedem* 33 (Jerusalem: Hebrew University Institute of Archaeology, 1992), 190–274. Of course, they also occur at Qumran, which suggests Essenes found them useful as well, but Hanan Eshel has demonstrated that the Qumran inhabitants believed that oil rendered stone vessels unclean. See H. Eshel, "CD 12:15–17 and the Stone Vessels Found at Qumran." http://orion.huji.ac.il/symposiums/3rd/papers/Eshel98.html (accessed Jan. 16, 2006).
5   Y. Magen (*The Stone Vessel Industry in Jerusalem during the Second Temple Period* [Jerusalem: Society for the Protection of Nature (Hebrew), 1988]), links stone vessels with the Pharisees. R. Deines (*Jüdische Steingefäße und pharisäische Frömmigkeit* [Tübingen: Mohr-Siebeck, 1923]), takes the position that these stone vessels are certainly Pharisaic, which remains unproven. For further analysis see Y. Magen, *The Stone Vessel Industry in the Second Temple Period: Excavations at Hizma and the Jerusalem Temple Mount* (Jerusalem: Israel Antiquities Authority, 2002); idem., "The Stone Vessel Industry during the Second Temple Period," in *Purity Broke out in Israel, catalogue no. 9, 7–28* (The Reuben and Edith Hecht Museum, University of Haifa, 1994); idem., "Jerusalem as a Center of the Stone Vessel Industry during the Second Temple Period," in *Ancient Jerusalem Revealed*, ed. H. Geva (Jerusalem: Israel Exploration Society; Washington, D.C.: Biblical Archaeology Society, 244–56).
6   L. Y. Rahmani, *A Catalogue of Jewish Ossuaries in the Collections of the State of Israel* (Jerusalem: Israel Antiquities Authority and the Israel Academy of Sciences and Humanities, 1994).
7   Magen, *Stone Vessel Industry in Jerusalem*, 94–103, 109.
8   The distribution of stone vessels from the north to the south of the country suggests that Pharisees are at the root of the custom, or that it is simply Jewish. We do not expect Essenes everywhere. For stone vessels at Qumran, see J. Magness, *The Archaeology of Qumran and the Dead Sea Scrolls* (Grand Rapids: Eerdmans, 2002), 211, 212, 213, 221.
9   Two of Cahill's bowl types ("Bowl Type I" [fig. 16:2–6] and "Bowl Type J" [fig. 16:7–16]) seem better interpreted as a cup.
10   Cahill, "Chalk Vessel Assemblages," 190–95.

11 S. Gutman and D. Wagner, "Gamla," in *Excavations and Surveys in Israel 1986*, vol. 5 of *Excavations and Surveys in Israel*, ed. A. Sussman and R. Greenberg (Jerusalem: Israel Antiquities Authority, 1987), 38–41.

12 Cahill, "Chalk Vessel Assemblages," 190–95, fig. 22. Four are shown in N. Avigad, *Discovering Jerusalem* (Nashville, Camden, New York: Thomas Nelson, 1983), 128, fig. 125.

13 R. Reich, "*Miqwa'ot* (Ritual Baths) at Qumran." *Qadmoniot* 114 (1997): 125–28. (Hebrew).

14 *m. Shek.* 8.2: "All utensils found in Jerusalem on the path down to the place of immersion must be deemed unclean; but [if they are found] on the path back they may be deemed clean; for the path by which they are taken down is not the same as that by which they are brought back." J. Neusner, *The Mishnah: A New Translation* (New Haven: Yale University Press, 1988), 264.

15 Sanders, *Judaism: Practice and Belief*, 226. A putative *otsar* at Jericho is visible in figure 5.

16 See *b. Ber.* 57b and *b. Ber.* 60b (when returning from a funeral or rising from sleep), *b. Ber.* 15a (before prayer), *b. Hul.* 105a (eating bread), *b. Hul.* 105a (before saying Grace), *b. Pesah.* 115a–b (before eating parsley on Passover).

17 A color plate of lavers found at Qumran appears in Y. Hirschfeld, *Qumran in Context: Reassessing the Archaeological Evidence* (Peabody, Mass.: Hendrickson, 2004).

18 Josephus, *Ant.* 18:14–18, *War* 2:163; Acts 23:1-11.

19 D. Ilan, "Burial Techniques," *OEANE* 1:384–86; R. Hachlili, "Funerary Customs and Art," chap. 4 in *Ancient Jewish Art and Archaeology in the Land of Israel* (Leiden, Brill, 1988); J. F. Strange, "The Art and Archaeology of Ancient Judaism," in *Judaism in Late Antiquity: The Literary and Archaeological Sources*, ed. J. Neusner (Leiden: Brill, 1995), 64–114.

20 A. Kloner, "Did a Rolling Stone Close Jesus' Tomb?" *BAR* 25 (1980): 3–29, 76.

21 See V. Fritz and R. Deines, "Catalogue of the Jewish Ossuaries in the German Protestant Institute for Archaeology," *IEJ* 49 (1999): 222–41. They follow Rachmani, *Catalogue of Jewish Ossuaries*, Appendix A, 53–55. Rachmani is in dialogue with E. M. Meyers, *Jewish Ossuaries: Reburial and Rebirth. Secondary Burials in their Ancient Near Eastern Setting* (Rome: Biblical Institute Press, 1971). R. Eyal argues that *ossolegium* reflects belief in individualism, not resurrection ("The Individualistic Meaning of Jewish Ossuaries: A Socio-Anthropological Perspective on Burial Practice," *PEQ* 133 [2001]: 39–49).

22 Clay ossuaries of the second and third centuries CE are also known in the Galilee; see M. Aviam and D. Syon, "Jewish Ossilegium in the Galilee," in *What Athens Has to Do with Jerusalem: Essays on Classical, Jewish, and Early Christian Art and Archaeology in Honor of Gideon Foerster*, ed. L. V. Rutgers, Interdisciplinary Studies in Ancient Culture and Religion 1 (Leuven: Peeters, 2002), 151–85.

23 Rachmani, *Catalogue of Jewish Ossuaries*, 20.

24   E. R. Goodenough, *Jewish Symbols in the Greco-Roman World*, abridged, ed. J. Neusner (Princeton: Princeton University Press, 1988); Rachmani, *Catalogue of Jewish Ossuaries*, 25–27.

25   Rachmani, *Catalogue of Jewish Ossuaries*, 28.

26   M. Hengel, "Proseuche und Synagogue: Jüdische Gemeinde, Gotteshaus und Gottesdienst in der Diaspora und in Palästina," in *The Synagogue: Study in Origins, Archaeology, and Architecture*, ed. J. Gutmann (New York: Ktav, 1975), 27–54.

27   Sanders, *Judaism*, 176, 450.

28   L. I. Levine, "The Nature and Origin of the Palestinian Synagogue Reconsidered," *JBL* 115 (1996): 425–48, and *The Ancient Synagogue: The First Thousand Years* (New Haven: Yale University Press, 2000). See chapter 13, "The Sages and the Synagogue," 440–70, where he recounts strong attachment to the synagogue among the sages, but mainly in the third century CE and later.

29   The plan of Capernaum in figure 5 is inferred from very limited data in the excavations of the Franciscans. See V. C. Corbo, "Resti della Sinagoga del Primo Secolo a Cafarnao," in *Studia Hierosolymitana in Onore di P. Bellarmino Bagatti*, Studium Biblicum Franciscanum, Collectio Maior III (1982), 314–57.

30   J. F. Strange, "Archaeology and Synagogues up to about 200 C.E.," in *Judaism and Christianity in the Beginning*, vol. 2 of Avery-Peck, Harrington, and Neusner, *When Judaism and Christianity Began*, 483–508.

31   J. F. Strange, "Ancient Texts, Archaeology as Text, and the Problem of the First Century Synagogue," in *The Evolution of the Synagogue*, ed. H. C. Kee and L. Cohick (Valley Forge: Trinity Press International, 1999), 27–45, and "The Synagogue as Metaphor," in *Judaism in Late Antiquity: Where We Stand* 4, ed. A. J. Avery-Peck and J. Neusner (Leiden: Brill, 2001), 91–120. The idea subsequently appeared in D. Binder, *Into the Temple Courts: The Place of the Synagogues in the Second Temple Period* (Atlanta: Society of Biblical Literature, 1999).

32   For the list of priestly courses see S. Klein, *Geographie und Geschichte Galiläas* (Leipzig: Rudolf Haupt, 1909). The list includes Yavnith, Meron, Sepphoris, Me'araia, Zefat, Selamen, Kefar Hanania, 'Arav (Gabara), 'Ailabon, Mamliah, Kefar Uziel, Migdal Nunia, Yodefat, Mafsheta, Kabul, Arbel, Bet Ma'on, Hammath, 'Ariah, Qana, Beth Lehem, 'Aithelu ('Ilut), and Nazareth. The possible exception is Qana, where the University of Puget Sound Excavations tentatively identify a structure as a second-century synagogue.

CHAPTER 10

1   In these respects, this chapter revisits those passages I analyzed three decades ago in J. Lightstone, "Sadducees versus Pharisees: The Tannaitic Sources," in *Christianity, Judaism, and Other Greco-Roman Cults: Studies for Morton Smith at Sixty: Judaism before 70*, ed. J. Neusner (Leiden: Brill, 1975), 3:206–17. In the thirty intervening years, we have learned far more about the literary

and rhetorical traits and the topical agendas of the documents in which these passages are found. It is in that light that this chapter revisits these same passages, while at the same time rehearsing the analyses undertaken thirty years ago.

2   This statement holds whether one favors (as I do) Neusner's view of the Tosefta (J. Neusner, *Tosefta: Its Structure and Its Sources* [Atlanta: Scholars Press, 1986]; *The Bavli that Might Have Been: The Tosefta's Theory of Mishnah Commentary Compared to the Bavli's* [Atlanta: Scholars Press, 1991]), which sees the Tosefta's composition and the formulation of much of its passages as dependent on the Mishnah; or Goldberg's view (A. Goldberg, "The Tosefta—the Companion to the Mishna," in *The Literature of the Sages, First Part: Oral Tora, Halakha, Mishnah, Tosefta, Talmud, External Tractates, Compendium Rerum Iudaicarum ad Novum Testamentum, Section 2.3*, ed. S. Safrai [Assen/Maastricht: Van Gorcum; Philadelphia: Fortress, 1987], 283–301), which sees the Tosefta as a "companion" collection of para-Mishnaic sources; or Friedman's or Hauptman's views (cf. S. Friedman, "The Primacy of Tosefta to Mishnah in Synoptic Parallels," in *Introducing Tosefta: Intertextual, Intratextual Studies*, ed. H. Fox, T. Meacham, and D. Kriger [Hoboken, N.J.: Ktav, 1999], 1–37; J. Hauptman, "Mishnah as a Response to Tosefta," in *The Synoptic Problem in Rabbinic Literature*, ed. S. J. D. Cohen, BJS [Providence, R.I.: Brown Judaic Studies, 2000]; J. Hauptman, *Rereading the Mishnah: A New Approach to Ancient Jewish Texts* [Tübingen: Mohr-Siebeck, 2005]) which argue that (some) Toseftan passages can be shown to be the very basis for, and source of, the Mishnah's treatment of the topic. For my own analysis of the relationship between the Tosefta and the Mishnah, see J. Lightstone, with an appendix by V. K. Robbins, *Mishnah and the Social Formation of the Early Rabbinic Guild: A Socio-Rhetorical Approach* (Waterloo, Ont.: Wilfrid Laurier University Press, 2002).

3   Why do I qualify "tannaitic" with the modifier "so-called?" I do so because the term has become ambiguous in my mind. It usually is taken to mean that the source so described comes from authorities who predate the production of the Mishnah. This meaning stems from the fact that these sources use attributions to named rabbinic figures who flourished in the second century CE or earlier. But clearly many of these sources are patently postmishnaic, since many of these passages can be shown to be dependent on Mishnaic pericopes as currently formulated in situ in the Mishnah. Clearly, then, the term "tannaitic" more accurately describes a "family" of texts and sources with certain literary traits—e.g., the traits of Toseftan passages and similarly formulated *beraitot* in the Palestinian and Babylonian Talmuds, the traits of the halakhic midrashim, and again, those *beraitot* in the Talmuds exhibiting these same literary traits. In short, tannaitic is problematic and equivocal (in the literal sense of the word); it can and does mean more than one thing, and these differences in meaning are crucial to the argument at hand.

4   This particular cautionary stance is foundational to J. Neusner's studies in the early 1970s of rabbinic traditions attributed to named rabbinic authorities—at least all such studies following, but not including, his *Life of Rabbi*

Yohanan ben Zakkai (Leiden: Brill, 1968). Neusner first propounded this stance in *Development of a Legend* (Leiden: Brill, 1970), which essentially repudiates forcefully the *Life*. As for my own personal scholarly experience, the general methodological stance articulated in the preceding paragraph has been consistently confirmed, beginning with "Sadoq the Yavnean," in *Persons and Institutions in Early Rabbinic Judaism* 1, ed. W. S. Green (Missoula, Mont.: Scholars Press, 1977), and *Yosé the Galilean: Traditions in Mishnah-Tosefta* (Leiden: Brill, 1979), through my more recent studies in *The Rhetoric of the Babylonian Talmud: Its Social Meaning and Context* (Waterloo, Ont.: Wilfrid Laurier University Press, 1994), and *Mishnah and Social Formation*. But let me be clear; trends and probabilities (the foundation of empirically founded methodologies) do not imply universality; there will always be counterexamples to trends in the evidence. See, for example, the studies of J. Hauptman and S. Friedman referred to above in note 2.

5   See essays in *Religious Rivalries and the Struggle for Success in Caesarea Maritima*, ed. T. Donaldson (Waterloo, Ont.: Wilfrid Laurier University Press, 2000); in *Religious Rivalries and the Struggle for Success in Sardis and Smyrna*, ed. R. Ascough (Waterloo, Ont.: Wilfrid Laurier University Press, 2005); and in *Religious Rivalries in the Early Roman Empire and the Rise of Christianity*, ed. L. E. Vaage (Waterloo, Ont.: Wilfrid Laurier University Press, 2006). As to contributions to this seminar, see my own "My Rival, My Fellow: Prolegomena to the Study of Rivalry and Cooperation among Religious Groups in the Galilee of Late Antiquity," in Vaage, *Religious Rivalries in the Early Roman Empire*, and "Urbanization in the Roman Levant and the Inter-religious Struggle for Success," in *Religious Rivalries and the Struggle for Success in Sardis and Smyrna*.

6   Consequently, it is predictable that in moments of perceived social vulnerability, we will expend significant creative energies arguing that we and they are not so different at all, even while at other times the very differences are stressed. Take, for example, the Letter of Aristeas's apology for Judaism or Judean society and culture; the author takes significant pains to argue that what is most characteristic of Judaic/Judean culture corresponds with that which is most valued in Hellenistic culture. Or consider, for that matter, the remarks of Tertullian (*Apol.* 42):

> [We Christians] live with you, enjoy the same food, have the same manner of life, and dress, the same requirements for life. . . . We cannot dwell together in the world without the marketplace, without butchers, without your baths, shops, factories, taverns, fairs, and other places of business. We sail in ships with you, serve in the army, till the ground, engage in trade as you do; we provide skills and services to the public for your benefit. (Trans. R. M. Grant, "The Social Setting of Second Century Christianity," in *Jewish and Christian Self-Definition*, vol. 1, *The Shaping of Christianity in the Second and Third Centuries*, ed. E. P. Sanders [Philadelphia: Fortress, 1980], 28)

Tertullian chooses to defend Christians, not by defending their distinctiveness, but rather by providing a list of shared aspects of civic life, which necessitate a highly shared framework of social norms and institutions that is highly shared with non-Christians.

7   See Rivkin, "Who Were the Pharisees?" in Neusner and Avery-Peck, *Judaism in Late Antiquity: Where We Stand*, 3:1–34.

8   See Neusner, *Judaism: The Evidence of the Mishnah*; on the literary-rhetorical traits of the Mishnah and comparisons of the same with the Tosefta, see Lightstone, *Mishnah and Social Formation*, chaps. 2 and 3.

9   On the literary nature of the composition of the Mishnah's "chapters," or "intermediate units" as Neusner calls them (because they do not necessarily coincide with the classical chapter divisions of Mishnah), see Neusner, *Judaism: The Evidence of the Mishnah*. Neusner based his conclusions at the time primarily on his work on the Mishnaic Division of Purities and the Mishnaic Division of Holy Things (cf. J. Neusner, *A History of the Mishnaic Law of Purities* 21 [Leiden: Brill, 1977], and J. Neusner, *A History of the Mishnaic Law of Holy Things* 3 [Leiden: Brill, 1979]. On the rhetorical-literary use of repetition, concatenation, and permutation of phrases and terms to "spin out" the "shank" of a Mishnah "chapter," see also Lightstone, *Mishnah and Social Formation*, chap. 2. See also W. S. Green, "Reading the Writing of Rabbinism," *JAAR* 51 (1983): 191–207. For a different view, see D. Zlotnick, *The Iron Pillar—Mishnah* (Jerusalem: Mosad Bialik, 1988).

10   See W. S. Green, "What's in a Name? The Question of Rabbinic Biography," in *Approaches to the Study of Ancient Judaism*, vol. 1, ed. W. S. Green (Missoula, Mont.: Scholars Press, 1979), 77–94.

11   As noted in Lightstone, "Sadducees versus Pharisees," 207 n. 1, E. Rivkin lists eight such pericopes ("Defining the Pharisees"). He includes *m. Yad.* 4:8, which refers in the standard printed edition to a "Galilean Sadducee"; however, the Parma, Kaufman, Lowe (Cambridge), Munich, and Naples MSS all read "a Galilean sectarian" (*myn glyly*). On this basis, we have excluded this pericope from consideration. It is likely that some scribe or printer has imported "Sadducee" at *m. Yad.* 4:8 from 4:6, where the term appears (in the pl.) in the major m. MSS as well as the standard printed edition.

12   See, for example, Rivkin, "Defining the Pharisees." In the analyses that follow of the passages at *m. Yad.* 4:6–4:7 and of their complementary passages in Tosefta, I have noted the oft-mentioned parallels to 4:6 and 4:7a in the Qumran texts 4QMMT. With respect to *m.* 4:6, see lines 24–35 and 43–44 of the composite text of 4QMMT produced by Strugnell and Qimron in F. G. Martinez, *The Dead Sea Scrolls Translated*, 2nd ed. (Leiden: Brill, 1996), 77–79. As regards *m.* 4:7a, see 4QMMT lines 57–61 of the same composite text.

    The question of what the 4QMMT parallels reveal about *m.* 4:6–4:7 or vice versa has been much discussed. It is facile to assume that the legal positions expressed in 4QMMT must be normative Sadducean views, that their opposite is Pharisaic, and, therefore, that when the Mishnah's laws oppose 4QMMT's, the Mishnah has preserved genuine premishnaic Pharisaic traditions. The analyses that follow demonstrate the complex literary, rhetorical, and redactional processes that have created the Mishnah texts in question. More than anything, then, these rabbinic passages reflect the work of the late second-century intrarabbinic processes that produced the Mishnah. What 4QMMT does indicate, however, is that the issues taken up at *m.* 4:6 and 4:7a specifically were not exclusively rabbinic preoccupations at the end of the second century. Others discussed them, and this substantially earlier than the end of the second century. See J. Baumgarten, "The 'Halakha' in Miqsat Ma'ase ha-Torah," *JAOS* 16, no. 3 (1966): 512–16; D. R. Schwartz, "MMT, Josephus, and the Pharisees," in *Reading QMMT: New Perspectives on Qumran Law and History*, ed. J. Kampen and M. J. Bernstein, SBLSS 2 (Atlanta: Scholars Press, 1996), 67–80; Y. Elman, "Some Remarks on 4QMMT and Rabbinic Tradition, or, When is a Parallel Not a Parallel?" in Kampen and Bernstein, *Reading 4QMMT*, 99–127; E. Regev, "Were the Priests all the Same? Qumran Halakhah in Comparison with Sadducean Halakhah," *DSD* 12, no. 2 (2005): 158–82.

13   Translations are my own, unless otherwise indicated. The translation of those in which both "Pharisees" and "Sadducees" are mentioned are based on my previous translations of these passages in Lightstone, "Sadducees versus Pharisees."

14   See discussions of this "narrative" in T. Zahavy, *The Traditions of Eleazar ben Azariah* (Missoula, Mont: Scholars Press, 1977), and R. Goldenberg, "The Deposition of Rabban Gamaliel II," in Green, *Persons and Institutions in Early Rabbinic Judaism* 1.

15   In passing, it is worth noting that what I have called a contrived narrative "riding the coattails" of a clause at *m.* 3:5b F ("on that day [בוֹ] that they seated Rabbi Eleazar ben Azariah in the Academy [as its president]") provided the core evidence for an alleged rabbinic "canonical council" at Yavneh, which fixed the rabbinic biblical canon of Scriptures; see J. Lightstone, "The Rabbis' Bible: The Canon of the Hebrew Bible and the Early Rabbinic Guild," in *The Canon Debate: On the Origins and Formation of the Bible*, ed. L. M. McDonald and J. Sanders (Peabody, Mass.: Hendrickson, 2002); and J. Lightstone, "The Formation of the Biblical Canon in Late Antique Judaism," *SR* 8, no. 2 (1979): 135–42.

16   Sometimes these underlying general legal principles are explicitly articulated, either as a "preface" to the "chapter," which then explores their porté under different hypothetical sets of circumstances; sometimes these principles are expressly presented as a "conclusion" to a composition (introduced by the formulary "this is the [general] principle [זה הכלל]").

17   See Lightstone, *Mishnah and Social Formation*, chap. 2; Neusner, *Judaism: The Evidence of the Mishnah*.

18   Indeed, parts of *m.* 4:1ff. appear elsewhere in the Mishnah, where in language and content they fit well. See, for example, *m. Kelim* 20:2 and *m. Zevahim* 1:1.

19   See Neusner, *Judaism: The Evidence of the Mishnah*; see also Lightstone, *Mishnah and Social Formation*, 33–78.

20   In this respect, I rely heavily on my previous work on the topic; see Lightstone, "Sadducees versus Pharisees."

21   See also *m. Toharot* 1:4 and *m. Hullin* 9:1.

22   Witness the fact that the traditional rabbinic commentaries make no effort to base the uncleanness of Scriptures on rabbinic purity law.

23   It stretches credulity to say that *m.* 4:6A provides an example of Pharisaic law based on extrabiblical tradition and is rejected for that very reason by *m.* 4:6's Sadducees—especially so since the Pharisaic position here does not interconnect with any discernable extrabiblical system of purity law.

24   As noted by classical rabbinic commentators, such as R. Ovadyah of Bertinoro, who points to Leviticus 11:36.

25   H. Albeck (*Shishah Sidré Mishnah, Toharot* [Jerusalem: Mosad Bialik, 1952], 609) notes that Hellenistic law typically holds masters responsible for damage done to another's property by their slaves. But one could not reasonably conclude from *m.* 4:7b that Sadducees are Hellenizers in comparison with the Pharisees (or early rabbis). Indeed, there is so much evidence that early rabbinic law—with respect to the Pharisaic law per se, we cannot say—was influenced by Hellenistic and Roman law that any characterization of Sadducees as, comparatively speaking, "legal Hellenizers" on the basis of this evidence would be ludicrous.

26   The meaning of מעבירים is a matter of considerable disagreement, as documented by the endnotes in H. Albeck, *Shishah Sidré Mishnah, Mo'ed* (Jerusalem: Mosad Bialik, 1952), 515. My own translation reflects the rendering of Rashi and of Ovadyah of Bertinoro, but I am in no sense married to this rendering or any other; simply put, *m. Hag* 3:8 is not my focus, and *t. Hag.* 3:35b is.

27   By contrast, *t. Hag.* 3:35b's "precedent narrative" is a complete non sequitur if read in the context of *t.* 3:35a. *T.* 3:35a deals with a *haver* who purchases utensils and dishes from, or transmits them for repair to, an artisan who is an *am ha'aretz*. For the Mishnah and Tosefta, one core operative distinction between the former and the latter is that a *haver* is one who takes upon oneself the obligation of observing outside the Temple cult certain laws of uncleanness normally in force while participating in that cult; the *am ha'aretz* observes these laws only when participating in Temple rites. Our precedent story clearly deals with matters taking place within the Temple, where the distinction between the *haver* and *am ha'aretz* as normally projected by the Mishnah and Tosefta have no relevance.

28   There is some question as to whether the reference to the menorah is a later accretion to *m. Hag.* 3:8C. For example, Yom-Tov Heller (Tosafot Yom Tov) maintains just this stance citing the Babylonian Talmud's discussion (*ad locum*) of *m.* 3:8 as probative evidence. Since *t. Hag* 3:35b is my focus, not *m. Hag.* 3:8, I shall not enter this debate other than to say that if "menorah" is a later accretion to *m. Hag* 3:8C, *t. Hag* 3:35's reference to the menorah may have provided some impetus for the interpolation in M.

29   J. Gereboff discusses many of the traits of early rabbinic precedent stories in "When to Speak, How to Speak, and When Not to Speak: Answers from Early Rabbinic Stories," *Semeia* 34 (1985); see also my own commentary on Gereboff's study in Lightstone, "When Speech is No Speech: The Problem of Early Rabbinic Rhetoric as Discourse," also in *Semeia* 34 (1985).

30 S. Lieberman makes an effort to provide some legal rationale for the
    Sadducean and Pharisaic legal differences underlying *t. Hag.* 3:35b by draw-
    ing attention to the *Hasdei David*'s claim that the Sadducees did not share the
    rabbinic (and presumed Pharisaic) view that contact with liquids rendered
    objects (more) susceptible to uncleanness. However, Lieberman seems to fall
    short of endorsing this explanation. See S. Lieberman, *Tosefta Mo'ed* (New
    York: Jewish Theological Seminary of America, 1962), 394.

31 For the edification of the reader, the two Toseftan passages presented syn-
    optically with their parallels in the Babylonian Talmud are found in the
    appendix.

32 See above at note 1. Here I both rehearse and go beyond my previously
    published conclusions.

33 I cannot agree with E. Rivkin's assertions in "Defining the Pharisees,"
    where he claims on the basis of these passages that each group evinces a dis-
    tinctive "approach to the Law" (212) or that these passages give indication
    that the parties' conflict "involved a basic irreconcilable principled conflict
    over the Law" leading the Sadducees to reject the Pharisees' "halakah sys-
    tem" (216). Yes, the texts in hand portray "irreconcilable . . . conflict" over
    specific laws. But the Mishnah and Tosefta also portray individual rabbinic
    authorities as having equally irreconcilable conflicts over specific laws. The
    legal differences between Sadducees and Pharisees on specific laws do not
    seem to be of a qualitatively different order. What is different is the rheto-
    ric of the Pharisees versus Sadducees passages; this rhetoric attempts to por-
    tray a conflictual relationship and engagement in mutual vilification, for
    which differences over specific laws provide the occasion. But I do not get
    the impression that Rivkin's assertions are so qualified. Presently, in the
    body of my discussion, I will return to the matter of rhetorical and literary
    traits.

34 Albeck, *Shishah Sidré Mishnah, Toharot,* 486.

35 J. Neusner has conclusively demonstrated this with respect to the Mishnah;
    see, for example, his *Judaism: The Evidence of the Mishnah;* see also Lightstone,
    Mishnah and Social Formation.

36 On whether the Tosefta at various junctures preserves some of the
    Mishnah's source materials, see above at note 2.

37 These are "those who immerse themselves at daybreak" in *t. Yad.* 2:20b,
    which passage is rhetorically modeled on *t. Yad* 2:20, analyzed above in this
    chapter. Elsewhere in M. and T., Pharisees appear in relation to "*am
    ha'aretz*" (the Jewish *pagani,* as it were), on the one hand, and "those who eat
    heave offering" (priests and their households), on the other. But Pharisees
    are not portrayed as in dispute or in confrontation with these groups.
    Rather, these passages are rabbinic attempts at "classification"; the
    Pharisees' practices with respect to purity define them as a legal category
    with respect to uncleanness somewhere in between the *am ha'aretz* and
    "those who eat heave offering." See *m. Hag.* 2:7.

38 I will not discuss here the machinations leading up to and during the
    Hasmonean dynasty, during which period the Saddokite clan's hegemony
    was challenged and usurped.

CHAPTER 11

1   See the following titles of mine for the texts referred to in this and the following chapters: *Rabbinic Traditions about the Pharisees; Formative Judaism: Religious, Historical, and Literary Studies, 3rd s., Torah, Pharisees, and Rabbis* (Chico, Calif.: Scholars Press for BJS, 1983); *The Pharisees: Rabbinic Perspectives, Reprise of Rabbinic Traditions about the Pharisees before 70*, 1–3 (New York: Ktav, 1985); as editor with W. S. Green, *The Origins of Judaism: Religion, History, and Literature in Late Antiquity* (New York: Garland Press, 1991). On the relationship between Pharisaism before 70 CE and rabbinic Judaism after 70 CE, see my *Eliezer ben Hyrcanus: The Tradition and the Man*, 2 vols. (Leiden: Brill, 1973; reprint, Eugene, Ore: Wipf & Stock, 2003).

2   Paul was educated under Gamaliel, according to Acts 22:3, but he does not state that Gamaliel was a Pharisee. In Acts 5:34 Luke, the author of Acts, speaks in his narrative of "a Pharisee named Gamaliel." On that basis I assume Gamaliel was a Pharisee.

CHAPTER 12

1   For debates on the matters covered in this chapter, see chapters 14 and 15. The matters are further spelled out in my contributions to the series *South Florida Studies in the History of Judaism* (Atlanta: Scholars Press): *Judaic Law; Are There Really Tannaitic Parallels to the Gospels? A Refutation of Morton Smith* (1993); *Why There Never Was a "Talmud of Caesarea": Saul Lieberman's Mistakes* (1994); *The Documentary Foundation of Rabbinic Culture: Mopping Up after Debates with Gerald L. Bruns, S. J. D. Cohen, Arnold Maria Goldberg. Susan Handelman, Christine Hayes, James Kugel, Peter Schaefer, Eliezer Segal, E. P. Sanders, and Lawrence H. Schiffman* (1995). These titles are now issued by University Press of America, Lanham, Md.

2   M. Smith, "The Dead Sea Sect in Relation to Ancient Judaism," *NTS* 7 (1961): 347–60.

3   Smith, "Dead Sea Sect," 353.

4   Smith, "Dead Sea Sect."

CHAPTER 13

1   That judgment must be modified, however, by the analysis of the traditions attributed to Eliezer b. Hyrcanus. See my *Eliezer b. Hyrcanus: The Tradition and the Man*.

2   See my *History of the Jews in Babylonia*, vol. 1, *The Parthian Period* (Leiden: Brill, 1965), 122–30.

CHAPTER 14

1   Catholic scholars during this period did not engage in historical study of antiquity. One exception would be J. Langen (*Das Judenthum in Palästina zur Zeit Christi* [Freiburg im Breisgau: Herder Verlag, 1866]), who criticized Geiger's study of the Pharisees and Sadducees as "silliness." Langen rejected the Talmud as a primary source, claiming it was too late to be use-

ful, and wrote that Jewish historians such as Geiger make use of the Talmud out of their "partiality" for Talmudic tradition.

2   Saldarini, "Pharisees," *ABD* 5:290.

3   G. Volkmar, *Die Religion Jesu* (Leipzig: F. A. Brockhaus, 1857), 60.

4   M. Wirth, *Die Pharisäer: Ein Beitrag zum leichtern Verstehen der Evangelien und zur Selbstprüfung* (Ulm: Stetten, 1824), iii; Langen, *Das Judenthum in Palästina*, 189; Anon., "Pharisäer," in G. B. Winer, *Biblische Realwörterbuch zum Handgebrauch für Studirende, Candidaten, Gymnasiallehrer und Prediger* 2 (Leipzig: Carl Heinrich Reclam, 1847, 1848), 2:244–48; C. F. von Ammon, *Die Geschichte des Leben Jesu: Mit stetiger Rücksicht auf die vorhandenen Quellen* (Leipzig: Vogel, 1842–1847), 1:225; E. Renan, *The Life of Jesus*, trans. C. E. Wilbour (New York: Carleton, 1864), 299.

5   Wirth, *Die Pharisäer*, 25.

6   Wirth, *Die Pharisäer*, iii.

7   "Heuchelei," "Ehrsucht," and "Pharisäer," in Winer, *Biblische Reclwörterbuch;* citation from von Ammon, *Die Geschichte des Leben Jesu*, 225.

8   J. S. Ersch and J. G. Gruber, *Allgemeine Encyklopädie* (Leipzig: J. F. Gleditsch, 1846).

9   A. Neander, *Geschichte der Pflanzung und Leitung der christlichen Kirche durch die Apostel*, 2 vols. (Hamburg: F. Perthes, 1832–1833); M. Schneckenburger, *Beiträge zur Einleitung ins Neue Testament und zur Erklärung seiner schwierigen Stellen* (Stuttgart: F. C. Löflund & Sohn, 1832); A. Gfrörer, *Das Jahrhundert des Heils*, 2 vols. (Stuttgart: E. Schweizerbart, 1838).

10 Neander, *Geschichte*, 2:529.

11 M. Schneckenburger, *Beiträge zur Einleitung ins Neue Testament und zur Erklärung seiner schwierigen Stellen* (Stuttgart: F. C. Löflund & Sohn, 1832), 69–75, 86–91. See also his *Vorlesungen über neutestamentliche Zeitgeschichte: aus dessen handschriftlichem Nachlass*, ed. T. Loehlein (Frankfurt: H. L. Brönner, 1862).

12 Gfrörer's views exerted negligible influence among Christian and Jewish theologians in his day, but he has been credited by more recent historians with presenting a sympathetic portrayal of tannaitic beliefs. See G. F. Moore, "Christian Writers on Judaism," *HTR* 14, no. 3 (1921): 197–254; and K. Hoheisel, *Das antike Judentum in christlicher Sicht* (Wiesbaden: Harrassowitz, 1978), 10–11.

13 I. M. Jost, *Geschichte der Israeliten* (Berlin, 1820–1828), pt. 2, 1:55–57.

14 Jost, *Geschichte der Israeliten*, 1:57.

15 Levi Herzfeld, *Geschichte des Volkes Israel von der Zerstörung des ersten Tempels bis zur Einsetzung des Makkabäers Schimon zum hohen Priester und Fürsten* (Braunschweig: G. Westermann, 1847–1857), 2:54, 57.

16 Moore, "Christian Writers on Judaism," 222–28.

17 H.-G. Waubke, *Die Pharisäer in der protestantischen Bibelwissenschaft des 19. Jahrhunderts*, Beiträge zur historischen Theologie 107, ed. J. Wallmann (Tübingen: Mohr-Siebeck, 1998), 58.

18 Gfrörer, *Das Jahrhundert des Heils*, 1:194–214.

19 Gfrörer, *Das Jahrhundert des Heils*, 2:167.

20 Gfrörer, *Das Jahrhundert des Heils*, 1:121.

21 Gfrörer, *Das Jahrhundert des Heils*, 1:132.

22   A. Geiger, *Urschrift und Übersetzungen der Bibel in ihrer Abhängigkeit von der innern Entwickelung des Judenthums* (Breslau: Julius Heinauer, 1857; 2nd ed., Frankfurt am Main: Verlag Madda, 1928), 149–50. The second edition was published with an introduction by P. Kahle, a postcript by N. Czortkowski, and a Hebrew essay by Geiger, reprinted from *Ozer Nechmad* 3 (1860): 1–15, 115–21, 125–28; in Hebrew translation, *Ha-Mikra v'Targumav*, trans. Y. L. Brukh (Jerusalem: Bialik Foundation, 1949; repr. 1972).

23   Geiger's theory is set forth in the *Urschrift*, especially on pages 150ff., 176ff., 423ff., 434ff.; also *JZWL* 1:19–39; 2:88–112; 8:278–91; and L. Geiger, ed., *Nachgelassene Schriften* (Berlin: L. Gerschel, 1875–1885), 2:121; 5:112–16, 118–20, 142–65.

24   Geiger, "Die Levirats-Ehe, ihre Entstehung und Entwickelung," *JZWL* 1 (1862): 19–39; "Neuere Mitteilungen über die Samaritaner," *ZDMG* 16 (1862): 714–28; "Sadducäer und Pharisäer," *JZWL* 2 (1862): 11–54; "Die Testamente der zwölf Patriarchen," *JZWL* 9 (1871): 123–25.

25   Geiger, "Die wissenschaftliche Ausbildung des Judenthums in den zwei ersten Jahrhundeten des zweiten Jahrtausends bis zum Auftreten des Maimonides," *WZJT* 1 (1835): 13–38, esp. 35; "Karäische Literatur," *WZJT* 2 (1836): 93–125; see also S. Posnanski, "Geschichte der Sekten und der Halacha," in *Abraham Geiger: Leben und Lebenswerk*, ed. L. Geiger (Berlin: Georg Reimer, 1910), 352–87.

26   Geiger, *Urschrift*, 35.

27   Geiger, *Urschrift*, 223. This particular statement of Geiger's gained widespread attention. Critics who opposed his interpretation of Pharisaism as a liberalization, in contrast to the Sadducees, argued that 2 Maccabees 2:17 describes not Pharisaism, but Israel's position vis-à-vis the heathen world. See Johann Wilhelm Hanne, "Die Pharisäer und Sadducäer als politische Parteien," *ZWT* 10 (1867): 239–63.

28   Geiger, "Sadducäer und Pharisäer," 41.

29   T. Keim, *The History of Jesus of Nazara*, trans. A. Ransom and E. Geldart (London: Williams & Norgate, 1876–1883), 1:342.

30   D. Schenkel, *The Character of Jesus Portrayed*, trans. W. H. Furness (Boston: Little, Brown, 1866), 2:6.

31   Schenkel, *Character of Jesus Portrayed*, 1:42.

32   Schenkel, *Character of Jesus Portrayed*, 2:9–10.

33   Schenkel, *Character of Jesus Portrayed*, 2:10.

34   Adolf Hausrath published several review essays in the *Protestantische Kirchenzeitung* presenting the results of Geiger's research and urging Christian scholars to read Geiger's work: A. Hausrath, "Die Resultate der jüdischen Forschung über Pharisäer und Saddukäer," *PKZ* 44 (1862): 967–78; "Jüdische Zeitschrift für Wissenschaft und Leben," *PKZ* 3 (1869): 88; "Jüdische Zeitschrift für Wissenschaft und Leben," *PKZ* 33 (1869): 781–82; "Jüdische Zeitschrift für Wissenschaft und Leben," *PKZ* 44 (1870): 983–84; [Anon.], "Abraham Geiger: Wissenschaft des Judenthums," *PKZ* 51 (1875): 1184–88.

35   A. Hausrath, *Neutestamentliche Zeitgeschichte* 1: *Die Zeit Jesu* (Munich, 1868), 145.

36   A. Geiger, "Innere Geschichte der zweiten Tempelperiode und deren Behandlung," *JZWL* 6 (1868): 253.
37   Letter from Geiger to Derenbourg, April 10, 1872, *JZWL* 10 (1872): 156–57.
38   Geiger to Derenbourg.
39   H. Graetz, *Geschichte der Juden von den ältesten Zeiten bis auf die Gegenwart*, vol. 4 first published in 1853, followed by vol. 3 in 1856; 2nd eds.: vol. 3 (Leipzig: Leiner, 1863), vol. 4 (Leipzig: Leiner 1866). See Graetz's review of Geiger's *Urschrift* in Anon., "Der jerusalemische Talmud im Lichte Geigerscher Hypothesen," *Monatsschrift für die Wissenschaft des Judentums* 20 (1871): 120–37. See Geiger's reviews of Graetz's *Geschichte der Juden* in *JZWL* 1 (1862): 68–75; *JZWL* 2 (1864): 290–91; *JZWL* 4 (1866): 145–50; *JZWL* 6 (1868): 220–22.
40   Deines, *Die Pharisäer*, 179.
41   Deines, *Die Pharisäer*, 181.
42   Graetz, *Geschichte der Juden*, 3:690.
43   A. Geiger, "Proben neuerer hebräischer Sprachgelehrsamkeit," *JZWL* 2 (1863): 230–31.
44   H. Ewald, *Geschichte des Volkes Israel* (Göttingen: Dieterischen Buchhandlung, 1864), 5:477, n. 1.
45   H. Ewald, letter to August Dillmann, 1872; cited by Waubke, *Die Pharisäer*, 219 n. 181.
46   For a discussion of F. Delitsch's responses to Geiger, see S. Heschel, *Abraham Geiger and the Jewish Jesus* (Chicago: University of Chicago Press, 1998), chap. 7.
47   J. Derenbourg, *Essai sur l'Histoire et la Geographie de la Palestine, d'apres les Thalmuds et les autres sources rabbiniques* (Paris: A l'imprimerie imperiale, 1867). Derenbourg changed a few details, making the Pharisaic struggle against the Sadducees primarily a religious conflict, without social and political components. For more on Derenbourg's career in France, and his scholarly dependence on Geiger's work, see P. Simon-Nahum, *Le cite investie: La Science du Judaisme francais et la Republique* (Paris: Les editions du Cerf, 1991). 99–108. K. Kohler, "Christianity in Its Relation to Judaism," 4:49–59; "Essenes," 5:224–32; "Jesus in Theology," 7:166–70; "Karaism," 7:446–47; "New Testament," 9:246–54; "Pharisees," 9:661–66; "Sadducees," 10:630–33; "Saul of Tarsus," 11:79–87, all in *Jewish Encyclopedia*, ed. I. Singer (New York: Funk & Wagnalls, 1902); D. Chwolson, *Das letzte Passahmahl Christi und der Tag seines Todes nach den in Übereinstimmung gebrachten Berichten der Synoptiker und des Evangelium Johannis* (St. Petersburg: M. Eggers, 1892); idem., *Beiträge zur Entwicklungsgeschichte des Judentums* (Leipzig: H. Haessel, 1910).
48   J. Wellhausen wrote in the foreword, "Ich habe mich hierüber, angeregt durch Geiger's Urschrift und Übersetzungen der Bibel, im Eingange meiner Arbeit ausgesprochen," *Der Text der Bücher Samuelis* (Göttingen: Vandenhoeck & Ruprecht, 1871), iii. Wellhausen goes on to agree with Geiger that deviations within the Masoretic text from orthographic rules are too numerous and too important to be viewed simply as scribal errors, but argues that seeing as many and as profound tendentious changes in the biblical text as

Geiger claims is exaggerated; see 29–33. Wellhausen concedes that Geiger is correct, for example, in seeing the animosity of the Pharisees toward the Sadducees in 1 Samuel 2:22; see 30. See Geiger's review, *JZWL* 10 (1872): 84–103.

49 There is a discrepancy about the date of the lectures. Wellhausen himself writes in the preface to *Die Pharisäer und die Sadducäer* that the lectures were held during the winter semester, 1871–1872, but records at the University of Greifswald indicate that the lectures were held on Saturdays from noon to one o'clock during the summer semester, 1873: University of Greifswald Archives, Hgb. 39 Bd. 29. Wellhausen's lectures were entitled "Über die jüdischen Parteien zur Zeit Christi." See also A. Jepsen, "Wellhausen in Greifswald: Ein Beitrag zur Biographie Julius Wellhausens," in *Festschrift zur 500-Jahrfeier der Universität Greifswald*, Festschrift zur 500-Jahresfeier der Universität Greifswald (Greifswald, 1956), 2:47–56; esp. 49.

50 J. Wellhausen, *Die Pharisäer und die Sadducäer: Eine Untersuchung zu inneren jüdischen Geschichte* (Greifswald: Bamberg, 1874; 2nd ed., Hannover: Orient-Buchhandlung H. Lafaire, 1924; 3rd ed., Göttingen: Vandenhoeck & Ruprecht, 1967).

51 The harsh tone Wellhausen adopted toward Geiger's work is not in itself significant, since it can be found in all of his criticisms of fellow scholars; Wellhausen seems to have been bombastic even when the difference in question was minor, as in his argument of the 1890s with Eduard Meyer. Wellhausen refers in his critique not only to Geiger, but to Christian scholars who had adopted his arguments, particularly Hausrath; Wellhausen writes concerning Hausrath, "Es ist eine übertriebene Bescheidenheit wenn Hausrath, weil er das Ganze nicht beherrscht, nur auch nicht wagt, sich über das Einzelne eine eigene Meinung zu bilden, sondern in Bausch und Bogen selbst einen Graetz als Quelle verwerthet," *Die Pharisäer und die Sadducäer*, 123. See C. Hoffmann, *Juden und Judentum im Werk deutscher Althistoriker des 19. und 20. Jahrhunderts* (Leiden: Brill, 1988), 159–65.

52 Wellhausen, *Die Pharisäer und die Sadducäer*, 17.

53 Wellhausen, *Die Pharisäer und die Sadducäer*, 21.

54 Waubke argues that Wellhausen is here following the lead of Heinrich Ewald; see *Die Pharisäer und die Sadducäer*, 181.

55 Nachlass Theodor Nöldeke, UB Tübingen, Md782-B 280; cited by C. Wiese, "Ein 'Schrei ins Leere'? Die Auseinandersetzung der Wissenschaft des Judentums mit dem Judentumsbild der protestantischen Theologie im Kontext der Diskussion über die Stellung der jüdischen Gemeinschaft im wilhelminischen Deutschland 1890–1914." Ph.D. diss., Faculty of Protestant Theology, Goethe University, Frankfurt. 1996, 89.

56 Wellhausen, *Die Pharisäer und die Sadducäer*, 73.

57 Wellhausen, *Die Pharisäer und die Sadducäer*, 17–18.

58 Wellhausen, *Die Pharisäer und die Sadducäer*, 19.

59 Wellhausen, *Die Pharisäer und die Sadducäer*, 19.

60 J. Wellhausen, *Israelitische und jüdische Geschichte* (Berlin, 1894), 297.

61 Wellhausen, *Die Pharisäer und die Sadducäer*, 19.

62 Wellhausen, *Die Pharisäer und die Sadducäer*, 128.
63 J. Wellhausen, *Prolegomena to the History of Ancient Israel* (New York: Meridan Books, 1957), 423.
64 Wellhausen, *Die Pharisäer und die Sadducäer*, 127.
65 Wellhausen, *Die Pharisäer und die Sadducäer*, 121.
66 Wellhausen, *Die Pharisäer und die Sadducäer*, 70.
67 Wellhausen, *Die Pharisäer und die Sadducäer*, 66.
68 Wellhausen, *Die Pharisäer und die Sadducäer*, 127.
69 Wellhausen, *Die Pharisäer und die Sadducäer*, 70.
70 Wellhausen, *Die Pharisäer und die Sadducäer*, 76; see A. Geiger, *Das Judentum und seine Geschichte von der Zerstörung des zweiten Tempels bis zum Ende des Zwölften Jahrhunderts. In zwölf Vorlesungen. Nebst einem Anhange: Offenes Sendschreiben an Herrn Professor Dr. Holzmann*, 2 vols. (Brelau: Schlettersche Buchhandlung, 1865), 1:75; *Urschrift*, 27–29, 37, 56–59.
71 Wellhausen, *Die Pharisäer und die Sadducäer*, 50.
72 For summaries of the criticisms, see D. A. Knight, ed., *Julius Welihausen and His Prolegomena to the History of Israel* (Chico, Calif.: Scholars Press, 1983).
73 R. Smend, "Wellhausen und das Judentum," *ZTK* 79, no. 3 (1982): 249–82. Smend cites a letter Wellhausen wrote to W. R. Smith, in June 1879: "Amüsant ist mir die Art wie die Juden über mich reden—sehr von oben herunter als wüßten sie alles viel besser. Nur Joseph Derenbourg macht eine Ausnahme, er wiegt freilich die anderen alle auf." [Amusing how the Jews speak about me—very condescending, as if they knew everything much better. Joseph Derenbourg is the only exception, he offsets all the others.]
74 H. D. Betz, "Wellhausen's Dictum 'Jesus was not a Christian, but a Jew' in Light of Present Scholarship," *ST* 45 (1991): 83–110. See also K. Berger, "Jesus als Pharisäer und frühe Christen als Pharisäer," *NovT* 30 (1988): 231–62; J. Meier, *Jesus von Nazareth in der talmudischen Überlieferung* (Darmstadt: Wissenschaftliche Buchgesellschaft, 1978); J. Meier, *Jüdische Auseinandersetzung mit dem Christentum in der Antike* (Darmstadt: Wissenschaftliche Buchgesellschaft, 1982).
75 See Hoheisel, *Das antike Judentum in christlicher Sicht*.
76 E. Schürer, *Lehrbuch der neutestamentlichen Zeitgeschichte* (Leipzig: J. C. Hinrichs'sche Buchhandlung, 1874); 2nd ed. published as *Geschichte des jüdischen Volkes im Zeitalter Jesu Christi* (Leipzig: J. C. Hinrichs'sche Buchhandlung, 1886–87; 3rd ed., 1898). See "Pharisäer und Sadducäer," 2:380–418; "Die Essener," 2:338, 556–84.
77 Schürer, *Lehrbuch*, 464; cited by Waubke, *Die Pharisäer*, 229; and Schürer, 391.
78 Hausrath, *Neutestamentliche Zeitgeschichte*.
79 See, for example, F. Perles, *Jüdische Skizzen*, 2nd ed. (Leipzig: G. Engel, 1920), 242–50; I. Abrahams, "Professor Schürer on Life under Jewish Law," *JQR*, n.s. 11 (1899): 626f. In his recent revision of Schürer's book, G. Vermes omitted that chapter; see Schürer, *History of the Jewish People*.
80 See the review by K. Wieseler in *TSK* 48, no. 3 (1875): 516–56.
81 S. Marchand, "Philhellenism and the Furor Orientalis," *Modern Intellectual History* 1, no. 3 (2004): 331–58.

82   W. Bousset, *Die Religion des Judentums im neutestamentlichen Zeitalter* (Berlin: Verlag von Reuther & Reichard, 1903).

83   Bousset, *Die Religion des Judentums*, 136.

84   These contradictions within Bousset's work are noted by I. Elbogen, *Die Religionsanschauungen der Pharisäer mit besonderer Berücksichtigung der Begriffe Gott und Mensch* (Berlin: 22nd Bericht über die Lehranstalt für die Wissenschaft des Judentums in Berlin erstattet vom Curatorium, 1904), 6.

85   W. Bousset, *Das Wesen der Religion* (Halle: Gebauer-Schwetschke, 1903), 87 and 360.

86   Bousset, *Das Wesen*, 116f., unchanged in the 2nd ed., p. 160.

87   F. Perles, *Boussets Religion des Judentums im neutestamentlichen Zeitalter kritisch untersucht* (Berlin: Wolf Peiser, 1903). Bousset wrote a response to Perles, *Volksfrömmigkeit und Schriftgelehrtentum: Antwort auf Herrn Perles' Kritik meiner "Religion des Judentums im N.T. Zeitalter"* (Berlin: Verlag von Reuther & Reichard, 1903). See also reviews of Perles by H. Holtzmann, *TLZ* 29 (1904): 43–46; W. Bousset, *TRu* 10 (1907): 380f. Among the Jewish scholarly responses to Bousset were I. Elbogen, "Die Religionsanschauungen der Pharisäer mit besonderer Berücksichtigung der Begriffe Gott und Mensch," *BHWJ* 22 (1904): 1–88; M. Güdemann, *Jüdische Apologetik* (Glogau: C. Flemming, 1906); and J. Eschelbacher, *Das Judentum im Urteile der modernen protestantischen Theologie* (Leipzig: G. Fock, 1907).

88   G. Beer, Pesachim (Ostern). *Text, Übersetzung und Erklärung* (Giessen, 1912). See the discussion in C. Wiese, *Challenging Colonial Discourse: Jewish Studies and Protestant Theology in Wilhelmine Germany*, Studies in European Judaism 10, ed. G. Veltri (Leiden and Boston: Brill, 2005), 381–88.

89   Deines, *Die Pharisäer*. 451.

90   P. Volz, "Pharisäer," *RGG* 4 (1930): 1178f. Cf. P. Fiebig, "Pharisäer und Sadduzäer," *RGG* 4 (1913): 1487–89.

91   This was in opposition to R. Leszynsky, who viewed the Damascus Document as a Sadducean text. See Leszynsky, *Die Sadduzäer* (Berlin: Mayer and Müller, 1912); J. Jeremias, *Jerusalem zur Zeit Jesu* 1: *Die wirtschaftlichen Verhältnisse* (Leipzig, 1923); 2: *Die sozialen Verhältnisse: A. Reich und arm* (Leipzig, 1924); *B. Hoch und niedrig; 1. Hauptteil: Die gesellschaftliche Oberschicht* (Göttingen, 1929); *2. Hauptteil: Die Reinerhaltung des Volkstums* (Göttingen, 1937; 2nd ed., 1958; rev. ed., 1962); on Pharisees, see Hoch und Niedrig, 115–40.

92   The work of Jeremias has been criticized for retaining anti-Jewish biases, despite its heavy reliance on rabbinic sources. See B. F. Meyer, "A Caricature of Joachim Jeremias and His Work," *JBL* 110 (1991): 451–62. In response, see E. P. Sanders, "Defending the Indefensible," 463–78.

93   For details, see S. Heschel, *The Aryan Jesus: Christians, Nazis, and the Bible* (Princeton: Princeton University Press, forthcoming).

CHAPTER 15

1   M. Smith, personal letter.

2   L. Baeck, *The Pharisees and Other Essays* (New York: Schocken Books, 1947).

3   R. T. Herford, *The Pharisees* (repr., Boston: Beacon, 1962).

4   G. F. Moore, *Judaism in the First Centuries of the Christian Era*, 3 vols. (Cambridge, Mass.: Harvard University Press, 1954).

5   G. H. Box, "Survey of Recent Literature on the Pharisees and Sadducees," *RTP* 4 (1908–1909): 129–51.

6   R. Marcus, "The Pharisees in the Light of Modern Scholarship," *JR* 32 (1952): 153–64.

7   S. Zeitlin, "Studies in Tannaitic Jurisprudence," *JJLP* 1 (1919): 297–311.

8   S. Zeitlin, "Les principles des controverses halachiques entre les écoles de Schammai et de Hillel," *REJ* 93 (1932): 73–83.

9   S. Zeitlin, "Prosbol: A Study in Tannaitic Jurisprudence," *JQR* 37 (1946): 341–62.

10   S. Zeitlin, "Hillel and the Hermeneutic Rules," *JQR* 54 (1963–64): 161–73.

11   S. Zeitlin, "The Pharisees and the Gospels," in *Essays and Studies in Memory of Linda R. Miller*, ed. Israel Davidson, 235–86 (New York, 1938).

12   S. Zeitlin, "The Semikhah Controversy between the Zugoth," *JQR* 7 (1916–17): 499–517.

13   S. Zeitlin, "Sameias and Pollion," *JJLP* 1 (1919): 61–67.

14   S. Zeitlin, *The Rise and Fall of the Judaean State: A Political, Social and Religious History of the Second Commonwealth*, 2 vols (Philadelphia: Jewish Publication Society, 1962, 1967).

15   J. Z. Lauterbach, *Rabbinic Essays* (Cincinnati: Hebrew Union College Press, 1951). "The Sadducees and Pharisees" is found on pages 23–50; "A Significant Controversy," 51–86; "The Pharisees and Their Teachings," 87–162.

16   S. W. Baron, *A Social and Religious History of the Jews: Ancient Times*, vol. 2 (Philadelphia: The Jewish Publication Society, 1952), 25–46, 342ff., nn. 43–53.

17   G. W. Buchanan, *The Consequences of the Covenant* (Leiden: Brill, 1970), 259–67.

CHAPTER 16

1   At issue is Sanders's *Jewish Law from Jesus to the Mishnah*.

2   One example: "Shall we call these 'oral law'? That is just the question. To get at it, I wish to make further distinctions: [1] between conscious and unconscious interpretation of the written law; [2] between interpretation and consciously formulated supplements, alterations, or additions, which are known not to be in the law at all. These distinctions are easier to state than to demonstrate, since exegesis can be fanciful and produce results which are now thought to be remote from the text, and since we have no direct access to what was 'conscious' and 'unconscious.' Nevertheless, if we bear these distinctions in mind and consider some examples, we shall improve our understanding of the problem" (*Jewish Law*, 102–3). The most powerful arguments against Sanders's distinctions are stated in his presentation of them: there is no evidence; we also do not know what was "conscious" and what was "unconscious." But these powerful considerations do not impede Sanders's progress. He simply dismisses them and moves on.

3   Sanders, *Jewish Law*, 111.

4 Sanders, *Jewish Law*, 244.
5 Sanders discusses so many groups that it is not at all clear how evidence drawn from any one of them pertains to the principal group under discussion.
6 Sanders, *Jewish Law*, 131.
7 Sanders, *Jewish Law*, 171.
8 But there are equally probative examples to be adduced (e.g., from Mishnah-tractate Tohorot chap. 2), which, like the passage at hand, place within a single continuum, so far as cultic cleanness of food in the Temple and not in the Temple is concerned, priests and nonpriests. That passage does not make explicit reference to the Pharisees, which is why I have given the present one as my single example, among countless candidates.
9 The hierarchical classification of all things defines the Mishnah's authorships' principal concern, as I have shown in my *Judaism as Philosophy: The Method and Message of the Mishnah* (Columbia: University of South Carolina Press, 1991).
10 Sanders, *Jewish Law*, 206–7, 234, 235..
11 I spell out this matter in my *Transformation of Judaism: From Philosophy to Religion* (Champaign: University of Illinois Press, 1991).
12 Sanders, *Jewish Law*, 236–42.
13 Sanders, *Jewish Law*, 240–41.
14 Sanders, *Jewish Law*, 240.
15 Sanders, *Jewish Law*, 245–46.

CHAPTER 17

1 *The Chambers Dictionary* (Edinburgh: Chambers Harrap, 1993), 1277.
2 The definition also suffers from conceptual confusion. "Sect" and "party," for instance, are not necessarily synonyms, and the definition's assertion that the Pharisees were simultaneously "democratic" and "legalistic" begs for clarification.
3 Happily, there is a record of strong scholarship that approaches this problem by differentiating the sources. See, for instance, Neusner, *From Politics to Piety*; Saldarini, "Pharisees," *ABD* 5 (Garden City, N.Y.: Doubleday, 1992), 289–303; and M. S. Jaffee, *Torah in the Mouth* (Oxford: Oxford University Press, 2001), esp. chap. 3.
4 A. I. Baumgarten has employed variations of this approach. His "The Name of the Pharisees" surveys an array of sources and suggests that "at least two interpretations [of the Pharisees' name] existed in antiquity, 'specifiers' and 'separatists' (in a hostile sense)" (426), but that "the original meaning of the name of the group may remain beyond our knowledge" (428). In "The Pharisaic Paradosis" he suggests, "When historical reconstruction of the nature of a person or group is carried out under ideal circumstances, we should have two kinds of evidence: we should know the self description of the subject, and be able to compare this self description with the way the subject was seen by others" (63). After a review of a range of sources, he concludes that "the terms *paradosis* of the elders and of the fathers were deliberate attempts by the Pharisees to give their tradition a

pedigree that it might have seemed to lack" (77). That is, the use of the term *paradosis* may suggest "how the Pharisees wanted to appear and were seen by their contemporaries in Palestine prior to the destruction of the Temple" (77). It does not, however, indicate the substance of Pharisaic teaching or tradition.

5 Jaffee, *Torah in the Mouth*, 44.

6 See, for instance, J. Baumgarten, "The 'Halakha' in Miqsat Ma'ase ha-Torah (MMT)," 512–16.

7 Regev, "Were the Priests All the Same?" 158.

8 Regev, "Were the Priests All the Same?" 159.

9 Regev, "Were the Priests All the Same?" 158.

10 See Schwartz, "MMT, Josephus, and the Pharisees."

11 I am grateful to Professor Lawrence Schiffman for helping me understand this argument. He bears no responsibility for my formulation of it.

12 Elman, "Some Remarks on 4QMMT and the Rabbinic Tradition."

13 Elman, "Some Remarks on 4QMMT and the Rabbinic Tradition," 99.

14 Regev, "Were the Priests All the Same?" 160.

15 Regev, "Were the Priests All the Same?" 161.

16 Regev, "Were the Priests All the Same?" 183.

17 Jaffee, *Torah in the Mouth*, 45.

18 A. I. Baumgarten, "The Pharisaic Paradosis," 77.

19 A. I. Baumgarten, "The Pharisaic Paradosis," 77.

20 As scholars have previously noted, since the story of the healing of the man with a withered hand is a miracle story that entails only speech, but no action, on Jesus' part, the Pharisees' objection to healing on the Sabbath cannot have Jesus' behavior as its object. Their comment is irrelevant to his act.

21 Jaffee, *Torah in the Mouth*, 47.

22 Schwartz, "MMT, Josephus, and the Pharisees," 73–74.

23 For the reasons given by Jacob Neusner above, the item on Strange's list most open to question as Pharisaic is the synagogue.

BIBLIOGRAPHY

Abrahams, Israel. "Professor Schürer on Life under Jewish Law." *JQR*, n.s. 11 (1899): 626–42.

Abrams, Dominic M., and Michael A. Hogg, eds. *Social Identity and Social Cognition*. Oxford: Blackwell, 1999.

Akenson, Donald Harman. *Saint Saul: A Skeleton Key to the Historical Jesus*. Oxford: Oxford University Press, 2000.

Albeck, Hanokh. *Shishch Sidré Mishnah, Mo'ed*. Jerusalem: Mosad Bialik, 1952.

———. *Shishah Sidré Mishnah, Toharot*. Jerusalem: Mosad Bialik, 1952.

Allegro, John Marco. "Further Light on the History of the Qumran Sect." *JBL* 75 (1956): 89–95.

———. *Qumrân Cave 4 I (4Q158–4Q186)*. DJD 5. Oxford: Clarendon, 1968.

Alon, Gedaliah. *Jews, Judaism, and the Classical World*. Jerusalem: Magnes Press, 1977.

Ammon, Christoph Friedrich von. *Die Geschichte des Leben Jesu: Mitsteitiger Rücksicht auf die vorhandenen Quelien*. 3 vols. Leipzig: Vogel, 1842–1847.

Anonymous. "Abraham Geiger: Wissenschaft des Judenthums." *PKZ* 51 (December 18, 1875): 1184–88.

———. "Der jerusalemische Talmud im Lichte Geigerscher Hypothesen." *Monatsschrift für die Wissenschaft des Judentums* 20 (1871): 120–37.

———. "Ersucht." In Winer, *Biblische Realwörterbuch*, 1.

———. "Heuchelei." In Winer, *Biblische Realwörterbuch*, 1.

———. "Pharisäer." In Winer, *Biblische Realwörterbuch*, 2.

Ascough, Richard, ed. *Religious Rivalries and the Struggle for Success in Sardis and Smyrna*. Waterloo, Ont.: Wilfrid Laurier University Press, 2005.

Attridge, H. W. *The Interpretation of Biblical History in the Antiquitates Judaicae of Flavius Josephus*. Missoula, Mont.: Scholars Press for HTR, 1976.

Aviam, Mordechai, and D. Syon. "Jewish Ossilegium in the Galilee." In Rutgers, *What Athens Has to Do with Jerusalem*, 151–85.

Avigad, N. *Discovering Jerusalem*. Nashville, Camden, New York: Thomas Nelson, 1983.

481

Baeck, Leo. *The Pharisees and Other Essays.* New York: Schocken Books, 1947.

Banks, Robert. *Jesus and the Law in the Synoptic Tradition.* Cambridge: Cambridge University Press, 1975.

Baron, Salo Wittmayer. *A Social and Religious History of the Jews: Ancient Times*, vol. 2. Philadelphia: The Jewish Publication Society, 1952.

Barrett, C. K. "John and Judaism." In Bieringer et al., *Anti-Judaism and the Fourth Gospel*, 401–17.

Bartsch, S. *Actors in the Audience: Theatricality and Doublespeak from Nero to Hadrian.* Cambridge, Mass.: Harvard University Press, 1994.

Basser, Herbert. "The Gospels and Rabbinic Halakah." In *The Missing Jesus: Rabbinic Judaism and the New Testament*, edited by B. Chilton, C. A. Evans, and J. Neusner. Leiden: Brill, 2002. 77–99.

Baumgarten, Albert I. *The Flourishing of Jewish Sects in the Maccabean Era: An Interpretation.* Leiden: Brill, 1997.

———. "Josephus and Hippolytus on the Pharisees." *HUCA* 55 (1984): 1–25.

———. "Korban and the Pharisaic Paradosis." *JANES* 16–17 (1984–1985): 5–17.

———. "The Name of the Pharisees." *JBL* 102, no. 3 (1983): 411–28.

———. "The Pharisaic Paradosis." *HTR* 80, no. 1 (1987): 63–87.

———. "Pharisees." In Schiffman and VanderKam, *Encyclopedia of the Dead Sea Scrolls*, 2:657–63.

———. "Seekers after Smooth Things." In Schiffman and VanderKam, *Encyclopedia of the Dead Sea Scrolls*, 2:857–89.

Baumgarten, Joseph M. "The 'Halakha' in Miqsat Ma'ase ha-Torah (MMT)." *JAOS* 16, no. 3 (1996): 512–16.

———. "The Unwritten Law in the Pre-Rabbinic Period." *JSJ* 3 (1972): 7–29.

Beare, Francis W. *The Gospel according to Matthew.* Peabody, Mass.: Hendrickson, 1981.

Beer, Georg. Pesachim (Ostern). *Text, Übersetzung und Erklärung.* Giessen, 1912.

Begg, C. *Flavius Josephus: Translation and Commentary.* Vol. 4 of *Judean Antiquities 5–7*, edited by S. Mason. Leiden: Brill, 2004.

———. *Josephus' Account of the Early Divided Monarchy (AJ 8,212–420): Rewriting the Bible.* Leuven: Leuven University Press/Peeters, 1993.

———. *Josephus' Story of the Later Monarchy.* Leuven: Leuven University Press/Peeters, 2000.

Bengtsson, H. *What's in a Name? A Study of Sobriquets in the Pesharim.* Uppsala, Sweden: Uppsala University, 2000.

Benko, Stephen. *Pagan Rome and the Early Christians.* Bloomington: Indiana University Press, 1986.

Berger, Klaus. "Jesus als Pharisäer und frühe Christen als Pharisäer." *NovT* 30 (1988): 231–62.

Bergmeier, R. *Die Essener-Berichte des Flavius Josephus: Quellenstudien zu den Essenertexten im Werk des jüdischen Historiographen.* Kampen: Kok Pharos, 1993.

Betz, Hans Dieter. "Wellhausen's Dictum 'Jesus was not a Christian, but a Jew' in Light of Present Scholarship." *ST* 45 (1991): 83–110.

Bieringer, R., D. Pollefeyt, and F. Vandecasteele-Vanneuville, eds. *Anti-Judaism and the Fourth Gospel: Papers of the Leuven Colloquium, 2000.* Jewish and Christian Heritage Series 1. Assen: Royal van Gorcum, 2001.

Binder, D. *Into the Temple Courts: The Place of the Synagogues in the Second Temple Period.* Atlanta: Society of Biblical Literature, 1999.

Birch, Bruce C. "The First and Second Books of Samuel." *NIB* 2. Nashville: Abingdon, 1998.

Black, M. "The Account of the Essenes in Hippolytus and Josephus." In *The Background of the New Testament and Its Eschatology,* edited by W. D. Davies and D. Daube. Cambridge: Cambridge University Press, 1956. 172–82.

———. "Judas of Galilee and Josephus's Fourth Philosophy." In *Josephus-Studien: Untersuchungen zu Josephus, der antiken Judentum und dem Neuen Testament: Otto Michel zum 70. Geburtstag gewidmet.* Göttingen: Vandenhoeck & Ruprecht, 1974. 45–54.

Bockmuehl, Marcus. "'Let the Dead Bury Their Dead'; Jesus and the Law Revisited." In his *Jewish Law in Gentile Churches: Halakhah and the Beginning of Christian Public Ethics.* Edinburgh: T&T Clark, 2000. 3–48.

Boring, M. Eugene. "The Gospel of Matthew." *NIB* 8. Nashville: Abingdon, 1995. 87–506.

Bousset, Wilhelm. *Das Wesen der Religion.* Halle: Gebauer-Schwetschke, 1903.

———. *Die Religion des Judentums im neutestamentlichen Zeitalter.* Berlin: Verlag von Reuther & Reichard, 1903.

———. *Volksfrömmigkeit und Schriftgelehrtentum: Antwort auf Herrn Perles' Kritik meiner "Religion des Judentums im N.T. Zeitalter."* Berlin: Verlag von Reuther & Reichard, 1903.

Bowersock, G. W. *Greek Sophists in the Roman Empire.* Oxford: Clarendon, 1969.

Bowie, E. L. "The Greeks and Their Past in the Second Sophistic." *Past and Present* 46 (1974): 3–41.

Bowker, J. *Jesus and the Pharisees.* Cambridge: Cambridge University Press, 1973.

Box, G. H. "Survey of Recent Literature on the Pharisees and Sadducees." *RTP* 4 (1908–1909): 129–51.

Braund, D. C. "Cohors: The Governor and His Entourage in the Self-Image of the Roman Republic." In Laurence and Berry, *Cultural Identity in the Roman Empire,* 10–24.

Brawley, Robert L. *Luke-Acts and the Jews: Conflict, Apology, and Conciliation.* SBLMS 33. Atlanta: Society of Biblical Literature, 1987.

Brown, Raymond E. *The Death of the Messiah: From Gethsemane to the Grave. A Commentary on the Passion Narratives in the Four Gospels.* 2 vols. ABRL. Garden City, N.Y.: Doubleday, 1994.

———. *The Gospel according to John.* 2 vols. ABRL. Garden City, N.Y.: Doubleday, 1966, 1970.

Brownlee, William. "Biblical Interpretation among the Sectaries of the Dead Sea Scrolls." *BA* 14 (1951): 54–76.

Buchanan, George Wesley. *The Consequences of the Covenant.* Leiden: Brill, 1970.

Bultmann, Rudolf. *Jesus and the Word.* Translated by L. Smith and E. Lantero. New York: Charles Scribner's Sons, 1934, 1958.

Burchard, C. "Die Essener bei Hippolyt: Hippolyt, REF. IX 18, 2–28, 2 und Josephus, Bell. 2, 119–161." *JSS* 8 (1977): 1–41.

Cahill, Jane M. "Chalk Vessel Assemblages of the Persian/Hellenistic and Early Roman Periods." In *City of David Excavations, Final Report III,* edited by A. De Groot and D. T. Ariel, Qedem 33. Jerusalem: Hebrew University Institute of Archaelogy, 1992. 190–274.

Carlston, Charles E. "The Things that Defile (Mark VII.14) and the Law in Matthew and Mark." *NTS* 15 (1968–1969): 75–96.

Carroll, John T. "Luke's Portrayal of the Pharisees." *CBQ* 50, no. 4 (1988): 604–21.

Carson, D. A. *Matthew 13–28.* Grand Rapids: Zondervan, 1995.

Carson, D. A., and Douglas J. Moo. *An Introduction to the New Testament.* Grand Rapids: Zondervan, 2005.

Carter, Warren. "Getting Martha Out of the Kitchen: Luke 10.38-42 Again." In *A Feminist Companion to Luke,* edited by Amy-Jill Levine. Feminist Companion to the New Testament and Early Christian Writings 3. London and New York: Sheffield Academic & Continuum, 2002. 214–31.

Catchpole, David. "Paul, James, and the Apostolic Decree." *NTS* 23 (1977): 428–44.

Chilton, Bruce. "Exorcism and History: Mark 1:21-28." *Gospel Perspectives* 6 (1986): 253–71.

———. *A Feast of Meanings: Eucharistic Theologies from Jesus through Johannine Circles.* NovTSup 72. Leiden: Brill, 1994.

———. "A Generative Exegesis of Mark 7:1-23." *JHC* 3, no. 1 (1996): 18–37.

———. *God in Strength: Jesus' Announcement of the Kingdom.* SNTSU 1. Freistadt: Plöchl, 1979. Reprinted in BibSem 8. Sheffield: JSOT Press, 1987.

———. "James in Relation to Peter, Paul, and the Remembrance of Jesus." In *The Brother of Jesus: James the Just and His Mission*, edited by B. Chilton and J. Neusner. Louisville, Ky.: Westminster John Knox, 2001. 138–60.

———. "Jesus and the Repentance of E. P. Sanders." *TynBul* 39 (1988): 1–18.

———. "Review: Jesus the Pharisee: A New Look at the Jewishness of Jesus." *ThTo* 42 (1985): 563–64.

———. *Mary Magdalene: A Biography*. New York: Doubleday, 2005.

———. *Pure Kingdom: Jesus' Vision of God*. Studying the Historical Jesus 1. Grand Rapids, Eerdmans, 1996.

———. "Purity and Impurity." In *The Dictionary of the Later New Testament and Its Developments*, edited by R. P. Martin and P. Davids. Downers Grove, Ill.: InterVarsity, 1997. 988–96.

———. *Rabbi Paul: An Intellectual Biography*. Garden City, N.Y.: Doubleday, 2004.

———. "Reference to the Targumim in the Exegesis of the New Testament." In *SBLSP*, edited by L. H. Lovering. Atlanta: Scholars Press, 1995. 77–82.

———. *The Temple of Jesus: His Sacrificial Program within a Cultural History of Sacrifice*. University Park: Pennsylvania State University Press, 1992.

Chilton, Bruce, and Craig A. Evans, eds. *James the Just and Christian Origins*. NovTSup 98. Leiden: Brill, 1999.

———. "Jesus and Israel's Scriptures." In *Studying the Historical Jesus: Evaluations of the State of Current Research*, edited by B. Chilton and C. A. Evans. NTTS 19. Leiden: Brill, 1994. 281–335.

Chilton, Bruce, and Jacob Neusner. *The Intellectual Foundations of Christian and Jewish Discourse: The Philosophy of Religious Argument*. London: Routledge, 1997.

———. *Judaism in the New Testament: Practices and Beliefs*. London: Routledge, 1995.

———. *Types of Authority in Formative Christianity and Judaism*. London: Routledge, 1999.

Chwolson, Daniel. *Beiträge zur Entwicklungsgeschichte des Judentums*. Leipzig: H. Haessel, 1910.

———. *Das letzte Passamahl Christi und der Tag seines Todes nach den in Übereinstimmung gebrachten Berichten der Synoptiker und des Evangelium Johannis*. St. Petersburg: M. Eggers, 1892.

Clarke, M. L. *Higher Education in the Ancient World*. London: Routledge and Kegan Paul, 1971.

Cohen, Shaye J. D. *Josephus in Galilee and Rome: His Vita and Development as a Historian*. CSCT 8. Leiden: Brill, 1979.

Cohen, Shaye J. D. "Josephus, Jeremiah, and Polybius." *History and Theory* 21 (1982): 366–81.

———. "The Rabbi in Second-Century Jewish Society." In *The Cambridge History of Judaism: The Early Roman Period*, edited by W. Horbury, W. D. Davies, and J. Sturdy, 3 vols. Cambridge: Cambridge University Press, 1999. 3:922–90.

———. "The Significance of Yavneh: Pharisees, Rabbis, and the End of Jewish Sectarianism." *HUCA* 55 (1984): 27–53.

Collins, John J. *The Scepter and the Star: The Messiahs of the Dead Sea Scrolls and Other Ancient Literature*. ABRL. Garden City, N.Y.: Doubleday, 1995.

———. "Sibylline Oracles: A New Translation and Introduction." In *OTP* 1, edited by J. H. Charlesworth. 2 vols. Garden City, N.Y.: Doubleday, 1983.

Conte, G. B. *Latin Literature: A History*. Baltimore: The Johns Hopkins University Press, 1994.

Conzelmann, Hans. *1 Corinthians: A Commentary on the First Epistle to the Corinthians*. Translated by J. P. Leitch. Hermeneia. Philadelphia: Fortress, 1975.

Cook, D. E. "A Gospel Portrait of the Pharisees." *RevExp* 84 (1987): 221–33.

Cooper, Joel, and Russell H. Fazio. "The Formation and Persistence of Attitudes that Support Intergroup Conflict." In *The Social Psychology of Intergroup Relations*, edited by W. G. Austin and S. Worchel. Monterey, Calif.: Brooks/Cole, 1979. 149–59.

Corbo, Virgilio C. "Resti della Sinagoga del Primo Secolo a Cafarnao." In *Studia Hierosolymitana in Onore del P. Bellarmino Bagatti*. Studium Biblicum Franciscanum. Collectio Maior III. 1982. 314–57.

Craddock, Fred B. *Luke*. IBC. Louisville, Ky.: Westminster John Knox, 1990.

Cranfield, C. E. B. *Epistle to the Romans* 2. ICC. Edinburgh: T&T Clark, 1979.

Cribiore, Raffaella. *Gymnastics of the Mind: Greek Education in Hellenistic and Roman Egypt*. Princeton: Princeton University Press, 2001.

Cross, Frank M. *The Ancient Library of Qumran and Modern Biblical Studies*. Garden City: Doubleday, 1958.

Culpepper, R. Alan. *The Anatomy of the Fourth Gospel: A Study in Literary Design*. Philadelphia: Fortress, 1983.

Darr, John. "Irenic or Ironic? Another Look at Gamaliel before the Sanhedrin (Acts 5:33-42)." In *Literary Studies in Luke-Acts: Essays in Honor of Joseph B. Tyson*, edited by R. P. Thompson and T. E. Philipps. Macon, Ga.: Mercer University Press, 1998. 121–39.

Daube, D. "Typology in Josephus." *JJS* 31 (1980): 18–36.

Davies, W. D. *Paul and Rabbinic Judaism: Some Rabbinic Elements in Pauline Theology*. London: SPCK, 1958.

Davies, W. D., and Dale C. Allison Jr. *A Critical and Exegetical Commentary on the Gospel according to Saint Matthew.* 3 vols. ICC. Edinburgh: T&T Clark, 1991.

de Boer, Martinus C. "The Depiction of the 'Jews' in John's Gospel: Matters of Behavior and Identity." In Bieringer et al., *Anti-Judaism and the Fourth Gospel,* 260–80.

———. "God-Fearers in Luke Acts." In Tuckett, *Luke's Literary Achievement,* 50–71.

de Lacey, D. R. "In Search of a Pharisee." *TynBul* 43, no. 2 (1992): 353–72.

Deeds, Leland R. *Cultic Metaphors: Sacrificial Ideology and Origins in Selected Scrolls from the Dead Sea.* Annandale, N.Y.: Bard College, 1996.

Deines, Roland. *Jüdische Steingefäße und pharisäische Frömmigkeit.* Tübingen: Mohr-Siebeck, 1993.

———. *Die Pharisäer: Ihr Verständnis im Spiegel der christlichen und jüdischen Forschung seit Wellhausen und Graetz.* WUNT 101. Tübingen: Mohr-Siebeck, 1997.

Derenbourg, Joseph. *Essai sur l'Histoire et la Geographie de la Palestine, d'apres les Thalmuds et les autres sources rabbiniques.* Paris: A l'imprimerie imperiale, 1867.

Dewey, Joanna. "The Literary Structure of the Controversy Stories in Mark 2:1–3:6." In *The Interpretation of Mark,* edited by W. Telford. Edinburgh: T&T Clark, 1995. 141–51.

Donahue, John, and Daniel Harrington. *The Gospel of Mark.* Collegeville, Minn.: Liturgical Press, 2002.

Donaldson, Terence L., ed. *Religious Rivalries and the Struggle for Success in Caesarea Maritima.* Waterloo, Ont.: Wilfrid Laurier University Press, 2000.

Doran, Robert. "The Pharisee and the Tax Collector: An Agonistic Story." Forthcoming.

Doudna, Gregory L. *4Q Pesher Nahum: A Critical Edition.* JSPSup 35/Copenhagen International Series 8. Sheffield: Sheffield Academic, 2001.

Dunn, James D. G. "The Embarrassment of History: Reflections on the Problem of 'Anti-Judaism' in the Fourth Gospel." In Bieringer et al., *Anti-Judaism and the Fourth Gospel,* 47–67.

———. "Jesus and Factionalism in Early Judaism: How Serious Was the Factionalism of Late Second Temple Judaism?" In *Hillel and Jesus: Comparative Studies of Two Major Religious Leaders,* edited by J. H. Charlesworth and L. L. Johns. Minneapolis: Fortress, 1997. 156–75.

———. "Judaism in the Land of Israel in the First Century." In *Judaism in Late Antiquity: Historical Syntheses,* edited by Jacob Neusner. Leiden: Brill, 1995. 229–28.

Dunn, James D. G. *The Partings of the Ways between Christianity and Judaism and Their Significance for the Character of Christianity*. London: SCM; Philadelphia: Trinity Press International, 1991.

Eck, Werner. *The Age of Augustus*. Translated by D. L. Schneider. Oxford: Blackwell, 2003.

Eckstein, Arthur M. "Josephus and Polybius: A Reconsideration." *CA* 9 (1990): 175–208.

———. *Moral Vision in the Histories of Polybius*. Berkeley: University of California Press, 1995.

Edmondson, J., S. Mason, and J. Rives. *Flavius Josephus and Flavian Rome*. Oxford: Oxford University Press, 2005.

Eisenman, Robert. *James the Brother of Jesus: The Key to Unlocking the Secrets of Early Christianity and the Dead Sea Scrolls*. New York: Viking, 1996.

Elbogen, Ismar. *Die Religionsanschauungen der Pharisäer mit besonderer Berücksichtigung der Begriffe Gott und Mensch*. Berlin: 22nd Bericht über die Lehranstalt für die Wissenschaft des Judentums in Berlin erstattet vom Curatorium, 1904.

———. "Die Religionsanschauungen der Pharisäer mit besonderer Berücksichtigung der Begriffe Gott und Mensch." *BHWJ* 22 (1904): 1–88.

Elliott, John H. "Temple versus Household in Luke-Acts: A Contrast in Social Institutions." In Neyrey, *Social World of Luke-Acts*, 211–40.

Elman, Yaakov. "Some Remarks on 4QMMT and the Rabbinic Tradition: or, When Is a Parallel Not a Parallel." In Kampen and Bernstein, *Reading 4QMMT*, 99–127.

Ersch, Johann Samuel, and Johann Gottfried Gruber. *Allgemeine Encyklopädie*. Leipzig: J. F. Gleditsch, 1846.

Eschelbacher, Joseph. *Das Judentum im Urteile der modernen protestantischen Theologie*. Leipzig: G. Fock, 1907.

Eshel, H. "Alexander Jannaeus." In Schiffman and VanderKam, *Encyclopedia of the Dead Sea Scrolls*, 2:16–17.

———. "CD 12:15–17 and the Stone Vessels Found at Qumran" (2003), http://orion.huji.ac.il/symposiums/3rd/papers/Eshel98.html (accessed January 16, 2006).

Esler, Philip. *Conflict and Identity in Romans: The Social Setting of Paul's Letter*. Minneapolis: Fortress, 2003.

———. *Galatians*. London and New York: Routledge, 1998.

Evans, Craig A., and Peter W. Flint, eds. *Eschatology, Messianism, and the Dead Sea Scrolls*. Grand Rapids: Eerdmans, 1997.

Ewald, Heinrich. *Geschichte des Volkes Israel*. 7 vols. Göttingen: Dieterischen Buchhandlung, 1864–1868.

Eyal, R. "The Individualistic Meaning of Jewish Ossuaries: A Socio-Anthropological Perspective on Burial Practice." *PEQ* 133 (2001): 39–49.

Falk, Harvey. *Jesus the Pharisee: A New Look at the Jewishness of Jesus.* New York: Paulist Press, 1985.

Falk, Zeev W. "Notes and Observations on Talmudic Vows." *HTR* 59 (1966): 309–12.

Farmer, W. R. *Maccabees, Zealots, and Josephus: An Inquiry into Jewish Nationalism in the Greco-Roman Period.* New York: Columbia University Press, 1956.

Feldman, Louis H. *Flavius Josephus: Translation and Commentary.* Vol. 3 of *Judean Antiquities 1–4.* Edited by S. Mason. Leiden: Brill, 2000.

———. *Josephus's Interpretation of the Bible.* Berkeley: University of California Press, 1998.

———. *Studies in Josephus' Rewritten Bible.* Leiden: Brill, 1998.

Feldman, Louis H., and Gohei Hata. *Josephus, Judaism, and Christianity.* Detroit: Wayne State University Press, 1987.

Fiebig, P. "Pharisäer und Sadduzäer." *RGG* 4 (1913): 1487–89.

Finkelstein, Louis. *The Pharisees: The Sociological Background of Their Faith.* Philadelphia: Jewish Publication Society of America, 1938.

Flesher, Paul. "The Fiction of Proselyte Baptism." In *Traversing Land and Sea: Proselytism in Judaism and Early Christianity,* edited by A.-J. Levine and R. Pervo. Forthcoming.

Freedman, D. N. *The Anchor Bible Dictionary.* 6 vols. Garden City, N.Y.: Doubleday, 1992.

Friedman, R. E. *The Bible with Sources Revealed.* San Francisco: HarperSanFrancisco, 2003.

Friedman, Shamma. "The Primacy of Tosefta to Mishnah in Synoptic Parallels." In *Introducing Tosefta: Intertextual, Intratextual Studies,* edited by H. Fox, T. Meacham, and D. Kriger. Hoboken, N.J.: Ktav, 1999. 1–37.

Fritz, V., and Roland Deines. "Catalogue of the Jewish Ossuaries in the German Protestant Institute for Archaeology." *IEJ* 49 (1999): 222–41.

Geiger, Abraham. *Das Judentum und seine Geschichte von der Zerstörung des zweiten Tempels bis zum Ende des Zwölften Jahrhunderts. In zwölf Vorlesungen. Nebst einem Anhange: Offenes Sendschreiben an Herrn Professor Dr. Holzmann,* 2 vols. Brelau: Schlettersche Buchhandlung, 1865.

———. "Die Levirats-Ehe, ihre Entstehung und Entwickelung." *JZWL* 1 (1862): 19–39.

———. "Die Testamente der zwölf Patriarchen." *JZWL* 9 (1871): 123–25.

———. "Die wissenschaftliche Ausbildung des Judenthums in den zwei ersten Jahrhunderten des zweiten Jahrtausends bis zum Auftreten des Maimonides." *WZJT* 1 (1835): 13–38.

Geiger, Abraham. "Innere Geschichte der zweiten Tempelperiode und
    deren Behandlung." *JZWL* 6 (1868): 247–77.
———. "Karäische Literatur." *WZJT* 2 (1836): 93–125.
———. Letter to Derenbourg. April 10, 1872. *JZWL* 10 (1872): 156–57.
———. "Neuere Mitteilungen über die Samaritaner." *ZDMG* 16 (1862):
    714–28.
———. "Proben neuerer hebräischer Sprachgelehrsamkeit." *JZWL* 2
    (1863): 229–38.
———. "Sadducäer und Pharisäer." *JZWL* 2 (1862): 11–54.
———. *Urschrift und Übersetzungen der Bibel in ihrer Abhängigkeit von der innern
    Entwickelung des Judenthums.* Breslau: Julius Heinauer, 1857. 2nd ed.,
    Frankfurt am Main: Verlag Madda, 1928.
Geiger, Ludwig, ed. *Nachgelassene Schriften.* 5 vols. Berlin: L. Gerschel,
    1875–1885.
George, Timothy. *Galatians.* NAC 30. Nashville: Broadman & Holman, 1994.
Gereboff, Joel. "When to Speak, How to Speak, and When Not to Speak:
    Answers from Early Rabbinic Stories." *Semeia* 34 (1985), 29–51.
Gfrörer, August. *Das Jahrhundert des Heils.* 2 vols. Stuttgart: E. Schweizerbart's
    Verlagshandlung, 1838.
Ginzberg, Louis. *An Unknown Jewish Sect.* Moreshet Series 1. New York: Ktav,
    1970.
Goldberg, Abraham. "The Tosefta—the Companion to the Mishna." In *The
    Literature of the Sages, First Part: Oral Tora, Halakha, Mishnah, Tosefta, Talmud,
    External Tractates, Compendium Rerum Iudaicarum ad Novum Testamentum, Section
    2.3,* edited by S. Safrai. Assen/Maastricht: Van Gorcum; Philadelphia:
    Fortress, 1987. 283–301.
Goldenberg, Robert. "The Deposition of Rabban Gamaliel II." In Green,
    Persons and Institutions in Early Rabbinic Judaism 1, 9–47.
Goldhill, Simon, ed. *Being Greek under Rome: Cultural Identity, the Second Sophistic,
    and the Development of Empire.* Cambridge: Cambridge University Press,
    2001.
Goodenough, E. R. *Jewish Symbols in the Greco-Roman World.* Abridged edition.
    Edited by Jacob Neusner. Princeton: Princeton University Press, 1988.
Goodman, Martin. "The Function of Minim in Early Rabbinic Judaism." In
    Geschichte-Tradition-Reflexion: Festschrift für Martin Hengel zum 70. Geburtstag.
    Band I: *Judentum,* edited by H. Cancik, H. Lichtenberger, and P. Schäfer.
    Tübingen: Mohr-Siebeck, 1996. 501–10.
Grabbe, Lester L. *Judaic Religion in the Second Temple Period.* London:
    Routledge, 2000.
———. *Judaism from Cyrus to Hadrian.* 2 vols. Minneapolis: Augsburg Fortress,
    1992.

————. "Sadducees and Pharisees." In Neusner and Avery-Peck, *Judaism in Late Antiquity: Where We Stand*, 1:35–62.

Graetz, Heinrich. *Geschichte der Juden von den ältesten Zeiten bis auf die Gegenwart.* 11 vols. Leipzig: Leiner, 1870–1897.

Green, Willam Scott. "Heresy, Apostasy in Judaism." In *The Encyclopedia of Judaism*, edited by Jacob Neusner, A. J. Avery-Peck, and W. S. Green. 3 vols. Leiden: Brill, 2000. 1:366–80.

————, ed. *Persons and Institutions in Early Rabbinic Judaism*, vol. 1. BJS 3. Missoula, Mont.: Scholars Press, 1977.

————. "Reading the Writing of Rabbinism: Toward an Interpretation of Rabbinic Literature." *JAAR* 51 (1983): 191–207.

————. "What's in a Name? The Question of Rabbinic Biography." In *Approaches to the Study of Ancient Judaism* 1, edited by W. S. Green. Missoula, Mont.: Scholars Press, 1979, 77–94.

Güdemann, Moritz. *Jüdische Apologetik.* Glogau: C. Flemming, 1906.

Guelich, Robert A. *Mark 1–8:26.* Dallas: Word, 1989.

Gundry, Robert H. *Mark: A Commentary on His Apology for the Cross.* Grand Rapids: Eerdmans, 1993.

Guthrie, Donald. *New Testament Introduction.* Downers Grove, Ill.: InterVarsity Press, 1970.

Gutman, S., and D. Wagner. "Gamla." In *Excavations and Surveys in Israel 1986*, vol. 5 of *Excavations and Surveys in Israel*, edited by A. Sussman and R. Greenberg. Jerusalem: Israel Antiquities Authority, 1987. 38–41.

Hachlili, Rachel. *Ancient Jewish Art and Archaeology in the Land of Israel.* Leiden: Brill, 1988.

Hagner, Donald A. *Matthew.* 2 vols. Dallas: Word, 1993.

————. "The *Sitz im Leben* of the Gospel of Matthew." In *Treasures New and Old: Recent Contributions to Matthean Studies*, edited by D. Bauer and M. Powell. Atlanta: Scholars Press, 1996. 27–68.

Hakola, Raimo. "Being the Same and Different at the Same Time: Social Identities and Group Phenomena in the Second Temple Period." In *Explaining Early Judaism and Christianity: Contributions from Cognitive and Social Science*, edited by P. Luomanen, I. Pyysiäinen, and R. Uro. Forthcoming.

————. *Identity Matters: John, the Jews and Jewishness.* NovTSup 118. Leiden: Brill, 2005.

————. "The Johannine Community as Jewish Christians? Some Problems in Current Scholarly Consensus." In *Reconsidering Jewish Christianity*, edited by Matt Jackson-McCabe. Minneapolis: Fortress, forthcoming.

Hamilton, David L., and Robert K. Gilford. "Illusory Correlation in Interpersonal Perception: A Cognitive Basis of Stereotypic Judgments." *Journal of Experimental Social Psychology* 12 (1976): 392–407.

Hanne, Johann Wilhelm. "Die Pharisäer und Sadducäer als politische Parteien." *ZWT* 10 (1867): 239–63.

Harrington, Hannah K. "Did the Pharisees Eat Ordinary Food in a State of Ritual Purity?" *JSJ* 26 (1995): 42–54.

Hauptman, Judith. "Mishnah as a Response to Tosefta." In *The Synoptic Problem in Rabbinic Literature*, edited by S. J. D. Cohen. Providence, R.I.: Brown Judaic Studies, 2000. 13–34.

———. *Rereading the Mishnah: A New Approach to Ancient Jewish Texts.* Tübingen: Mohr-Siebeck, 2005.

Hausrath, Adolf. "Die Resultate der jüdischen Forschung über Pharisäer und Saddukäer." *PKZ* 44 (November 1, 1862): 967–78.

———. "Jüdische Zeitschrift für Wissenschaft und Leben." *PKZ* 33 (January 23, 1869): 88.

———. "Jüdische Zeitschrift für Wissenschaft und Leben." *PKZ* 33 (August 14, 1869): 781–82.

———. "Jüdische Zeitschrift für Wissenschaft und Leben." *PKZ* 44 (October 29, 1870): 983–84.

———. *Neutestamentliche Zeitgeschichte.* 4 vols. Munich: Bassermann, 1868–1878.

Hegermann, Harald. "The Diaspora in the Hellenistic Age." In *The Cambridge History of Judaism: The Hellenistic Age*, edited by W. D. Davies and L. Finkelstein. 3 vols. Cambridge: Cambridge University Press, 1989. 2:115–66.

Heil, John Paul. *The Meal Scenes in Luke-Acts: An Audience-Oriented Approach.* SBLMS 52. Atlanta: Society of Biblical Literature, 1999.

Hengel, Martin. *Die johanneische Frage: Ein Lösungsversuch.* WUNT 67. Tübingen: Mohr-Siebeck, 1993.

———. "Jakobus der Herrenbruder—der erste 'Papst'?" In *Glaube und Eschatologie. Festschrift für Werner Georg Kümmel zum 80. Geburtstag*, edited by E. Grässer and O. Merk. Tübingen: Mohr-Siebeck, 1985. 71–104.

———. "Proseuche und Synagogue: Jüdische Gemeinde, Gotteshaus und Gottesdienst in der Diaspora und in Palästina." In *The Synagogue: Study in Origins, Archaeology, and Architecture*, edited by J. Gutmann. New York: Ktav, 1975. 27–54.

———. *The Zealots: Investigations into the Jewish Freedom Movement in the Period from Herod I until 70 A.D.* Edinburgh: T&T Clark, 1989.

Hengel, Martin, and Roland Deines. "E. P. Sanders' 'Common Judaism,' Jesus, and the Pharisees." *JTS* n.s. 46, no. 1 (1995): 1–70.

Herford, R. Travers. *The Pharisees.* Reprint, Boston: Beacon, 1962.

Herzfeld, Levi. *Geschichte des Volkes Israel von der Zerstörung des ersten Tempels bis zur Einsetzung des Makkabäers Schimon zum hohen Priester und Fürsten.* 3 vols. Braunschweig-Nordhausen, 1847.

Heschel, Susannah. *Abraham Geiger and the Jewish Jesus.* Chicago: University of Chicago Press, 1998.

———. *The Aryan Jesus: Christians, Nazis, and the Bible.* Princeton: Princeton University Press, forthcoming.

Hezser, Catherine. *The Social Structure of the Rabbinic Movement in Roman Palestine.* TSAJ 66. Tübingen: Mohr-Siebeck, 1997.

Hinton, Perry R. *Stereotypes, Cognition and Culture.* Psychology Focus Series. Philadelphia: Taylor & Francis, 2000.

Hirschfeld, Y. *Qumran in Context: Reassessing the Archaeological Evidence.* Peabody, Mass.: Hendrickson, 2004.

Hoffmann, Christhard. *Juden und Judentum im Werk deutscher Althistoriker des 19. und 20. Jahrhunderts.* Leiden: Brill, 1988.

Hogg, Michael A. "Social Categorization, Depersonalization, and Group Behavior." In *Blackwell Handbook of Social Psychology: Group Processes,* edited by Michael A. Hogg and R. Scott Tindale. Oxford: Blackwell, 2001. 56–85.

Hoheisel, Karl. *Das antike Judentum in christlicher Sicht.* Wiesbaden: Harrassowitz, 1978.

Hölscher, Gustav. "Josephus." *PW* 18:1934–2000. Munich: A. Druckenmüller, 1916.

Horgan, Maurya P. *Pesharim: Qumran Interpretations of Biblical Books.* CBQMS 8. Washington, D.C.: Catholic Bible Association of America, 1979.

Ilan, D. "Burial Techniques." *OEANE* 1:384–86. Oxford: Oxford University Press, 1996.

Isaac, Benjamin. *The Invention of Racism in Classical Antiquity.* Princeton: Princeton University Press, 2004.

Jaeger, Werner. *Paideia: The Ideals of Greek Culture.* 2 vols. Oxford: Oxford University Press, 1973.

Jaffee, Martin S. *Torah in the Mouth.* Oxford: Oxford University Press, 2001.

Jepsen, Alfred. "Wellhausen in Greifswald: Ein Beitrag zur Biographie Julius Wellhausens." In *Festschrift zur 500-Jahrfeier der Universität Greifswald,* Festschrift zur 500-Jahresfeier der Universität Greifswald. Greifswald, 1956. 2:47–56.

Jeremias, Gert. *Der Lehrer der Gerechtigkeit.* SUNT 2. Göttingen: Vandenhoeck & Ruprecht, 1963.

Jeremias, Joachim. *Jerusalem in the Time of Jesus.* Philadelphia: Fortress, 1969.

———. *Jerusalem zur Zeit Jesu.* 2 vols. Leipzig and Göttingen, 1923–1924, 1929, 1937.

Jervell, J. *The Unknown Paul: Essays on Luke-Acts and Early Christian History.* Minneapolis: Ausburg, 1984.

Johnson, Luke Timothy. *The Gospel of Luke.* SP 3. Collegeville, Minn.: Liturgical Press, 1991.

Jokiranta, Jutta. "Social Identity Approach: Identity-Constructing Elements in the Psalms of Pesher." In *Defining Identities: Who is the Other? We, You, and the Others in the Dead Sea Scrolls. Congress Proceedings of 10QS, July 25–28 2004, Groningen,* edited by F. G. Martínez. Leiden: Brill, forthcoming 2006.

Jost, I. M. *Geschichte der Israeliten.* 9 vols. Berlin, 1820–1828.

Kalmin, Richard. "Christians and Heretics in Rabbinic Literature of Late Antiquity." *HTR* 87 (1994): 155–69.

———. *The Sage in Jewish Society of Late Antiquity.* London and New York: Routledge, 1999.

Kampen, J., and M. J. Bernstein, eds. *Reading 4QMMT: New Perspectives on Qumran Law and History.* SBLSS 2. Atlanta: Scholars Press, 1996.

Keener, Craig S. *A Commentary on the Gospel of Matthew.* Grand Rapids: Eerdmans, 1999.

Keim, Theodor. *The History of Jesus of Nazara.* 6 vols. Translated by A. Ransom and E. Geldart. London: Williams & Norgate, 1876–1883.

Kennedy, G. A. *A New History of Classical Rhetoric.* Princeton: Princeton University Press, 1994.

Kermode, Frank. "Matthew." In *The Literary Guide to the Bible,* edited by R. Alter and F. Kermode. Cambridge: Harvard University Press, 1987. 387–401.

Kimelman, Reuven. "*Birkat Ha-Minim* and the Lack of Evidence for an Anti-Christian Jewish Prayer in Late Antiquity." In *Aspects of Judaism in the Greco-Roman Period,* vol. 2 of *Jewish and Christian Self-Definition,* edited by E. P. Sanders, A. I. Baumgarten, and A. Mendelson. Philadelphia: Fortress, 1981. 226–44.

Klein, Samuel. *Geographie und Geschichte Galiläas.* Leipzig: Rudolf Haupt, 1909.

Klines, David J. A., ed. *Dictionary of Classical Hebrew,* 5 vols. Sheffield: Sheffield Academic, 1993–1998.

Kloner, Amos. "Did a Rolling Stone Close Jesus' Tomb?" *BAR* 25 (1999).

Knight, Douglas A., ed. *Julius Wellhausen and His Prolegomena to the History of Israel.* Chico, Calif.: Scholars Press, 1983.

Kohler, Kaufmann. "Christianity in Its Relation to Judaism." In Singer, *Jewish Encyclopedia,* 4:49–59.

———. "Essenes." *JE,* 5:224–32.

———. "Jesus in Theology." *JE,* 7:166–70.

———. "Karaism." *JE,* 7:446–47.

———. "New Testament." *JE,* 9:246–54.

———. "Pharisees." *JE*, 9:661–66.

———. "Sadducees." *JE*, 10:630–33.

———. "Saul of Tarsus." *JE*, 11:79–37.

Krauss, Samuel. *Talmudische Archäologie: Grundriss der Gesamtwissenschaft des Judentums*. 3 vols. Leipzig, 1910–1912. Reprint, Hildesheim: G. Olms, 1966.

Ladouceur, D. J. "Josephus and Masada." In Feldman and Hata, *Josephus, Judaism, and Christianity*, 95–113.

Lake, Kirsopp. "The Apostolic Council of Jerusalem." In *The Beginnings of Christianity* 5, edited by F. J. Foakes Jackson and Kirsopp Lake. Grand Rapids: Baker, 1979. 195–212.

Lane, William L. *The Gospel according to Mark*. Grand Rapids: Eerdmans, 1974.

Langen, Joseph. *Das Judenthum in Palästina zur Zeit Christi*. Freiburg im Breisgau: Herder Verlag, 1866.

Laqueur, Richard. *Der jüdische Historiker Flavius Josephus: Ein biographischer Versuch auf neuer quellenkritischer Grundlage*. 1920. Reprint, Darmstadt: Wissenschaftliche Buchgesellschaft, 1970.

Laurence, Ray, and Joanne Berry, eds. *Cultural Identity in the Roman Empire*. London: Routledge, 1998.

Lauterbach, Jacob Z. *Rabbinic Essays*. Cincinnati: Hebrew Union College Press, 1951.

Lebeau, Paul. *Le vin nouveau du Royaume: Etude exégétique et patristique sur la Parole eschatologique de Jésus à la Cène*. Paris: Desclée, 1966.

Leszynsky, *Rudolf. Die Sadduzäer*. Berlin: Mayer & Müller, 1912.

Levine, Lee I. *The Ancient Synagogue: The First Thousand Years*. New Haven: Yale University Press, 2000.

———. "The Nature and Origin of the Palestinian Synagogue Reconsidered." *JBL* 115 (1996): 425–48.

———. "The Political Struggle between Pharisees and Sadducees in the Hasmonean Period." In *Jerusalem in the Second Temple Period: Abraham Schalit Memorial Volume*, edited by A. Oppenheimer, U. Rappaport, and M. Stern. Jerusalem: Izhak ben-Zvi, 1980.

Lieberman, Saul. *Tosefta Mo'ed*. New York: Jewish Theological Seminary of America, 1962.

Lightfoot, J. B. *The Apostolic Fathers* 1. London: Macmillan, 1890.

Lightstone, Jack N. "The Formation of the Biblical Canon in Late Antique Judaism," *SR* 8, no. 2 (1979): 135–42.

———. *Mishnah and the Social Formation of the Early Rabbinic Guild: A Socio-Rhetorical Approach*. With an appendix by V. K. Robbins. Waterloo, Ont.: Wilfrid Laurier University Press, 2002.

Lightstone, Jack N. "My Rival, My Fellow: Prolegomena to the Study of Rivalry and Cooperation among Religious Groups in the Galilee of Late Antiquity." In Vaage, *Religious Rivalries in the Early Roman Empire and the Rise of Christianity.* Waterloo, Ont.: Wilfrid Laurier University Press, 2006. 85–105.

———. "The Rabbis' Bible: The Canon of the Hebrew Bible and the Early Rabbinic Guild." In McDonald and Sanders, *Canon Debate,* 163–84.

———. *The Rhetoric of the Babylonian Talmud: Its Social Meaning and Context.* Waterloo, Ont.: Wilfrid Laurier University Press, 1994.

———. "Sadducees versus Pharisees: The Tannaitic Sources." In *Christianity, Judaism, and Other Greco-Roman Cults: Studies for Morton Smith at Sixty: Judaism at 70,* edited by J. Neusner. 3 vols. Leiden: Brill, 1975. 3:206–17.

———. "Sadoq the Yavnean." In *Persons and Institutions in Early Rabbinic Judaism* 1, edited by W. S. Green. Missoula, Mont.: Scholars Press, 1977, 49–148.

———. "Urbanization in the Roman Levant and the Inter-religious Struggle for Success." In Ascough, *Religious Rivalries and the Struggle for Success in Sardis and Smyrna.* Waterloo, Ont.: Wilfrid Laurier University Press, 2005. 211–41.

———. "When Speech is No Speech: The Problem of Early Rabbinic Rhetoric as Discourse." *Semeia* 34 (1985), 53–57.

———. *Yosé the Galilean: Traditions in Mishnah-Tosefta.* Leiden: Brill, 1979.

Lim, Timothy H. "Kittim." In Schiffman and VanderKam, *Encyclopedia of the Dead Sea Scrolls,* 1:469–71.

Loader, William R. G. "Jesus and the Law in John." In *Theology and Christology in the Fourth Gospel: Essays by the Members of the SNTS Johannine Writings Seminar,* edited by G. van Belle, J. G. van der Watt, and P. Maritz. BETL 184. Leuven: Leuven University Press, 2005. 135–54.

Lumby, J. Rawson. *The Acts of the Apostles.* CGTSC. Cambridge: Cambridge University Press, 1904.

Luz, M. "Eleazar's Second Speech on Masada and Its Literary Precedents." *Rheinisches Museum* 126 (1983): 25–43.

Luz, Ulrich. *Matthew 8–20.* Translated by J. Crouch. Minneapolis: Fortress, 2001.

MacMullen, R. *Enemies of the Roman Order: Treason, Unrest, and Alienation in the Empire.* London: Routledge, 1966.

Maddox, Robert. *The Purpose of Luke-Acts.* SNTW. Edinburgh: T&T Clark, 1982.

Magen, Y. "Jerusalem as a Center of the Stone Vessel Industry during the Second Temple Period." In *Ancient Jerusalem Revealed,* edited by H. Geva. Jerusalem: Israel Exploration Society; Washington, D.C.: Biblical Archaeology Society, 1994. 244–56.

————. "The Stone Vessel Industry during the Second Temple Period." In *Purity Broke Out in Israel, catalogue no. 9*, 7–28. The Reuben and Edith Hecht Museum, University of Haifa, 1994.

————. *The Stone Vessel Industry in Jerusalem during the Second Temple Period.* Jerusalem: Society for the Protection of Nature [Hebrew], 1988.

————. *The Stone Vessel Industry in the Second Temple Period: Excavations at Hizma and the Jerusalem Temple Mount.* Jerusalem: Israel Antiquities Authority, 2002.

Magness, Jodi. *The Archaeology of Qumran and the Dead Sea Scrolls.* Grand Rapids: Eerdmans, 2002.

Maier, Gerhard. *Mensch und freier Wille: Nach den juedischen Religionsparteien zwischen Ben Sira und Paulus.* Tübingen: Mohr-Siebeck, 1981.

Malina, Bruce, and Jerome Neyrey. "First-Century Personality: Dyadic, Not Individualistic." In Neyrey, *Social World of Luke-Acts*, 67–96.

Mann, C. S. *Mark.* Garden City, N.Y.: Doubleday, 1986.

Marchand, Suzanne. "Philhellenism and the Furor Orientalis." *Modern Intellectual History* 1, no. 3 (2004): 331–58.

Marcus, Ralph. *Josephus: Jewish Antiquities.* 9 vols. LCL. Cambridge, Mass.: Harvard University Press; London: Heinemann, 1966–1971.

————. "The Pharisees in the Light of Modern Scholarship." *JR* 32 (1952): 153–64.

Marincola, John. *Authority and Tradition in Ancient Historiography.* Cambridge: Cambridge University Press, 1997.

Marrou, H. I. *A History of Education in Antiquity.* Madison: University of Wisconsin Press, 1956.

Martyn, J. Louis. *History and Theology in the Fourth Gospel.* NTL. 3rd ed. Louisville, Ky.: Westminster John Knox, 2003.

Mason, Steve. "Contradiction or Counterpoint? Josephus and Historical Method." *RRJ* 6 (2003): 145–88.

————. "Early Jewish and Christian Uses of Philosophy." In *The Columbia History of Western Philosophy.* edited by R. H. Popkin. New York: Columbia University Press, 1999. 111–18.

————. "Figured Speech and Irony in T. Flavius Josephus." In Edmondson et. al., *Flavius Josephus and Flavian Rome*, 243–88.

————. "Flavius Josephus in Flavian Rome: Reading on and between the Lines." In *Flavian Rome: Culture, Text, Image*, edited by A. J. Boyle and W. J. Dominik. Leiden: Brill, 2002. 559–89.

————. *Flavius Josephus on the Pharisees: A Composition-Critical Study.* StPB 39. Leiden: Brill, 1991.

————, ed. *Flavius Josephus: Translation and Commentary.* Vol. 9 of *Life of Josephus.* Leiden: Brill, 2001.

Mason, Steve. "Josephus, Daniel, and the Flavian House." In *Josephus and the History of the Greco-Roman Period*, edited by F. Parente and J. Sievers. Leiden: Brill, 1994. 161–91.

———. "Pharisees." In *Dictionary of New Testament Background*, edited by C. Evans and S. Porter. Downers Grove, Ill.: InterVarsity, 2000. 782–87.

———. "The Problem of the Pharisees in Modern Scholarship." In *Approaches to Ancient Judaism*, n.s. 4, edited by Jacob Neusner. Atlanta: Scholars Press, 1993. 103–40.

———. "Revisiting Josephus's Pharisees." In Neusner and Avery-Peck, *Judaism in Late Antiquity: Where We Stand*. 2:23–56.

———. "Was Josephus a Pharisee? A Reconsideration of *Life* 10–12." *JJS* 40 (1989): 31–45.

May, James M. *Trials of Character: The Eloquence of Ciceronian Ethos*. Chapel Hill: University of North Carolina Press, 1988.

McDonald, Lee M., and James Sanders, eds. *The Canon Debate: On the Origins and Formation of the Bible*. Peabody, Mass.: Hendrickson, 2002.

McKnight, S. *A Light among the Gentiles: Jewish Missionary Activity in the Second Temple Period*. Minneapolis: Fortress, 1991.

Meeks, Wayne A. "Breaking Away: Three New Testament Pictures of Christianity's Separation from the Jewish Communities." In *"To See Ourselves as Others See Us": Christians, Jews, "Others" in Late Antiquity*, edited by J. Neusner and E. S. Frerichs. Studies in the Humanities 9. Chico, Calif.: Scholars Press; 1985. 94–115.

Meier, Johann. *Jesus von Nazareth in der talmudischen Überlieferung*. Darmstadt: Wissenschaftliche Buchgesellschaft, 1978.

———. *Jüdische Auseinandersetzung mit dem Christentum in der Antike*. Darmstadt: Wissenschaftliche Buchgesellschaft, 1982.

Meier, John P. "Is There *Halaka* (the Noun) at Qumran?" *JBL* 122 (2003): 150–55.

———. "The Quest for the Historical Pharisee: A Review Essay on Roland Deines, Die Pharisäer." *CBQ* 61 (1999): 713–22.

———. *The Vision of Matthew: Christ, Church and Morality in the First Gospel*. New York: Paulist Press, 1979.

Mellor, R. *Tacitus*. London: Routledge, 1993.

Meredith, A. "Later Philosophy." In *The Roman World*, edited by John Boardman, Jasper Green, and Oswyn Murray. Oxford: Oxford University Press, 1988. 288–307.

Meyer, Ben F. "A Caricature of Joachim Jeremias and His Work." *JBL* 110 (1991): 451–62.

Meyer-Zwiffelhoffer, E. Πολιτικῶς ἄρχειν: *Zum Regierungsstil der senatorischen Statthalter in den kaiserzeitlichen griechischen Provinzen*. Stuttgart: F. Steiner, 2002.

Meyers, E. M. *Jewish Ossuaries: Reburial and Rebirth. Secondary Burials in Their Ancient Near Eastern Setting.* Rome, Biblical Institute Press, 1971.

Michel, O. *Der Brief an die Römer.* Göttingen: Vandenhoeck & Ruprecht, 1966.

Millar, Fergus. "Last Year in Jerusalem: Monuments of the Jewish War in Rome." In Edmondson et al., *Flavius Josephus and Flavian Rome*, 101–28.

Miller, Stuart S. "The Minim of Sepphoris Reconsidered." *HTR* 86 (1993): 377–402.

―――. "New Perspectives on the History of Sepphoris." In *Galilee through the Centuries: Confluence of Cultures*, edited by Eric M. Meyers. Duke Judaic Studies Series 1. Winona Lake, Ind.: Eisenbrauns, 1999. 145–59.

Moehring, H. R. "Joseph ben Matthia and Flavius Josephus." In *Aufstieg und Niedergang der Römischen Welt*, edited by H. Temporini and W. Haase. Berlin: Walter de Gruyter, 1984. 2.21.2, 864–917.

―――. "Novelistic Elements in the Writings of Flavius Josephus." Ph.D. diss., University of Chicago, 1957.

Moloney, Francis J. "Israel, the People and the Jews in the Fourth Gospel." In *Israel und seine Heilstraditionen im Johannesevangelium: Festgabe für Johannes Beutler SJ zum 70. Geburtstag*, edited by M. Labahn, K. Scholtissek, and A. Strotmann. Paderborn: Ferdinand Schöningh, 2004. 351–64.

Momigliano, Arnaldo. *Quarto Contributo alla Storia degli Studi Classici e del Mondo Antico.* Rome: Edizioni di Storia e Letteratura. 1969.

Moore, George F. "Christian Writers on Judaism," *HTR* 14, no. 3 (1921): 197–254.

―――. "Fate and Free Will in the Jewish Philosophies according to Josephus." *HTR* 22 (1929): 371–89.

―――. *Judaism in the First Centuries of the Christian Era.* 3 vols. Cambridge, Mass.: Harvard University Press, 1954.

Mørkholm, Otto. "Antiochus IV." In *The Cambridge History of Judaism: The Hellenistic Age*, edited by W. D. Davies and L. Finkelstein, 3 vols. Cambridge: Cambridge University Press, 1989. 2:278–91.

Moxnes, Halvor. "Patron-Client Relations and the New Community in Luke-Acts." In Neyrey, *Social World of Luke-Acts*, 241–68.

Murphy-O'Connor, Jerome. *Paul: A Critical Life.* Oxford: Clarendon, 1996.

Neander, August. *Geschichte der Pflanzung und Leitung der christlichen Kirche durch die Apostel: als selbständiger Nachtrag zu der allgemeinen Geschichte der christlichen Religion und Kirche.* 2 vols. Hamburg: Friedrich Perthes, 1832–1833.

Neusner, Jacob. *The Bavli that Might Have Been: The Tosefta's Theory of Mishnah Commentary Compared to the Bavli's.* Atlanta: Scholars Press, 1991.

―――. *Development of a Legend.* Leiden: Brill, 1970.

―――. *Eliezer ben Hyrcanus: The Tradition and the Man.* 2 vols. Leiden, 1973: Brill. Reprint, Eugene, Ore.: Wipf & Stock, 2003.

Neusner, Jacob. "The Fellowship (חבורה) in the Second Jewish Commonwealth." *HTR* 53 (1960): 125–42.

———. *Formative Judaism: Religious, Historical, and Literary Studies. Third Series. Torah, Pharisees, and Rabbis.* BJS 91. Chico, Calif.: Scholars Press, 1985; Now: Lanham, Md.: University Press of America.

———. *From Politics to Piety: The Emergence of Pharisaic Judaism.* Englewood Cliffs, N.J.: Prentice Hall, 1973. Reprint, New York: Ktav, 1979.

———. *A History of the Jews in Babylonia.* Vol. 1: *The Parthian Period.* Leiden: Brill, 1965.

———. *A History of the Mishnaic Law of Holy Things* 3. Leiden: Brill, 1979.

———. *A History of the Mishnaic Law of Purities* 21. Leiden: Brill, 1977.

———. "Josephus' Pharisees: A Complete Repertoire." In Feldman and Hata, *Josephus, Judaism, and Christianity,* 274–92.

———. *Judaic Law from Jesus to the Mishnah.* Atlanta: Scholars Press, 1993.

———. *Judaism as Philosophy: The Method and Message of the Mishnah.* Columbia: University of South Carolina Press, 1991.

———. *Judaism: The Evidence of the Mishnah.* Chicago: University of Chicago Press, 1981.

———. *Life of Rabbi Yohanan ben Zakkai.* Leiden: Brill, 1968.

———. *The Mishnah: A New Translation.* New Haven: Yale University Press, 1988.

———. *The Mishnah: Social Perspectives.* Leiden: Brill, 1999.

———. "Mr. Maccoby's Red Cow, Mr. Sanders's Pharisees—and Mine." *JSJ* 23, no. 1 (1992): 81–98.

———. *The Pharisees: Rabbinic Perspectives. Reprise of The Rabbinic Traditions about the Pharisees before 70.* Vols. 1–3. New York: Ktav, 1985.

———. *The Rabbinic Traditions about the Pharisees before 70.* 3 vols. Leiden, Brill, 1971. Second printing, Atlanta: Scholars Press for South Florida Studies in the *History of Judaism,* 1999. Now: Lanham, Md.: University Press of America.

———. *Reading and Believing: Ancient Judaism and Contemporary Gullibility.* BJS. Atlanta: Scholars Press, 1986.

———. *Religious, Historical, and Literary Studies, 3rd s., Torah, Pharisees, and Rabbis.* Chico, Calif.: Scholars Press for BJS, 1983.

———. *Tosefta: Its Structure and Its Sources.* Atlanta: Scholars Press, 1986.

———. *Transformation of Judaism: From Philosophy to Religion.* Champaign: University of Illinois Press, 1991.

———. *Uniting the Dual Torah: Sifra and the Problem of the Mishnah.* Cambridge: Cambridge University Press, 1990.

Neusner, Jacob, and A. J. Avery-Peck, eds. *Judaism in Late Antiquity: Where We Stand.* 5 vols. Leiden: Brill, 1999.

Neusner, Jacob, and William Scott Green, eds. *The Origins of Judaism: Religion, History, and Literature in Late Antiquity*. 20 vols. New York: Garland Press, 1991.

Newport, Kenneth G. C. "The Pharisees in Judaism Prior to A.D. 70." *AUSS* 29, no. 2 (1991): 127–37.

Neyrey, Jerome. "Ceremonies in Luke-Acts: The Case of Meals and Table-Fellowship." In Neyrey, *Social World of Luke-Acts*, 361–87.

———, ed. *The Social World of Luke-Acts: Models for Interpretation*. Peabody, Mass.: Hendrickson, 1991.

———. "The Symbolic Universe of Luke-Acts: 'They Turn the World Upside Down.'" In Neyrey, *Social World of Luke-Acts*, 271–304.

Nicklas, Tobias. *Ablösung und Verstrickung: "Juden" und Jüngergestalten als Charaktere der erzählten Welt des Johannesevangeliums und ihre Wirkung auf den impliziten Leser*. RST 60. Frankfurt am Main: Peter Lang, 2001.

Nock, A. D. *Conversion: The Old and the New in Religion from Alexander the Great to Augustine*. London: Oxford University Press, 1933.

Oakes, Penelope J., S. Alexander Haslam, and John C. Turner. *Stereotyping and Social Reality*. Oxford: Blackwell, 1994.

Oakes, Penelope J., S. Alexander Haslam, and Katherine J. Reynolds. "Social Categorization and Social Context: Is Stereotype Change a Matter of Information or of Meaning?" In Abrams and Hogg, *Social Identity and Social Cognition*, 55–79.

Overman, J. Andrew. *Matthew's Gospel and Formative Judaism: The Social World of the Matthean Community*. Minneapolis: Fortress, 1990.

Otis, Brooks. "The Uniqueness of Latin Literature." *Arion* 6 (1967): 185–206.

Palmer, Leonard R. *The Greek Language*. London: Faber, 1980.

Parsons, Mikeal C., and Richard I. Pervo. *Rethinking the Unity of Luke-Acts*. Minneapolis: Fortress, 1993.

Pelling, Christopher. *Plutarch and History*. Swansea: Classical Press of Wales, 2000.

Perkins, Pheme. *The Gospel of Mark*. NIB 8. Nashville: Abingdon Press, 1995. 509–733.

Perles, Felix. *Bousset's Religion des Judentums im neutestamentlichen Zeitalter kritisch untersucht*. Berlin: Wolf Peiser, 1903.

———. *Jüdische Skizzen*, 2nd ed. Leipzig: G. Engel, 1920.

Poirier, John C. "Why Did the Pharisees Wash Their Hands?" *JJS* 47 (1996): 217–33.

Posnanski, Samuel. "Geschichte der Sekten und der Halacha." In *Abraham Geiger: Leben und Lebenswerk*. edited by Ludwig Geiger. Berlin: Georg Reimer, 1910. 352–87.

Powell, Mark Allan. "Do and Keep What Moses Says (Matthew 23:2-7)." *JBL* 114, no. 3 (1995): 419–35.

———. *Fortress Introduction to the Gospels*. Minneapolis: Fortress, 1998.

Rabbinowitz, Noel S. "Matthew 23:2-4: Does Jesus Recognize the Authority of the Pharisees and Does He Endorse Their Halakhah?" *JETS* 46, no. 3 (2003): 423–47.

Rabin, Chalm. "Alexander Jannaeus and the Pharisees." *JJS* 7 (1956): 3–11.

Rahmani, L. Y. *A Catalogue of Jewish Ossuaries in the Collections of the State of Israel*. Jerusalem: Israel Antiquities Authority and the Israel Academy of Sciences and Humanities, 1994.

———. "Ossuaries and Bone-Gathering in the Late Second Temple Period." *Qadmoniot* 11 (1978): 102–12 (Hebrew).

Rajak, Tessa. *Josephus: The Historian and His Society*. London: Duckworth, 1983.

Rappaport, Uriel. "Onias." *ABD* 5:23–24. New York: Doubleday, 1992.

Rapske, Brian. *The Book of Acts and Paul in Roman Custody. The Book of Acts in Its First-Century Setting* 3. Grand Rapids: Eerdmans, 1994.

Rasp, Hans. "Flavius Josephus und die jüdischen Religionsparteien." *ZNW* 23 (1924): 27–47.

Ravens, David. *Luke and the Restoration of Israel*. JSNTSup 119. Sheffield: Sheffield Academic, 1995. 247–57.

Reed, Jonathan L. *Archaeology and the Galilean Jesus: A Re-examination of the Evidence*. Harrisburg: Trinity Press International, 2000.

Regev, Eyal. "Were the Priests All the Same? Qumranic Halakhah in Comparison with Sadducean Halakhah." *DSD* 12, no. 2 (2005): 158–82.

Reich, Ronnie. "*Miqwa'ot* (Ritual Baths) at Qumran," *Qadmoniot* 114 (1997), 125–28 (Hebrew).

———. "Miqwa'ot at Khirbet Qumran and the Jerusalem Connection." In *The Dead Sea Scrolls Fifty Years After Their Discovery*, edited by L. Schiffman, E. Tov, and J. L. VanderKam. Jerusalem: Israel Exploration Society in cooperation with the Shrine of the Book, Israel Museum, 2000. 728–31.

Reinhartz, Adele. *Befriending the Beloved Disciple: A Jewish Reading of the Gospel of John*. New York: Continuum, 2001.

———. "The Johannine Community and Its Jewish Neighbors: A Reappraisal." In *"What is John?": Literary and Social Readings of the Fourth Gospel*, edited by F. F. Segovia. SBLSymS 7. 2 vols. Atlanta: Scholars Press, 1998. 2:111–38.

Renan, Ernest. *The Life of Jesus*. Translated by C. E. Wilbour. New York: Carleton, 1864.

Richards, G. C. "The Composition of Josephus' Antiquities." *CQ* 33 (1939): 36–40.

Ringe, Sharon. *Luke*. Westminster Bible Companion. Louisville, Ky.: Westminster John Knox, 1995.

Rivkin, Ellis. "Defining the Pharisees: The Tannaitic Sources." *HUCA* 40 (1969): 205–49.

———. *A Hidden Revolution: The Pharisees' Search for the Kingdom Within*. Nashville: Abingdon, 1978.

———. "Who Were the Pharisees?" In Neusner and Avery-Peck, *Judaism in Late Antiquity: Where We Stand*, 3:1–34.

Rohrbaugh, Richard L. "The Pre-industrial City in Luke-Acts: Urban Social Relations." In Neyrey, *Social World of Luke-Acts*, 125–49.

Rosivach, Vincent J. *The System of Public Sacrifice in Fourth-Century Athens*. ACS 34. Atlanta: Scholars Press, 1994.

Roth, Cecil. "The 'Chair of Moses' and Its Survivals." *PEQ* 81 (1949): 100–101.

Rudich, Vasily. *Dissidence and Literature under Nero: The Price of Rhetoricization*. London: Routledge, 1997.

———. *Political Dissidence under Nero: The Price of Dissimulation*. London: Routledge, 1993.

Rutgers, Leonard V. *What Athens Has to Do with Jerusalem: Essays on Classical, Jewish, and Early Christian Art and Archaeology in Honor of Gideon Foerster*. Interdisciplinary Studies in Ancient Culture and Religion 1. Leuven: Peeters, 2002.

Saldarini, Anthony J. *Matthew's Christian-Jewish Community*. Chicago: University of Chicago Press, 1994.

———. "Pharisees." *ABD* 5 (Garden City, N.Y.: Doubleday, 1992), 289–303.

———. *Pharisees, Scribes and Sadducees in Palestinian Society: A Sociological Approach*. Wilmington, Del.: Michael Glazier, 1988.

Sanders, E. P. "Defending the Indefensible." *JBL* 110 (1991): 463–78.

———. *Jesus and Judaism*. Philadelphia: Fortress, 1985.

———. *Jewish Law from Jesus to the Mishnah: Five Studies*. London: SCM Press; Philadelphia: Trinity Press International, 1990.

———. *Judaism: Practice and Belief, 63 BCE–66 CE*. Philadelphia: Trinity Press International, 1992.

Sanders, Jack T. *The Jews in Luke-Acts*. Philadelphia: Fortress, 1987.

———. "The Pharisees in Luke-Acts." In *The Living Text: Essays in Honor of Ernest W. Saunders*, edited by D. Groh and R. Jewett. Lanham, Md.: University Press of America, 1985. 141–88.

Satran, D. "Daniel: Seer, Prophet, Holy Man." In *Ideal Figures in Ancient Judaism: Profiles and Paradigms*, edited by J. J. Collins and G. W. E. Nickelsburg. Chico, Calif.: Scholars Press, 1980. 33–48.

Schechter, S. *Aspects of Rabbinic Theology: Major Concepts of the Talmud*. New York: Schocken Books, 1961.

Schenkel, Daniel. *The Character of Jesus Portrayed*. 2 vols. Translated by W. H. Furness. Boston: Little, Brown, 1866.

Schiffman, Lawrence. "The Pharisees and Their Legal Traditions according to the Dead Sea Scrolls." *DSD* 8 (2001): 262–77.

Schiffman, Lawrence H., and James C. VanderKam, eds. *Encyclopedia of the Dead Sea Scrolls*. 2 vols. Oxford: Oxford University Press, 2000.

Schneckenburger, Matthias. *Beiträge zur Einleitung ins Neue Testament und zur Erklärung seiner schwierigen Stellen*. Stuttgart: F. C. Löflund & Sohn, 1832.

———. *Vorlesungen über neutestamentliche Zeitgeschichte: aus dessen handschriftlichem Nachlass*. Edited by Theodor Loehlein. Frankfurt: H. L. Brönner, 1862.

Schneiders, Sandra M. *The Revelatory Text: Interpreting the New Testament as Sacred Scripture*. 2nd ed. Collegeville, Minn.: Liturgical Press, 1999.

Schürer, Emil. *The History of the Jewish People in the Age of Jesus Christ (175 B.C.–A.D. 135)*. 3 vols. Revised and edited by G. Vermes, F. Millar, and M. Black. Edinburgh: T&T Clark, 1973–1987.

———. *Lehrbuch der neutestamentlichen Zeitgeschichte*. Leipzig: J. C. Hinrichs'sche Buchhandlung, 1874; 2nd ed. published as *Geschichte des jüdischen Volkes im Zeitalter Jesu Christi*. Leipzig: J. C. Hinrichs'sche Buchhandlung, 1886–87. 3rd ed., 1898.

Schwartz, Daniel R. "Josephus and Nicolaus on the Pharisees." *JSJ* 14 (1983): 157–71.

———. "MMT, Josephus, and the Pharisees." In Kampen and Bernstein, *Reading 4QMMT*, 67–80.

Schwartz, Seth. *Josephus and Judaean Politics*. CSCT 18. Leiden: Brill, 1990.

Schweizer, Eduard. *The Good News according to Matthew*. Translated by D. Green. Atlanta: John Knox, 1975.

Segal, Alan F. "Judaism, Christianity, and Gnosticism." In *Anti-Judaism in Early Christianity: Separation and Polemic*, edited by S. G. Wilson. Studies in Christianity and Judaism 2. Waterloo, Ont.: Wilfrid Laurier University Press, 1986. 133–61.

Senior, Donald. *What Are They Saying About Matthew?* New York: Paulist Press, 1996.

Setzer, Claudia. *Jewish Responses to Early Christians: History and Polemics, 30–150 C.E.* Minneapolis: Fortress, 1994.

Sherman, Steven J., David L. Hamilton, and Amy C. Lewis. "Perceived Entitativity and the Social Identity Value of Group Membership." In Abrams and Hogg, *Social Identity and Social Cognition*, 80–110.

Shutt, R. J. H. *Studies in Josephus*. London: SPCK, 1961.

Sievers, Joseph. "Josephus and the Afterlife." In *Understanding Josephus: Seven Perspectives*, edited by S. Mason. Sheffield: Sheffield Academic, 1998. 20–31.

———. "Josephus, First Maccabees, Sparta, the Three Haireseis—and Cicero." *JSJ* 32 (2001): 241–51.

Simon-Nahum, Perrine. *Le cite investie: La Science du Judaisme francais et la Republique.* Paris: Les editions du Cerf, 1991.

Singer, Isidor, ed. *The Jewish Encyclopedia.* 12 vols. New York: Funk & Wagnalls, 1901–1906.

Smend, Rudolf. "Wellhausen und das Judentum." *ZTK* 79, no. 3 (1982): 249–82.

Smith, Christopher R. "Literary Evidences of a Fivefold Structure in the Gospel of Matthew." *NTS* 43 (1997): 540–51.

Smith, D. Moody. "The Contribution of J. Louis Martyn to the Under-standing of the Gospel of John." In *History and Theology in the Fourth Gospel*, edited by J. Louis Martyn. NTL. 3rd ed. Louisville, Ky.: Westminster John Knox, 2003. 1–19.

Smith, Morton. "The Dead Sea Sect in Relation to Ancient Judaism." *NTS* 7 (1961): 347–60.

———. "The Description of the Essenes in Josephus and the Philosophoumena." *HUCA* 35 (1958): 273–93.

———. "The Occult in Josephus." In Feldman and Hata, *Josephus, Judaism, and Christianity*, 236–56.

———. "Palestinian Judaism in the First Century." In *Israel: Its Role in Civilization*, edited by M. Davis. New York: Harper, 1956. 67–81.

———. "The Pharisees in the Gospels." In Neusner, *From Politics to Piety*, 155–59.

Squires, John T. *The Plan of God in Luke-Acts.* SNTSMS 76. Cambridge: Cambridge University Press, 1993.

Steele, E. S. "Luke 11:37–54—a Modified Hellenistic Symposium?" *JBL* 103 (1984): 379–94.

Stemberger, Günter. *Jewish Contemporaries of Jesus: Pharisees, Sadducees, Essenes.* Translated by Allan W. Mahnke. Minneapolis: Fortress, 1995.

Stern, Sacha. *Jewish Identity in Early Rabbinic Writings.* AGJU 23. Leiden: Brill, 1994.

Strange, James F. "Ancient Texts, Archaeology as Text, and the Problem of the First-Century Synagogue." In *The Evolution of the Synagogue*, edited by H. C. Kee and L. Cohick. Valley Forge, Pa.: Trinity Press International, 1999. 27–45.

———. "Archaeology and Synagogues up to about 200 C.E." In *Judaism and Christianity in the Beginning*, vol. 2 of *When Judaism and Christianity Began:*

Essays in Memory of Anthony J. Saldarini, edited by A. J. Avery-Peck, D. Harrington, and J. Neusner. Leiden: Brill, 2004. 483–508.

Strange, James F. "The Art and Archaeology of Ancient Judaism." In *Judaism in Late Antiquity: The Literary and Archaeological Sources*, edited by J. Neusner. Leiden: Brill, 1995. 64–114.

———. "The Synagogue as Metaphor." In Neusner and Avery-Peck, *Judaism in Late Antiquity: Where We Stand*. 4:91–120.

Swain, Simon. *Hellenism and Empire: Language, Classicism, and Power in the Greek World, AD 50–250*. Oxford: Oxford University Press, 1996.

Syme, Ronald. *The Roman Revolution*. Oxford: Oxford University Press, 1939.

———. *Tacitus*. Oxford: Clarendon, 1958.

Talbert, Charles H. *Reading Luke: A Literary and Theological Commentary on the Third Gospel*. New York: Crossroad, 1992.

Taylor, Vincent. *The Gospel According to Mark*. Grand Rapids: Baker Book House, 1966, 1981.

Thackeray, H. S. J. *Josephus: The Jewish War*. 9 vols. LCL. Cambridge, Mass: Harvard University Press; London: Heinemann, 1926–1965.

———. *Josephus: The Man and the Historian*. 1929. Reprint, New York: Ktav, 1967.

Theobald, Michael. "Abraham – (Isaak –) Jakob: Israels Väter im Johannes-evangelium." In *Israel und seine Heilstraditionen im Johannesevangelium: Festgabe für Johannes Beutler SJ zum 70. Geburtstag*, edited by M. Labahn, K. Scholtissek, and A. Strotmann. Paderborn: Ferdinand Schöningh, 2004. 158–83.

Tigerstedt, E. N. *The Legend of Sparta in Classical Antiquity*. 2 vols. Stockholm: Almquist & Wiksell, 1974.

Tilley, C.Y. *Metaphor and Material Culture*. Oxford: Blackwell, 1999.

Tolmie, D. François. "The Ioudaioi in the Fourth Gospel: A Narratological Perspective." In *Theology and Christology in the Fourth Gospel: Essays by the Members of the SNTS Johannine Writings Seminar*, edited by G. van Belle, J. G. van der Watt, and P. Maritz. BETL 184. Leuven: Leuven University Press, 2005. 377–97.

Tomes, R. "Why Did Paul Get His Hair Cut? (Acts 18.18; 21.23-24)." In Tuckett, *Luke's Literary Achievement*, 188–97.

Tuckett, C. M., ed. *Luke's Literary Achievement: Collected Essays*, JSNTSup 116. Sheffield: Sheffield Academic, 1995.

Turner, John C. "Some Current Issues in Research on Social Identity and Self-Categorization Theories." In *Social Identity: Context, Commitment, Content*, edited by N. Ellemers, R. Spears. Oxford: Blackwell, 1999. 6–34.

Twelftree, G. H. "Scribes." In *Dictionary of New Testament Background*, edited by C. Evans and S. Porter. Downers Grove, Ill.: InterVarsity, 2000. 1086–89.

Vaage, L. E., ed. *Religious Rivalries in the Early Roman Empire and the Rise of Christianity*. Waterloo, Ont.: Wilfrid Laurier University Press, 2006.

VanderKam, James C. "Pesher Nahum and Josephus." In *When Christianity and Judaism Began: Essays in Memory of Anthony J. Saldarini*, edited by A. J. Avery-Peck, D. Harrington, and J. Neusner. JSJSup 85. 2 vols. Leiden: Brill, 2004. 1:299–311.

———. "Those Who Look for Smooth Things, Pharisees, and Oral Law." In *Emanuel: Studies in Hebrew Bible, Septuagint, and Dead Sea Scrolls in Honor of Emanuel Tov*, edited by S. Paul et al. VTSup 94. Leiden and Boston: Brill, 2003. 465–77.

Vermes, Geza. *The Complete Dead Sea Scrolls in English*. New York and London: Penguin, 1997.

Volkmar, Gustav. *Die Religion Jesu*. Leipzig: F. A. Brockhaus, 1857.

Volz, Paul. "Pharisäer." *RGG* 4 (1930): 1178f.

Wacholder, B.-Z. "A Qumran Attack on the Oral Exegesis? The Phrase מרקס דומלתב רס in 4 Q Pesher Nahum." *RevQ* 5 (1966): 575–78.

Wächter, L. "Die unterschiedliche Haltung der Pharisaeer, Sadduzaeer und Essener zur Heimarmene nach dem Bericht des Josephus." *ZRGG* 21 (1969): 97–114.

Wahlde, Urban C. von. "'The Jews' in the Gospel of John: Fifteen Years of Research (1983–1998)." *ETL* 76 (2000): 30–55.

———. "The Relationships between Pharisees and Chief Priests: Some Observations on the Texts in Matthew, John, and Josephus." *NTS* 42 (1996): 506–22.

Wansbrough, Henry, ed. *Jesus and the Oral Tradition*. Sheffield: Sheffield Academic, 1991.

Wardman, A. *Rome's Debt to Greece*. Bristol: Bristol Classical Press, 1976.

Waubke, Hans-Günther. *Die Pharisäer in der protestantischen Bibelwissenschaft des 19. Jahrhunderts*. Beiträge zur historischen Theologie 107. Edited by J. Wallmann. Tübingen: Mohr-Siebeck, 1998.

Wellhausen, Julius. *Der Text der Bücher Samuelis*. Göttingen: Vandenhoeck & Ruprecht, 1871.

———. *Die Pharisäer und die Sadducäer: Eine Untersuchung zu inneren jüdischen Geschichte*. Greifswald: Bamberg, 1874; 2nd ed., Hannover: Orient-Buchhandlung H. Lafaire, 1924; 3rd ed., Göttingen: Vandenhoeck & Ruprecht, 1967.

———. *Israelitische und jüdische Geschichte*. Berlin, 1894.

Wellhausen, Julius. *Prolegomena to the History of Ancient Israel.* New York: Meridian Books, 1957.

Wengst, Klaus. *Bedrängte Gemeinde und verherrlichter Christus: Ein Versuch über das Johannesevangelium.* 4th ed. Munich: Kaiser Verlag, 1992.

Westerholm, Stephen. "Pharisees." In *Dictionary of Jesus and the Gospels,* edited by J. Green and S. McKnight. Downers Grove, Ill.: InterVarsity, 1992. 609–14.

Wiese, Christian. *Challenging Colonial Discourse: Jewish Studies and Protestant Theology in Wilhelmine Germany.* Studies in European Judaism 10. Edited by Giuseppe Veltri. Leiden: Brill, 2005.

———. "Ein 'Schrei ins Leere'? Die Auseinandersetzung der Wissenschaft des Judentums mit dem Judentumsbild der protestantischen Theologie im Kontext der Diskussion über die Stellung der jüdischen Gemeinschaft im wilhelminischen Deutschland 1890–1914." Ph.D. diss., Faculty of Protestant Theology, Goethe University, Frankfurt, 1996.

Williams, D. S. "Josephus and the Authorship of *War* 2.119–161 (on the Essenes)." *JSJ* 25 (1994): 207–21.

Winer, Georg Benedikt. *Biblische Realwörterbuch zum Handgebrauch für Studirende, Candidaten, Gymnasiallehrer und Prediger.* 2 vols. Leipzig: Carl Heinrich Reclam, 1847–1848.

Wirth, Michael. *Die Pharisäer: Ein Beitrag zum leichtern Verstehen der Evangelien und zur Selbstprüfung.* Ulm: Stetten, 1824.

Wise, Michael, Martin Abegg, and Edward Cook, eds. *The Dead Sea Scrolls: A New Translation.* San Franscisco: Harper, 1996.

Wiseman, T. P. *Death of an Emperor: Flavius Josephus.* Exeter: University of Exeter Press, 1991.

Wojciechowski, M. "Le naziréat et la Passion (Mc 14,25a; 15:23)." *Bib* 65 (1984): 94–96.

Wright, N. T. *Romans.* NIB 10. Nashville: Abingdon, 2002.

Zahavy, Tzvee. *The Traditions of Eleazar ben Azariah.* Missoula, Mont.: Scholars Press, 1977.

Zeitlin, Solomon. "Hillel and the Hermeneutic Rules." *JQR* 54 (1963–1964): 161–73.

———. "The Pharisees and the Gospels." In *Essays and Studies in Memory of Linda R. Miller,* edited by Israel Davidson. New York, 1938. 235–86.

———. "Les principes des controverses halachiques entre les écoles de Schammai et de Hillel." *REJ* 93 (1932): 73–83.

———. "Prosbol: A Study in Tannaitic Jurisprudence." *JQR* 37 (1946): 341–62.

―――. *The Rise and Fall of the Judaean State: A Political, Social and Religious History of the Second Commonwealth*. 2 vols. Philadelphia: Jewish Publication Society, 1962, 1967.

―――. "Sameias and Pollion." *JJLP* 1 (1919): 61–67.

―――. "The Semikhah Controversy between the Zugoth." *JQR* 7 (1916–1917): 499–517.

―――. "Studies in Tannaitic Jurisprudence." *JJLP* 1 (1919): 297–311.

Ziesler, J. A. "Luke and the Pharisees." *NTS* 25 (1978–1979): 146–57.

Zlotnick, Dov. *The Iron Pillar—Mishnah*. Jerusalem: Mosad Bialik, 1988.

Zumstein, Jean. "The Farewell Discourse (John 13:31–16:33) and the Problem of Anti-Judaism." In Bieringer et al., *Anti-Judaism and the Fourth Gospel*, 461–78.

ABOUT THE CONTRIBUTORS

BRUCE D. CHILTON is Bernard Iddings Bell Professor of Religion and director of the Institute of Advanced Theology at Bard College, Annandale-on-Hudson, New York.

WILLIAM SCOTT GREEN is professor of religion, Philip Sm Bernstein Professor of Judaic Studies, and dean of the college, University of Rochester.

RAIMO HAKOLA is adjunct professor (docent) in New Testament studies at the University of Helsinki and works as a postdoctoral researcher in the Department of Biblical Studies.

SUSANNAH HESCHEL is Eli Black Associate Professor of Jewish Studies in the Department of Religion at Dartmouth College.

AMY-JILL LEVINE is E. Rhodes and Leona B. Carpenter Professor of New Testament Studies at Vanderbilt University Divinity School and Graduate Department of Religion in Nashville, Tennessee.

JACK N. LIGHTSTONE recently joined Brock University (St. Catharines, Ontario) where he is president and vice-chancellor, and professor of history. Previously, he was professor of religion at Concordia University (Montreal, Quebec), where he also served as provost.

STEVE MASON is Canada research chair in Greco-Roman Cultural Interaction and professor in humanities at York University, Toronto.

JACOB NEUSNER is research professor of theology and senior fellow in the Institute of Advanced Theology at Bard College, Annandale-on-Hudson, New York.

MARTIN PICKUP is associate professor of biblical studies at Florida College, Temple Terrace, Florida.

ADELE REINHARTZ is associate vice-president for research at the University of Ottawa, Canada, where she is also professor in the Department of Classics and Religious Studies.

JAMES F. STRANGE is Distinguished University Professor in the
Department of Religious Studies at the University of South Florida.

JAMES C. VANDERKAM is the John A. O'Brien Professor of Hebrew
Scriptures at the University of Notre Dame.

DATE DUE